Revolution and Its Past

Identities and Change in Modern Chinese History

R. Keith Schoppa

Doehler Chair in Asian History
Loyola College in Maryland

Prentice
Hall

Upper Saddle River, NJ 07458

Library of Congress Cataloging-in-Publication Data

Schoppa, R. Keith

   Revolution and its past : identities and change in modern Chinese history / R. Keith Schoppa.

    p. cm.

  ISBN 0-13-022407-3

    1. China—History—19th century.   2. China—History—20th century.   3. Revolutions—China—History.   4. National characteristics, Chinese.   I. Title: Identities and change in modern Chinese history.
II. Title.

  DS755.S294 2002

  951′.033—dc21   00-140083

Acquisitions Editor: *Charles Cavaliere*
Associate Editor: *Emsal Hasan*
Production Editor: *Joe Scordato*
Prepress and Manufacturing Buyer: *Lynn Pearlman*
Cover Design Director: *Jayne Conte*
Cover Designer: *Bruce Kenselaar*
Cover Photo: *Fallender/SIPA Press*

Excerpt on back cover from "Heirs of the Dragon" by Hou Dejian from *New Ghosts, Old Dreams* by Geremie Barmé and Linda Jaivin, Eds., copyright © 1992, by Geremie Barmé and Linda Jaivin. Used by permission of Times Books, and division of Random House, Inc.

This book was set in 10/12 Times Roman by The Composing Room of Michigan, Inc. and was printed and bound by RR Donnelley & Sons. The cover was printed by Phoenix Color Corp.

 © 2002 by Pearson Education, Inc.
Upper Saddle River, New Jersey 07458

Printed in the United States of America
10 9 8 7 6 5 4 3 2 1

ISBN 0-13-022407-3

Prentice-Hall International (UK) Limited, *London*
Prentice-Hall of Australia Pty. Limited, *Sydney*
Prentice-Hall Canada Inc., *Toronto*
Prentice-Hall Hispanoamericana, S.A., *Mexico*
Prentice-Hall of India Private Limited, *New Delhi*
Prentice-Hall of Japan, Inc., *Tokyo*
Pearson Education Asia Pte. Ltd., *Singapore*
Editoria Prentice-Hall do Brasil, Ltda., *Rio de Janeiro*

Contents

——————
——
——
–

Part 3:   Revolution and Identity: Social
Revolution and the Power of Tradition,
1928–1960

Part 4: From "Politics in Command" to the Glory of Getting Rich: Contemporary Change and Identity, 1961–2000

Preface

————————

————

———

—

In October and November 2000 the central Chinese coastal city of Hangzhou sponsored an international fair. Named the West Lake Millennial Exposition for the city's most famous tourist attraction, it was designed to showcase the new China in its international contexts. In the midst of China's emergence as a growing world power, the exposition and its environs pointed to China's profusion of political and economic identities at the opening of the twenty-first century. Though there were several sites in the city where exposition events were held, the center of the fair was a new spectacularly modern stadium whose design reminded the onlooker of two enormous bridgeheads—and almost symbolically of the passage to a new China. The stadium complex included a hotel and huge glistening shopping emporiums. Yet little more than a decade ago the stadium site was rice paddies—so rapid has been the city's modernization. For all the glitz of the stadium, streets within a block were lined with the hovels of workers. The shopping emporiums stocked the latest in brand names from the West—clothing, cosmetics, and all manner of consumer products, while the overwhelming aroma emanating from the woks of street peddlers, like that of a century ago, was the pungent smell of *chou doufu* or stinky tofu. Though China persists in calling itself Communist, all the money for the exposition came not from the government or party but from private sources. The exposition trumpeted the international context of China's growing modernity (no fewer than thirty-one Italian furniture makers were on hand, for example), yet at two archives I was denied access to materials because I was a *waiguoren* (foreigner). China is moving into the modern world with such speed that it is understandable that there are inevitable time warps. But such anomalies point to the transcendent questions of what China is and where China is going. These questions are crucial to us because in the twenty-first century China is a significant player in world affairs; if we hope to deal intelligently with China and its people, we must understand their past and present.

It is a truism (though one frequently forgotten in the presentist American culture) that one cannot understand the present and its identities without understanding the past. Many Chinese today are acutely aware of their past—as individuals, as country, and as culture. Even popular culture in the last years of the twentieth century celebrated the link between past and present. The hugely popular "Heirs of the Dragon" by rock star Hou Dejian pointed to the power of the dragon, the symbol of traditional Chinese civilization, over today's Chinese:

> Under the claws of this mighty dragon I grew up
> And its heir I have become.
> Like it or not—
> Once and forever, an heir of the dragon.

But what has it meant and what does it mean for the Chinese to be "heirs of the dragon"? What does it signify for the world entering the new century? This book, which is comprehensive in scope, explores these questions and examines the fundamental aspects and developments of the Chinese past. I have used the broad and important theme of "identities" to help shape much of the presentation—analyzing traditional identities under the "dragon" and various modern identities that its heirs have tried to shape or have experimented with. It is a natural theme given the fact that the discourses of history and identity both attempt to delineate a meaningful past for a particular present. Further, in the making of history, individual and state actions depended in large part on how individual and state perceived their identities and how they were perceived by others with whom they had to interact.

This study begins in the last two decades of the reign of one of China's greatest emperors, the Qianlong emperor (1736–1795). While early textbooks of "modern" China often treated the salvoes of the Opium War (1839–1842) as the beginning of the "modern" period, recent work has shown that important changes foreshadowing developments in the nineteenth and twentieth centuries were underway in the late eighteenth century. Thus a date (though somewhat arbitrary) around 1780 seems to make historical sense. Starting then, when Chinese wealth and power were perhaps at their imperial peak, also provides us with a baseline of sorts to provide important context for understanding China's rapid decline in the nineteenth and part of the twentieth century. In that period of decline and throughout its twentieth century revolution, one of the most important problems facing individual Chinese and China as a nation was choosing appropriate political, social, cultural, and economic identities as contexts and situations changed.

Above all, this is a story of men and women whose choices shaped modern Chinese history in the often-startling directions it seemed to lurch. It is a dramatic story filled with some triumph but more often than not tragedy. It is a tale frequently bloody and violent, alternately soaring with hope and plunging into bleak despair. It compels our interests both as a history of an ancient civilization developing into a modern nation-state and as an account of how the heirs of the dragon have struggled and are continuing to work to find their identity in the modern world.

I would like to thank Dilip Basu of the University of California, Santa Cruz, Victor

Xiong of Western Michigan University, Winston W. Lo of Florida State University, Deborah Buffton of the University of Wisconsin-La Crosse, Madeline Hsu of San Francisco State University, and Prasenjit Duara of the University of Chicago, who reviewed earlier versions of the manuscript for this book, for their helpful suggestions.

R. Keith Schoppa
Baltimore, Maryland

Notes on Pronunciation

In writing about Chinese developments before 1949 and in the People's Republic since that time, I use the pinyin system of romanization in general use today. Names in pinyin are pronounced generally as written, with vowels often taking on the phonetic value of vowels in European romance languages and German. Consonants are generally pronounced as consonants in English; but there are three exceptions.

> *Q* is pronounced as *CH*—as in the name of the last Chinese dynasty, Qing, pronounced as if it were written Ching.
>
> *X* is pronounced as *HS,* in effect a softer version of *SH,* with the *H* producing a slight hiss—as in the name of China's late twentieth-century reformer Deng Xiaoping.
>
> *C* is pronounced as *TS*—as in the name of important cultural leader Cai Yuanpei.

I have not used pinyin for Sun Yat-sen and Chiang Kai-shek who are better known by these names than by their names in pinyin (Sun Yixian and Jiang Jieshi, respectively).

In writing about Chinese developments in Taiwan and about those men and women closely involved with Chiang Kai-shek's government in the 1930s, I have used Wade-Giles romanization. This choice was to respect the fact that the regime in Taiwan has not adopted the pinyin system and generally uses Wade-Giles, though romanization in Taiwan tends to be highly variable. Vowels, as in pinyin, generally take on the value of vowels in Spanish, Italian, and German. Most consonants are pronounced as in English, with these exceptions.

When the following consonants have an apostrophe after them, they are pronounced as in English: *ch', k', p',* and *t'.* When they do not have an apostrophe, *ch* is pronounced as *j; k* is pronounced as *g; p* is pronounced as *b;* and *t* is pronounced as *d.* Further, *j* is pronounced as *r.*

1

Personal Identities

———
——
—

There are over 1.2 billion Chinese living in the People's Republic of China today. In Western minds over the years, images of these masses have often been focused on the sameness—the "hordes" moving in "human wave" assaults in the Korean War, the "blue ants" mindlessly carrying out the bidding of their Communist overlords in mass campaigns of the 1950s, the mobs of Red Guards screaming in demonstration marches in the 1960s, enraged students attacking the U.S. embassy in 1999. Indeed, in all these images, all Chinese seemed to look alike! But the identities of Chinese, like people of every country and ethnic group, are as different as the number of Chinese who exist. Thumbnail sketches of a quartet of Chinese figures point to the kind of stark individuality seen amid the masses throughout China's modern history.

Zeng Guofan was a stolid Confucian conservative in the mid-nineteenth century. With the highest civil service degree under his belt, he became perhaps the most important Chinese official serving the alien Manchu dynasty. What mattered to him most were his family, his family's farm, and his culture. He organized an army to defend his home province Hunan against the threat of the Taiping rebellion led by a man who claimed to be the younger brother of Jesus Christ. During his leadership of this army, he, as the elder brother, wrote letters to his brothers in Hunan, urging them, in good Confucian terms, to pay attention to their duties at home. Although he was impressed with modern Western technology, when he was old and infirm, he refused to seek Western medical treatment, preferring to be treated with traditional Chinese medicine.

Qiu Jin, a thirty-two-year-old woman, was beheaded at dawn on July 15, 1907. She had left her husband and children several years earlier to go to Japan to study. She had a reputation for wearing men's clothes and riding horses in men's style. She was photographed wielding an unsheathed dagger. She antagonized locals by having female students at her school train in military drills. She became involved in an elaborate plot that included assassinating the governor of a province and staging an uprising against the government. But she was arrested before she could rebel and paid the bloody price.

Soong Meiling, the daughter of a wealthy Chinese merchant, attended Wellesley College in Massachusetts, spoke excellent English, and was a Christian. In 1927 she was married to Chiang Kai-shek who would become the leader of the Republic of China, first on the mainland (1928–1949) and then on Taiwan (1949–1975). Madame Chiang became the darling of the American press and political elites during World War II, when she addressed a joint session of Congress stressing China's plight. In 2000, with a home maintained in Taiwan, she was still living in New York City.

Cui Jian is China's most famous rock star of the late 1980s and the 1990s. While the government tried to keep him off television and to cancel his concerts, this longhaired, often open-shirted cultural rebel became a hero to the youth of China. His song lyrics scandalized government leaders and censors. One line in a song on a 1991 recording says, "Look—we've come to the end of the Golden Road"—Golden Road being slang for Communism. An American journalist commented that Cui's "raspy outbursts of alienation [became] the anthems of his generation."[1]

Qiu, Song, Zeng, and Cui—all put the lie to the stereotype that Chinese were faceless and colorless masses with minds benumbed by powerful authorities whether emperors, military generals, or Communists. As the world entered a new millennium and China found itself in the midst of vast change, one question was raised with increasing frequency: What does it mean to be Chinese? What attributes, ethical and cultural values, attitudes, and worldviews are "typically" Chinese? Most important here, what is the shared history of the Chinese that gives them their identity?

This book focuses on the history of modern China, that is, China's history from the late eighteenth century to the present. It is concerned with Chinese characteristics, customs, idiosyncrasies, past experiences, and relationships. It probes the identities China and the Chinese have assumed and the identities that others have ascribed to it and to them. It analyzes the changes seen over time. Above all, this is a story of people—men and women who shaped China's identity and history and, in turn, were shaped by it. This chapter sets the stage for the study of Chinese identities by focusing on the cultural commonalities that were the foundation for Chinese society and the dynamics of social relations, actions, and interactions. Because these cultural elements often played key roles in historical events and developments, understanding them is a first step for understanding the Chinese and their past.

HISTORY AND IDENTITY

A person's identity comes from many sources. Contextual sources are important: time and place of birth, ethnic heritage, parents' occupations and socioeconomic status, the nature of local community, schools, and friends. Perhaps equally significant components are personal characteristics—appearance, personality, and habits. But people's identities are fundamentally their personal history, what has happened to them during their lifetime; that history has created each person as he or she is at the present time. Understanding someone's past or the

Zeng Guofan

past of any institution or political and social body—nation, town, neighborhood, school, church, company, organization, sports team—is recognizing a person's or its identity. In other words, the shape of the past gives meaning to the present.

There are three important corollaries to seeing the relationship between history and identity. Take, as an example, a college senior in a fraternity. On an individual level, he has his own characteristics, personality, habits, and history that give him an identity through which he sees and understands himself. But ultimately in the world outside himself, his identity is given or bestowed by others; a fraternity brother, a freshman classmate, a girl-friend, a professor would likely all bestow on our hypothetical fraternity man substantially different identities. Sometimes how he is perceived might be as or perhaps more important for those around him than what he really is.

So it is with China's past and its identity. Over the last two hundred years, China has acted on its own for its own reasons and on its own standards. But the outside world has often perceived Chinese actions and motivations in entirely different ways, sometimes through direct reactions to Chinese events or policies or actions, sometimes unfortunately through bias and stereotype. Thus, the violent crackdown of the Chinese government on student demonstrators in 1989 has continued into the twenty-first century to shape and color views of American politicians and journalists about the goals and motives of the Chinese government. This particular "coloration" has remained despite changes in Chinese politi-

Qiu Jin

cal leadership and more than a decade of nothing short of staggering economic and consequent attitudinal changes.

Second, a person's identity may be bestowed by people with biases and ulterior motives as well as by those seeking to truly understand what kind of person he or she is. Thus, our fraternity man may be judged on the basis of race, ethnicity, religion, gender, sexual orientation, or social group. Because different people with different agendas are bestowing different identities, it follows that every individual will have many identities. So too with China and the Chinese. Thus in the early twenty-first century, China could be seen primarily as a rapidly developing nation, as a country with an immense population problem, as an increasing military threat, as a potential leader in East Asia, as a country with a rich old culture, as a nation obsessed with "getting rich." Just as in any perception of an individual's identities, some of the variety of identities or all of them may apply in a variety of combinations.

Third, because identity comes in large part from history and because a person's present and future will become a part of that history, a person's identity is continually evolving and developing. He or she might react to a new situation in a way that would be seen as totally "out of character" with what others would have expected of him or her. Yet that reaction would help others redefine that person and give him or her a new identity. Identity is therefore very fluid and unset. Identities are provisional and tentative. Again, such is the

Soong Meiling

case with China and the Chinese. Each new event and reactions to events shape anew our understanding of Chinese attitudes and goals. My work as historian—and the goal of this book—is to try to reach and present an understanding of the Chinese historical identity that reflects as closely as possible China's culture and past experiences.

ASSOCIATIONAL IDENTITIES: LINEAGES AND FAMILIES

It is a truism that while the basic social unit in the modern West is the individual, in China that foundational unit is the group. There is probably no clearer illustration of the relationship of the Chinese individual to the group—and here the most important group, the family—than in the nature of Chinese names. Many (though not all) Chinese personal names are composed of three characters and pronounced in three syllables. Traditionally the surname came first, pointing clearly to the priority of the surname group, the family or, taken more largely, the lineage (sometimes called a clan), that is, all Chinese descendants of a single patriarch in the past. Take the name Zeng Guofan. The surname is Zeng. The second name, Guo, is a generational name. For those families deeply rooted in the Chinese tradition of the extended family, all brothers and cousins of one generation should ideally share a common name. Thus, Zeng's brothers were named Zeng *Guo*quan, Zeng *Guo*hua, and Zeng *Guo*huang.[2] It follows that only the last character in the three-character name is the

Cui Jian

individual's own. The family, the generation, and then *and then only* the individual—a marked difference from the modern West where the individual name precedes all others.

Such a Chinese naming pattern suggests the role of the individual in the family—he or she was submerged in the group with implicit responsibilities to that group. There was not a concept of an individual's rights within the family in the traditional cultural view: when Qiu Jin's parents arranged her marriage to a bland, conventional man with whom she had little in common, she did not assert herself against the family's decision (though, later showing considerable spunk, she eventually left him). An assertion of individual rights would immediately throw family harmony and solidarity into jeopardy. Elder brother Zeng Guofan set off bitter quarreling with his brothers by insisting that they remain home, tending family needs, instead of serving in the military campaigns against the Taiping. At least two brothers saw him as blocking their individual careers and possible paths to higher status and prestige.[3] This situation reveals an important facet of family structure: it was hierarchical, and, as in the case of any hierarchy, there were superior and subordinate ranks. Elder brother Zeng Guofan could tell his brothers what they should do and the younger brothers were expected to comply. The elder brother-younger brother relationship was one of five "Confucian bonds" that defined cardinal relationships in Chinese society. Three were familial. Joining elder brothers in the superior ranks were fathers and husbands who could direct and control sons and wives, respectively. Clear in these "bonds" was that maleness and age outranked femaleness and youth.

Within the family "responsibility" was the watchword. Both superiors and subordinates had responsibilities, superiors to direct, train, provide for, and control and subordinates to be obedient, compliant, and respectful. For sons and daughters the proper family ethic, filial piety, had a number of aspects. First and foremost, it meant doing whatever was necessary to provide for the physical and psychological needs of parents in a spirit of respectful obeisance. Stories abound, many likely apocryphal, about the dimensions of such action. There was the filial son who cut off flesh from his own thigh to feed a starving parent; there was the filial daughter who breast-fed an elderly parent for nourishment; there was the seventy-year-old son who clowned around on the floor to lift his elderly parents' depression. There was the story of one Guo Ju, desperately poor and trying to support his wife, son, and mother. When there was no way for all to survive, he decided it best for his son to die so his mother might have enough to eat. But this extreme solution was aborted, for while digging the grave for his son, he dug up buried treasure, which allowed all to live and prosper. The moral: upholding filial piety will bring solutions to a family's bleakest plights and ultimately happiness and prosperity.

A second component of filial piety was protecting one's body as a gift from one's parents. A Confucian disciple once fell off a porch and injured his leg; from that point he walked around with a continual hangdog expression on his face. When someone asked him why, he replied his fall showed that he had not been properly filial, that one should not forget his parents in taking a single step or in saying a single word. While it is unlikely that few Chinese were so totally constrained, it is likely that such teachings produced some hesitance before one acted recklessly and, as a consequence, helped give rise to a markedly conservative Chinese social culture.

A third aspect of filial piety was carrying on the family line. The second-generation Confucian thinker Mencius argued that the most unfilial thing was to have no children, for it meant that the ancestors who ultimately produced the present generation would have no one to remember them properly. This remembrance of deceased family members constituted a fourth important aspect of filial piety. Remembrance came in various ways. The best-known method of remembrance for ancestors was ancestor reverence: Rituals were held on birthdays and death days of parents and key ancestors where food was presented for the sustenance of the ancestors in their other life. The graves of ancestors were traditionally swept on the Qing Ming festival (April 5 or 6).

Mourning periods for one's parents were prescribed to last up to three years. Marked by various restrictions in lifestyles, they were taken very seriously and were obligatory even for men in important positions. In the middle of the campaigns against the Taiping, Zeng Guofan had to retire twice, once on the death of his mother in 1852 and then following his father's death in 1857, the latter retirement lasting almost two years. Remembrance also came through the most auspicious siting of the graves; for if the graves of the deceased were sited poorly, the spirits of the dead might play a negative role in the lives of their descendants. So it was that in 1858, because of a series of family mishaps and tragedies, Zeng and his brothers relocated the graves of their parents to try to change their fortune for the better.[4] It was a task for Daoist geomancers, or specialists in the art of fengshui (literally "wind-water" and pronounced something like fung-shway) to discover the best grave sites. Daoism was an indigenous Chinese philosophical and religious tradition that focused on nature and on aligning oneself in various ways with the forces of nature and the natural state.

Though the extended or joint family (including grandparents, parents and siblings, children and cousins) was the ideal, financial realities probably made it quite rare. An estimated 60 percent of the Chinese in late imperial times lived instead in small or nuclear families composed of parents and their unmarried children. Another ideal was the lineage, in which all the descendants of one patriarch in the past would live in the same area and provide a support base for their relatives. Ideally the lineage would own joint property; the proceeds of harvests from that land provided an economic safety net for lineage members or money for special projects or undertakings. The lineage would periodically publish genealogies as a way to express its unity and significance.

The strength and importance of lineages varied across China. They were strongest in the south. Anthropologists argue over the reason. Some say strong lineages developed there to deal with the labor-intensive irrigation facilities crucial in southern rice paddy agriculture. Others suggest that since the south was China's frontier area, strong lineages developed for protection in an often violent and unpredictable context. Whole villages in southern areas were—and still today are—composed of members of one lineage. Often the lineage surname simply became the name of the village; thus in east central China a village inhabited mostly by the Sun lineage was known simply as Sun Village on the Lake. If lineages were a source of solidarity in south China, they were also a scourge in some areas when a strong lineage might be pitted against another strong lineage in bloody and costly feuds. Feuds, especially common in the southeastern provinces of Fujian and Guangdong, could begin over any issue, but were often ignited by disputes over water rights and boundaries.

ASSOCIATIONAL IDENTITIES: SOCIAL CONNECTIONS

Basic social identity comes not only from a person's family and his or her place in it, but from social connections and the networks that develop from them. An American journalist has written that the Chinese "instinctively divide people into those with whom they already have a fixed relationship, a connection, what the Chinese call *guanxi,* and those that they don't. These connections operate like a series of invisible threads, tying Chinese to each other with far greater tensile strength than mere friendship."[5] Connections and their next step, networks, were established in various ways.

Some were surefire. Friends obviously had close connections; the only one of the five Confucian bonds that was a bond nearing equality rather than one of hierarchy was friendship. Certainly for this reason friendship was more celebrated in Chinese literature than any other social relationship. Friendship also provided connections to the friend's family. If a person came from the same hometown or county or even province (called in Chinese, "native place"), he or she had an automatic connection with anyone else from that place; the connection was stronger the more local the common place—county or town or village, for example. Thus, among all the Chinese students living in Japan during the first decade of the twentieth century, Qiu Jin (executed for her role in the 1907 assassination plot) developed her most important revolutionary ties to two men from her native place of Shaoxing, men whom she had not known previously.

Academic and scholarly ties were also significant sources of connections. The men who received civil service degrees in the same year shared a type of alumni connection. An example of the power of such a connection: in a famous sixteenth-century case, an official who received his degree the same year as a murdered fellow official became a surrogate father to the victim's son, even to the point of coaching him for a revenge attack on the guilty.[6] Teacher-student relationships provided connections for life, taking on an almost master-disciple dynamic. When he chose someone to lead the Anhui provincial army against the Taiping, Zeng Guofan not surprisingly selected one of his former students and protégés, Li Hongzhang.[7]

Though social connections are important in every culture, Chinese culture has developed them to the nth degree. They are immensely practical social realities; put more bluntly, they are a *must* to get things done. From the bureaucracy of the traditional state to the bureaucracies of the Communist state and post-Communist state, people have used their personal social connections to get what they want or need. Li Hongzhang nurtured his connections to Zeng Guofan, theoretically his superior, through doing various acts of kindness and by supportive actions. Zeng, in turn, responded in kind with acts of kindness, generosity, and support shown to Li (a key example was selecting Li to head one of the provincial armies). In the process, Li's social debts to Zeng increased. His repaying those debts through reciprocal actions further nurtured the connection that they shared, making its "tensile strength" very great indeed. The accumulation and repaying of obligations was a continual social reality.

China's most famous twentieth-century sociologist Fei Xiaotong wrote about the importance of connections and networks for the working of Chinese society. Networks might encompass many people, but their structure was based on the connections of two people, and then two others, and so on. The strength of any two connections varied. Similarly, individuals found themselves to be a part of a number of networks; and the strength of the personal connections to people in each network also varied. This situation had definite ethical implications. Noting that Chinese society was structured as "webs woven out of countless personal relationships," he argued that "[t]o each knot in these webs [was] attached a specific ethical principle." In this society, "general [ethical] standards [had] no utility. The first thing to do [was] to understand the specific context: Who [was] the important figure, and what kind of relationship [was] appropriate with that figure? Only then [could] one decide the ethical standards to be applied in that context."[8] Thus, there was no universal ethic to be applied across the boards to all people and in all situations. Ethics in China were traditionally determined by connections; and they varied with particular people and situations.

These kinds of social realities gave Chinese social life considerable fluidity. Not only did a person's place in society largely depend on those to whom he was connected, but the way he treated others and the way he was treated depended on those connections. In addition, the power of connections was such that a person might be moved to act in ways or participate in efforts that he might ordinarily have been reluctant about. In the end, the disheartening fact was that if that person with whom he had spent years establishing and cultivating connections was kicked out of power, lost his job, was incapacitated, or died, then he would be back to square one in trying to establish his own social position. Developing and nurturing personal connections was understandably a full-time, lifetime undertaking, for it was those connections that gave a person his social identity.

ASSOCIATIONAL IDENTITIES: RELATIONS TO THE "OTHER"

In a real sense, if a person's social identity came in large part from those with whom he or she was connected, the obverse was also true. Identity came in a negative way from those with whom a person had no connections—call them the "Other." By lifestyle, habits, religious practices, and language, a person shows or tells society in various ways, "I am not one of them; I am different from the Other." Since one had no connections to the Other, there were no special ethical responsibilities to them. Thus, for example, a person can cut in line in front of them or push and shove them getting on or off the bus. Fei gives the example of the wretched state of many public toilets as an example of the lack of sense of ethical responsibility to the public with whom one has no special connections. It must be stressed that this is a general cultural tendency, not a necessary inevitability. The Buddhist concept of karma, that a person's deeds in this life would determine how he or she was reborn in the next life, may have played a role in the ethical views of many. In traditional Chinese social thought, there was no sense of equality among people, only connections or their lack. The philosopher, Mencius put it this way: "That things are unequal is part of their nature. . . . If you reduce them to the same level [that is, to equality], it will only bring confusion to the empire."[9]

Though one owed the Other no special concern or treatment, the Other was potentially frightening, possibly dangerous, and almost always suspicious precisely because they did not owe those to whom they were unconnected any special concern or treatment. Thus, the Other had best be kept at arm's length. In the world of folk spirits, the most threatening beings were the "hungry ghosts," ancestors of someone who were no longer being remembered and revered; that is, no one living was providing them with the necessities for existence in the spirit world. In the language of connections, no one in the world of the living was maintaining the proper connections with them. These ghosts were reported to be mean and dangerous, more than willing to create all sorts of misfortune for those who were not providing them with their needs. As with connections and the Other in the land of the living, in the spirit world the spirits of ancestors being reverenced by one family were for another family the "Other," in this case ghosts to be avoided.

In society, strangers were always suspect. The short-term transients—beggars and vagrants—and the more long-term and uprooted—the homeless and refugees—were potential threats. Their presence and their passing through an area suffering a famine or experiencing the violence of banditry, rebellion, or war only heightened the fluid danger latent in society. Even more serious than these passing strangers were permanent Others with whom Chinese had to deal, ethnic minorities. While one might avoid those transient strangers, state and society had to come to grips with how to deal with the permanent Others.

China is a country of several dozen sizable ethnic minorities; in 1990, there were in fact nine minorities with a population of four million or more.[10] The home of many of these—Mongols, Tibetans, Uighurs—has been and continues to be near the periphery of the Chinese nation. Yet groups like the Zhuang, Hui, Miao, and Yi have remained more within the Chinese geographical core, living scattered among the Han people, those considered the ethnic Chinese. Contemporary social scientists have pointed out that terms like race and ethnicity do not describe discrete or even meaningful categories, that there is much fluidity and complexity in these concepts. Ethnicity is seen today more as a system of relationships. In the words of one historian, "ethnicity, or ethnic belonging, is not something that one is but something that one does."[11] Instead of being in either this or that ethnic group, there is a large spectrum of possible ethnic identities.

And yet the traditional Chinese state and the Han Chinese elite continued to see the Other as a noun, not as a verb in process; and as a noun, the Other was to be classified and then controlled as the "barbarians" they were until they could be assimilated into Han Chinese culture. From early in Chinese history, ethnicity—based more on language, customs, and culture than on race—was a rationale for keeping the ethnic Other separate. It is important in this regard to realize that the category of Han Chinese itself was not homogeneous. Some Han Chinese, like the Hakka, who centuries earlier had migrated from the north into central and southern areas, the Hui who were Muslim Chinese, and people from Subei, the northern part of Jiangsu province, were treated with suspicion and contempt.

SPATIAL IDENTITIES: NATIVE PLACE

A person's native place was crucial for his or her identity. It is generally the site where a person's ancestors were buried and where eventually he or she would be interred as well. It provided "home," a retreat from life beyond: people returned to mourn for parents, to renew old ties, in between career positions, and at stressful and traumatic periods of life. Native place was and is the indispensable information provided in newspaper accounts and biographies in local histories and yearbooks. It is one of the first things a Chinese asks about when meeting someone else.

As we have seen, shared native place is one of the most important bases for connections, and by extension, networks. In turn, native place connections and networks played crucial roles in politics, culture, and the economy. In the economy, certain native places became associated with particular trades and professions and sent men out, in some cases, around the country to carry on their activities. In the late empire, merchant bankers from Shanxi province, for example, dominated the world of banking, becoming as it were bankers for the central government. The city of Shaoxing in Zhejiang province became known as a supplier of lower officials and clerks who staffed many government offices and the central government boards. Merchants from the city of Ningbo, also in Zhejiang province, came to dominate the economic and social life of the city of Shanghai.

Even in the realms of the non-elite and non-rich, native place came to be connected with particular roles. In the central Zhejiang river port of Quzhou, where docks stretched almost two miles along the bank, men from two relatively nearby counties in Zhejiang and one in neighboring Jiangxi province dominated stevedoring. In another example, in the city of Shanghai, people from northern Jiangsu (Subei) provided the bulk of unskilled labor.

When elites and non-elites alike traveled or "sojourned" away from their native places to other cities or ports, they could often depend on "native place associations" there as a home away from home to provide lodging, meals, advice, and a general helping hand. When a person sojourned or traveled, he or she became the Other in relation to the native populace. The native place associations in a sense softened that Other status; they provided assistance both to anyone from the native place passing through and to sojourners, say merchants, who lived semi-permanently in their non-native place. Native place associations could serve people from whole provinces or they could serve a particular city or county or prefecture. Take as an example the river city of Quzhou, where in the early twentieth century sojourning outsiders dominated the commercial population—bankers, merchants, stevedores, freight brokers, commission agents, and warehousemen. Altogether there were sixteen native place associations in the county; in the city itself there were six, four of them by the 1930s nearing the end of their second century of existence: two provincial associations, Jiangxi (established in 1746) and Fujian (1801); one two-prefecture association, Ningbo and Shaoxing (1752); and one prefectural association, Huizhou (1756).

Native place identities were also part and parcel of politics. Networks in which native place was often a critical component flourished in political decision making and action. In the fluid world of politics where connections were the name of the game, networks, especially if they were tightly cohesive, tended to become factions or cliques. When Chiang Kai-shek who hailed from the province of Zhejiang assumed control of the country in 1928, men from Zhejiang appeared in many positions of importance. Political factions in Chiang's Nationalist party—the CC clique and the Western Hills faction—were based in large part on native place. The Guangxi clique was a military faction from that southern province that became a potent political force and frequent antagonist of Chiang Kai-shek. Other considerations—kinship, friendship, personality, ideology, and context—certainly played important roles in politics, but native place was a basic building block.

Cultural developments were also often linked to locality and the native place of those instrumental in those developments. Studies, for example, have shown that the "evidential research" scholarship that marked Confucianism in the seventeenth and eighteenth centuries was centered in the Lower Yangzi (Jiangnan) region. Various subsets of this "school," like the Zhedong (Eastern Zhejiang) school developed in different geographical subregions.[12]

SPATIAL IDENTITIES: VILLAGE AND MARKETING COMMUNITIES

Before the late 1960s, social scientists studying China generally considered the village to be the basic geographical unit in Chinese society. In the countryside, the usual housing pattern was the village; only in Sichuan province did one find the pattern of the solitary farm home sited on the farm itself. Farmers then generally lived together in villages and went out to farm their lands that were typically divided among several small plots not at all contiguous with each other. Villages ranged in size from only a few households to several thousand, with a common range between perhaps two and four hundred inhabitants. Because they were generally quite small and because of the relatively large population in most areas, villages tended to be clustered fairly closely. Nevertheless in his study of rural China in the first half of the twentieth century, sociologist Fei Xiaotong painted a picture of villager isolation. Village life centered on the village; there was not much interaction with other villages nearby. Villagers did not tend to travel, and there was little contact with the world beyond the village confines. The focus of life was the village and the life and affairs of villagers. It was in Fei's words, "a society without strangers,"[13] a social and cultural world that would perhaps predispose its inhabitants to see what was at hand as the norm and as good and consequently to be fearful and distrustful of the Other. When, especially in villages in the south, villagers were all members of the same lineage or clan, the tightness and closedness of the village to outsiders might tend to be even stronger. If one were to ask a villager with this sort of life about his or her spatial identity, he or she would almost certainly have responded with the name of the village.

But many scholars today believe that the most basic geographic unit shaping the horizons of the Chinese villager was what has been called a marketing community. If this is the case, then, contrary to the views of Fei, the world of the villager did extend beyond the village. A market town served a marketing community composed roughly of six to forty villages whose population was too small to support a market; further, since many traditional village families were almost self-sufficient, even the market town did not have to maintain a market all the time. Part of a hierarchy of market towns, stretching from large city all the way down, the lowest level marketing town, often called the standard market, tended to hold its market on mornings according to certain patterns. Traditional China did not use a seven-day week, having instead a basic time frame of ten days. A market town thus might open its market on days one, four, and seven of the ten-day cycle; or on days two, five, and eight; or days three, six, and nine.

Imagine Li Village on the first cycle, Wang Lane on the second, and Lin Lake on the third. On the first day of the cycle, Mr. Sun who lived in a small village two miles away from Li Village would walk there early in the morning. Traveling merchants would have already arranged their goods in stalls along streets or on the temple grounds. Others selling services—doctors, dentists, barbers, fortune-tellers—would set up booths. Local restaurants, teahouses, and taverns would be open for the villagers who came to buy and in some cases to sell goods. On the next day, both Mr. Xiao whose village was oriented to Wang Lane would do his marketing, and the following day Mr. Jiang whose village was oriented to Lin Lake would follow suit. Because of the rather close clustering of villages in populated areas, even the farthest village from the market town was probably in the range of only three miles.

All three villages would be a part of the larger intermediate marketing community, say, of Greenfield. An intermediate marketing town, Greenfield would have a larger population, and the goods at its market would include more specialized and harder-to-get products. While the standard market generally served only retail functions, the intermediate market town served both wholesaling functions for the standard market traveling merchants and retailing functions for its own merchants' businesses. The other higher-level marketing centers shared these wholesaling-retailing functions. If Sun, Xiao, and Jiang were unable to find what they needed at the standard markets, they could travel to the intermediate market or make arrangements with an itinerant merchant to bring the item from the intermediate market on the next standard market day.

Apart from its obvious commercial and economic significance, the marketing community provided the general social and cultural horizons for the farmers in its villages. It is likely that Sun, Xiao, and Jiang did not go beyond the standard marketing community many times in their lives. When they went to the market, not only did they buy and sell, but they likely conversed with friends and acquaintances along the streets or in teahouses. They caught up on the news from neighboring villages, asking questions about spreading rumors from other villages and passing on the latest gossip from their own. They would talk about the weather, political news, new farming techniques. In the marketing community, the same dialect would be spoken and village inhabitants would generally share the same culture. It is not, of course, that people never ventured beyond their marketing community, but for many it defined their economic, social, and cultural world.

SPATIAL IDENTITIES: MACROREGIONS AND PROVINCES

Provinces were the largest political and administrative units in the Chinese system, composed (moving down the administrative ladder) of prefectures, counties, and townships. (Provinces were roughly the size of states in the United States; and Chinese counties and townships were roughly equivalent to their U.S. counterparts.) In the Qing (1644–1912), there were eighteen provinces within (that is, south of) the Great Wall, a sporadic two thousand-mile structure built at various times in the Chinese past to try to keep the Other out. Provincial boundaries had largely been set in Ming times (1368–1644); many of their names reflected their geographical situation (e.g., Hubei [north of the lake] and Hunan [south of the lake], Shandong [east of the mountains] and Shanxi [west of the mountains]). Provinces were the largest "native place" to which Chinese could claim residence, and thus they were still a source of connections—even though much weaker than connections formed in village, town, county, or prefecture. As such, they were an important part of the constellation of attributes making up the Chinese identity.

In the 1970s, anthropologist G. William Skinner, whose earlier work had focused on the standard marketing community, argued that Chinese economic, social, cultural, and perhaps political history might be better understood in terms of the history of natural economic regions than in artificial political units (provinces, prefectures, counties). Skinner described a number of "macroregions," many of them structured around the basin(s) or valley(s) of a river or of several rivers and often surrounded by mountains. The scope and boundaries of these macroregions have little relationship with provinces; in fact, some provinces are divided into different macroregions (on Map 2, see the province of Zhejiang for example). Skinner argued that these large natural regions were more coherent systems, where transportation and communications links as well as social and political networks were denser than those between macroregions or within provincial borders drawn by humans, often with political purposes in mind. Thus, to understand Chinese historical trends and developments more systematically and therefore more realistically, a student should look at the past of macroregions.

For purposes of analysis, macroregions have been divided into "cores"—areas of denser population, greater commercial activity, and higher degrees of urbanization and economic development—and "peripheries"—areas of sparser population, lesser commercial activity, and lower levels of urbanization and economic development. The nature of life in the cores and peripheries of each macroregion varied considerably and most assuredly affected how resident Chinese elites at least saw themselves and their world.

A brief survey of the nature of each macroregion will set the stage for our study of the key patterns and trends of Chinese history. As you read through the descriptions of each region, try to imagine the key or pressing issues that life in that area brought and how they may have given a person's identity a particular flavor. Note such things as the natural environment, the topography, the crops and growing season. How easy would it have been to make a living? Note the social realities—the existence or non-existence of kinship groups (lineages) and whether there was ethnic homogeneity or diversity. Note the orientation of the region: to the sea, to the interior, to an important river, to a city. The purpose of this section, other than to lay the context for our study, is to underscore in your mind from the beginning that there are many Chinas and that to understand China of the past and of the present we must begin to see it in its fascinating diversity. Though many of these characteristics endure to the present, the presentation uses the past tense.

North China

In part because it contained Beijing, the capital city throughout most of the late imperial and modern periods, the North China region, bordered on the north by Manchuria and Mongolia, played a central role in China's history. Its most prominent topographical feature was its large plain constituting large parts of three provinces, Zhili (now called Hebei), Shandong, and Henan, bordered by mountains on three sides and low-lying swampy land to the south. Its most prominent natural waterway was the Yellow River. Traditionally it has been called "China's sorrow" because of its propensity to flood. Early in its journey to the sea, it traversed loess lands where it picked up huge amounts of silt. East of Xi'an, after it made its greater than right angle turn toward the sea, the gradient of the riverbed became very slight, dropping less than a foot per mile as it flowed the five hundred miles to the sea. Thus, the velocity of the water dropped precipitously, and with it immense quantities of silt, something on the order of 100 million tons a day, sank to the riverbed. Because of this continual build-up of sediment, the river flowed between ten and forty feet above the flood plain; therefore dike building and repair to prevent flooding at times of heavy rains required constant vigilance. Inevitably, at times of state economic weakness, political crisis, or administrative corruption, the dikes were not adequately maintained. The price was disastrous floods, destroying people and property and devastating cropland. Like the Yellow River, most other rivers and streams in this region were not navigable. The most important north-south waterway was the human-constructed Grand Canal which ran from the south-central city of Hangzhou to near Beijing.

Because of the general absence of abundant water resources, farmers depended on

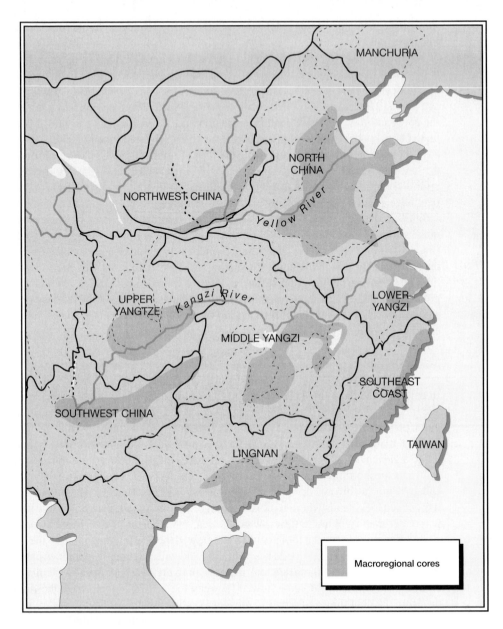

Late Imperial China, Its Macroregions and Their Cores

rain for the key crops—wheat, barley, millet, and sorghum. Draft animals were horses, mules, even camels. The settlement pattern was in small clustered villages. Differences in dialects across the region were small. Compared to other regions, subethnic differences were minor, and there was consequently less violence. As might be expected in relatively

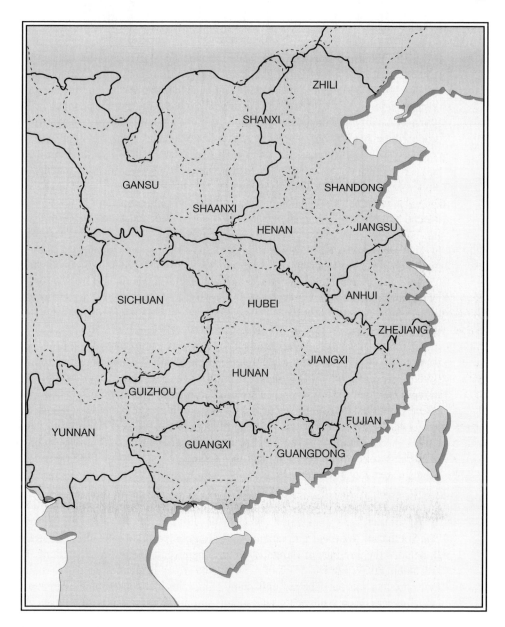

Macroregions in Relation to Provinces

consistently flat terrain, there was considerable mobility in the population. Because of the presence of the country's capital and the trade on the Grand Canal and between the North China region and the steppe to the north, there were many sojourning merchants and government. The region had many native place associations from around the country.

Lower Yangzi

Mostly flat plains, the Lower Yangzi had in abundance what the North China region did not: sufficient water resources for irrigation and for easy transportation. Composed of southern Jiangsu, northern Zhejiang, and southern Anhui, it was, in the late imperial and modern periods, the region with the highest level of urbanization and the densest population. The Yangzi River, which for this area did not constitute the same kind of flood threat as the Yellow River, produced the delta that has made the region one of China's most significant rice baskets. It produced not only great quantities of rice but also tea, silk, and wine, which were sent to markets across much of the country. A measure of its economic centrality was that in the Qing dynasty over a quarter of the land tax that was paid to the government came from this region. Its economic importance was more than agricultural and commercial, for it was an important industrial base since the Ming and Qing dynasties when silk and cotton textile mills flourished.

The region's generally high level of wealth allowed more families here than perhaps in other regions to set aside and use resources to help talented young men study for the famous civil service examinations; if they passed, they might rise to become an official in the Chinese governmental bureaucracy (see Chapter 2). Education and the scholarly tradition were, therefore, emphasized. It is then perhaps not surprising that six of the nine prefectures in the whole country producing the largest number of Ph.D.-equivalent degrees (*jinshi*) were in this region.[14]

Villages, generally larger than in the north, were often clustered along canals and waterways. Many villages were made up of a single lineage. Although regional lineages published more genealogies than other regions, lineage roles here seemed "softer-edged" than in regions to the south where lineage power frequently led to violence. There were small ethnic groups, islands in the sea of Han Chinese in this region, but they did not play a major social role. Because of the trade and the general wealth of the region, merchant sojourners were abundant. A very large number of native place associations set up alongside restaurants, teashops, taverns, and gardens helped make the style of life especially in cities sophisticated and eminently livable.

Southeast Coast

The Southeast Coast was a mountainous region composed of the valleys of several rivers. It included the province of Fujian, southern Zhejiang, and eastern Guangdong. It had several hallmarks. While two crops of rice could be grown in areas along the coast, its most famous product was tea. The region's many mountains had necessitated intensive use of the land. Tea was often produced on mountain- and hillside terraces with villages clustered in opportune sites.

Another important hallmark was the involvement of the region in high volume trade, both with other regions along the coast and especially with overseas ports. Chinese who ventured abroad whether in late traditional or modern times to Southeast Asia or to Chinatowns in the United States and Europe generally came from this region or from that of Lingnan to its south. The advanced degree of trade helped foster the relatively high degree of urbanization in the Southeast Coast core; overall, there was also a high population density.

The society here was much more disparate and violent than in North China or the Lower Yangzi. There were a larger number of ethnic groups; though some were partially assimilated, the tendency was for such groups to separate themselves and maintain a coherence that could intimidate and perhaps fend off opponents. The most serious troubles often involved Hakkas who maintained their own exclusive identities through their occupations, customs, language, and dress. They clashed with both Han Chinese and other ethnic minorities. Even the Han Chinese in this region were more disparate, speaking a wider number of distinct dialects. Another stimulus of social unrest was the power and unruliness of lineage groups, whose feuds over such things as property boundaries and water rights, were notorious around the country. In addition, this region was the origin of various blood brotherhoods, like the Triads, who might function as mutual support groups but could transmute in gang-like fashion to involvement in organized crime. It is little wonder that in such a violence-prone situation walled villages and even fortresses were not uncommon.

Lingnan

Lingnan was the drainage basin of the East, North, and West Rivers in the provinces of Guangxi and most of Guangdong. Just as North China was dominated by the capital Beijing, there was a dominant city in Lingnan as well—Canton (in Chinese, Guangzhou). A city that in the eighteenth and nineteenth centuries became a symbol of overseas trade with the West, Canton underscored the importance of overseas trade for the region. As indicated above, Lingnan and the Southeast Coast were the regions most turned to the sea and those beyond the sea; Lingnan joined the Southeast Coast in contributing the largest number of Chinese from all the regions to settle abroad.

Its mild subtropical-tropical climate joined with rich alluvial soils in the Pearl River delta to produce flourishing crops and bountiful harvests; rice could be triple-cropped, for example. Agriculture in the interior mountains and their river valleys was, however, markedly poorer. The contrasts between production and life styles in the two areas were stark.

Like the Southeast Coast, society in Lingnan was diverse and often rancorous. In addition to the fact that people in the region speak six major dialects of Chinese, there was a heterogeneous population of Han Chinese, Zhuang, Yao, Tanka, Miao, Hakka, and Muslim. As in the Southeast Coast, Hakkas often found themselves in disputes with the locals. While single-lineage villages in Lingnan were as common as in much of southern China, there were also single-ethnicity villages. Lineages were strong social forces and often based their power on estates owned by the lineage as a type of corporation. So strong was the emphasis upon kinship that in this region so-called clans were organized to join all persons having the same surname on the basis that, going back far enough, they would have shared the same ancestor.

Northwest China

This corridor for trade with central Asia and the upper valley of the Yellow River was separated from the rest of China by mountains to the east and south. Composed of Gansu,

Shaanxi, and western Shanxi provinces, this region, semiarid in nature, was often the site of severe drought. With few navigable waterways, transport was difficult and costs were high.

Population density was one of the lowest in China. Even so, diverse ethnicities and religions, let alone dialects, gave rise to considerable internal disunity. Han Chinese, Hui (Han Chinese Muslims), Mongols, and Tibetans intermingled, often with notable antagonisms. The Han Chinese population was heaviest in cities and river valleys. Muslims comprised over a third of the population in Gansu province by the end of the nineteenth century. Many Muslims had outwardly assimilated into Han Chinese culture, choosing Chinese names and adopting speech and habits of dress, but they retained their own separate neighborhoods, their religious leaders, and their restrictions on eating pork.

On the whole, life was hard here. In traditional times, Han Chinese and Muslims often lived in caves carved into the loess hillsides while Tibetans and Mongols made their homes in tents. In this region, lineages were not strong. As a result in part of the economic situation, this region did not produce large numbers of scholars.

Middle Yangzi

In contrast to the aridity of Northwest China, the Middle Yangzi was focused on water. The region, including parts of no fewer than nine provinces, got its identity from the over five hundred miles of Yangzi River that flowed through it and from the Yangzi's four major tributaries. Those tributaries and the mountains that border them form clearly defined subregions; yet all were oriented to the Yangzi. Water was a focus in three ways. Its abundance meant irrigated paddies in contrast to the dryland farming of north and northwest China. On the downside, it presents an almost continual problem with flooding; severe floods in 1990 and 1998, for example, left many dead and many more homeless. Finally, the Yangzi, cutting west to east across central China, and its tributaries, running north and south, were important arteries of trade. The political, social, and cultural life of many cities along the rivers was dominated by merchant groups involved in a flourishing trade. In late imperial times because of its commercial importance the role of the government was perhaps less than in other regions.

The region did experience some ethnic conflict. Before the Han Chinese migrated into the area in the third and fourth centuries, it was inhabited by non-Chinese who the immigrants in many cases pushed up into the mountains during their settlement of the area. As in the relationship between settlers and native Americans in the American West, the relations between the Han and non-Han remained uneasy with sporadic outbreaks of violence. The situation was exacerbated by the presence of large numbers of Hakkas in the south who often feuded both with Han and non-Han.

Upper Yangzi

Known as "heaven's storehouse" because of its favorable climate and rich productive farmland, the Chengdu basin was the core of the Upper Yangzi region. In this area which included the eastern two thirds of Sichuan province and contiguous mountains in Gansu to the north and Yunnan and Guizhou to the south, the chief products were agricultural—rice, wheat, potatoes, maize, and timber products. Yet this region on the periphery of the Chinese state was tied to other more central regions through trade on the Yangzi. The river indeed served as the lifeline to the province: the only natural entrances into this mountain-contained region were the Yangzi River gorges and a pass to the northeast.

The population was diverse—a large Muslim population, Tibetan tribes living in the west, sojourning merchants, and other ethnic groups. Yet hostilities were not such an important feature as in other regions; and the cities were noteworthy for the lack of animosities among their ethnic groups. Following massive depopulation in bloody early seventeenth century unrest and rebellion, this region was one of the least urbanized in late imperial times.

Southwest China

Composed mostly of the provinces of Yunnan and Guizhou with a small portion of southern Sichuan, Southwest China was peripheral in many ways. Its rivers were mostly not navigable, making travel and transportation difficult and expensive. Population settlements were small. The region was not well incorporated into the Chinese cultural mainstream; indeed there was more fundamental cultural diversity than in any other region. Tribal peoples made up roughly half of the population in late traditional times; they were joined by a host of various ethnic and subethnic groups.

The most important non-agricultural occupation was mining deposits of copper, silver, zinc, lead, cinnabar, coal, and iron. This was a lure to Han Chinese from outside the region. The Han Chinese population was dominated by male sojourners, coming into the area to make their fortune. For the indigenous population, these Han Chinese immigrants were a destabilizing force in the local economy and society; conflicts between these migrants and the locals were prevalent and frequently bloody.

Taiwan

The island of Taiwan, ninety miles from the mainland, was the eastern frontier of the Southeast Coast. Chinese, mainly from Fujian province across the strait, had begun to migrate to the island in the sixteenth century; many of the first immigrants were sojourning males. The island was not brought firmly under Chinese government control until 1683, the year when the Manchus defeated the Ming loyalists who had fled to the island in the 1640s. In that year, there were approximately 100,000 aboriginal peoples of Malayo-Polynesian stock from over a dozen ethnolinguistic groups who were mostly hunters but who also cultivated rice and millet; there were also approximately the same number of Han Chinese immigrants. By the end of the eighteenth century, the numbers of Han Chinese had reached about a million, including large numbers of Hakkas. As in the Middle Yangzi area, the Han Chinese settlement pushed the aboriginal groups into the mountains of the central and eastern parts of the island where they remain to the present. The presence of Han Chinese, Hakkas, and aborigines created the same combustible ethnic mix apparent in such other regions as the Southeast Coast and Lingnan.

As more settlers came from the mainland, they transformed the wild grasslands of the western part of the island into the richly productive coastal plain that came to resemble the rice paddy terrain of southeast China. Taiwan would remain under firm control of the Manchu government until it was taken as a war trophy by Japan in 1895.

Manchuria

Like the frontier of Taiwan in late imperial China, Manchuria, the homeland of the Manchus, remained largely frontier until the twentieth century. A region of rich soil and important natural resources—mineral, timber, and water—Manchuria was off-limits to Chinese immigration from 1668 onward. The Manchus, in their concern over their identity (as we will see in the next chapter), restricted Chinese migration in order to preserve the area as their haven.

The fertile core of the region in the south was the valley of the Liao River which entered the Bo Hai west of the Liaodong peninsula, less than seventy miles from the Shandong peninsula. In other words, this area was easily accessible to Chinese merchants, who, despite the closed-off political status of the region, were able to link it commercially to other regions of China. Its bordering on Korea made it strategically important to the Chinese regime, as was the more remote northern area of Heilongjiang that bordered on Russia.

Xinjiang

Yet another frontier area was China's far west, known in traditional times as the "Western regions."[15] Won militarily by troops under the Qianlong emperor in 1759, the area was three times the size of France. The immense area was composed of two large basins that essentially were deserts; they were separated by the rugged Tianshan mountains. The northern basin was called Zungharia; successful farming occurred only in mountain river valleys and at the base of the mountains. The southern basin, called most often the Tarim Basin, and sometimes, Chinese Turkestan, has been called "one of the most forbidding places on earth" (see Map 20-1). The Taklamakan Desert at the basin's center has an average annual rainfall of less than two-thirds of an inch and towering sand dunes ranging from over three hundred to one thousand feet. Yet where irrigation is possible near the mountains, agriculture has been productive. Two main passes through the Tianshan Mountains link the two basins. The most agriculturally productive part of Xinjiang was the so-called Eastern March between Urumchi, which became the region's main economic center, and Suzhou (today, named Jiuquan). There sometimes using underground aqueducts for irrigation, farmers produce cotton, melons, grapes, and other fruit.

The mostly Muslim population of Xinjiang was predominantly Turkic-speaking Uighurs. Although Xinjiang had held most of the famous oases along the old silk route, it was not until after the 1759 conquest that Chinese merchants became actively involved in what developed as thriving commercial activity. In 1884 the Qing made Xinjiang a province, after which Chinese immigration increased substantially. At the establishment of the People's Republic in 1949, only 5.5 percent of Xinjiang's population were Han Chinese;

by 1970 that number had skyrocketed to 40 percent. During that time period, the Tarim Basin became the main site for China's nuclear testing.

The cultural and regional stage has now been set for historical action.

Notes

[1] Nicholas D. Kristof and Sheryl Wudunn, *China Wakes* (New York: Random House, 1994), p. 286.

[2] William James Hail, *Tseng Guo-fan and the Taiping Rebellion* (New York: Paragon Book Reprint Corp., 1964), pp. 417–419.

[3] Ibid., pp. 164, 209, and 335–336.

[4] Ibid., pp. 146, 200, and 344.

[5] Fox Butterfield, *China: Alive in a Bitter Sea* (New York: Times Books, 1982), pp. 74–75, cited in Ambrose Yeo-chi King, "Kuan-hsi and Network Building," *Daedalus,* 120, 2 (Spring 1991), p.64.

[6] R. Keith Schoppa, *Xiang Lake—Nine Centuries of Chinese Life* (New Haven: Yale University Press, 1989), pp. 46–54.

[7] Frederic Wakeman, Jr., *The Fall of Imperial China* (New York: Free Press, 1975), p. 173.

[8] Fei Xiaotong, *From the Soil: The Foundations of Chinese Society* (Berkeley: University of California, 1992), pp. 78–79.

[9] Ibid., p, 79.

[10] Robert E. Gamer, Ed., *Understanding Contemporary China* (Boulder: Lynne Rienner Publishers, 1999), p. 231.

[11] Jonathan M. Lipman, "Hyphenated Chinese: Sino-Muslim Identity in Modern China," in Gail Hershatter, Emily Honig, Jonathon Lipman, and Randall Stross (Eds.), *Remapping China* (Stanford: Stanford University Press, 1996), p. 99.

[12] Benjamin Elman, *From Philosophy to Philology: Intellectual and Social Aspects of Change in Late Imperial China* (Cambridge: Harvard University Press, 1984), pp. 91 and 233.

[13] Fei, p. 41.

[14] Susan Naquin and Evelyn S. Rawski, *Chinese Society in the Eighteenth Century* (New Haven: Yale University Press, 1987), p. 149.

[15] This description is based upon James A. Millward, *Beyond the Pass* (Stanford: Stanford University Press, 1998), pp. 20–25.

2

Chinese and Manchus

When the outsiders from the northeast, the Manchus, took power in China in 1644 and established the Qing dynasty, it was not the first time that non-Chinese had donned imperial yellow court clothing. From China's earliest history there had been a continual pas de deux between Chinese within the wall and those outside, the peoples of the steppe—Mongols, Turks, Manchus. In certain periods the steppe-dwellers pursued a more active China policy, initiating raids and outright invasions. Seven centuries before the Manchu conquest a more active pattern of outsider involvement had begun with various ethnic groups from outside the wall taking parts of north China; then in the late thirteenth century all of China fell into the hands of the great Mongol conquerors Genghis and Kublai Khan. While the Mongols controlled China under the Yuan dynasty for less than a century (until 1368), throughout the Han Chinese Ming dynasty (1368–1644), Mongols from the north and west sporadically continued to threaten the Chinese political order.

In the late sixteenth and early seventeenth centuries, two exceptionally able leaders emerged among Manchu clans, groups that had a strong sense of descent from a mutual ancestor and were the main social units in Manchu society. Nurhaci (1559–1626) and his son Hong Taiji (1592–1643) put in place the organizational framework that led to the Manchu seizure of China. Most crucial early on was the establishment of the banner system. Specifically they assigned Manchu warriors to various "banners," identified by particular colored flags that would serve as units for military and civilian bureaucratic mobilization. Over time the banner organization weakened the clans and funneled loyalty away from clans and to Nurhaci and son. As Mongols and even Chinese along the border defected to the Manchus, the Manchu leadership formed both Mongol and Chinese banners as well. By the early seventeenth century, the Manchus displayed clear dynastic pretensions by copying the broad structural outlines of the Ming governmental administration.

This growing and organized force from outside the wall emerged at the same time as a Ming dynasty tailspin with all the ills traditionally associated with a dying regime: governmental inertia and corruption, the exercise of arrogant power by imperial eunuchs (the keepers of the harem), the depletion of the national treasury, factionalism, and rebellion. When one of the rebels succeeded in taking the capital in the spring of 1644 and the last Ming emperor dramatically hanged himself on a hill immediately north of the Forbidden City, it seemed as though another Han Chinese dynasty would emerge. But then the Manchus swept into China through the pass between the Great Wall and the sea, sweeping before them the would-be-emperor rebel and seizing the Dragon Throne for themselves. Ming resistance lasted almost four more decades, but by 1683, the minority Manchus had become masters of the majority Han Chinese and the realm's various ethnic minorities.

PRESERVING A MANCHU IDENTITY

Outnumbered about one hundred to one, the Manchus had won the kingdom, as the cliché put it, "on horseback." But it took much more to establish successful long-term rule. At the heart of such rule was the tricky and precarious balancing act of adopting sufficient aspects of Chinese cultural identity to be acceptable to the Chinese majority while maintaining enough distance to preserve their own cultural identity.

At the heart of a person's identity are the cultural values that he or she lives by. The Manchus were clan-based peoples who stressed martial values based on skills of horsemanship and archery—a stark contrast to Chinese society that stressed civilian values based on skills of the writing brush. The first Manchu leaders were "gripped with this anxiety [:] ... that hereafter our sons and grandsons will forget the old regulations and do away with horseback riding and archery in order to copy Han customs."[1] From the beginning, the fear of loss of native identity was strong. But if the fear was strong so, too, was the knowledge that they could not rule China without the assistance of the Chinese.

Probably the greatest emperor of the dynasty and perhaps in all of imperial China, the Kangxi emperor (1654–1722), Nurhaci's great-grandson, grappled with the dilemma. He was nothing short of a role model in holding to that old Manchu identity by preserving the martial vigor and skills that had made possible the conquest. He was in charge of the final military campaigns that had ended Ming resistance in 1683. He personally led military campaigns against Mongol and Tibetan forces. He insisted that the military ethos be preserved symbolically through hunting expeditions he led north of the Wall throughout his reign. But he also reached out to the Chinese, many of whom were embittered by Manchu brutality during the conquest. When some scholars boycotted the regular civil service exams, he offered them a special examination as an enticement to join the Manchu regime. He made it a point of showing his concern for the welfare of the people by visiting areas where flooding had occurred and where dikes were being repaired. At one point in his reign, in an edict, he declared that he saw no difference between Manchus and Chinese and their ability to serve in the state. Identity was a paramount concern for this emperor and his grandson, the Qianlong emperor (1711–1799), as well.

One way to uphold martial identity was to maintain the vehicles of Manchu military success, the banner forces. After the Manchus defeated Ming forces, they preserved these former enemies as the Army of the Green Standard, a constabulary force assigned to garrisons around the country. Though the 500,000 Green Standard forces were at least double the size of the Manchu banners, the banner forces were positioned more strategically: as examples, whereas in the eighteenth century there was only one banner garrison in the commerce-focused Middle Yangzi region, there were many garrisons in the newly-conquered central Asian frontier territory of Xinjiang—where numbers of bannermen were clearly a major factor in China's political control. While civil officials controlled the Green Standard, military governors controlled the banners.

Yet another strategy in maintaining martial values was to set aside Manchuria as a permanent Manchu homeland. That had been the military base from which the conquest took shape; the territory itself was thus inextricably linked with the source of the Manchus military expertise. Further, by making Manchuria off-limits to the Han Chinese, the leadership may have been saying that even if life among the Han Chinese within the Wall might dull Manchu military ardor, Manchuria would always remain as a place where those military values could be revived and rejuvenated.

Once in control in China, the Manchus also continued to maintain and promote their native shamanism, a policy that clearly differentiated them from Chinese ways and the Chinese themselves. A shaman was a person who was thought to have had a spiritual death and rebirth and could thus easily move to the world of the supernatural where he or she could influence events. Using spirit poles to symbolically connect heaven and earth in order to communicate with clan spirits, Manchus conducted shamanic state rituals, processions, and dances in the Forbidden City into the twentieth century.

In addition, the Manchus patronized Yellow sect Lamaism in Mongolia and Tibet. In Mongolia, patronage of Lamaism became a method of controlling Mongol tribes who had converted to that religion in the seventeenth century. Lamaism was overseen by the Dalai Lama in Lhasa, Tibet; thus Manchu interests in exercising control in Mongolia through this religion naturally fostered its interests in exercising control in Tibet from the 1720s onward. From the late seventeenth to the late eighteenth century, the Manchu regime constructed or restored thirty-two Tibetan temples in Beijing and eleven in the Manchu summer capital of Chengde north of the Great Wall.

The Manchu regime tried to prevent close association between Chinese and themselves by forbidding intermarriage and outlawing business partnerships. They stepped into the realm of customs so as to differentiate Manchus from Chinese physically. For example, they forbade Manchu women to bind their feet, as most proper Chinese women did. The custom had begun centuries earlier when fascination with a ballerina of the court led many young women to desire tiny feet, no more than three inches long, known as "golden lilies." Girls, roughly five to eight years old, had their feet tightly bound with cloth so that the arches were broken and pushed upward. "As the arch [was] gradually broken, the flat of [a girl's] heels and the balls of [her] foot . . . [were] gradually moved from horizontal to perpendicular, facing each other, so that an object like a silver dollar [could] be inserted in the narrow space between them. The result [was] that [she would] never run again and [could] walk [only] on the base of [her] heels . . . with [great] difficulty."[2] This cruel and curious custom supposedly lent sophistication to its victim, making good marriage

Manchu bannermen
Source: Wellcome Library, London

matches more likely. The patriarchal family system defined by male domination perpetuated the custom, though, as has been pointed out, "without the cooperation of the women concerned, footbinding could not have been perpetuated for a millennium." It has been called "a central event in the domestic women's culture," "an exclusively female affair."[3] Be that as it may, it hobbled women, keeping them from gallivanting. "Golden lilies" even became used in sex play. Though not all Chinese women in all places bound their feet (Hakka women, for example, did not), footbinding continued into the twentieth century. The Manchus chose to differentiate their women from Chinese women in this obviously significant physical way.

The Manchu desire to keep themselves distinct from the Chinese co-existed with their need to assert that they were China's rulers. As a physical expression of that overlordship, they ordered that all Chinese men adopt the Manchu hairstyle: shave the front parts of their heads, let the hair in the back grow longer, and then plait that hair into queues or pigtails. In essence that hairstyle physically marked the Chinese as subjects of the Outsider Manchus. The order was particularly scandalous to Chinese who had been used to growing their hair long; it has been suggested that many saw the new hairstyle as something like "tonsorial castration," a mutilation of their physical wholeness and their manhood.[4]

In the arena of official ruling, the Manchus gave themselves preferential treatment in

Woman with bound feet

the examination system, in official appointments, and in the justice system. Although their small numbers relative to the Chinese population meant that they had to work with the Chinese, appointment to governmental positions went more or less equally to Manchus and Chinese. If there was balance in that way, the fact remained that the Manchus were careful to check Chinese power. While Chinese might be appointed to serve as governors of provinces, governors-general, who oversaw two or three provinces, tended to be Manchu. The trump card, of course, was that the ultimate arbiter and decision-maker—the emperor—was always Manchu.

BUYING INTO CHINESE CULTURE

The Civil Service Examination

The Qing, for all their Manchu identity, accepted the heart of the Chinese political, social, and cultural system—the imperial civil service examination and the Confucianism on which it was based. Developed over many centuries, this system aimed to bring into government positions the best and the brightest, men who brought to their ruling tasks both wisdom and virtue. China's government personnel system was then not generally based on birth but rather on merit measured through an examination system based on what today we would call the humanities—Confucian philosophical texts and commentaries, history, and literature. Thus, it produced generalists, not specialists. While at times of economic crisis men might enter the civil service "irregularly" by purchasing degrees or positions, in normal times, the vast majority of men who served took the examination. Thus, most of China's officials were trained in the same body of principles, rules, and norms which, while it could never produce uniformity of thought, did provide a common base of learning with clearly understood standards for ruling. Therefore, the examination did more than simply test; the study required to pass the examination shaped ways of thinking about dealing with problems of governance.

Confucianism, the foundation of the Han Chinese cultural system, was based on the teachings of Confucius (Kong fuzi [551–479 B.C.E.]) and key followers, especially for late imperial times, Mencius (Mengzi [372–289 B.C.E.]). Confucius and Mencius both taught at a time when Chinese society and politics were in disarray. Their prescription for a more harmonious, smoothly functioning polity was to get wise and virtuous men who could transform politics and society and restore the situation to what it had been in the golden age of a mythic past. These best and brightest would be motivated to rule the state benevolently through high principles, a profound sense of morality, and a thoroughgoing empathy with the people. In Confucius's eyes, education was the key to developing sages who could so rule the state.

If a Chinese family noted a son who had strong intellectual abilities, they might make efforts to hire a tutor who could oversee his preparations for taking the examination. This decision certainly depended in part on the family's economic situation. Poor farm families, for example, would have had less cash available for such an undertaking and would, in the first place, not have been likely to want to lose an extra farmhand to the long study necessary to be successful. In areas where strong lineages dominated, lineage estates might provide precocious young men, even of poorer families, the money to study for the examination.

The exams themselves took several days to complete. Candidates were ushered into tiny cubicles placed in long rows in the examination area. There they wrote essays and poetry in answer to various questions. In different periods, the examination's substance differed; for example, questions relating to practical administration were dropped in 1757, but they were added again by the late nineteenth century. The form of the answer was important: Essays had to follow a particular format of presentation; the essay's length was prescribed. Poetry was stressed: A provincial director-of-studies said that inferior ability in poetry carried with it the "smell of village mediocrity."[5] Calligraphy was also important because it was seen as indicative of a person's morality. Throughout the centuries questions were raised about how these kinds of examination practices could produce men who were capable of handling the messy problems of day-to-day governance. But, despite these concerns, the examination remained central into the twentieth century.

Success in major examinations, offered at three levels, brought degrees. Preceded by a preliminary exam at the county seat, the lowest-level exam was offered twice every three years in prefectural capitals. Successful candidates received the *shengyuan* (government student) degree; studies have shown that the vast majority received their degrees between the ages of twenty and thirty. Pass rates for all examinations were roughly 1 to 2 percent. Receiving the *shengyuan* degree did not entitle the degreeholder to an official position; however, it brought him and his family considerable status and marked him as an elite member of his resident community. The *juren* (provincial graduate) degree was bestowed on those passing the second-level examination at the provincial capital, an exam offered once every three years; the average age for this accomplishment in the nineteenth century was about thirty-one. This degree provided an entryway into officialdom, not to the highest positions but to magistracies of counties and prefects of prefectures, and sometimes to ad hoc appointments. The highest degree, the *jinshi* (metropolitan graduate), came from success at the imperial capital; here the examination itself was followed by an examination at the palace, administered by the emperor himself. In the nineteenth century the average age for the attaining of this degree was thirty-three to thirty-six. It opened all official career doors immediately—from governorships to important imperial commissionerships to membership in the Hanlin Academy, the government's policy-making think-tank.

Attaining any of these degrees brought legal, economic, and social privileges. A degreeholder could only be judged in a legal case by someone who was educationally superior. They were legally protected from insults by commoners. They were protected against corporal punishments. They were freed from official labor service that was required of all commoners. All degreeholders wore buttons on their hats that were based upon particular degree held—the *jinshi* and *juren,* plain gold; the *shengyuan,* plain silver. Degreeholders wore black gowns bordered in blue. They alone were allowed to wear furs, brocades, and fancy embroidery. Despite the personal privileges and the status that attaining a degree brought generally to the successful candidate's family, he could not pass the honor on to his son; if his son wanted such status, he had to pass the examination himself. At any time in the nineteenth century there were something over 800,000 *shengyuan* degreeholders (roughly 1.8 to 2.4 percent of the population), 18,000 to 19,000 *juren,* and about 2,500 *jinshi* degreeholders.

Rituals, Religion, and Values

The adoption of Ming state rituals was a crucial way for Manchu rulers to assert their legitimacy by linking themselves to the former legitimate imperial state. These included sacrifices to gods and the imperial ancestors; political rituals, like receiving envoys and reviewing troops; and imperial household and lineage rituals, focusing on marriage and death. Performing such rituals symbolically spoke the Confucian "idiom," generally underscoring the regime's support for the Confucian ethical and political values and practice that connected it to the Han Chinese past.[6]

Whether Confucianism was a religion or a philosophy depends on one's definition. Though Confucius himself had refused to get involved in questions about an afterlife ("we do not yet know about life; how can we talk about what happens after death"), his teachings on the continuity of the family over generations and of ancestors raised issues often thought of as religious. Central here was ancestor reverence. The Qing erected both their ancestral tablets for state sacrifices in Beijing and their familial tablets within the Forbidden City. The practice especially pointed to the value of filial piety or filiality to which Qing emperors explicitly committed themselves. The Kangxi emperor (1662–1722) noted, "We rule the empire with filial piety. That is why I want to exemplify this principle for my ministers and my people—and for my own descendants."[7] Such a central Confucian conception seemed to resonate in the actions of the most important Qing emperors—from the care of the Kangxi emperor for his beloved grandmother to the Yongzheng emperor's (r. 1722–1736) filiality to his father to the Qianlong emperor's (r. 1736–1795) ostentatious show of filial piety for his mother which included building in the capital replicas of her much-beloved southern China streets that she could putter around in.

The patronage of Lamaist Buddhism not only was a way of controlling ethnic subjects but also linked the regime with Buddhism, borrowed by the Chinese from India over fifteen hundred years earlier. Though the power of Buddhism in Chinese society had greatly diminished after the ninth century, it was still a part of many Chinese lives. The construction of Buddhist temples by the regime in both Beijing and Chengde was a visible linkage of the Manchu outsiders with an important Chinese religious tradition.

DEALING WITH THE OTHER

Since they themselves were "Other" to the Chinese, the Qing regime in its policies toward China's "others" seemed to be acutely aware of differences in those "others." It developed two starkly different approaches to dealing with those outside the Chinese cultural realm. Even before it established its rule in China, in 1638 it organized the Court of Colonial Affairs (*Lifanyuan*) to handle its relations with the Mongols. This Court became the organ in charge of relations with the peoples north and west of "China within the wall"—Mongols, Uighurs, Tibetans, and Russians. Triumphant mid-eighteenth century military campaigns extended Chinese control into the central Asian Tarim Basin, bringing control over Xinjiang in 1759 and six million square miles of grasslands, desert, and scattered oases into the empire. The Qing considered it a "strategic frontier zone" and did not allow Chinese colonization. Three interventions in Tibet from the 1720s to the 1750s made that state a Chinese protectorate. The Lifanyuan supervised the affairs of Lamaist organizations in the Qing efforts to control both the Mongols and the Tibetans through their patronage of Lamaism. Acculturation was not the name of this game. On the contrary, Qing policies toward the peoples of this region, as one historian suggests, brought economic, social, and cultural changes "that encouraged the growth of ethnic identities" among these peripheral peoples.[8] Doing so fit into the self-chosen identity of the Qing emperors, ethnic outsiders themselves. They were not simply the Chinese Sons of Heaven but emperors of an Asian multi-ethnic, multicultural empire.

Over the centuries the Chinese state had developed a different system of dealing with foreigners who did not come from the northern and western steppes; the Qing regime inherited it. Though the Chinese themselves had no name for its various procedures, Western scholars have called it the tributary system. In surveying the "barbarians" who ringed the country, Han Chinese elites saw China as The Civilized Country. Early in China's past, the

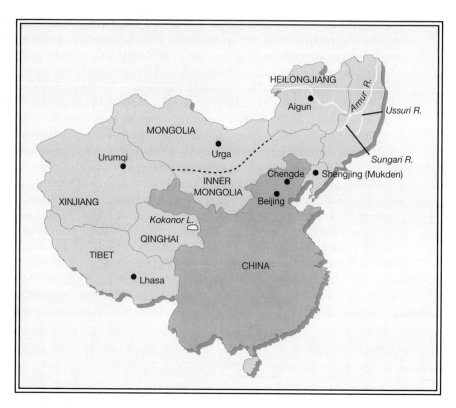

The Qing Empire, Early Nineteenth Century

country had been known as Everything Under Heaven—that is, everything that's worth anything. Another name often used was the Central Country—central specifically in terms of culture. The Chinese believed that their role was to train and educate the Others, not by physically forcing them to accept the Chinese way, but, as elder brothers to younger brothers, making it possible for them to participate in certain controlled ways in the blessings that Chinese believed their culture had to offer. The goal then was acculturation, at least to some degree. Like any sort of connections, the strength of China's ties to various countries and peoples varied in intensity. Relations with the kingdoms of Korea and Vietnam, located along Chinese borders, were strongest.

But for the present, as an example of the tributary system, let's take Japan, a close tributary state of China in the Ming dynasty (1368–1644). As with traditional ethnic minorities (and as with elder brothers treating younger brothers), a crucial goal throughout was control. The Board of Rites, not the Court of Colonial Affairs, managed this system, for at the core of the system was ritual. The Ming regime allowed Japan to send to China one tribute mission every three years. The mission came bringing tribute composed of native Japanese products, gems, animals—whatever the Japanese ruler deemed appropriate. The Chinese specified the port of entry, in this case Ningbo, south of Shanghai on the East China

Sea. The Japanese mission was met at Ningbo by a Chinese delegation that accompanied the Japanese to Beijing via the Grand Canal. Along the way the Japanese were repeatedly banqueted and showered with costly gifts of silks and jades. Once they arrived in the capital, they had to bide their time until the arrival of the most auspicious date when they would be ushered into the presence of the Chinese emperor.

At that meeting they would perform various rituals, the most famous being the kowtow (*ketou*) in which the foreigners were to prostrate themselves on the floor three times and with each prostration they were to knock their heads on the floor three times. Three prostrations, nine head-knockings. It was a ritual of extreme obeisance, one that at least theoretically every Chinese child performed before his parents each New Year's Day. Apart from the deep meaning of submission evident in the kowtow, the performance of this same ritual performed by children for their parents in a sense connected the foreigners, the Others, with the larger Chinese "family" and its culture. After the rituals, the foreign mission was allowed to remain in Beijing and trade for a period before being accompanied back to Ningbo and the trip home. For the Others, the episode offered the bestowal of expensive presents and the lucrative opportunity to trade, continual rounds of feasting and celebrations, and probably what was the experience of a lifetime. For the Chinese, it provided corroboration of their view of themselves as the superior, generous, paternalistic elder brother, offering the Other the opportunity, as the Chinese phrase went, "to come and be transformed [*laihua*]."

IDENTITY AND CHANGE: THE QIANLONG EMPEROR IN THE LATE EIGHTEENTH CENTURY

Historians frequently assert that traditional China reached the height of its power and wealth during the reign of the Qianlong emperor (1736–1795). Indeed, there is much to support that view. His successful military conquest of inner Asian frontiers more than doubled Chinese territory. With peace and prosperity the order of the day within China, South, Southeast, and East Asian states regularly sent tributary missions. Economic prosperity, prompted by efficient and effective government in the earlier reigns of the dynasty, flourished. The state treasury in the first year of the Qianlong emperor's reign had a surplus of twenty-four million taels of silver; fifty years later the surplus had been more than tripled. Probably nothing reveals the extraordinary fiscal situation better than the fact that the Qianlong emperor was able to cancel the collection of annual taxes four times. The increasingly significant availability of regional cash crops—cotton, tea, and tobacco—pointed to the expansion of trade between regions. Foreign trade also thrived: southeastern coastal provinces traded on a large scale with Southeast Asia and Taiwan; Europeans and Japanese merchants came to China for its much-valued silk, tea, and porcelain. New crops imported from the New World—sweet potatoes, maize, peanuts—permitted cultivation of previously untillable sandy or mountainous land.

Agricultural diversification and trade helped stimulate economic growth that brought many changes to Chinese society. That taxes were now usually paid in money rather than in kind (as in earlier dynasties) pointed to the increasing importance of money in the economy. The credit and transfer needs of long-distance interregional trade fueled the development of native banks and new fiscal institutions. The new prosperity brought marked social changes: elite status came to depend more and more on wealth; occupational differentiation gave rise to new opportunities; the number of markets increased, linking farmers in villages to towns and cities in new commercial relationships.[9]

One important social development in the Lower Yangzi region especially was the emergence of elite women writers. Studies have shown that already in the seventeenth century in the midst of commercialization and urbanization, "[t]hrough writing and reading, elite women developed new spheres of influence, expanding the domain of kinship and friendship beyond domestic space, mastering the tools of learning that had been the domain of men . . . "[10] In the eighteenth century, shifts in gender relations were underscored by the debates about the degree of learning that women in scholarly families should endeavor to attain. Through their writings, women sought "to assert and extend their authority in the family and to reach beyond the domestic realm to criticize the commercial sex markets of their time."[11] They also wrote to make connections to other women to share "what they valued, to celebrate what they admired, and to lament what they lost."[12] In the world of work in the economically prosperous years, the Qing state heralded household textile handicraft production in the domestic sphere controlled by the wife; yet the commercial trends of the time, especially the development of the urban artisan class, tended to undercut household fiscal power. Nevertheless, the emergence of elite women through their learning and by their writing cautions us about overly general conclusions about the completely bleak world inhabited by Chinese women.

Certainly the social development resulting from economic growth that had most impact on China as a whole was a monumental increase in population. Available data reveal that the population rose sharply from over 177 million in 1749 to over 301 million in 1790, an increase of 70 percent in little more than forty years.[13] What gave rise to such a soaring population is not completely clear, though food crops from the Western hemisphere and techniques like double-cropping helped support the increase. Both a declining mortality rate and rising birth rate may also have been factors during these years. Scholars have seen population growth as both a "reflection of—and a contributor to—prosperity."[14] It contributed to prosperity, for example, by providing more field workers to increase harvest yields and more immigrants to develop regions of previously untilled or underpopulated land.

Overall, the picture that emerges is of economic well-being and abundance. In the view of one eighteenth century writer: "Houses cluster together like fish-scales and people are as numerous as ants. Since local administration is simple, the district is often quiet. While everywhere on the fields mulberry, hemp, and various cereal crops are grown, the streams abound with carp and other fish."[15] The reality of environmental and historical differences in macroregions must cause us to keep in mind that this picture of China as a whole at the zenith of its traditional strength is generalized. Despite general state prosperity, many areas were not sites of plenty and wealth. One historian has noted that "one did not have to travel far from the commercialized cores to find abject poverty, unemployment, and disorder."[16] Our knowledge of the variety, diversity, and complexity of China's macroregions, cores, and peripheries must surely temper this view.

On the whole, the glories of China were sought for and emulated in the late eighteenth-century West. Chinese products—silk, cloisonné, porcelains, fans, tea, rhubarb—were not simply sought after, but many things Chinese became the European rage. They copied Chinese wallpaper, interior decor, and furniture; elite homeowners in Versailles and London created Chinese gardens with Chinese pavilions. European royalty and Enlightenment philosophers were excitedly enthusiastic about the perceived Chinese model of rule, "enlightened" or "benevolent" despotism.The musings of Benjamin Franklin today seem both naive and quite chilling in its implications: "Could we be so fortunate as to introduce the industry of the Chinese, their arts of living and improvements in husbandry, ... America might become in time as populous as China."[17] It is unfortunately likely, as an American historian suggested, that "literate Westerners knew more about China in the eighteenth century than they [did] in the twentieth."[18]

IDENTITY CRISIS

The Emperor's Roles

The issue that loomed larger and larger for the Qianlong emperor in the years after the Qing's last act of expansion, the seizure of Xinjiang in 1755, was a growing identity crisis. At base, who were the Manchus? Were they outsiders who in their capacity as the heads of a Chinese dynasty were in effect actually becoming acculturated Chinese? Or were they primarily rulers of a multi-ethnic empire in which the Chinese were only one part and because of which their identity as Manchus had to remain predominant?

In many ways, as we have seen, the Manchus bought into Chinese traditions, upholding the examination system, Confucianism, filial piety and ancestor reverence, and the body of family and state rituals. The Qianlong emperor himself performed rituals before ancestral tablets in the Forbidden City and in Manchuria at the reputed site where the Manchus originated. In addition, he took on the scholarly and artistic roles of the Chinese sage, serving as patron to Chinese scholars and artists. He collected about eight thousand paintings and calligraphy in an imperial collection, on a number of which—as indicative of his questionable lack of taste and judgment—he made notations on the painting itself. He added fifty-four inscriptions to one hand scroll and pressed his seal thirteen times on a single painting. His tastes, which leaned to the showy, theatrical, and monumental, had a great impact on the artistic trends of his day. He was also enormously productive himself, though quantity is no obvious indicator of quality. He wrote about forty-three thousand poems and, it is said, ninety-two books of prose. That he took the abilities of and devotion to the role of a Chinese scholar seriously is underscored by his daily schedule. Rising at 6:00 A.M., he spent the morning reading official reports and memorials, consulting with his advisors, and receiving and dispatching officials. Afternoons, however, were devoted to reading, painting, and writing poetry.

Had he, then, as has been said in some sources, become "more Chinese than the Chinese"? It is abundantly clear that he had not. In actions to reinvigorate the Manchu identity, Qianlong aimed his policies at the Manchu elites, the bannermen scattered around the realm in city-based garrisons, who had been the foundation of imperial power. The emperor saw

The Qianlong emperor
Source: Lang Shih-ning (Giuseppe Castiglione), Chinese, 1688–1768, Qing Dynasty, "Inauguration Portraits of Emperor Qianlong, The Empress, and the Eleven Imperial Consorts," 1736. Handscroll, ink and color on silk, 52.9 × 688.3 cm. The Cleveland Museum of Art. John L. Severance Fund, 1969.31.

that in those garrisons bannermen's livelihoods were in general economic decline, a situation that produced low morale. Because the situation was serious enough garrison commanders had begun to allow bannermen to live outside the garrison, purchase homes and businesses there, and participate in city life. For the emperor such a change opened the bannermen to a dangerous urban diversity that threatened the integrity of Manchu identity. One of the emperor's obsessions in the last two-thirds of his reign became to restore and protect Manchu traditions; he was in the words of one historian "bent on authentic Manchuness."[19] This meant an active revival of the Manchu language among bannermen, especially among the imperial Aisin Gioro clan; it involved establishing standard tests for military skills; and it included rejuvenating the spiritual and cultural roles of the clans. For all bannermen, the government promoted education that stressed the reading and writing of Manchu, astronomy, mathematics, riding, and shooting.

In addition to his concern with the bannermen, the Qianlong emperor chose to uphold the Manchu character of the imperial household and clans. Whereas his grandfather, the Kangxi emperor, had participated in autumn hunts north of the Great Wall, his father, the Yongzheng emperor, had never done so. The Qianlong emperor restored the practice, developing the hunting "preserve to its fullest extent."[20] He insisted on sponsoring archery contests for both banner and Green Standard troops and boasted about his ability to kill deer with one shot. He directed the publication of Manchu genealogies, the writing of a history of the eight banners, and laying out in detail myths about the origins of the imperial Aisin Gioro clan. Fearful that shamanism was disappearing and desiring to preserve this traditional Manchu religion, he ordered its being written down and disseminated among the Manchus.

The Qianlong emperor also asserted his Manchu-ness as a ruler of a multi-ethnic empire by continuing the early-dynasty championing of Tibetan Buddhism. He continued the construction of Tibetan Buddhist temples in Beijing and in Chengde, site of the summer palace. He sponsored the translation of Buddhist sutras, which he then distributed to temples and monasteries. He had a Buddhist chapel built in the Forbidden City and reportedly practiced meditations every day. He had himself painted by court painters not only as a great warrior and a sage, but significantly as the Buddha and as a Buddhist monk. At the summer palace, he built a replica of the Potala, the Dalai Lama's residence at Lhasa. Most persuasive of his commitment to Buddhism was the tomb that he designed for himself. On the ceiling of the crypt directly over where his coffin was laid was a symbol of the *cakravartin,* "the wheel-turning king"—"an earthly ruler who by his conquests in the name of the Buddha would move the world toward the next stage in universal salvation."[21] In addition, he had Sanskrit prayers for the wheel-turning king carved in the tomb walls.

Clearly in his religious efforts he was trying to impress the non-Han Chinese in the empire and to assert his multi-cultural moral legitimacy. His multi-lingualism was also part of this effort. He began to learn Mongolian in 1743, Uighur in 1760, Tibetan in 1776. In his description of his language ability, he continued, "In 1780, because the Panchen lama [the chief spiritual adviser of the Dalai Lama] was coming to visit, I also studied Tangut. Thus, every year when the [emissaries] of Mongols, Uighurs, and Tibetans came to the capital for audience, I used their own language and did not rely on an interpreter. . . ."[22]

Literary Inquisition

The question of Manchu-ness and Chinese-ness became most strained and dangerous when posed in the context of the Manchu conquest. In some areas of China and some sectors of Chinese society, bitterness about the conquest and the violence with which it was carried out did not lie too far beneath the surface. The Manchus were alert from the beginning about any writings that hinted at resistance or insurrection; and there were occasional cases that emerged.

One that served as a harbinger of sorts for a spectacular literary inquisition from 1772 to 1782 and that underscores the identity obsession that the Qianlong emperor developed was the case of one Zeng Jing. During the reign of the Qianlong emperor's father, Zeng had read the anti-Manchu writings and rantings of a Han Chinese scholar named Lu who had died in the 1680s. Zeng had been so agitated by what he read that he contacted a general in the area to try to get him to launch a rebellion against the government. The general promptly turned Zeng in, and in 1730 the case reached the Yongzheng emperor. The emperor's response was an exhibition of the benevolence of the Confucian sovereign: he ascribed Zeng's actions to the gullibility and naiveté of youth, taken in by Lu's abusive and overdrawn rhetoric. Zeng's interrogation was printed and published along with his recantation and an essay by court scholars on Lu's errors. Zeng was released and, as a mark of the emperor's mercy, was even given a minor local position. In his response, the emperor had suggested that Lu's original attack on the Manchus was misplaced because the Manchus had been transformed by their long-term exposure to the civilizing force of Confucianism.

Such a position had apparently rankled the soon-to-be Qianlong emperor. As one historian put his likely thoughts on the subject, "[W]as it really necessary that the emperors of the great Qing empire continue to humble themselves before the image of Confucius, still placidly denying the culture of their ancestors in order to curry favor with those whom they had conquered?"[23] On taking the throne, the Qianlong emperor reopened the Zeng case, ordering the destruction of the published record of the interrogation and recantation. Zeng was retried, found guilty of sedition, and sentenced to death by slicing. The case revealed that the Qianlong emperor was determined, as soon as he took the throne, both to stifle anti-Manchu expressions and to reassert the Manchu-ness of the regime.

In 1772 the emperor ordered the collection of all existing books and manuscripts, whether held in libraries or owned privately. The goal was to bring them to the capital, review them, and recopy the most outstanding in new editions in order to insure the preservation of important, valuable, and, in some cases, rare literary and historical treasures. The collection, known as the *Four Treasuries,* because it was grouped in four sections—classics, history, philosophy, and miscellaneous literary works—was immense. Fully 3,593 works were recopied, filling 36,000 manuscript volumes; in addition the *Four Treasuries* included an annotated catalogue of 10,680 extant titles. In initiating this vast undertaking, the emperor was clearly giving evidence of his Chinese persona: here, the opening lines of his edict. "[In our rule] We have always been mindful of precedent, revered the writings of the past, relied on the brush to govern and ruled in accordance with principle. We have been diligent from day to day in our study."[24]

The huge project was facilitated by intellectual trends in the late eighteenth century when a philosophical movement called Han learning or "evidential research" (*kaozheng*) was the rage. Beginning in the seventeenth century this movement emphasized getting at the truth through analyzing old texts and, if need be, revising them on the basis of skills that scholars gained from such fields as epigraphy, philology, historical investigation, and textual criticism. The goal was to abandon speculation and to search for the truth in actual facts (*shishi qiushi*), in effect to reestablish classical learning on a firmer foundation. In the *Four Treasuries* project, *kaozheng* scholars played the leading role. Because of their interests, many such scholars in the Lower Yangzi macroregion were tied into networks of bookstores and book sellers, a fact that eased collection of books. Many books for the project, for example, came from Hangzhou libraries. But, more important, they controlled the editorial process in combing through the texts and therefore in shaping the project's outcome.

Although not abundantly clear from the beginning, the project became a full-blown campaign of censorship or, as it has been called, a literary inquisition. In this regard, the Qianlong emperor was acting in his Manchu persona. A little more than a year after inaugurating the project, the emperor noted that some provincial governors had not been sending many books to the capital and mused about whether it might be because they were of a "rebellious or seditious nature."[25] This speculation is indicative of the emperor's Manchu-defensive assumptions. By late 1774, these assumptions were declared forcefully: the fact that not any book thus far collected had any hint of sedition suggested to him that books were being hidden; they had to be found. From 1776 on, more and more time of the men involved in the project was spent examining books closely for an indication of anti-Manchu thoughts or language; the censorship campaign seemed to develop its own momentum. From 1780 until 1782, the central government took firmer control of the effort, establishing centralized censorship boards and issuing lists of banned books and criteria for determining sedition. Up to twenty-four hundred works were destroyed in this literary inquisition; and there were an estimated four hundred to five hundred that were edited following official decree. This movement reflects the almost schizophrenic government attitude toward Chinese and Manchu identities, as it also likely reflects growing factionalism at the court between Chinese and Manchu factions. It clearly highlights the late eighteenth century identity crisis epitomized in the policies of the Qianlong emperor.

EMERGING PROBLEMS

For subsequent Chinese the literary inquisition left a bitter taste of Manchu autocracy, certainly a downer of an experience amid what many have perceived as traditional China's most glorious period. There were, however, other political, economic, and social indicators that pointed to a host of emerging problems, some fraught with danger as China headed unawares into confrontation with the West.

Although the expansive military campaigns in central Asia had ended, the country was faced by a seemingly increasing series of social explosions. A 1774 religion-inspired rebellion in Shandong province was followed in the 1780s by a secret society-based uprising in Taiwan, by two Muslim revolts in Gansu province, and by rebellions by aboriginal Miao tribesmen in southwest China. The military's efforts to douse the flames of rebellion began to erode the full treasury. The strongest test for the Chinese military was the White Lotus Rebellion (1796–1804), a religious-based movement to establish a utopia on earth, which raked across north central China. It took eight long years for the Chinese military to put this threat down. Not only did the state reportedly spend one hundred million taels (or 30 percent more than the government's annual revenue) in suppressing this rebellion, but, perhaps even more serious, the Chinese military was tentative and ineffective.[26] Corruption and poor morale had already substantially weakened the banner forces by the mid-eighteenth century. The Green Standard forces, though battling the same social problems, seem to have maintained somewhat better fighting ability. Nevertheless, an undisciplined and generally incompetent military coupled with a weakening economy did not bode well.

The population surge itself, which we have earlier seen as a marker of the general prosperity, was ironically also the greatest long-term danger. The population increase far exceeded what could be supported by the newly-cultivated crops from the western hemisphere. Estimates suggest that the population tripled from about 1685 to 1780, but during that time the amount of cultivated land only doubled. The problem of too many people and not enough land was made worse by Chinese inheritance customs. The Chinese practiced a partible inheritance system where land was divided equally among all the sons. Landholdings in China tended to be tiny to begin with; in the North China macroregion, for example, in the late eighteenth century the average farm was only 2.5 acres. Given that figure and a hypothetical farmer on the North China plain with three sons, each son would inherit only .83 acres of land. With the huge population increase, land per capita was shrinking dangerously; when coupled with partible inheritance, the odds of farmers who were once economically viable falling into bankruptcy and poverty escalated sharply.

Indeed, regions of the country were differentially affected by the population increase, since demographic growth occurred at different rates. It is also likely that economic problems were more serious in the peripheries, which had far fewer human and natural resources, than in the cores. But the demographic situation affected to greater or lesser extent the whole country, not only with economic but political implications. The larger population put greater strain on an already fiscally-weakened government to provide various services for the people. Two crucial services were public works and the distribution of charitable grain relief at times of poor harvest or famine. In the last years of the Qianlong emperor's reign, public works were not being maintained as they should have been; sections of the Grand Canal, for example, were silted up. Floods were in the offing. More serious, charitable relief granaries were often empty.

The political implications were perhaps even more crucial than the short-term economic effects. In ascending the throne, the Chinese emperor was said to have received the Mandate of Heaven. As part of the mandate to rule as the "Son of Heaven," he had to rule benevolently and carry out his proper ritual functions. Natural disasters—droughts, floods, earthquakes, insect plagues—were interpreted as signs that the emperor was not performing his functions properly and that his mandate was in jeopardy. Emperors who were believed to be inattentive to the people's needs were in danger of losing the Mandate, that is, being overthrown. When poor harvests in an area created hunger and even starvation, empty relief granaries were visible and potent evidence that the emperor was not seeing after the needs of those over whom Heaven had given him charge.

One other political reality that made the population explosion dangerous was that the state bureaucracy was already spread very thin. In the Qianlong reign, the empire was twice as large as the Ming state yet the numbers of magistrates serving in counties remained the same. Often called the "father-mother official," the magistrate was the main conduit for the emperor's benevolence on the local scene. When this crucial position was understaffed and (with the growing economic difficulties) often underfunded, the ability to respond to the needs of a rapidly-growing populace was greatly diminished, while the likelihood of corruption (to gain additional operating funds) increased. In such situations, to survive, the magistrate had to make connections and work with local bigwigs who might be scholar-gentry, merchants, or even local gangsters or toughs; such alliances also obviously affected the perception of the government by the people.

Part of the difficulties of the last decades of the century can be chalked up to the personal decisions of the Qianlong emperor himself. Emulating his grandfather the Kangxi emperor, he took a number of tours down the Grand Canal to the Lower Yangzi area. At least two of these were undertaken for his mother's sake, a notably public display of filial piety. But the expenses of these Southern Tours were ten times those of his grandfather, and they were accompanied by significant disruptions of life along the Grand Canal. Triumphal arches and temporary palaces were built; the Grand Canal had to be repaired to insure the safety of crowds; grain that ordinarily would have been shipped north was kept for the imperial retinue in the south. Such conspicuous display of government power was generally for the glory of the emperor (and his mother). Yet, the Yellow River overflowed some twenty times during the Qianlong emperor's reign and not once did he make a personal visit as a ritual inspection of the dikes or to express concern for the flood victims. In short, the emperor's sense of perspective on both the appearance and the substance of rule seemed to be wanting.

Perhaps nothing illustrates what might best be called a loss of perspective than his doting on a handsome court favorite, Heshen. Beginning in 1775, when he was sixty-five and Heshen was twenty-five, the emperor handed much power over to this man who was said to have reminded him of his father's concubine with whom as a youth he had been infatuated. Whether this was a homosexual relationship or not, Heshen was able to parlay his ruler's patronage into extensive personal power. He held many important posts, including minister and vice-minister of key boards and director of the *Four Treasuries* project. His son was married to the emperor's daughter. He was able to appoint cronies to key bureaucratic posts around the empire; he and they engaged in many corrupt activities from which they made millions of taels to enrich themselves. When the Jiaqing emperor, the Qianlong emperor's son, forced Heshen to commit suicide in 1799, his personal treasury held the equivalent of two year's of the realms revenue. Corruption had a way of spreading like a cancer on the body politic, metastasizing far beyond Heshen and his gang, in the end harming the people themselves. When each level of the bureaucracy took more and more from the levels below, it ultimately robbed not only economic resources but eroded the respect that the people ideally should have maintained for their rulers.

THE DAOGUANG EMPEROR

After he returned to the Forbidden City from the summer palace in early October 1813, the thirty-one year old prince who would become the Daoguang emperor in 1821, encountered a remarkable scene. With the help of unscrupulous eunuchs, a rebel band had entered the Forbidden City. Once the alarm had sounded, the prince acted quickly and courageously, grabbing a pistol and shooting two rebels as they tried to scale a wall. He then assisted in the roundup and capture of the remaining rebels. Such decisive action might lead one to think that as emperor, he would, in the words of one biographer, be "one who could be relied on to restore the dynasty's fortunes in the face of crises spawned by the Heshen scandals and the fiscal strains unleashed by demographic crisis."[27] But the Daoguang emperor was of different mettle from his grandfather, the Qianlong emperor, and, above all, the times and the context were different.

The Daoguang emperor as a boy and teenager had participated in hunts north of the wall with his grandfather and father, the Jiaqing emperor (1796–1820); on a hunt at the age of nine he killed a deer with his bow and arrow, reportedly greatly pleasing his grandfather. He thus knew his Manchu roots, being trained in martial skills and military values. He was also adept in the customary activities of a Chinese sovereign/Confucian sage: studious and especially knowledgeable about Chinese literature, he was the author of ten volumes of prose and twenty-four volumes of poetry. The obsession with the Manchu-Chinese identity crisis had generally died with the Qianlong emperor; with his death efforts to stop Manchu assimilation into the Chinese realm were abandoned. Like his father, the Daoguang emperor was less concerned about the Manchu identity of bannermen and more concerned about keeping them in the garrison compounds and away from opium, the black market, and banditry. The word best describing Manchu life among the banner population even at the center of the Manchu world in Beijing was "decline": dilapidated housing, general poverty, and spreading opium usage.

In the realm at large, at the beginning of his reign, the Daoguang emperor had some military success in putting down a Muslim uprising in Turkestan (1825–1828), but he did not pursue Muslim allies in further western campaigns, likely because it would have been too costly. Most believe that such a possible policy was aborted by cost. For the crucial reality that he faced was the depletion of the treasury which meant an ongoing financial crisis that strangled any government attempts to act forcibly. Many important public works for example, were now largely in disrepair. Whereas his grandfather's gaze had been the multiethnic empire from the forests of Manchuria to the Mongolian and Tibetan grasslands to the Xinjiang deserts, the eyes of the Daoguang emperor had to focus on internal developments within the wall.

It is not that this emperor had no ability. Though earlier studies had suggested that he was weak, conservative, and unimaginative, more recent accounts have shown him to be conscientious, flexible, and even innovative. He was ready to experiment in trying to help deal with the financial crisis. He repeatedly admonished bureaucrats to tighten their fiscal belts. He set an example by cutting back on his own personal expenditures. In trying to find ways to finance crucial public works, he worked closely with regional and local officials, cajoling officials to take the initiative and working toward consensual center-local arrangements.

The most important of these public works for the overall health of the state was repairing the crucial waterway, the Grand Canal. The Grand Canal had been constructed in the Sui (589–618) and Ming (1368–1644) dynasties to link the northern capital region to the Lower Yangzi macroregion, one of China's chief rice baskets. The canal had been constructed because China's main rivers ran from west to east and the sea route along the coast was notoriously treacherous. Running from Hangzhou to near Beijing, the canal served as an essential artery not only for commerce but especially for the transport of tax grain, important at any time but especially at this time of financial desperation. The Grand Canal system was an extraordinarily complex system composed of the canal itself, tributary streams, dikes and embankments, floodgates, and drainage channels. At one place the canal briefly joined the Yellow River; at the junction site there was an elaborate system of embankments, locks, and lock gates. The whole system was in disrepair, with the canal itself shallow and silting up. Indeed, the basic problem was that the Yellow River itself was in the process of shifting its channel from south of the Shandong peninsula to its north—a disaster that has happened about once every six hundred years.

The emperor's technique in ruling was to listen to men in the field, to compromise and work toward consensus, and to be flexible: "I manage the country as a whole and search out information from everyone. Then I select a good plan and follow it. Moreover, I do not go into the planning process beforehand with a prejudiced view."[28] He came to see that he could not control the project from Beijing and that, while the fiscal realities called for a central government-regional collaboration, the careful analysis and actual repair of the waterworks systems had to be conducted by men on the scene. This is a less assertive and autocratic kind of approach than the Qianlong emperor used, say, in the *Four Treasuries* project; but the reality of the times called for different ruling tactics. In this crisis, however, the Daoguang emperor did take the generally bold initiative in pushing for a one-year experiment of transporting the grain by the sea route; that effort was successfully designed, enlisting Shanghai merchant vessels, and carried out in 1826.

If the concerns and contexts of the Daoguang emperor's reign bore little resemblance to that of his grandfather, neither did his style. The arrogance and ostentation of the reign in the late eighteenth century was replaced by humility and frugality. In his will, he requested that no tablets praising his accomplishments be set up at his tomb and that his clothing be distributed to his courtiers (in contrast to the usual custom of preserving imperial clothes in sealed chests). During his reign he made it known that he even wore mended clothes as part of his effort to hold down expenditures. One wonders whether the Daoguang emperor ruled at a time that was indeed more difficult than it was for his grandfather who had full treasuries, military triumphs, and unprecedented prosperity. The Daoguang emperor's original name, "Mianning," means "unbroken peace." Unfortunately his reign would forever come to be associated with war; it was his fate "to be the first Emperor of China to be humiliated by a Western power."[29]

Notes

[1] Quoted in Frederic Wakeman, Jr., *The Great Enterprise* (Berkeley: University of California Press, 1985), Vol. 1, p. 209.

[2] John King Fairbank and Merle Goldman, *China, A New History* (Cambridge: Harvard University Press, 1998), p. 174.

[3] Dorothy Ko, *Teachers of the Inner Chambers* (Stanford: Stanford University Press, 1994), pp. 149–150.

[4] Wakeman, *The Great Enterprise,* pp. 648–650.

[5] Quoted in Chang Chung-li, *The Chinese Gentry* (Seattle: University of Washington Press, 1955), p. 177.

[6] The phrase "Confucian idiom" comes from Pamela K. Crossley, *The Manchus* (Oxford: Blackwell), p. 106.

[7] Quoted in Evelyn S. Rawski, *The Last Emperors* (Berkeley: University of California Press, 1998), p. 208.

[8] Ibid., p. 301.

[9] See the discussions in Susan Naquin and Evelyn S. Rawski, *Chinese Society in the Eighteenth Century* (New Haven: Yale University Press, 1987), especially Chapters 1, 2, 4, and 6.

[10] Susan Mann, *Precious Records* (Stanford: Stanford University Press, 1997), p. 7.

[11] Ibid., p. 120.

[12] Ibid., p. 226.

[13] Jonathan Spence, *The Search for Modern China* (New York: W. W. Norton, 1990), p. 94. These figures come from Ho Ping-ti, *Studies on the Population of China, 1368–1953* (Cambridge: Harvard University Press, 1959), p. 281.

[14] Naquin and Rawski, p. 223.

[15] Quoted in Frederic Wakeman, Jr., "High Ch'ing: 1683–1839" in James B. Crowley, Ed., *Modern East Asia: Essays in Interpretation* (New York: Harcourt, Brace and World, 1970), p. 5.

[16] Philip A. Kuhn, *Soulstealers: The Chinese Sorcery Scare of 1768* (Cambridge, 1990), p. 39.

[17] Quoted in Harold Isaacs, *Scratches on our Minds* (New York: John Day Co., 1958), p. 95.

[18] Ibid., p. 94.

[19] Pamela K. Crossley, *Orphan Warriors: Three Manchu Generations and the End of the Qing World* (Princeton: Princeton University Press, 1990), p. 21.

[20] Rawski, p. 21.

[21] Crossley, *The Manchus,* p. 112.

[22] Quoted in Rawski, p. 255.

[23] Crossley, *The Manchus,* p. 111.

[24] Quoted in R. Kent Guy, *The Emperor's Four Treasuries* (Cambridge: Harvard University Press, 1987), p. 35.

[25] Ibid., p. 159.

[26] Naquin and Rawski, p. 219.

[27] Jane Kate Leonard, *Controlling from Afar* (Ann Arbor: University of Michigan Press, 1996), p. 54.

[28] Ibid., p. 195.

[29] Arthur W. Hummel, *Eminent Chinese of the Ch'ing Period* (Washington, D.C.: U.S. Government Printing Office, 1943), p. 575.

3

The Opium War and the Treaty System: Challenges to Chinese Identity

_____

_____

___

If only in terms of territorial size, the drive of European states to establish colonies in Asia seems quite surprising. China and India are huge countries on the Eurasian landmass while Europe is only a small peninsula on that same body of land. But European expansion was impelled by imperialism's three "Ms": merchants, missionaries, and the military. Commercial motives drove the merchant class that had emerged during the rise of capitalism; they sought to profit from bringing commodities—rice, spices, sugar, cotton—from East Asia, items that were not naturally prolific in the narrow span of European latitude (from 35 to 55 degrees north). Convinced that it possessed the Truth, the Christian church sent out missionaries to gather in the souls of benighted heathen like so many crops to be harvested. In many countries the merchant and the missionary were the advance men, preparing the way for the military, the arm of state power, to come for the biggest harvest of all, that of territory and people. All three groups were propelled by a missionary-like urge to spread the gospel of Western capitalism, Western religious truth, and Western state power.

THE EARLY WESTERN ROLE

In 1600 the British government granted the East India Company a monopoly on trade east of Africa's Cape of Good Hope to South America's Straits of Magellan; made perpetual in 1609, this monopoly over all trade in the Indian and Pacific oceans lasted until 1834. Others had come before without such grandiose dreams. In 1517 the Portuguese made a horrific start in southernmost China when they followed their African practice of kidnapping adolescents to take as slaves; the Chinese forbade them to return. The Spanish arrived in the 1570s, trading along the southeast coast and setting up a base in Taiwan. The Dutch came in the early seventeenth century, supplanting the Spanish by the 1640s. The famous Italian Jesuit missionary Matteo Ricci reached Beijing in 1601 and was followed by more Jesuit priests who oversaw a substantially successful mission operation. It foundered when the Dominican and Franciscan orders attacked it for allowing converts to continue practicing rites of ancestral veneration. A papal bull in the 1740s was the Jesuit mission's coup de grace.

Most of the West's most active early phase of exploring East Asian waters came during the collapsing Ming regime and the bloody Manchu conquest, a disorienting and chaotic time for the Chinese state. The threat of Ming loyalists, based in Taiwan, compelled the Qing to close coastal ports in 1662; but when the threat was suppressed in 1685, four ports were re-opened. Traditional state cultural and economic attitudes had denigrated merchants and trade. Confucianism had called agriculture the root of the state. In contrast, commerce was simply trading and trying to profit on what others had produced; its practitioners, the merchants, thus exhibited some parasitic characteristics (living on what others had produced), and were the lowest legitimate social grouping, following scholars, farmers, and craftsmen. Further, within its own self-perception, China was "everything under Heaven" (*tianxia*), by definition self-sufficient, and therefore needing nothing from outside. China's allowance of trade probably came in small part from its traditional paternalistic outlook toward "barbarians," but more likely it resulted from the government's desire to profit from the trade even as it outwardly frowned on it.

Even with the opening of four ports, much of the trade gravitated to Canton (Guangzhou). Beginning in the 1720s Canton merchants dealing with Western trade established their own guild, the Cohong (from *gonghang,* or cooperative merchant companies), to monopolize trade; the guild was composed of thirteen "hong" (from *hang,* or company) merchants. The government made them guarantors for the behavior of foreigners and payment of transit fees. In 1759, the East India Company sent James Flint to undertake talks with the government about the trading situation at Canton. Flint violated Chinese restrictions by sailing to northern ports and presenting petitions using incorrect procedure. In retaliation, the court decreed that Canton from that time would be the only open port and that Europeans could trade only with the Cohong under the general control of a Superintendent of Maritime Customs (the "hoppo"). If the government was going to be compelled to trade, it was going to make certain that it gained some profit. In this case the profit came from the hong merchants who both had to buy their positions and then make extensive annual presents and contributions as well. In 1834, for example, the worth of these contributions and presents totaled over 456,000 taels. Hong merchant willingness to pay such a sum points to the lucrative nature of the monopoly and their ability to profit from it.[1]

Over time a procedure of trade and barbarian management called the Canton system evolved. Essentially it was an effort to fit Western merchants into the traditional tributary state framework; as such, the system set various rules and regulations that outsiders had to obey. All purchased goods had to be paid for in cash. Foreigners could not enter the walled city of Canton, could not be taken in sedan chairs, could not learn the Chinese language, and could not bring weapons or women to the thirteen Western "factories" or trading posts located on the bank of the Pearl River outside the city walls. They could only deal with hong merchants and could attempt no direct communications with Chinese officials; any communication with officials went first to the Cohong and had to include the character for "petition." Finally, if a regulation was violated or other problems developed, the Chinese halted all trade, as in the traditional tributary system, until the outsiders came to their senses and followed Chinese directions. The Westerners were generally willing to dance to the tributary tune that the Chinese played and thus were able to continue to purchase primarily the tea, silk, and porcelains that European and American customers desired.

By the turn of the century, tea made up 80 percent of Chinese exports to Europe. From the picking of tea buds and leaves to the delivery of tea chests in British ports, the tea trade was an arduous and lengthy undertaking. Black teas were harvested in Fujian province, approximately four hundred miles northeast of Canton; green teas came from even further away, five hundred to six hundred miles, in Zhejiang, Jiangxi, and Anhui provinces. From the Chinese side, limiting Western trade to Canton made the tea business more difficult and costly. The tea had to be carried by porters over mountain trails until rivers could be reached to boat the tea to Canton; in addition to transport costs, money had to be paid out to toughs along the way for the protection of the cargo. There were at least three tea-pickings per year, in March–April, May, and June. The early spring picking began to arrive in Canton in October, with most arriving from November to January. It was stored in warehouses near the Western factories until Western ships took it. Western ships generally left London in the early spring for the four- to six-month voyage to Canton. They were usually at that port in October and out to sea again by January. The round trip from London to Canton took over a year.

Despite such a long haul and the hassles of the Canton system, the eighteenth and early nineteenth centuries saw trade continually expanding; from 1719 to 1833 the tonnage of foreign ships increased more than thirteen times over. And perhaps little wonder, given the fact that in the late 1820s enough tea was imported into England to give every man, woman, and child two pounds a year. But despite the flourishing trade, Westerners were unable to change the terms and procedures of the trade. In 1793, the British East India Company sent Lord George Macartney to try to expand trading privileges, open more trading ports, and establish diplomatic residence. But the Qianlong emperor treated the effort as a tributary mission; and there were no changes in Chinese policy. An 1816 follow-up mission, led by Lord Amherst, was not even formally received.

Recent studies have cautioned against seeing what happened in encounters between the representatives of China and those of foreign countries, such as in the Macartney mission, as a clash of cultures or of civilizations.[2] Just as we have been reminded repeatedly that there are many Chinas, so there were many Western countries with their own structures, outlooks, and practices. And there were, to focus on Macartney's land, many Britains and Britishers, all of which or whom may have been related, but all of which or whom would have had their own approaches, outlooks, and styles. Historical analysis must dissect the realities of each moment and not assume that one abstracted variable, say, culture explains what happened. Thus, in any close study of the 1793 mission, Macartney should be seen as "an exemplar of a specific stratum of late eighteenth-century British society rather than a 'Westerner' in some undifferentiated, timeless sense."[3] These points are especially important in understanding people trying to deal with the "Other," for the tendency was to overgeneralize and make the Other undifferentiated.

CHINA AND THE WEST: MUTUAL PERCEPTIONS

To the Chinese, Western merchants and diplomatic emissaries, coming to the east coast of the country, were first simply "eastern barbarians." Indeed, in the 1860s, after two decades of treaty making, the British ambassador was still referred to in Chinese sources as the "English barbarian chieftain."[4] There was great confusion in Chinese minds over the separate identity of Western countries, likely in part a reflection of Chinese inability to perceive much physical difference among Westerners. They all looked alike—with their big noses, generally light-colored eyes and hair, ruddy complexions, and hairy bodies. The last contributed to their repulsive body odor especially after months on board ships in the tropics; it was a sickening smell that the Chinese who have comparatively little body hair and odor had trouble tolerating. Rumor had it that because of their light-colored eyes, Westerners could not see at night. Others said that Westerners could not bend their knees or stretch out their legs or feet like Chinese could. It is surely the case that the confusion and ignorance came from lack of contact, lack of interest, and a strong repugnance—realities that also gave rise to reporting only superficial characteristics that seemed strikingly different from Chinese attributes. One writer, for example, noted that "their flesh is dazzling white, and their noses are lofty . . . their custom is to esteem women and think lightly of men . . . The men are violent and tyrannical and skilled in the use of weapons. They wear short coats and tip their black felt hats as a sign of politeness. The Swedes and the Englishmen like to take snuff, which they carry in little containers made of golden thread." At best, Westerners were quaint curiosities; at worst, they were morally and intellectually inferior or even savages—foreign devils—who lived "as a herd of cattle." An important Manchu official reported on England: "This is naturally a country of barbarians, with the nature of dogs and sheep, fundamentally ignorant of rites and of modesty; how can they know the distinction between ruler and subject, and upper and lower?"[5]

Views of China in the abstract among Western intellectuals and some statesmen in the late eighteenth century, as we have seen, had been positive, even enthusiastic. Once merchants and then missionaries went to China to deal with Chinese on a day-to-day basis, the labor and stresses of cultural interaction began to color the views of some, though not all. One with negative views whose musings were published and who allegedly helped create a growing anti-Chinese feeling in the West was British Commodore George Anson. Anson asserted that he had been treated badly by Chinese—given the bureaucratic runaround and overcharged—when he had entered Canton harbor in 1743 for repair work on his ship. As a result, he paid the Chinese back with bitter assessments of the people: "Indeed, this much may undoubtedly be asserted, that in artifice, falsehood, and an attachment to all kinds of lucre, many of the Chinese are difficult to be paralleled by any other people."[6] Anson accused Chinese of being innately dishonest, of being second rate in handicraft arts, and of suffering confusion from the "infinite obscurity" of the language. Missionaries, as we will see, brought their own brand of verbal abuse. Suffice it to say, the perceptions that developed on both sides when Westerners interacted with Chinese helped to shape actions and reactions then and later, sometimes tragically so.

OPIUM: THE PROBLEM AND THE WAR

The serious trade problem for Western merchants was that they had nothing that the Chinese wanted to buy. At Canton, stevedores would unload the cargo: from Britain, woolens and lead; and from goods picked up in India and stops in Southeast Asia (in what was known as the "country trade"), camphor, tin, cotton piece goods, rattans, birds' nests, fish maws, and spices. Had it not been for the South Asian and Southeast Asian items, the British position would have been a complete disaster. Woolens, the main British export, hardly appealed to Chinese in tropical Canton and its environs. Even with the country trade, there was a severe trade imbalance. British ships arrived in Canton with 90 percent of their stocks composed of bullion, mostly silver. The annual flow of silver into China reached over 3 million taels in the 1760s but soared to 16 million twenty years later. But then opium came to the rescue.

The Chinese had begun to smoke opium in the seventeenth century, first mixing it with tobacco in a regular pipe, a practice perhaps first introduced by the Dutch in Taiwan. Smoked in this way, each pipe gave the smoker about 0.2 percent of morphine by volume. By the mid-eighteenth century, Chinese had begun to smoke pure opium by heating refined opium paste and inhaling it through a long-stemmed pipe; this method provided the smoker with 9 or 10 percent of morphine. Opium smoking renders its users inert and dormant. French writer Jean Cocteau described the drug as "the only vegetable substance that communicates the vegetable state to us."[7] Those who sought some kind of escape from stress and boredom in their lives were most attracted to the drug. Its use stretched across the social landscape from rich to poor, from high officials to clerks and runners in county government offices, from eunuchs and bureaucrats in the Forbidden City to peasants, from merchants and coolies to soldiers. The most serious implications for China's political and social health was the reported high number of smokers in the military and in government offices, the first, because inert soldiers cannot fight; and the second, because secretaries, clerks, and runners were the "government" with which most people came into contact on a daily basis: finding them "stoned" would not have filled people doing government business with great confidence in their government.

Estimates of numbers of smokers vary, though about 10 percent of the population was a commonly accepted figure; numbers of addicts may have reached 3 to 5 percent of the population.[8] The personal tragedy was addiction. Without daily fixes, the user experiences the hellish misery of withdrawal with all kinds of wretched physical and psychological symptoms. Cocteau, himself a addict, wrote that the person experiencing withdrawal should "bury his head in his arm, to glue his ear to that arm, and wait. Catastrophe, riots, factories blowing up, armies in flight, flood—the ear can detect a whole apocalypse in the starry night of the human body."[9] In patterns well known from contemporary society, it is apparent that the addict will do whatever it takes to get opium—from using all his household's money to various criminal activities. Addiction, then, led to a host of social problems.

In 1800 and 1813, new imperial edicts (which followed earlier prohibitions in 1729 and 1796) forbade opium importation, production, and consumption. While the Cohong had handled the purchase of opium until then, the new edicts made it impossible for such above-board purchase. Consequently opium importation became opium smuggling. Western ships would anchor off the marshy delta with its many small bays and criss-crossing creeks and streams to unload opium chests either onto a receiving ship that served as a floating warehouse or onto well-armed but shallow draft Chinese boats that delivered the goods to networks in the delta and beyond Canton. The numbers of chests smuggled into the country grew dramatically from four thousand to five thousand chests around 1820 to eighteen thousand in 1828 to forty thousand in 1839.[10] The smuggling got a huge boost when the East India Company's monopoly of trade was abolished in 1834; then more individual shippers got into the smuggling business. There were many sides to the developing tragedy. Perhaps the most ironic was that some—large numbers of Chinese *and* the British as a whole—were becoming economic addicts of the drug, as it were. As the numbers of chests increased, the numbers of Chinese involved in the smuggling trade grew, increasingly dependent on it for their economic livelihood. For the British the opium trade meant that their unfavorable trade balance had been righted; now, indeed, the trade imbalance was on the Chinese side, with silver bullion leaving Chinese coffers to pay for opium. Other countries joined in the trade; United States' firms, for example, picked up opium in Turkey.

The outflow of silver has been estimated as up to 9 million taels annually in the early 1830s, an almost five-fold increase from the 1820s. Such a huge outflow destabilized the Chinese economy, based as it was on a bimetallic system of silver and copper. As silver left the country, it became more expensive in terms of copper. While daily purchases were made in copper, copper coins had to be changed into silver for the payment of taxes. Thus, taxes in the form of necessary copper coins were driven up by the outflow of silver. In the province of Shandong, far from the site of the smuggling, in 1800, it took between 1,450 and 1,650 copper cash to equal 1 silver tael; in 1830, it took 2,700.[11] This growing economic pressure was made worse by years of bad harvests in the first half of the 1830s, a situation that created food shortages and rising prices.[12] The crisis of international relations and the opium-induced social and cultural crisis thus helped create an economic crisis as well.

The Daoguang emperor, having successfully fended off the takeover of the Forbidden City by rebels in 1813, could not so easily and decisively deal with the opium crisis. He had issued anti-opium edicts in 1821, 1822, 1823, 1828, 1829, 1831, 1832, 1834, 1835, 1838, and 1839. This year-by-year listing suggests the persistence of the throne's actions, but they were to little avail. The emperor was especially filled with anger on learning that the imperial clan, key banner officers, and high civil servants were using opium. The court debated the course of action. Some advocated legalizing the drug so that it might be traded and taxed, with the goal of taxing it so greatly that the expense might decrease some of the use; at the least, such a policy would make up for the outflow of silver. Others argued that legalization would only make the social problems stemming from opium greater.

In the end, in early 1839 the emperor decided that the opium trade had to be wiped out. He had found the advice of an official, Lin Zexu, persuasive—that the importers and distributors of the drug, rather than the users, had to bear the principal force of government actions. To suppress the opium traffic, the emperor in March appointed Lin as imperial commissioner. It was an appointment that seemed a good bet to deal with the problem successfully, for Lin had the highest credentials and a reputation for incorruptibility—for which he was known as Lin, the Blue Sky. In trying to quash the distribution system, Lin rapidly mobilized gentry and local officials to name opium dealers and distributors. By July 1839, he had arrested about seventeen hundred Chinese and confiscated forty-four thousand pounds of opium and over seventy thousand opium pipes.

In trying to deal with the problem of importation, Lin demanded that the foreigners turn over their opium stocks. He tried to reason with the British and use shame to get them to surrender the drug. His plaintive words in a message to Queen Victoria: "The wealth of China is used to profit the barbarians . . . By what right do they then in return use the poisonous drug to injure the Chinese people? Even though the barbarians may not necessarily intend to do us harm, yet in coveting profit to such an extreme, they have no regard for injuring others. Let us ask, where is your conscience?"[13] Such appeals had little effect: the British first ignored the order, then refused. Following the logic of the tributary system, Lin then stopped all trade and set up a siege of the factories and their 350 foreigners. They held out for six weeks, blasting the action as a "piratical act against British lives, liberty, and property."[14] When they finally delivered over 21,000 chests to Lin, he had 500 laborers dig 3 immense trenches—7 feet deep, 25 feet wide, and 150 feet long, line them with flagstones on the bottom and timber on the sides, fill them with two feet of water, put in the more than 2,600,000 pounds of opium, decompose it using salt and lime, and flush it out to the sea. This monumental task took 22 days to complete. He composed a prayer to the God of the Sea, apologizing for polluting the waters and endangering sea creatures. He had won what seemed a moral victory over the opium-smuggling foreigners.

But it was a pyrrhic victory. Because the British superintendent of foreign trade had been, since 1834, a representative of the crown and not a merchant company, the siege and the seizure of opium were treated by the British as a national affront and a cause for war. Hostilities began with clashes between war junks in fall 1839 after incidents in the summer had ratcheted up tensions. The Daoguang emperor who had been impressed with Lin Zexu's memorials on the opium problem was not pleased by the results of his policy. In comments to Lin's explanation of what had gone wrong, the emperor wrote that Lin had "caused the waves of confusion to arise" and "a thousand interminable disorders" to grow. "In fact you appear as if your arms were tied, without knowing what to do. It appears that you are no better than a wooden image."[15] With that, Lin was exiled to Turkestan for four years.

The war itself was an on-again, off-again struggle against a backdrop of negotiations between the two sides. Serious talks began in the fall of 1840 with a settlement reached in early 1841. But both the Daoguang emperor and Prime Minister Palmerston were upset that the settlement was too lenient for the other side. The fighting then dragged on for a year and a half longer before the signing of the Treaty of Nanjing in August 1842 ended it with the surrender of the Central Country to the English barbarians.

For the Chinese, it was a military disaster, underlining the reality that imperial forces were desperately outmoded. The British not only had large traditional men-of-war but also touted steam-driven, shallow-drafting crafts that could glide up inland streams. The Chinese, in stark contrast, had no navy at all. There was simply no way that they could compete with the steam-powered warship that one day in early 1841 with withering long-distance artillery destroyed nine war junks, two military stations, five forts, and a shore battery. In land fighting it was the same. The British, sporting the latest in technology, fought the Chinese with self-firing rifles. The banner forces had matchlocks, in which the gunpowder had to be ignited by hand; most troops had only cold weapons—knives, swords, clubs, and spears. Mid-century official Zuo Zongtang probably summed it up best: "the land troops could neither ride nor shoot and the water troops could not sail or fire a cannon."[16]

The Opium War was the opening salvo of a century of aggression by Western nations against China, a century of conflict between very different cultures with sharply differing values; yet each clash would have its own particulars and realities. Some eventual war may have been inevitable, but it was particularly tragic that this first conflict centered on questions of international morality, specifically, England's demand that it had a "right" to smuggle opium into China no matter what it was doing to China or many of its people. For a number of Chinese this pivotal first confrontation with the West indeed marked the West as amoral, if not immoral: the plaintive question of Lin Zexu echoes—"Let us ask, where is your conscience?" Indeed, one of the consequences of the war was that foreign nations continued to import opium into the country despite Chinese laws forbidding its sale and use. While the number of chests smuggled into China in 1839 was about forty thousand, by 1884, the number brought into the country had more than doubled to eighty-one thousand.[17]

THE UNEQUAL TREATY SYSTEM AND ITS IMPACT ON CHINESE IDENTITY

The Treaty of Nanjing was the first of many treaties between China and foreign nations that were called "unequal" because China did all the giving and received nothing in return. The treaties began to erode China's sovereignty. In the beginning China deluded itself by rationalizing that its "generosity" matched its traditional tributary benevolence. It was only over time that they realized the insidious nature of the treaties. A cornerstone of the system was the application of the most-favored-nation principle, put in place in a supplementary treaty Britain and China signed in 1843. It promised that each country would receive every right and privilege that every other country received even if it were not specified in their particular treaty. For example, the Treaty of Nanjing did not contain provision for renegotiations. The U.S.-Chinese Treaty of Wangxia of 1844 did, however, provide that possibility in ten years time. The British then used the most-favored-nation clause to claim that right and demanded renegotiation of their treaty in 1852. From the Chinese perspective, as benevolent tributary elder brother, it was simply providing the same privileges magnanimously to all Western countries.

The early treaties were signed under the leadership of a group of Manchus at the court who had come to favor greater conciliation in dealing with the West. Led by the chief councilor Mujangga, this group dominated diplomacy relative to the West from 1840 to 1850 under the banner of avoiding at all costs actions that might incite a new military conflict. They were opposed by groups of Han Chinese literati who supported stronger resistance against the West and opposed any treaty that would give the West more trading rights. During the opium crisis these groups were strong proponents of Lin's cutting off trade with Britain in 1838 and of fighting the British with local militia units that allegedly had a more resistant and determined spirit than banner forces. The Manchu-Han Chinese hostility at the top of the government was also apparent in Lin Zexu's exile, which Mujangga demanded and which the Han Chinese opposed. This difference in policy outlook should not be taken to suggest that the Manchus were "easy" on the West because they were outsiders themselves. For the Manchus it was a choice over which strategy was least dangerous for the country until it could more effectively meet the challenge of the West. For the Han Chinese, who saw themselves as upholding the principle of protecting the morality of the state and culture against the attack of immoral barbarians, the Manchu policy was disgustingly weak and had to be morally censured.

When the Daoguang emperor's son, the Xianfeng emperor, took power in 1850, he dismissed Mujangga, whom he personally detested, as well as his allies. As if to underscore the shift from his father, he appointed Lin Zexu to deal with growing social unrest in the south and brought back to policy-making positions Han Chinese whom Mujangga had earlier ousted. Once in power, they did not try to undo the treaty system under construction but downplayed appeasement in their dealings with the West.

Foreign Concessions

The series of treaties opened up more ports for trade and foreign residence. The Treaty of Nanjing, for example, opened up four new ports (Xiamen [Amoy], Fuzhou, Ningbo, and Shanghai) to join Canton as site for foreign settlements and continuous trade. Each port was chosen for its role in the already existent maritime trade. Xiamen was a center of the junk trade with southeast Asia; Fuzhou was the main tributary port for Taiwan and the Ryukyu Island tributary missions; Ningbo was the traditional port involved in trade with north China, Korea, and Japan. Shanghai had long been an important port at the Yangzi's mouth. Other treaties opened more ports, first along the coast, then on inland rivers, especially the Yangzi.

Foreign concessions were areas carved out of existing Chinese cities where foreigners now became the rulers. In these areas where many Chinese still lived, foreigners assessed the taxes and collected them; foreign police and troops patrolled there; foreign law was the authority there. Thus, Chinese residents of foreign concessions were uprooted from their native country without moving an inch; and Chinese sovereignty over these former citizens was ended. Yet the Chinese did not react strongly to the situation; they could point to the precedent in past dynasties when Arab traders in particular lived with their own laws in designated parts of port cities.

The numbers of foreigners were small, growing at the five ports from about 450 in 1846 to around 600 in 1854. Most of these people had been resident for some time before the war at Canton so that there was a sense among the treaty port foreigners of being one community, a sense that may have been heightened by some Chinese cultural hostility. The British, having "opened" China, led the way in the creation of the treaty system and in the life of the ports. Approximately half of the foreign populace, predominantly men, was from the British Isles with another quarter from India, so that treaty port life was reflective of the British-Indian culture of the time.

The foreign population was made up mostly of merchants with a fairly small number of missionaries. The most important merchant houses were two British firms, Jardine, Matheson, and Company and Dent and Company; the major American firm was the Boston-

The Opium War and Initial Treaty Ports

based Russell and Company. All three had been involved in the opium trade; in the new treaty ports, they still brought in opium but participated as well in legal commerce and expanded their interests into such areas as banks and insurance, godowns (warehouses) and shipyards. The head of a foreign firm had to rely completely on a Chinese middleman, or comprador, who spoke enough pidgin English (a mixture of Portuguese, Chinese, and English) to converse with the foreigner and who could fulfill the needs of the firm through his contacts in the Chinese community, overseeing transactions and being responsible for the firm's Chinese personnel. Many compradors grew to be extremely wealthy men.

Extraterritoriality with Consular Jurisdiction

Another treaty "right" established by the West was extraterritoriality with consular jurisdiction by which a foreigner accused of a crime would be tried not in Chinese courts but in one presided over by his national consul. The Western rationale was that Chinese law was barbaric. Certainly the gulf between Western and Chinese culture over the general concept of law was wide. Western culture had made law the centerpiece of its political, social, and economic life ever since the deity had handed it down. Chinese culture had denigrated law as the last recourse for people who could not deal with their fellow men in proper moral fashion. China had no independent profession of law nor were there lawyers. No independent judiciary existed. The county magistrate served to investigate cases, to preside as court judge, and to deliver judicial decisions. In criminal cases, punishments were prescribed; since extenuating circumstances were not considered, magistrates had to follow them. Suspects were presumed guilty and were treated severely; torture and beating were expected if the suspect did not confess. Those who had passed even the lower-level civil service examination were exempted from physical punishment in such cases. At times of local social disturbances, those involved in the action might be subject to summary execution. In homicide cases, the Chinese system firmly upheld an "eye for an eye" policy. There was little consideration if the death was an accident, no possible lesser charge, as in the West, of "involuntary manslaughter." If a life was taken, a life must be given. If the killer was not findable, then a family member or someone connected to the killer would substitute.

Western experience with the Chinese legal system stretched back to the early eighteenth century, but the two most famous cases related to two ships, the British ship, *Lady Hughes* in 1784 and the Baltimore-based American ship *Emily* in 1821. The country-trading *Lady Hughes* sailed up to Canton with very important people on board. The gunner fired a salute, the discharge from the shot killing two Chinese. When the ship's captain refused to tell the Chinese which gunner fired the shot, they arrested the ship's business manager who was then threatened with punishment, an associate, as it were, of the gunner. When the gunner was eventually turned over to the Chinese, he was, in accord with China's eye-for-an eye homicide law, strangled. His death following the killing that most British felt was accidental underscored in foreign minds the barbarism of the Chinese legal system. In a similar case, a sailor on the *Emily* was responsible for the death of a Chinese woman on a boat; though there are different accounts of the nature of the death, the sailor was taken and executed. Because of these experiences, when drunken British sailors went ashore near Hong Kong and beat a Chinese villager to death in the summer of 1839, the British refused to turn them over to Chinese authorities. The episode ratcheted up tensions already high over the opium crisis. Westerners took the position that extraterritoriality was necessary until the Chinese amended their legal system.

Initially there was no strong Chinese reaction to this loss of control over foreign citizens. For one thing, it meant that the Chinese did not have to burden themselves with learning all the languages of these barbarians. As with the establishment of foreign settlements, China could find a precedent for such an arrangement: they had allowed Tang dynasty Arab traders in Canton to hold extraterritoriality. But difficulties came to the surface quickly, when, as in foreign settlements, some Chinese also gained protection from their own government under extraterritoriality. This happened among different groups. For example, when compradors or other key Chinese personnel of Western business firms were accused of a crime, the officers of the firm understandably would become highly agitated. If he were tried in Chinese courts, he would almost certainly be found guilty. With imprisonment or worse, he would then be lost to the firm. Since compradors were the key to business success, performing the crucial middleman role, in such cases Western firms faced financial losses or even bankruptcy. To find a new comprador would take much time, and for a new comprador to make the required business connections and arrangements would take much longer. Thus, officers of Western firms began placing key personnel under the umbrella of extraterritoriality. If accused of a crime, they would be tried in courts presided over by the consul of the country of the firms' officers, presumably in sessions that would be much friendlier to the firm and its protégés.

Western missionaries also offered such protection to their accused protégés, Chinese converts. In this case, missionaries may have worked many hard years for only a dozen or so converts. Imagine the chagrin when, say, the first convert and leader of the congregation was accused of a crime. Missionaries would want to vouch for the man and in many instances they claimed the right of extraterritoriality for him. When, as it happened more than once, missionaries resorted to having their consuls dispatch gunboats to force their way on this matter in difficult cases, extraterritoriality became not simply a legal dispute but a matter of brute force. Essentially, through the "right" of extraterritoriality there came to be a category of Chinese who were more privileged than others, a particularly galling situation for the non-privileged.

According to the treaties, China also lost its sovereign right to set, control, and collect its own tariffs. Tariff rates were set at about 5 percent of the value of the goods, not raising a red flag in Chinese minds because they were not notably out of line from traditional tariff rates. But the times were not traditional. Unable to raise the tariff, the Chinese could not, for example, keep out unwanted items. Perhaps more importantly China's enforced paralysis relative to the tariff had serious implications for China's efforts to industrialize. During the Opium War China came face to face with modern technology in the form of ships and weapons; the experience was a catalyst for some Chinese to begin to think initially about buying them from the West and ultimately to consider manufacturing them themselves. But Chinese efforts to establish modern industry, both heavy and light, were hampered by their inability to raise tariffs to protect its infant industry. In the twentieth century, Communist thinkers and activists were especially condemnatory about the loss of tariff control, for they argued that it prevented China from entering the capitalist era, thereby short-circuiting China's passage through the "scientific" evolution of history described by Marx.

Not only did China lose control of its tariff, but it also lost the right (of any sovereign state) to collect those customs duties. In the 1850s in the middle of the turmoil of the Taiping Rebellion in the vicinity of Shanghai, the British began collecting customs duties to insure their collection. This collection became institutionalized in the Chinese Maritime Customs Service. Even though long-time director Robert Hart was effective and dedicated, seeing himself essentially as part of the Chinese bureaucracy, the collection of customs for one county by another was a humiliating loss of sovereignty. China would not gain control of the tariff or its collection until 1933.

Another sovereign right of a nation is to control its rivers and streams, specifically to have control over who can sail up those waterways into its interior regions. This right is obviously critical for a country's security and defense. Yet, according to the treaties, China could not make any inland waterway off limits to foreign ships nor could it restrict ships from any nation from penetrating its space via its rivers.

Foreign Ambassadorial Residence

The main structure of the treaty system was completed by the Treaty of Tianjin (1858) and its follow-up, the Convention of Beijing (1860). These agreements came in the midst of another war waged by Britain and France against China. Called the *Arrow* War and sometimes the second opium war, this struggle began with the British accusation that a Chinese ship (the *Arrow*) under British registry had been illegally searched by Chinese officers searching for a Chinese pirate. Overreactions to a series of incidents led to fighting and to British calls for upholding its honor and interests abroad. In the end, France joined the campaign, using as an excuse the murder of a French missionary in an area that was off limits to foreigners. It is hard to avoid the conclusion that both countries were simply looking for a pretext to force further political and economic demands on China.

The British and French took Canton in December 1857 and then sailed north, seizing in summer 1858 the coastal Dagu Forts that served as strategic protection for key cities in the capital region and taking the city of Tianjin. Negotiations ensued, producing the treaty that bears the city's name. It expanded the treaty system and established two more exceptionally significant "rights." As for expanding the system, it opened ten new treaty ports, four of them ports on the Yangzi River. It allowed anyone with a passport to travel anywhere in the country, and passports were not even required for travel up to thirty miles from treaty ports.

One of the new "rights" set forth in the treaty was that ambassadors of foreign states would reside permanently in Beijing. An important aspect of the tributary system had been to designate ports of entry far away from the capital in order to keep foreigners' Chinese "home port" at a distance. They were escorted to the capital and, following the prescribed

Chinese dead at the Dagu fort during the Arrow War
Source: George Eastman House/Felice Beato/Hulton Getty Collection/Archive Photos

rituals, were allowed to remain in Beijing for only a specified period. There was no ongoing presence of foreigners in the capital or in China. Now diplomatic representatives from all "barbarian" nations could live near the Forbidden City. This the Chinese could not abide. Even after the treaty was signed, they continued the fight. In the summer of 1859 the British again attacked the forts, but were repulsed. When a British negotiating team was sent to Beijing, it was arrested and some members were killed. The British commander, Lord Elgin decided strong measures must be taken in revenge and to force compliance with the treaty. He sent his troops to occupy Beijing; the emperor fled the capital for his hunting lodge north of the Great Wall. In October 1860, Elgin's troops marched northwest of the city to the Summer Palace (Yuan Ming Yuan), a complex of over two hundred pavilions and pagodas built during the reign of the Qianlong emperor. There they looted its thrones, furniture, porcelains, robes; and then Elgin gave orders for them to burn the whole ten square mile area. Chinese resistance against aggressive Western armies had turned beauty to ashes. The words of an Englishman with Elgin's army: "But whenever I think of beauty and taste, of skill and antiquity, while I live, I shall see before my mind's eye some scene from those grounds, those palaces, and ever regret the stern but just necessity which laid them in ashes."[18]

Six days after the torching, the Chinese agreed in the Convention of Beijing to the permanent residence of ambassadors in the capital. One minor stipulation of the treaty was that from that time on, China could no longer use the character for "barbarian" (*yi*) in referring to the British. What underlay this stipulation and the demand for permanent diplomatic residence was the Western state model of equality among nations, a model with which the traditional tributary system with its hierarchy of superior/subordinate could never coexist. Though it would take decades for the system to die in Chinese thinking, for all practical purposes the centuries-long tributary system was dead. While China never became a full-fledged "colony," its loss of sovereignty over its own territory and people created what has been called a semi-colony, subject to the demands and pressures of not one but many foreign nations.

THE MISSIONARY AND CULTURAL IMPERIALISM

The Treaty of Tianjin granted another crucial "right" to Western nations, the guarantee that Christianity could be openly taught and practiced. Missionaries could travel anywhere, purchase property for church and school, and spread their message at will. The record of the impact of nineteenth-century missionaries is complex: each missionary naturally had his or her own motives; they came from a variety of countries which each had its own approaches to China and attitudes toward the mission effort. Yet missionaries shared one thing: their conviction that they possessed absolute truth. Largely because of this, the story of the relationship between missionaries and Chinese was by and large not a happy one. The political and social landscape of the dynasty's last half century is marked by episode upon episode of turmoil and violence touched off by the actions of missionaries in communities across China.

While Jesuit missionaries had enjoyed some success in their sixteenth- and seventeenth-century efforts to convert scholar-gentry elites, the Yongzheng emperor (1722–

1736) outlawed Christianity. From that time on Christianity had to operate underground; in the early nineteenth century persecutions with arrests, punishments, and executions were frequent. As a measure of the control exercised in this area, only one new missionary came into China during the years 1801 to 1829—Protestant Robert Morrison, entering Canton with the protection of the East India Company. Beginning in the late 1810s Catholic missionaries began to build Catholic communities around the country; the first American Protestants came in 1830. Others followed. One, German Karl Gutzlaff, is not a symbol of all missionaries at the time, but his actions point to something all missionaries shared—a willingness to use any means necessary to spread the gospel. Gutzlaff became a translator on opium ships plying the China coast. From these ships dispensing opium, Gutzlaff also distributed Christian tracts. The message the Chinese ultimately picked up from this mix of Christ and opium must at the least have distorted the Christian intent.

In viewing the Chinese, the missionaries were convinced of their own superiority and the total Truth of their message. The Chinese, in their estimation, were benightedly superstitious, greedy, and materialistic. In that state, they desperately needed what the Christian message offered. But these early missionaries were frustrated by the prohibition against the open practice of Christianity and frequently attacked Chinese policies regarding the West and Western merchants. By the late 1830s some missionaries were calling for armed invasion by the West "to break down the barriers which prevent the gospel of Christ from entering China."[19] Once the Opium War broke out and battles led to scenes of slaughtered Chinese, one missionary opined: "I regard such scenes . . . as the direct instruments of the Lord clearing away the rubbish which impedes the advancement of Divine Truth."[20] While this missionary saw the Chinese people as "rubbish," others used other adjectives: imbecilic, ignorant, conceited, weak, heathen, pagan. It does not take much imagination to realize how these conceptions of the people they wanted to save would affect their approach.

In 1844, as part of a general treaty with France, the Qing government removed its proscription against Christianity. The 1860 treaty further solidified the toleration toward the Western religion. The numbers of missionaries entering China grew quickly. By 1870, 250 Catholic missionaries represented a number of orders; at least 350 Protestant missionaries were in China by that year. Yet the Catholics, who had a long history of mission work in China, were far ahead of Protestants in terms of conversions. In 1870 there were approximately 400,000 Catholic converts as opposed to about 6,000 Protestants. The Catholic mission at that time had spread throughout China, while the Protestant effort was concentrated in treaty ports mostly along the coast.

Unhappily the missionaries retained the same attitudes to the Chinese people as they had shown during the Opium War period. Their approach in all daily matters was that they were the privileged who had to have their own way in every matter—especially in dealing with the rabble Chinese. That approach raises the question of whether a missionary could be sincerely tolerant of a society that he or she wanted to change to some degree; even if sympathetic, was it not the case that rejection of that society as it existed was at the heart of his or her approach? Missionaries frequently wanted to protect their converts by extending the Western right of extraterritoriality to them; they felt they could rely on the support of their national consuls who had the treaties behind them. In extreme situations, a missionary called for his consul to send a gunboat for a show of force or firepower if he was being thwarted by local officials in his demands. The government of France, which saw the Catholic establishment in China as the vehicle for furthering its national interest, became the demanding protector of the Catholic mission. In one famous case, the governor of Guizhou province was accused of ordering various anti-Christian moves. The Catholic bishop lobbied French diplomats to have them pressure the Chinese government first to have the governor removed and then to have him executed; the French legation in Beijing did so. From the perspective of the French, they still had to rid themselves of the "rubbish" impeding their way. From the perspective of the Chinese government, here were foreigners demanding the transfer and execution of a Chinese provincial governor, a matter over which outsiders should have no say in another sovereign state.

The Chinese reaction to missionaries and their work grew out of reactions to foreigners in general and the missionaries' message and approach in particular. Although Chinese elites did not necessarily speak for all Chinese, elite attitudes filtered down to the masses, affecting their reactions. Educated Chinese generally saw all non-Chinese and their ideas as barbarian. While the Chinese saw themselves as grounded in realistic pragmatism, some Christian teachings such as a virgin birth and a father allowing his son to be crucified seemed not only superstitious but downright scandalous. Further, the Chinese saw missionaries in their daily activities maneuvering to purchase the best sites for their churches and pronounced them materialistic and grabbing. Many Chinese scholar elites found missionaries to be direct threats in their local communities. Products of the Chinese civil service examination, scholar gentry were the locality's teachers, mediators, authorities, and charity providers. When missionaries moved into an area and converted Chinese, they were the obvious leaders of their congregations. In that capacity, they performed the same functions for their congregations—teaching, mediating, providing charity—that gentry did for society at large. Therefore, not only were gentry upset by this usurpation of their roles, but, just as the treaties had done with foreign concessions and extraterritoriality, the missionary presence and roles separated some Chinese from others.

Chinese elites did not have access to gunboats or instruments of force to deal with offensive missionaries; but they did wield the writing brush. They wrote propaganda tracts about missionaries and their work with the intent to tar the missionary with the broad brush of sexual immorality. This was a tactic that traditionally had been an important weapon in the Chinese political attack inventory. Here is a sample from a tract, "A Record of Facts to Ward Off Heterodoxy" [*Bixie zhishi*], first published in 1861 but reprinted many times in the decades following:

> During the first three months of life the anuses of all [Christian] infants—male and female—are plugged up with a small hollow tube, which is taken out at night. They call this "retention of the vital essence." It causes the anus to dilate so that upon growing up sodomy will be facilitated. At the junction of each spring and summer boys procure the menstrual discharge of women and, smearing it on their faces, go into Christian churches to worship. They call this "cleansing one's face before paying respects to the holy one" and regard it as one of the most venerative rituals by which the lord can be worshipped. Fathers and sons, elder and younger brothers, behave li-

centiously with one another, calling it "the joining of the vital forces". . . . There are all sorts of things of this nature that cannot be fully related. Hard as it may be to believe, some of our Chinese people also follow their religion. Are they not really worse than beasts?[21]

Such scatological tracts were widely circulated, painting for elites and non-elites who heard the tales pictures of despicable depravity and perversity. Certainly they helped incite suspicion, anger, and fear among the Chinese populace. Indeed, Chinese authorities in at least three provinces, sensing its incendiary possibilities, banned this particular tract. Missionaries blamed these tracts for anti-Christian violence that erupted in numerous localities against themselves and their converts.

A paroxysm of violence in the northern treaty port city of Tianjin on the afternoon of June 21, 1870 underscores the cultural gulf and the fragility of relations that existed between foreign missionaries and Chinese. Tianjin was a city where relations with the West had set Chinese nerves ajar. It was there, following the signing of the 1858 treaty, that French and British troops had been based from 1860 to 1863. Having seized a former imperial mansion to serve as consulate and having built a cathedral on the site of a former Chinese temple, the French were seen as arrogant and especially detested by the local populace. As if the latent animosity were not enough, in 1869 and 1870, anti-Christian writings had appeared in the area.

French Catholic nuns managed an orphanage in the same compound as the large new cathedral of Notre Dame des Victoires. They were especially eager to be able to baptize sick children and administer last rites to those who might be near death. The orphanage thus saw a higher mortality rate than normal, a reality made worse by an epidemic that raced through the orphanage in June 1870. Suspicion spread about goings-on behind the compound's walls. Rumors abounded: Orphans, it was said, were being killed, with their body parts used to make aphrodisiacs for priests and nuns in their alleged sex play. Chinese mistrust of French motives was heightened because the nuns had a policy of giving a small sum of money to people who turned children in to the orphanage. In addition, once children were placed under the nuns' control, the nuns did not allow them to be reclaimed by anyone, even if they represented themselves as parents or relatives. This situation helped fuel the rumor that scoundrels were kidnapping children to turn them in to make some cash. The confession of a man arrested on June 18 that he had kidnapped several children and sold them to a janitor who worked for Catholic institutions in the city raised tensions to an almost palpable level.

As rumors swirled, Chinese began to demand to search the orphanage. The search of the premises by a high local official, his being able to disprove the kidnapper's confession, and his announcement that all seemed in order at the orphanage did not still the increasing agitation. When a fight broke out at the cathedral between converts and onlookers, the official dispatched soldiers to quash the disturbance. At the same time, the French consul and his chief secretary charged into the official's office, the consul carrying two pistols. Incredibly, the consul shot at the official. When he missed, attendants seized him. The official calmly advised that he not go back on the streets where a huge angry crowd was forming. Saying that he was not afraid of any Chinese, the consul walked into the crowd. When he spotted the local magistrate coming toward him, he totally lost control, opening fire again; he missed the magistrate but hit and killed his attendant.

The killing transformed the crowd into an angry mob who killed the consul and his officer on the spot and nineteen others including twelve priests and nuns. The French victims were mutilated: after being raped, the nuns had their breasts sliced off and their eyes gouged out before they were burned alive. Several dozen Chinese converts were also killed. The cathedral, along with four American and British churches, was burned. French demands followed. The settlement included a large sum for reparations, the execution of eighteen mob leaders and hard labor for twenty-five others, the exile of the high official and magistrate of Tianjin, and the sending of a mission of apology.[22] The violent episode often stands as a symbol of the seeming haplessness of amicable relations between these two sides.

If the faces of imperialism in its 3M onslaught—merchants, missionary, and military—differed as to motive, approach, and national and individual purpose, they all had some common features. They all believed that what they had to bring to the Chinese was infinitely better than what the Chinese had. Acting for the capitalist countries of the West, the merchants believed that they could shake China awake from its self-sufficient dream world into the system of multi-state trade and that they could take advantage of the fabled China market. The military with its power had no doubt that it could blast the neanderthalic and outmoded regime and culture, thereby making possible the expansion of "enlightened" Western civilization. The missionary had the Truth to save Chinese from eternal damnation.

But they were dealing with a culture that gloried in its long history and vaunted traditions, with an intellectual elite who was absolutely certain of the superiority of their culture. In depth of commitment to their transcendent civilizational goals, these cultures were seemingly two immovable forces. The difference for the two sides in this confrontation was the timing of the Western arrival. The West's military power came in force at a time when China's military power was on life support. The historical game of "what if" often provides insights: *what if* the West's military had come during the military heyday of the late eighteenth century? We will never know for sure, but it is likely that the course of world history would have been markedly different, and it is likely that China's modern history would not have been so tragic.

Notes

[1] See Chang Hsin-pao, *Commissioner Lin and the Opium War* (Cambridge: Harvard University Press, 1964) p. 14.

[2] James Hevia, *Cherishing Men from Afar* (Durham: Duke University Press, 1995), pp. 24–26.

[3] Paul Cohen, "Review of *Britain in China* by Robert Bickers," *Journal of Asian Studies,* 59, 2 (May 2000), 401.

[4] This discussion is based on John King Fairbank, *Trade and Diplomacy on the Chinese Coast* (Cambridge: Harvard University Press, 1954), pp. 9–20.

[5] Ibid., p. 19.

[6] Quoted in Jonathan D. Spence, *The Chan's Great Continent* (New York: W. W. Norton, 1998), p. 53.

[7] Quoted in Peter Ward Fay, *The Opium War, 1840–1842* (Chapel Hill: University of North Carolina Press, 1975), p. 9.

[8] Ibid., p. 154.

[9] Ibid., p. 10.

[10] Jonathan Spence, "Opium Smoking in Ch'ing China," in Frederic Wakeman, Jr. and Carolyn Grant, Eds., *Conflict and Control in Late Imperial China* (Berkeley: University of California Press, 1975), p. 151. A chest usually contained 133 English pounds.

[11] Chang Hsin-pao, p. 39.

[12] James Polachek, *The Inner Opium War* (Cambridge: Harvard University Press, 1992), p.79.

[13] "Lin Zexu's Moral Advice to Queen Victoria, 1839" in Ssu-yu Teng and John K. Fairbank, Eds., *China's Response to the West* (Cambridge: Harvard University Press, 1954), p. 25.

[14] The phrase is Immanuel C. Y. Hsu's in *The Rise of Modern China* (New York: Oxford University Press, 1970), p. 228.

[15] Peter Ward Fay, *The Opium War, 1840–1842* (Chapel Hill: University of North Carolina Press, 1975), p. 268.

[16] Paraphrased in John K. Fairbank, Edwin O. Reischauer, and Albert M. Craig, *East Asia, The Modern Transformation* (Boston: Houghton Mifflin, 1965), p. 142.

[17] Spence, p. 151. He notes that by 1900 the imports had leveled off at about fifty thousand chests per year.

[18] Quoted in Wakeman, *The Fall of Imperial China,* p. 158.

[19] Stuart Creighton Miller, "Ends and Means: Missionary Justification of Force in Nineteenth Century China" in John K. Fairbank, Ed., *The Missionary Enterprise in China and America* (Cambridge: Harvard University Press, 1974), p. 252.

[20] Ibid., p. 255.

[21] Paul Cohen, *China and Christianity* (Cambridge: Harvard University Press, 1963), p. 51.

[22] The amount of reparations vary according to source. Jonathan Spence, *The Search for Modern China* (New York: W. W. Norton, 1990) says that they totaled 250,000 taels (p. 205). Immanuel Hsu puts the sum at 400,000 (p. 363). Paul Cohen in *China and Christianity* notes that a total of 280,000 taels of reparations were paid (250,000 to France and 30,000 to Russia) with additional sums of 212,000 taels to France and England to pay for property losses (p. 246).

4

An Age of Rebellion: Defiance of and Commitments to Traditional Chinese Identities and Approaches

——————

——————

——

Beset and besieged by Western powers, the Qing government faced an even more desperate threat in a series of mid-nineteenth century domestic rebellions that one scholar says "constitute[d] what was probably the greatest wave of peasant wars in history."[1] The devastation wrought by the largest of these, the Taiping War (1851–1864), was almost unfathomable: in the words of one observer, "smiling fields were turned into desolate wildernesses; 'fenced cities into ruinous heaps.' The plains . . . were strewn with human skeletons; their rivers polluted with floating carcasses; wild beasts descending from their fastnesses in the mountains roamed at large over the land, and made their dens in the ruins of deserted towns."[2] Not only were foreigners destroying Chinese life and property, but Chinese themselves were turning productive land into moonscapes and slaughtering themselves in vast numbers.

"TRADITIONAL" REBELLIONS

The nineteenth century was born in domestic rebellion, mostly of the guerrilla variety. The rebellion of Miao aborigines (1795–1806) against the ever-increasing encroachment of Han settlers sandwiched the century mark. Buddhism gave rise to the White Lotus Rebellion, that strove to establish a utopia on earth and that also straddled the turn of the century (1796–1804), and to the 1813 rebellion of Lin Qing, which reached the Forbidden City in its aim to assassinate the Jiaqing Emperor. Though each had its own context and meaning, there were similar patterns of setting, historical actors, agenda, and Qing dynasty responses. They prefigure patterns in the great mid-century rebellions.

Setting

These traditional rebellions were born in provincial border regions. Practically such a setting made sense since bandits and rebels could quickly cross provincial boundaries to another province if they were being pursued. While authorities in the other province might eventually pursue them, it is obvious that the rebels did not cross the border where there were military garrisons or police posts. Many provincial border regions were known for their natural wildness—mountains, forests, deserts, areas where the population might be less sedentary and stable, often (especially in central, south, and southwest China) where the population was ethnically mixed. If there was ethnic diversity and accompanying language differences, ethnic consciousness often produced among each group a strong sense of the Other's presence. To maintain order or bring peace in areas marked by such social diversity and such environmental challenges often necessitated a substantial degree of militarization. The mix—ethnically diverse peoples, with a consciousness of that diversity, militarized, and potentially in trouble with the law—could easily become combustible if ignited.

The Miao rebellion began along the mountainous border between Hunan and Guizhou, but even more significant, along the border between the Middle Yangzi and both the Upper Yangzi and Southwest China macroregions. At higher altitudes, they practiced slash-and-burn agriculture; at lower elevations, they farmed. The rebellion was ignited by the Qing dynasty efforts to extend their political control in the area, a policy accompanied by a large influx of Han Chinese settlers. The White Lotus Rebellion took shape in the mountainous and forested lands on the borders of Hubei, Sichuan, and Shaanxi—or, again, more apropos, the borders of three macroregions, Northwest China, the Upper Yangzi, and the Middle Yangzi. A utopian Buddhist ideology fueled this rebellion. Lin Qing's 1813 rebellion that the Daoguang emperor helped to quell does not fit the macro-regional border pattern and thus points to the range of possibilities for rebellious activity. It erupted with the impetus of Buddhist beliefs in Shandong and near Beijing in the North China macroregion; but the world of its leader Lin Qing was the economically peripheral world of the poor North China peasant and the poverty stricken urban underclass.

The Historical Actors and their Agendas

Any rebellion required leaders. A leader might emerge from almost any social type—peddlers, Daoist or Buddhist monks, laborers, failed examination candidates, boatmen, charcoal burners, geomancers. Yet all leaders had compelling messages or were charismatic or both. During his life, Lin Qing had many odd jobs—night watchman, clerk, coolie, construction worker, nothing in short to indicate exceptional talent. Yet after his arrest, a relative told the Qing authorities that the secret of his success was his convincing descriptions of how he would succeed and why people should contribute money to his cause. White Lotus Rebellion leader Liu Zhixie was reportedly charismatic, an able strategist who was able to mobilize numerous congregations of White Lotus followers.

In addition to leaders, of course, a rebellion needed masses of people who were organized and mobilized at least to some degree. The social structures and substance of rebellions varied geographically. In north China during the late Qing a number of such social upheavals, including the White Lotus rebellion, were inspired by belief in the coming of the Buddha of the Future who, it was thought, would establish a paradise on earth. Such ideas were promoted by the White Lotus sect, a cult organized into local communities based on congregations. At times of social trouble and disorder, these communities would join in defensive efforts by forming militia groups; in this way they could quickly become the building blocks for rebellion. For disturbances to grow into major rebellions, leaders of these communities had to have links to other groups who were involved in the world of violence—for example, groups that practiced traditional martial arts. The White Lotus Rebellion spread in the beginning because of the links that sect communities had to bandits who made their lair the forests of the three-province border region.

In south China the building blocks of rebellion tended to be "lodges" in a secret blood brotherhood called the Triads. The Triads spread throughout the Southeast Coast and Lingnan macroregions in the eighteenth century and to the Lower Yangzi by the early nineteenth century. Composed mostly of the underclasses—laborers, pirates, smugglers, yamen clerks and runners, boatmen, and peasants, Triad organizations did not seek to overthrow legitimate society but to exploit it for what it could. A slogan put it this way: "The people of the top class owe us money; those of the middle class should wake up. Lower classes come with us! It is better than hiring an ox to plow poor land!" There was nothing revolutionary about the Triads. They looked back to the Ming and, with anti-Manchu venom, called for restoring the Ming to power. Like the White Lotus sects in the north, the Triads organization found a ready audience because of a growing social malaise brought on by changes coming from urbanization, migration, and expanding networks of domestic and foreign trade. In time of peace they served as mutual assistance organizations; they readily accepted women as members. In the south the presence of strong and often feuding lineages further encouraged the growth of the Triads.

Qing Government Response

In the case of the White Lotus Rebellion, the government sent regular banner forces against the guerrilla enemy. A key goal was capturing leaders, the theory apparently being that a leaderless movement could be dealt with more quickly. The struggle then turned into what in the twentieth-century Vietnam War would be called search and destroy operations, with destruction often falling most heavily on civilians in their villages. The war dragged on with local communities often left in charge of their own defense. There were two elements to the defense. First was utilizing an old tradition of "strengthening the walls and clearing the countryside"—that is, building to fortify the walls of urban settlements, bringing people and grain from the countryside into these "strategic hamlets." Such a policy brought a more secure civilian population and deprived the rebels of food. The second element of defense was the establishment of local militia units by local elites who also served as militia heads. These policies—and both meant relying on local solutions—eventually successfully met the threat of the rebellion.

THE TAIPING WAR (1851–1864): ATTEMPTING
TO REVOLUTIONIZE IDENTITY

Though traditionally called a rebellion, this largest, most destructive such explosion in world history, might best be considered a civil war that devastated much of east central and southern China and militarily embroiled to greater or lesser degree sixteen of the eighteen provinces within the Great Wall. A rebellion is defined by the established powerholders who are under siege; rebels endeavor to unseat existing rulers. A civil war, in contrast, pits armies composed of combatants without necessarily presuming that one is in a privileged position.[3] Even more pertinent to the themes of this book is the revolutionary threat of the Taiping to traditional Chinese cultural identity: Taiping ideology and practice struck at the very heart of the Confucian framework and substance that so much created Chinese identity. It was also an event that underlined in blood one pernicious effect that Western Christianity came to play in the social tinderbox of south China. For the rebellion was the brainchild of Hong Xiuquan whose sickbed visions left him with the perverted conviction that he was the younger brother of Jesus Christ and that he had a holy mission to accomplish.

Regional Context

The historical and spatial contexts provided Hong with the people and the support that made his movement a threat not only to the ruling Manchus but to traditional Chinese civilization as well. The Taiping movement was born in the Canton region in the troubled years following the Opium War; it grew in large part because of the destabilization of the region from the opium scourge and the war itself. For several decades, opium smuggling, trafficking, and smoking had been a major problem in the region. In their daily lives, people in the area had experienced the full impact of ballooning taxes caused by the currency instability that resulted from the outflow of silver to pay for the opium. There were other longer-term political problems for some in this region. Two centuries earlier, this had been the last region conquered by the Manchus, and many areas had not—even after all that time—ever reconciled themselves to the control of these outsiders. In that context of distrust and contempt, this area had then seen the pitiful performance of the regime's military forces in the Opium War. It is almost certainly the case that such a humiliating defeat brought to some people in the region thoughts and perhaps talk about the Mandate of Heaven. Was it beginning to slip from the dynasty's grasp? Further, the treaty system itself opened up to Westerners not only the walled city of Canton (which had been off limits to the West earlier) but the interior; to see a "foreign devil" was an immediate reminder that the Manchus had not been strong enough to forestall this development. Given such a reality, Manchus, their military, and their bureaucrats could become obvious targets.

The new treaty system itself made the possibilities of social unrest in the region more likely. In the rapid growth of trade with the West in the late eighteenth century, tea and silk had been the West's prime objectives. Though some were produced in the Canton area, the main tea and silk producing regions were in Zhejiang, Jiangsu, and Fujian provinces. In the eighty years (1760s to 1842) when Canton was the only port open to the West, overland and riverine trade routes had developed from the Lower Yangzi and Southeast Coast macroregions to Canton. Shippers and brokers were involved along these routes, as were local toughs who were enlisted to protect the expensive commodities; they all made their living from this domestic trade. They were generally men who by the nature of their occupations knew how to deal with dangerous situations and handle themselves amid potential violence and criminal behavior. With the opening of the treaty ports of Ningbo (Zhejiang province) and Shanghai (Jiangsu province) in the Treaty of Nanjing, tea and silk could much more easily and quickly be carried to these closer new ports. No longer needed, the old trade routes dried up and, with them, the livelihood of the transporters and security guards who had worked the routes. The unemployment of these transport workers—many of whom were roughnecks at best—created a new potentially destabilizing factor in the region.

The introduction of another unsettling population increased the tinderbox situation in the region. Pirates had been a traditional threat along the southeast coast. Because the ports opened with the Treaty of Nanjing were along this coast, Western ships plying these waters became the objects of pirate raids and attacks. The British therefore began a policy of suppressing the maritime pirates. This pirate suppression campaign was on the whole successful, allowing for safer ocean travel, but it forced the now-unemployed maritime pirates into the interior where they were transformed into land-based and river-based bandits who preyed on the local Chinese population.

In addition to these new forces there were old ethnic rivalries that tore at the region's social amity. There were Hakkas, "guest people," Han Chinese immigrants from north China centuries earlier, who remained separate from the locals. They spoke their own dialect. Hakka women did not bind their feet as any "respectable" and sophisticated Han Chinese woman would have. Thus, women joined men in working the fields. Hakkas often worked the poorer land since the area had already been settled when they moved in; there were frequent clashes with locals over land use and irrigation rights and even over patterns of residence. Yet even Hakkas fit in more easily with the longtime resident Han Chinese than the Miao and Yao tribesmen who inhabited the mountainous areas. Hakkas often found themselves in competition and skirmishing with the Miao and Yao peoples. The ethnic diversity in the area increased the likelihood of social unrest.

There were, then, considerable social tensions brought by ethnic divisions, poverty, the presence of a variety of unruly and criminal types, and contempt for the Manchus and Westerners. But until there was some vehicle to express this malaise and give it shape, it was amorphous and aimless. Beginning in the mid-1830s, those vehicles began to appear in the form of secret societies and religion-based sects. A 1836 rebellion led by a Yao minority tribesman who was also leader of a White Lotus community was only the first of several uprisings that eventually involved the Triad society. Like this one, mini-rebellions in 1847 and 1849 were put down. When secret societies and religious sects became involved in the increasingly bitter rivalry between Hakkas and locals, social tensions and violence threatened social fragmentation.

The Rebellion Takes Shape

It was into this world that Hong Xiuquan, a Hakka, was born in 1814, the son of a poor farmer. Since he seemed to be a bright child, his family arranged for Hong to be tutored so that he might take the civil service examination. He failed the first two attempts to pass the examination. In 1836, when he was in Canton to try again, he was handed a collection of Biblical passages and explanatory sermons called "Good Words for Exhorting the Age." The author was one Liang Afa, a convert to Christianity early in the century, who had become an evangelist. The work was explicit in asserting that moral decline was putting Chinese society in great peril; its "stark fundamentalist message hammer[ed] home the omnipotence of God, the degradation of sin and idolatry, and the awesome choice between salvation or damnation."[4] Hong reportedly did not read the material but took it home and set it aside. The next year he failed the examination for the third time. Overcome with humiliation and shame, he reportedly spoke at length with his parents about his feelings of worthlessness. And then he fell ill; how much was physically related and how much a nervous breakdown, is not certain.

During his illness, he had a vision. He ascended to Heaven where he was purified and his body regenerated with new internal organs. A venerable man with golden hair and beard and dressed in black robes handed him a sword and emblems of royalty, instructing him to kill the demons. Feeling as righteous and powerful as he had felt worthless before, Hong set out on quests that spanned the cosmos carrying out the golden-haired man's orders. Accompanying him on these missions was a middle-aged man whom Hong thought to be his older brother. When his illness abated, Hong turned to teaching in the village school, though he clearly remembered his hallucinatory vision. In 1843 he tried to pass the civil service examination once more, and once more he failed. Angry with himself but more so with the system, he returned home.

At this point he apparently read the Christian tracts that he had brought home seven years earlier. It was a eureka experience explaining his earlier vision. The venerable old man was none other than God, and the middle-aged man was Jesus. God addressed Hong as the heavenly younger brother; he was, in effect, God's Chinese son. And it was God who instructed Hong to slay the demons. Yet, in his comprehension of the vision, Hong did not immediately see any political import. His writings in the years after 1843 depicted his charge as one of converting Chinese to Christianity. Further, Hong seemed to want to merge the Christian message, which in his hands meant primarily worship of the One God, with Confucianism, especially an emphasis on living an upright and morally orthodox life. Hong's impassioned beliefs led him to begin to convert family and friends and to antagonize his community by destroying statues of gods in the local temple.

In 1844 Hong and one of his earliest converts, close friend Feng Yunshan, left his native village and journeyed to the hill country of southern Guangxi to begin proselytizing. Hong returned to his home village in late 1844 and spent the next two years writing and teaching about his new beliefs; he studied for two months in 1847 with American Baptist missionary Issachar Roberts in Hong Kong. Feng in the meantime proved himself to be a master missionary and organizer, by 1850 converting many Hakka communities. He organized local congregations and linked them together in multi-village networks stretching into over a dozen counties; they comprised the God Worshipping Society.

In many ways, this organization was a secret society, founded, like the White Lotus sect, on religious ideas. The context of communal struggle and vendettas among ethnic groups, serious famines in 1847 and 1849, and the consequent appearance of many bandits helped fuel the spread of the God Worshippers. God Worshippers, who were in the main Hakkas and Miao tribesmen, began to set up their own militia units for self-defense; in the tense atmosphere, they frequently had fights with militia units formed by non-Hakka, non-Miao local inhabitants. Members of the Triad Society began to join the God Worshippers, adding a contingent to the organization that actively called for the overthrow of the Manchus. It was in this context that Hong's message began to become politicized with many coming to see that the demons God had ordered exterminated were Manchus.

History often turns on contingencies. In late 1848 Feng was seized by a local militia leader, accused of sedition, and sent to Guangdong to the governor-general's office; Hong left also to argue Feng's case. They were gone for seven months, a critical period in the movement's development because it allowed other leaders to emerge. Probably the most powerful was a local bully from Thistle Mountain, the headquarters of the God Worshippers—Yang Xiuqing, an illiterate maker of charcoal. His crony Xiao Chaogui was also a charcoal maker. Two others came from wealthier backgrounds: Wei Changhui of aboriginal stock came from a landlord pawnshop-owning family and Shi Dakai, from a wealthy farm family. Of these four only Shi had some education. Yang and Xiao took a page from the divinity book of Hong Xiuquan. Whereas Hong was the Heavenly Younger Brother, Yang announced—as an obvious reflection of his ambition—that when he spoke it was the voice of God the Father and Xiao alleged that his voice was that of Jesus. These developments had all the makings of future trouble: when divinity clashed with divinity, who would mediate?

In July 1850 the leaders called all God Worshippers, about twenty-thousand strong, to Thistle Mountain. They had left their homes behind; all their movable possessions they brought to put into a common treasury. They had been farmers, charcoal makers, miners, Triads, and pirates. Now they made up a vast military camp. The Qing government recognized the threat as serious: a Christian cult had militarized and was now forming an army. In response, it sent the state's army which was promptly defeated by the God Worshippers in several engagements. With victories under their belts, in January 1851, the God Worshippers declared the establishment of a new dynasty, the Heavenly Kingdom of Great Peace (*Taiping tianguo*). As a visible symbol of their anti-Manchu identity, they abandoned the Manchu hair style, letting their hair grow long all over their heads; people called them the "long-haired rebels." So-coifed, they set out in military campaign to realize the Heavenly Kingdom on earth now.

The year and a half between the Taiping seizure of the small city of Yongan in Guangxi province and the capture of Nanjing in March 1853 saw the rapid growth of the movement, in many cases because the Qing armies, disorganized and poorly disciplined, could not execute any coordinated military strategy. The Taiping suffered serious defeats; in one, the movement's most prolific proselytizer and best organizer, Feng Yunshan was killed in summer 1852. Then in the fall Xiao Chaogui, the voice of Jesus, died of wounds suffered in battle, a death which, taken on its face, should have created a theological crisis of major proportion. But no one seemed to notice.

In their march north to the Yangzi River, a key was crossing over from the Lingnan macroregion (with its east-flowing rivers) to the Middle Yangzi with its vast Yangzi River tributary network. As transportation was made easier after the crossing, triumphs seemed to come the same way. They took the Hunan provincial capital, Changsha in September 1852; the Hubei provincial capital, Wuchang on the Yangzi River in January 1853; and then, Nanjing. With each victory the numbers of Taiping swelled: after Changsha, an estimated 120,000; after Wuchang, possibly 500,000; after Nanjing, perhaps 2 million. On the taking of Nanjing, the Taiping leadership followed the orders the golden-haired man had given Hong long ago back in his native village: They began to exterminate the demons. In an act that might be called the first Nanjing massacre, all of the 40,000 Manchus who lived in Nanjing who were not killed in the fighting were stabbed to death, drowned, or burned alive.

The Taiping Revolution

The Qing dynasty had enough problems with the Taiping Rebellion that exploded out of the Guangxi hills and transformed itself into the Taiping War once it gathered momentum in the Yangzi River valley. But it was the Taiping ideology and its political, social, and economic systems that made up the Taiping Revolution that posed the most serious threat to the regime and that eventually gave rise to the forces that would crush the whole Taiping movement.

Underlying Taiping Christianity was the basic idea of the equality of human beings before God, creating a universal brotherhood-sisterhood. The world and all in it belonged to God. It followed that the brotherhood-sisterhood used the natural world and its products, but that there was no private ownership. Further, economic competition, exploiting the world's resources, and acting selfishly were condemned. Implicit, of course, was a clear economic leveling that made extremes of poverty and wealth untenable. The social ideal was embodied in the 1853 land system which specified that all men *and women* received equal shares of land. That women could receive land is the first indication of the gender revolution that the Taiping were willing to engineer. The land grants were not owned but rather cultivated in common by a grouping of twenty-five families, the basic social-political unit in Taiping society. In keeping with the primitive economic communism that was a hallmark of the new regime, each grouping of families shared a common treasury. The grouping was headed by a "sergeant" who performed multiple roles. He kept records of production and of the common treasury. He mediated disputes and served as judge. He managed the education of the families' children. As the grouping's military leader, he selected militiamen to serve for the unit's defense. He oversaw church services on the Sabbath. The structure of this commune-like system came in large part from an old traditional Chinese work, the *Rituals of Zhou;* but since much of the ideology was based on Christian idealism, the system was clearly a hybrid. It is perhaps not surprising, given the commune-like structure and the primitive form of economic communism, that twentieth century Communists have seen the Taiping movement in a positive light.

The social roles and position of women in Taiping society were markedly superior to those of women in Qing society. As part of the Hakka heritage, footbinding was not permitted. Women were allowed to take the new civil service examinations based upon the Bible and the various writings of Hong Xiuquan. Women could, as a result, hold some offices in the bureaucracy. Women could participate in active military units. In the hands of the Taiping policymakers, a revolution in gender relations seemed a likely development.

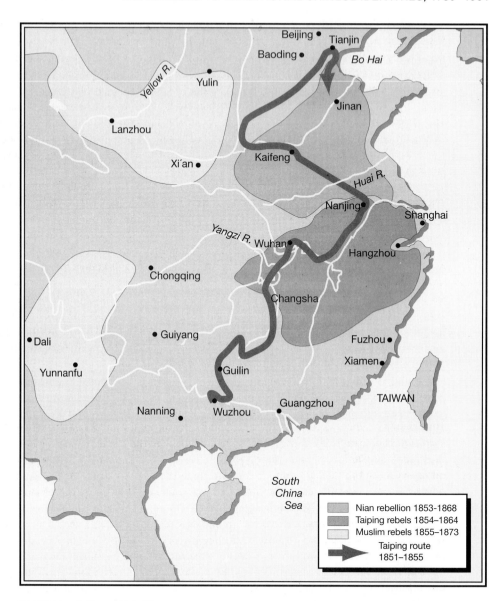

Mid-Nineteenth Century Rebellions

In some areas of social policy, the puritanism of fundamentalist Christianity rein-forced a native Chinese puritanism. The use of alcohol, tobacco, and opium was forbidden. Gambling, witchcraft, prostitution, and adultery were taboo. With regard to sexual relations, the Taiping instituted a policy of strict abstinence, even between husbands and wives. If one thought of a universal brotherhood and sisterhood, sexual relations of any sort would be in-cestuous. It is obvious that the Taiping could not end sexual intercourse permanently, for no newborn Taipings ultimately would mean the end of the movement. But leaders wanted chastity the rule in order to preserve order and discipline until after the heavenly kingdom was firmly established. Therefore, men and women lived in strictly segregated housing; having sex brought with it the penalty of execution. Not surprisingly, because of massive morale problems the policy of sexual segregation was abandoned by 1855.

The Taiping Revolution was a potent threat to the traditional Chinese Confucian system. Taiping-ism provided an all-embracing cosmology, linking the three component parts of the traditional Chinese universe—Heaven, earth, and humans—in a new way. God in a Christian Heaven replaced the impersonal force of Heaven which endowed the Chinese emperor with his mandate to rule and which reflected events on earth by the forces of nature (e.g., storms, plagues, earthquakes). Now earth and its resources were to be shared by humans equally in a universal siblinghood—a startlingly different social arrangement from the traditional Confucian vision of social hierarchy with elites dominating society and its resources. Further, specific social and political policies undercut traditional Chinese norms. The centrality of the family disappeared into the twenty-five family grouping, with the power of the father taken by the sergeant and the family losing its economic and social preeminence. Economic competition was abolished. The new state received a new kind of legitimacy—from the Christian God—and delved deeper into personal lives than ever before: prescribing daily economic, social, and religious roles for people, even forbidding sexual intercourse between husbands and wives. It is little wonder that some Chinese, trained in the glories of traditional Confucianism, might have begun to feel their cultural identity and that of China threatened by the Heavenly Kingdom.

Why the Revolution Failed

Historians speculate whether the Taiping could have swept the Qing away if they had kept their remarkable military momentum and moved to the north. But they did not know where to proceed, so Nanjing became their capital. In the end, it became their tomb. During their eleven-year stint in the city, they tried generally unsuccessfully to implement their vision of politics and society even as they wreaked havoc and destruction on forays in all directions but especially in the Lower Yangzi region.

The eventual collapse came for many strategic reasons. Probably most important was the disintegration of the central leadership. In the days at Thistle Mountain, six men had emerged as leaders, first called "marshals," but after reaching Nanjing, "kings." Two, the South King (Feng) and the West King (Xiao) had been killed in the campaign. That left the powerfully ambitious East King (Yang), the North King (Wei), the Assistant King (Shi), and the Heavenly King (Hong). While egalitarianism was prescribed for the masses by the Taiping kings, the kings themselves had numerous perks and privileges, perhaps the most notable being heavily populated harems, in which they could have sex whenever they wanted. Living luxuriously in palaces that took years to construct, the kings could expect commoners to fall on their faces in a show of obeisance whenever they passed in their sedan chairs. If a commoner did not comply with this expectation, he could become a "celestial lamp," that is, burned alive, or, alternatively, he might by torn apart after being tied to five horses.

Because political power was so concentrated at the top, whenever problems developed among the kings, they had life and death import for the whole movement. Almost from the time of reaching Nanjing, bad blood developed between Hong and Yang, the East King. In a moment of rage, Hong had kicked one of his concubines. Yang, claiming that God the Father spoke through him, demanded that Hong be punished by beatings with a bamboo rod. Later, when Hong had agreed to submit, God graciously canceled the sentence. But from that time they were on bad terms. Yang, continuing to try to one-up Hong, also let it be known that he was not only the voice of God the Father but the incarnation of the Holy Ghost. In 1856, he (in his God the Father voice) demanded that Hong give him the title of "10,000 Years," the traditional title of the Chinese Son of Heaven. This was too much for Hong, who could see a coup in the making. He enlisted Wei, the North King, to kill Yang. Wei's actions were like using a bomb to kill a fly: in a bloody massacre, he slaughtered not only Yang and his family but twenty thousand followers to boot. Shi, the Assistant King, was horrified and denounced Wei's actions, but then discovered that he was next on Wei's list. Though Shi escaped over the city wall, Wei wiped his family out. Hong, now fearing the madman he had unleashed, had Wei and two hundred of his supporters killed. Although there was a regime revival of sorts with the appointment of a raft of new kings, "[i]n this arena of carnage, greed, and paranoia perished whatever remnants of its original vision the Taiping movement might have retained."[5]

Another reason for the failure of the Taiping revolution was that the land reform and commune-like grouping systems were never really put in place in areas that the Taiping controlled. The Taiping, however visionary, were not skillful administrators. The envisioned revolution faced huge practical obstacles, not the least of which was insufficient time to install so radical a program. Even if there had been, there was not enough manpower to penetrate to the local level where entrenched social patterns had to be eradicated. Thus, those people who staffed most of the local governments had been there before the Taiping and had little loyalty to the regime or its program.

A basic reason for the failure can be found in the very identity of the Taiping effort. It was a fanatical totalitarian religious movement which promised utopia but delivered nothing beyond hard work, strict discipline, no sex, and a harsh existence. Once the bloodshed between the kings started, once one's friend became a "celestial lamp," once the discrepancy between the lifestyles of the kings and their entourages and the masses became known, then resentment began to replace the hope that had driven the movement. In short, when promises of future rewards, which had given the movement aim and direction, were not forthcoming, the commitment of people to the regime vanished. In some areas, especially those to which the Taiping came late in the life of its regime, there was not much commitment to the Taiping anyway.

Strategically, the Taipings can be faulted in many ways. Instead of keeping their substantial momentum and moving to the north where Qing political power lay, they had holed up in Nanjing—where the movement eventually was snuffed out. They were not adept at trying to enlist possible collaborators who might join in a common drive to overthrow the Manchus. For example, there were two other serious uprisings that occurred concurrently with the Taiping, the Nian in north China and the Red Turbans in south China. There was cooperation on frequent occasions with the Nian, but never any efforts to pursue the possibility of a long-term strategic alliance, a situation which in any case may have been made doubtful by the religious nature and claims of the Taiping. Similarly, one can point to the Taiping lack of foresight in trying more directly to curry favor with Western nations. Initially Western missionaries were interested and intrigued by the possibility of a "Christian" revolutionary movement seizing power. When many of them visited Nanjing, however, they were shocked by the substance of Taiping Christianity. In addition, just as the Chinese in various tracts had alleged that Western missionaries and their converts practiced sodomy, now Western missionaries alleged that Taiping leaders were involved in homosexual activities. Thus, seeing their ideology and alleged practices, Western missionaries were repulsed; they wanted nothing to do with the Taiping. Western merchants were put off by the Taiping refusal to allow opium into their realm. Western nations, that initially might have been interested in the Taiping as a regime that could possibly be more open to the West and its demands than the Qing, rallied instead to the Qing in order to save Shanghai from Taiping conquest. Late in the rebellion, Western-led mercenary troops, the "Ever-Victorious Army," led first by American Frederick Townsend Ward and then by Charles "Chinese" Gordon, fought Taiping troops in their efforts to take the city.

Despite the multiple internal faults and weaknesses that help explain the Taiping collapse, probably the most important reason for the failure of the Taiping Revolution was military defeat at the hands of Chinese civil servants who were deeply committed to traditional Chinese culture and who saw the Taiping as spearheading an attack on their way of life. In 1852 the Xianfeng emperor named some militia commissioners whose job was to bring together gentry-led local militias into federations that could protect local society from the rebels. Important official Zeng Guofan accepted the appointment. Zeng was one who was outraged by the Taiping threat to traditional culture. His proclamation against the Taiping in 1854 reads in part: "Scholars may not read the Confucian classics, for they have their so-called teachings of Jesus and the New Testament. In a single day, several thousand years of Chinese ethical principles and proper human relationships, classical books, social institutions and statutes have all been completely swept away. This is not just a crisis for our Qing dynasty, but the most extraordinary crisis of all time for the Confucian teachings . . . "[6]

With the permission of the court, Zeng took his appointment as militia commissioner and ran with it straight to the formation of his own provincial (Hunan) army, which he recruited from networks of gentry connections. Throughout the chain of command, Zeng's army was built on Confucian principles—"duty to one's neighbors, piety to one's family, and personal loyalty to one's commander."[7] It was largely funded by a new tax, the *lijin,* collected on shipped commercial goods at customs barriers along key routes. Zeng's protégé, Li Hongzhang, set up a counterpart provincial army in Anhui province. Both men purchased some foreign cannon and arms for their forces. These armies, not the Manchu banners, played the key role in battles leading up to the final Taiping collapse. It was Zeng's Hunan army that was the key in the seizure of Nanjing in July 1864. The Heavenly King had died a few weeks earlier; none of the original leaders of the movement were around at the end.

The destruction wrought by the rebellion was appalling. Population estimates for just the Lower Yangzi macroregion suggest that population in 1843 had reached 67 million, but that a half century later in 1893 it had fallen to 45 million.[8] Fully fifty years after Hong's capital went up in flames, a reporter from a Shanghai newspaper described the great destruction still apparent in the Zhejiang prefectural capital of Yanzhou: "At the southeast corner of the city what are today grazing lands were once the site of a bustling, crowded quarter."[9] Yet the movement had great historical significance apart from the horrific death toll and the destruction. "More than any other rebellion of their day, they addressed themselves directly to the crisis of the times and offered concrete measures for resolving it. Their vision of a new system of property relations, a new mechanism of local control, and a new relationship between the individual and the state was an authentic response to the distinctive problems of the late imperial age."[10]

GUERRILLA WARFARE: THE NIAN REBELLION (1853–1868)

The Nian Rebellion was the only one of the four major mid-century rebellions that did not have a religious dynamic. It developed in the bleakly poor, sandy Huaibei region of north central China along the Anhui-Henan-Jiangsu border, an area much subject to severe flood and drought. As in the Taiping, the region was populated with a huge cast of potential rebels. Some were the "human debris of the White Lotus Rebellion"[11]: White Lotus adherents and perhaps rebels themselves, but, more importantly, mercenary soldiers who had been recruited in Huaibei to fight the White Lotus rebels farther in the interior and who returned to the area after the rebellion. Other potential elements of the population that might have had a predilection toward social violence included peasants propelled toward belligerence by the harsh existence and ruffian-like salt-smugglers and guards for the salt traffickers. A prized and essential commodity produced along the Jiangsu seacoast, salt was a government monopoly. There were always large numbers of men who attempted to make money by smuggling outside the bounds of the monopoly. Studies have also shown that the rate of female infanticide in the area was higher than in some areas of China and that as many as 20 percent of marriage-age men remained unmarried. The availability of large numbers of such unattached males (called "bare sticks"), free to participate in social unrest, was also a destabilizing factor.

In this perennially poverty-stricken area, disaffected types joined groups in various predatory practices—banditry, smuggling, theft, plunder, kidnapping, and organized feuds. Some of these groups were Nian bands that began to appear around the turn of the century; in the beginning they were often structured around families and lineages. Although the origins of the word *nian* remain somewhat unclear, the term came to be applied to groups of bandits who took a blatantly Robin-Hood approach: a folksong of the time put it this way: "The poor men's hearts are happy to see him [the Nian leader], and the moneybags' bones go soft with terror."[12] By about 1850 Nian bands had become firmly ensconced in villages across the Huaibei area with whole communities participating in banditry and plunder. Natural disaster helped to weld these bands together in what became known as the Nian Rebellion. Severe floods in 1851 heralded the beginning of the tragic shift of the Yellow River from the south to the north of the Shandong peninsula; though the major collapse of the dikes did not occur until 1855, the years from 1851 on brought famine and economic calamity. In the context of crisis more and more people joined Nian bands. In guerrilla strikes they plundered for their livelihood as they protected and fortified their home communities.

In 1852, Zhang Luoxing, a local landlord and member of a powerful local lineage involved in salt-smuggling, was chosen to lead a federation of Nian communities. When he was elected "Lord of the Alliance" in 1856, the Nian organized themselves in five units under red, yellow, blue, white, and black banners; each may have contained up to twenty thousand men, though the total number of Nian is unknown. Later the number of banners was increased, but the organization remained loose. Though Zhang's leadership never approached the centralized control of Hong Xiuquan, the banner system did bring greater coherence to the movement. As an indicator of the still-haphazard nature of the movement, however, some Nian bands in Henan province did not even join the federation.

The first phase of the rebellion until about 1864 took the form of what one writer has called seasonal militarization. Even after the formation of the alliance, the Nian continued to fight in small guerrilla units, notably mobile on horseback. As any guerrilla force, they were dependent on the local populace for support. Rebels maintained their fortified base communities and tended to be sedentary in the summer and winter months. In the spring and autumn they moved into the military phase of banditry, raiding, and plunder. They utilized the traditional policy the Qing regime had used in fighting the White Lotus Rebellion, "strengthening the walls and clearing the countryside." This meant keeping rebel communities protected, sometimes with cannon, while gathering all the grain and other food items from the countryside and bringing them into the earth-walled settlements.

This policy created a scorched earth situation in the countryside, which deprived government troops of what they needed to subsist during their efforts to quell the rebellion. A French missionary who accompanied government troops in the early 1860s described the situation. "Almost everywhere, when we were not strong enough to intimidate the villages we had to go through, we were refused even water for our horses; if we asked if we could buy a measure of millet or a feed of corn, we were invariably told that there was none. It seemed as if we were in a wilderness, while, when the rebels approached, everyone rushed to entertain them and to procure what they needed." Most of the rebellion's plundering occurred in Shandong, Henan, and northern Jiangsu in an area of about 100,000 square miles. The Qing regime began to take the movement very seriously when in the mid-1850s Zhang assumed threateningly suggestive titles like the "Great Han Prince with the Heavenly Mandate"; when the rebels adopted secret society symbols, oaths, and rituals; and when the rebels cooperated with the Taiping on a number of occasions.

The Qing government first utilized troops from the Army of the Green Standard who had difficulty coping with the Nian's guerrilla warfare. When Mongol prince Senggerinchin, a descendant of Genghis Khan, was appointed imperial commissioner to deal with the Nian in late 1860, he brought with him not only Green Standard troops but banner cavalry and infantry. Known for his aggressive leadership, he ordered that those he captured have their ears and noses cut off and sent to Beijing as war trophies. Under his direction, Zhang Luoxing was captured in 1863. In his confession before his execution, Zhang noted the handful of times he had cooperated with the Taiping in joint military operations, and at age fifty-three, resignedly recognized his fate and the rebellion's rather dire straits: "In these past few years I have plundered too many places to remember all of them clearly. My wife has been chased off by government troops and I do not know where she is. My son and adopted son have both been captured together with me. My brother Zhang Minxing, leading several thousand men, has taken off for the Southwest and I do not know his where-abouts. As for [four other leaders], they have all been killed by the government troops."[13]

In 1864 a second more dangerous phase of the rebellion began—a war that ranged sporadically over the North China plain, a war fought by the increasingly expert Nian cavalry. In part, this second wind of the Nian may have stemmed in part from the Nian's being joined by Taiping troops who survived the defeat at Nanjing. The ambush death of Senggerinchin in May 1865 led the Qing government to appoint Zeng Guofan, the scholar official hero of the Taiping War, to lead the suppression of the Nian movement. Zeng focused first on the central Nian base. His goal was to establish a water blockade formed by rivers and canals and to establish four major government bases on all sides of the nest area. Having thus isolated the Nian base, government troops invaded it, digging ditches and trenches in order to hamper the Nian use of horses and painstakingly separating each walled village from its neighboring settlements. The goal was to register the population and appoint new village chiefs, then in effect quarantine each "cleansed" village from Nian rebels.

Then government forces attempted to turn the tables on the Nian and utilize the strategy that the rebels had used so successfully—scorched earth and fortified settlements. The first denied rebels their resources; the latter protected villages from rebel seizure. In the end, Zeng was not as successful as in his struggle against the Taiping. He had trouble getting the cooperation of the governors of the provinces involved; and, having demobilized many of his best Hunan provincial forces, he was dependent on troops from the Anhui army of his protégé, Li Hongzhang, many of who were not personally loyal to Zeng. In the end it was simply Nian mobility that allowed many of the rebels who were still in the base area to escape.

Because of these difficulties, the government appointed Li to finish the job in late 1866. The rapid mobility of Nian forces and their effective guerrilla activity still produced two more years of fighting before Li's forces were finally able to wear the rebels down. Eventually victory came through the use of modern British-made guns that Li purchased and the importation of forty-nine hundred experienced and skillful cavalrymen from Manchuria and Inner Mongolia. In contrast to the Taiping, the Nian were no challenge to the traditional value system or to traditional cultural identity. The nature of their warfare, diffuse guerrilla attacks, made them very difficult to suppress: Li had reported that they moved "as freely as mercury." Whereas the Taiping had moved in large military campaigns to take new territory, the Nian were embedded in local villages among lineages, intimately linked to local society. Their rebellion was not so much an attack on Qing political and ideological legitimacy as it was an attempt in the Nian nest area to cast off government authority.

MUSLIMS VERSUS CHINESE: CLASHES IN ETHNIC IDENTITY

Muslims had lived in China for many centuries. Since the Tang dynasty (618–907), Muslims had settled in communities at the eastern end of the silk road in the northwestern provinces of Gansu and Shaanxi. The other site of great Muslim population concentration was in the far southwest province of Yunnan, which had been settled first in the thirteenth century. But there were Muslims elsewhere as well. Muslim Arab traders since the Tang period had lived in ports along the Guangdong and Fujian coasts. By mid-nineteenth century, there were an estimated million Muslims in the region of the Nian Rebellion. Han Chinese Muslims were called *Hui*. While they maintained their own mosques and religious practices, Muslims saw themselves as subjects of Chinese authorities. Muslims could take the civil service examination and receive bureaucratic posts. The early Qing emperors had handled relations with Muslims and their communities with respect.

Beginning in 1762, however, the Qianlong emperor announced a series of anti-Muslim laws. Penalties for crimes committed by Muslims, for example, became harsher than for Han Chinese who had committed the same crime. Problems began to develop when Han Chinese started to move into areas where Muslims had been the majority population and controlled the region's resources. Competition between Han Chinese settlers and Hui over land and commercial opportunities led to animosity and heightened tensions. Court cases erupting over disputes relating to these issues usually found the Muslims on the losing side, discriminated against by Han Chinese and Manchu alike.

The Panthay Rebellion (1855–1873)

Concurrent with the Taiping and Nian conflagrations were two bloody rebellions waged by Muslims in southwest and northwest China. The Panthay rebellion in Yunnan province grew from a mix of ethnic and religious tensions, but the spark which ignited the problem was economic rivalry. Yunnan's greatest natural resource was its copper, gold, and silver mines which had long been controlled by Muslims. Han Chinese settlers had worked some mines which over the years had become depleted. By the beginning of the nineteenth century, they thus lusted after the Muslim mines, a desire that escalated into feuding and violence. In 1856, at the behest of a Manchu official, between two and three thousand Muslims in the provincial capital of Kunming were massacred. Han Chinese in the countryside began to form militias to kill Muslims. Muslims fought back, assassinating Chinese officials and capturing the city of Dali. There an educated devout Hui named Du Wenxiu established the kingdom of Panthay, claiming for himself the title of sultan. Du oversaw a bureaucracy manned primarily by Han Chinese officials and a military with a strong minority of Han Chinese officers. He believed that Islam was compatible with Confucianism; indeed, he proclaimed that all three religions in Yunnan—Islam, Confucianism, and the folk religions of aboriginal tribes—should be revered. Du's forces controlled almost half of Yunnan. He was challenged until 1862 by another Muslim faction that controlled much territory in central and southern Yunnan.

The Qing military response was weak and incompetent. The terrain was rugged and military campaigning rigorous. In the end, the government was able to play off opposing Muslim factions one against the other and depend militarily especially upon local forces and leaders. The rebellion continued in the western part of the province until 1873, where it was marked by siege warfare of over fifty walled cities that Du controlled. Most of the seizures of the cities resulted in bloody massacres by Qing troops. Du was captured and executed.

Northwest Muslim Rebellion (1862–1873)

The northwest rebellion that spread from near Xi'an in Shaanxi province westward into Gansu province was more serious from a strategic viewpoint than the Panthay rebellion. Located between Mongolia and Tibet, regions crucial, as we have seen, in the Qing empire, and reaching to the Russian border, this area was the main corridor between Beijing and Xinjiang, the vast region won by conquest in the mid-eighteenth century. It was also the main passageway through which Chinese Muslims could have contact with the Islamic world to the west. Thus, it was here, more than in Yunnan, where Islamic currents from the west continually reinvigorated or challenged religious thought and faith.

In the mid-eighteenth century a Chinese Muslim had introduced into the area a practice from the mystical Muslim school of Sufism. Known as the New Teaching, it challenged the traditional method of "ridding the mind of all thinking except that focused on God." In the 1780s it inspired several uprisings against the Qing, who put them down, executing the sect leader and banning the sect, actions which turned the leader into a saint and sowed the seeds of a bitter ill will. It was Muslim networks of supporters of the New Teaching that became the main factor in the rebellion that erupted in 1862. Yet it was not so much the New Teaching that was at the root of the violence, but rather simple Muslim–Han Chinese antagonism.

In that year a brief Taiping expedition close to Xi'an had set off unrest. It was the pretext for both Han Chinese and Muslim communities to engage in the rapid formation of militias ostensibly for defense. But the volatile situation quickly led to each side attacking the other, burning villages and murdering their inhabitants. The Qing military was able to suppress the violence in Shaanxi province by early 1864, in part because so many Muslims had fled west to Gansu carrying the message that the Qing was planning a huge massacre of Muslims. The number of adherents of the New Teaching sect, now led by Ma Hualong, were greater in Gansu. Joined by other rebels not of the New Teaching sect, they quickly mobilized. By 1867 all of Gansu save for a few cities and the provincial capital were in Muslim hands; Qing power had been effectively overthrown.

In the fall of 1866 the Qing court appointed Zuo Zongtang (1812–1885) to be governor-general of Shaanxi and Gansu provinces. A scholar who had failed three times in his attempts to pass the highest level civil service examination, Zuo was a serious student of geography and agriculture. In the 1840s he bought a farm to experiment with methods of producing tea and silk. In the first years of the Taiping he became involved in military affairs, rising rapidly in the esteem of fellow officials; and in 1860 he was charged by the court to raise his own army to fight the Taipings, alongside the armies of Zeng Guofan and Li Hongzhang. Named governor-general of Zhejiang and Fujian provinces in 1863, he was an excellent administrator and showed his forward-looking approach by experimenting with steam boats and selecting the site for the Fuzhou shipyard (see Chapter 5). On his way to the northwest to deal with the Muslim uprising, he received orders to help in the final campaigns against the Nian.

Much of the struggle that Zuo faced was siege warfare, attacks on walled urban centers for which his army, most of whom were provincial forces who had had experience fighting the Taipings or the Nians, had large siege guns, including some imported from the German firm of Krupp. In approaching the Muslims, Zuo was guided by the Qing policy: "The only distinction is between the innocent and the rebellious, there is none between Han and Muslim."[14] Because he likened the New Teaching to the heterodoxy of the White Lotus sect, he refused to grant clemency to any active supporter of the New Teaching. As Zuo and his forces moved westward in the campaign, there was great loss of life. His aim was focused on Ma Hualong's stronghold of Jinjibao near the border between Gansu and Inner Mongolia, supposedly protected by more than five hundred forts. Zuo tightened the noose, slowly starving the walled city; by the time Ma surrendered and the siege was lifted, Jinjibao's inhabitants had been reduced to eating grass roots and flesh from the dead. Ma and adult males from his family were executed by slicing, and almost two thousand of his staff and troops were massacred. Zuo then continued the campaign, the final walled city siege coming in October 1873. The campaign took five years, and it saw widespread slaughter of the inhabitants of the besieged cities. But with this suppression, the county was generally free of rebellion and at peace for the first time in over two decades.

All in all, the four mid-century rebellions created vast devastation in six of the nine macroregions, killed tens of millions of people, and destroyed hundreds of towns and cities. They all reflected the ballooning crisis that China faced. Three raised issues of identity. The Taiping championed a completely new identity for China that would have constituted a revolution had it been successful. The Muslim rebellions brought to the fore issues of ethnic identity, so crucial a fact in the Qing multi-ethnic empire, yet an extremely volatile factor with potential not only to rip the fabric of society but to gut out state control. Two openly challenged the Qing dynasty with calls for a new dynasty: the Taiping's Heavenly Kingdom of Great Peace and the Nian's guerrilla campaigns against the government. With the exception of the Panthay rebellion, the mid-century rebellions were suppressed not by Qing generals but by scholar-officials, civilians who had upper degrees in the civil service system. They were military generalists, not professionals, who applied Confucian moral and political principles, insisted on serious training for and discipline among their troops, and used some Western technology, particularly guns and ships. They faced both toward the Chinese past, trying to save their culture from the Taiping version of Christianity, the Nian plunderers, and the Muslim crusaders, and toward the Chinese future, taking the first gingerly steps toward what became known as "self-strengthening," that is, using Western technology to bolster the Chinese defense. In one sense the military actions of the scholar-officials were cases of ethnic Chinese saving Manchu overlords; but more accurately it was an effort of scholar administrators imbued with Chinese culture aiding their rulers also committed to that culture.

Notes

[1] Jean Chesneaux, *Peasant Revolts in China, 1840–1949* (New York: W. W. Norton, 1973), p. 23.

[2] Thomas W. Kingsmill, "Retrospect of Events in China and Japan during the Year 1865," *Journal of the North China Branch of the Royal Asiatic Society* 2 (1865), 143.

[3] In using "civil war," I am following the lead of Pamela Crossley in *The Manchus;* see p. xv.

[4] Philip A. Kuhn, "The Taiping Rebellion" in Fairbank, Ed., *The Cambridge History of China, Volume 10: Late Ch'ing, 1800–1911, Part 1,* p. 267.

[5] Ibid., p. 295.

[6] "Zeng Guofan: A Proclamation against the Bandits of Guangdong and Guangxi, 1854" in Pei-kai Cheng and Michael Lestz with Jonathan Spence, *The Search for Modern China: A Documentary Collection* (New York: W. W. Norton, 1999), pp. 147–148.

[7] Wakeman, *The Fall of Imperial China,* p. 170.

[8] G. William Skinner, "Regional Urbanization in Nineteenth Century China" in G. William Skinner, Ed., *The City in Late Imperial China* (Stanford: Stanford University Press, 1977), p. 229.

[9] *North China Herald,* 1914/8/1, p. 336.

[10] Kuhn, p. 317.

[11] Ibid., p. 310.

[12] Quoted in Chesneaux, p. 33.

[13] Quoted in Elizabeth J. Perry, *Rebels and Revolutionaries in North China, 1845–1945* (Stanford: Stanford University Press, 1980), p. 266.

[14] Quoted in Kwang-ching Liu and Richard Smith, "The Military Challenge: The North-West and the Coast" in Fairbank and Liu, p. 228.

5

The Power of Traditional Cultural Identity: Chinese Reactions to Continuing Threats

For a culture so deeply rooted in the glories of the past the bloody and violent nightmares of the mid-nineteenth century were wrenching for they seemed such a cataclysmic rupture from the past. Chinese culture had always focused on the past. Even for Confucius the golden age had been in that past, a time when society was harmonious and the country was peaceful. The goal of statesmen throughout the centuries was to restore something of that splendid past, even though no one thought that it could ever really be done. The past framed and confined the present so that any change in state and society had to be rationalized in terms of that past, whether the particularly relevant past was the policies of a recent emperor or one's family traditions.

Previous foreign invaders had come to China on horseback, wielding bows and arrows. To greater or lesser degree, China had been able to rein them in, incorporating them into the Chinese cultural world. But these foreign invaders had come by sea with big ships and powerful cannon. They offered no indication that they would ever accept the Chinese cultural tradition. The break with the past was dramatically clear. The Central Country was being buffeted by radical challenges that it could not control; humiliation seemed to grow by the day. The crises of the nineteenth century therefore presented Chinese leaders with a life-and-death decision: how to overcome their military and strategic impotence so that they might begin to compete with these foreigners on a more equal playing field.

Scholar-officials varied considerably in their reactions and in their prescriptions about what should be done. Yet no one reacted that the Chinese political system or its institutions might somehow be too weak or ill arranged or at fault. All reactions were defensive. Even the most liberal reaction, to move to self-strengthening, was based on the premise that the system and its institutions must be saved.

UNWILLING TO CHANGE (OR HOLDING TO THAT OLD-TIME IDENTITY)

Some argued that China's only vehicle to restored strength was in revitalizing its incomparably great culture which had given rise to the glories of the past. Above all, these culturalists argued, barbarian weapons and machines were not the answer. Use of such implements of war would contaminate the Chinese hands that wielded them. If tools of war were to be part of the answer to China's problems, then Chinese should use those from the Chinese repertoire of warfare from the past.

One of these archconservatives and a famous teacher, official, and man of letters, Yu Yue (1821–1907) looked at China in the late nineteenth century and wrote about his three fears. His first fear brings us face to face with the issue of China's identity: if the current involvement of Western nations in China continues, Yu was afraid that "it will not be long before she loses her identity as the 'Central Nation.'"[1] Second, if scholars begin to study Western things, "Confucianism will be undermined and eventually destroyed." Third, with technology beginning to use up natural resources, "the universe as we know it may end soon." The common denominator in these fears is *fear of change* and the impact it might have on the world that Yu, holder of the highest civil service degree and member of the Hanlin Academy, had come to know.

Yu was not alone in his fears. A host of influential men in the Beijing bureaucracy and in positions of power came to oppose any compromise in dealing with the West or adopting Western things. Perhaps the most influential in the 1860s was the famous Mongol official Woren. Like Yu Yue, he held the highest degree and served in the Hanlin Academy. In addition he held a variety of high official posts—Grand Secretary and president and vice president of several Boards (or ministries) where he established connections with and enjoyed considerable influence over key figures in the capital. He has also been called "one of the two or three great transmitters" of Neo-Confucian thought during the nineteenth century.[2] And he was probably the staunchest opponent of any dealing with the West. He is said to have wept when he was appointed to serve in a new governmental body, the Zongli Yamen, set up to deal with the West. When his attempt to resign was not permitted, he intentionally threw himself from his horse on the first day on the job, injuring himself. He then used the injury as an excuse that he could not walk and thus could not serve on the Yamen; although he received several sick leaves, he did not recover until he was allowed to resign.

Woren (and others) made arguments like the following. "The foundation of a nation lies in the virtues she possesses" rather than in technology; no nation, he claimed, "has ever become strong by relying on achievement in technology."[3] At the heart of the answer for the crisis facing China was dependence on Confucian moral principles and unfailingly continuing to exhort the people to follow these principles. Anathema to Woren was dealing with the West, which he described as treacherous, as mere technicians—"foreigners have always been our enemies." If we have to be taught this science, math, and technology, Woren asserted, find Chinese experts to do the job: "Why do we have to employ foreigners? Why do we have to honor them as our teachers?" Foreigners were devoid of civilization, simply put, barbarians; many archconservatives even saw them as closer to beasts—dogs and sheep—than to men.

But, the arguments on technology went on, we should not have to borrow at all. China had never borrowed from the West; why begin now? Just because technology was good for the West, did not mean that it would have the same meaning in China, for China had different values and realities. The West, for example, might need machines to make up for a labor shortage; but move the machines to China with its vast population, and the machines would only make unemployment a greater problem.[4] Even if China would be convinced that it must borrow technology from the West, would not the West, for military reasons, only sell China obsolete guns and cannon. In that case China would be cheated as well as humiliated. A number of officials claimed that the benefits of technology had clearly been exaggerated. Further they argued that the use of technology would deplete the natural resources that were used to power and feed machines. Finally, they worried that introduction of Western technology and Western things in general would interfere with and wreck the existing cosmic order. Since the cosmic and human worlds were intimately connected and mutually reflective, Western imports like railroads and telegraph poles, for example, would by their nature make the "spirits of wind and water" (*fengshui*) go awry with negative and perhaps catastrophic results.

SELF-STRENGTHENING

Rationale and Fallacy

The so-called self-strengtheners, those who wanted to strengthen China with a view to fending off Western imperialists, had a far different line on technology. Li Hongzhang, the commander of the anti-Taiping Anhui army, minced no words: "I firmly believe that to strengthen herself as a nation, China must learn Western technology."[5] While self-strengthening involved a multi-pronged effort in the spheres of diplomacy, education, technology, and the military, advances in military technology—guns, ships, and armaments—were usually taken as a yardstick of successful self-strengthening for they were most clearly related to defense.

But how to rationalize these changes that to archconservatives only raised fears? Self-strengtheners started with the premise that Western weapons and ships were simply inanimate machines, culture-neutral, as it were. They argued that foreign weapons and ships could therefore be bought or manufactured without cultural pollution. Indeed, they argued that in the extreme crisis facing China, foreign military implements were the *means* by which the crucial *end*—protecting traditional Chinese culture—could be achieved. In other words, Western guns and ships were the techniques by which the substance of Chinese civilization could be protected and maintained. By this formula, self-strengtheners rationalized change as the only way to protect the culture of the past and to realize some restoration of that past. Even for these "reformers" the past was the lens making possible appropriate views of the present.

Simply stated, this formula seemed tame enough, but it contained a serious logical fallacy. Foreign machines might look culture-neutral (that is, anyone can turn a switch, pull a trigger, or pilot a ship), but they came with a host of culture-specific scientific and worldviews. To build ships and weapons at the new Jiangnan arsenal or the recently constructed Fuzhou shipyard would require the study of engineering and technology. Reading these scientific texts would take the student into a new world where old assumptions about the natural world would almost certainly be challenged. If a Chinese entered that world and then returned to the Chinese classics, he would again almost certainly see those classics in a broader context and ask new questions of them. For that student, their meaning and indeed the substance of Chinese culture had been changed. In short, means do affect ends.

Or, taking up more practical issues, if arsenal and shipyard schools have been established with engineering and foreign language courses, how could they attract able young men to study these "barbarian" things? After all, the ladder to success in imperial China remained the civil service examination. Li Hongzhang had an answer: "One of the measures we can take is to introduce a new category in the civil service examination, namely the category of technology." But that strategy would mean that a traditional degree which had always been based on the classical humanities tradition could now be obtained with at least part based on something from outside that tradition. Clearly, if this were the case, the practical requirements for successful self-strengthening clearly gave evidence that the means had come to have an immense impact on the ends. Borrowing Western technology had a way of undercutting traditional Chinese cultural substance. The logical fallacy of the self-strengtheners was one that would begin to open China up to new, often unpredictable forces. It was also one that would appear again more than a century later when China opened itself up to computers and high-technology in the late twentieth century.

The Self-Strengtheners

In the bureaucracy at Beijing, the key supporters of self-strengthening were Manchu leaders Prince Gong and Wenxiang. Prince Gong was the sixth son of the Daoguang emperor. He negotiated, at age twenty-five, the 1858 Treaty of Tianjin and the 1860 Convention of Beijing; his conduct of foreign affairs in the 1860s into the 1880s was known for his conciliation. In 1861, after the death of his brother, the Xianfeng emperor, he played a key role in the coming to power of the late emperor's concubine, Cixi, who emerged in a coup d'etat as regent for her young son, the Tongzhi emperor. Though considered spoiled and not averse to seeking bribes from office-seekers, Prince Gong was especially close to Wenxiang, one of the most talented, conscientious, and respected Manchu metropolitan officials. A *jinshi* degree-holder, Wenxiang became a member of the Grand Council, the most important policy and personnel body in the central government.

Among Chinese officials, the triumvirate that had been instrumental in suppressing the mid-century rebellions, Zeng Guofan, Li Hongzhang, and Zuo Zongtang, were important leaders in the self-strengthening effort. Zeng was a model of the Confucian official, the most important Chinese official at mid-century. A *jinshi* degreeholder and member of the Hanlin Academy, he served with distinction in various capacities. His Hunan army, which he formed in the conscientious way that was his hallmark, was the chief agent of the Qing victory over the Taiping. He became a Grand Secretary in 1867 and governor-general of Zhili province in 1868. Known for his foresight, incorruptibility, and great perseverance,

Prince Gong

he was an excellent judge of men: Many of the more than eighty men who served on his personal staff later became famous in their own right.

Li Hongzhang was a protégé of Zeng, though in many ways Li was as flashy as Zeng was gray in his stolidity. A *jinshi* degreeholder, Li became the most powerful official in the last thirty years of the nineteenth century and was involved in many of the major events and developments of the times, including every important international issue. His most important official post was as governor-general of Zhili province (the capital province) from 1872 until his death in 1901. He amassed great power and wealth; in the process, he was often awash in an aura of corruption. (A brief biographical vignette of Zuo Zongtang, the central hero in the suppression of the northwest Muslim rebellion, is in Chapter 4.) There was a host of second tier reformers, but one other should be mentioned: Feng Guifen, a Hanlin Academy scholar and local administrator, who might be called the best publicist for self-strengthening. In 1860 he published a collection of about fifty essays discussing the political, social, and economic issues facing China and calling for reform. He noted especially the rationale for self-strengthening—that Western learning was useful in a framework of Chinese values. Feng had considerable influence in the self-strengthening thinking and proposals of Li Hongzhang.

Reforms

Though self-strengthening did not call for institutional change, emphasizing instead already existing institutions and policies, an important new institution was established in 1861. Established principally at the initiative of Prince Gong and opposed by the conservatives, the Zongli Yamen ("Office for General Management") was the general coordinating bureau for all "Western affairs" (*yangwu*). These included diplomacy and trade, missionary problems, and, most important in the context of reform, overseeing and managing all projects and programs that involved Western matters or technology. Prince Gong headed the Zongli Yamen for twenty-seven years (1861–1884, 1894–1898). Indicative of its centrality in governmental decision making was the fact that from 1861 to 1884, it functioned in reality as a committee of the Grand Council, with Grand Councilors serving concurrently on the Yamen. From 1861 to 1868, three of the five Councilors served on the seven-man Yamen; from 1869 to 1875, four of the five served on the ten-man Yamen; and from 1876 to 1881, all of the Councilors served on the twelve-man Yamen, with the number of Councilors from 1880 at six.

In the sphere of diplomacy, the Zongli Yamen sponsored the establishment of a school to train diplomats to handle relations in the new international order China had to face. The Tongwenguan (Interpreters College) was formed in 1862 to offer foreign language instruction. When Prince Gong and Wenxiang undertook an initiative to seek out Western science teachers for the school in 1866, conservatives shot down the trial balloon. However, in 1869, the school developed an eight-year course of study with a curriculum focused on languages and science. Most of China's diplomats were trained there. It was headed by American missionary W. A. P. Martin, who also co-translated a major work on international law, Henry Wheaton's *Elements of International Law*. Published under the auspices of the Zongli Yamen, translations like this began to acquaint diplomats and the Zongli Yamen's members with Western concepts and practices of international relations. Robert Hart, the longtime inspector-general of the Imperial Maritime Customs Service, served as leading foreign advisor to the Yamen.

The major diplomatic step managed by the Zongli Yamen was the sending of diplomats abroad, not a small accomplishment given the shame and contamination, that many Chinese associated with dealing with Western "barbarians." Zongli Yamen members were frequently referred to as "devil's slaves." The first "Chinese" ambassador abroad was actually an American, Anson Burlingame, who had been serving as the American minister in China. Sent in 1868, on the advice of Robert Hart, Burlingame's mission was to dissuade Western nations from being too insistent in upcoming treaty revision talks. Traveling to the United States and European capitals with Chinese and Manchu co-envoys, Burlingame was able to achieve the mission's objective: Countries were at least temporarily moderate in their approach to treaty revision. Burlingame himself was not so fortunate: He died of pneumonia in Russia. His co-envoys made it back to China in late 1870, but they were treated as if the trip had contaminated them. Both were sent far away from Beijing, almost as if in exile—one to a position in Mongolia, and the other, to a remote post in western China.

That treatment paled in contrast to the treatment received by Guo Songtao, the first *Chinese* ambassador, sent abroad in 1877. Guo had been a Hanlin Academy scholar who had thought long and hard about China's dealings with the West. He became an advisor to Li Hongzhang in the early 1860s. In the self-strengthening camp, he wanted to discover the secrets of Western wealth and power. He was also persuaded that successful policy toward the West could only come when Western realities were understood; he firmly believed that the application of longheld Chinese principles in any crisis would end negatively if they were taken without reference to the specific circumstances of the crisis. When he accepted an appointment to serve as minister to Great Britain, he was roundly condemned for his decision by conservative officials. One wrote in his diary, "Guo Songtao stands out for his learning and literary talents, but he should not have accepted the mission to the West! I am truly regretful for him."[6] He was leaving the world of Confucian sages to go serve the devils. In Guo's hometown in Hunan province, people felt that he had brought such shame on his native place that they attempted to demolish his house.

During his two-year stay in London, he was awed by the British system of governance and especially by the modernization begun by the Industrial Revolution. In letters back to China, he extolled the virtues of railroads, telegraphs, machines, and electricity. Guo talked of Great Britain's Great Leap Forward in a letter to Li Hongzhang: "From the beginning of England's rise [following the Industrial Revolution], it has been only several decades; while China was weak and declining, they covered a distance of 70,000 li in the wink of an eye. . . . Chinese scholars and officials are presumptuous in their sanctuary and are trying to obstruct the changes of the universe; they can never succeed."[7] The vituperation and threats that Guo received led him to cut short his service as ambassador. Although he had intended to publish his diary under the auspices of the Zongli Yamen, the court, receiving great pressure from the ultra-conservatives, ordered the seizure and destruction of the printing blocks. Fearful for his life, Guo retired—and might as well have been in exile for all the impact he had on Chinese developments. Permanent diplomatic missions were sent to the United States, Japan, Russia, Germany, and France for the first time in 1879, fully eighteen years after Western ambassadors had begun to live in Beijing, a time gap that underscores the difficulty, acrimony and sense of shame that underlay China's moving into the international arena. It was all a question of identity: China's identity as the Central Kingdom had been lost forever. China had been decentered and was now simply one in a large family of nations.

In his arguments about self-strengthening, Feng Guifen had asserted certainly with tongue-in-cheek that "what we then have to learn from the barbarians is only the one thing, solid ships and effective guns."[8] Certainly weapons for defense were first on China's borrowing priority list. The first steps toward attaining military technology was through the Zongli Yamen with the establishment of arsenals, shipyards, and machine shops. Key here were also the scholar-administrator heroes of rebellion suppression. In 1865 at Shanghai, Zeng and Li established the Jiangnan Arsenal, which produced ships, gunboats, muskets, howitzers, shrapnel, ammunition, tools, and machinery. The following year Zuo built the Fuzhou Shipyard at which 2,000 Chinese craftsmen, 900 laborers, and an administrative staff of 150 labored to produce larger ships than did the Jiangnan Arsenal. Fifteen were produced from 1869 to 1874.

There were educational programs established at both the shipyard and the arsenal. The shipyard school was established in 1867, having enrolled over a hundred pupils under thirteen years of age. For political correctness sake, they had to take a Chinese curriculum and enter either a French or English division. In the English division, cadets took courses in nautical astronomy, plane and spherical trigonometry, geography, and English, all under a three-year "major" of theoretical navigation. Then they went on board a training ship. The French division focused on naval construction and design with courses on analytical geometry, calculus, physics, mechanics, and French. After five or six years they took on major responsibilities at the shipyard. The arsenal had a more varied educational program. A translation department published manuals, textbooks, and treatises on science and technology; at least fifty-four volumes were published by 1877. There were various courses of study, including Chinese studies, English, French, math and science; but the study was more haphazard and not as directed to specific ends as the program at Fuzhou.

Finally, part of the self-strengthening educational program was sending students abroad for training so that they could return and assist in China's modernizing effort. The most famous of these was the mission of Yung Wing, a Cantonese who had been educated at Yale with the support of missionaries. Between 1872 and 1875 with the approval of Zeng, Li, and the Zongli Yamen, four groups of thirty boys, ages twelve to sixteen, went to the Connecticut Valley. Originally they were to stay for fifteen years, attending school, living with families, and spending two weeks every three months at Hartford being tutored in a Chinese curriculum. The latter was not to much avail in preventing the boys from becoming thoroughly Americanized. The program was ended in 1881 because of many reasons, including a growing anti-Chinese movement in the United States. On their return, many of the boys-turned-men made contributions in the technological and business sectors.

For the technological, diplomatic, and educational progress made under the leadership of the self-strengtheners from the early 1860s into the 1880s, the speed of progress and the possibility of bolder initiatives was greatly hampered by the ultra-conservatives. Many officials on all levels dragged their feet on carrying out policies. Conservatives attacked the famous self-strengthening proponents and secondary figures as traitors. As we have seen, just dealing with foreigners at all could bring the wrath of the conservatives. Cultural inertia held back change. Feng Guifen's collection of essays on reform, published in 1860, was not presented to the emperor for his reading until 1889. Another key early work explaining the West, Wei Yuan's 1843, *Illustrated Treatise on the Maritime Kingdoms,* was not presented to the court until 1858.

If one needs further evidence at the negative and destructive impact of the ultra-conservative culturalist, he need only look at the course of railroad development. In 1876, a less-than-twenty mile line from Shanghai to Wusong was started by Westerners. In 1877 Chinese officials purchased the line and ripped up the tracks. Railroad construction from Beijing to the town of Qingjiangpu planned by official Ding Richang, who worked closely with both Zeng and Li, had to be aborted because of conservative opposition. Likewise, a plan as late as 1889 to run a line from Tianjin to Tongzhou, about ten miles east of Beijing, was forcibly discarded. Guo Songtao rightly predicted the outcome of such outmoded thinking: "After several decades foreigners will arrive and then they will gradually build railroads and develop (natural resources) for us . . . Then both the ownership and the profits will fall into the hands of foreigners and China will have nothing to depend upon."[9]

HOLDING TO THE TRIBUTARY MENTALITY: KOREA

In the twenty-one years from 1874 to 1895, China lost its three most important tributary states, the Ryukyu Islands (Liuqiu in Chinese), Vietnam, and Korea. Aggressive actions by

Japan in the first and third and by France in the second pointed to a new wave of imperialism in the closing quarter of the century. The first two cases resulted from China's naiveté and inexperience in managing foreign relations in the system of Western international law. All three cases underscore how deeply the tributary mentality continued even though on paper it had been dead since 1860. It is most likely the case that for the Chinese the treaty system and the tributary system co-existed, relating to each other in various ways in different places and situations.

The Loss of the Ryukyu (Liuqiu) Islands

For China the Ryukyus were an important tributary state; since 1372, China had regularly received tribute missions from the islands. But China was completely unaware of the islands' relationship to Japan. In 1609 the feudal lord of the Japanese domain of Satsuma on Kyushu's southeast coast had conquered the islands. From that point—even before the establishment of the Qing dynasty—Japan ruled the northern part of the islands directly with the rest indirectly under the titular control of the Ryukyuan king. The islands thus paid tribute to Satsuma and even to the shogun in Edo. Since Satsuma wanted to participate in trade with China, however, it ordered the Ryukyus to continue to participate in the tribute system with China.

Late in 1871 over fifty shipwrecked sailors from the Ryukyu Islands were killed by aborigines in eastern Taiwan. In 1873, the Japanese claimed that they had the sole right to speak for the islands and in 1874 undertook a naval expedition to Taiwan to punish the aborigines. China responded in amazement, declaring that both Taiwan and the Ryukyus were Chinese. The Japanese asserted that they had had to act because the aborigines' action clearly revealed that the Chinese did not in fact exercise sovereignty over the island. When face-to-face diplomacy did not achieve a solution to the dispute, the British minister served as arbiter. In the end, China paid 500,000 taels for the victims of the killings and for some Japanese barracks built in Taiwan and promised also not to condemn the Japanese expedition. Both actions pointed to diplomatic obtuseness: going along with the expedition was at base a recognition of Japan's position (and control) over the Ryukyus, and the payment to Japan amounted, in the words of the British ambassador to Japan, to a "willingness to pay for being invaded."[10] In 1879, Japan annexed the islands, and they became Okinawa prefecture.

Troubles in Korea

Korea was one of China's closest tributary states. Whereas many tributary states sent tributary missions once every so many years, in the Qing Korea sent four tributary missions every year. China had occupied the northwestern part of the peninsula during the Han dynasty and had tried without long-term success to seize the country again in the Sui and Tang dynasties. Despite that history of aggression, the Koreans took Chinese institutions as the models for their cultural and political institutions; by the Yi dynasty (1392–1910), Korea was in many ways a smaller replica of the Chinese system. Koreans called its relations with China, "serving the great" while its relations to others, for example Japan, were denoted "neighborly relations."

A tragic fact of Korea's history has been its geographical position. Caught between Japan and the huge land powers of China and Russia, Korea has served as the bridge for land powers to Japan (in the thirteenth-century Mongol invasions) and for Japan to the land powers (in the late-sixteenth century invasion of Japanese leader Hideyoshi). Viewed in the context of potential threats from the mainland, Japan, in a stock phrase, contended that Korea was a "dagger pointed at its heart." It is not surprising that in the nineteenth century Korea tried to isolate itself for protection, turning itself into what became known as the "hermit nation."

From 1866 to 1873 Korea had been ruled by a regent for the minor king who had been adopted into the line of succession because there was no direct heir. The regent, known as the Taewon'gun, was in reality the king's biological father and would remain one of the political lightning rods around which many would rally from the 1860s into the 1880s. The king had in his early teens been married off to an ambitious older woman of the powerful Min family who emerged as the other political lightning rod. Since the rivalry between China and Japan in Korea would be played out in the context of the struggle between the Taewon'gun and Queen Min, their positions regarding foreign affairs are important. "The Taewon'gun had a simple foreign policy: no treaties, no trade, no Catholics, no West, and no Japan. He viewed Japan's progressive reforms as yet more evidence of how far it had fallen from the way, how little the island people really understood the virtues of a Sinic [Chinese] world order."[11] But the king took over in 1873, and with him, his assertive wife, more open to dealing with the outside world.

In the first half decade following the overthrow of the Tokugawa shogunate in 1868, some government leaders in the new Meiji regime saw Korea as an opportunity. By military action in Korea, Japan could establish itself on the continent, prevent other countries from gaining territory or a colony so close to Japan, and provide a chance for former samurai to get the fighting blood out of their system by turning them on Korea as retaliation for a Korean rebuff to Japanese vessels. Though that plan came to naught, Korea, located only a hundred miles across the Sea of Japan, began to play an important role in Japan's conception of its role in northeast Asia.

In 1875 after Japanese gunboats had already leveled a Korean fort on Kanghwa Island near Inchon, and well aware of the tributary relationship between China and Korea, Japan sent emissaries to sound out China about its reactions to greater Japanese involvement in Korea. Li Hongzhang's tributary-framed answer was that "though Korea is a dependent country of China, it is not a territorial possession; hence in its domestic and foreign affairs, it is self-governing." Emboldened by China's implicit permission to talk to Korea about opening trade, the Meiji government proceeded to "open" the hermit nation by the signing of a treaty in 1876. As to Korea's status, the treaty stated that "Korea, being an independent state, enjoys the same sovereign rights as does Japan." China interpreted "independent" as "autonomous," but it is clear from subsequent events that Japan saw things differently.

When Japan annexed the Ryukyu Islands in 1879, China seemed to suddenly become aware of the threat that an unchallenged Japan posed in Korea. In 1880 Korean relations were taken away from the Board of Rites which oversaw the tributary system and given to Li Hongzhang. Li encouraged the Korean government to sign treaties with Western powers

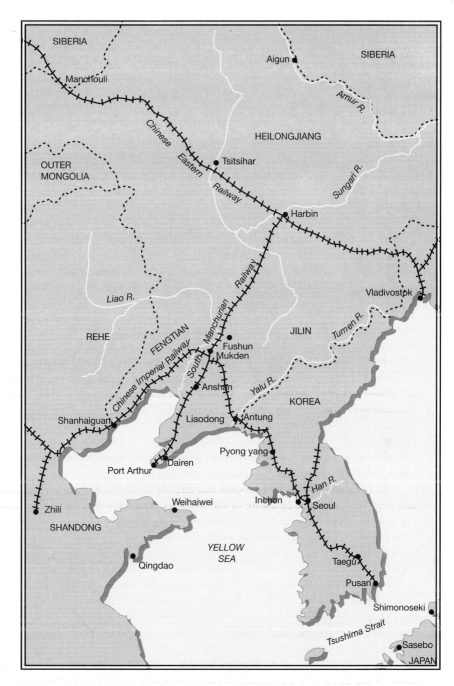

Northeast Asia, Late Nineteenth, Early Twentieth Century

and thereby to encourage a foreign policy of using barbarians to control barbarians. Indeed, when there was some hesitance on the Korean part, Li negotiated the United States-Korean treaty and presented it to the Koreans to sign: Thus the tributary elder brother acted to pull the younger brother into the international community. Another way to see this is that Li Hongzhang had simply taken over the making of Korean foreign policy, a view that is underscored by the fact that he followed up the American treaty with two more, with the British and the Germans.

Despite Li's efforts, the period was one of increasing tensions between China and Japan on the Korean peninsula; with both keeping some nationals in the country, the situation was always ripe for problems. Firmly in power, Queen Min supported reform, specifically hiring Japanese military officers to train the nucleus of a modern Korean military. The Taewon'gun was determined to break her power. In 1882 he reportedly incited a Korean army mutiny over the better provisions that the Japanese-trained unit received. The mutineers attacked the palace (with Queen Min barely escaping) and burned the Japanese legation. The Taewon'gun again took the reins of government. Both China and Japan sent forces "to restore peace."

The Chinese then exercised the big brother act once again. Informed of the Taewon'gun's complicity in the mutiny, the Chinese arrested him and threw him in jail in China because he had moved against the queen, whom the Chinese recognized as the proper authority. This act, the arrest of a Korean leader by Chinese diplomats and his incarceration in China, trumpeted the tributary mentality for all the world to hear. Clearly not dead, the tributary system continued to function through the cultural inertia that was so much of the response to reform, or more accurately, to change. The upshot of the crisis was that the Japanese maintained a permanent guard at their legation in Seoul; the Chinese kept three thousand soldiers in the country, sent arms and Chinese instructors to the Korean military, and posted advisors to the Korean government. These actions too were those of the elder brother.

In the mid-1880s, different Koreans looked in different directions for the path that the country should follow, some to China, some to the United States, some to Japan. A number of youthful Koreans had gone to Japan to study and had become passionately enthusiastic about the course of Meiji reforms. In 1884, they attempted a coup against a Korean regime that now seemed clearly in the Chinese camp. The conspiracy was joined by the Japanese ambassador with Japanese legation guards ready for action. The plan: take advantage of a large public gathering—a dinner attended by foreign diplomats and key Korean officials in celebration of the opening of the new post office—to assassinate important leaders. The reformer-conspirators were successful in murdering seven people. They then set fire to the city; Japanese guards rushed the palace and seized the king and queen. But with Queen Min's urgent appeal, the Chinese military leader Yuan Shikai advanced on the palace, freed monarch and spouse, and suppressed the coup. But Japan sent forces and demands both for an indemnity and an apology over damage to the Japanese legation (which had, in fact, been torched by the fleeing Japanese ambassador). Japanese leader Ito Hirobumi was sent to China to negotiate an end to the crisis with Li Hongzhang. Each country withdrew its forces and promised to notify the other if it was planning to send forces in the future. Presumably if that would happen, joint consultations would mean that cooler heads would prevail and another crisis could be averted. This Li-Ito convention brought another decade of peace, in which the new Chinese Resident General, Yuan Shikai, sought to preserve the forms of Chinese suzerainty. But the agreement also made Korea a virtual co-protectorate of China and Japan. The trouble was not over.

HOLDING TO THE TRIBUTARY MENTALITY: VIETNAM

Vietnam, the northern part of which China had controlled directly from the Han through the Tang dynasties, was a close tributary in the Ming and Qing dynasties. Though it fought off Chinese political control, it continued in the Chinese cultural orbit, like Korea, borrowing its most important political and cultural institutions. From the Chinese perspective, the tributary relationship with Vietnam was a crucial reality. The Chinese established Vietnamese emperors in office and sent troops to help its tributary "younger brother" put down unrest. Certainly by the 1880s after China's experience with foreign invasion and pressures, in addition to her tributary concerns, China was also aware of the strategic importance of Vietnam for its own security. In the words of one official, "The border provinces are China's gates; the tributary states are China's walls. We build the walls to protect the gates, and protect the gates to secure the house. If the walls fall, the gates are endangered; if the gates are endangered, the house is shaken."[12]

French interest in Vietnam began with Jesuit missionaries in the seventeenth century, but the French Revolution and the Napoleonic wars put East Asian involvement on hold. At the turn of the nineteenth century, the French became briefly involved, offering crucial support for Nguyen Anh in the establishment of the Nguyen dynasty (1802–1945). The Nguyen emperors championed and emphasized Chinese cultural models and forbade trade and intercourse with the West and the spread of Christianity. In the late 1850s the French began to take more concerted action to extend their interests, beginning with a military campaign in southern Vietnam as revenge against anti-missionary riots. By 1862, they had taken Cochin-China, the three southernmost provinces of the country, and forced the Vietnamese government to cede it to them.

A treaty in 1874 further extended French influence, permitting French shipping on the Red River in the country's northernmost section, Tonking, and seizing control of Vietnamese foreign relations. Part of France's intention in this treaty was to try to establish the independence of Vietnam from China, an obvious precondition if France was taking control of Vietnam's foreign affairs. Thus, the treaty recognized "the sovereignty of the King of Annam [Vietnam] and his complete independence of all foreign powers."[13] The Chinese responded to this treaty by saying that Vietnam had been a tributary state of China for centuries, and that China would look into the matter; but it did not do so. Even worse, when the Chinese response was translated into French, "had been a tributary" was translated into the past perfect tense which implied that the tributary relationship was completely over. Therefore, the French took this as Chinese tacit acceptance of what was essentially a French protectorate. Feeling free to act forcefully, the French stepped up their aggressive actions in northern Vietnam whereupon the Vietnamese government, in the role of tributary "younger brother," sent a tributary mission to China and asked the Chinese for help. With

Southeast China and Vietnam

the situation "as precarious as piled eggs," the Chinese sent in irregulars known as the Black Flags, who began to skirmish with French troops in 1882.[14] The next year the Chinese without fanfare dispatched regular troops.

THE WAR WITH FRANCE AND THE IMPACT OF SELF-STRENGTHENING

As war clouds thickened, Chinese policy was halting and uncertain. A rancorous policy dispute over the proper reaction to the Vietnamese crisis had broken out. On one side were so-called "realists" like Li Hongzhang who contended that Chinese self-strengthening, specifically coastal defenses and the naval program, had not yet reached the point where China could realistically repel France. This group called for negotiations since, they argued, China could not annul the treaties France had signed with Vietnam nor could they force France from Vietnam. Open war would only end in certain Chinese defeat and French demands on China itself. Though Li had the support of the Zongli Yamen's Prince Gong, the opposition was shrill and vociferous. Offering *qingyi,* literally meaning "public opinion" but having the strong sense of "moral censure," this group, which I will call the censure faction, attacked Li's position as appeasement. This faction, made up of men mostly born about the time of the Opium War, was carrying on the tradition and positions of men who had called for a strong anti-British stand in the 1830s and 1840s and who had opposed the conciliatory stand of the Manchu negotiators during treaty negotiations in the 1850s. All except one of the faction's nucleus held the *jinshi* degree and had been members of the Hanlin Academy; most of the group had no experience either in foreign policy or military affairs. In essence their argument was "enough is enough": If China would make one great effort, then all of China's foreign policy humiliations would come to a halt. In practical terms this meant that if China made a huge concerted effort to fight the French until they were defeated, the action would so deter other foreign nations that they would cease bullying China. The faction's arguments often stressed the special morality of China, the bravery of the Chinese, and that "battles are determined even more by men's hearts than by weapons."[15]

It seems clear that the Empress Dowager was to some degree immobilized by the clashing policy lines of the realists and the censure faction. The court let the skirmishing in Vietnam continue even as it ordered Li Hongzhang to negotiate. In the next few months two potential peace treaties were scuttled, the first by the French and the second by the French and the censure faction, which flooded the court with almost fifty calls for Li's removal. On the reception of a French ultimatum that Chinese forces withdraw from Vietnam and with the threat of a French attack on China, the Empress Dowager went over to the side of the censure faction, appointing two of its leaders to key positions in south China, one to the command of the Fujian fleet based at the city of Fuzhou.

In August the skirmishing between the Chinese and French became a war. The French began to sail ships up the Min River twenty miles to Fuzhou, home port of one quarter of the Chinese navy and site of the Fuzhou Shipyard. All the ships, including their largest vessel in Chinese waters, sailed past numerous Chinese batteries with modern guns and cannon purchased from European firms, all exhibits of the self-strengthening program. Early in the afternoon of August 23, the French fleet made target practice not only of the Chinese fleet but disastrously of the shipyard itself. In a quarter hour all but two of the twenty-three Chinese war junks and men-of-war were sunk or were burning; the shipyard was demolished. Approximately three thousand Chinese were killed. The censure faction commander of the Fujian fleet was one of the first to flee and watched the conflagration from hills overlooking the port. For the debacle he was exiled.

The summer afternoon had revealed the emptiness of the self-strengthening efforts: Without organization, coordination, and leadership, all the modern machines and weapons that might be manufactured or bought were ineffectual. The presence of the French fleet at Fuzhou at a time of an increasing likelihood of war in the area should have alerted Chinese authorities to the imminent danger. Garrisons along the river bank should have been prepared to prevent the ships from coming upstream. The tragic irony was that the court had attempted to force two of its other fleets to participate in actions against the French, but their leaders, one of whom was Li Hongzhang, refused. Li's refusal can be seen as a statement of displeasure at having the Empress Dowager side with the censure faction or, more certainly, as a desire to keep his fleet out of a battle that he believed would almost certainly be a defeat and intact so that it might be ready if necessary in Korean waters.

The disaster at Fuzhou brought the Empress Dowager more solidly into the censure faction camp. But when, three months later, there were no gains and fears began to spread that Japan would take advantage of the situation by wreaking havoc in Korea, the Empress Dowager went back to the negotiating route. The end of the war came with an agreement in mid-1885 in which China ended its centuries-long tributary relationship by recognizing French control over Vietnam. Part of the blame for the loss had to be placed on the censure faction and its naiveté; only one of its proponents, Zhang Zhidong, survived to play any important public role in the years following the war.

The self-strengthening movement had been an ignominious failure to this point: China was not in the least capable of fighting off aggressors. Political decision-makers had not been able or willing to make the institutional and personnel decisions that could have provided the appropriate context for self-strengthening success. Unfortunately, moreover, they did not take the necessity for institutional and personnel changes as the main lessons of the war. The incorrect lesson they learned instead was that there had simply not yet been enough self-strengthening.

Therefore, the decade following the loss of Vietnam saw an expanded menu of self-strengthening. A key figure in the effort was none other than censure faction leader Zhang Zhidong, who, anti-foreign as he continued to be, was converted by the war into a forceful self-strengthener. He wrote, "If we wish to make China strong and preserve Chinese learning, we must promote Western learning. But unless we use Chinese learning to consolidate the foundation and to give our purpose a right direction, the strong will become rebellious leaders and the weak, slaves. The consequence will be worse than not being versed in Western learning. . . ."[16] In Zhang's thinking, China had to emphasize both the old and the new: Only if Chinese maintained a firm grounding in Chinese traditional thought would self-strengthening using Western technology and science not eradicate Chinese identity.

Although Zhang established an arsenal and a mint in Canton, his main base was the metropolis of Wuhan (made up of the three cities of *Wu*chang, *Han*kou, and *Han*yang) in the Middle Yangzi where he served as governor general of Hunan and Hubei provinces from 1889 to 1894 and 1896 to 1907. At Wuhan he set up an iron foundry, and he founded two schools of Western studies, one focusing on the sciences and international law, the other, on commerce and Western languages. In keeping with his conviction that the old must be studied as well as the new, he established a traditional academy which became involved in publishing over 175 volumes written during the Qing period.

One institutional innovation that especially portended greater changes was the establishment of military academies. Li Hongzhang had set up a naval academy at Tianjin in 1880 and 1881, modeled on the school that functioned at the Fuzhou shipyard. Its first dean was Yan Fu, a graduate of the Fuzhou school and soon to become China's most important translator of major Western works. Apparently prompted largely by the Sino-French war, Li established the Tianjin Military Academy in 1885 where men selected from his Anhui army were trained in military affairs. Li hired German officers as teachers in the two-year curriculum that included science, mathematics, surveying, fortifications, and military drilling; classes were conducted mostly in German. Approximately fifteen hundred men received training from 1885 to 1900. Li added a special five-year officers training program in 1887. In 1885, Zhang Zhidong also established a military training school, the Guangdong Naval and Military Officers' Academy. While the military innovations in mid-century, the founding of the personal provincial armies of Zeng Guofan and Li Hongzhang, had been established under a Confucian ethos, these institutional changes were the first steps toward the establishment of a modern Chinese military, setting up curricula focusing on military science. Significantly, many important military leaders in the early twentieth century were trained at these academies.

In the wake of the naval disaster at Fuzhou, the government established a Board of Admiralty to centralize navy functioning and build naval power. But this board was soon moribund because of the system of personal connections and corruption that sank any efforts to reform. Efforts to centralize the fleets foundered on the desires of men in charge of specific fleets to maintain their own control; Li created the strongest fleet, the Beiyang or northern fleet. The naval self-strengthening program was also undercut by lack of funds, a problem made worse by actions of the Empress Dowager. In a story that has become classic in its disturbing irony, much of the appropriation earmarked for naval expansion was used by the Empress Dowager for rebuilding the Summer Palace which had been destroyed during the Arrow War. Apparently, part of those naval appropriations was used to fund the renovation of the infamous Marble Barge on which the Empress Dowager liked to picnic—at a time when no ships whatsoever were added to the main Chinese fleet, she poured money into one that would not float.

IDENTITY AND PERCEPTION: THE ROLES OF
THE EMPRESS DOWAGER

From her emergence in 1861 to her death in 1908, the Empress Dowager, Cixi, was the most powerful figure in China. She is also perhaps the most controversial figure in modern Chinese history. Certainly part of her reputation comes from the traditional Chinese negative attitude toward women rulers. Women should not rule: "The hen does not herald the coming of the morning." Women rulers in the past, like the Tang dynasty's Empress Wu, have been morally tarred with salacious stories about their sexual appetites and promiscuity. There have been sexual whisperings about Cixi as well. Another part of her negative reputation comes from her unscrupulous political manipulation (and worse) of two emperors for whom she served as regent and her unwillingness to relinquish power. Yet another part of her reputation comes from the disastrous problems that China experienced "on her watch." Domestic turmoil, state bankruptcy, humiliation by foreign powers, and war have been blamed to greater or lesser degree on her narrow-mindedness, authoritarian nature, and corruption. Certainly others in addition to Cixi were to blame. Just to take the wretched state of China's finances as an example, already by 1850, over a decade before she took power,

The Empress Dowager, Cixi

the Qing government was taking in only about 10 percent of what it was spending. In the end, all the criticisms and rumors about her indeed make it difficult to disentangle her actual identity from her perceived or attributed identity.

In 1861, she became regent for her son the Tongzhi emperor who ascended the throne at the age of five. For twelve years she ruled outright for him, and after he began to rule for himself, she constantly interfered in matters of state and in his private life. He apparently resented her actions and in turn enraged her by choosing for his bride someone other than her own choice. Rumor had it that she or at least eunuchs close to her encouraged the young emperor to visit brothels and engage in a dissolute lifestyle. Some accounts have suggested he may have contracted venereal disease. In November 1874, however, he became ill with smallpox, which may have been the cause of his death in January 1875. Without either a son or brother, the Tongzhi emperor's demise left Cixi again in the driver's seat.

She chose her nephew, who was four years old at the time and who was indeed her closest male relative, to become the Guangxu emperor. This choice infuriated some conservatives at the court because it violated the precedents and tradition of dynastic succession, particularly that a succeeding emperor come from a generation younger than the deceased emperor. The ideal of filial piety necessitated such a choice. The new emperor was, however, from the same generation as the Tongzhi emperor. Cixi was able to survive the criticism, and she achieved her main goal—to be able to serve as regent once again, in effect to serve as the sole ruler.

When the Guangxu emperor achieved his majority in 1889, Cixi officially retired to the Summer Palace where she might loll away her afternoons on her Marble Barge. But she had held power too long to give it up. She insisted, for example, that all memorials be sent to her for her perusal; she retained decision-making power in key appointments to the six Boards and to the Grand Council. Reportedly at moments of crisis she held court with the emperor. Just like the earlier relationship between mother and son (the Tongzhi emperor), the relationship between aunt and nephew became very strained. The Guangxu emperor's ideas about China and the West began to diverge sharply from Cixi's and feelings of suspicion and mistrust grew between them.

What were the sources of Cixi's power over the emperor and her continued centrality in the court? First, as the empress dowager, she was the emperor's "official" mother even if not his biological mother. Therefore, the emperor had to treat her with the proper respect and filial piety; certainly he could never show her open hostility. Further, the emperor was not a natural heir; Cixi had selected him. Beholden to her for his position, he could not rid the court of her presence or do away with her efforts to control him. Any such actions would only incense many of the high court officials who were also beholden to Cixi for their positions; their connections to her made most of them personally loyal to her. The emperor could not have taken any bold action in his relationship with the Empress Dowager because he would have alienated the very people he needed in order to rule. Since the court was filled with her supporters, it made her continued involvement all the easier. As yet one other indication of Cixi's stranglehold, it was traditional for a new emperor to make his own appointments to the Grand Council. But for four years after the Guangxu emperor took power, only Cixi's appointees staffed the council; and even after that, those who were appointed to the Council had gotten their career starts with her patronage.

Thus, as China entered the 1890s, a decade that would come to take on the terrifying aura of a nightmare, at the top of the government there was an ominous split. The fifty-five-year old Empress Dowager, who was used to being in control, was now trying to hold onto as much power as possible and continuing to cultivate ties to those at the court and in the top ranks of the bureaucracy. The nineteen-year old emperor, on the other hand, had while a child been so fearful and timid (perhaps because of Cixi's overbearing qualities) that on hearing the sound of thunder he reportedly hid his head in his tutor's lap. Now, however, he had begun to try to assert himself, to take up the responsibilities of the Son of Heaven, and to stake out his own intellectual and political positions. The troubles of the nineties would only make their mutual resentment and distrust more intense.

Notes

[1] Quoted in Dun J. Li, *China in Transition, 1517–1911* (New York: Van Nostrand Reinhold, 1969), p. 164.

[2] Ting-yee Kuo and Kwang-ching Liu, "Self-Strengthening: The Pursuit of Western Technology" in Fairbank, Ed., *The Cambridge History of China, Volume 10: Late Ch'ing, 1800–1911, Part 1*, p. 529.

[3] These quotations from Woren are taken from Li, pp. 162–163.

[4] This example comes from Yen-p'ing Hao and Erh-min Wang, "Changing Chinese Views of Western Relations, 1840–1895" in Fairbank and Liu, p. 174.

[5] Li, p. 142.

[6] Hao and Wang, p. 183.

[7] "A Letter of Guo Songtao from London, 1877" in Ssu-yu Teng and John K. Fairbank, Eds., *China's Response to the West* (Cambridge: Harvard University Press), p. 99.

[8] Feng Guifen, "On the Manufacture of Foreign Weapons" in Teng and Fairbank, p. 53.

[9] "A Letter of Guo Songtao from London, 1877," p. 102.

[10] Fairbank and Liu, p. 88.

[11] Bruce Cumings, *Korea's Place in the Sun* (New York: W. W. Norton, 1997), p. 100.

[12] Quoted in Lloyd E. Eastman, *Throne and Mandarins* (Cambridge: Harvard University Press, 1967), p. 38.

[13] Ibid., p. 33.

[14] This phrase was used by the governor-general of Yunnan-Guizhou. It is cited in Lloyd E. Eastman, "Ch'ing-I and Chinese Policy Formation During the Nineteenth Century," *Journal of Asian Studies,* XXIV, 4 (August 1965), p. 602.

[15] Ibid.

[16] Zhang Zhidong, "Exhortation to Learn," cited in J. Mason Gentzler, *Changing China* (New York: Praeger, 1977), p. 102.

6

The Devastating Nineties: Destroying Traditional Identities

Bookends of a tragic decade.

In 1891 a brilliant *jinshi* degreeholder, Kang Youwei dropped the intellectual equivalent of a bomb on the Chinese intellectual community. He argued in a book that the version of the Confucian classics that had been considered the philosophical canon and used for centuries as the basis for the civil service examination was a forgery. The fallout was the same as if some Western scholar were to prove that the Bible as the West has known it is a forgery. Kang had shattered the Chinese intellectual identity; how was it to be re-formed?

In 1900, a scene in Tianjin. "On this day someone saw a corpse on the slope. . . . It was a man who had been killed by the [Boxer] bandit chief Cao Futian. His testicles had been cut off and his head severed and placed between his thighs, facing upward stiff and motionless. These people regard life as a trifling matter. When they kill a person, they rarely dispatch him with a clean blow of the sword; more often they slash indiscriminately with their swords and chop the body into pieces. The horror of the slaughter they perpetrate is even worse than that of the punishment of death by dismemberment."[1]

In many ways the 1890s saw the bitter culmination of challenges to traditional Chinese identities and self-perceptions. From the intellectual shocks brought by Kang and others to the bloody terror of the Boxers, the question that kept coming was "what does it mean to be Chinese?" In between there were other shocks—a startling military defeat, Western nations coming to carve up the "Chinese melon," and an aborted political reform effort that ended with the Empress Dowager putting the Guangxu emperor under permanent house arrest. It was a decade that at last proved to most Chinese that for China to survive radical changes had to occur.

IDEOLOGY FOR CHANGE: KANG YOUWEI'S INTELLECTUAL BOMB

Rationalizing change in the name of the past was the quintessential Chinese way of looking to the future. The self-strengtheners were out to protect the past by using modern Western technology. In addition to the ideas of the self-strengtheners, there were other more mechanical ways of using the past to allow change. One argument, based on patterns of cyclical change, asserted that it had been two thousand years between the time of the ancient sage kings of Yao and Shun and the establishment of the empire in 221 B.C.E. Because the late nineteenth century was about two thousand years after that axial event, it was thus cyclically appropriate that a new momentous change could occur. Another argument proposed that Western science and technology could be legitimately borrowed from the West because mathematical and chemical ideas current in the West had first appeared in early Chinese history. This approach brought up the question of why and how, if this knowledge was so critical for the development of modern science, China had somehow lost it.

A key motive force in the modern Western world, emerging in the Enlightenment in the late eighteenth century, was the idea of progress. With humans using their brains and the realities of modern technology and science, they had the power to make progress inevitable. It was a view of history that was ever onward, ever upward, a strong contrast with the Chinese view of history which envisioned a trend cyclically downward from a past golden age. Above all, the Chinese worldview was marked by an acceptance of fate, not, as in the modern West, by the potentiality of human action. In the 1890s, scholar Kang Youwei gave to the Chinese intellectual world its own idea of Progress, building a rationale, as always *based upon the past,* for radical institutional change. Notably his prescribed changes went far beyond self-strengthening. They were no longer to preserve traditional Chinese culture (as the self-strengtheners wanted to do) but, most basic, to preserve China. Put another way, Kang moved beyond what is often called "culturalism" to the borders of a modern "nationalism."

In order to build new ideological structures, Kang first had to destroy the old edifices. The shocking forgery thesis in the 1891 book was a major part of that demolition. Kang claimed, based on textual criticism, that the true Confucian teachings were found not in the texts that had been the basis for the School of Han Learning since the seventeenth century. Rather they were found in the so-called New Texts from the earlier Han dynasty. Kang's purpose was to undermine the School of Han Learning, whose textual and philological focus he believed had taken serious thinkers away from the central point of Confucianism which should be political concern and institutional reform. Though today Kang's interpretation is not seen as credible, the impact on the intellectual world of the 1890s, already buffeted by realities of imperialism and rebellion, was shattering. If the traditional canon was shown to be false, there was no firm intellectual ground on which to stand, indeed there was not even a firm past to rationalize in the name of.

A second major ideological contribution was Kang's 1897 book *Confucius as a Reformer,* a book he began in 1886. It contributed both to the demolition of the old and to the construction of something new. During his lifetime, Confucius himself had claimed that he was not a creator but simply a "transmitter" from the past. This idea Kang tried to demolish. In its place, he structured a new Confucius as a great innovator, "a messianic, forward-looking 'sage king,'" a man who used the past to call for major institutional change in the present. Kang was not only proposing a new Chinese identity; he was questioning the meaning of China's traditional identity. In another work, he then set forth his rationale for progress, using primarily ideas from the West, but placing them in categories that he found in the "real" Confucian New Texts.[2] His ideas set forth a unilinear view of history similar to that in the post-Enlightenment West. He found three axial ages through which history moved: the Age of Disorder, the Age of Approaching Peace, and the Age of Universal Peace. He argued that the world had been stuck in the Age of Disorder but that it could move to the next axial age, that of Approaching Peace, if his reform ideas were adopted. In essence, Kang was using the past to break away from the past. His reform proposals advocated basic institutional change, which included a state constitution and assemblies where rule by the people might be exercised.

Although many in the intellectual and political worlds judged him a heretic from Confucian orthodoxy, his proposals for institutions based on and infused with Western ideas began to excite, as nothing had before, an interest in Western things beyond simply guns and ships. Kang's works thus began to prime the pump for greater change. Perhaps even more significant, Kang's reinterpretation of Confucianism had a major impact, the shock waves of which would continue for decades. The reason? Kang's treatment of Confucius and his thought essentially changed Confucianism from "what so far had been the unquestioned centre of faith into an ideology, the basic character of which was problematic and debatable."[3] Once Confucianism became an ideology, for example, it could be interpreted as a tool that elevated certain social types (fathers, husbands, parents, elder brothers) and degraded other social types (sons, wives, children, younger brothers). Kang's work in essence was the revolutionary first step, however little he intended it, in the deposing of Confucius and his thought as the foundation of Chinese culture, the first step in the dismantling of traditional Chinese identity.

POLITICAL AND CULTURAL EARTHQUAKE: DEFEAT BY THE "DWARF PEOPLE"

From the mid-1880s an uneasy calm between China and Japan existed on the Korean peninsula. Their agreement in 1885 to abstain from sending troops without notification to the other had held into the 1890s. Chinese Resident General Yuan Shikai had developed close relations with powerful Queen Min, whose reputation for corruption had become almost legendary. But Japanese determination to act decisively in any further crisis or simple opportunity had become firmer.

Beginning in the 1860s an eclectic religion called *Tonghak* (Eastern Learning) had begun to grow in southwest Korea. In many ways, especially in its promise of a utopian regime, it was reminiscent of the Taiping movement. In the early 1890s it gave rise to a rebellion that grew out of an array of political, social, and economic problems besetting the Korean countryside. In the summer of 1894 with the rebellion spreading, the Korean government, still operating under its tributary mentality, asked the Chinese government to send troops to help quell the disturbance. Following the guidelines of the Li-Ito convention, the

Chinese government notified Japan of its plan to send fifteen hundred troops but to withdraw them as soon as the rebellion was suppressed. The Japanese answered by sending around eight thousand troops. Li Hongzhang desperately tried to negotiate a settlement; he was well aware that any war would be fought with his Anhui army and Beiyang navy. But when his efforts to use Britain and the United States as mediators went nowhere, he decided that reinforcements had to be sent. On July 25, the Japanese sank a British steamer that had been chartered by the Chinese, drowning 950 Chinese troops. Both countries declared war on August 1.

The war was the first test for the Chinese military after ten years of what might be called accelerated self-strengthening. In the climactic naval battle off the Yalu River on September 17, of the twelve Chinese ships involved, four were sunk, four were crippled beyond repair, and four fled. All twelve Japanese ships survived without major damage. The results, in short, were the same as those in the war with France a decade earlier: complete and humiliating defeat on both land and sea. A nation comprised of what earlier Chinese had contemptuously dismissed as "dwarf people" had smashed the Central Country. Many nations were astonished by the outcome, having assumed that the land giant would overwhelm the tiny island nation. But the result should not have been surprising. Japan had been rapidly modernizing since the 1870s, and its war effort was driven by national fervor. China's efforts at modernizing had been fitful, eroded by counterproductive policies. When war came, it was indeed fought mostly by Li Hongzhang's Beiyang fleet and his provincial army. "China had no clear demarcation of authority, no unity of command, and no nationwide mobilization. Conflicting advice from the Tsungli [Zongli] Yamen, provincial authorities, and irresponsible [censure faction] officials rendered the court indecisive."[4] This post mortem could have been written about the Sino-French War.

The settlement might have been even worse from the Chinese perspective had two contingencies not occurred. First, peace envoy Li Hongzhang was shot in the head by a Japanese terrorist. Though he survived, the Japanese were horrified and most of all frightened that this insane act might jeopardize their spoils of victory. They thus withdrew some of their most overweening and expansive demands, specifically that they be given control of three cities in the Beijing area. The second unexpected development came after the conclusion of the Treaty of Shimonoseki, which ceded Taiwan and the Liaodong peninsula in southern Manchuria to Japan. Russia, Germany, and France joined in what became known as the Triple Intervention to force Japan to return the Liaodong peninsula to China. In spite of that return, China lost Taiwan and had to give up forever any tributary-related claims to Korea.

With the Sino-Japanese War, imperialism entered a far more perilous phase. The cession of Taiwan was the first major loss of Chinese territory. Japan acquired the right to build and operate factories in the treaty ports, a "right" that was soon taken by all the Western nations. More ominously, Japan successfully imposed a huge indemnity (230 million taels) on China to defray the costs of the war—an action that deepened China's financial crisis (its annual revenue was only about 89 million taels) and thereby further eroded the government's chances to undertake any needed policy initiatives. It also meant the necessity of borrowing money from foreign firms. From 1895 to 1898, loans were arranged from Russia, a French-Russian consortium, and an Anglo-German consortium; they were secured against customs revenues. From this point until the establishment of the People's Republic of China in 1949, China was continuously in debt to foreign countries.

It is certainly the case that no event to this point in the nineteenth century had created such a widespread shock and such deep humiliation as the loss of this war to a people that many Chinese had traditionally scorned. Any critically thinking Chinese could no longer believe that things could go on as they had or that business as usual would somehow muddle through. Had there been protest demonstrators carrying signs emblazoned "The end is near," they would likely have captured the despair felt by many Chinese. As it was, there was a protest in Beijing following the signing of the treaty. Because it was the time for the metropolitan examination for the highest degree in the civil service system, large numbers of candidates thronged the capital. Kang Youwei and his closest disciple Liang Qichao drew up a long memorial, calling on the government to repudiate the treaty, to continue the war and move the capital farther into the interior, and to institute reforms. Thirteen hundred examination candidates signed the petition. But the government did not respond. The country apparently had to be abased even further before the government would act to redress the situation.

A NEW PHASE OF IMPERIALISM: CARVING THE MELON

In the aftermath of one foreign policy disaster came another crisis between China and the foreign powers. It initially involved Germany and Russia. Since it was Russian interest in Manchuria and Korea that in part drove Japan to fight China for predominant rights in Korea and since it was Russia who spearheaded the Triple Intervention, a look at the Russian role and interests with regard to China is essential. The Sino-Russian relationship seems most atypical when comparing it to China's other international relationships.

Russia had been active in East Asia since the seventeenth century, a logical extension of its interests in Siberia. Treaties in 1689 and 1727 had established the border between the two countries and essentially regularized relations. From the beginning, China treated Russia differently from other Western nations. The treaties were signed as between equals; the tributary system did not seem to come into play. Although Chinese documents indicate that Russian ministers kowtowed to the Chinese emperor, Qing records never officially named Russia as a tributary state. Russia "was the only foreign country with which China maintained treaty relations, the only 'Western' state to which China sent diplomatic missions, and the only foreign power granted religious, commercial, and educational privileges" in Beijing.[5] From 1693 on, Russian merchants were permitted to come to Beijing every three years. In addition, the Chinese government authorized and paid for the travel of Russian priests to Beijing every ten years in order to minister to Russians in the capital; the government also picked up the cost of living expenses for the priests. Following the treaty in 1727, Russia was allowed to send students to learn Chinese and Manchu at a language school in Beijing; the Chinese government helped pay the costs of travel and, once in the capital for decade-long stays, subsidized living expenses including providing clothing and food at no charge. Although all these special concessions and considerations were bestowed by the Qing in order to insure Russian neutrality as the Qing tried to strengthen their hold on the north and northwest frontiers, they persisted long after those frontiers were stabilized. Russia monopolized this special status in Beijing until the Treaty of Tianjin in 1860 opened the capital to general diplomatic residence.

In that 1860 treaty, in fact, the Russian ambassador helped mediate disputes between Prince Gong and British and French representatives. He also had his own goals to further the Russian agenda in central and northeast Asia. From the early 1850s, the Chinese had allowed Russians to trade, build storage facilities, and set up consulates in northern Xinjiang. The Russians had also been pushing in eastern Siberia, building garrisons along the Amur River. In a treaty concluded in 1860, Russians showed themselves as aggressive as the Western Europeans, demanding and receiving land north of the Amur River and all land east of the Ussuri River, the latter comprising what became known as the Maritime Province. Altogether these territorial gains totaled between 300,000 and 400,000 square miles. In addition, more cities in Xinjiang were opened to Russians: these chickens came home to roost when the Russians seized the northern part of Xinjiang in 1878, but negotiations led in 1881 to their withdrawal and the reduction in the number of their consulates in the region.

But Russian interests in northeast Asia did not diminish. The terminus of the Trans-Siberian Railway, begun in 1891, was to be Vladivostok on the Sea of Japan. The Russians could have chosen a route totally in Russian territory, that is running along the north bank of the Amur River. But that route was about 350 miles farther and with much rougher terrain than a route that would cut across Manchuria in a straight shot from Cita. For the less expensive route, the Russians obviously needed Chinese permission. This they received in negotiations with Li Hongzhang, sent to St. Petersburg in 1896 as China's imperial commissioner at the coronation festivities of Nicholas II. With their railroad, the Chinese Eastern Railway, cutting through Manchuria just to the north of Korea, Russian interests in the area were substantially enhanced.

It was just about this same time that other European powers had also begun to enhance their own standings in China. It was Germany that put into motion what has been called the "scramble for concessions" or the establishment of "spheres of influence" or, more graphically, "carving up the Chinese melon." Germany had been interested in establishing a Chinese naval base for some time; by 1896, it had focused its lustful eyes on Jiaozhou Bay on the southern coast of Shandong for reasons both of its excellent deep-water port and its location generally near Shandong's mineral resources. All it needed was a pretext to act with demands and, if need be, force. It came in November 1897, when two German missionaries of a particularly aggressive Catholic order were hacked to death by a band of Chinese while they were visiting a third missionary. In response, Germany occupied the bay and its city, Qingdao. In March 1898, it forced the Chinese government to lease the port and surrounding area for ninety-nine years; the leasehold included Germany's right to build two railroads and hold mining rights.

Driven by imperialist rivalry, the rest of the nations followed suit. Russia used the pretext of protecting China from Germany to occupy Port Arthur and Dalian on the tip of the Liaodong peninsula in December 1897 and signed a twenty-five year lease in March 1898. As part of the leasehold, Russia also acquired the right to build a railroad from these two ports up to the Chinese Eastern Railway; it would come to be called the South Manchurian Railway and would play a crucial role in China's subsequent history. To check the Russians, Britain countered with a twenty-five year lease of the port of Weihaiwei directly across the Bohai Straits from Port Arthur and Dalian; in June 1898, it also leased the so-called New Territories of Hong Kong for ninety-nine years. France forced a lease of Guangzhou Bay for ninety-nine years in April 1898, thus setting up its sphere of influence in Lingnan and Southwest China. Italy, the United States, and Japan were frozen out of the carving competition: Italy's late demands were refused; the United States was interested in a particular site but was occupied with its war with Spain; Japan was focusing on its role in Korea.

In the aftermath of the scramble and with no sphere of influence of its own, the United States government issued the Open Door notes, statements by which it hoped to insure continuing and equal commercial opportunity. Not an altruistic policy, it was obviously intended to insure that countries with spheres would not freeze the United States out of treaty ports or areas of natural resources that were within those spheres. Though no country obligated itself to the notes, the United States Secretary of State Hay asserted that they had. In any case, the fact that the land-grabbing had stopped did not develop from this policy but rather "because the imperialists feared rivalry and conflict among themselves. The resultant equilibrium saved the [Qing] empire from immediate collapse."[6]

At the time, of course, the Chinese were not aware that the Westerners would cease their carving competition. The making of treaty ports had thus escalated to the seizure of considerable territory with substantial economic rights. In this scramble for more and more of China and its resources following so closely the disastrous war with Japan, imperialism had thus reached a more virulent level that boded greater danger for China's future. It is not surprising that alarm about the incipient demise of the Chinese nation spread among elites all over China.

THE REFORM MOVEMENT AND THE HUNDRED DAYS: CLASHING IDENTITIES

The scramble for concessions formed the backdrop for one of the compelling dramas of the late nineteenth century—the Hundred Days from June into September 1898, when breakneck, breathtaking reforms promised a new China but delivered beheadings, forced flight, and imprisonment. The Hundred Days reform effort did not emerge suddenly full-blown. The ideas that infused the movement and the institutions that gave it momentum had developed in the aftermath of the loss of the war with Japan. Its leaders were Kang Youwei and Liang Qichao.

Liang's writings are important because many elements of his thought would remain central in the discourse of change throughout much of the twentieth century. He believed that self-strengthening efforts had focused too narrowly on technological innovations at a time when the essential agenda necessitated political reforms. His prescription for the foundation of such change was the traditional cultural approach of educational reform, specifically fostering the spread of literacy. This goal could clearly not be accomplished through the traditional examination system. Since it was obvious that as long as the examination system remained in place no other system could be successfully carried out, Liang favored

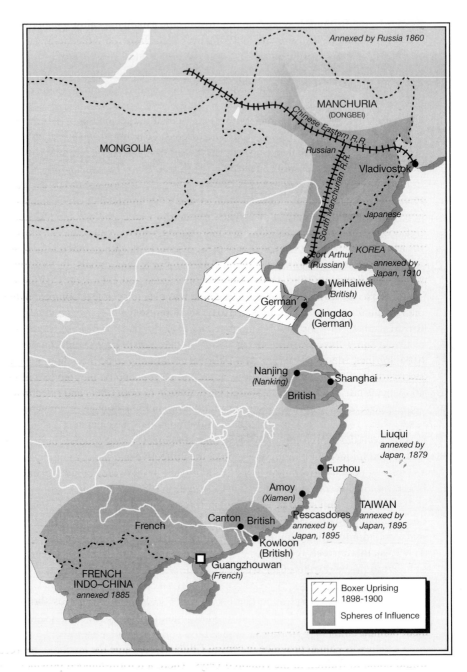

Foreign Spheres of Influence and the Boxer Uprising

abolishing the examination and moving toward the establishment of a national school system. In that system, with students studying both ideas from the West and Chinese traditions, intellectual development and political consciousness would be fostered.

Beyond educational reform, Liang supported Kang's emphasis on the essentiality of significant institutional change to move China forward. A cardinal concept in Liang's thought about what China needed to do was "grouping"—an idea that involved several aspects of change.[7] At its most basic level, this meant the formation of associations of concerned elites who would meet to study and discuss the political and social changes that had to be undertaken; in a real sense such associations would *mobilize* (the key word!) the intellects and energies of China's leaders.

But the concept had another deeper, more revolutionary thrust as well. China's predicament necessitated national solidarity and a commitment of the people as a whole to solving the desperately urgent problems. Implicit in Liang's arguments was the belief that traditional Chinese political culture and institutions, with their emphasis on individual identity and personal connections and networks, discouraged and inhibited a more general social solidarity and any sort of energetic commitment to wider goals. In addition, the traditional state was authoritarian: its policies constrained and even repressed the people and prohibited a free flow of information. If China was ever to be able to compete with the West, Liang contended, such constraints had to be shattered so that Chinese political culture could develop an all-important "collective dynamism."

Certainly there was the strong flavor of nationalism here even if he did not use the word. Further, Liang called for a new political community to be the center of a reconceived and restructured state. This new state would not be founded on the rule of a monarch over his subjects but would feature a shared participation of both rulers and ruled in a system of popular sovereignty. For the first time Liang brought the language of democracy into Chinese political discourse. The concept of "grouping" thus capsulated in a fundamental way ideas of political community, the nation, and democracy. Liang's radical political discourse, which championed mobilizing the people, the collective and the community and installing a system of popular sovereignty, would become the watchwords of subsequent Chinese reformers and revolutionaries from Sun Yat-sen through Mao Zedong.

The practical efforts of institutional reformers, led by Kang and Liang, began with the establishment of "groupings" in particular study associations. The ultimate goal was to remake China by giving it a new national identity. As a first step, the study associations were to facilitate greater contact and social integration among official and non-official elites and, through the study process, to educate elites and mobilize their energies. The first study societies were established in Beijing and Shanghai in the second half of 1895. Since the Manchus had forbidden the formation of private societies in the 1650s and this ban still held, the study societies' establishment was illegal; indeed by the next spring, the government banned both study societies.

But it was Hunan province in central China that became the incubator for reform that would come to fruition in the Hundred Days. There a reform-minded provincial administration sponsored in mid-decade the formation of a number of important new industrial, commercial, and educational institutions. In the provincial capital of Changsha, for example, electric lights were installed and paved (macadamized) roads became a reality. A telegraph line was erected between Changsha and the important Yangzi port of Hankou. With encouragement and sometimes loans from the government, local elites established a match factory and a steamship line to link Hunan and Hubei.

A fervent champion of reform in the provincial administration was Huang Zunxian who had served in many diplomatic posts and was "a leading expert on foreign affairs." Huang prompted administrative, judicial, and prison reforms as well as instituting training programs for officials to keep them informed of current affairs. In that vein, a School of Current Affairs was established in the fall of 1897 in a joint effort by the provincial government and elites. The curriculum was a mix of Western studies (sciences, history, politics) and Confucian classics. What made the school more radical was its teaching staff. Huang recommended that Liang Qichao be made the head lecturer; three other young scholars—all disciples of Kang Youwei—were made Liang's assistants. The thrust of the teaching was primarily political; anti-Manchu ideas were spread to the students through seventeenth-century texts condemning despotism and describing the Manchu massacre at the city of Yangzhou during the Manchu conquest.

The most famous study association in Hunan was the Southern Study Society, founded by the more radical reformist gentry; it was the largest of the fourteen study societies founded in Hunan in 1897 and 1898. At its height it had over twelve hundred members, both official and non-official elites. Nominally a private voluntary organization, it escaped being banned because the Changsha government had supported its formation and even participated in its functioning. Provincial officials received proposals from its members on matters of public policy for consideration and possible implementation; and in researching current issues, members could petition the government to see public records. Commenting on the Society after it had closed, Liang noted that "though nominally a study society, the Southern Study Society had all the makings of a local legislature."[8]

Another crucial aspect of the reform activity was the publication of newspapers, the beginnings of what would in the coming decades become an explosion in the number of newspapers, most short-lived, but almost all focusing on questions relating to the identity of the new China. They were published by the early Beijing and Shanghai study societies and well as those in Hunan. The first paper, *Hunan Study* [Xiangxue bao], began to be published in early 1897; it was joined by the *Hunan Daily* [Xiang bao]. Both papers became crucial vehicles for publicizing and propagandizing reformist and radical thought. Most of Liang Qichao's essays appeared in these newspapers. They were distributed mostly free of charge, not only in Hunan but along the southeast coast as well.

In early 1898, the teachings of Liang Qichao and various writings in newspapers linked to the Southern Study Society became notably radical, taking on staunchly nationalistic positions with considerable anti-Manchu slant. Conservatives and even moderate reformers who had been involved in provincial reform activities became apprehensive. A struggle erupted between reformers and more conservative forces. The question at issue was "what is the Chinese identity." While for the reformers the answer was increasingly becoming Han Chinese nationalists subordinated to a depraved and ineffective Manchu minority, for the conservatives the answer was simple: the supporters of traditional Chinese cultural values—which they felt duty-bound to protect against the heterodox views of the reformers. The abrasive staying power of the past was at work eroding the possibilities of institutional change.

A bitter ideological attack on Kang and Liang spread as a stream of accusations poured into the court, condemning both their ideology and reform agenda as heresy from the Confucian orthodoxy. Kang and Liang were condemned for their open criticism of Chinese political culture and tradition and for their negative treatment of the Manchus. Kang's reinterpretation of Confucius and the classics were especially upsetting. The call in the writings of Liang and others for people's rights and equality clashed head-on with the traditional Confucian bonds and the Confucian ideas of social hierarchy. For those in the camp of the anti-reformers, the reformers were as much cultural enemies of Chinese traditions as the Taiping had been forty years earlier. By the summer, most reformers were expelled from Hunan, with the majority of Hunanese gentry mobilized not for the construction of a new state and society but against the reformers. By late summer the governor of Hunan petitioned the court in Beijing to destroy the printing blocks for Kang's *Confucius as a Reformer* and to ban its publication.

At the very time that Kang and company were bearing the attacks in and being hounded out of Hunan he was to come closest to wielding substantial national power. The surprising development was that Kang had found a powerful supporter in the Forbidden City—the Guangxu emperor himself. The twenty-seven year old emperor had been won over to the cause of reform through his long-time tutor, Weng Tonghe. In 1889 Weng had encouraged the emperor to read Feng Guifen's 1860 collection of essays on reform. The emperor was so impressed with the possibilities of using Western learning for Chinese benefit that in the early 1890s he studied English in the Forbidden City with teachers from the Interpreters College. He was especially interested in the contemporaneous writings of advocates of reform. In 1895, the Empress Dowager, well aware of the emperor's burgeoning interests in Western things, halted his language study and allowed him to have tutorials only on traditional Chinese materials.

Weng Tonghe's interests in reform had naturally led him to Kang as the leader in calls for institutional change. Kang had sent memorials to the court as early as 1888, pointing out the need for reform. When Kang formed the eventually banned study society in Beijing in 1895, Weng Tonghe had been a member. Weng was not an advocate of radical reform, but the radical nature of Kang's ideas came to be known only gradually: Many of Kang's most extreme views and positions were set forth only in 1898. In any event, Weng recommended Kang to the emperor who established direct communications with the reformer. On January 24, 1898, the emperor arranged an open meeting at the Zongli Yamen between Kang and high officials at the court, including Weng, Li Hongzhang, and Ronglu, one of the Empress Dowager's trusted confidants. An exchange revealed Kang's goal of remaking the Chinese identity.

Ronglu: "The institutions of the ancestors cannot be changed."

Kang Youwei: "We cannot preserve the realm of the ancestors; what is the use of their institutions?"

Li Hongzhang: "Shall we abolish all the Six Boards and throw away all the existing institutions and rules?"

Kang: "The laws and governmental system . . . have made China weak and will ruin her. Undoubtedly they should be done away with."[9]

In the aftermath of the meeting, Kang sent three memorials to the emperor detailing his plan of action. They included following the reform models of Meiji Japan and Russia under Peter the Great and establishing a constitution and national assembly. To facilitate change, the emperor should announce openly that reform was the order of the day and he should establish new bodies to work to that end, thereby avoiding working through the cumbersome and conservative government bureaucracy. On June 11, the emperor showed whose camp he was in, announcing, as Kang had suggested, that reform had become state policy. Five days later, Kang had his first audience, a five-hour marathon, with the emperor. The emperor appointed Kang to the Zongli Yamen and permitted him to submit memorials directly to the emperor instead of through the regular bureaucratic channels. From June 11 to September 21, in what has come to be known as the Hundred Days, the emperor, with Kang providing the agenda, issued over a hundred decrees calling for institutional reforms in almost every policy arena. It is certainly the case that the national context in early 1898—the Western scramble for concessions through the new approach of "leasing" territory—created in the minds of many the sense that some kind of substantial change was necessary to keep the country from being eaten alive.

Taken as a whole, the political, economic, military, and educational reforms called for in the wave of reform edicts would have drastically restructured the Chinese polity. They included revamping the examination system and establishing a national school system; restructuring the government and abolishing sinecure positions; modernizing the military, police, and postal systems; setting up new institutions to promote agriculture, commerce, and industry; and establishing rewards for inventions. Significantly, the emperor did not decree the centerpieces of Kang's plan—the setting forth of plans for a constitution and national assembly.

But even as it was, the reforms threatened the entire status quo, specifically the world of the Empress Dowager and her supporters. Changing the examination system was unsettling to all those already in the examination "pipeline." Suggestions that Buddhist temple complex buildings might be used as schools stepped on the toes of Buddhists. Restructuring the government threatened those in current positions as did abolishing those posts for which men were paid yet for which they did no or little work. Military reforms meant changing or perhaps abolishing existing armies. It also did not help the cause with Manchus that the only Manchu involved in the effort was the emperor. The Empress Dowager's continuing power behind the scenes was the crucial reality that would bring everything to a violent halt.

Even from the opening of the Hundred Days, the Empress Dowager revealed her opposition to the emperor and the reform group. Already on June 15, she had dismissed Weng Tonghe. She then bided her time, let anti-reform bitterness fester, and made certain of her support. Then on September 21, with the help of the military under Yuan Shikai, she staged a coup d'etat, seizing all power from the emperor and putting him under house arrest. She then began her third regency, one that would last to her death a decade later. Five days after the coup all the reform edicts were revoked. While Kang was able to escape to Hong Kong and Liang, to Japan, six young reformers, including Tan Sitong, were executed. Tan, a brilliant thirty-three-year old intellectual, had been a leader of the reform efforts in Hunan, editing a newspaper and heading a study society. He was assigned to be a secretary to the Grand Council in order to facilitate the reforms only on September 5. When the Empress Dowager's coup came, he had only been on the job for less than three weeks. He refused to flee, saying "I wanted to kill the robbers, but lacked the strength to transform the world. This is the place where I should die. Rejoice, rejoice!"[10] He was beheaded for treason on September 27.

The reform effort was put down quite easily, a fact which is often used to argue that in China change at this time could not likely come from the top. Chinese political leaders seemed unable to change the system in order to deal effectively with the crises; perhaps they were not even yet able to realize the state's dire peril. And yet, despite the coup against it, the reform movement had considerable historical import. It did, as one historian argues, "usher in a new phase of Chinese culture—the era of ideologies." The ideas of Kang and Liang, with their taking Western thought seriously and their dethroning of Confucianism from a way of life to an ideology, "raised the curtain on the cultural crises of the twentieth century."[11] Elites began to join together in associations, debating issues and starting to deal with problems in new contexts; since many involved political activity, the amount of political participation on the part of elites increased. Newspapers began to sprout up and proliferate, in the stock Chinese phrase, "like bamboo shoots after a spring rain"; perhaps their most outstanding feature was evidence of a growing sense of nationalism. The discourse they began was essentially the beginning of modern Chinese public opinion. Elites placed educational reform at the center of the public agenda, and that reform would come to fruition in the next decade. Finally, the reform era gave rise to the birth of the modern intelligentsia; Unlike the old scholar-gentry, the new intelligentsia were "free-floating intellectuals,"[12] not tied to localities and lacking a symbiotic relationship with the government. Further, the new intelligentsia, unlike the old scholar elites, struggled with problems of alienation from the government and above all of cultural identity, caught between the old and the new, East and West.

THE BOXER CATASTROPHE: WHICH IDENTITY NOW?

The collapse of traditional state and civilization was punctuated at century's end by an outrageous constellation of events in north China. From a culture of poverty in Shandong province came a social explosion. Led by so-called "Boxers," a name taken from the martial art rituals, or boxing, that they performed, the movement was composed of mostly young farmers, laborers, and out-of-work drifters. The roving Boxer groups also included women's groups (called Red Lanterns).

Natural disasters—flood and drought—formed the context for the rise and the spread of the Boxer movement. In August 1898, a month before the Empress Dowager's coup against the reformers, a flood broke the Yellow River dikes in three places, sending torrents of water into thirty-four counties, covering over two thousand villages, and making at least temporary refugees out of millions. Crops were ruined and in some places the devastation wrought by the flood was so severe that crops could not even be planted the next spring.

Government corruption in the dispersal of relief grain meant that large numbers of people, even those living relatively close to cities, did not receive any aid. "Many peasants were still huddled on the dikes [where they had taken refuge] eating leaves, bark, or weeds fully three months after the flooding began."[13] In such cases anti-government or anti-official feelings could begin to rise quickly. Drought was a factor in expanding the Boxer movement as we will see.

Anti-Christian hostility was a crucial cause of the uprising. In the area where the Boxer movement began, German Catholic missionaries of a stridently militant order had been very active. The killings of the two missionaries that had served as Germany's pretext to seize Jiaozhou occurred in this area. A missionary, named Georg Stenz, who they were visiting at the time of their murders escaped death—ironically, since he was the likely object of the armed attack. A word about him reveals some dynamics behind the anti-Christian hostility. The aggressive nature in the missionizing approach of this order Stenz reveals in his autobiography when he describes his "mission cross which was to be at once weapon and banner in my fight for the Kingdom of God." His contempt for the Chinese drips from his description of Shanghai: "An entirely new world now opened before us. Crowds of slit-eyed Chinese swarmed about the harbor—prominent merchants in their rustling silks and poor coolies in ragged clothes that did not hide their filthy bodies. . . . Cunning, pride, and scorn flashed from the eyes that met our inquiring looks."[14]

But more upsetting to Chinese than attitudes of superiority, arrogance, and contempt for those they were trying to save were the actions of missionaries with regard to their converts. They were particularly active in interfering in their converts' lawsuits, claiming the applicability of extraterritoriality in some cases and frequently pressuring magistrates. They also demanded that magistrates punish people for alleged offenses against the church or church property. They forbade converts from participating in or contributing to village festivals which often featured processions following a statue of the local god; such participation the missionaries called idolatry. In the name of preventing that evil, they were rupturing the Chinese community by asserting their own values and in the process in effect taking away at least a part of the Chinese identity of their converts. Non-convert Chinese were offended and embittered by this action.

Therefore, from their start in 1898 and 1899, Boxers attacked the property and persons of Christian converts and missionaries. Most pockets of Boxer activity in the beginning were in Shandong. But the governor of the province, Yuxian, was able generally to crush the unrest in the southern part of Shandong by the spring of 1899. Growing Boxer activity in the province's northwest along with Western pressure on the government got him cashiered in late 1899. Yuan Shikai succeeded him in Shandong and was able to crush the Boxers there.

In the winter of 1899–1900, the movement began to spread and grow—into Zhili, Henan, Shanxi, and even inner Mongolia and Manchuria. There was no central leadership; Boxer bands would coalesce, attack Christian converts, fade away. One historian has argued that in part the movement spread quickly because of the dynamic of spirit possession. "The empowerment possession conferred made it enormously attractive to those at the bottom of the Chinese social scale, regardless of locale. Also, the possession ritual [which involved boxing, incantations, breathing through clenched teeth, and foaming at the mouth], by placing individuals in direct communication with their gods and enabling them, when in a possessed state, to in effect become gods, placed a major barrier in the way of the creation of a more centralized, structured, and perhaps durable movement."[15] The expansion of the movement also depended on the attitude of the officials. Yuan Shikai's no-nonsense approach in suppressing the northwest Shandong Boxers contrasted sharply with Yuxian's encouragement of Boxers in Shanxi in the summer of 1900.

But perhaps the most important dynamic in the Boxer growth was the drought that began after the Yangzi River floods in late 1898. It freed up many young field hands who ordinarily would have been working in the fields to join the Boxers. An attraction of the Boxers as food became scarce was that they usually had good supplies of grain, gained in their pillaging of Christian households and sometimes their extortion from the wealthy. Psychologically the drought created a problem of hunger anxiety, of growing nervousness, restlessness and hopelessness. And the drought became linked in many Chinese minds with the presence of the Westerners, particularly the missionaries. "In one placard after another, the Chinese people are enjoined to kill off all foreigners and native Chinese contaminated by foreigner or foreign influence. Only after this process of physical elimination of every trace of the foreign from China has been completed will the gods be appeased and permit the rains once again to fall."[16] It is little wonder that missionary anxiety moved in the direction of panic over the continuation of the drought.

Western nations, frightened by the continuing attacks on and murder of missionaries, as well as property losses, demanded that the Qing court act to suppress the uprising. Since the Boxers had championed a slogan supporting the Qing ("Revive the Qing; destroy the foreigner"), the Empress Dowager was reluctant to undertake such suppression. Wall posters hung up in villages and towns shouted the Boxer goal:

> When at last all the Foreign Devils
> Are expelled to the very last man,
> The Great Qing, united, together,
> Will bring peace to this our land.[17]

The Empress Dowager echoed the Confucian line, "Heaven sees as the people see; Heaven hears as the people hear," alluding to the Mandate of Heaven. The whole situation had turned her into something of a populist; in that vein, she argued that "China is weak; the only thing we can depend upon is the hearts of the people. If we lose them, how can we maintain our country?"[18] With Western pressure on the court becoming stronger, the Empress Dowager quite incredibly threw her support behind the Boxers—slowly at first, in January 1900 ordering local authorities to distinguish between lawful local militia formation and bandit activity. Westerners thought that the purpose of that decree was to give the Boxers some cover. The Qing did send military forces against the Boxers, but there was not concerted or sustained action that might have halted the unrest. Boxers nearing Beijing in late spring were attacking railroad lines, ripping out the track and burning stations, and tearing down telegraph lines. The political and policy bankruptcy of the Qing, in permitting and even condoning this action, was clear.

Western nations and Japan determined that they would have to act to save missionaries and stop the bloodshed. On June 10, 1900, Boxers beat back a British relief force marching from Tianjin; they were eventually joined by Qing imperial troops. On June 17, pro-Boxer Manchus told the Empress Dowager that the foreign nations were demanding that she retire and that the Guangxu emperor be returned to the throne. If there had been any question about her siding with the Boxers before, there was not anymore. On June 20, the German minister on his way to a meeting with the Zongli Yamen was shot dead on the street. The next day, in a scene that conjures up the theater of the absurd, the Empress Dowager declared war on the eight foreign powers. Having been repeatedly defeated by one country at a time, the Qing had now decided to battle eight. The Manchus who throughout the dynasty had identified themselves with Chinese and Chinese culture were now identifying themselves and putting their fate into the hands of adolescent warriors. Two of the emperor's brothers were reportedly seen leading Boxer forces in their attacks.

The ambassadorial legation quarters in Beijing and the Northern Cathedral two miles northwest of the legations had become the havens to which missionaries and converts fled. In late June, the Boxers besieged the legation quarters and cathedral, acts that gave rise in the Western press to the phrase "yellow peril." The worst Boxer violence occurred in Shanxi province, where Governor Yuxian, having lost his Shandong governorship due to Western pressure, encouraged Boxer attacks on Westerners. In early July he called forty-four missionaries and their families—men, women, and children—to Taiyuan, the provincial capi-

Western military forces entering the Forbidden City

tal, for their protection. On July 9, under his person supervision, he had them executed. Other missionaries in the province suffered similar fates, along with some two thousand Christian converts.

The war was localized in the north because of actions of key central and southern governors-general and by Yuan Shikai serving as Shandong governor. They simply ignored the declaration of war. An eight-nation force of about twenty thousand men arrived in the capital on August 14 to lift the siege. Most Boxers disappeared into the north China countryside. The Empress Dowager decided to flee southwest. She decided the emperor had to be taken. When the emperor's favorite consort suggested that he be allowed to remain in Beijing in order to negotiate peace, the Empress Dowager had her thrown down a well for her presumptuousness. Disguised and under armed guard, the empress dowager and the emperor took flight in a cart. En route, edicts were issued in the emperor's name in which he took full blame for the disaster. In late October they reached the ancient capital of Xi'an in Shaanxi province, some eight hundred miles from Beijing. They would remain there until January 1902.

Over the next six months, Western troops joined missionaries in making raids out to surrounding cities and towns, pillaging Chinese property. The missionaries were quite enthusiastic about revenge. One missionary, D. Z. Sheffield, wished that more American troops be sent: "It is not bloodthirstiness in missionaries to desire to see further shedding of [Chinese] blood, but an understanding of Chinese character and conditions, and a realization that the policy of general forgiveness means the loss of many valuable native [Christian] and foreign lives."[19] Sheffield's remarks were par for the missionary course. But for sheer outrageousness, the essay "The Ethics of Loot," written by missionary Gilbert Reid for *Forum* magazine in 1901, takes the cake. Reid argued that "To confiscate the property of those who were enemies in war may be theoretically wrong, but precedent had established the right. For those who have known the facts and have passed through a war of awful memory, the matter of loot is one of high ethics." He even said he was sorry that he had not looted more himself. In his capacity as a conspicuous Christian, he had the audacity to ponder the question of "whether the sacking and burning of the entire city of [Beijing] might not 'have been the greatest good for the greatest number.'"[20]

By late 1900, forty-five thousand foreign troops were in north China. They spent their time on search and destroy missions, trying to ferret out Boxers and kill them. But, as in any guerrilla-type action, how does one identify the enemy? The upshot was many innocent killed. One American commander noted that "it is safe to say that where one real Boxer has been killed since the capture of [Beijing], fifty harmless coolies or laborers on the farms, including not a few women and children, have been slain."[21] Troops staged "punitive picnics," affairs that featured menus of arson, rape, and looting.

The signing of the Boxer Protocol in September 1901 brought the lowest point of the Qing court in its relations with the West. The West, like its missionaries, was out for revenge: they called for the execution and punishment of officials who had participated in the war; the Manchu Yuxian, who had egged the Boxers on in Shanxi, was executed, and five others were allowed to commit suicide. The foreign nations punished the whole elite class of would-be officials by suspending the civil service examinations for five years in forty-

Foreigners troops with decapitated Boxers (Note Japanese soldier wiping blood off his sword)
Source: Neg./Transparency no. 336289. (Photo Copied by P. Goldberg). Courtesy Dept. of Library Services, American Museum of Natural History.

five cities. They ordered over two dozen forts destroyed and a dozen railroad posts occupied so that Western troops could have ready access to Beijing. They expanded the legation quarters and ordered it permanently fortified. They put a two-year prohibition on China's importation of arms.

But the most disastrous was an indemnity which was staggering in its immensity.[22] For damage to foreign property and lives the Chinese were forced to pay 450 millions taels (about $333 million in 1901), a sum truly *staggering* since by this time the complete annual Qing income was only about 250 million taels. The indemnity was to be paid annually in thirty-nine installments in gold, with interest rates that by the date of the full payment of the debt (the end of 1940) would total about one billion taels. For a government that could not move with any certainty into the modern world in part because of lack of money, the indemnity was a crushing burden.

The extremely harsh nature of the protocol, the miserable showing of the Chinese military, the insane policy of attempting to use the Boxers as instruments of policy, and the mortifying overland flight of the country's sovereigns were on view for the whole world to see. The apex of Qing wealth and power under the Qianlong emperor had been just a century earlier, yet the state now entered the twentieth century in degradation, poverty, and humiliation.

Notes

[1] Cited in Paul Cohen, *History in Three Keys* (New York: Columbia University Press, 1997), p. 174.

[2] Hao Chang, "Intellectual Change and the Reform Movement, 1890–98" in Fairbank and Liu, p. 288.

[3] Ibid., p. 290.

[4] Immanuel C. Y. Hsu, "Late Ch'ing [Qing] Foreign Relations, 1866–1905" in Fairbank and Liu, p. 109.

[5] Hsu, *The Rise of Modern China,* p. 163.

[6] Hsu, "Late Ch'ing [Qing] Foreign Relations, 1866–1905," p. 115.

[7] This discussion of Liang Qichao's thought is based on Hao Chang, *Liang Ch'i-chao and Intellectual Transition in China, 1890–1907* (Cambridge: Harvard University Press, 1971), pp. 73–120.

[8] Quoted in Hao Chang, "Intellectual Change . . . ", p. 308.

[9] Fairbank, Reischauer, and Craig, pp. 391–392.

[10] Quoted in Jonathan Spence, *The Gate of Heavenly Peace* (New York: Viking Press, 1981), p. 53.

[11] Ibid., p. 329.

[12] The wording is from Hao Chang, p. 337.

[13] Joseph Esherick, *The Origins of the Boxer Uprising* (Berkeley: University of California Press, 1987), p. 179.

[14] Ibid., p. 125.

[15] Cohen, *History in Three Keys,* p. 34.

[16] Ibid., p. 89.

[17] Esherick, p. 300.

[18] Fairbank, Reischauer, and Craig, pp. 397 and 400.

[19] Stuart Creighton Miller, "Ends and Means: Missionary Justification of Force in Nineteenth Century China" in John K. Fairbank, *The Missionary Enterprise in China and America* (Cambridge, 1974), p. 274.

[20] Ibid., pp. 279–280.

[21] Quoted in Esherick, p. 310.

[22] See as examples, Ibid., p. 403; Spence, *The Search for Modern China,* p. 235; and Wakeman, *The Fall of Imperial China,* p. 221.

7

The Revolutionary Manchus

During their exile in Xi'an, the Empress Dowager reported, "We [the emperor and herself] were both clad in the meanest of garments, and to relieve our hunger we were scarcely able to obtain a dish of beans or porridge. Few of our poorest subjects have suffered greater hardships of cold and hunger than befell us in our pitiful plight."[1] Despite the laughable exaggeration in Cixi's description, she was probably reflecting much of what she felt. Taken together, her Xi'an experience of over a year and the memory of the Boxer nightmare and subsequent Western revenge had awakened her to China's danger with all the subtlety of a bucket of icy water thrown in her face. The total experience changed Cixi from being an obstructionist conservative into a leading reformer, initiating change in all the areas that the reformers of the Hundred Days had dreamt about. The reforms focused openly and without apology on adopting the strong points from foreign countries in order to make up for China's weaknesses. In substance they varied from mildly reformist to quite radical, even revolutionary. When the Manchu world ended with their abdication in early 1912, it was after a decade-long bang of activity rather than the whimper of those who, resigned to the forces of history, do nothing.

THE STIRRINGS OF A NEW CHINA IN MACROREGIONAL CORES

During the course of the reforms up to the 1911 revolution, the first signs of a new China began to be seen—from modern-style economic developments to outbursts of nationalism to the appearance of new social forces. Certainly, if the Manchu reform effort was stimulated by China's plight vis-à-vis the outside world, it was also prompted by the increasing evidence of marked internal developments and change.

From the start it should be noted that the stirrings of a new China were spatially uneven. Macroregional core areas of greater urbanization and higher degree of economic development, often situated along the coasts or important river systems, exhibited the greater degree of modern change; peripheral backwaters, the least. The rate of change tended to create different experiences, attitudes, and "worldviews" among the people of areas of varying development. Cities were always the sites of greatest change. They were now being paved, lighted, and policed. They were the homes for wide-ranging reformist voluntary associations to deal with social problems like foot-binding and vices like opium-smoking and gambling. Newspapers and magazines were being produced in greater number, focusing on current issues and developments. With regard to social change during these years, it has been estimated that the numbers of letters, newspapers, and magazines sent and received in 1910 were twenty-five times that in 1901.[2] Such an increase most certainly came primarily in the macroregional cores.

Increasingly common in the cores during these years were evidences of nationalism, expressed often as fears of national dismemberment and even of the obliteration of the Chinese people. Public meetings and demonstrations dot the political landscape—about British threats to Tibet and by extension even the province of Sichuan, Russian influence in Mongolia and Manchuria, and French pressure in the southwest. School songs and plays urged the government to stand up to all foreign pressure. Nationalism as resistance to foreign powers perhaps reached its high point in the 1905–1907 anti-U.S. boycott for its immigration restriction law and its mistreatment of Chinese who attended the 1904 World's Fair in St. Louis.

Nationalism was also expressed against Western intrusion into matters within China. A growing number of rancorous treaty port incidents exploded from cases of Westerners' "right" of extraterritoriality. Though some provinces had eliminated the cultivation of opium, the British argued that until the drug was completely eradicated from the country at large it still could import it. In angry response, there was talk in some Chinese circles of another opium war. A dramatic "rights recovery" movement developed to win control over mines that were foreign-owned and railroads that were foreign-built and foreign-controlled. Recovering the railroads seems to have captured the attention of core society as a whole. People from all social classes in pertinent core zones—from gentry and rich merchants to students and shopkeepers to coolies and even beggars—pledged and contributed money to recover China's railroad rights. Key railroads targeted included the Canton-Hankou line, the Shanghai-Ningbo line and lines in Sichuan province. Some contributors, increasingly upset by foreign control, even threatened to commit suicide in front of foreign embassies in Beijing. Their patriotic shout: "To die for one's country is glorious."

Another important group in the recovery movement, and in Chinese politics and economics in general, was overseas Chinese, particularly those in Southeast Asia (but also the United States and Europe) who came to be seen by elites in China as a source of considerable financial and moral support for reformist and revolutionary causes. One feature of the Chinese diaspora had always been the continuing interest of those abroad in their homeland and especially by their desire to be buried in their ancestral native place. The early twentieth century saw the birth among overseas Chinese communities of a more committed political interest in developments in the "home country," a development that would remain a reality throughout the twentieth century.

In these public displays of nationalism new social groups for the first time were finding public voices, joining the old leaders of society, the scholar-gentry and a new group that appeared in the sources in the last years of the nineteenth century, the gentry-merchants. Youth emerged as a vocal and enthusiastic force, specifically the students who went abroad to Japan, Southeast Asia, America, and Europe. China had sent students to Japan beginning in the late 1890s, many on provincial government scholarships; in 1899 there were two hundred; by 1903, about one thousand; and by 1906, there were some thirteen thousand. In Japan, students formed associations, many of them based upon common provincial origin; there were, for example, associations for students from Jiangsu, Hubei, and Zhejiang that published their own newspapers. Seeing rapidly modernizing Japan, already a growing world power, these students naturally asked what was wrong with China. One student newspaper noted that "Japanese schools are as numerous as our opium dens, Japanese students as numerous as our opium addicts."[3] Those who studied in Japan and Southeast Asia became enamored of Western liberal and radical ideas and returned to China ready to reshape the world. Those who studied in Europe and America tended to concentrate on more technical subjects; while they might not have reentered the Chinese scene with the political commitment that others evidenced, they were still affected by life in more modernized states.

Another traditionally subordinated social group, women, stepped into the world of public affairs in the cores as never before. They joined in nationalistic demonstrations, organized patriotic societies, contributed jewelry for the revolutionary cause, and joined Sun Yat-sen's revolutionary organization, the Revolutionary Alliance. They ran the gamut from the upper crust (court women read *Peking Woman* which talked about the equality of all human beings) to the masses (Canton boatwomen went to the revolutionary front-line in 1911 to serve as the first nurses ministering to combat troops). Women spokespersons advocated the feminist and revolutionary ideas they saw in the model feminist-revolutionary Qiu Jin, executed in July 1907 for her role in anti-government plotting. In urban cores, the practice of footbinding began to decrease. Newspapers reported on the suicides of women whose mothers-in-law forbade them to unbind their feet.

The caveat in all this is that these sweeping revolutionary-sounding changes were largely restricted to macroregional cores. There was a huge gap between the cores and peripheries in terms of the extent of political, social, and economic change; that gap would continue to have a substantial impact on the life of the populace in each zone and on the rate and nature of change in the future.

THE MANCHU REFORM MOVEMENT: EDUCATION

As the Empress Dowager took the Qing into the reform arenas, this flurry of activity in cities and core zones had to have been part of the reality prompting her to act. Reform was necessary as a tactic to build Chinese strength to fend off the West and to maintain leadership in China. In its reformist efforts, the government turned first to education, at the heart of any change that Confucian China might try to undertake.

Examination Reform

It is clear that the Empress Dowager and her officials meant business. Traditionally the function of education had been to train future officials, inculcating them with Confucian values. The proof was in the examination which had varied considerably over the years as to the coverage of questions (sometimes more relevant to current issues, other times, not). A hallmark of the examinations since the Ming period, however, was that the essays had to be written in a formulaic format known as the "eight-legged essay," a structure which artificially strait-jacketed the writer's presentation and his creativity. From Xi'an in August 1901 came Cixi's edict banning the eight-legged essay and calling for examinations that would in part test knowledge of foreign governments and sciences. Note that this was less than three years from the end of the Hundred Days reform attempt. The reformers—some dead, some in exile, with their emperor supporter under house arrest—may have ultimately have had much more impact on subsequent political thinking and developments than the events in September 1898 might first suggest.

One Chinese historian has described the significance of these changes as "epoch-making." Indeed the following questions and topics asked on the "foreign" portion of the 1903–1904 civil service examination for the *jinshi,* or highest degree, tend to show that the thought and actions of Kang, Liang, and others had substantially altered the thinking of "conservative" Qing officials.

Topic 1: "Western countries attach great importance to foreign study tours. How can we define the purpose and contain the time span [of such tours] in order to obtain the maximum benefits with the least costs?"

Topic 2: "Japan Westernized its system of learning with great rapidity. In its initial rush to change, Japan invariably encountered problems from deliberately skipping over normal steps. Yet Japan can still be called a Confucian country. What are suitable goals [for Japan] that preserves strengths while rejecting weaknesses?"

Topic 3: "Chambers of Commerce and modern banks are the main features of a modern fiscal system for which budgeting and balancing accounts are fixed practices. In order to put [modern fiscal practices] into effect, the[se] fundamental components are necessary."

Topic 4: "A modern police system is closely linked to a modern political system. We should obtain foreign police codes and proceed to implement their practice."

Topic 5: "Industry, modern shipping, and railways augment military strength. All countries that have achieved wealth and power have done so using these means. Should we therefore adopt these things? What about the foundational values of a nation?"[4] It is likely that the bodies of arch-conservatives like Woren were spinning in their graves with the reality that Western institutions and values had become such an integral part of the highest level civil service examination.

A National School System

Whether Kang's and Liang's reformist ideas of popular education had hit their mark or whether the Empress Dowager was influenced from elsewhere, in October 1901 she championed the establishment of a national school system. It would be structured as a hierarchy of schools located at each territorial level of government administration: county, prefecture, province, and capital. It would run alongside and feed into traditional examinations, in essence becoming another route to traditional degrees. The hope was that within perhaps a decade the new school system could supersede the examination system. But this approach did not work. There was no incentive for men to choose the new route to examination success. Private tutoring for the old examination was cheaper and more familiar than untried schools. Even more serious, there were no provisions for financing the new schools or for obtainining teachers and textbooks.

In 1904, a more detailed plan for a national school system was laid out. It specified, for example, such particulars as how many kindergartens and primary schools should be established per numbers of families in a community, where middle schools and high schools should be established, and what should be taught. But the plan still allowed the civil service examination to continue for three more years. Therefore, even with the greater details of the 1904 plan, the new government schools died on the vine while the examination system continued to flourish.

The Most Revolutionary Act of the Century

The year 1905 was crucial in what became the program of Qing reforms. That year Japan defeated Russia in war, the first victory ever of an Asian country over a European country. Japan's great success in its entrance into the modern world and its roles on the world stage, in contrast to China's pitiful performance, was a spur to a more widespread reform effort. Another forceful impetus was the organization of anti-Qing revolutionary groups in Japan. In Tokyo in 1905, Sun Yat-sen formed his Revolutionary Alliance with the specific goals of overthrowing the dynasty and establishing a republic. From the Manchu perspective, leading the reforms might very well be the only way to save the dynasty from its antagonists.

In August 1905 the most powerful provincial officials, led by Yuan Shikai, urged the abolition of the civil service examination system. In an act that should be heralded with trumpet fanfares to mark its extraordinary significance, the Empress Dowager accepted the advice and ordered the examination cast into the dustbin of history. *It was the most revolutionary act of the twentieth century.* Why? The examination had been at the heart of traditional culture: It had been the chief vehicle of orthodox state and social ideology; it had given birth to the political elites who took the posts at all levels of the imperial bureaucracy; it had given birth to the social elites, the scholar-gentry, who provided essential leadership at local levels of society.

Now, with the abolition of the examination, there was no way to convey an official ideology. Indeed there was no longer an official ideology of state. What were left were questions without answers. From now on, what would give state and society its direction and its values? From now on, how would political and social leaders be produced? From now on, what would hold China together? Indeed, it is the case that once the civil service examination was gone, there was no way to stop, divert, or even slow the tides of change.

From 1906, then, education had to succeed or fail with the new government school system. The problems—insufficient school buildings, inadequate funding, and paucity of able teachers and textbooks—had not gone away. Likely because of the great traditional stress placed upon education, local elites took it upon themselves to open and teach in schools. The school system in any particular locality was hostage to two factors—the degree of local economic development and the presence of interested elites. The system, as it developed, tended to remain weak at its base: local elites could achieve greater prestige setting up a high school than an elementary school so some communities had no elementary schools. Similarly kindergartens and elementary schools lacked teachers because most potential instructors preferred the prestige (and salary) of teaching at a higher level school. Despite the immense problems, the education system was quickly, if very haphazardly, revolutionized. Perhaps most revolutionary were the curriculum with both Chinese and Western studies replacing the classics and the social impact, as students now met daily in the classroom with other students as peers instead of studying with one's tutor. Studies have shown that core zone counties tended to have fairly well-developed school systems while poorer peripheral counties had fewer schools and students; nevertheless even in wealthier areas conservative traditional outlooks sometimes retarded school construction and development.[5]

THE MANCHU REFORM MOVEMENT: MILITARY CHANGE

A well-known Chinese proverb says, "Good iron is not beaten into nails; good men are not made into soldiers." Chinese civilization had through the centuries hailed and stressed the virtues of civilian rule and civil values. The empire could be won on horseback, the platitude went, but it had to be ruled with the writing brush. There was an imperial military examination that theoretically paralleled the civil service examination, but it had little prestige. By late imperial times it had become mostly contests of strength and physical prowess and knowledge of centuries-old manuals. If one were a man of ability and ambition, he simply did not route his future into the military. However, one of the major changes wrought by China's nineteenth- and twentieth-century history is, as we will see, the revaluation of the military amid the increasing militarization of Chinese politics and society.

At the opening of the century there were several types of military organizations. The oldest were the weak and useless banner and Green Standard forces. Not much better by the end of the century were the regional armies formed during the Taiping, now mainly vested interests of their leaders. In these armies there was no set numbers of troops; ranks were often peopled with vagrants; and officers, who had no knowledge or interest in modern weapons, did not train their troops and embezzled the money which was to have been paid to those troops. Li Hongzhang's Anhui army had done the fighting against Japan in 1894–1895; at the time about 60 percent of the troops had guns; the other 40 percent used swords, spears, and pikes.

There were also two "new armies," established in the mid-1890s to be used against Japan; but the war had ended before these armies, trained by German military officers and equipped with modern weapons, could be deployed. In 1895, Zhang Zhidong established the Self-Strengthening Army in Nanjing while Yuan Shikai formed the Newly-Established

Army near Tianjin. Both men tried to avoid the situations existing in the foundering provincial armies. Zhang, for example, recruited men between the ages of 16 and 20 from peasant families in the vicinity of Nanjing; he required that their character be vouched for by neighbors and that they have a physical examination by a foreign doctor before being accepted. Yuan established similar procedures. Both new armies paid their men well; and Yuan insisted that part of the salary be sent to the men's families. In July 1901, the Manchus transferred control of Zhang's "new army" to Yuan, making him the key army builder in the country and, until his transfer to Beijing in 1907, the head of what came to be called the New Army.

In late 1903 a Commission for Army Reorganization was appointed to modernize all the country's military institutions. They mandated troop regulations like those Zhang and Yuan had initiated and ordered that each province establish a modern force manned by residents of that province. They set up a system where New Army divisions were stationed at crucial locations across the country. Despite these reforms, central direction of the army remained fragmented. Military centralization in a real sense was made impossible because of political realities—China was fragmented into regional and provincial political interests and domains. In addition, funding for a fully modernized force was completely inadequate.

New military academies were established beginning in 1904 in Beijing and in the provinces of Shaanxi, Zhili, Jiangsu, and Hubei; they joined the ranks of the modern Baoding Academy founded by Yuan Shikai after the Boxer uprising. All the academies came to use Japanese instructors, instead of the more expensive Germans. They began to produce cadets who were inculcated with patriotic ideas, who brought together modern military expertise with a sense of acting for the good of the country. Increasing numbers of graduates of these academies began to travel for further study at Japanese military academies, including future leader Chiang Kai-shek. There, like students in other Japanese schools, they began to talk about the nature of China's problems. By the time they returned to China to be assigned to their posts, many of them were filled with the anti-Manchu and revolutionary ideas of Sun Yat-sen and others.

More able men began to choose military careers after the abolition of the civil service examination system. The army seemed to present a new ladder that they could climb to social prestige and considerable power. Studies have shown that peripheral (but not the most peripheral) regions tended to produce the highest proportional share of young men attending new military academies, like that at Baoding.[6] These were regions that traditionally did not typically produce many civil service degreeholders. Thus in these areas there seemed likely a conscious awareness of the new and prestigious career possibilities in the military.

Because of the power of connections in Chinese society and the importance of the teacher-student relationship, the men at Baoding Military Academy became personally connected to Yuan Shikai through his leadership. His command came to be known as the Beiyang (Northern) Army. As a mark of the changed roles of military men in the early twentieth century, among his Beiyang officers, ten would become military provincial governors after 1912 and five would become presidents or premiers of Republican China. The military had arrived as a legitimate and even determinative factor in Chinese society and politics.

THE MANCHU REFORM MOVEMENT: CONSTITUTIONALISM

The Chinese did not see the victory of Japan over Russia in 1905 as simply a triumph of Asia over Europe, but more significantly as an indicator of what its path of political modernization should be: Japan, a constitutional power, had decisively defeated Russia, an authoritarian country. In thinking about the source of Western wealth and power—and now seeing Japanese success in emulating the West—it was not farfetched to believe that somehow one of the sources might be constitutionalism. In addition, Qing policymakers saw a very practical reason for wanting to move in that direction: constitutional forms might very well be a vehicle for strengthening their control over localities and their elites, tying provinces and localities more closely to the central government.

What the court saw as it looked back over the previous half century was a country whose regions, provinces, and localities were spinning out of the control of the Center in centrifugal fashion. Much of the problem came from the political and military weakness and economic bankruptcy of the central government. Thus, when the Taiping war had begun to wreak its destruction, the center had to ask civilian officials to form provincial armies to save the Center. Power flowed out to the provinces—and those armies were still around almost fifty years later. Then, when it was time for reconstruction following the rebellions, the Center had no money for the immense task, so that it had to rely on local elites to take the lead. Studies have shown that during the rebellions and in their aftermath local elites emerged as significant leaders in establishing and managing local militia, rebuilding public works, sponsoring charitable undertakings, underwriting educational expenses, and contributing to and superintending the renovation of water control facilities. Power had "devolved" from the Center to the local arenas. From the Qing perspective, constitutional bodies, directed and controlled ultimately by the throne, might be vehicles to bring local and provincial elites back into a firmer relationship with the Center.

With this in mind, in 1905 the Empress Dowager decided to send missions abroad to study constitutional systems in Europe, the United States, and Japan. The study mission lasted from late 1905 to late summer 1906 (one wonders whether the first "foreign" topic on the 1903–1904 civil service examination was asked with such a mission in mind). On their return, the clear choice was the Japanese model—retaining the monarchy which itself would bestow the constitution; the court sensed that this model would actually strengthen the throne's power. On September 1, 1906, the Empress Dowager proclaimed:

> The wealth and strength of other countries are due to their practice of constitutional government, in which public questions are determined by consultation with the people. The ruler and his people are as one body animated by one spirit, as a result of which comprehensive consideration is given to the general welfare and the limits of authority are clearly defined. . . . Under these circumstances, we can . . . adopt a constitutional polity in which the supreme authority shall be vested in the crown, but all questions of government shall be considered by a popular assembly.[7]

Celebrations broke out in cities around the country following the Empress Dowager's proclamation.

The edict of September 1 had also called for the complete revamping of the central government structures. Though this reform ignited considerable resistance among conservative officials, by November the new forms were on the books, if not yet fully implemented. The traditional Six Boards which had existed since the Tang dynasty (618–907) were to be abolished and in their place new ministries established. The Board of Revenue became the Ministry of Finance; the Board of Punishments, the Ministry of Justice; the Board of Works joined with the Board of Commerce (established in 1903) to become the Ministry of Agriculture, Industry, and Commerce—and so on. One can be skeptical and wonder whether these were simply name changes without any substance; but it is important to understand that these name changes were shucking off forms that had been around for over a millennium and that in China forms can ultimately be as important as substance, forms indeed can become substance. The establishment of the new ministries was followed by a massive reshuffling of official posts and by a move to restructure provincial governments.

In the fall of 1907 the Empress Dowager announced that a national deliberative assembly and provincial deliberative assemblies would be established. Local assemblies were also to come into being. In August 1908 the Empress Dowager set forth a nine-year calendar of tutelage during which specific constitutional forms would be established. For example, provisional provincial assemblies would be set up in 1909, with a provisional national assembly, in 1910; each year the state would take a new step toward the full realization of a constitutional system in 1917.

Had she lived, the Empress Dowager might have been able to lead China into that new system, but she died in November 1908. The Guangxu Emperor, age thirty-seven and under house arrest since the 1898 coup, died the day before she did. Though one report suggests that he suffered from Bright's disease, most historians believe that Cixi had him poisoned. She had already decided on his successor, the three-year-old grandson of her closest Manchu official (and some say her lover) Ronglu. Since the new Xuantong Emperor was only three years old, his tenure as Son of Heaven was controlled by his father as regent. While he and other Manchu princes whom he allowed to have considerable power did not undo the constitutional schedule, many of their actions in ruling were ignorant and inept. Their chief goal seemed to be maintaining and enhancing their own power. One wonders why the adeptly political Empress Dowager left power in such unfit hands.

Strong officials who had served the Empress Dowager well were dismissed on flimsily absurd pretexts. The most able Manchu official, Duan Fang, was sent packing in late 1909 "for taking photographs on the way [of Cixi's state funeral], for moving about in his sedan chair with undue freedom and for making use of the trees at the Mausolea for telegraph poles."[8] This followed the dismissal early in the year of the most able Chinese official Yuan Shikai who suddenly found from the official edict dismissing him that he was ill: "Unexpectedly [Yuan] is suffering from leg disease and walks only with difficulty. He is, therefore, incapacitated for office. Let him vacate his post and return to his native place for treatment."[9] Unexpectedly indeed! With the absence of the Empress Dowager and the main officials who had propelled the reforms, the reforms seemed to languish.

Local Self-government

The "local" in local self-government is relative; everything not national was considered local; thus, local self-government includes the arenas of the province, the county, and the township. Elections for the provisional provincial assemblies were held from February to June 1909, the first Chinese elections ever for representative bodies. Many Chinese, suspicious and not completely understanding what was happening or its significance, were apathetic; bribery in the elections was common. Because of educational or economic requirements both for candidates and voters, the number of people voting relative to the entire population was very small, averaging about .42 percent, barely over 4 people per 1000. Yet, given the fact that this was the first election in a country where elections were unknown, the elections were markedly significant events. The elected twenty-one assemblies, averaging 78 representatives each, were generally bodies of provincial notables with the vast majority being civil service degreeholders. In the fifteen provincial assemblies on which there is complete data, 89.1 percent of assemblymen held degrees.[10] But the backgrounds of the elected chairmen of the assemblies showed that the bodies were a mix of the old and the new forces in Chinese society. There were 63 speakers and deputy speakers in the twenty-one assemblies: 51 were upper degreeholders and 7 held lower degrees; 6 had studied abroad. Indeed, of the 1643 assemblymen, 167 (10.2 percent) had attended modern schools or gone abroad; 105 or 6.4 percent had studied in Japan. The average age of all assemblymen was in the early forties.[11]

When the assemblies met, they discussed among other things education, local self-government, trade and industry, and police affairs. They were not cowed by provincial officials and quickly became bold and demanding. The chairman of the Jiangsu assembly called a meeting of representatives from the provincial assemblies in Shanghai in November 1909; 51 representatives from 16 provinces met to draw up a petition calling for the immediate convening of the national assembly. Three times in 1910 similar petitions were presented with the number having signed the petition increasing with each attempt—reportedly 200,000 signed the first, 300,000 the second, and 25 million the third. As one historian says, almost underplaying the stunning nature of this development, "This 'mass movement' was an unprecedented event."[12] The regent refused to grant the petition, stating that the establishment of the National Assembly should not be rushed.

The preliminary steps to establish county level self-government bodies also began in 1909 with the setting up of offices to oversee the formation of county seat, town, and township councils. In Zhejiang province, for example, they were elected by the third lunar month of 1911 for two year terms. County seat and town councils had twenty to fifty men; township councils six to eight. These councils in turn chose the executive boards of the county seat and town (generally six members) and the township manager and his assistant. County seat, market town, and township councils and boards were meeting in the core zones and in most counties of the periphery by the late summer of 1911. On the whole, the revolutionary quality of these political changes, initiated by the Manchus, is nothing short of astonishing. If the Manchus saw these changes as a way to reestablish tighter control over the localities and their elites, local elites saw the new institutions as a way to solidify and enhance their own political leadership positions that had grown in the aftermath of the nineteenth century rebellions.

In addition to the self-government bodies, the Qing mandated the establishment of other elite associations to be established in counties to assist in the modernization process. Many of them were based on foreign models. In 1903 came edicts calling for the formation of Chambers of Commerce "to perform various managerial and mediational functions in the local economy 'in addition to the duties discharged by the chambers of commerce in foreign countries.'"[13] These were followed by mandated education associations (1906), agriculture associations (1907), lawyers' associations (1912), and bankers' associations (1915). In all matters they were under government control. The government saw these associations, like self-government bodies, at least in part as control mechanisms over local elites. Unlike self-government bodies, the actual dates of the establishment of these associations were more dependent on local conditions and degree of economic development. It is clear that counties in the peripheries did not have enough commercial activity to warrant the early establishment of Chambers of Commerce. While the average date for the establishment of Chambers of Commerce in Zhejiang's most developed core area, the inner core, was 1906, in the outer core the average date came a year later, in 1907. In the more developed areas of the periphery the average date was 1909, but in the least developed they did not appear on average until 1917 or later. Similar patterns are evident with education and agriculture associations. Other less developed areas lagged behind these dates. Location and relationship to economic development thus played a major role in a locality's timing and experience of revolutionary change.

National Self-Government

The provisional national assembly met in Beijing on October 1, 1910 (thirty-nine years to the day later would see the establishment of the People's Republic of China). Composed of two hundred members, one hundred elected by the provincial assemblies and one hundred chosen by the Throne, the assembly's mandate was to discuss such issues as the national budget, taxes, industrial development, and insurance and transportation regulations. They were initially barred from discussing the adoption of the constitution. But the assembly, like provincial assemblies a year earlier, threw caution to the winds and first debated, then voted on October 24 to telescope the nine-year constitutional schedule. Two days later as part of a bitter factional struggle between the regent and a new empress dowager, the government's Finance Minister came out in favor of an immediate full-fledged national assembly. On November 2, the provincial assembly representatives again tried to present their petition for an immediate national assembly, with some men showing the depth of their determination by cutting off their fingers to write their petitions in blood. A sense of urgency, of the necessity of a "great leap" ahead, of the imperative of "seizing the hour, seizing the day" seemed to sweep over Chinese in the drive to realize the institutions of a modern state.[14]

And then it happened. The Throne caved in on November 4 and promised a full-fledged national assembly by 1913. In little more than a month the provisional national assembly had shown itself to be the master of the court. But 1913 was not soon enough. "Now" was the cry. In December, street demonstrations broke out: over two thousand students in Tianjin paraded to government offices calling for the immediate establishment of a national assembly. The appearance of court weakness only encouraged more demands. In November the assembly condemned the chief government executive organ, the Grand Council, for approving of a government loan without the approval of the assembly; assemblymen argued that the Council should be subject to the assembly or a Cabinet. In the context of increasingly persistent political interests and demands on the part of the assemblies, the Throne looked totally politically inept when in May 1911 it announced the formation of a cabinet of thirteen comprised of eight Manchus, one Mongol bannerman, and only four Chinese. Many Chinese perceived such a make-up as a slap in the face.

By the summer of 1911 many Chinese elites and students were riding a political roller coaster with hopes for rapidly realizing constitutional bodies and rights zooming high and then plummeting with the caution and ineptitude of the court. When one puts these developments in the context of rising anti-Manchu bitterness (see below), the situation was quite volatile and dangerous. The assemblies indeed emerged as revolutionary organs on the provincial and national scene.

Analysis of the last decade of the Qing suggests that the court reformed itself out of existence. Every reform that it initiated and oversaw hastened its own end. Ending the civil service examination opened the floodgates, leaving major ideological, political, and social questions without answers. Educational reforms in the sending of students abroad put the students together with their peers to question the legitimacy of Manchu rule. Military reform produced a new kind of soldier, trained in military academies and inculcated with nationalism. Administrative reform brought the reconstruction of centuries-old government institutions and raised questions about state ends. Finally, constitutionalism opened the political door to the citizens at the local, provincial, and national levels, giving the people forums in which to debate, legislate, maneuver, and vociferously demand. In these arenas it is surely not an exaggeration to call the Manchus "revolutionary."

THE ANTI-MANCHU REVOLUTIONARY MOVEMENT

While the Manchus were undertaking revolutionary reforms, anti-Manchu sentiment had grown both in China and abroad among Chinese who believed that the day for reform, particularly "Manchu" reform, had passed and that revolution was the only way to save China. Nationalism was emerging as a strong force in core areas and among students in Japan; in any discussions about the nation or nationalism, "Manchus" often ended up being lumped with foreigners as the "Other."

The first decade of the twentieth century was dotted with small scale attempts at local rebellion with the rationale that a single spark might set off a raging conflagration. Many of these were initiated by Sun Yat-sen and his Revolutionary Alliance. The son of a poor farmer in Guangdong province, Sun (1867–1925) as a teenager had studied in Honolulu where his brother had emigrated. Though trained in medicine in Hong Kong, he quickly tired of medical practice and began to devote his time and thought to reversing China's plight. In 1894, he formed the Revive China Society with the ostensible goal of undertaking reforms to revitalize China but with the actual aim of organizing a revolt against the Manchu government. In the fall of 1895, he attempted to launch the first of what, extending to 1911, would become ten revolts. This one, like all the others, seemed almost tragicomic—failing from various combinations of inadequate planning, confusion, bad timing, weapons not arriving, or the discovery of the plot before it could begin.

When he was not planning revolts, Sun spent his time focusing on two things. The first was raising money for the revolutionary cause in overseas Chinese communities around the world—an effort where a major competitor was no less than the former reformer Kang Youwei who was raising money for his Protect the Emperor Society aimed at getting rid of the Empress Dowager. The second was putting ideological flesh onto the skeleton of political aims set forth in the rationale for the founding of the Revolutionary Alliance. Sun's essential points became known as the Three Principles of the People and would become the guiding principles of the later incarnation of the Revolutionary Alliance, the Nationalist Party (*Guomindang*). The three principles were "nationalism," which meant ending both the rule of the Manchus and the presence of the foreign imperialists; "democracy," which, according to Sun, especially included election, initiative, referendum, and recall; and "socialism" or, as Sun expressed it, "people's livelihood," the least fleshed out principle that focused primarily on equalizing land ownership and controlling capital.

Sun's Revolutionary Alliance was not the only organization established for revolution against the Manchus. In 1903, Huang Xing, a *shengyuan* degreeholder from Hunan who studied briefly in Japan, established the Society for the Revival of China (*Huaxinghui*); also strong in the organization was his fellow Hunanese, twenty-one-year-old Song Jiaoren. The next year, Zhejiang scholar Cai Yuanpei, who had attained the *jinshi* degree at the remarkably young age of twenty-two and had served in the Hanlin Academy in the 1890s, formed the Restoration Society (*Guangfuhui*). Huang's and Song's society merged with the Revolutionary Alliance at its formation in 1905 while the Restoration Society maintained its own integrity—though individuals did choose to become members of both groups.

In addition to the formation of revolutionary associations, individuals emerged to voice in various ways their strong protests against the Manchus. Eighteen-year-old Zou Rong, who had studied in Japan, wrote *The Revolutionary Army* in 1903. Zou argued that the Chinese were slaves to the Manchu "bandits," that Zeng Guofan, Zuo Zongtang, and Li Hongzhang who had helped the Qing crush the mid-nineteenth-century rebellions were "Chinese traitors," and that a revolution must sweep the Manchus out and usher in a republic with a constitution modeled on the American constitution.[15] Several tens of thousands of the tract were distributed across China and in overseas Chinese communities; it was the most influential and widely circulated revolutionary piece of the decade. Zou was imprisoned in the International Settlement for distributing inflammatory literature; he died of natural causes in prison at age nineteen.

Other protests were more violent. In 1907, Qiu Jin, the revolutionary feminist, joined with fellow native-placer and fellow student in Japan, Xu Xilin, a knight-errant type, in a plot to assassinate the Manchu governor of Anhui province. Both were members of the Restoration Society and both had been involved in heading a school that functioned as a front for revolutionary planning and activity. Xu and two accomplices were able to assassinate the governor, though they were seized and executed immediately. When Qiu's involvement came to light, troops from the provincial capital stormed her school, seized her, and beheaded her. Today Qiu is seen as a national heroine, the leading earliest feminist, and a great poet; her most famous line was allegedly written just before her execution: "The autumn wind and the autumn rain will make me die of sorrow."

Other revolutionary efforts hit closer to the home of the Manchu national leadership. Wang Jingwei had won both the *juren* degree at age twenty and a government scholarship to study in Japan. He became a member of the Revolutionary Alliance and was a frequent contributor to the alliance's newspaper. In early 1910, he went to Beijing with the intent of assassinating the prince regent in hopes of stirring the Chinese to revolt. The plot: to set off a bomb placed under a bridge on the prince regent's route. But a mistake by his fellow conspirators tipped the police off. Wang was arrested and imprisoned. Saved from execution by Manchu hopes that, amid their growing weakness, going lightly with such political criminals might take some of the heat off themselves, Wang was released when the revolution broke out in the fall of 1911. His courage to act and to freely tell his captors what he was about made him at least temporarily, in the words of an historian, "the golden boy of Chinese nationalism."[16]

It is noteworthy how Japan served as the incubator of revolution. Not only was the key revolutionary organization formed there; but, more importantly, young Chinese men and women coming to Japan to study at both civilian and military schools, often on government scholarships, were turned into anti-government revolutionaries. They saw the immense difference in the degree of modernization in Japan, and it contrasted in humiliating ways with what they saw in China. Japan gave them a milieu in which their revolutionary fervor could openly grow and in which they could increase mutual revolutionary ardor. It is little wonder that they then returned home to China to become the Zou Rongs, Qiu Jins, and Wang Jingweis.

THE 1911 REVOLUTION

The climactic act of the decade-long revolutionary drama was the revolution itself. Like many events in history that shatter the status quo, the revolution was shaped by timing and contingency as much as by planning. The setting for the beginning of the drama was the city of Wuchang on the Yangzi River in the Middle Yangzi macroregion; it was not only the site of an important New Army garrison but also of the yamen of the governor-general of Hunan-Hubei. The first contingency was that the military garrison had been weakened with the transfer of three battalions of New Army troops to deal with fighting that had erupted between military forces and citizens in Sichuan province over the issue of railroad rights recovery. If the garrison had been at full strength, the revolution may not have succeeded.

The actors in this first act were not members of the Revolutionary Alliance, but were active in two organizations that had had contact with it; they had been at work enlisting the support of New Army troops for a planned revolt. In late September, they sent messages to Huang Xing and Song Jiaoren, asking them to come participate in their planned uprising. Neither complied. Sun Yat-sen was on a fund-raising trip in the United States. He would read about the revolution he had tried to ignite for so many years in a newspaper on a train outside of Denver. There were thus no recognized revolutionary leaders present. Then, on October 9, while the revolutionaries were putting gunpowder into shells, one was careless enough to allow ashes from a lighted cigarette to fall into the powder, creating an explosion. Police came running and found revolutionary insignia and membership lists, including the names of large numbers of New Army troops. The Manchu governor-general and the commanders of the Eighth Division and the cavalry battalion (Li Yuanhong) began an intensive effort to halt any possible revolt by arresting and imprisoning the people on the lists.

Facing arrest and certain execution, the revolutionaries decided their only choice was to proceed with the revolt. It began on the rainy and windswept evening of October 10. If the governor general and the commander of the Eight Division had steeled themselves to the task and not fled, it is possible that the revolt would have failed. But they did flee along with most of the city's civil and military officials. By the morning of October 11, the revolutionaries were in charge of the city. But they had no leader. Someone mentioned the possibility of enlisting Li Yuanhong, the New Army leader. He was certainly no revolutionary or friend of one; indeed in the first burst of fighting he was approached by a man dispatched from the rebels asking him to throw his lot and his battalion in with the rebels. He promptly took out a knife and stabbed the man to death. When the fighting took a turn for the worse for the government, Li, fearful of what rebels might demand of him, went to hide at the home of one of his staff. Eventually found, he was asked to be their leader. When he refused, they threatened him, at least figuratively putting a gun to his head. "I am your leader," he replied. Li would go on to become the only man ever to serve twice as president of the republican government at Beijing.

The Qing responded by ordering the Minister of War to plan and oversee an attack on the rebel forces at Wuchang. The logical person to lead these Beiyang forces was their old leader Yuan Shikai, who had been rudely dismissed for a fictitious leg illness. They decided to appoint Yuan as the governor-general of Hunan-Hubei. His response: "Unfortunately my leg disease has still not healed, so I can't help you." Obviously two could play the sorry game concocted two years earlier by the regent. Yuan was biding his time to see which way the winds would blow. The battle results showed strong anti-Qing winds, with defeat following defeat. With their backs up against the wall, the Qing court was eager to learn Yuan's terms for stepping in to deal with the situation. He still did not respond when the court appointed him imperial commissioner in complete charge of the army and navy. He only agreed to lead the campaign against the revolutionaries when, on November 1, they consented to appoint him as premier of the government with the right to name his own cabinet. In essence, the Manchus were steering China in the direction of a constitutional monarchy.

But that was not to be; revolutionary events were spiraling out of control. In coups in provincial and prefectural capitals and in county seats across China, mostly in cores but in some more developed peripheries, New Army troops were joining the old scholar-gentry, rich merchants, and returned students from Japan to declare the beginning of the republic. By late November fifteen provinces had seceded from the Qing dynasty. Yuan emerged as key power broker in the struggle. As Yuan whittled down the power of the court, forcing the regent's retirement in early December, he tried to get peace talks going with the revolutionaries in order to determine what he might be able to gain from negotiations with them. Battles played key roles in determining the political situations. The revolutionaries would not talk with Yuan's emissaries until after he defeated them decisively at Hanyang in late

November. But, in turn, the court's cause was dealt a deathblow by the defeat of its forces in Nanjing in early December after weeks of brutal fighting.

In early December the revolutionaries, in the person of Huang Xing, offered Yuan the presidency of the republic if he would support that political system and bring about the abdication of the Qing emperor. Yuan leapt at the opportunity. It was a decision that the revolutionaries would come to regret. In his career, Yuan had been a powerful and capable dynastic official serving effectively in many capacities. Yet he had had no experience with republicanism. Why did the revolutionaries give him the republic on a silver platter? Most historians believe that the revolutionaries agreed to this in order to stop the fighting as quickly as possible so as to forestall the possibility that foreign powers in their treaty ports and concession areas might take advantage of the unrest to increase various kinds of imperialistic pressures and demands.

Signs of ever more threatening foreign imperialism were all around. In October 1911 the Chinese government defaulted in their Boxer indemnity payments. The British Foreign Office meeting with representatives from the powerful Hong Kong and Shanghai Banking Corporation agreed that in order to secure their loans they would likely have to take control of crucial institutions in the Chinese government. Here was the specter of Western nations seizing part of the Chinese government. Or, perhaps even worse: "It did not seem to matter how great the Chinese interest in a given case; every treaty right was once again supreme." Thus a provincial governor could not stop the export of beans at a time of famine because a 1902 agreement had stipulated that China "had no right to interfere in the bean trade."[17] Because of such a foreign presence and threat, the Chinese were very skittish about any actions that might incur foreign wrath and retaliation. They were careful in their fighting that they not damage foreign property lest foreigners use it as a pretext to take more. Thus, fighting in the Yangzi port of Hankou had to be carefully controlled so that foreign warehouses were not hit. And in the crucial fighting in the area between Nanjing and Shanghai, revolutionary troops felt they had to walk alongside the Shanghai and Nanjing Railroad tracks rather than ride the train or, much bolder, seize the train for their use—because Great Britain owned the line and the revolutionaries did not dare risk damaging British property. With such realities, it is not surprising that the revolutionaries turned to Yuan.

Sun Yat-sen returned to China on December 25. Though he was elected the provisional president of the Republic of China by the representatives of sixteen provincial assemblies (an act that angered Yuan), Sun was aware of Yuan's greater power. He supported the earlier deal that had left Yuan in charge. The only remaining task for Yuan was bringing the dynasty to an end, a task helped along in late January by a telegram sent to Yuan's cabinet from over forty commanders in the Beiyang army asking for the establishment of a republic. The abdication of the Manchus came on February 12, 1912, with the announcement that the six-year-old Xuantong emperor (Puyi) and his family could continue to live in the Forbidden City, receive a payment of four million dollars each year, as well as own the treasures of the imperial palace.

In localities, the contours and the meaning of the revolution varied according to particular location. In most areas the revolutionary acts were like coups d'etat, with local civilian leaders and/or military units seizing control. In some areas, reformist scholar-gentry and other elites who had been involved in reforms, like recovering railroad rights or serving in

Chambers of Commerce and local self-government bodies, simply stepped in to lead and staff temporary military governments. New Army men were often in the forefront of directing revolutionary action. In some areas revolutionary organizations, like the Restoration Society or the Revolutionary Alliance, sometimes joined by secret societies and even underworld figures linked to criminal activity, were pivotal. In yet other areas usually more peripheral than core, political and social disorder was the order of the day. People in many areas, core and periphery, hung white flags in memory of the Ming, the last Chinese dynasty, and declared what was happening "restoration," that is, the return of rule from Manchu to Han Chinese. The date of the beginning of the revolution—the tenth day of the tenth month or Double Ten—has been celebrated as National Day since by the Republic of China on the mainland until 1949 and after, on Taiwan.

The meaning of the events from October 1911 to February 1912 was extraordinarily revolutionary. The abolition of the civil service examination had begun the process of destroying traditional China by demolishing the recruitment structure for political and social elites. Now the abolition of the monarchy demolished the whole political structure. In place for over two thousand years, the Son of Heaven and the empire were gone, along with all the traditional political principles, laws, customs, and morality. In its place was an untried republic, as yet only a name without substance, to be led by a man who had never supported

Cutting the queue as a sign that the Manchu regime was over

such a system. As China entered the spring of 1912, it was beginning the process of constructing a new Chinese identity, of building a new state and nation—the new China—in a completely uncharted, unmarked future.

Notes

[1] Cited in Maribeth E. Cameron, *The Reform Movement in China, 1898–1912* (New York: AMS Press, 1931), p. 56.

[2] Mary Clabaugh Wright, "Introduction: The Rising Tide of Change" in Mary Clabaugh Wright, Ed., *China in Revolution: The First Phase, 1900–1913* (New Haven: Yale University Press, 1968), p. 30.

[3] The report in the *Beijing xinwen huibao* (September 26, 1901) is quoted in Douglas R. Reynolds, *China, 1898–1912: The Xinzheng Revolution and Japan* (Cambridge: Harvard University Press, 1993), p. 62.

[4] Fan Peiwei, "*Qing mo guimao jiachen ke huishi shulun*" (A review of the late Qing metropolitan examinations of 1903–1904, *Lishi dang'an* (History Archives, 3 (1993), pp. 105–110. Translated by Douglas R. Reynolds in *China, 1895–1912: State-Sponsored Reforms and China's Late-Qing Revolution* (Armonk, N.Y.: M. E. Sharpe, 1995), p. 94.

[5] R. Keith Schoppa, *Chinese Elites and Political Change* (Cambridge: Harvard University Press, 1982), pp. 121–122.

[6] Ibid., pp. 123–124.

[7] Quoted in Cameron, p. 103.

[8] *North China Herald,* November 27, 1909, quoted in Cameron, p. 119.

[9] *North China Herald,* January 9, 1909, quoted in Cameron, p. 117.

[10] Of these, 4.4 percent were *jinshi* degreeholders, 21.3 percent were *juren* degreeholders, and 62.5 percent held lower degrees.

[11] This data comes from Chang P'eng-yuan, "The Background of Constitutionalists in Late Qing China" in Eto Shinkichi and Harold Z. Schiffrin, Eds., *China's Republican Revolution* (Tokyo: University of Tokyo Press, 1994), pp. 66–68.

[12] Peng-yuan Chang, "The Constitutionalists" in Wright, *China in Revolution: The First Phase, 1900–1913,* p. 161.

[13] Schoppa, *Chinese Elites and Political Change,* p. 34.

[14] The phrase comes from a poem by Mao Zedong. It is quoted, and the whole phenomenon is discussed in Zhang Kaiyuan, "The 1911 Revolution and 'Seize the Hour, Seize the Day'" in Eto and Schiffrin, pp. 77–88.

[15] See the excerpt, "Zou Rong on Revolution, 1903" in Pei-kai Cheng and Michael Lestz with Jonathan Spence, Eds., *The Search for Modern China, A Documentary Collection* (New York: W. W. Norton, 1999), pp. 197–202.

[16] Howard L. Boorman, Ed., *Biographical Dictionary of Republican China* (New York: Columbia University Press, 1970), vol. 3, p. 370.

[17] Wright, "Introduction: The Rising Tide of Change," p. 58.

8

Selecting Identities: The Early Republic

If there is one figure from modern Chinese history who has drawn almost universal condemnation, that person is Yuan Shikai. A leading Communist spokesman, Chen Boda, in 1946 published a book, *Yuan Shikai, The Great Thief who Stole the Nation;* a Chinese historian based in the West subtitled his study of Yuan, "Brutus Assumes the Purple." Yuan has been tarred with the charge that he betrayed the republic, and almost universally he has been saddled with the title "father of the warlords." Yet at the time, he received considerable praise. The American ambassador to China, Paul Reinsch, reported that "The President is very cordial and genial in his manner. He speaks fluently and to the point and loves to give a humorous turn to his thought . . . Nothing escapes his eye [;] . . . he evidently has a grasp and mastery of details."[1] No less a person than Liang Qichao said that because of his affable personality being with Yuan was "like drinking champagne."[2] It is obvious that the problem was not Yuan's personality or ability but his policies. Whatever the historical judgment, his record should be seen in the context of the times.

LEGACIES OF THE REVOLUTION

Yuan assumed power at a time when almost everything in the political realm seemed up for grabs. There were no "how-to" manuals that could answer the difficult basic questions raised by the collapse of the two millennia-long traditional civilization. What did republicanism mean in the Chinese context and how was it to be implemented? In the new China, what constituted the legitimacy of a government or its elites?

In addition, the revolution and its aftermath left a serious and basic question: "Who had won?" Certainly the revolutionaries did not rake in many of the spoils of victory. Their demand to have the capital relocated to Nanjing, nearer their power base and as a graphic symbol of change from the centuries-long imperial capital, was not satisfied; Yuan would not leave Beijing. The official positions meted out to revolutionaries were few and did not include crucially powerful posts like the Minister of Finance or the Minister of the Army. Sun Yat-sen was named national director of railroad development.

In the provinces, though there were fourteen provincial revolutionary governments established, only three had the most important position, that of military governor, filled by a former member of the Revolutionary Alliance. In part this was a reflection of the pre-revolutionary situation when the alliance's national leaders did not have much contact with what was going on in the provinces. Organizationally the alliance had been loose, lacking solidarity through its many geographical arenas. Further, in many areas, old elites who had been active in politics in the self-government movement or other public bodies took the political plums. Thus, though the revolutionaries came out on top in overthrowing the monarch, a more accurate answer to the question of who won would be Yuan Shikai and the already-ensconced elites.

Another legacy of the revolution and its aftermath was the rise of a potent provincialism, a development that was especially troubling to Yuan and his goal of a stronger centralized government. The revolution had taken the shape of individual provinces declaring their independence from the Qing dynasty. When the republic was established, a strong sense of loyalty to province continued. Listen to the words of Zhejiang's pro-Yuan military governor, Zhu Rui in speaking of the province: "Protecting our local area [is] a heaven-ordained duty"; therefore he vowed that troops from other provinces would not be allowed to enter the province.[3] It is not that this provincialism was necessarily antithetical to nationalism; they could coexist: one could show allegiance to both province and nation. But for many at a time of considerable political uncertainty and lack of clarity, one's native province, and that all-important sense of native place, was a closer-to-home way of thinking about political loyalty. In addition, some provinces were led by men who were suspicious of Yuan and were reluctant to be drawn into closer relationships with Beijing. As one historian has said, the political reality of the early Republic was a "de facto confederation of provinces."[4] Sun Yat-sen meant his depiction of China as a "sheet of loose sand" to describe the political coherence of the masses, but it could also have been an apt description for the lack of political coherence of the nation in these years.

THE PRESIDENCY OF YUAN SHIKAI

Yuan had built his reputation as a military reformer, though in his stints as Shandong governor and Zhili governor-general, he had also initiated reforms in education, commerce, and industry. Though he had never traveled beyond Korea (for his post as resident general) and did not know any foreign languages, he recruited men who had foreign education or experience, and he nurtured connections to foreigners. In his policies he sought to blend old and new, though in his personal life he was a thoroughly traditional Chinese man, having more than twelve wives and at least thirty children. Despite his geniality, he could be cold-bloodedly ruthless, willing to kill for political purposes almost at the drop of a hat. Thus a West-

President Yuan Shikai

ern description of his appearance at his inauguration as provisional president speaks to his short plump build but not the reality of his political determination: Yuan "came in wobbling like a duck, looking fat and unhealthy, in Marshal's uniform, the loose flesh of his neck hanging over his collar."[5]

His political ideals were order, control, and rigid devotion to regulations. In his presidency, he worked continually to realize these ideals as part of his efforts to centralize in order to modernize the country. To his mind, the political world that he inherited—a republic with political parties and representative bodies at the county, provincial, and the national levels—was too messy, too disorderly, too spontaneous, and so completely unpredictable that it could not in reality serve as a solid base on which to build the reforms that would make a new China. If assemblies at whatever level went off and did their own things, there could not be the kind of careful planning and directing that a strong head of state assisted by focused bureaucrats needed in order to build a modern nation-state. Yuan and those who had turned the republic over to him were thus on a collision course from Day One.

Sun Yat-sen turned his Revolutionary Alliance into a political party, the Nationalist Party (Guomindang), to field and support candidates in the December 1912 National Assembly elections. He also named thirty-year-old Song Jiaoren, longtime member of the alliance, to manage the party organization; Song hoped that if the Guomindang gained the majority seats in the Assembly he could emerge as Prime Minister. Three other parties (one led by 1898 reformer Liang Qichao) were also formed to compete in the elections, which were also held for provincial and county assemblies. As in the late Qing assemblies, there were age, gender, educational, and economic qualifications for voting and serving: males, twenty-one and over, graduates from elementary school, who owned five hundred dollars in property and paid at minimum two dollars in taxes. Women did not get the right to vote. While National Assembly elections were marked by some corruption, they were remarkable for the relative smoothness with which they were carried out. They have been the high point of electoral democracy in the twentieth and twenty-first centuries on the Chinese mainland and in Taiwan until the late 1980s. The Guomindang won approximately 43 percent of the vote, a plurality among the multiple parties; they took 269 of 596 House of Representative seats and 123 of 274 Senate seats: they would control 45 percent of the seats in each house.

But the euphoria was short-lived. In March 1913, as he was leaving for Beijing to form the new government, party leader Song Jiaoren was shot and killed at the Shanghai train station. Yuan was implicated in the assassination: the man who hired the killer had been in communication with the secretary of Yuan's prime minister. Shock and outrage swept the country. A Wuchang newspaper offered bitter condemnation: "Yuan Shikai! The measure of your iniquity is full, and the time has come to answer for it."[6] To add insult to tragedy, Yuan on his own without even a nod to the national assembly's constitutional involvement negotiated a huge loan of about $100 million from a foreign consortium. In May he proceeded to remove from their posts the major military governors who were supporters of the Nationalist Party. By the summer an open revolt of pro-Guomindang forces began against Yuan's regime. This so-called "second revolution" ended in the military rout of the revolutionaries and the flight of Sun and others to Japan.

Yuan then set to work to construct what historians have seen as his dictatorship. In October, he first forced the National Assembly to ratify his election as president for a five-year term. In November he brazenly outlawed the Guomindang, evicting its members from the assembly. Then in February 1914, he simply abolished all the assemblies—national, provincial, and county. He had made short shrift of China's democratic experiment. There is little wonder that he has been seen by later Chinese as a thief and a betrayer. As a contemporary historian has noted: "What an affront to the educated and propertied classes who had participated in building this structure of representation!"[7]

In addition to these actions, after the second revolution, Yuan militarily occupied the provinces from which his troops had been kept out. He also attempted to silence some of the expressions of provincial autonomy by dismissing independent-minded provincial officials and reasserting Beijing's authority to make provincial appointments. A 1914 law tightened general press censorship. Chamber of Commerce regulations were also tightened so that the government had more control over these organizations. In steps that smacked of a police state, police could open the mails and search luggage at train stations. With a heavy hand, Yuan was trying to combat "the consequences of a new, participatory, radicalizing nationalism."[8]

In domestic policies under his dictatorship, Yuan carried on some of the initiatives from the last decade of Qing reforms. He called for "universal education" for all males, which meant four years of free primary school; in the area of mass education he encouraged literacy campaigns using alphabetized Chinese. He was very successful in suppressing the domestic cultivation of opium. In many ways he appeared much the self-strengthener, adopting economic policies that would build Chinese wealth and development. He put some government resources, for example, into agricultural experimentation in such areas as cotton growing, forestation, and livestock breeding. He worked toward an independent judiciary to help create a legal system that the West would see as more enlightened and thus might move to ending extraterritoriality.

One hallmark of Yuan's domestic reforms was his efforts to blend old and new. He restored some imperial symbols and ceremonies. He reinstituted tradition in the form of Confucianism as a state religion. In primary school textbooks, *Mencius* and the *Analects* replaced pictures and accounts of Sun Yat-sen and Huang Xing. In short, Yuan, like the self-strengtheners, was a reformer firmly rooted in traditional ways. But the context had changed from the days of Zeng Guofan, for then the traditional culture had been very much alive. With all the changes of the early years of the century, Yuan's attempts to put old wine into new bottles seemed not very appropriate.

One historian has suggested that when Yuan looked at the problems of his presidency, he diagnosed them as "imperial under-nourishment: the emperor was missing."[9] To remedy that situation, in August 1915, Yuan helped launch a campaign to have himself declared emperor; he would take the throne on the first day of 1916 as the "Grand Constitutional Emperor." In his mind must have been the thought: what better way to rebuild the centralized state and handle society's messy new forces than with the institution of the monarchy with its time-honored traditions and ethos? But it was a mistake. Even though the monarchy had been gone barely three years, reactions showed that the Chinese political culture had already left it far behind in their memories.

A National Protection Army directed against Yuan was launched by military forces in southwest China in late December 1915. It effectively used guerrilla attacks against Beiyang forces in Sichuan while from the coast came attacks by Sun Yat-sen and his allies. In the meantime many of Yuan's Beiyang forces were ambivalent at best about Yuan's imperial initiative. Foreign nations were not supportive; Japan, especially aware of the great unpopularity of Yuan's actions among Chinese elites, even helped fund the rebels. Very quickly Yuan realized his power was collapsing. By March 22, he backpedaled to his fallback position as president, but, with more provinces declaring themselves independent, he could not stanch the bloodletting. His June 6 death from uremia in the midst of rebellion was undoubtedly from a personal standpoint a merciful ending. But for the country it was the moment of collapse into a national nightmare of bloodletting that would extend for more than a decade ahead.

TO GET RICH IS GLORIOUS: CAPITALISTS TO THE FORE

The first years of the Republic were also the first years of what one historian has called "the golden age of the Chinese bourgeoisie," by which she meant modern-style businessmen, financiers, and industrialists, in short, capitalists.[10] Aspects of two early Republican buildings suggest cardinal aspects of the world of the bourgeoisie. The first was located in Shanghai. Completed in 1917 by an entrepreneur who made millions in medicine, the Great World was a huge, six storied Shanghai amusement palace, described as "a kind of Crystal Palace and Coney Island" rolled into one. "The third floor," for example, "had jugglers, herb medicines, ice cream parlors, photographers, a new bevy of girls, their high-collared gowns slit to reveal their hips . . . and under the heading of novelty, rows of exposed toilets, their impresarios instructing the amused patrons not to squat but to assume a position more in keeping with the imported plumbing. . . ."[11] The other building was one of the most imposing edifices in the city of Shaoxing on the southern coast of Hangzhou Bay, southwest of Shanghai. Built from 1915 to 1917, it was the headquarters of the city's Chamber of Commerce and served as an unofficial political-social-economic center for the city. It had a huge hall, offices, meeting rooms, and garden; organizations from all over the city rented meeting rooms there.

A first thing to note is the location of the Great World in Shanghai, the largest and most important of the treaty ports set up along the coast and inland rivers in the nineteenth century. Established to facilitate trade, treaty ports served as transit points between foreigners on China's coast and Chinese in the interior; these cities experienced increasing trade in the last half of the nineteenth century, exports primarily of tea and silk and imports of textiles, kerosene, and sugar. By the early twentieth century that trade, as the description of the Great World shows, had even come to include Western-style toilets. Since foreigners knew neither Chinese nor local customs, Chinese merchants played key roles, managing most transactions while financing them through native Chinese banks.

The Great World Pleasure Palace in Shanghai
Source: R. Barz, "Shanghai: Sketches of Present-Day Shanghai." N.p.: Centurion Printing, n.d.

Modern industrial development did not begin in Chinese cities until near the actual end of the nineteenth century. The Treaty of Shimonoseki (1895) gave the Japanese the right to establish factories in the treaty ports. Other foreign nations leapt at the chance to establish textile mills in these cities where the cheap Chinese labor and lower costs of local raw materials made manufacturing more profitable than in the home country. Competition from Chinese businessmen in this industry was practically nil. Despite the development of factories in cities, interior parts of the country were not affected to any appreciable degree. It is likely the case that the Lower Yangzi macroregion was the only region where economic changes had progressed far enough at this time for there to be even an incipient capitalist class.

Chinese had begun to establish their own "modern" firms during the early days of self-strengthening. They are noteworthy because they reveal the close relationship between business and government that became a hallmark of economic development both under the Nationalist government of the 1920s through the 1940s and the Communist government. In 1872 Li Hongzhang established the China Merchant Steamship Navigation Company to end the foreign domination of coastal shipping. It operated according to the formula of "government-supervision, merchant-management," getting much of its income from government contract for the transport of tax grain.

In many ways this model of business organization was similar to the centuries-old imperial salt monopoly where the government monopolized salt production and sales but farmed out to merchants the roles of managing production and distribution. These new enterprises were not government monopolies, but in Li's company and others—the Kaiping Mining Company in Zhili province (1877) and the Shanghai Cotton Cloth Mill (1890), to name two—government support in the form of loans, tax breaks, and/or a production monopoly played a crucial role in getting the firms started. Private merchants were slow to invest in these companies which merchants managed generally without intrusion from the government. By the end of the dynasty, the Chinese bourgeoisie was composed of merchants, bankers, compradores (Chinese who were employed by Western firms to serve as middlemen to Chinese suppliers and distributors), a few industrialists, and overseas Chinese. Politically they played increasingly important roles as major participants in antiforeign boycotts (such as the one against the United States in 1905–1907). In the 1911 revolutionary period, their roles varied depending on local circumstances, but they were generally not pivotal players in the local coups that made up the revolution.

World War I and the peace that followed served as catalysts for a prosperous period for Chinese business and industry. During the war from 1914 to 1918 Western eyes were temporarily averted from China to the horrors of the Western Front. That relative Western absence first gave Chinese entrepreneurs an opportunity to become involved in the flourishing wartime trade. Imports from the West dropped dramatically; values of imports from Britain, for example, fell from 96 million taels in 1913 to 49 million in 1918. On the China side, silk exports increased by more than 50 percent. It is little wonder that China's trade deficit fell from 166 million taels in 1913 to only 16 million in 1919.

Second, the war years gave Chinese entrepreneurs the opportunity to more assertively begin to develop modern business and industry that did not use the "government-supervision, merchant-management" model. During the last years of the war into the early 1920s,

coastal cities, especially Shanghai, saw such a rapid growth rate of modern light industries—spinning, flour, and oil mills and cigarette factories—that it was not equaled again
until the 1950s. The number of textile mills went from 22 in 1911 to 109 in 1921; the number of flourmills increased from 67 in 1916 to 86 at the end of the war. Tonnage of coal produced increased from about 13 million in 1913 to over 20 million in 1919; iron production
almost doubled during the war. The development of modern Chinese banks also dates from
this period; while there were only 7 at the time of the establishment of the Republic, the
number soared to 131 in 1923.

Two examples of famous industrialists point to the economic boom and the kind of
men who became leaders. Like the Great World, Zhang Jian, from Jiangsu province in the
Lower Yangzi, merged the old and the new. He was an old-style *jinshi* degreeholder who
served as Minister of Industry under Yuan Shikai. In his home of Nantong, about sixty miles
northwest of Shanghai, he established the Dasheng Cotton Mills in 1899. Evident of the
early Republican boom, he was able to double the number of spindles at the mill from 1914
to 1922. The cotton mills were part of Zhang's efforts to make Nantong a national model
which involved not only the establishment of industry but educational, philanthropic, and
conservational reforms as well. The other industrialists were two brothers, Rong Zongjing
and Rong Desheng, who came from a family of merchants and minor officials in the Yangzi
delta city of Wuxi. In Shanghai they built the Maoxin Flour Mills and the Fuxin Flour Mills
in 1901 and 1913, respectively. As a mark of the rising tide of prosperity amid China's capitalists, between 1914 and 1920, they opened eight new factories and broadened their interests into textiles, opening the Shenxin Spinning Mill.

The flurry of mostly treaty port business and industry led to a new business culture
in the cities. New businessmen's associations sprang up, like the Chinese Cotton Millown-
ers Association (1918) and the National Bankers Association (1920). They provided arenas
for joint discussions about the economic situation, industrial problems, relations with foreigners (since many businesses and industries lay within foreign settlements), and relations
with the government. In addition, many of these associations began to publish their own
magazines to discuss these same issues. Indeed, the claim that, at least until the 1990s, the
years 1917 to 1923 were the "golden age of Chinese capitalism" seems well taken.[12]

The rising power of merchants was not only a development in treaty ports, but in the
macroregional cores as well. Powerful entrepreneurs or groups of them were active in establishing textile mills, paper mills, and telephone and electric companies in core zone
provincial capitals, county seats, and even larger market towns. As an example of the range
of entrepreneurial undertakings, a powerful merchant named Jin in 1919 petitioned the Zhejiang Industry Ministry for the right to build an industrial complex at the market town and
river port of Linpu, fifteen miles southeast of Hangzhou. Included would be factories producing paper, textiles, bamboo and wood products, brushes, and tiles.[13]

Local businessmen increasingly depended on Chambers of Commerce to facilitate
their business enterprises, to mediate between businesses and businessmen, and to serve as
a conduit between business and government. Here the second building of our entree into
the world of capitalism, the Shaoxing Chamber of Commerce, comes into play. Chamber
of Commerce activity becomes an index of the power of merchants and entrepreneurs on
the local scene. The government in 1917 limited the number of Chambers per county to two,

recognizing their potential power on the local scene. But by the early 1920s, Chambers had begun to get around the restrictions by establishing branch chapters. In what may be a particularly egregious example, by 1924, Jiaxing county in Zhejiang province had no fewer than thirteen branch chambers.

On the local scene economic muscle was often easily translated into political clout. A foreign observer noted that "With the downfall of the Manchu regime . . . the government of almost every city in China was for months virtually carried on by the Chambers of Commerce and associated guilds."[14] On the agenda of one of the branch chambers in Jiaxing county much later in 1924, for example, were items in regard to education, sanitation, and the town's winter defense. The fact that people in Shaoxing saw the Chamber of Commerce building as *the* place in the city to hold their various meetings suggests the important place that the organization held in local minds. In some cases, in the 1920s Chambers became unofficially the main local decision-makers, taking power from local assemblies and other bodies. Indeed, the flexing of capitalist muscles during the early Republic puts the economic expansion of China in the 1990s and the first decade of the twenty-first century into important historical perspective.

THE POWER OF THE GUN

If the merchant, businessman, banker, and financier were beginning to play more than bit parts on the Chinese stage during the early Republic, the stars of the show were military commanders with their supporting casts of thousands of soldiers. As long as Yuan Shikai was alive and maintained the power that he had taken, he was able to control the generals who had been trained under his command in the New Army; he had been their patron and they, his students. With his overplaying the imperial hand and the sudden erosion of his power in the spring of 1916, however, China began to collapse in confusion. Yuan's opponents were not united. There were only clusters or groupings of military men tied together by various connections. When Yuan died, the destructive genie of military competition was freed to wreak havoc over the land. The goal of this warring competition was to seize Beijing and its government institutions and through that military success to be recognized as president of the Republic. This struggle among what became known as warlords produced one of the most tragic and chaotic periods in twentieth-century China. Although it technically ended in 1928 when the country was again nominally unified, what has been called "residual warlordism" persisted into the 1940s.

Before the warlord situation became bleakest in the early and mid-1920s, there was one last attempt to restore the monarchy. The effort points with exclamation points to the clashing public identities on the Chinese political scene at this time of substantial change. Zhang Xun had been a senior military officer under Yuan since the formation of the New Army. Even though he served Yuan, his ultimate loyalty was to Chinese traditions and the monarchy. As for traditions, he was one of the most outspoken supporters of maintaining the official cult of Confucius. As a visible symbol of his loyalty to the monarchy, he insisted on keeping his queue and ordered that his troops maintain theirs as well. Foreigners dubbed him the "pig-tailed general." (For purposes of graphically visualizing the clashing identities of the early Republic, imagine Zhang Xun at the Great World with the Rong brothers.)

In early July 1917, Zhang restored Aisin Gioro Puyi, the last Qing emperor, then eleven years old, to the Dragon Throne. He used the opportunity of being asked by the president of the Republic, Li Yuanhong, to intervene in a dispute between the current government premier, military leader Duan Qirui, on the one side, and Li and the National Assembly, which had been reestablished after Yuan's death, on the other. Zhang badly misjudged the likely reactions of the Beiyang commanders who sent troops to storm the capital and end the less than two-week reign. Never again would anyone attempt to restore the monarchy, though the chaos and destruction of the period as late as 1922 led people at least in some localities to express the opinion, as Yuan had and as Zhang surely would, "that the emergence of the rightful Son of Heaven would solve local and national problems."[15] The aborted 1917 restoration episode did reveal that the governmental institutions in the capital—the bureaucracy and the National Assembly—were not really the main players on the political stage. Those roles increasingly belonged to the military. Zhang, using military forces, had restored the emperor; but opposing military forces had ousted him (and Zhang to boot). Within the less than six years since Double Ten, struggles between military forces had four times determined the identity of the Chinese government (1911–1912, 1913, and twice in 1917).

It is apparent that in the 1920s governmental institutions became pawns in the warlords' struggle for military control of the capital and by extension the country. The concerns of civilian politicians and bureaucrats focused more and more on keeping their positions and maintaining their own political power, often through cultivating connections with warlords. In this context, corruption tended to become the crucial dynamic and often decided elections and policies. In perhaps the most infamous case, Cao Kun, a civilian official in the hip pocket of a leading warlord, won the presidency of the Republic in 1923 by spending Mex. $13,560,000 to bribe National Assemblymen to vote for him (at $5,000 per vote). As one scholar has noted about the affair, "in the act of purchase, the presidency was devalued."[16] The sorry spectacle was that from mid-1916 until the spring of 1926, China had six different presidents and twenty-five cabinets. The high hopes of a productively functioning Republic lay in shambles: the Republic indeed had become an empty shell.

In the shaping of political culture, a republican ethos—carrying the voice of the people into the halls of government—had been aborted; in its place flourished the ethos of the military. In these years militarization began to emerge as a major dynamic in twentieth-century China. While all warlords were military men and held territory of varying size, the name "warlord" covered many different military types with differing goals. Some warlords perhaps actually had the abilities, character, and potential to unite the Chinese nation and become a head of state. Central China's Wu Peifu, who emerged to head the Zhili clique, one of the central warlord coalitions, for example, was a man who had received the lowest-level civil service degree. He was also a graduate of Yuan Shikai's Baoding Military Academy. A writer who had a deep love for traditional Chinese culture, he was a student of the Buddhist canon and the Confucian classics. Or, as another example, there was north China's Feng Yuxiang, a self-taught Christian convert who indoctrinated his troops with Christian and traditional Chinese values and was said to baptize his troops with a fire hose. He was a committed social and educational reformer, establishing, for example, in areas that he came to control orphanages, rehabilitation centers for drug addicts, and public education facilities. Yan Xishan of Shanxi province was a third potential candidate for heading the nation. He had briefly studied the classics, graduated from a Japanese military school, had joined Sun's Revolutionary Alliance, and rose to the position of military governor in the 1911 revolution. His reforms, his careful attention to rule, and his concern for promoting public morality contributed to his being called the "Model Governor."

Warlords like Wu, Feng, and Yan vied for the top; others had lesser goals, some regional, others local. Some warlords were simply thuggish. One of the more notorious, for example, was Zhang Zongchang, the "Dog-Meat General." A famous journalist described him as having "the physique of an elephant, the brain of a pig, and the temperament of a tiger." As a measure of the man, it is said that Zhang had his "'three don't knows': he did not know how much money he had, how many troops he had, or how many women he had in his harem."[17] His Shandong military troops, which included four thousand White Russians (dubbed "soldiers of misfortune") and a unit of several thousand boys whose average age was ten, were notorious for their practice of "opening melons," that is, splitting skulls, and for hanging strings of human heads on telegraph poles to elicit respect for their power.

Warlords striving for national power often put together coalitions in order to have greater troop strength and a broader availability of resources. Such coalitions were by their nature unstable, for most often they were formed as part of a strategy to accomplish short-term or intermediate goals. Among the warlord players on the national level, coalitions did not have ideological bases. Nor were they usually based upon close personal connections; a frequent pattern, in fact, was that today's ally often became tomorrow's enemy. All coalition-building, as well as the shaping of policies, was driven by mercenary and power considerations. Coalitions would therefore collapse if one or more coalition member(s) were lured away for a better deal from a rival warlord; the lure of money or position to bring about the defection of a militarist or military commander was known as "silver bullets." Their use made any sort of long range planning difficult and caused at least one militarist to predict, "We shall undoubtedly win. It is simply a matter of waiting for treason."[18] One other method to destroy coalitions was by assassinating coalition members. Reportedly a common approach was to invite the proposed victim to a banquet where he was then murdered—a practice that one presumes would have led anyone invited to a banquet to have second thoughts about accepting.

The Beiyang militarists were separated into two main cliques that formed around Yuan Shikai's two chief lieutenants, the Anfu clique led by Duan Qirui and the Zhili clique led by Feng Guozhang. The first major war broke out between them in 1920; when the warlord of Manchuria Zhang Zuolin sided with the Zhili clique it quickly defeated the Anfu clique. This victory, however, simply set the stage for the next war between the victorious Zhili forces and the Fengtian forces of Zhang Zuolin, waged in 1922. Although the Zhili forces defeated Zhang's Fengtian troops, they did not have enough power to oust him from his Manchurian base. The third major war, again between Zhili and Fengtian forces, was fought in 1924; it ended quickly when Zhili general Feng Yuxiang defected to Zhang's forces and the Zhili troops were defeated. But by 1925 Feng and Zhang were at each other's throat in north China, a struggle that ended the next year with Zhang in charge of Beijing.

But these were only the major wars. One historian has counted more than 140 wars fought between 1916 and 1928.

These were bloody affairs that grew bloodier as the years progressed. Though many of the officers were graduates of military academies and could be seen as professional mil-

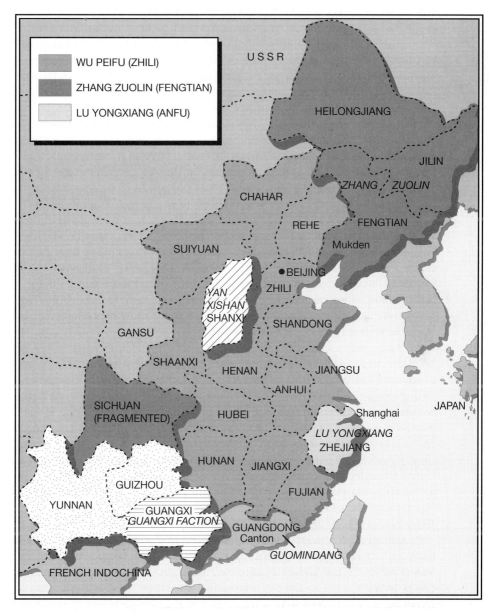

Spheres of Warlord Power, Mid-1920s

itary men, the soldiers themselves were in many cases recruited from rural areas. Each army was tied together by the typical social bonds—linkages through family, marriage, and friendship and teacher-student and patron-protégé ties. Recruits enlisted to make a living and were in the army for an indefinite period; though national regulations specified that they were to be nineteen to twenty-six years old, commanders frequently took them at all ages, as the case of Zhang Zongchang indicates. Fatalities in battle were high, a situation made worse by the lack of medical care where even light wounds could end in death.

Among the populace the warlord scourge included loss of life, rapes by military victors and losers, destruction of crops, cropland, and agricultural infrastructure, and widespread economic dislocation and property destruction. Troops lived off the areas they occupied or moved through, looting and pillaging. One warlord reported, "My men would surround a village before dawn and fire several shots to intimidate the people. We told them to come out and give up. This was the classic way of raiding a village. Sometimes we killed and carried away little pigs. . . . We took corn, rice, potatoes, taro." Peasant carts and labor were regularly commandeered. Cities were special targets for looting. A British official reported on the 1920 looting of Yuzhou in Hunan, "I have never seen more thorough work. Every shop, every house in this beautiful and prosperous city has been literally stripped. There is not a vestige of any usable commodity from one end of the city to the other. . . ."[19]

But there was more. Warlord armies needed weapons and supplies, necessities that demanded money. Two sources of money that emerged as critical to the warlord campaigns were opium and taxes. In the late Qing the cultivation of opium had been practically eradicated in most areas. Its capacity to bring in huge profits, however, made it attractive to warlords who forced farmers in many areas to plant opium instead of food crops. In some places warlords forced opium cultivation by placing the land tax so high that opium was the only feasible crop to plant. While the acreage of cultivated land devoted to opium production lay at 3 percent in the years from 1914 to 1919, it had shot up to 20 percent in the period 1929 to 1933.

The other source of money was taxation. Extraordinarily high taxes were placed on every conceivable item, from consumer goods to licenses to lifetime situations (getting married, owning a pig, going to a brothel). Land taxes were collected far (perhaps more than ten years) in advance. Taxes on commodities in transit were exorbitant: a Hankou newspaper reported, for example, that "a shipment of paper worth $1,350 when landed at Shanghai was shipped up the Yangzi to Chengdu. It passed through eleven tax stations . . . and the illegal taxation collected on it by regional authorities totaled $2,150."[20] With taxes reaching confiscatory levels and without recourse, the economy of affected communities was wrecked; the people's livelihood was, as it were, left for dead. Finally, like typhoons spawning tornadoes, warlord wars gave rise to widescale banditry. In many cases what warlords did not succeed in destroying or taking, the bandits did.

One of the tragedies of the warlord struggles was that many battles were made possible and certainly more destructive because various Western nations supplied ammunition and guns, "by the gun and by the shipload," to warlords. An American suggestion in 1919 that nations join in an embargo of weapons sales to China in order to put a halt to the fighting led to an Arms Embargo Agreement, but it was so conspicuously violated that it was abrogated within ten years. Some countries, especially Japan and Russia, were interested in aiding those warlords that they thought were the best bets to seize state power. Obviously, if their pet warlord then did become president, the likelihood that they would receive privileges from his regime would be increased. The Japanese provided large loans to the Anfu clique and continual monetary and material support to Manchuria's Zhang Zuolin. Likewise, the Russians gave Feng Yuxiang money, military instructors, and arms and materiel. Great Britain maintained exceptionally close relations with Wu Peifu but did not reportedly offer government support of his rule, though British firms did offer Wu loans. In the late 1910s and early 1920s British and American diplomats applied some pressure on the Beijing government to end the warlord strife and bring about domestic peace; in part this effort represented foreign governments' desire to see the military disruptions of trade and the economy in general ended.

Historians have seen the warlords, ironically arising from a context of growing nationalism, to be the very antithesis of nationalism. Though some warlords aspired to unite the nation, their activity actually radically fragmented a state whose identity had not really developed after traditional civilization collapsed. They contributed to the growing militarization of Chinese society. Reliance on foreign arms and aid undercut the identity of a new nation standing on its own and was retrogressive in light of late Qing rights recovery. The very nature of warlordism produced a demoralized and devastated populace, a situation that weakened a patriotism that might have inspired commitment to build a new China. Further, many aspects of the warlord period seriously damaged the economy and inhibited economic progress.

Finally, warlords and their activities conflicted with the new forces of Chinese society, frequently producing more bloodshed and tragedy. An example was the massacre of students near the Gate of Heavenly Peace on March 18, 1926. In the 1925–1926 warlord struggle between Feng and Zhang, Feng's forces had mined the sea approaches to Tianjin to keep Zhang from landing there. The Japanese, Zhang's main patrons who saw the Tianjin area as their sphere of influence, protested the mining because of its impact on their trade; they ordered the mines removed. Beijing students protested the Japanese ultimatum as interference in Chinese domestic affairs. Though government troops dispersed them on March 17, on the next day more students came out to demonstrate. When they tried to march to the head of state's office, police opened fire and killed forty-seven students. Sidney Gamble, an American social scientist in Beijing to do social research for the YMCA, was an eyewitness:

> The shooting of the students on March 18th was a terrible tragedy. . . . Just how much the students threatened to use force at the Cabinet office we do not know, but once the guards started firing they kept it up for fifteen or twenty minutes. The soldiers used their bayonets on the wounded and robbed the bodies of the dead. Even glasses were snatched from one of the girls as she was getting out through a back gate.[21]

Zhu Ziqing, on the faculty at Qinghua University, participated in the march and left a much more personal description of his actions upon hearing the gunshots.

> One or two minutes later, the red-hot blood of the person on top of me streamed down the back of my hand and onto my jacket. I understood immediately that the massacre had begun. The only thing I knew was that I did not want to die; I only wanted to

live. . . . I rolled down a hill of corpses. Later, when I realized that I had walked on corpses, I shuddered with fear for a long time.[22]

Warlord wars had thus precipitated a crisis that, because of foreign interests in China, had brought Japanese intrusion into Chinese affairs and the nationalistic student demonstration. As tragic as the loss of student lives on the Beijing streets, their numbers paled when seen against the deaths of the thousands of Chinese who died in the warlord struggles. Lu Xun, China's most important twentieth century writer, summed up the despair and sense of futility created by the age of the warlords with specific reference to the March 18 tragedy.

Time flows eternally on: the streets are peaceful again, for a few lives count for nothing in China. . . . As for any deeper significance, I think there is very little; for this was only an unarmed demonstration. The history of mankind's battle forward through bloodshed is like the formation of coal, where a great deal of wood is needed to produce a small amount of coal.[23]

CHINA TOTTERS ON THE WORLD STAGE

The outbreak of World War I placed China in imminent danger of becoming a battleground for European powers which had spheres of influence on Chinese soil. To forestall that possibility, China hastily declared its neutrality. That action did not stop Japan from invading the German leasehold in Shandong province in response to ally England's request to seize German properties in China. The war took imperialist Western nations out of competition with Japan in China. Japan set out to make imperial hay while the sun of World War I shone, expanding the former German holdings almost as soon as it had taken them.

Then in January 1915, as European powers were preoccupied with the war, Japan acted to strengthen its hand in China, presenting Yuan's government with the Twenty-One Demands. This was a list of five categories of demands, mostly economic rights and privileges in Shandong, Manchuria, Inner Mongolia, the Yangzi valley, and Fujian province. But the fifth group of demands cut more deeply into Chinese sovereignty: it required that the Chinese attach Japanese advisers to the key governmental executive, military, financial, and police bodies, making China in effect a protectorate of Japan. This group of demands also specified that China had to purchase at least half of its munitions from Japan. The spring of 1915 saw a wave of anti-Japanese protests and rallies sweep the country. When the Japanese eventually modified the demands by dropping the ominous fifth group and then issued Yuan an ultimatum to accept the rest, Yuan acceded. The day of agreeing to the demands, May 7, was commemorated in subsequent years as National Humiliation Day.

The Shandong Issue

Having largely had its way with China, Japan set out to solidify its gains in Shandong during the remainder of the war. As a starter, The Twenty-One Demands included confirmation of Japan's position in the former German leasehold. Japan then proceeded to gain through secret treaty from each Allied power—Russia, Britain, France, Italy, and the United States—recognition of Japan's position and predominant interests in Shandong. When the matter would come before the Versailles Conference at the end of the war, Japan would thus be certain of Western support for its remaining in Shandong. The flagrant nature of imperialist control and decision-making is underscored by these secret treaties. China's future was being decided by outsiders who did not even consult Chinese leaders. The disdain with which the imperialist powers, including Japan, dealt with the world's colonies and (in China's case) its semi-colonies did not bode well for the postwar world.

But the event which drove the final nail in the coffin of the Chinese case for kicking the Japanese out was a secret treaty that Japan made with the Chinese government itself in 1918. In exchange for Japan's offering China's warlord government a twenty million yen loan, the Beijing government gave Japan the right to build two railroads in Shandong, to station troops there, and to train and oversee Chinese train guards. China could thus not point to the Twenty-One Demands as being forced on them, for in this agreement the government had given recognition of Japan's special role in Shandong of its own free will— and all for twenty million yen.

People all over the world had been affected by the wartime rhetoric of U.S. President Woodrow Wilson. The "war to make the world safe for democracy" and the "war to end all wars" had also been one that was supposed to bring the "self-determination" of peoples to control their own destiny inside their chosen homelands. For many colonized peoples, the message, infused with high idealism, also brought high hopes they might once again be able to control their lives and their countries. The Chinese delegation to the Versailles Conference went with such high hopes—the goals, to recover Shandong province and to eliminate the unequal treaty system. However, since the conference had convened only to deal with issues that were resulting from the war, the disposition of the unequal treaties was not included on the conference agenda.

The Chinese argued that Shandong, the home province of Confucius, and therefore a very special area for all Chinese, should be returned. They pointed to the original agreement of the German leasehold from 1898 which specified that there could be no "subletting" of the leasehold; therefore, Japan could not lay stake to the territory. They pointed out that Chinese agreement to the Twenty-One Demands had been coerced and had not been ratified by the National Assembly. But these arguments were to no avail because of the secret treaty China had signed with Japan in 1918. Japan was also bound and determined to have its way completely in Shandong. It had come to the conference with two objectives— holding onto Shandong and former German Pacific islands and getting a racial equality clause accepted into the Covenant of the League of Nations. The defeat of the racial equality clause was engineered mostly by countries in the British Empire, fearful of an international body's becoming involved in domestic issues of immigration and citizenship. Whatever the reason, it was a defeat for Japan, and the Japanese delegation began to make noises that it just might walk out of the conference—as Italy had done a few days earlier. Wilson, faced with the specter of the collapse of the conference and believing that the Shandong issue could be taken up in a functioning League of Nations, caved in to Japanese pressure. But it is obvious that Japan had all the legal arguments and the political turns at the conference going its way. In China the reaction was swift and fierce, inaugurating a major political explosion discussed in the next chapter.

The Washington Conference

In late 1921 and early 1922, nine world powers met in Washington, D.C.: the United States, Great Britain, France, Italy, Japan, China, the Netherlands, Belgium, and Portugal. The main goal of the Western nations, in light of predictions that war with Japan was looming in the future, was to try to limit Japan's freedom of action in military matters, specifically taking efforts to halt a naval race and to limit fortifications of territory in the Pacific, East, and Southeast Asia. Also included on the agenda were China and the permanent disposition of Shandong. The Chinese delegation basically called on the other nations to begin respecting Chinese rights, specifically its political independence and its territorial integrity; they also called for reviewing the unequal treaty system.

The conference produced three treaties, the most important of which for China was the Nine-Power Treaty. It said all the right things: the nations "agreed to respect China's territorial integrity and political independence, to renounce further attempts to seek spheres of influence, to respect its neutrality in time of war, and to honor equal commercial opportunity for all."[24] But it was toothless; there was no way to enforce the agreement or to take action against some country that violated the terms. An agreement, mediated by Great Britain and the United States, was reached regarding Shandong. Japan would return Shandong but it would continue to keep economic interests, including maintaining property for use by Japanese living in the area, having Japanese serve as advisors in various businesses and industries, and having Japanese hold key leadership positions for five more years in the railroad that the Japanese had built from Qingdao to Jinan. According to the treaty, the Chinese would buy that railway from the Japanese using a Japanese loan. In short, though China received the lion's share of what it wanted, the Japanese could keep their fingers in the pie.

China did make other small, but in the historical context of its relationship with the West, not insignificant gains at the conference. Great Britain agreed to give up their leasehold of Weihaiwei, due to expire in any case in 1923. The powers allowed the Chinese to raise the customs tariff from 3.5 percent of the value of the goods to 5 percent; in addition, there was stipulation that China would eventually gain complete control over the tariff and that extraterritoriality would be abolished. But no specifics were offered on how this would be accomplished and, even more important, when it would occur. Two years after the conference, Russia on its own gave up the right of extraterritoriality and Boxer indemnity payments even as it also allowed the return to China of its concessions in two cities.

Continuing Evidence of Imperialist Power

Despite these gains, the imperialist powers continued to appoint men to serve in Chinese governmental structures, specifically the Chinese Maritime Customs Service, the Salt Revenue, and the Chinese Postal Service. Foreign settlements in treaty ports and concessions and leaseholds still dotted the Chinese landscape with foreigners continuing to make demands. Great Britain maintained its grip on Hong Kong through which it had a command-ing control over trade throughout southern China. Japan was increasingly predominant in Manchuria, controlling the South Manchurian railway and its environs.

Three episodes point to the humiliating power that imperialists maintained, a threat that created, in the words of the inaugural address of President Xu Shichang on Double Ten in 1918, "a crisis of national existence."[25] After the 1911 Revolution, foreign involvement in the Maritime Customs Service expanded from assessment and accounting to the very col-lection of the revenue. Furthermore, after collection, the revenue was deposited in foreign banks before it was disbursed for payment of Chinese debts; thus foreigners were able to earn interest on what was really Chinese money. In addition, the foreign diplomatic corps in Beijing had been made "trustee" of the money before it was disbursed from foreign banks. Customs revenue was earmarked for interest payments on loans that had been secured on the basis of that customs revenue. During World War I with the growth of Chinese trade, the customs revenue collected was more than needed for the interest payments. The diplo-matic corps began to control that surplus. In 1917 it let the surplus go to the Chinese gov-ernment for general administrative expenses. But in 1918, it tightened the control noose around the Chinese government, telling the government specifically how the surplus could be spent. In other words, foreigners were telling the Chinese government how it must spend its own money.

In 1922 the French government, having seen the value of its Boxer indemnity decline because of depreciating French paper currency, demanded that the indemnity be paid in gold. Such a policy, if adopted, would be to the strong disadvantage of China, specifically creating huge financial losses. In December the government referred the case to Wang Kemin, the governor of the Bank of China and former Chinese director of the Sino-French joint venture, the Banque Industrielle de Chine. After the French government tried to sweeten the deal by reopening the Banque which had been closed a year earlier, Chinese fi-nanciers who had had deposits in the Banque lobbied the Chinese government to accept. With such pressure and with Wang's own past involvement with the bank, Wang's advice to the government—to pay the indemnity in gold—looked corrupt and anti-nationalistic: it was advice that was profitable for Wang and investors but harmful to China. It looked in short to be evidence of the unholy alliance that existed between imperialist powers and the warlord governments. There was a huge public outcry. In Wang's home city of Hangzhou, a crowd attacked and destroyed his family's ancestral shrine, hacked up the shrine's ances-tral tablets into seven pieces, and threw them into West Lake where they disappeared. Such was the depth of hatred for the warlord and imperialist collaboration.

In May 1923 bandits stopped an express train at Lincheng in Shandong province; they held up and kidnapped many on the train. Among the two hundred held captive were some two dozen foreigners who were held for ransom for over a month. Foreigners and the for-eign press in China reacted with outrage. A Shanghai paper noted that "[f]ailure of the gov-ernment to check banditry has made possible an occurrence which cannot but cause a feel-ing of deep humiliation to the people of a government that has a shadow of self-respect. That which is called a government in China . . . has not and is not functioning in a manner and to a degree worthy of the name."[26] But words of condemnation were not enough for the foreign population. A note from the diplomatic corps of all the powers demanded not only penalties and indemnities, but that "Chinese railways [be put] under the powers' joint supervision in order to reform railway fiscal and management policies."[27] Such foreign oversight supposedly would prevent any future act of banditry or warlordism that would result in the seizure of money slotted to pay foreign debts. Imperialist powers saw a weak and divided China with an ineffectual government; in response they insisted in a host of arenas that they knew what was best for China. In a frankly racist book, *What's Wrong with China?*, written in 1926, the author, Rodney Gilbert, gives his opinion: "What is really wrong with China and will continue to be wrong with her is that the Chinese are children, that their world is a child's make-believe."[28] What Gilbert and the powers did not know was that forces were underway, even as they spoke their imperialist and paternalistic platitudes, that would not only put the lie to Gilbert's opinion but would begin the eviction of imperialists from China altogether.

Notes

[1] Quoted in Ernest P. Young, *The Presidency of Yuan Shih-k'ai* (Ann Arbor: University of Michigan Press, 1977), p. 51.

[2] Quoted in Young, p. 243.

[3] R. Keith Schoppa, "Politics and Society in [Zhejiang], 1907–1927: Elite Power, Social Control, and the Making of a Province," doctoral dissertation, University of Michigan, 1975, pp. 155–156.

[4] Ernest P. Young, "Politics in the Aftermath of Revolution: The Era of Yuan Shih-k'ai, 1912–1916" in Fairbank, Ed., *The Cambridge History of China, Vol. 12, Part 1,* p. 213.

[5] Quoted in Young, *The Presidency of Yuan Shih-k'ai,* p. 51

[6] Quoted in Young, *The Presidency of Yuan Shih-k'ai,* p. 118.

[7] Young, "Politics in the Aftermath of Revolution," p. 242.

[8] Ibid., p. 244.

[9] Ibid., p. 246.

[10] See Marie-Claire Bergère, *The Golden Age of the Chinese Bourgeoisie, 1911–1937,* trans., Janet Lloyd (Cambridge: Cambridge University Press, 1990).

[11] Quoted in R. Keith Schoppa, *Blood Road: The Mystery of Shen Dingyi in Revolutionary China* (Berkeley: University of California Press, 1995), p. 53.

[12] Marie-Claire Bergère, "The Chinese Bourgeoisie" in Fairbank, Ed., *The Cambridge History of China, Vol. 12, Part 1,* p. 745.

[13] Schoppa, *Chinese Elites and Political Change,* p. 65.

[14] Quoted in Marie-Claire Bergère, "The Role of the Bourgeoisie," in Wright, *China in Revolution, The First Phase, 1900–1913,* p. 268.

[15] Schoppa, *Chinese Elites and Political Change,* p. 95. The opinion came from elites in Fenghua county in Zhejiang province.

[16] Andrew J. Nathan, *Peking Politics, 1918–1923* (Berkeley: University of California Press, 1976), p. 220.

[17] Boorman, volume 1, p. 124.

[18] Cited in James Sheridan, *Chinese Warlord* (Stanford: Stanford University Press, 1966), p. 21.

[19] The two quotations are quoted in James E. Sheridan, *China in Disintegration* (New York: Free Press, 1975), p. 91.

[20] Cited in Sheridan, *Chinese Warlord,* p. 26.

[21] Quoted in Jonathan Spence, *Chinese Roundabout* (New York: W. W. Norton, 1992), p. 64.

[22] Quoted in Vera Schwarcz, *The Chinese Enlightenment* (Berkeley: University of California Press, 1986), p. 157.

[23] Cited in Spence, *The Gate of Heavenly Peace,* p. 197.

[24] Hsu, *The Rise of Modern China* (New York: Oxford University Press, 2000), 6th edition, p. 532.

[25] Nathan, p. 129.

[26] Quoted in John Fitzgerald, *Awakening China* (Berkeley: University of California Press, 1996), p. 142.

[27] Nathan, p. 214, n.54.

[28] Quoted in Fitzgerald, p. 140.

9

Constructing a New Cultural Identity: The May Fourth Movement

————

————

——

A story from the late Qing:

> Chaste Woman Ni . . . at the age of seventeen [was] married to Ni Dechang . . . After three months she was widowed and afterwards unceasingly and with great care served her parents-in-law. After eight years, her parents-in-law, because of the family's poverty, sought to marry her . . . The day before the marriage they told Woman Ni. She pretended to agree. . . . At midnight she jumped into the river and died. . . . The next year, an edict of imperial praise adorned the gate of this family.[1]

A story from 1919: Miss Zhao of Nanyang Street in Changsha, Hunan, was unwillingly betrothed by her parents to a Mr. Wu. On her wedding day, as she was being carried to the groom's home in a sedan chair, the bride, dressed in festive red, pulled out a dagger hidden in the chair and slit her throat.

Though studies have shown that at least elite women in the early and mid-Qing dynasty structured their own spheres of assertiveness and influence, most Chinese women labored in the centuries-old social hierarchy that placed them near the bottom. That reality and those of the others who were socially subordinated came center-stage in a cultural revolution that swept over macroregional cores and into the peripheries in the late 1910s and early 1920s. Called the May Fourth Movement, it was one of the pivotal turning points in China's modern history. If the abolition of the civil service examination and the monarchy brought the destruction of the traditional political and social structures, the May Fourth Movement struck a paralyzing blow at traditional cultural norms and structures. In one of Lu Xun's most famous stories, "The Diary of a Madman," an official, suffering an obsessive paranoia that everyone wants to kill and eat him, discovers an old history book: " . . . my history has no chronology and scrawled over each page are the words: 'Virtue and Morality.' Since I could not sleep anyway, I read intently half the night, until I began to see words between the lines, the whole book being filled with the two words—'Eat people.'"[2] This was a savage indictment of traditional Chinese society—that it parrots the proper Confucian pieties which only mask the reality that Confucian values destroy human lives by crushing them beneath a social hierarchy of superiors.

Lu desperately believed that something had to be done to wake the Chinese to what he saw as the destructiveness of traditional culture. Personally that meant a career change for him from medicine to writing. For the Chinese people as a whole it was something more risky. Lu captured both the danger and the opportunity in one of his strongest metaphors.

> Imagine an iron house without windows, absolutely indestructible, with many people fast asleep inside who will soon die of suffocation. But you know since they will die in their sleep, they will not feel the pain of death. Now if you cry aloud to wake a few of the lighter sleepers, making those unfortunate few suffer the agony of irrevocable death, do you think you are doing them a good turn?
>
> But if a few awake, you can't say there is no hope of destroying the iron house.[3]

THE NEW CULTURE MOVEMENT: "DOWN WITH CONFUCIUS AND SONS"

While Confucianism as an ideology had officially ended with the abolition of the examination system, it retained its stranglehold on social relationships and ethics in Chinese society. In family life, the ancient Confucian social bonds emphasizing the importance of age and male-ness retained their sway, elevating the status and power of parents over children and of men over women. At the core of the New Culture Movement was the rejection of traditional culture and efforts to define a new cultural base and direction. The most influential vehicle for the expression of contempt for the old and hope for a new social and cultural world was the journal *New Youth.* Established in 1915, it was edited by traditional degreeholder, returned-student from Japan and France, and participant in the 1911 revolution, Chen Duxiu. With a circulation of up to sixteen thousand copies, the journal provided a forum where students in all parts of the country could discuss issues.

In the lead essay of *New Youth,* "Call to Youth," Chen championed the young as China's saviors.

> The Chinese compliment others by saying, "He acts like an old man while still young." Englishmen and Americans encourage one another by saying, "Keep young while growing old." Such is one respect in which the different ways of thought of the East and West are manifested. Youth is like early spring, like the rising sun, like trees and grass in bud, like a newly sharpened blade. It is the most valuable period of life. The function of youth in society is the same as that of a fresh and vital cell in a hu-

man body. In the processes of metabolism, the old and rotten are incessantly eliminated to be replaced by the fresh and living.[4]

Those who revere mostly the past, as Chinese had done into the twentieth century, will, in Chen's estimation, "be lodged in the dark ditches fit only for slaves, cattle, and horses." In practicality, pitting youth against age meant targeting filial piety in its various aspects. In part, it meant eliminating ancestor reverence as it had traditionally been practiced. Ancestors and the continuing roles they supposedly might play in people's lives cast a conservative shroud around the living. One did not dare act to bring shame upon the family, itself a gift of the ancestors. Thus, the Hangzhou students who destroyed banker Wang Kemin's ancestral tablet were making a strong statement not only against the marriage of imperialists and warlords but also one of considerable contempt for this Chinese tradition.

But in the present for most young Chinese, targeting filial piety meant targeting father and mother who had immense control over their children's lives—from career decisions to marriage to life-style patterns. These years saw countless rebellions of young Chinese against their fathers in particular. Sons disregarded parental wishes and even outright orders regarding various life decisions. In 1919, a young man from Zhejiang province, Shi Cuntong wrote an article, "Against Filial Piety" attacking the coerciveness of this traditional value. In another essay Shi described how he had personally felt the arbitrariness and domination of his father. "My family life was like hell to me . . . I suffered enormously in a home of utter darkness, abused by an ignorant father of vile temper. My father often beat me up for no good reason."[5] In the famous essay itself, Shi claimed that filial piety was the same as "the virtue required of a slave" and that "[t]o invoke the imperatives of filial piety these days is for the elders to demand absolute obedience from the younger generation."[6] A writer noted the widespread rebellion against the family system.

> I know a young man who abandoned his own name and substituted the title "He-you-I." Later when I went to Beijing, I met . . . a friend of mine accompanied by a young girl . . . "May I ask your family name?" I asked her. She stared at me and screamed, "I don't have any family name!" There were also people who wrote letters to their fathers saying, "From a certain date on, I will not recognize you as my father. We are all friends, and equal."[7]

The most popular novel of the 1930s, Ba Jin's melodramatic *Family,* looked at the May Fourth generation and described the struggles of three brothers against the patriarchal extended family system and its old traditions upheld by old men.

Women were also victims in Ba Jin's novel. Traditionally girls were seen as close to being burdens on the family. Female infanticide was sometimes practiced especially by the poor. Girls would be provided for by their natal families until they were sent off to be married and then perhaps never seen again. Children were betrothed by matchmakers in marriages for the benefit of families, not to satisfy the desires of individuals; sometimes the result, as with Miss Zhao above, was tragic. If one's fiancé died before marriage or if one's husband died early, the unmarried or widowed woman was required to remain forever chaste, choosing death rather than risking becoming once again intimately involved. Lu Xun, with his typical incisive commentary noted that

> There are two . . . types of chaste women: one kills herself when her husband or fiancé dies; the other manages to commit suicide when confronted by a ravisher, or meets her death while resisting. The more cruel her death, the greater glory she wins. If she is surprised and ravished but kills herself afterwards, there is bound to be talk . . . no man of letters will want to write her biography and, if forced to, he is sure to end on a note of disapproval.[8]

In addition to having praise from the emperor, parents whose daughters committed suicide might erect memorial arches to women who by that means retained their chastity. Some parents were known to pressure their daughters to kill themselves in order to reap praise from the community.

In one of Lu Xun's most famous short stories, "The New Year's Sacrifice," a poor widow, known only as Xiang Lin's wife, is forced to remarry against her will. She did so literally kicking and screaming because of the dominating concern for chastity that women had incorporated in Confucian culture. When her second husband died as well, Xiang Lin is tortured by the fear that in the afterlife she will have to be split in two because she had had two husbands. Some young women in this period were also forbidden by mothers-in-

Xiang Lin's Wife from Lu Xun's "The New Year's Sacrifice"
Source: Courtesy of the Library of Congress

law to unbind their feet or even to attend school. A young woman in the distant interior of Gansu province threw herself down a well rather than deal with a mother-in-law who forbade her to unbind her feet. Suicide rates tell the tragic story: Among Chinese women, they were highest among those in their late teens and twenties; in the early twentieth century, suicide rates of women this age were more than double the rates in Japan and ten times more than in Sweden. The power of "Confucius and sons" was literally that of life and death.

With the collapse of former "established truths" and institutions and with the rise of new social and political alternatives, there should be little surprise that slogans like "Down with Confucius and sons" began to fill new newspapers and journals and to echo in street demonstrations. Editor Chen of *New Youth* led the way: "Emancipation means freeing oneself from the bondage of slavery, [and it should be clear that] loyalty, filial piety, chastity, and righteousness are a slavish morality."[9] As a sign of the times, in Xiaoshan county, Zhejiang province, the characters on an arched memorial—"Respect chaste women and filial sons"—were blotted out and replace with new characters: "Long live women's liberation." Also added was a couplet that reminds one of Lu Xun's madman.

> Beyond doubt in the Twenty-four Histories are written the ethical
>   teachings of those who eat people.
> Beneath this memorial arch there are the ghosts of I don't know
>   how many crushed women who have been wronged.[10]

During the period roughly from 1917 to 1921, intellectual discussion and emphasis on individualism and achieving individual goals reached its greatest point of any time in modern China's history. The absence of a powerful state structure and the wide-open search for a new social, political, and ideological Way created a liberating context for the young. But most important was the rebellion of youths, both male and female, against the cultural shackles of patriarchy and family authority. Liberation from that system, when it could come, promised to bring individual emancipation, the expression of individual wills, and the realization of individual desires.

LANGUAGE AND LABORATORIES FOR A NEW CULTURE

Before 1917, *New Youth* was written in classical or literary Chinese like all printed materials, whether books, newspapers, or journals. The classical style was difficult: it valued conciseness, often omitting subjects and objects; it was marked by characters that were particles giving the sentence a tone or a particular turn; and it used no punctuation. Traditional scholars had believed that anyone intelligent enough to read the classical language should be intelligent enough to know how to punctuate it. But because of the conciseness, the particles, and the lack of punctuation, it was not only difficult but very ambiguous. It was thus a great obstacle to increased literacy among the Chinese masses. Because the development of a modern Chinese nation state required a more literate public, language reform was crucial. In addition, constructing a new political and social culture simply necessitated a new language; it was impossible to construct a new culture on a language intimately connected to and expressive of the old culture of "eating people." In Lu Xun's story of the madman, the short opening segment, which tells of the madman's "recovery" and his return to a "people-eating" bureaucratic position, is written in classical Chinese while the diary itself, which the reader comes to see is not that of a madman but of one enlightened, is written in the vernacular.

When Chen chose to use the vernacular or *baihua* in *New Youth* in 1917, one of its strongest proponents was Hu Shi. Hu had received his undergraduate degree at Cornell University and his doctorate from Columbia University, studying there with famous pragmatist philosopher John Dewey. Already during his years at Cornell, he had written about the viability of *baihua* to bring about a literary revolution. He later wrote, "A dead language can never produce a living literature; if a living literature is to be produced, there must be a living tool. . . . We must first of all elevate this [vernacular] tool. . . . Only with a new tool can we talk about such other aspects as new ideas and new spirit."[11]

This literary revolution was slowly successful. Not only did *New Youth* publish in the vernacular but so did all new literary magazines. In 1921 the government's Ministry of Education announced that from that point all texts used in primary schools would be published in the vernacular. There were some protests but they were belated and lacked any compelling force. The literary revolution joined the anti-Confucian cultural revolution as the two centerpieces of the May Fourth Movement. The speed of monumental change in the first years of the century was nothing short of mind-blowing: within about a dozen years, the examination system and the monarchy had been dismantled, the traditional language made into a museum piece, and traditional culture trashed.

Both Chen Duxiu and Hu Shi became colleagues at Beijing University, which became one of the main laboratories of the New Culture Movement. When it was established in 1898 as Imperial University, its students were high-ranking officials and degreeholders. It was renamed the National University of Beijing in 1912. It did not have a reputation as a serious institution of study or research; rather, an education there was seen as a ticket to a governmental bureaucratic position. Professors were judged by their official rank, not their teaching ability, and were called "their excellencies." The campus lifestyles of both professors and students featured both gambling and whoring; among the university's nicknames, as indications of the nature and reputation of the institution, were "the Gambling Den" and "the Fountainhead of Ribaldry and Bawdiness."

In 1916, Cai Yuanpei was appointed chancellor of the school. Cai, whom one scholar has called the "moral leader of the new intelligentsia and one of the greatest educators and liberals in modern China," held the highest degree under the traditional examination system and had spent substantial time studying in both Germany and France. He was determined to change the university's reputation and its reality. He believed that if a new language would form the basis for a new culture which was to be forged by the young, then Beijing University should be the central laboratory where that culture should be shaped.

In his revamping of the university, Cai insisted on three points. First, the purpose of the university was academic research which had as its crucial goal the creation of a new culture; such research, Cai believed, should be critical of Western civilization and Chinese traditional civilization alike. Second, students should get rid of the idea that a diploma from Beijing University was their ticket to a job; the university, he argued, was not simply a replacement for the old examination system. Third, if the university was a laboratory in which to chart a new civilization, there had to be complete academic freedom. Divergent ideas had to be expressed openly and sincerely so that the new Chinese Way could be found. Deliberation, study, and debate should lead the way to the new Way. Cai thus brought to the university scholars of all intellectual and political stripes—from reactionaries on the right to radicals on the left—to discuss possibilities for the new China, to debate ideas about the form and shape of China's modern state, and to argue and contend in an atmosphere of unfettered academic freedom. A Chinese writer noted that "all the most . . . gifted among the younger members of the Chinese intelligentsia flocked to take a place under his leadership. The result was the creation, within a few years, of an incredibly productive intellectual life, probably unparalleled in the academic history of the world."[12] Among faculty and students trying to devise a blueprint for modern China, the excitement was electric.

Although the phrase came to be linked with a policy of Mao Zedong in the 1950s, the New Culture Movement, extending into the mid-1920s, was an era when "a hundred schools of thought" contended. It was essentially an intellectual revolution. In classroom and debating hall, in study societies and literary organizations, in restaurants and taverns, in several hundred new newspapers and journals, men and women, old and young met and contended, their ideas set forth to battle antagonistic thoughts, to complement similar strategies, to challenge the status quo, and to propose remedies for the future. Monarchists, anarchists, socialists, Christians, atheists, Buddhists, Confucianists, anti-Confucianists, Marxists, pacifists, pragmatists, scientists, metaphysicists, poets—the list could go on—all debated the potential viability and validity of new values.

The keyword was "new," the adjective that was used to modify various nouns to produce the names of many magazines: *Youth, Tide, Life, Literature and Art, Society, Epoch, Tides of Zhejiang.* The sense of having entered a new historical epoch where people had to act in new ways was pervasive among those involved in the culture debates. In an essay called "The Year 1916," Chen Duxiu rhapsodized

> The epoch in which you are living, what epoch is this? . . . To live in the present world, you must raise your head and proudly call yourself a person of the 20th century and not confine yourself to following the 19th. For the evolution of human civilization is replacing the old with the new, like a river flowing on, an arrow flying away, constantly continuing and constantly changing.[13]

During the late 1910s and early 1920s, the spirit and excitement of intellectual quest was enhanced by lecture tours of foreigners coming with divergent intellectual positions. Hu Shi's Columbia University professor and adviser John Dewey spent 1919 and 1920 living and lecturing in China, spreading his message of pragmatism in eleven provinces; editors of newspapers and journals eagerly published his lectures. In 1921 and 1922, British philosopher Bertrand Russell lectured widely not only on his intellectual interest of mathematical logic but also on pacifism, a subject that in the violent warlord period must have had hundreds of eager listeners. In 1922, Margaret Sanger, feminist and birth control advocate, lectured at Beijing University (with Hu Shi interpreting) on "The What and How of Birth Control"; her ideas, which fed into the period's emphasis on women's liberation, also stirred the first Chinese interest in the issue of birth control. The visit of Indian Nobel laureate Rabindranath Tagore in 1924 touched off a heated debate because of his message praising Asian cultures and warning about importing too much Western civilization. Such foreign lectures served to validate some of the new ideas emerging in the intellectual debates and to stimulate more ideas. Perhaps most important, the lectures and their coverage in the press brought greater and greater numbers of people into the debates.

Despite the extolling of the East by Tagore and his supporters, there were louder supportive calls for two "men" whose backgrounds were clearly in the West and whose names became watchwords at the time and a siren song in China for much of the twentieth century. They were Mr. De and Mr. Sai. Mr. De(mocracy) became the rallying cry of those angered and humiliated by the wretched state of the Chinese state over which warlords and their corrupt politician and bureaucratic allies had run roughshod. Even though the memory of the brief burst of democracy in 1912 and 1913 was fading, the potential for democracy seemed heightened by the victory of the "democratic" Allied powers in World War I and by the 1917 Bolshevik Revolution in Russia.

Mr. Sai (Science) was leading the march into the modern world. He enlightened the darkness of ignorance and superstition. Since whatever was "scientific" seemed progressive, the essential route to realize the best for the future of the individual and the nation was the scientific road. A few intellectuals, like Liang Qichao condemned the West's use of science for the construction of sophisticated weapons of destruction during World War I. But the vast majority of Chinese saw science as a panacea for the country's ills. The emphasis on science was not so much on pure research in an academic discipline as it was its impact on popular thinking—that science was the very essence of the meaning of "modern." Thus, when Shanghai's Commercial Press published a four-volume collection of "scientific" subjects, the Table of Contents read like a blend of serious scientific topics and Ripley's Believe It or Not: "The Structure of the Atom," "Einstein's Theory of Light and Energy," "The Unimaginable New Discoveries in Astrology," "Strange Reptiles," "Four-Legged Birds," "New Cures for Tuberculosis," and "Bicycles on Water." Science at this stage, in short, often took the form of undisciplined knowledge.

THE MAY FOURTH INCIDENT AND ITS AFTERMATH

The New Culture Movement is part of what is generally known as the May Fourth Movement, an amorphous range of political and cultural activities that can be dated from the founding of *New Youth* in 1915 to roughly 1923 or 1924 and that, taken together, can be considered a cultural revolution. It takes its name from a primarily student demonstration in Beijing on May 4, 1919, an incident fueled by nationalistic fervor that substantially changed the direction of the whole cultural revolution movement. Prompted by the Allied decision to allow the Japanese to retain control of Shandong, the incident was the beginning of a marked increase in the politicization and political involvement of students.

A year before on May 21, 1918, about two thousand students from a number of Beijing colleges had joined in a protest demonstration against a series of agreements that China was signing with Japan—the contents of which were largely kept secret because of what

Chinese leaders were willing to give up to Japan (like the right to station troops in northern Manchuria and Inner Mongolia). They marched to the office of China's president to ask for both the content and the annulment of the treaties. President Feng received thirteen students who trustingly accepted his word that nothing would be done to harm China's interests. Similar demonstrations took place in Shanghai, Fuzhou, and Tianjin. Although the protests died down quickly, they were, in effect, "rehearsals" for the May Fourth incident.

By May 1919, the college population at Beijing University was composed of an estimated 20 percent (of 2,228) or close to 450 students who were politically active, as opposed to students mainly interested in studies not politics and residual gamblers and partyers. When word came about the decision at Versailles, the activists, who were members in a number of student organizations, met to plan a demonstration for May 7, the anniversary of the signing of the Twenty-One Demands. Four other Beijing colleges and universities agreed to participate. However, rumors and bitter anger about the turn of events led students to move the demonstration up to May 4. Some students were so outraged that they were moved to write anti-Japanese denunciations in blood on the walls of university dormitories and lunchrooms. Supported by faculty, about three thousand students from thirteen universities and colleges massed at the Gate of Heavenly Peace in front of the Forbidden City. Government representatives tried to end the protest, but to no avail. A manifesto "of all the students of Beijing," distributed at the demonstration read in part, "This is the last chance for China in her life and death struggle. Today we swear two solemn oaths with all our countrymen: (1) China's territory may be conquered, but it cannot be given away; (2) the Chinese people may be massacred, but they will not surrender."[14]

Once the students left the square to march to the home of one of the three Chinese officials who were seen as Japanese collaborators, the orderliness of the protest broke down. Shouting, "The traitors! The traitors!" they invaded his house, and, before torching it, smashed all the furniture. One of the other suspected collaborators was seized and beaten. Fighting lasted for several hours, at the end of which thirty-two students were arrested. After the arrests, the driving goal of the unarrested students was getting the release of their fellow-demonstrators. To accomplish it, students went on strike; protest telegrams poured in from around the nation. On May 5, Beijing students established a citywide student union bringing together students from middle and high schools with those from colleges and universities; women students were for the first time specifically included.

Ironically, after the arrested students were released on May 7 and the student strike was cancelled, there was a steady escalation of tensions. The government issued new restrictions on all further student meetings and protests; further, Cai Yuanpei was forced to resign as Beijing University chancellor. Almost immediately more students were arrested. Professors and teachers formed their own alliance. Word came that a pro-warlord official was named to head the Ministry of Education and that the government was determined to crackdown on student organizations. Then on May 19, the Student Union declared a general strike, demanding, among other things, that China's president refuse to sign the Versailles treaty, punish the alleged pro-Japanese traitor-officials, and restore Cai to his position.

The next two weeks saw the government policy toward the students waver from harsh to lenient; the harsh periods came mostly because of Japanese pressure for the government to crush anti-Japanese demonstrations. Students continued their strike and set out in clusters

The May 4, 1919 demonstration at the Gate of Heavenly Peace, Beijing
Source: Courtesy of the Kautz Family YMCA Archives and the YMCA of the USA.

all over Beijing to give impromptu anti-Japanese lectures on street corners. John Dewey reported on June 4, "We saw students making speeches this morning about eleven, . . . and heard later they had been arrested. . . . There are about ten thousand striking in Beijing alone."[15] By June 4 (a date that seventy years later would feature a bloody massacre of students on these same streets), over eleven hundred students had been arrested. On June 5, more than a thousand women students from the Beijing area, in unprecedented action, marched to the presidential palace demanding the release of the prisoners and freedom of speech.

By this time what was going on in Beijing was simply part of a larger nation-wide protest movement. The Beijing Student Union served as prototype for similar organizations in cities like Shanghai, Wuhan, and Tianjin and ultimately for a Student Union of the Republic of China, established in June. Students served as the yeast, as it were, for a rising nationalistic ferment. At Shanghai especially, patriotic sentiment was strong. The Shanghai Student Union issued the following rationale for their actions.

Throughout the world, like the voice of a prophet, has gone the word of Woodrow Wilson, strengthening the weak and giving courage to the struggling. And the Chinese have listened, and they too have heard. . . . They have been told that in the dispensation which is to be made after the war, unmilitaristic nations like China would have an opportunity to develop their culture, their industry, their civilization unhampered. They have been told that secret covenants and forced agreements would not be recognized. They looked for the dawn of this new era; but no sun rose for China. Even the cradle of the nation was stolen.[16]

Ten thousand attempted to march in demonstration in the city on May 7. The Shanghai Student Union launched a boycott against Japanese goods. Students sent from Beijing reported on government repression in the capital and further fired up the anger of Shanghai-nese. Whereas the Beijing unrest had continued to center on teachers and students, in Shanghai by late May the nationalistic fever had spread to businessmen, merchants, and laborers. The demonstrations and boycott culminated in a general strike that began on June 5. Its goal: to try to force the Chinese delegation at Versailles to refuse to sign the peace treaty. The trump card of the Shanghai general strike was that the city was the economic heart of the Republic of China and that a long general strike could bring an already weak economy to its knees. Bankers were warning the government that "the financial market cannot be maintained tomorrow, if the problem is not solved today."

On June 6 industrial workers joined the strike, first printers, then textile workers, and, most important, streetcar workers, whose participation paralyzed the city. The extent of the rising tide of nationalism can be seen in that even the notorious underworld organizations, the Green and Red gangs, ordered their members not to disrupt the strike. The strike continued until June 12 when it was learned that the three offending pro-Japanese officials had been dismissed. Demonstrations continued to punctuate city life until the announcement came on July 2 that the delegation at Versailles had refused to sign the treaty.

Significant as that point was—that the Chinese delegation was asserting China as a nation in a forceful way—even more important on the domestic front was that political victory had gone to the people through the efforts of the student unions and those involved in the general strike. In cities, the movement was really a mass protest by students, the urban professional class (journalists, teachers, doctors, lawyers, and engineers), leaders and managers of business and industry, shopkeepers, and the urban working class. Acting together, they had forced the government to change its positions, not only to oust the officials that it had in the beginning strongly supported but also to refuse to sign the treaty.

POLITICAL CHANGE FIRST, CULTURAL CHANGE WILL FOLLOW

Such a positive result of direct, in-your-face political action from the perspective of patriotic Chinese had crucial implications for the direction of the May Fourth Movement. Two main camps began to emerge in what would become a struggle over the direction of the movement. Some began to point to the events in the spring and summer of 1919 as what could be accomplished through direct political action. In order to change China, they argued, why not continue this kind of political action? How, they asked, can we build a modern Chinese culture (a task which even if possible would have to take generations) at a time when the people who hold political power have the power to jail and even shoot down those who are offering alternatives to present policies? First, they asserted, we must alter the political system to make it more conducive to other modern changes. Direct, even violent, political action must become the central focus of activity, the main tool for revolutionary change. A leading spokesman for this view was Chen Duxiu, *New Youth* editor and Dean of the School of Letters at Beijing University.

Political tools that received increasing attention for their potential in dealing with China's problems were Marxism and, after the success of the Bolsheviks in 1917, Leninism. One of the early converts to Marxist-Leninist thought was Li Dazhao. Brought to Beijing university by Cai Yuanpei to serve as head of the university library, Li eventually taught history, political science, and economics. On the editorial board of *New Youth,* he became one of the most influential and popular faculty figures at the university; he was always ready to talk with students about everything from personal problems to politics. Li's first attraction to Marxism-Leninism may have been a case of "nothing succeeds like success," in this case the success of Marxism-Leninism in the Russian Revolution. A year after the Bolshevik success, he commemorated the anniversary in *New Youth* with an essay, "The Victory of Bolshevism." Six months later, in May 1919, he devoted a complete issue of the journal to articles on Marxism.

By late 1919 he had become not only supportive of its aims, but had become something of a true believer in its main doctrines. The summer of 1920 began to see the formation of study societies that would become the building blocks for political organizations. In Beijing, Li established the Society for the Study of Marxism at whose meetings he and other faculty lectured on Marxism. Mao Zedong, a student whom Li had befriended at Beijing University by finding him a job in the library, returned to his home in Hunan province to form such a study group. Chen Duxiu, who had been imprisoned briefly in the aftermath of the May Fourth incident and who had moved to Shanghai in 1919, was one of eleven intellectuals and journalists who formed a Marxist Study Society in that city to discuss socialism and Marxism. In their meetings, punctuated by personal animosity and ideological disagreements, they discussed news that they exchanged with the Beijing study group and a new one in Guangzhou, prepared for the expansion of propaganda work, and talked about the development of a more permanent organization. The organizations were the forerunners of the Chinese Communist Party.

At the opening of the twenty-first century, when Communism in most areas of the world has collapsed following a miserable record throughout the twentieth century, it may seem hard to understand the appeals of Marxism-Leninism to the Chinese of the early 1920s. On a most basic level, the "nothing succeeds like success" adage provides one answer: this ideology had been tried and was successful in providing the base for overthrowing autocratic rule in Russia. Chinese intellectuals also felt strongly inclined to the Soviet model after the apparently generous 1919 offer by the Soviet government in the Karakhan Declaration. This declaration promised to return all the privileges that the czars had won in unequal treaties as well as to renounce Russia's share of the Boxer indemnity. These acts clearly marked the Soviet Union as a cut above the other imperialists who at the Versailles Conference had so recently thumbed its collective nose at China and its plight.

Then there was the intellectual attractiveness of Marxism for the May Fourth generation: Above all, it was "scientific." Marx's idea of historical materialism explained history and the chief dynamic of historical development: history moves through stages—from slave to feudal to capitalist to socialist to communist, propelled from stage to stage by classes struggling for control of the means of production. Such an explanation offered a vision of where a particular society was in its march forward in revolutionary progress toward the communist utopia. Leninism explained China's plight as a semi-colony of the imperialist powers, arguing that for Western capitalism to survive Western nations had to develop empires with raw materials and cheap labor. Cut off the support from their colonies and, Lenin claimed, Western capitalism would wither. Leninism further provided the all-important revolutionary vehicle, a tightly organized and controlled party; and in addition, it offered an individual revolutionary ideal shaped by patriotism and self-sacrifice. The most important appeal of Marxism-Leninism was that it seemed to offer a sweeping systemic solution to China's myriad problems. "[I]t provided a self-consistent, universalistic, and "scientific" view of the world's history which enabled one to reject the imperialist West in the name of Western "scientific thought" and explain China's humiliating backwardness as due to her bondage to "capitalist imperialism." . . ."[17]

CULTURAL CHANGE FIRST, POLITICAL CHANGE WILL FOLLOW

If Chen, Li, and others were moving quickly toward the establishment of a political party that might become an important revolutionary tool, the other camp that developed in the aftermath of the May Fourth incident staked out a very different approach. They contended that any meaningful political change had to be preceded by and therefore had to be built upon cultural change. By the nature of things, cultural change cannot be engineered rapidly by tools like violence; it is a slow effort based more on evolutionary rather than revolutionary dynamics. One of the most important advocates of this path to change was Hu Shi whose own personal tendencies and education under Dewey must certainly have inspired this solution. Pragmatists saw a world of "problems" that needed solving. They searched for solutions to each problem. Since problems diverged in different areas, among different kinds of people, in different arenas of life, careful study should reveal the solution to each problem, which would then serve as the "truth" in each circumstance. Solving that problem through reform was the key. Hu argued that "[t]here is no liberation *in toto* or reconstruction *in toto*. Liberation means liberation from this or that institution, from this or that belief, for this or that individual; it is liberation bit by bit, drop by drop."[18] For this reason, Hu attacked what he called "isms"—like Marxism and Leninism—as overarching creeds, blueprints, systems, or "fundamental solutions" that seemed to offer a way out of China's predicament.

Many Chinese had difficulties with this approach. Certainly, for a civilization in crisis, this "bit by bit, drop by drop" solution focusing on education and evolutionary change was not in the least intellectually satisfying. But more important, this approach would take many years, perhaps decades, even a century or more; even then, its adoption would bring with it no guarantee that it could remake China before China might indeed disintegrate and fall completely into Western hands. As one May Fourth intellectual, Shen Dingyi, put it,

"Under the present circumstances, part of the Chinese people and their land has become fish and pork on the cutting board... [P]owers ... hold their knives [in readiness]. ... We should take over the knife, kick away the cutting board, and refuse to be fish and pork."[19] For many Chinese intellectuals and students, so recently enamored of individual liberation, the emerging priority came to be the fate of the nation, the thinking being that without national liberation individual liberation would ultimately be meaningless.

Thus, from 1919 on, and picking up steam into the early 1920s, the direction of the May Fourth Movement changed. Its focus on enlightenment and individual liberation through the shattering of traditional cultural hierarchical bonds was swallowed up by an emphasis on national salvation, that is, on liberating the nation from imperialist and warlord control. For this reason, one Chinese historian has called the movement "an abortive revolution because its intellectual goal of enlightenment was unrealized" when the "revolutionary imperative of national salvation eclipsed demands for enlightenment."[20] It is also significant that, as in traditional times, during the New Culture Movement intellectuals were in charge. Initially in the switch to direct political action at the time of the May Fourth incident and after, intellectuals remained in the forefront. But by the late 1920s they would begin to lose their leadership positions. Once the Nationalists and Communists were ensconced in power, intellectuals would no longer be in the historical forefront; instead they became a distrusted social group that was continually subject to all sorts of repression and mistreatment. The revolution, as it developed, had all sorts of major implications for Chinese society and social groups.

NEO-TRADITIONALISM

Both those who favored big system solutions and those who preferred pragmatic approaches nevertheless were in agreement that traditional culture was at the heart of China's problems and that a new China had to be created. For those wanting to build a Chinese nation, this position presented a problem in itself. From the late eighteenth century on when nations have been constructed, they have usually been based upon the history and the traditional myths and culture of the society building the nation. Both the big systems proponents and the pragmatists were rejecting those traditional myths and culture. Upon what foundation then was the new nation to be built? There was not at the time much agreement on the nation's new building blocks.

In contrast to the "isms" and the "problems" advocates, there were scholars who were adamant opponents of rejecting traditional Chinese culture. They argued that Chinese culture could, indeed must, be the basis for the nation. There were three such neo-traditional "schools" of thought. All of them shared several positions. They were all suspicious and distrustful of Western values—individualism, materialism, and utilitarianism—and their validity for China's development. They all believed that traditional Chinese values which came to constitute a "core of truth" were in fact antithetical to Western values. The anti-Western slant of these views fit well the anti-imperialist thrust beginning to emerge in the early 1920s and contrasted with the Western-oriented solutions that were offered by the advocates of systemic solutions and pragmatism. These three "schools" actually predated the

May Fourth Movement, having emerged out of the radical rethinking of Confucianism and Chinese culture in the late 1890s reform movement.

The "national essence" school sought to find elements in traditional culture other than Confucianism that might serve as ideas or practices that could be used in the building of a nation. There were, for example, different philosophical and religious traditions: non-Confucian schools of thought, most of which had risen with Confucianism in the middle and late Zhou dynasty (1122–221 B.C.) and the important religious import from India, Buddhism. On a somewhat different level, there were the "knight errant" tales with their tradition of action and "heroic violence"—popular ideas that had penetrated among the Chinese masses. There thus came to be a populist thrust in this school that broke through the elite-controlled images and practices of standard Confucianism. In essence this school gutted the authority of the Confucian classics, making them simply a part of the larger body of Chinese literature. If this school was against the old Confucian orthodoxy, it was also strongly anti-Western; its arguments struck deep into Western assumptions and practices. For example, "national essence" adherents contended that the very basic idea that had inspired Western attitudes and approaches since the Enlightenment—the idea of progress—was a delusion, little more than a "modern superstition."[21] The Western drive for power and wealth was destructive of the "inner life" of a culture and its inhabitants. China, they contended, must build a nation using its own "internal spiritual powers of renewal."

Cai Yuanpei brought a number of these "national essence" scholars to Beijing University in his effort to have open debates over divergent ideas that could potentially be used for the making of the new China. During this time, these scholars were most vocal in opposing the replacement of classical Chinese with the vernacular. One, in answer to the argument that the vernacular would benefit China because it would facilitate literacy, responded that "the language most popularly used was not necessarily a better one. More bread and jam were consumed than roast turkey throughout the world; yet could we say that the latter was less delicious and nutritious than the former only because it was rarer and that we should all eat 'only' bread and jam?"[22] Charitably, it could be said that most "national essence" arguments were not so lacking in depth.

The 1898 reformer Liang Qichao was the leading advocate and thinker in the so-called "national character" school. Unlike the "national essence" thinkers who searched the past for a non-Confucian basis for a new China, Liang sought to uncover a living national character of the Chinese people. He argued that "nations have a nature like people and that their fate depends upon this intangible quality, visible in religion, customs, and language."[23] The key for Liang was the strengths of the family system—the very system under so much attack in the May Fourth movement. In it Liang found elements that he claimed were crucial for the building of a new China. Respect for rank and concern for future generations were important aspects of the system that Liang stressed as especially important for the formation of a modern nationalism. Further, he claimed that the ideal of reciprocity—that the claims of authority on the part of males and elders were balanced by moral claims of the subordinates against those in authority—should undercut the vehement May Fourth attack on familism. Like the "national essence" school, Liang attacked the West and its values. Liang had gone to France to be an observer at the 1919 Versailles Conference. He had come away with a completely negative impression of the West as morally bankrupt and degenerate. He saw Western life dominated by an emphasis on science and technology, a focus that he claimed helped produce economic and social systems that led directly to hedonism, corruption, and greed. His was the voice of a Cassandra, prophesying a disaster for China if it followed the Western path into the modern world.

The third neo-traditionalist approach sought to set forth the modern relevance of Confucianism. From the 1898 reform movement until the death of Yuan Shikai, this effort focused on attempting to make Confucianism a state religion. But by the May Fourth period this attempt seemed no longer credible amid arguments by secularists that, in the context of scientific progress, religion for society at large would soon become obsolete. Confucianism's great champion and the most influential neo-traditionalist thinker in the May Fourth period was Liang Shuming, invited by Cai to join the Beijing University faculty in 1917. He set forth his major ideas in his book, *Eastern and Western Civilizations and Their Philosophies.* He argued that Western civilization was based on two legs: one was rational calculation focusing on the external world, a process that gave rise to the development of science and to trying to master the environment; the other was rational calculation focusing on individual self-interest, an effort that led to democracy and, in its communal arena, communism. Throughout, Western thought had stressed skepticism and utilitarianism.

China's culture, Liang asserted, was much the superior. It was shaped by the living force of the cardinal Confucian virtue of *ren,* a word that is difficult to translate but means something like "human empathy" or "human heartedness." Under its umbrella, Chinese society had been "tolerant and flexible, frugal and agrarian, cooperative and nourishing of human sentiments."[24] In short, Liang argued that Confucian values were superior because they recognized that reality is fluid and experience is often intuitive; thus the Western emphasis on rational analysis is found faulty and misleading. Of all the neo-traditionalists, Liang was probably most conservative. While the "national essence" and "national character" thinkers set forth their ideas as the foundation for the Chinese nation, Liang's ideas hearkened back to the traditional pre-nationalist views of the primacy of culture or what has been called culturalism. It is also important to note that none of the neo-traditionalists schools concentrated on the individual, the focus of the initial phase of the May Fourth Movement.

THE HISTORICAL SIGNIFICANCE OF THE MAY FOURTH MOVEMENT

Historians have generally ranked the May Fourth Movement with the abolition of the civil service examination and the overthrow of the monarchy and imperial regime as one of the most significant revolutionary milestones in China's twentieth-century revolution. While the first two milestones cast off the old and made necessary the as-yet-unknown new, this third milestone, while also discarding the old, initiated an earnest search for the new. It is certainly an important demarcation in the intellectual and cultural history of China. Scholars have called it China's Renaissance, in part because the vernacular first came to be used then. It was in the Western Renaissance that writing in the Western vernaculars—French, Spanish, Italian, etc., as opposed to Latin—first came into practice. Scholars have also called it the Chinese Enlightenment, a term recalling the important role of science and experimentation and the casting out of tradition. It may also be called an intellectual and cultural revolution, where the old and traditional were discarded—even trashed—and various kinds of bold experimentation with new ideas and methods were attempted. It was the first of a series of attempts to dismantle traditional culture.

Because it discarded traditional Chinese culture, the May Fourth Movement has drawn strong reactions from various Chinese political forces. The identities of these forces have almost necessarily had to reflect their stand on the meaning of the traditional culture for a modern Chinese nation state. For the Nationalist regime of Chiang Kai-shek and his successors, it seemed too radical a movement, destroying much good that lay in Chinese tradition; further, with its increased emphasis on direct political, often violent, action, it was linked too closely with the rise of Chinese communism. The Nationalists viewed the movement with considerable distrust and suspicion. The Communists, whose party grew out of the intellectual ferment and issues of the time, have looked more kindly on the May Fourth period, but have looked with jaundiced eye at the first phase which emphasized the role of intellectuals in enlightening society so as to realize individual aspirations. Condemning emphasis on the individual as "bourgeois," the Communists throughout their history have attacked those who maintained such a mentality and at intellectuals in general who seemed by nature to be tainted with the toxin of individualism. Thus, the reaction of both major political parties has been colored with negativism about this crucial modern movement.

Finally any postmortem must stress that the time given to these cultural revolutionaries to make major social and cultural changes was absurdly short. Their efforts were largely aborted—overtaken as they were by the sweep of revolutionary political events. The movement for cultural criticism and renewal was swallowed whole by the movement for national salvation.

Notes

[1] Cheng and Lestz with Spence, p. 235.

[2] Lu Hsun, "A Madman's Diary" in *Selected Stories of Lu Hsun* (Beijing: Foreign Languages Press, 1972), p. 10.

[3] Lu Hsun, "Preface to the First Collection of Short Stories, 'Call to Arms'" in *Selected Stories,* p. 5.

[4] Teng and Fairbank, p. 240.

[5] Quoted in Yeh Wen-hsin, *Provincial Passages* (Berkeley: University of California Press, 1996), p. 111.

[6] Ibid., p. 181.

[7] Quoted in Chow Tse-tsung, *The May Fourth Movement* (Stanford: Stanford University Press, 1960), p. 184.

[8] Lu Xun, "My Views on Chastity," in Cheng and Lestz with Spence, p. 236.

[9] Teng and Fairbank, p. 241.

[10] Schoppa, *Blood Road,* p. 108.

[11] Leo Ou-fan Lee, "Literary Trends I: The Quest for Modernity, 1895–1927" in Fairbank, Ed., *The Cambridge History of China, Vol. 12, Republican China, 1912–1949, Part 1,* p. 467.

[12] Quoted in Chow, p. 52.

[13] Quoted in Leo Ou-fan Lee, "Modernity and its Discontents: The Cultural Agenda of the May Fourth Movement" in Kenneth Leiberthal, et. al., Eds., *Perspectives on Modern China, Four Anniversaries* (Armonk, N.Y.: M. E. Sharpe, 1991), pp. 161–162.

[14] Quoted in Chow, pp. 106–107.

[15] Ibid., pp. 149–150.

[16] Quoted in Joanna Waley-Cohen, *The Sextants of Beijing* (New York: W. W. Norton, 1999), p. 207.

[17] Fairbank, Reischauer, and Craig, p. 670.

[18] Cited in Fairbank, Reischauer, and Craig, p. 669.

[19] Schoppa, *Blood Road,* p. 65.

[20] Quoted in Leo Ou-fan Lee, "Modernity and its Discontents: The Cultural Agenda of the May Fourth Movement," p. 173.

[21] The phrase and many of these arguments come from Charlotte Furth, "Intellectual Change: From the Reform Movement to the May Fourth Movement, 1895–1920," in John K. Fairbank, Ed., *The Cambridge History of China, Vol. 12, Republican China, 1912–1949, Part 1,* p. 361.

[22] Quoted in Chow, p. 281.

[23] Furth, p. 362.

[24] Ibid., p. 370.

10

Drawing the Sword: The Politicization of Identity

In the last years of the twentieth century, nationalism became a hot topic. World trouble spots such as the Balkans, the Middle East, and Northern Ireland raised questions about the meaning of nationalism and its relationship to ethnicity. Scholars opened new inquiries into the meaning and dynamics of nationalism and its relationship to not only ethnicity, but to class and gender as well. For Chinese early in the twentieth century, nationalism was a new lens through which to see their identity. In imperial times there had been China the central country with that centrality situated clearly in its culture. But the nineteenth century nightmare of foreign invasion and military defeat had effectively made shambles of China's assumed cultural superiority. Events had forced Chinese political, social, economic, and intellectual leaders by the early twentieth century to see China simply as one of many nations and as one of the weakest. In their view the most outstanding characteristic of the Chinese nation in the context of continuing imperialist pressure was a thoroughgoing and humiliating impotence. That view came to be drummed into the population at large through such annual public commemorations as National Humiliation Day, the anniversary of China's 1915 acceptance of the Twenty-One Demands. The question of the early twentieth century thus became how to build national power as quickly as possible so as to prevent not only continuing national humiliations but even dismemberment.

THE BIRTH OF THE CHINESE COMMUNIST PARTY

A strong government was essential. To establish such a government meant building political parties to serve as the engine and military forces to serve as the vehicle by which to defeat the warlords and their supporters and then expel or, at the least, deal more effectively with the imperialists. Since this is the story of the seeds of revolution, a blow-by-blow account highlights the relative slowness of developments and the complex, often intricate, usually tense dance between the Chinese Communist Party, Sun Yat-sen's Guomindang, and advisors sent from the Communist International in Moscow. This chapter might be entitled "How to Make a Revolution," but the story it tells does not adhere to the neat outline that historians often structure to show the macro-trajectory or large course of revolution. Instead it was a messy, often unclear, and always muddled process. For a revolution is made by people who, in the process of revolution, do not know the end results; therefore, their choices and decisions were often shaped by personalities, emotions, and reactions to contingencies and day-to-day realities.

The Communist Party was established first. As the last chapter showed, a number of things—the intellectual attractiveness of Marxism-Leninism, the success of the Bolshevik revolution, and the apparent generosity of the Karakhan Declaration—predisposed some Chinese intellectuals and journalists to favor the Soviet model. Another essential element in moves to form a Communist party was the initiative of the Communist International or Comintern, an organization that Lenin established to incite and direct world revolution. A mission led by twenty-seven year old laborer-turned Comintern agent Gregory Voitinsky arrived in Beijing in April 1920; he had what has been called a "winning personality," a characteristic that facilitated his work with Chinese students and intellectuals. In the capital, he met intellectuals including Li Dazhao; Li gave Voitinsky a letter of introduction to Chen Duxiu then living in Shanghai. The Comintern delegation traveled to Shanghai to meet Chen and others in the Marxist Study Society. In September 1920, Chen Duxiu turned *New Youth* into a Communist journal, subsidized by the Comintern.

By summer 1920 a Communist cell group was functioning in Shanghai, overseeing the establishment of a Russian language school, the beginning efforts to organize labor unions, and the formation of a Socialist Youth Corps, later to be known as the Communist Youth Corps. By January 1921, eight Socialist Youth Corps organizations with about three hundred members were reportedly established in a number of cities. Other Communist cell groups were formed in Beijing, Canton, Hankou, Jinan, Changsha (established by Mao Zedong), and by Chinese students in Japan and France. Each was initially composed of only a handful of men and women. The revolution started bit by bit, drop by drop.

A word about the students in France. In the years 1919 and 1920 over a thousand Chinese male and female students participated in work-study programs there. The goal of the programs was to join study with manual labor. This was a pointed break with past traditions when Chinese scholars grew their fingernails long to underline the fact that they did not work with their hands. In a practical sense, working in factories covering the gamut from bean curd to automobile production paid the costs of studies and of daily life. Ultimately the goal of work-study was to offer training and some knowledge of technology that could be of use upon their return to China. For many students, however, life in France above all further politicized them, introducing them to socialist doctrine and Marxism-Leninism, as well as labor strikes. It was this kind of context that led to the founding of Chinese Communist cells in Europe. Two of the most important Communist leaders in the mid- and late twentieth century—Zhou Enlai and Deng Xiaoping—participated in the work-study program.

Back in China, in November 1920 Voitinsky met with Sun Yat-sen. Sun had fled to Japan after the brief "second revolution" against Yuan Shikai in 1913. In the next few years he came to see that establishing the strong government of a full-fledged republic would require a strong party and some effective military apparatus. In Japan he had experimented with setting up a more tightly organized party with party members swearing personal loyalty to him; this demand alienated too many people so Sun dropped the idea. When he returned to China in 1916, he spent most of his time in Canton, reorganizing his parliamentary style Guomindang still as an open party and trying to link himself to the warlord in the area whose forces might be used for Sun's purposes. But his party reorganization had little import and various attempted military arrangements did not work. During these years, Sun was clearly spinning his wheels; he was thus ready to make contact with the Comintern agent to see whether there might be anything to gain.

Meeting Sun was an important development in the eyes of the Comintern. In summer 1920 at the Second Comintern Congress, policies regarding Communist movements in colonial and "backward" countries were on the agenda. Given the very small number of Communists in any of these countries (many did not yet even have Communist parties) and the reality that they had insufficient power to accomplish much, should Communists adopt the short-term tactic of joining bourgeois parties for national ends in a united front against common enemies? Lenin said yes: A temporary united front made tactical sense; once the common enemies were defeated the united front would end and the former allies would then become enemies. Others in the Comintern (the Indian M. N. Roy and later the Soviet Union's Leon Trotsky) argued that national ends should play no role because the real struggle was the class struggle of workers and peasants around the world against the forces of feudalism and capitalism. Lenin's position carried the day. Voitinsky's meeting with Sun was thus in line with the recently decided Comintern policy initiative.

Twelve delegates attended the founding congress of the Chinese Communist Party (hereafter, CCP) which met in the Shanghai French Concession in July 1921; the party had only between fifty and sixty members. At the congress, the delegates elected the central executive committee and chose Chen Duxiu as secretary-general. They came down very firmly in what looked to be an uncompromising decision that they could have no relationships with other parties. Attending the congress as Comintern representative was a Dutch Communist, Hendricus Sneevliet (also known as Maring), every bit as aggressive and stubborn as Voitinsky was mild and unassuming. Since Comintern agents had to tutor and work closely with the Chinese, their personalities and approaches were significant for the success of their work. From the perspective of the still small group of committed Communists, both Comintern revolutionary expertise and financial assistance were crucial. Following Moscow's policy, Sneevliet began to urge the Communists to join Sun Yat-sen's Guomindang, still an open parliamentary-style party. The young CCP did not initially support such a move, but the sway of the Comintern on the infant Chinese party was strong.

Pressure from Moscow in this regard became stronger with the meeting of the Congress of the Toilers of the East in January and February 1922. There the focus was East Asian countries and their "revolutionary liberation . . . and solidarity with proletarian Russia."[1] To bring about this liberation, speakers argued, required both the development of strong proletarian movements of workers and peasants and cooperation with "bourgeois nationalists." The Guomindang was singled out as the Chinese party that might be crucial for the development of the revolutionary effort in China.

In December 1921 Sneevliet had journeyed to south China to meet Sun Yat-sen to discuss China's situation and its relationship to the Soviet Union. Whether they discussed cooperation between the CCP and Guomindang is uncertain, but since Sneevliet had become one of cooperation's biggest supporters it is probable that it was at least mentioned. Sun reportedly had many positive things to say about the Soviet Union and its new system. In April 1922 Sneevliet opened a hornet's nest with his advice to Socialist Youth Corps and CCP members to join the Guomindang. CCP leader Chen Duxiu said, in essence, "No way!" CCP members even questioned the idea of a united front. But by June the party, mindful of the discussions at the earlier Congress of the Toilers of the East and coming to see that the Guomindang was "relatively revolutionary and democratic," issued a manifesto that it was ready to join with the Guomindang. The decision to participate in a united front was confirmed at the second party congress in July 1922. The united front took dead aim on two opponents—the warlords and the imperialists: Defeat the warlords once and for all, and kick out the imperialists, ending the reign of the unequal treaty system.

Most Chinese Communists favored an outright alliance between the parties, but Comintern agents' talks with Sun about some sort of united front had made clear that he opposed an alliance of separate parties because he ultimately did not want two major parties vying with each other. Sun favored letting individual CCP members join his party, forming what came to be called a "bloc within" system. CCP members adamantly opposed that possibility, arguing that a "bloc within" would blur class organization and cut down on the CCP's independence. In essence CCP members were contending that the political identity of the party and of themselves was at stake in such a decision. But when push came to shove, Sneevliet weighed in: "The Comintern has already decided on the 'bloc within'; will you obey the decision?" Given its dependence on the Comintern, the CCP had no choice but to obey. Thus, from the very beginning, the key decision for the united front was made primarily by Sun and the Comintern with the CCP forced into a decision by its Comintern adviser. The "bloc within" was ratified at the third party congress in the summer of 1923.

GIVING THE GUOMINDANG A NEW IDENTITY

In August 1922, Sun met Adolf Joffe a top Soviet diplomat who had been sent to China for high level governmental discussions but who quickly made arrangements to see Sun. The two talked at length in late January 1923 and apparently set down basic approaches for greater cooperation between the Soviets and the Guomindang. Sun asked for financial aid and for advisers on "military and political problems." He announced his intention of sending a military mission to Moscow to study government and party organs. The talks did produce a joint statement noting that although the Soviet system could not be introduced into China, Russia would support China's national independence and reunification. Sun followed up his talks with Joffe by sending one of his most trusted aides, Liao Zhongkai, to Japan for extended discussions with Joffe who was in Japan on assignment.

The main thrust of Soviet support was tutorial: Russia would provide advice and training for Sun to restructure his party and to form a party army. In autumn 1923, the Comintern dispatched Michael Borodin to help reorganize the Guomindang. A Russian Jew, Borodin had lived in the United States from 1905 to 1917, had returned to Russia at the time of the revolution, and had since served as Comintern agent in Mexico and several European countries. Many sources describe him as almost larger than life—a big, husky man with a magnetic personality and great intelligence. In China Borodin used his ability to build substantial power quickly.

As a political party, the Guomindang was open, often factionalized, frequently unruly, and without anything to keep it directed and coherent. In short, it was not the kind of organization that would serve to pull off a revolution. Thus, Borodin drafted a new Guomindang constitution, translated into Chinese by Liao Zhongkai. It restructured the party in Leninist fashion according to the concept of "democratic centralism" which envisions a hierarchical party structure. Debate and discussion ("democracy") occur in each level of the hierarchy with recommendations passed up the hierarchical chain of command. Once the topmost level (in the party, the Central Executive Committee) reaches a decision, there is no more discussion and the decision must be carried out ("centralism"). In short, it is a structure that presents a facade of democratic-style discussion; but in substance at the end of the process, it is really centralized autocracy. Further, because of surveillance operatives at every hierarchical level and in every arena of party activity, such a party is extraordinarily difficult to subvert. By early 1924, then, China's two parties were both Leninist-style organs.

There is evidence that the reorganization was not popular with many Guomindang members. In the late fall many meetings were held at which Borodin and Liao explained the reasons for the restructuring. Borodin even had to defend the changes in meetings with members of the CCP and the Socialist Youth Corps. From men connected with the Guangdong party office Sun received a petition claiming that the revised party constitution had really been drafted by Borodin and CCP leader Chen Duxiu; they argued that the bloc within was a plot for the CCP to take over the Guomindang. Sun rejected the petition, saying that the constitution had been "prepared by Borodin at my request and checked by myself. . . . Chen Duxiu had no part in this." He went on to explain that "the capitalist countries will never be sympathetic to our Party. Sympathy can only be expected from Russia, the oppressed nations, and the oppressed peoples."[2] Thus, the united front proceeded with constant backbiting, fear, suspicion, and distrust.

The party's ideology, in contrast to its structure, was more homegrown. In 1923 and 1924 Sun had set down his own thinking about the direction and goals of the party and state; he had spoken of many of these ideas since the days of the Revolutionary Alliance. Known as the Three Principles of the People, they championed nationalism, democracy, and socialism (vaguely described as "people's livelihood"). For Sun the realization of nationalism had more meaning than simply asserting China's national rights. He argued

> Only when imperialism is eliminated can there be peace for all mankind. To achieve this goal, we should first rejuvenate Chinese nationalism and restore China's position as a sovereign state. Then, with morality and peace as the ideological foundation of our foreign policy, we can help to bring about a unified world and brotherhood among men. This . . . is . . . the true spirit of Chinese nationalism.[3]

Sun's description of democracy uses many of the distinctions used by Communist leaders in the late twentieth century regarding the issue of human rights. He claimed that

There is a difference between the European and Chinese concept of freedom. While the Europeans struggle for personal freedom, we struggle for national freedom. As far as we are concerned, personal freedom should never be too excessive. In fact, in order to win national freedom, we should not hesitate to sacrifice our personal freedom.

Democracy for Sun meant "that all people . . . should enjoy the same political rights" and he enumerated those rights as the right to vote, to recall officials, to undertake initiatives, and to hold referendums. While the people have four major political rights, the government holds five powers—executive, legislative, judiciary, examination, and censorship.

In his discussion of "people's livelihood," Sun took on the Marxists who argued that China's central social and economic problem was uneven distribution of wealth; Sun asserted that the real problem was the "grinding poverty of the Chinese people." He called for some socialist solutions—the equalization of land ownership and the development of government-owned enterprises. But he also called for other reforms, including rent reductions for farmers and gaining control of the tariff in order to protect native Chinese industry. A centerpiece of his economic package was an idea he borrowed from the American economist Henry George: a tax on the increase in value of landed property, in Sun's term, the "unearned increment"—since whoever held the land had done nothing to earn the amount that increased in value over time.

In addition to a restructured party and an ideology that gave the polity direction, the other essential prerequisite for building a strong government and nation was a capable military force. That would be important for any seizure of power, but even more so when the nation was ruled by an array of warlords and when society had become increasingly used to political decisions made by force of arms. With a view toward beginning the building of an army, Sun sent a delegation led by Chiang Kai-shek (mandarin pronunciation, Jiang Jieshi) to Russia from August to November, 1923. Chiang had attended military schools in both China and Japan before the establishment of the Republic. A member of the Revolutionary Alliance, he participated in the 1911 revolution in Shanghai and was involved in anti-Yuan Shikai activities until 1916. After that time he "lingered in Shanghai," working as a stockbroker and making close ties with the Green Gang, Shanghai's and the Lower Yangzi's underworld secret society. It was not until 1921 that Chiang began to work for Sun Yat-sen; it is little wonder that he was, in the words of one historian," a somewhat irregular member of Sun's entourage." There were many others much closer to Sun than Chiang. The purpose of Chiang's mission to Moscow was to study Soviet government and party institutions and to inspect military academies with a view to understanding military organization and training. A more general goal of the mission was developing closer relations between the Guomindang and Soviet leaders. However, the longer he remained in Moscow, the more disillusioned Chiang became about any long-term alliance between Russia and China.

The cornerstone of a modern army, *loyal above all to the party,* was a military academy. In 1924 under Borodin's and Liao Zhongkai's leadership, one was established at

Huangpu (usually called Whampoa), ten miles downstream from Canton. Reportedly the Soviet government contributed three million rubles for setting up the school and its initial running expenses; in addition, Borodin subsidized it on the order of 100,000 Canton dollars every month. Though he was not Sun's first choice, Chiang Kai-shek was appointed commandant in May. Almost 500 cadets formed the first class, beginning in June 1924; between seventeen and twenty-four years old, those who were admitted had to pass an entrance examination. The academy's course of study was six months. Upon graduation, the cadets had to serve in the army a year for every two months they were students at the academy.

In his address at opening ceremonies on June 16, 1924, Sun set forth the goals of the academy.

> What is our hope in starting this school today? Our hope is that from today on we will be able to remake our revolutionary enterprise and use students of this school as the foundation of a revolutionary army. . . . Without a good revolutionary army, the Chinese revolution is doomed to failure. Therefore . . . our sole hope is to create a revolutionary army to save China from extinction.[4]

Sun's Three Principles of the People was the ideological core of their training. Sun appointed Liao Zhongkai to be senior political officer in control of political training and in-

Sun Yat-sen and Chiang Kai-shek

doctrination. Faculty and administrative staff were balanced between Communists and Nationalists, with many of the former being part of the bloc within. Zhou Enlai, for example, who would become a pivotal member of the leadership of the People's Republic after 1949, was a political instructor at Whampoa. Despite the conspicuous presence of Communists and Comintern advisers (there were about a thousand Russian military advisors in China by early 1925), the cadets became fiercely loyal to Chiang who supervised the training of the first three classes. Many would come to play roles as his generals in the 1930s and 1940s and almost all would become his avid backers as members of his strongest supporting faction, the Whampoa clique.

THINGS FALLS APART: SUN'S DEATH AND
THE MAY THIRTIETH MOVEMENT

The realities of Chinese social and political culture tended to produce political parties that were composed of factions based on personal connections. The glue of connections that holds personal networks together—based on kinship, native place, alumni connections, friendship, teacher-student ties, political patron-client ties—is the strongest political binding agent. Sometimes the political landscape saw factions or personal networks coming together as coalitions. Such coalitions tended to be much less cohesive than personal-connection factions; they tended to be held tenuously together perhaps by ideology or strategy or long- or short-term goals. Sun Yat-sen, named Guomindang leader for life and the most prominent national figure in China, headed a party with many factions and networks even though it had been restructured in the Leninist mode. Party members owed personal loyalty and support to him; many had followed him since the Revolutionary Alliance days in the early years of the century. But among the factions and networks, there was considerable competition, even bitter disagreement about policy and ideology.

There were surely party members all along the political spectrum from right to left, but, for our purposes, seeing the basic split between right (conservative) and left (liberal) clarifies the general elements of disagreement. On the political right were those who believed that the Russians had too much power in shaping the Chinese revolution, that Borodin had become a much too powerful decision-maker, and that the "bloc within" was basically a bad policy that had to be eliminated. These were people like Dai Jitao, Sun Yat-sen's personal secretary from 1916 on. Graduate of a Japanese university, Dai had become one of the most active popularizers of Sun's ideas and had been a part of the Shanghai Marxist Study Society. But the course of events convinced him that Russians and the CCP were becoming chief beneficiaries of CCP-Guomindang cooperation in the united front. Especially irritating to the rightists was the tendency of Communists who had joined the Guomindang as individuals to cohere in separate groups, almost as if they were a party within the larger party.

On the political left were those whose political positions were similar to those of the Communists, offering some support for social and economic as well as political revolution, though they may have had doubts about the extent of power of Soviet advisors. These were men like Liao Zhongkai and Wang Jingwei, both extremely close associates of Sun Yat-sen. American born and Japanese educated, Liao had been with Sun since 1903, had with his wife been members of the Revolutionary Alliance, and had played an important role in shaping the cooperation between the Comintern and the Guomindang. He worked with Borodin closely on a number of projects and, as we have seen, Sun sent him to Japan for further talks with Joffe about the Soviet system. Wang, once the "golden boy of Chinese nationalism" for his 1910 attempt at assassinating the Manchu prince regent, had been one of the most active members of the Revolutionary Alliance. From 1917 on, he was a member of Sun's entourage, renowned for his handsomeness, "a humbler of female hearts."[5]

In the center were those like Chiang Kai-shek who was not as close to Sun as Dai, Liao, and Wang. The centrists made their own way, supporting Sun and his working with the Soviets, but capable of going to the right or left depending on contingencies. The continual presence and important roles of the Communists within the party kept the issues regarding the pros and cons of the united front alive and usually but not always just below the surface of day-to-day activities. While the political right carped about surface issues like the power of Borodin in day to day decisions, the basic difference in outlook over what the revolution was to be was not broached.

In June 1924 a group of conservatives took the case of Communists in the Guomindang coalescing into units to Sun and the Central Executive Committee. They pointed out that they did not object to individual CCP members joining the Guomindang, but that it was not proper for there to be a party within the Party. They pointed to the relatively large numbers of Communists who held positions on the Guomindang Central Executive Committee and to the successful efforts of Communist units within the party to get Communist ideas at the forefront of party publications. The Central Committee decided in late summer to leave things as they were. In a sense Sun added insult to the conservatives' injury, so to speak: when he established a new party organ, the Political Council to advise on political issues, he named none other than Borodin as its head. While the surface calm remained, conservatives were rankled by Borodin's and the CCP's seeming domination of Sun and the Guomindang left. For their part CCP members were nervous and irritated by the continual rumblings of Guomindang discontent. The united front was clearly ill, but Sun was still holding it together.

But then he died. On a trip to Beijing in late 1924 and early 1925 to discuss the national situation with Zhang Zuolin, the Manchurian warlord currently controlling the capital, he became ill. Surgery showed incurable liver cancer, and he died on March 12. On the day before he died, Sun signed two documents, one a testament drafted by Wang Jingwei and the other a statement to the Soviet Union. The latter read in part

> I leave behind me a party which, as I always hoped, will be allied with you in its historical task of liberating China and other suppressed peoples from the yoke of imperialism. . . . I therefore charge my party to maintain permanent contact with you. I cherish the firm belief that your support of my country will remain unaltered.[6]

His message for continued support from the Soviet Union certainly does not indicate that Sun was aware at the time of his death of the seriousness of the united front's ill health.

Death transformed Sun; he became a potent symbol of patriotism and unfinished revolution. But, for all its power, a symbol cannot hold parties together. The situation was worsened by what has become known as the May 30th Movement. At a Japanese-owned textile mill in Shanghai, a Chinese worker was killed by a Japanese guard after he and other workers had broken into the factory during a strike lockout and wrecked some machines. Demonstrations of public outrage led to the arrest of several students. On May 30, thousands of demonstrators massed before the police station to demand their release. With little warning, a British inspector gave orders to fire on the crowd; eleven were killed and at least twenty wounded. Furor erupted in cities and towns around the country in the form of street demonstrations, incendiary articles in newspapers, and strikes. It was an unprecedented anti-imperialist explosion that considerably increased the visibility of the CCP and the Guomindang; the numbers of people who were Communist party members reportedly rose from one thousand in May to around ten thousand near the end of the year. In the aftermath, the CCP was able to organize the Shanghai General Labor Union during its leadership of a Shanghai protest strike in early June. The May Shanghai killings, however, were compounded by more bloodshed. On June 23, British troops in Canton opened fire on demonstrators protesting the May 30 deaths, killing fifty-two and wounding over one hundred more. These shootings galvanized the deepening sense of national peril; demonstrations of rage and revolutionary fervor swept the country. In Canton and Hong Kong anti-British outrage produced a sixteen-month strike and boycott of British goods.

The contingencies of Sun's death and the May 30 Movement put great pressure on the parties. The May 30 Movement especially increased the likelihood that the military phase of the revolution itself was near and that revolutionary goals (which might safely remain vague or substantially undiscussed if the revolution was still in the distant future) now had to be sharpened. But such honing of goals necessarily drove greater wedges between the factions and networks that already existed. The remainder of the year saw an increasingly malevolent polarization. As identities were politicized into right or left, conservative or radical, revolutionaries began drawing the sword. In August, Liao Zhongkai, so instrumental in the united front, was assassinated in Canton on his way to attend a meeting of the Central Committee; though the identity of the killers was never made certain, party members from the right wing were implicated in the killing. Liao's murder ironically had the effect of turning the revolution more to the left, since key right-wingers who had ties to those apparently involved in the killing left the province.

From November 1925 into January 1926, a group from the right wing met in the Western Hills section of Beijing before Sun's coffin to demand that Borodin be dismissed and that the bloc within, indeed any relationship with the Communist party, be dropped. But at the second Guomindang congress in January 1926, 60 percent of the 278 delegates were leftists or Communists, 23 percent might be termed centrists, and only 16 percent were rightists. In reaction to the domination of the congress by the left wing, and further indicative of the politicized polarization, in March the rightists held their own party congress in Shanghai, charting their own direction for the future. In the Guomindang itself within a year of Sun's death, politically things had fallen apart.

THE BEGINNINGS OF MASS MOBILIZATION

In the face of bitter competition in the united front, one thing that kept the CCP cooperating was the opportunity that the front gave them to work to mobilize workers and farmers under a Guomindang cover. Marx had believed that the motive force of revolution came from the urban working class (the proletariat). This was still the basic outlook and approach of the Communist Party, though since at least the Congress of the Toilers of the East, there had been the strong conviction that the peasantry would have to become important players in the revolutionary game. First the workers.

The first major effort of the Communists at organizing unions was a tragic disaster. In the fall of 1922, workers, demanding better pay and the recognition of unions, struck various railroads and mines in north China. Various associations approximating unions sprang up over the region. Communists, having formed labor clubs along the Beijing-Hankou railway, wanted to unite them into a national federation under the logic of "in numbers, there is strength." Representatives of these clubs met in the city of Zhengzhou in Henan province to finalize a constitution drafted earlier. Even though the warlord of the area, Wu Peifu, forbade the meeting, they came to the city and essentially found themselves locked out by troops and police. They reacted by calling a general strike on February 4, in effect shutting the railway down. Wu Peifu, angry at this action that was costing him fifty thousand dollars per day from railroad revenues, brutally broke the strike, killing thirty-five workers and injuring many more. Among laborers the Communist party received failing marks for its leadership.

The main geographical focus for sustained organizing of both workers and farmers was, as might be expected, in Canton where the party and army were headquartered, as well as its surrounding areas and its province of Guangdong. In the spring of 1924 Guomindang leader Liao Zhongkai, in an effort to begin to unite separate labor organizations in the city, had arranged a May Day rally to which all unions were invited and at which there was a large turnout. Sun Yat-sen's address pointed to tensions in the united front, as he tried to shift the CCP's emphasis from class struggle to the hurtful economic privileges of foreigners. Despite the turnout, when conferences were later slated to discuss larger unions, workers initially gave the cold shoulder to the initiative. Workers were embedded in their local organizations, could not see the advantages of being grouped in organizations they did not know, and were distrustful of organizers. Organizing unions was not easy work.

In May 1925 the CCP called into being in Canton a National Labor Congress in another attempt to unite unions into a single labor federation. They succeeded with the formation of the National General Labor Union. Though its membership nationwide had risen to 1.2 million by May 1926, the most important branch in Shanghai had to go underground by the fall of 1925. The unionization situation was not on the whole healthy. In the aftermath of the 1923 tragedy on the Beijing-Hankou railroad line, only one railway in northern China as of late 1926, the Beijing-Suiyuan line, had a union. The seamen's union operated only on ocean liners. The Anyuan miners union, where organizers like Communists Liu Shaoqi and Li Lisan had done earlier work, had been totally suppressed. Thus, the record of Communists in organizing labor unions during the years 1923 to 1926 was on the whole quite bleak.

The earliest attempt to organize farmers came in Zhejiang province in the fall of 1921. There local political activist Shen Dingyi, a member of both the CCP and the Guomindang, organized a rent-resistance movement which local authorities easily crushed. In 1922 and 1923 Socialist Youth Corps organizer Peng Pai successfully set up active farmers associations in several counties east of Canton along the South China Sea. The Guomindang took the first steps toward actively organizing farmers into associations in summer 1924, establishing a Farmers Bureau that could train special deputies to be sent to the countryside to investigate the conditions, propagandize about farmers associations, and form those associations. The CCP moved quickly to take over this effort when the Farmers Bureau was replaced by a more permanent Farmers' Movement Training Institute. It was also not easy work. Without connections, it was hard to be able to enter villages for the work of organizing; farmers were distrustful and uncooperative. The attitude of village elites was especially hostile, because farmers associations were their potential enemies; thus elites attacked potential organizers using local militia units or just plain local toughs.

Borodin believed that progress in the establishment of farmers associations would be the key to a successful military campaign north through northern Guangdong and Hunan provinces. The presence of large numbers of associations would facilitate the march of troops through the area by creating a more supportive population. Thus, he began to subsidize the Farmers' Movement Training Institute with about fifteen hundred dollars per month, to help pay salaries and the costs of printing pamphlets and posters. The first five classes at the training institute produced 545 men who were trained to do the work of rural organizing. They were sent to Guangdong and Hunan (targeted for military purposes), with a few dispatched to the provinces of Guangxi, Fujian, Anhui, Henan, and Shandong. Once established, the associations focused on reducing rents paid by tenant farmers to landlords and lowering various taxes that hit some localities very hard.

Even if associations were established (and it was sometimes over the dead bodies of local powerholders), problems with their functioning were continual. There was not much discipline to keep associations in line; they often did what they wanted and did not report to the center. Their local actions were dogged by poor local leadership and by members refusing to pay their local dues. Elites, who stood to suffer financially from the efforts of farmers associations, sometimes joined them in order to subvert them. The numbers of farmers brought into the associations increased dramatically in 1926, the beginning year of the military Northern Expedition as the Table below shows. But the huge increase in some areas meant large-scale fighting between farmers and landlords. In most cases, county governments usually sided with landlords.

The role of the Northern Expedition itself in the organizing that accompanied and followed it is remarkable. In June 1926, one month before the beginning of the Northern Expedition, 66 percent of all farmers in associations (647,766 out of 981,442) were in Guangdong province. The farmers organized in Hunan and Hubei during and immediately after

Membership in Farm Associations

Provinces	May 1925	June 1926	December 1926
Guangdong	210,000	647,766	n.a.
Henan	n.a.	270,000	n.a.
Hunan	n.a.	38,000	1,200,000
Hubei	n.a.	7,200	287,000

the military campaign soared. Two interesting sidelights of the organizing was (1) that the relatively large numbers in Henan province (where CCP membership also rose swiftly) represented work among the secret society Red Spears: whole Red Spear organizations were brought into associations at one time; and (2) that Mao Zedong served as principal of the Farmers' Movement Training Institute from May to October 1926.

THE EMERGENCE OF CHIANG KAI-SHEK AND
THE NORTHERN EXPEDITION

In the meantime Commandant Chiang at Whampoa was becoming more suspicious of the aims of the Communists. In his diary, criticisms of Russian advisers become more numerous in early 1926; he wrote, "I treat them with sincerity but they reciprocate with deceit. It is impossible to work with them."[7] Guomindang and the Russian advisers disagreed over when the military campaign to defeat the warlords should begin, with the Guomindang ready to go but the Russians urging caution. In early March Chiang became aware that there seemed to be developing an orchestrated campaign to get rid of him with Wang Jingwei most often named as the leader. In that context of considerable distrust and even paranoia on Chiang's part, on March 20, during the Shanghai congress of the rightist Guomindang, a gunboat commanded by a Communist officer mysteriously neared Whampoa island. Chiang, reportedly fearful that a coup against him was underway, undertook his own coup against Communists in the area. Although Borodin was not in Canton, Chiang arrested over thirty Russian advisors and declared martial law. As a result of these actions, Borodin later agreed to a substantial decrease of Communist power and prerogative in the party, allegedly because of pressures from Stalin, leader of the Soviet Union, who evidently did not perceive the growing dangers to the Communist effort. With the immediate presumed political threat under control, Chiang continued plans for the military campaign to unite the country. The episode did reveal Chiang's active suspicion about Communist intentions, although he still favored cooperation in the united front; it also pointed clearly to the intra-party feuding that repeatedly saw drawn swords.

In July 1926, at the head of his National Revolutionary Army (NRA), Chiang began the Northern Expedition, a two-pronged campaign to reach the Yangzi River and gain south and south central China for the Guomindang. The armies on the western route moved up through Hunan province which had been "softened" by the mass mobilization, most quickly reaching their goal. They were already fighting in the Yangzi area in late August, and they took the key metropolis of Wuhan on October 10. Units from this western route then turned to Jiangxi province, capturing its capital by November 8. Despite some serious problems— summer floods, cholera, and transport difficulties, the success of the NRA was remarkably rapid. There are a number of reasons. The nature of the Army itself was crucial. Trained solidly for two years and filled with national feeling, this new military force was strictly forbidden to prey upon the population by looting and raping, the usual way warlord armies operated. Russian advisors played key positive roles. Credit for the general strategy has been given to Russian general Blyukher; further, each corps and even some divisions had Russian advisors. Rivalries among four warlords in Hunan province also allowed the NRA to hasten their conquest. In addition, success seemed to breed success as the early military victories brought competent troops from Guizhou warlords into the Nationalist effort.

But perhaps the most important reason for the rapid military victory in the area, as I have stated, was the political work that preceded and accompanied the campaign. Mao Zedong, active in the mass mobilization in Hunan, his home province, reported that from January to June 1926 the organizational activity was underground, but that it became open with the arrival of the NRA.[8] In addition to the army's good treatment of the people and their property this activity helped to win over the local population to the Nationalist cause. Farmers association members served as scouts, guides, and porters for the army; people along the campaign route offered baked sweet potatoes and other foodstuffs and water to the troops; farmers assisted by harassing the enemy's rear.

Coinciding with and following the successful campaign was a frenzy of mass mobilization of farmers and laborers. Before the Northern Expedition in Hunan, Hubei, and Jiangxi, farmers association membership numbered less than 50,000, but Communist leaders claimed by the end of 1926 that there were 1.5 million organized farmers in 91 counties of Hunan and Hubei alone. Likely some exaggeration, this figure nevertheless points to a gigantic increase in farmers now politically mobilized, even if for some it was in name only. The organizers toned down the rhetoric of class struggle, focusing instead on lowering rents and taxes, reducing food prices, and opening grain storage facilities at time of shortages. But this agenda naturally stirred up the hostility of landlords who took retaliatory and of-

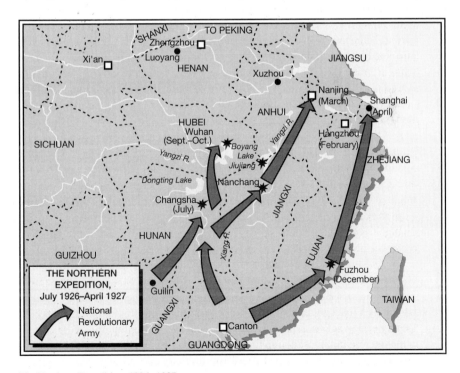

The Northern Expedition, 1926–1927

ten violent actions against tenants, responses that in turn elicited violent tenant reactions in an ever-escalating struggle between the classes. Violent outbursts also marked the spread of labor mobilization. In the wake of the military victory mostly Communist organizers formed dozens of unions. Agitation for higher wages and better working conditions led to a wave of strikes in November 1926. By spring 1927, an estimated 400,000 workers were in unions, 90,000 of them in industry. Participating with unions and the farmers associations in rambunctious public demonstrations were women and students, who took to the streets to denounce imperialism and to march for the coming of a new Chinese nation.

Such mass activity raised the crucial question of where the revolution was headed: should it take on social and economic goals as the Communists desired, or should it remain primarily political in its call for ousting warlords and imperialists? Increasingly in fall 1926 those two ideological stances became associated with particular places. Wuhan, to which Borodin, CCP members, and adherents to the Guomindang left had traveled, became the center of the mass mobilization and leftist activity. The city of Nanchang in Jiangxi province, which Chiang Kai-shek had made his military capital, also became the capital of sorts of the Guomindang right, an ideological position to which Chiang himself was rapidly heading. In late 1926, relations between Borodin and Chiang became icily hostile.

Borodin later pointed to the Chiang-inspired Central Committee decision in early January 1927—to keep party headquarters and governmental capital in Nanchang and away from the radicalism of Wuhan—as the first sign that a break with Chiang was inevitable. The impasse over the location of the capital caused the already tense relationship to deteriorate rapidly. It even strained relations between Comintern agents. When Voitinsky traveled to Nanchang to try to save the united front and work things out with Chiang, Borodin attacked him as an "anti-revolutionary compromiser," while Voitinsky charged that Borodin was "harming the Chinese revolution and the position of Soviet Russia."[9] In March 1927 Borodin and the Guomindang left named Wang Jingwei as Guomindang leader in direct challenge to Chiang. In response, Chiang struck out at Communists and leftists in several Jiangxi cities.

Disagreements over military strategy only made worse what had become an unbridgeable rift. In the spring of 1927, the immediate goal of the NRA was the capture of Shanghai, then controlled by warlord Sun Chuanfang. Powerful warlords—Feng Yuxiang and Zhang Zuolin—remained in the north, and there were concerns about whether they might ally themselves with Sun Chuanfang. Russian advisors advocated pushing north toward the city of Zhengzhou to link up with Feng Yuxiang's forces before heading toward Shanghai. Chiang, in contrast, was negotiating with Zhang Zuolin and preferred a move directly toward Shanghai.

As Chiang's forces made their way to Shanghai from the southwest, Communists and Guomindang leftists, who had organized and now led Shanghai labor unions, initiated an uprising against Sun Chuanfang. In late February as the NRA took the city of Hangzhou, workers staged a general strike to undercut Sun's power and thereby make NRA seizure of the city easier, action that might be likened to the "softening up" of the Hunan route by precampaign organizing. Though the six-day strike was broken brutally by Sun's men (swordsmen were sent into the streets to perform summary executions), it politically mobilized hundreds of thousands of workers and revealed the strength of Communist power. It also increased the conviction among Shanghai businessmen and adherents of the Guomindang right wing that the Communists had to be stopped. Then on March 21, as the NRA was nearing the southern edge of the city, the Communist-led General Labor Union called another general strike, involving over 600,000 workers: heavy fighting erupted as workers cut electrical and telephone lines and occupied railway and police stations. The workers' strategy seemed to be not only to make the NRA takeover easier but also to seize and hold Chinese areas of the city. The commander of the NRA, Bai Chongxi, ended the strike when he took the city on March 24.

Chiang, already suspicious and worried over the import of the actions of leftists in Wuhan, was now faced with a potentially explosive situation of leftist and labor power in Shanghai. The General Labor Union was attempting to turn the situation against the imperialists by demonstrating for the seizure of the city's foreign concession areas, action that would most certainly have brought some sort of strong Western response. Western nerves were already on edge, for on March 24, the American, British, and Japanese consulates in Nanjing had been looted, and there had been attacks on foreigners resulting in at least six deaths. After discussions with city business elites, Guomindang veterans who still had ties to the Left wing of the party, and the underworld Green Gang, with whom he had had ties since the 1910s, Chiang moved to attack those who had made it easier for him to seize the city.

On the night of April 11 the Communist head of the General Labor Union was invited for dinner at the home of Green Gang leader Du Yuesheng; there he was murdered. Early the next morning, Green Gang members and forces loyal to Chiang attacked all union headquarters; protests about these attacks led to NRA soldiers opening fire on civilians. In this Red Purge hundreds were mowed down by machine guns in the bloody attacks; survivors described how, on that rainy day, the streets ran with blood. An estimated five thousand were killed; thousands more fled the city in panic. The Shanghai slaughter, for some, came to signify Chiang's treachery—turning brutally on those who had helped him take the city. This tragedy was the beginning of what from the perspective of the left is called the White Terror, an effort to destroy the power of the left and especially the Communists who had attained so much power through their "bloc within" party membership. The rationale of Chiang and the Guomindang conservatives was set forth right after the events in Shanghai.

> [S]ince the beginning of the Northern Expedition, while members of the Guomindang have been laboring faithfully either on the field of battle or elsewhere, and while the militarists of the country have been gradually eliminated, the Communists, taking advantage of our success, have seized important cities as their centers for propaganda and usurped the power of the Party. . . . For the welfare of the Revolution as well as that of the Guomindang, we are forced to adopt this strong measure to purge the Party of all undesirable elements.[10]

The terror spread over the country in almost all the major cities and continued well into 1928. In Zhejiang province alone almost one thousand people were executed in April 1927; though the numbers of victims dropped during the summer, another wave of terror swept the province late in the year and into the next. The revolution was destroying its own; millions of young idealistic Chinese were losing their heads. The battle over ideology and the direction of the Chinese revolution was being fought with executioners' weapons.

The purge and its disarray forced choices on the Communists and the Guomindang left in Wuhan. Stalin argued that the purge had clarified the China situation by having Chiang show his true colors. Almost as if he were blindfolded to what was happening, he continued to call for the Communists to work with the Guomindang left and to strike out at those allied with Chiang. Given the political realities of the purge, CCP General Secretary Chen Duxiu cynically said that these orders were "like taking a bath in a toilet."[11] For its part, the left began to doubt the intentions of the Communists especially after one agent showed leftist leaders one of Stalin's telegrams. When these leftists began discussions with Chiang early in the summer, the Communist effort was doomed. Russian advisors and some of Borodin's staff began to leave in late June. The final split between the CCP and left GMD came in mid-July. Borodin himself, after four years of substantial power on the Chinese scene, left at the end of July. Hated by Chiang, who had put a price on his head, Borodin did not dare go down the Yangzi toward Nanjing and Shanghai; he went overland to the north and then across the Gobi Desert to the Soviet Union. He would end up dying as a political prisoner in one of Stalin's Siberian gulags in 1948.

The last months of 1927 saw several Communist efforts to rise up and establish CCP-led regimes, but they were all short-lived and ineffective. The Nanchang (Jiangxi) uprising began on August 1 (celebrated today as the founding of the Red Army). It was initially a quick success militarily with the seizure of the city. But then the new "regime" seemed not to know what to do next. Its armies marched south toward Guangdong in devastatingly oppressive heat and quickly became plagued by desertion and disease; equipment was lost; the populace offered no support; and the whole effort simply disintegrated. There were several so-called Autumn Harvest Uprisings slated to begin on September 10 in Hunan and Hubei. The Hubei uprising collapsed almost as soon as it began. Mao Zedong was in charge of the Hunan uprising where the participants were an army of farmers, miners, soldiers, and bandits. But the effort petered out when he could get only about two thousand "troops" to attack the city of Changsha and when even these began fighting among themselves. Mao prevailed upon many of his "soldiers" to travel with him to the famous bandit lair and stronghold on Jinggangshan on the Hunan-Jiangxi border. In all these late summer-early fall uprisings, there were simply insufficient planning, leadership, and manpower.

By far the most tragic of the Communist attempts to stage rebellions during the White Terror was the "Canton commune," founded by Communists and workers in that southern city. The decision to stage the uprising was made by the Communist provincial committee who planned to recruit about 2000 workers and some Communist cadets from Whampoa; the difficulty with the plans was their shortage of arms. Then the date of the uprising had to be moved up when police found the rebels' cache of bombs. The effort started out fairly effectively with the seizure of most police stations, the railroad station, telegraph and post offices, government offices, and Guomindang headquarters. There was much looting and burning of property (police later reported that 900 buildings had been gutted). But there was not much popular support: only about 3000 workers out of an estimated 290,000 in the city area participated. Between 3000 and 4000 were killed in the two-day Canton commune, many by execution squads that roamed the streets, often nabbing completely innocent people in an "orgy of revenge." Historians often point to this disaster as the low point of Communist fortunes; the CCP itself has called it the "heroic battle in the retreat of a revolutionary high tide."[12] It was the last CCP urban uprising for the next twenty years.

Two other noteworthy casualties in 1927 were Li Dazhao and Chen Duxiu, the cofounders of the Chinese Communist Party. On April 6 Beijing city police raided a building in the Soviet embassy compound on a tip that Chinese Communists were using it to plan an uprising. The thirty-six Chinese found there were arrested; among them was Li, who had taken residence there in December 1926 when the rabidly anti-Communist warlord Zhang Zuolin seized the capital. Despite the appeals of prominent north Chinese citizens, he was executed by strangling at the age of thirty-eight. In the summer of 1927, Chen was deposed as secretary-general of the CCP by Comintern agents—ultimately by Stalin—and blamed for everything that had happened to it. He was guilty, they declared, of "opportunism," though he had only been following their orders. He was formally expelled from the party in 1930. In 1932 he was arrested by Chiang's Nationalist government, tried and sentenced to fifteen years in prison. He was paroled at the start of the war with Japan in 1937, and he died in obscurity in a small town in Sichuan province in 1942.

By August 1928, Chiang and the NRA reached Beijing. The Nationalist Revolution had grown out of the uneasy united front collaboration of the two Leninist-style parties, the Chinese Communist Party and the Guomindang or Nationalist Party. After Sun's death and the May Thirtieth movement political positions (and therefore, identities) had tended to become more inflexible. Political polarization between left and right inhibited revolutionary

Summary execution, defeat of the Canton Commune, December 1927

progress as CCP and Guomindang Left and Right tended to turn in on themselves, drawing swords to strike out against their perceived foes and, they would have said, the foes of revolution. Now in the success of the Northern Expedition the CCP was vanquished, seemingly dead after a short life of six years, one of its founders dead, the other deposed. Stalin's policy of trying to "call the shots" from Moscow had been a tragic mistake; but Communists and especially Stalin had difficulty accepting personal responsibility for mistakes. Chinese Communist history is thus littered with scapegoats. Yet in many ways the important role of Russian aid and advisors was a harbinger of other foreign aid that would come to China later, from the United States in the 1940s and the Soviet Union again in the 1950s. The Communist party would rise again, but its leaders would be of a different sort than the May Fourth intellectuals who had formed and given life to the party in this, its first incarnation.

Finally, at least on the map, China was unified for the first time since the death of Yuan Shikai had given birth to the warlords. The Nationalist Revolution had been the springboard for Chiang Kai-shek to rise to power: now he was faced with the immense tasks of reconstruction after years of war and of the construction of a new viable Chinese state.

Notes

[1] C. Martin Wilbur and Julie Lien-ying How, *Missionaries of Revolution* (Cambridge: Harvard University Press, 1989), p. 31.

[2] Ibid., p. 92.

[3] Sun Yat-sen, "The Three Principles of the People," in Dun J. Li, *The Road to Communism: China since 1912* (New York: Van Nostrand Reinhold, 1969), p. 118. The quotations below from the same source.

[4] Quoted in Cheng and Lestz with Spence, Eds., pp. 253–254.

[5] Quoted in Wilbur and How, p. 219.

[6] Quoted in Wilbur and How, p. 124.

[7] Ibid., p. 250.

[8] Mao Zedong, "Report on an Investigation of the Peasant Movement in Hunan" in *Selected Readings from the Works of Mao Tsetung* (Beijing: Foreign Languages Press, 1971), pp. 24–25.

[9] Wilbur and Howe, p. 387.

[10] Quoted in Cheng and Lestz with Spence, Eds., p. 264.

[11] Quoted in C. Martin Wilbur, *The Nationalist Revolution in China, 1923–1928* (Cambridge: Harvard University Press, 1983), p. 131.

[12] Boorman, *Biographical Dictionary of Republican China,* Vol. 1, p. 112.

11

Revolution in Retreat:
The Nanjing Decade

After the Northern Expedition, Wen Yiduo became professor of English and American literature at Nanjing University. Having studied at the Art Institute of Chicago and Colorado College, he had developed ambivalent views about the West. But his poetry also revealed considerable ambiguity about China. One of his most famous poems, "Dead Water," set forth one vision of China at the opening of what has become known as the Nanjing Decade (1928–1937), when the Chinese capital was located in Nanjing.

> Here is a ditch of hopelessly dead water.
> No breeze can raise a single ripple on it.
> Might as well throw in rusty metal scraps
> or even pour left-over food and soup in it.
>
> Perhaps the green on copper will become emeralds.
> Perhaps on tin cans peach blossoms will bloom.
> Then, let grease weave a layer of silky gauze,
> and germs brew patches of colorful spume.
>
> Let the dead water ferment into jade wine
> covered with floating pearls of white scum.
> Small pearls chuckle and become big pearls,
> only to burst as gnats come to steal this rum.
>
> And so this ditch of hopelessly dead water
> may still claim a touch of something bright.

And if the frogs cannot bear the silence—
the dead water will croak its song of delight.

Here is a ditch of hopelessly dead water—
a region where beauty can never reside.
Might as well let the devil cultivate it—
and see what sort of world it can provide.[1]

Wen could describe a China left for dead after twelve years of warlord and revolutionary destruction as "hopelessly dead water"—littered with scraps of rusty metal, scum, and germs. Cleaning up the mess—the gargantuan task of reconstruction and transformation—might take a superhuman (here Wen says "the devil"), and it is possible that beauty can never again reside there; but there is at least the element of hope that Wen shared with many Chinese that China could be transformed from dead water to the better day of emeralds, jade wine, and songs of delight.

CHIANG KAI-SHEK

The man upon whom the task fell was Chiang Kai-shek. He had been tried in the arena of military leadership, warlord politics, and factional party struggle and emerged at the top. Now the question was, could he lead the country on to construct a modern nation state that could keep at bay foreign threats and enemies as it bettered the lives of its own citizens. Chiang was a cold, aloof, and distant man. He was determined, even single-minded, intolerant, and afflicted with a fierce temper. As one historian suggested, "People did not love Chiang Kai-shek, but they were impressed by him."[2] He saw himself as selfless and moral. As time passed he came to identify himself more and more with China and to see anyone who opposed him as betraying China in clearly immoral fashion. There could, in short, be no loyal opposition. In terms of his rule, such qualities meant that he did not know how to delegate, that he often paid little attention to chains of command, and, perhaps the worst tendency of a military figure, that he thought force could triumph over every obstruction.

In December 1927 Chiang married Soong Meiling, daughter of a Chinese businessman who had been a longtime financial supporter of Sun Yat-sen. Indeed, Meiling's next older sister had married Sun, and her oldest sister was married to financier H. H. Kung, soon to become an important player in Chiang's government. Moreover, the three sisters' brother T. V. Soong would also become an important government figure. The marriages of two Soong sisters to the key leaders of the Guomindang, Sun and Chiang, and the close-knit family group at the top of the government were quite remarkable. Soong Meiling was a good match for Chiang. A graduate of Wellesley College, she spoke English fluently. She was attractive and urbane; and she was able to some degree to soften or, at the least, to conceal some of Chiang's hard edges.

The marriage was controversial because Chiang was still married to his first wife; his son by that marriage, Chiang Ching-kuo (Jiang Jingguo) was a student in Moscow at the time of the wedding. To get approval for the marriage, especially since the Soong family was Christian, Chiang had to promise that he would "investigate Christianity." Following that pledge, he was baptized in Shanghai in October 1930. "Soong Meiling stood beside her husband at that ceremony and repeated vows with him to dramatize their joint dedication to Christian principles and to the rejuvenation of China."[3]

It could be said that Chiang's power lay in three positions that he held. As head of state (his specific title was chair of the State Council), he had the power to set domestic policy and to deal with foreign powers. As chair of the party's Central Executive Committee, he controlled the organ that, in line with the thought of Sun Yat-sen, was to serve as tutor for the people until they eventually could move into a full-fledged republic. Significantly, the length of this period of "party tutelage" was not spelled out. As commander-in-chief of the party army, he held military power as his most important resource. Holding these three posts made Chiang look supreme, but as time went on, it was the man himself who seemed to emerge supreme as the institutions of party and state shrank before his apparent indispensability. But in the beginning, he looked anything but indispensable.

MILITARY POWER, PARTY FACTIONALISM, AND RESIDUAL WARLORDISM

The influence of the military in Chinese politics and society had seemingly grown exponentially since the 1911 revolution. While the army at the end of the Qing had numbered about 400,000, by 1922, there were 1,200,000 men under arms; by 1929 that number had shot up to 2,000,000. In 1929 over half of the 630,000 Guomindang party members were soldiers; even more crucial, in terms of party rule, in 1935, 43 percent of the Central Executive Committee were soldiers. On the provincial leadership level during the Nanjing decade, 25 of the 33 men who served as provincial chairs were generals. Revealing Chiang's commitment to the military was the fact that during the period fully 66.7 percent of national government expenditures were funneled to the military and to payment on debts.

While the Northern Expedition had technically united the country and ended the warlord scourge, "residual warlordism" remained a problem, a dangerous political and military challenge. That danger was compounded by the reality that Chiang did not have really firm control of the party apparatus until near the end of the Nanjing decade. Before surveying the civil wars that continued to rake across China in the 1920s and 1930s, it is important to understand the party challenges Chiang faced. When he had risen to power, Chiang had had to face the party's left-wing challenge posed by the government at Wuhan led by Wang Jingwei. Indeed, in late 1927 to mid-1928, leftists controlled many provincial and local regimes. In Zhejiang, for example, the government sponsored a rent-reduction campaign; while in Jiangsu, in the name of eliminating superstitions, temples were confiscated and turned into welfare centers.

While Wang was in Europe in 1928–1929, others of the left, specifically journalist and former Communist Chen Gongbo, carried on the fight for their program that continued to call for mass organizations that could give the new regime a popular base. In late 1928 Chen founded the Society of Comrades for Guomindang Reorganization. It and its leftist members came to be called the Reorganizationist Clique, with its own constitution, its own party headquarters in Shanghai, and branches around the country. Its formation came at a time when Chiang and the party were cracking down on local and provincial leftist power. The general approach of ridding the party of "undesirables" was to institute party re-registration during which the unwanted simply would not be allowed to register as party members. But violence was also a tactic to get rid of perceived threats to Chiang's party control: the assassination of maverick Zhejiang party leader Shen Dingyi in August 1928 is only one example. Chiang played his trump card against the left at the party's third congress in March 1929, when he changed the rules to prevent a strong presence of the left by appointing 75 percent of the delegates. At the congress, left-wing leaders were expelled from the party, some (like Chen Gongbo) for "forever" and others for a specified number of years; because of his stature, Wang Jingwei was simply reprimanded for "straddling parties." Chiang's efforts to defeat the left could weaken and humble the once-strong faction, but as events would show the left would not disappear.

Warlords were still around, waiting in the wings for opportunities, because Chiang had co-opted them into the Northern Expeditionary armies instead of defeating them. During the Northern Expedition, the important warlords had been named heads of branch political councils as a way of gaining their support. Chiang and his advisers had determined that these had to be abolished and that there had to be a demobilization of the bloated armies. Chiang's own army had to be reduced from its 240,000 man size, for the cost of supplying it and keeping it in the field was 60 million yuan more than Chiang's government revenues. But a demobilization meeting of the chief warlords that Chiang called in early 1929 was a fiasco. When Chiang appeared to be asking sacrifice for the militarists but not so much for himself, the conference disintegrated and in effect led to a series of costly civil wars. These were no small affairs. Since there were so many similarities to the mammoth warlord wars of the early and mid-1920s, one can legitimately ask whether the warlord period was over, and, alternatively, whether, in fact, during this stage of his career, Chiang Kai-shek was simply the biggest (and ultimately, the last) warlord.

The very first war in this new series of struggles began the month (March 1929) that Chiang set for abolishing the branch political councils. What follows is a catalogue-like descriptive outline of these wars, set down in this fashion to underline the ongoing nature of the challenges Chiang faced. Added also are the five military campaigns Chiang launched against a revived Communist threat in southeastern China and the campaign against the Japanese in Manchuria—both of these will be discussed at length in the two succeeding chapters. As you read this list, do not become concerned about remembering the complex details; the important point is to give you some understanding of the instability, even chaos, that occupied the attention of the Nanjing government; of the challenges to Chiang from a wide array of enemies; and of the fragility with which Chiang held power.

(1.) March to May 1929—Militarists of the Guangxi clique (in southern China) rebelled against Chiang's control. With 230,000 men they seemed by themselves a formidable force. But there were rumors that they were going to ally with northern warlord Feng Yuxiang. Chiang, using the typical warlord ploy of the "silver bullet," bought Feng off with a bribe of two million yuan and a promise that Feng could take charge of Shandong province. Chiang won the war in two months.

(2.) May 1929—When Chiang went back on his Shandong promise to Feng, Feng challenged Chiang. Chiang seemed the master warlord tactician, offering key outfits in Feng's army massive silver bullets. Over 100,000 of Feng's army defected to Chiang. The war was thus mercifully short.

(3.) October to November 1929—Feng's army fought Chiang's forces in Henan province.

(4.) February to September 1930—Longtime master strategist, warlord Yan Xishan announced that he would side with Feng against Chiang in a Northern Coalition. Not only did the Guangxi clique say that it would coordinate its activities with this coalition, but two Guomindang factions, Wang's Reorganizationist clique and the Western Hills faction supported this serious challenge. Fighting raged from May into September, with a new national government formed at Beiping (the new name, "northern peace," given to the city of Beijing or "northern capital" when Nanjing became the capital) with Yan as head of state. The final success of this campaign against Chiang would have been determined by whether the Manchurian warlord Zhang Xueliang would join the coalition. Continuing the brilliance of his silver bullet campaign, Chiang bought Zhang off with a ten million yuan bribe. The coalition thus failed. Zhang, emboldened, immediately led 100,000 of his men into north China to dominate that region.

(5.) December 1930—First "Extermination" Campaign against a revived Communist movement in Jiangxi province failed.

(6.) February 1931 to January 1932—Almost a year of cold war that threatened to break out into a hot war. It began with Chiang's arrest of Hu Hanmin, head of the main legislative body in the government. In support of Hu, militarists in Guangxi and Guangdong, backed by Wang Jingwei, the Western Hills group and others, established a breakaway government in Canton on June 1. A civil war would likely have broken out if Japanese aggression in Manchuria had not exploded into a war. As it was, Chiang resigned his posts, and a new government under Sun Yat-sen's son Sun Fo lasted for twenty-five days in January 1932 before Chiang returned to power.

(7.) May to June 1931—Second "Extermination" Campaign against the Jiangxi Communists failed.

(8.) September to December 1931—Manchurian campaign against Japanese aggressors.

(9.) July to October 1931—Third "Extermination" Campaign against the Communists failed.

(10.) January to March 1932—Campaign in the Shanghai metropolitan region against the Japanese invasion.

(11.) January to March 1933—Fourth "Extermination" Campaign against the Communists failed.

(12.) March 1933—Japan seized the Inner Mongolian province of Rehe

(13.) August 1933—Japan took the eastern part of the Inner Mongolian province of Chahar.

(14.) October 1933 to October 1934—Fifth "Extermination" Campaign against the Communists succeeded.

Indeed, this is an appalling list. It shows that from October 1928 when Chiang first became head of state until the ending of the successful campaign against the Communists in October 1934, Chiang's forces were involved in actual warfare or on the brink of potential warfare for forty-five of the seventy-two months—roughly 62.5 percent of the time. Further, at some times as in 1931, Chiang faced up to three struggles concurrently. In trying to understand the Nanjing decade and Chiang's role in it, this context of hot war and cold war upon which Chiang had to focus is extraordinarily important. Even though some of the internecine warfare may have been to some degree his responsibility, its reality meant that the needed tasks of transforming the dead water, of reconstructing Chinese society had to wait for another day.

SECRETS OF CHIANG'S ABILITY TO RETAIN POWER

Military Sources

Given the immense political and military opposition he had to face and the obstacles he had to overcome, it is more than just a minor miracle that Chiang was able to keep the reins of power. What were his sources of power? Most basic was that he was a military man at a time when military force was the sole arbiter of power. He was also a master of warlord politics, flexibly linking himself to different factions at different times and freely using silver bullets to blast apart coalitions of warlords. In practical terms, the teacher-student bonds he built up at the Whampoa Military Academy were crucial; he had served as hands-on commandant for four Whampoa classes that produced about five thousand soldiers—all of whom shared those special master-disciple *guanxi* or connections. Chiang would come to depend on the Whampoa clique in many ways, as we will see.

The active core of the clique was known as the Blue Shirts, an organization formed at the prompting of young officers upset about the state of the nation. Concerns focused on ills of the party and the state. They argued that the party which had been the vehicle of revolution "now seem[ed] to have dissipated the hopes of the masses."[4] Indeed, victory in the Northern Expedition had swelled party ranks from 150,000 in 1926 to 630,000 in 1929, with a third of those members under twenty-five years old—people without much historical memory of major revolutionary changes: They would have been only seven or eight at the time of the 1911 revolution and about fifteen at the time of the May Fourth Incident. Party victory understandably attracted thousand of opportunists, ready to seize whatever prize they might. Chiang's Chief of Staff, He Yingqin, already in early 1928, had worried about what a huge influx of party population might do to the party: "Party headquarters at all levels are concerned only about the quantity, and pay no attention to the quality [of the new members]. The spirit of the party becomes more rotten by the day."[5]

Another complaint, of similar nature, focused on the governmental bureaucracy, men charged with executing crucial policies. Many were bureaucrats who had served old-style warlord regimes and who now crowded into Nanjing to grab up the spoils of victory—new official posts. Though some may have been motivated by a desire to serve, most seemed to be mainly concerned with making money and seeking power. The upshot was an administration that featured two of the three bête-noires of sound and effective government—an ineffectual and unresponsive bureaucracy and uncontrolled open corruption. (The third bête-noire, political repression, will appear momentarily.)

The problems with bureaucracy were certainly known in China prior to this regime, but bureaucratic delay and obstacles seem to have become even more egregious. One observer noted that "a document arriving at a provincial government office was transmitted through thirty-seven steps, each of which consumed from a few hours to a few days . . . A reply after a half year's time was a surprise to no one. Not a few documents perished on their long and dreary journey, buried alive in someone's desk drawer. . . ."[6] As for corruption, it was omnipresent. In 1935 author Lin Yutang aptly noted that "The commonest conjugation in Chinese grammar is that of the verb 'to squeeze' [to be corrupt]: '*I squeeze, you squeeze, he squeezes, we squeeze, you squeeze, they squeeze.*' It is a regular verb."[7] There was a penetrating sense in many circles that the existing structures were no longer revolutionary. Indeed, Chiang himself admitted in 1932: "The Chinese revolution has failed." His hope was "to restore the revolutionary spirit that the [party] had in 1924."[8] In that vein, Chiang welcomed the establishment of the Blue Shirts.

The Blue Shirts saw fascism as the way to restore China. Many had become familiar with German Nazism from contact with the German military advisory mission that Chiang brought to China to manage and advise on military academy education. In addition, hundreds of Chinese soldiers went to Germany and Italy to study military science. Hitler's rise seemed to signal to many that fascism was in the vanguard of historical progress. Chiang himself argued, "Can fascism save China? We answer: yes. Fascism is now what China most needs . . . fascism is a wonderful medicine exactly suited to China, and the only spirit that can save it."[9] In a very real way, the Blue Shirts were the political institutional reaction against the May Fourth Movement. Chiang again made the point: "In the last several decades we have in vain become drunk with democracy and the advocacy of free thought. And what has been the result? We have fallen into a chaotic and irretrievable situation."[10] The remedy: fascism with its emphasis on the "total exaltation of the nation," the "total abnegation of the individual," and "obedience to the supreme leader."

The Blue Shirts were a dominant force in many of Chiang's programs. They were in charge of political training in the army, government, and schools; they were involved in public security operations; they were active in setting up people's militia units. There were in addition two major efforts in which the Blue Shirts were intimately involved. One was "Special Services," the government organ charged with intelligence-gathering and responses to perceived enemies of state. Headed by notorious Dai Li, the Military Commission's Bureau of Investigation and Statistics became infamous for its active involvement in spying, sabotage, kidnapping, assassination, and terror. Dai was something of a honorary member of the Whampoa clique since he never graduated from the academy but was held in such esteem by Chiang that he received a diploma "through special dispensation." A measure of the importance of Dai's work for the regime and of the increasing political repression—the third bête-noire of sound and effective government—was the ballooning size of Dai's Bureau. In 1932, when it began, it had 145 operatives; three years later, it had over 1700; and at the end of World War II there were between 40,000 and 50,000. The Blue Shirts themselves were disbanded in 1938, but they quickly reappeared under a new name, the Three People's Principles Youth Corps.

A second major effort of the Blue Shirts was in Chiang's New Life Movement, a campaign that began in 1934 in order to spread the fascist spirit and challenge the anti-traditionalism of the May Fourth period. Chiang apparently hoped that New Life's ideological appeal to a resuscitated Confucianism might prove a potent alternative to Communism. It is hard to imagine how Chiang could have ever seriously believed that appeals to a "sloganized Confucianism"—calling for the upholding of "propriety, justice, honesty, and sense of self-respect"—would have been able to catch the attention of and engage most Chinese. Chiang also restored Confucianism as a state religion and made Confucius's birthday a national holiday.

The vagueness of the Confucian virtues for any meaning for day-to-day life was clarified somewhat by the issuance of ninety-five rules by which people were to live their lives, rules like

> Everyone should keep himself clean all the time.
>
> Do not spit in the streets.
>
> Shoes should be worn correctly.
>
> Walk and sit with correct posture.
>
> Do not write on walls.
>
> Say good morning to others every morning.
>
> Do not make noise while eating and drinking.
>
> Do not urinate as you please.
>
> Do not laugh while others have funerals.
>
> Keep to the left when walking on the street.

To be sure, some of these things—maybe all—were not bad; but, given the seriousness of China's problems, these slogans, maybe appropriate for a military academy, were laughable. But Chiang contended, perhaps not too compellingly, that they were central to the New Life Movement. He claimed, "If we are to have a new life that accords with ['propriety, justice, honesty, and sense of self-respect'], then we must start by not spitting heedlessly. If we are to restore the nation and gain revenge for our humiliations, then we need not talk about guns and cannon, but must first talk about washing our faces in cold water."[11] Chiang's vision of the movement's goals showed all how far he had traveled on the road to fascism. The New Life Movement

> is to thoroughly militarize the lives of the citizens of the entire nation so that they will cultivate courage and swiftness, the endurance of suffering and a tolerance for hard work, and especially the habit and ability of unified action, so that they will at any time sacrifice for the nation.[12]

Financial Base

Another important reason for Chiang's ability to dominate potential rivals was his superior financial base in Shanghai. During the 1910s, when he worked as a stockbroker in that city,

Mass wedding ceremony during the New Life Movement at which loyalty to the Guomindang and legacy of Sun Yat-sen was pledged

he developed very close ties with bankers and financiers, on one hand, and with the underworld Green Gang, on the other. For his putting down the labor unrest in his bloody April 12, 1927 coup, he received 3 million yuan from Shanghai business interests; their contributions continued. Since Chiang's military expenses were at least 20 million yuan each month and since his Shanghai supporters were not committed enough to come up with the money voluntarily, Chiang had to resort to forced contributions. His agents, for example, demanded 500,000 yuan from the Nanyang Tobacco Company and 250,000 yuan from the Sincere Company Department Store. When businesses and industries refused, they were threatened, faced extortion, or their leaders were abducted. A Western observer noted that "[w]ealthy Chinese would be arrested in their homes or mysteriously disappear from the streets. . . . Under no previous regime in modern times had Shanghai known such a reign of terror."[13] Many of the "legitimate" taxes also reached government coffers through Shanghai: during the decade taxes on trade and industry produced up to 85 percent of total revenue.

Political Skills and Authoritarianism

We have already seen how skilled Chiang was in navigating the tricky and dangerous waters of warlord politics. Those same skills put him in good stead with the equally tricky factional politics in the Guomindang. Not only were there the Reorganizationists, the Western Hills faction, and the Whampoa clique, but two other factions maintained substantial power.

The CC (for Central Club) clique was built by two brothers, Chen Guofu and Chen Lifu, who were nephews of 1911 revolutionary Chen Qimei, a close associate of Chiang. The government bureaucracy was their base; they controlled many bureaucratic organs and agencies, youth organs, and labor unions. In contrast, the power of the Political Study clique lay not in positions but in its relationship to Chiang. Its two central members were sworn brothers of Chiang, and as a result, this clique could wield great power. It stressed "technical expertise and bureaucratic professionalism." Tensions between cliques were great, for there was continual jockeying for power among them. As examples, the Blue Shirts thought all the civilian cliques were corrupt; they especially opposed the CC clique for many of the functions performed by both cliques overlapped; the CC clique, in turn, was especially resentful of the Political Study clique because of its close relationship with Chiang.

By the middle of the 1930s, Chiang had become the indispensable man while both party and government became increasingly enfeebled. There were the five branches of government envisioned by Sun Yat-sen: the Executive Yuan, the most powerful, made up of ten ministries and overseeing the bureaucracy; the Legislative Yuan, a law-making body, but not in the mode of a Western-style parliamentary body; the Judicial Yuan, the highest judicial body; the Control Yuan, serving as censorate; and the Examination Yuan, dealing with civil service examinations. But as a measure of the languishing of government, only 8 to 13 percent of the budget in the 1930s went toward the functions of the bureaucracy. Chiang's hands were everywhere; as one commentator put it, "In terms of authority, he was the head of everything."[14]

With such a centralized structure the relationship between the center at Nanjing and localities across the country was problematical. This relationship was complicated both by elements of culture and recent history. With cultural emphasis on family, personal networks, native place, and local gods, the natural focus of Chinese civilization was still on the local. But in addition, historical developments since the late Qing had only enhanced the power of the locality and its elites. The weakened central regime during the late nineteenth century and the politically and socially fragmented period between 1911 and 1927 had given local elites in institutions like self-government bodies and Chambers of Commerce increasingly important political roles in their communities. The important thing is that they had been undirected and undeterred by the central government (when it even existed).

Chiang shared the view of Yuan Shikai, that considerable local autonomy and local elite initiative were not conducive to rapid nation-building and could potentially lead to further social and political fragmentation. Thus, Nanjing was determined to penetrate society more deeply than the imperial state had done. In the imperial state, the lowest level of government penetration, that is, where an official in the state bureaucracy served in official capacity, had been the county. Townships which made up counties had local leaders. Under Chiang's government, county was once again the lowest level where a state official ruled. But beneath the county, the Center established a system of wards composed of townships, which were made up, in turn, of rural villages and urban neighborhoods. The heads of each of these units were appointed by the magistrate in bureaucratic fashion, not chosen by the people in the units. The whole structure was undergirded by the traditional *baojia* system of group mutual surveillance in which groups of families were made responsible for the actions of others in their group. Despite numerous tinkering with local level administration and despite claims that the ward-township-village-neighborhood apparatus could serve as the framework for democracy, this regime's vision of nation-building remained top-down.

Chiang's authoritarianism is evident not only in his public roles but even more so in his reaction to dissent. Individual dissenters often had unwanted appointments with Dai Li's assassins. In 1933 Yang Quan, secretary-general of Academia Sinica, China's highest study and research organization supported and controlled by the government, was ambushed. The reason came from the other hat that Yang wore, as secretary general of the China League for Civil Rights, a role that brought him in conflict with Chiang's policies. In reaction to the killing, Cai Yuanpei, the former chancellor of Beijing University during the May Fourth period and now president of Academia Sinica, resigned all his posts and left China for Hong Kong, but not before he denounced Chiang's government publicly. In 1934, Shi Liangcai, Shanghai civic leader and editor of the important newspaper the *Shenbao* was gunned down; he had been critical of Chiang's policy toward Japanese aggression.

If the dissenters were plural, as in students, Chiang did not send assassins but police. There was enough distrust of the possibility of student disruptions that in 1930 all campus non-academic organizations were forbidden unless they were tightly controlled by the Guomindang. Beginning in 1931 students began to protest Chiang's acquiescence to Japanese seizure of territory and non-stop demands. In the repression that followed, some students were killed. But Chiang generally reacted to student demonstrations by sending forces in pre-dawn raids on student dormitories and making arrests and/or forcing the expulsion of students from the schools. Political repression became Chiang's seemingly inevitable reaction to any challenge. Journalists were frequently arrested and newspapers and magazines censored. Already in 1930 a Western newspaper reported that "[c]ontrasted with the enthusiasm of less than eighteen months ago, the sense of hopelessness . . . among all Chinese today is perhaps the worst feature of all."[15]

CHIANG'S RECORD

Given the gigantic tasks of reconstruction that China faced, the large numbers of political and military enemies that continued to dog Chiang, and the limitations, miscalculations, and failures of his government, any progress toward realizing the establishment of a modern nation state during the Nanjing decade may seem remarkable. There were, however, positive aspects to Chiang's record, though each accomplishment was tinged with a downside.

Chiang had risen to power under the banner of nationalism, the goals of his revolution having been, on the one hand, to eliminate warlords and unite the nation and, on the other, to expel the imperialists and liberate the nation. With his victory against the warlords, Chiang thus had the opportunity to begin to negotiate the end of the almost century-old unequal treaty system. One of the most continually irritating aspects of China's semicolonial position under the system was its loss of ability to set and collect its own tariffs. This meant that it could not protect its own nascent industry by raising rates to keep out cheaper Western-made products. Between July 1928 and May 1929, China successfully negotiated its tariff autonomy with seven major powers and gained control of the Maritime Customs Service. Through negotiations it was also able by the 1931 to reduce the number of foreign concessions from thirty-three to thirteen. Because it set forth new law codes (as demanded by the West), it was able to begin to negotiate the issue of extraterritoriality for the first time. The downside of these negotiations was that it was not until 1943 when extraterritoriality was finally abolished, and then not so much because of negotiations but as a gesture from the United States and Great Britain to a wartime ally.

Despite the continued political and military challenges, Chiang was able to stop the warlord period trend toward territorial fragmentation. But it was a slow go and not completely successful. In 1934, Chiang firmly controlled only seven of eighteen provinces (Henan, Hubei, Jiangxi, Anhui, Jiangsu, Zhejiang, and Fujian). He was able to seize the opportunity of his campaigns against the Communists on the Long March (see the next chapter) to solidify his control over four others (Hunan, Guizhou, Sichuan, and Yunnan). When war broke out with Japan in the summer of 1937, there were, however, one third of the Chinese provinces (six) that were still beyond Chiang's control (Guangdong having been corralled in late 1936).

Economic Development

To build a modern nation state required not only reconstruction from the years of war but large-scale development in industry, utilities, and mining. In 1933 this sector of the economy accounted for less than 4 percent of the net domestic product. Even though the modern sector of the economy grew from 1931 to 1936 at a rate that compared well with that of other countries, the problem was the very small base with which China began its development. At the time of Chiang's victory in 1928, China had only about 1220 miles of railroad. Its output of electric power was just .88 million megawatts, only 1 percent of the output in the United States and less than 18 percent produced in Russia. With such small bases, even moderate rates of industrial growth would appear large. Thus, by the end of the decade, China's mileage of railroad had grown by what sounds like a whopping 47 percent—all the way up to twenty-three hundred miles.

In many ways Chiang could be seen as the heir to the long line of self-strengtheners stretching from nineteenth-century leaders like Li Hongzhang and Zhang Zhidong through Yuan Shikai in the early Republic. Though he was called by two Western commentators, "an economic ignoramus," he knew generally what he wanted to do, that is, to modernize China's economy, often using Western models, in order to preserve a state that he increasingly envisioned as based on traditional values.[16] Like Yuan, he believed that central control and decision making were keys for modernizing the economy and the state. Chiang turned to the areas of communications, transportation, and manufacturing for most of his development focus because development in these areas would provide crucial infrastructure for defense and a significant base for further modernization.

Unfortunately progress in the arena of industrial development was minuscule. Blueprints for a large-scale four-year plan to industrialize the Yangzi valley had to be shelved because the state could not fund the prescribed construction of communications and factories. State plans to build four new steel mills shriveled into the construction of only one small plant. By 1937, China with its 400 to 500 million population had less industrial production than the 8 million people of Belgium. Even with the attention focused on construction of highways, railroads, and telegraphs, the little that was accomplished is rather shocking: By 1937 China had the same mileage of modern highways as Spain, one third of the telegraph lines as France, and less railroad mileage than the state of Illinois.

Why such "drop-in-the-bucket" accomplishments? The political and military challenges were, of course, significant here, but other serious challenges also curtailed significant reconstruction and development. Economic and fiscal difficulties were debilitating. The worldwide depression was anything but a stable context in which to realize economic development and expansion. From 1929 to 1931, because of the currency situation, China actually experienced an economic boom. China was the only large country in the world that had a currency based on silver. When the stock market crashed in 1929, the world price of silver dropped, making China's currency worth less than previously. This depreciation meant that other countries' goods were too expensive for Chinese to purchase, so that for the time being foreign competition in China was no problem. Silver also flowed into the country with foreign investments in the low-priced Chinese economy. With huge silver reserves, Chinese banks offered Chinese entrepreneurs loans for business expansion at low interest rates. But then in 1931 Great Britain and Japan went off the gold standard in order to make their goods more marketable, setting up direct competition with the Chinese. The depression then hit China. Even worse was to follow. The bottom fell out of the economy following action by the United States. In 1934 the U.S. Congress passed the Silver Purchase Act, making the U.S. government a huge purchaser of silver in order to drive up prices for the benefit of Western silver-producing states. The effect was to drain China precipitously of its silver reserves and send the economy tailspinning into deeper depression.

Even more serious for China's economic reconstruction and development was its insufficient and poorly structured tax base. Traditionally the crucial tax for the Chinese central government was the land tax. But collecting it after so many years of war and turmoil was problematical. With the considerable disruption of local economies and the upheaval of population flight and resettlement over the previous decades, land ownership in many areas was unclear. The situation necessitated a census before taxes could be collected; but a census was both too time-consuming and too expensive. Because of this, Chiang and the government decided simply to write off the land tax: If provinces wanted to collect it, they could do so.

The national government thus became dependent on tariffs, excise taxes, and borrowing. The taxes were counterproductive. Fully 50 percent of the government's revenue came from customs duties (as opposed to 1 percent at the time in the United States). The tariffs handicapped trade and industry, the modern sector that the government wanted to develop, by making it more expensive for purchasing machinery or items needed in manufacturing (during the decade total purchased manufacturing equipment reached 500 million Chinese dollars). The government in Nanjing also levied the salt tax, tobacco tax, a stamp tax, and the "consolidated taxes," which were collected at the time of manufacture on about fifteen items like flour, kerosene, matches, rolled tobacco, cotton yarn, and cement. In the main these taxes were regressive, hitting hardest those least able to pay. With such a tax base, it is hardly surprising that much industrial development was stillborn. Other than these taxes, the government was dependent on borrowing. The pitfall here was that to attract capital the government had to offer a high rate of return on bonds and loans; and when they offered the attractive rates, these government options attracted 70 percent of the nation's available investment capital. Thus, there was such a paucity of capital to invest in non-governmental industrial and commercial enterprises that they had to pay up to 20 percent interest in order to attract capital. Like the tax reality, borrowing was also counterproductive to the larger goal of economic development.

One other tactic that the government used to garner funds for development and to spur that development itself was to become directly involved in setting up and managing economic enterprises. A private stock company, the China Development Finance Corporation was established by T. V. Soong in 1933 with the goal of marshalling funds from Chinese and foreign investors in order to foster economic development. This corporation offered loans and jointly managed utilities and water control and mining enterprises. In addition, the Bank of China, headed by Soong, and the Ministry of Industries became involved in commercial and light industrial enterprises—all in a quest for government revenue and, most assuredly, for their own enrichment as well.

Probably the arena of development in which there was most success was in communications and transportation. There was construction on two major railroad trunk lines. In 1935, the east-west Longhai line that ran from the seacoast in northern Jiangsu to near the Gansu-Shaanxi border was extended west of Xi'an. The north-south Canton-Hankou line was completed in 1936. The construction of an iron bridge over the Qiantang River just south of Hangzhou linked two other rail lines, the Zhejiang-Jiangxi and the Shanghai-Hangzhou-Ningbo. Highway construction produced over 115,000 kilometers of paved roads by 1936. Modern airlines with regular air routes were established. Telegraph lines went up after having met much destruction in the warlord period; long distance telephone communication expanded.

Agriculture: the World of the Chinese Farmer

A British economic historian reporting on the Chinese agricultural situation in the early 1930s noted that "[t]here are districts in which the position of the rural population is that of a man standing permanently up to the neck in water so that even a ripple is sufficient to drown him."[17] Although historians debate whether Chinese farmers were becoming more deeply mired in poverty or, as the word is used, "immiserized," the fact of life for Chinese farmers, who made up at least 80 percent of the population, was a numbing poverty that could only give rise to a brutalized existence. Two examples. The first from the core zone of the Lower Yangzi macroregion, the richest area of China. The place is a village in Xiao-shan county across the river from Hangzhou; the time, the 1920s.

> The inside of all thatched roof farm homes . . . were the same: black rafters, gray walls, a dirt floor, a kitchen table, a bench, farm implements, and amulets from the local temple. There was generally nothing on the walls. . . . "The floors were covered with chicken shit; and people walked through it with their bare feet." Amid such conditions, the popular saying in the area: "Nothing to eat, nothing to wear—those things still go to the little king [the landlord]."[18]

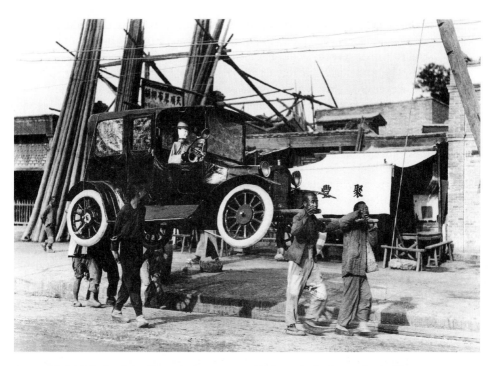

A paper Model A Ford and chauffeur to be burnt at graveside for use in the deceased's afterlife

The second comes from far western China, a peripheral region on the border between Sichuan and Shaanxi provinces; the time, the early 1940s.

> The peasants up and down the valley lived and died in their special fashion . . . The father of one family died. Since his wife had been failing and the family was very poor, they decided not to bury him right away. Perhaps the old woman would die, too, before really warm weather came and the old man began to smell. Then they could save by burying both with one funeral. The old lady agreed, so they stored the coffin in their darkest, coldest room, the old woman's sickroom, and piled stones on its lid to keep the dogs out.[19]

It is perhaps not surprising that the death rate in China in 1930 was 250 percent higher than in the United States and even substantially higher than in India. In part it resulted from the appallingly bleak poverty; in part from malnutrition and starvation. In part it also stemmed from the use of night-soil, human and animal excrement, for fertilizer; night soil carried many often lethal parasites—hookworm, liver fluke, and blood fluke. If night soil is not properly fermented to kill these worms, they become a great danger. If, for example, fecal-borne hookworm eggs hatch, the worm can pass through the skin of a farmer's leg as he, wearing only shorts, slogs through a rice paddy. The half-inch worm eventually finds its way to the farmer's intestinal wall where it lives sucking blood; if joined by hundreds of its blood-sucking kin, they can devour a half-pint of the farmer's blood daily, causing anemia and eventually death. Indeed, it is estimated that close to a quarter of all deaths in China resulted from infection by these parasites.

The most difficult reality farmers faced was nature; against it there was no protection. Will it ever rain? Will it ever stop raining? How do we deal with the rice driven into the mud by the high winds? What about the cotton destroyed by hail? In pre-insecticide days, how do we deal with pests like the rice borer and grasshoppers? A pertinent example were the Yangzi River floods in 1931 when days of torrential rain raised the river an unprecedented fifteen feet above its normal levels. Dikes broke, flooding "an area the size of New York state" with water at "an average depth . . . of nine feet. . . . And over twenty-five million people—a population approximately equivalent to the entire farm population of the United States—were displaced and suffered losses from the flood."[20]

The problem is that 1931 was not all that anomalous. Rain, wind, hail, and drought in 1934 and 1935 made those years nightmares as well. As a result, the rice harvest was down by a third from 1931, soy beans by 36 percent; and wheat by 7 percent. A farmer planted his crop, having borrowed money for the seeds; he worked from dawn to dusk. When natural disaster struck and his crop was wiped out, he had the bills for the seeds and other expenses waiting to be paid. Thus, it meant a trip to the pawnbroker, if there was indeed anything to pawn. If natural disasters came in twos or in bunches, the farmer could very easily lose all that he had. His and his family's only choice might be abandoning their village and emigrating elsewhere—a chilling possibility given the fact that all their connections were in their home area and they would be moving to an area peopled only by the Other.

Even if his crop was harvested, if he was a tenant farmer, he had not only the outstanding bills to pay, but the rent to the landlord as well. It is estimated that about 50 percent of all farmers rented all or some of their land, though the extent of tenancy varied throughout China. In the north tenancy was less and many farmers were small-landholders. In central and southern China, as well as Sichuan, tenancy was more widespread (though not as high a rate as in countries like France, Ireland, and Denmark). Since the Chinese practiced partible inheritance in which the inheritance was divided equally among the sons of the family, each succeeding generation would have less and less land to farm, making livelihood ever more precarious.

For its part, Chiang's government put regulations on the books in the Land Law of 1930 that limited rents to 37.5 percent of the harvest. For tenants who had been paying 60 to 70 percent, such a change was obviously helpful. Unfortunately, like so many plans and laws set forth by the Nanjing government, the law—which even stipulated that tenants could buy the land from an absentee landlord if they farmed it for a decade—was never implemented. Reports indicate that rents thus remained in the 50- to 70-percent range. Beyond this stillborn law, the government was afraid to go, for its fear of social unrest and its desire to maintain generally good relations with rural elites prevented further action. Some have said that the decision not to collect the land tax for the national government was a pointed indication that Chiang was unwilling to tackle the mammoth problems of farmers and the countryside or to do something to rein in local elites whose power had also risen during the government-weak warlord period.

The government did set forth certain programs to try to increase agricultural productivity, funding and sponsoring research on new varieties of seed and on fertilizers and pesticides. Attention was paid as well to developing disease-resistant silkworms and tea and cotton plants and then to marketing their products more effectively. The "infrastructure" of agricultural production began to be renovated as some rivers were dredged and some irrigation systems constructed. In dealing with agricultural issues, the government continually faced an immense country whose localities and conditions were incredibly varied. Agricultural problems differed from locality to locality, and methods of dealing with them of necessity had to vary.

Rural Reconstruction Efforts

Another approach at trying to come to grips with agricultural problems was promoting projects of rural reconstruction. These were efforts to undertake various rural reforms in specific areas; in essence, they were holistic attempts to develop an area. Interestingly in light of the government's inability and unwillingness to engage the rural populace in basic change, these were initially begun by private citizens. The first to be undertaken, while lesser known, was the East Township Self-Government Association in Zhejiang province. There in 1928 reformer Shen Dingyi inaugurated the economic, educational, and political development of the township through, among other things, the establishment of mass organizations and self-government bodies, the setting up of cooperatives and schools, and the initiation of programs of conservation, medical care, sericulture reform.

Two more well-known efforts at rural reconstruction focused on education as the key to remaking China. James Yen's Mass Education Association in over sixty market towns and villages in Ding county (Hebei province) set up "people's schools" to offer some practical education for the masses with an emphasis on public ethics. He expanded his work in the creation of a "model village" with an emphasis not only on education but on public health, agricultural reform, and economic development. The Nanjing regime gave considerable latitude to noted Confucian scholar Liang Shuming in his management of the Shandong Rural Reconstruction Institute. This body oversaw development efforts in two counties with a focus on education and particularly with a view toward bringing about good class relations between elites and masses; Liang's program developed out of his strong hatred of the Marxist idea of class struggle. The Nanjing government itself also became involved in setting up two short-lived experimental counties as models of bureaucratic reform. The creators of all these rural reconstruction efforts envisioned them as models of local development with the potential for serving as models for the nation. Liang, for example, believed that his Shandong experiment would catch fire and spread across the nation. In the end, all these efforts of model-building for the nation were, like so many plans during the Nanjing decade, stillborn. It remained for them to be destroyed completely in the fires of war with Japan.

The Cooperative Movement

One effort to deal with rural economic problems, especially the lack of available credit, was establishing cooperative associations. The first cooperatives in China dated from

1918, established mostly in Hebei province under the auspices of the China International Famine Relief Commission. The commission had been formed after the North China famine of 1920–1921 and was involved, with heavy missionary participation, in spearheading various rural improvement efforts like building roads and dikes and digging wells. Other cooperatives were begun by individuals: Zhejiang's first cooperatives, for example, appeared in 1928 with the rural reconstruction experiment of Shen Dingyi. After 1928 provincial governments encouraged the establishment of cooperatives; Nanjing got behind them only beginning in 1934. Official patronage shot the number of cooperatives up nationwide 1181 percent to 46,983 (with 1.5 million members) on the eve of war with Japan. Of these, though there was a variety of types of cooperatives—production, retailing, as well as credit, the last were the most numerous: In Zhejiang, for example, 91.2 percent in 1932 were credit cooperatives. There was simply an urgent rural need for institutions to provide loans at reasonable rates of interest; in 1931 the annual rate of interest on loans in rice-producing areas was 28 percent; in wheat-producing areas, 38 percent. Local residents, mostly elites, created a fund whose monies could be loaned out at cheaper interest rates than the standard creditors—pawnbrokers, merchants, and rich farmers and landlords.

Despite the increasing numbers, several aspects of the Chinese cooperative scene suggest that they are misleading in terms of meaningful change in the countryside. Studies have shown that during the 1930s, when cooperatives might have been significant institutions that would have fulfilled the urgent rural credit need, the increase in cooperatives did not stem from any groundswell of local enthusiasm over their potential. Their surge in numbers came rather from government stimulus; in other words, this is another example of the Nanjing decade's top-down phenomenon. Certainly it seemed from the case of East Township cooperatives that such local bodies needed outside impetus, even patronage, to organize and to function effectively; there various cooperatives flourished under Shen Dingyi's leadership, but all collapsed within a few years after his death.

On a more negative view of the question of leadership, cooperatives were dominated by elites, often for the benefit primarily of elites. Local farmers did not necessarily perceive that buying shares into the cooperative would greatly benefit them. But the most negative aspect of the cooperative was that at the height of the cooperative fever under the Nanjing government, not even 3 percent of the total money loaned out to farmers came from cooperatives; over 97 percent came from traditional rip-off (in terms of interest rates) sources. The cooperative effort even became a sort of bureaucratic boondoggle as each county with cooperatives got a new county official, the director of cooperatives.

By the end of the Nanjing decade Wen Yiduo was writing no more poetry. It was clear that the "dead water" of his 1928 vision had just become filled with more debris and that the world had not been transformed into a better place. During the decade, Wen had become politically passive, calling on his students at Qinghua University to shun involvement in politics. As if trying to avoid looking at the turmoil around him, he turned his attention ever farther back into the Chinese past, to serious study of early Daoist writings and to explications of Tang dynasty poetry. When war broke out against Japan in 1937, he joined his family whom he had sent on ahead to far southwest China to avoid the conflagration. He could not have then known that he would soon regain his interest in current affairs and that eventually it would be the cause of his death.

Notes

[1] Quoted in Leo Ou-fan Lee, "Literary Trends: The Road to Revolution, 1927–1949," in Fairbank and Albert Feuerwerker, Eds., *The Cambridge History of China, Vol. 13, Republican China 1912–1949, Part 2,* pp. 457–458.

[2] Lloyd E. Eastman, *The Abortive Revolution* (Cambridge: Harvard University Press, 1974), p. 279.

[3] Boorman, Vol. 3, p. 139.

[4] Eastman, p. 32.

[5] Lloyd E. Eastman, "Nationalist China during the Nanking Decade, 1928–1937" in Fairbank and Albert Feuerwerker, p. 118.

[6] Eastman, *The Abortive Revolution,* p. 12.

[7] Ibid., p. 14.

[8] Eastman, *The Abortive Revolution,* p. 1.

[9] Quoted in ibid., p. 40.

[10] Quoted in ibid., p. 42.

[11] Quoted in ibid., p. 67.

[12] Quoted in ibid., p. 68.

[13] Eastman, "Nationalist China during the Nanking Decade, 1928–1937," p. 132.

[14] Eastman, *The Abortive Revolution,* p. 280.

[15] Eastman, "Nationalist China during the Nanking Decade, 1928–1937," p. 138.

[16] Quoted in Eastman, *The Abortive Revolution,* p. 281.

[17] R. H. Tawney, *Land and Labor in China* (Boston: Beacon Press, 1966), p. 77.

[18] Schoppa, *Blood Road,* pp. 100–101.

[19] Graham Peck, *Two Kinds of Time* (Boston: Houghton Mifflin, 1967), p. 208.

[20] Eastman, *The Abortive Revolution,* p. 188.

12

Revolution Reborn: The Communists in the 1930s

_____

_____

__

A study of the Communist movement in the 1930s points to at least two unfortunate elements of history. First, the trouble with the history of a revolution (actually of any history) is that we see the finished product, but we don't see the "roads not taken." The lives of people, parties, governments, and nations have many crossroads, some like superhighways, others like small lanes that, if taken, would have produced a very different history. Going back to look at those crossroads and their nature can get us to see that nothing about the finished product was inevitable. The Communist party's efforts to resuscitate itself following Chiang Kai-shek's White Terror in 1927 and 1928 were marked by many possibilities of different paths, as we will see. A second unfortunate fact about the history of revolution is that the winner gets to decide on and shape the revolution's past and thus create the "standard" way of seeing that past. For the Communist revolution in the 1930s, Mao Zedong emerged by mid-decade as the first among his peers; by the end of the decade he was writing the canonical works for the party. It is little wonder that for much of the rest of the century the history of the Communist movement in the 1930s was seen either as one with Mao at center-stage or as one that bore Mao's imprimatur. This phase of the revolution, as we will see, was considerably more complex.

THE PARTY: "SO WIDELY SCATTERED AND SO BADLY MAULED"[1]

The policy choices that the CCP had made in the 1920s had left it dying on the side of the revolutionary road. The "bloc within," which had looked like a Trojan horse from which to destroy the Guomindang, had stirred up rightist Guomindang fears that grew into an unimagined tidal wave. Repeatedly, specifically after Chiang's March 1926 coup against

Soviet advisors and his April 1927 massacre of leftists and CCP members in Shanghai, Stalin had chosen to have the CCP continue its united front with the Guomindang—each time with very negative consequences. The party's Autumn Harvest uprisings and Canton commune in the second half of 1927 were total disasters. Party membership that had reached about sixty thousand in April 1927 had collapsed to less than ten thousand by year's end. The party was in shambles.

But ironically, the Comintern, largely responsible for the CCP's bitter fate, would for the next four years wield even greater power than it had during the united front period. It helped reconstruct the Communist party with its shattered leadership and its scattered membership, which had taken flight in all directions in late 1927. To make matters even more difficult than earlier in the 1920s was that now the party was outlawed: it could not operate in the open. From the Comintern side, the initial step of rebuilding, the choice of a new general party secretary, was shepherded by Comintern representative Besso Lominadze. The work of rebuilding the party after 1928 fell largely to Pavel Mif, who had attended the CCP's fifth National Congress in summer 1927 and who held the key Comintern positions relating to China.

Beginning in late 1927 there were key shifts both in party leadership and in party members in general. Each man who emerged as party leader was a generation or more younger than now-discredited CCP general secretary Chen Duxiu, who had been born in 1879: Mao Zedong, the oldest, born in 1893; Qu Qiubai (b. 1899); Li Lisan (b. 1900), Chen Shaoyu [a.k.a., Wang Ming] (b. 1907), and Qin Bangxian [a.k.a., Bo Gu] (b. 1907). Less grounded in traditional China, all except Mao had studied abroad, Qu, Chen, and Qin in the Soviet Union and Li in France. The major shift in party membership was a large influx of peasants and a decline in the numbers of intellectuals and urban workers; it was a shift that gave rise to considerable anxiety among established party members for it almost certainly portended changes in policies and styles. One scholar has asserted that

> "[h]istory might have been very different if the original leaders of the Chinese Communist party" had not been killed or later expelled. "They were civilized and sophisticated urban intellectuals, holding humanistic values, with cosmopolitan and open minds, attuned to the modern world . . . Their sudden elimination marked an abrupt turn in the Chinese revolution."[2]

Though this view of the original leaders may be over-romanticized, it is true that when the party rose again, its personnel and its agenda were sharply different.

A word about the word "peasants." To this point in this book, I have refrained from using this word for "farmers" or for the "farming population." Both of the latter are, I would argue, more neutral terms. "Peasant" has about it more primitive overtones. A "peasant" somehow seems cruder, less developed, more elemental than a "farmer." While "peasant" has been used in other geographical contexts, it is used most by the "developed" world to describe a social type in the "non-developed" world. The use of the word seems patronizing on the part of the modern West. Why didn't the United States, even in its non-developed days, have "peasants"? They were, it seems, always "farmers." In any event, my preference would be to continue to use "farmers." But, almost ironically, the Communists have translated the term *nongmin* as peasant and have used the term in dividing the farm population into groupings (rich peasant, middle peasant, and poor peasant). To substitute "farmer" in this case would not seem appropriate.

Qu Qiubai served as party leader only in the last half of 1928; a prolific writer and fluent in Russian, Qu had the misfortune to take over when the party was still disintegrating. He contributed to his own fall from Comintern grace with his call for the seizure of Canton. The failure of that goal plus the bloodbath that ended the Canton commune led to his ouster and recall to Moscow in mid-1928. The problems of direction for the party and of its organizational difficulties were staggering. With many peasants now joining the party, what directions should the party take? How could the scattered membership be reconstituted while the White Terror was still going on? How could the party put the lid on factionalism that bedeviled it especially badly at times of defeat when all were looking for scapegoats? How could the party bind itself together as it concurrently rebuilt when just the sheer geographical dispersal of its members alone made communications difficult? It took from six to nine months for communications to reach certain remote areas. It is said, for example, that the commander He Long, based in western Hunan and Hubei provinces (called the Xiang-exi base area), did not hear about decisions made at the July 1928 Sixth Party Congress until the spring of 1929.

He was one of the military figures who with other CCP members had retreated far from the cities to remote areas that they could use as bases. In these so-called "base areas," they could organize and mobilize the people, living off the land, and building their strength. Mao put it this way: "While working for the revolution, we cannot simply run here and there; otherwise we will get into all sorts of difficulties. The base area is our home from which we carry on revolutionary struggles against the enemy. If he does not come, we train soldiers and mobilize the masses here; if he comes, we fight him from our home."[3] Indeed, Communist groups who did try to maintain guerrilla activity without building bases simply disintegrated. Other Communist leaders began to form their own base areas. Zhang Guotao became the head of the Eyuwan base area on the borders of Hunan, Anhui, and Hebei. Mao himself retreated to Jinggangshan on the border between Hunan and Jiangxi, where in early 1928 he and Zhu De established a rural base area. Other base areas developed as well, all of them like bandit lairs in traditional times on the borders of different provinces. They all began insignificantly. Zhang in the Eyuwan base did not take his first county seat until the winter of 1929, an indication of the remoteness and poverty of his base. When He Long established his base, he had only twenty men armed with eight rifles. Mao, somewhat more fortunate, was able to take two county seats in mid-1928.

Mao Zedong, who would become one of the giants of the twentieth-century world, was born in Hunan province, the eldest son of a wealthy peasant with whom Mao did not get along. Educated at the village primary school, he went on to study at several higher level schools where he was introduced to some Western political and philosophical works. He briefly joined a volunteer military unit to fight in the 1911 revolution. In 1913 he began study at the Hunan First Normal School in Changsha, the provincial capital. Turned on by *New Youth,* the radical journal edited by Chen Duxiu, he had an essay on physical fitness and its relation to the nation published in the journal's April 1917 issue. Mao served as director of the Changsha Student Association in 1917 and 1918 and graduated from the First Normal School in June 1918. Three months later he was in Beijing, working in the Beijing

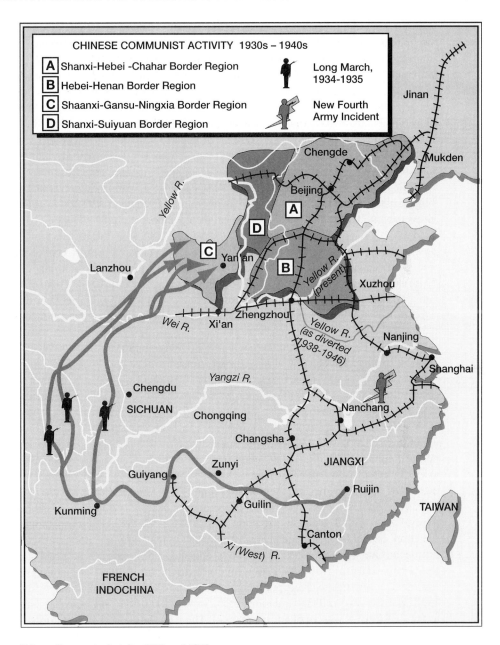

CHINESE COMMUNIST ACTIVITY 1930s – 1940s

A Shanxi-Hebei -Chahar Border Region
B Hebei-Henan Border Region
C Shaanxi-Gansu-Ningxia Border Region
D Shanxi-Suiyuan Border Region

Long March, 1934-1935

New Fourth Army Incident

Jinan

Chengde

Mukden

Beijing

A

D

C   Yan'an

B

Yellow R.

Lanzhou

Yellow R. (present)

Xuzhou

Wei R.   Xi'an   Zhengzhou

Yellow R. (as diverted 1938-1946)

Nanjing

Shanghai

Yangzi R.

Chengdu

SICHUAN

Chongqing

Nanchang

Changsha

Zunyi

JIANGXI

Guiyang

Ruijin

Guilin

TAIWAN

Kunming

Canton

Xi (West) R.

FRENCH INDOCHINA

Chinese Communist Activity, 1930s and 1940s

University library under founding CCP member Li Dazhao and auditing some courses. Though in the capital city only about six months, he reportedly was "deeply influenced" by Li's vision of a new China.

He returned to Changsha where he was active in May Fourth activities, founding his own journal, the *Xiang River Review,* in the summer of 1919. Forced to leave because he had antagonized the provincial warlord by organizing a student strike against him, Mao went back to Beijing for discussions with Li Dazhao and then to Shanghai for conversations with Chen Duxiu. He read the *Communist Manifesto* and wrote later that by September 1920, "I considered myself a Marxist." In January 1921, he organized a branch of the Socialist Youth Corps. He was one of the two Hunan representatives at the CCP's First Party Congress in July 1921. In the next several years he worked at organizing party activities and labor strikes in Hunan. Under the "bloc within" option, Mao joined the Guomindang and at the Guomindang's first party congress was elected as a alternate member of the Central Executive Committee. In 1925 and 1926 he threw himself into organizing peasants into associations, serving in Canton as the director of the important Farmers' Movement Training Institute. In 1927 he went to Hunan to assess the revolutionary potential of the peasant situation. He predicted that

> [w]ithin a short time, hundreds of millions of peasants will rise in central, south, and north China with the fury of a hurricane; no force, no matter how strong, can restrain them. They will break all the shackles that bind them and rush to the road of liberation. All imperialists, warlords, corrupt officials, and bad gentry will meet their doom at the hands of the peasants. All revolutionary parties and comrades will be judged by them.[4]

At the base at Jinggangshan to which Mao fled in late 1927, he worked closely with Zhu De, so closely in fact that among Jiangxi peasants, Zhu Mao "was an all-powerful personage who wanted to make the people happy."[5] Zhu had studied at a number of modern schools in his native Sichuan and graduated from the Yunnan Military Academy in 1911, where he later became instructor. He participated in the 1911 revolution, in the campaign against Yuan Shikai in 1916, and in warlord struggles in Sichuan until 1921. He was in Germany from 1922 until 1926, studying intermittently and building a police record through political agitation—ending up expelled from the country. Having joined the Guomindang in 1912, he became an officer in Chiang's Guomindang army in 1926; but he left it in summer 1927, making known his membership in the CCP which he joined in Germany.

He met Mao for the first time in 1928 when he became commander of the Fourth Red Army. His main charge was to further organize and expand the Red Army. Communists had seen how crucial the Guomindang army had been in that party's victory and set out to duplicate the Guomindang's success. Composed mostly of illiterate peasants and workers, the Red Army gave priority to political training. To do so, the army was structured with parallel organizations, one to direct political work and the other to command the military. In late 1928, Guomindang military pressure forced evacuation of the Jinggangshan base and led to the Red Army's seizure of Ruijin, Jiangxi. There on the Jiangxi-Fujian border, Mao and Zhu began to organize and expand their control.

FINDING ITS WAY: THE PARTY'S FACTIONS

Despite the slowly-growing base areas in rural and mostly mountainous areas, the Comintern and the CCP central leadership, still located in Shanghai, continued to stress that the Communist movement had to be led by urban workers. The Sixth Party Congress was held in Moscow in mid-1928. It decreed that the new "instrument" of CCP political power would be the "soviet" or council, a decision-making and control body. The congress called for CCP members to "proletarianize" the party by making workers the bulk of the membership and leadership. Indeed the nominal general secretary of the party from 1928 to 1931 was one-time coolie turned labor organizer Xiang Zhongfa, the only urban worker to lead the party before the establishment of the People's Republic. But he was overshadowed immediately by long-time labor organizer Li Lisan and then from late 1930 by the so-called 28 Bolsheviks.

Li Lisan is mostly known for his "line" or policy plan for the party, that national revolution could be ignited if he could mobilize urban workers to rise up in key cities and support them with the Red Army. He argued that the proletariat, not the peasantry, was the key to revolution. He received support for this "line" from the CCP Central Committee in Shanghai. The essence of his strategy was to attack major central Chinese cities in order to win the ultimate prize of Wuhan. He therefore had Mao, Zhu, and their army attack Jiangxi's capital, Nanchang, but they quickly had to withdraw without success. In late August, Communist forces led by commander Peng Dehuai seized Hunan's capital, Changsha, but held it for only seven days; another attempt to take the city in September also failed. With these humiliating defeats, the Li Lisan line, basically the line of the Comintern, collapsed. Li lost his position in the party in the fall of 1930 and was sent packing to Moscow, where he remained for the next fifteen years.

Quickly stepping into the party's leadership vacuum was a group with the unlikely nickname of the "28 Bolsheviks." These were men who had been chosen by the CCP in the mid-1920s to attend newly formed Sun Yat-sen University in Moscow for training as party cadres. Most remained in Moscow for four years, during which time they became known for their staunch support of Stalin's China policy. They also became the favorite students of university head Pavel Mif. In mid-1930 when Mif was named Comintern representative to China, the 28 Bolsheviks returned with him and became actively involved in efforts to oust Li Lisan. When they succeeded, leaders of the group were catapulted into power with the support of Mif. In January 1931, twenty-four-year-old Wang Ming (Chen Shaoyu) became CCP general secretary and proceeded to pack the CCP Politburo with more of the 28 Bolsheviks. When he left in 1932 to be CCP representative to the Comintern, his close ally Bo Gu (Qin Bangxian) became general secretary; he served in that capacity until 1935. In 1931, the Bolsheviks, still located in Shanghai, set out to establish firmer control over the rural base areas than had been exercised by Li Lisan in an effort solidify their control over the party. The base areas or rural soviets had been governed to that point by "front committees"; from this point on they were to be controlled by a central bureau that owed responsibility directly to the Politburo in the hands of the 28 Bolsheviks.

From his Jiangxi or Central Soviet, Mao Zedong warily watched first the leadership of Li Lisan and then of the 28 Bolsheviks at the Shanghai Party Center. He shared Li's sense that revolution was imminent. In a famous letter he wrote to military commander Lin Biao in January 1930, he argued that

> China is in such a state of constant trouble and anarchy that the anti-imperialist, anti-warlord, and anti-landlord revolutionary high tide is inevitable and will come very soon. China is littered with dry firewood that can quickly turn into a raging fire. The

phrase "A single spark can start a prairie fire" is an apt description of the current situation.[6]

But he greatly opposed Li's efforts to get him to put his army under more central control in order to carry out Li's line. Twice in mid-1930, he essentially sat on his hands, not carrying out military orders, and twice he received stinging rebukes from the Party Center in Shanghai. Mao's power and that of his soviet was growing strongly as the 28 Bolsheviks tried to assert more control over the rural soviets. Political realities were rapidly undercutting the power of the Shanghai Party Center and the Comintern. "The constant shift in Comintern line, the enormous 'scissors' between the Comintern line and the Chinese realities, and finally the imposition of the [28] Bolsheviks as leaders of the party had simply undermined the faith of party members."[7] By early 1931, the Shanghai Party Central Committee, in the words of one scholar, "was reduced to little more than a liaison organization relaying instructions from the Comintern to the soviets."[8] But it was not until 1933 when the Shanghai leaders finally moved out to the Jiangxi Soviet, a signal at last that the revolution's focus had shifted away from the cities and to the rural soviets.

THE JIANGXI SOVIET

Chiang Kai-shek, too, was especially worried about the rising strength of Mao Zedong's Jiangxi soviet. Thus, he launched his first extermination campaign against it in December 1930; it ended the same month, a failure. That same month Mao had his own crisis to deal with. In his drive for power and in his capacity as general political commissar of the Jiangxi Soviet Red Army, he had angered some local Communists (native to Jiangxi province) by ousting them from military posts and replacing them with his own men. When they formed an anti-Mao group, Mao moved against them, arresting about seventy and imprisoning them at the town of Futian. An infuriated local commander and several hundred troops stormed the prison and freed about twenty; they then rebelled against Mao. Mao's Red Army subsequently captured and massacred hundreds.

This conflict clearly revealed the tensions between locals and outsiders (even though political allies, still the "Other"); it was a problem that the Communists would face repeatedly in the years before 1949. The Futian incident also showed that Mao's rise to power from the very beginning was marked by "harsh and bloody conflict." It is also interesting that at this early stage Mao turned what was a basic political struggle into an ideological crusade of sorts. He asserted that his opponents were members of "a nationalist secret organization known as the 'A.B. League' (Anti-Bolshevik League)" whose existence threatened the revolution. He would return to this pattern many times in his career, charging political opponents with treason.[9] In reaction to this bloody Futian Incident, Mao was criticized at the Jiangxi Soviet's First Party Congress in early November 1931 for his unduly violent handling of the affair; he lost his position as the army's political commissar and was given a position in the soviet government.

By 1931 over a dozen soviets were located in parts of some three hundred Chinese counties. Most were located in the foothills regions of central China, between the plains to the north and east and the higher mountains to the south and west. In November 1931 came the landmark meeting of the First All-China Soviet Congress held at Ruijin in Mao's Jiangxi Soviet. The congress established a national regime, the Chinese Soviet Republic. Mao was appointed chair of the new government, with Zhang Guotao, head of the Eyuwan soviet, and Xiang Ying, a former Li Lisan supporter, appointed vice-chairs. Mao did not, however, control the party; that power still lay in the hands of the Shanghai-based 28 Bolsheviks.

The Chinese Soviet Republic was a state within the state. It called itself "the democratic dictatorship of the proletariat and peasantry"—even though, of course, there were no urban workers in the soviets that comprised the Soviet Republic: the Comintern fiction and that of the Party Center still in Shanghai had to be kept ideologically alive. Most importantly, for the first time the CCP had its own "state" where it could begin to experiment with social revolution. It adopted a constitution; in the area of its rule it issued laws and maintained political and military control. By early 1932 that area, containing about three million people, was about fifteen thousand square miles in seventeen counties (the more than a dozen smaller soviets scattered throughout central China had a population of about six million).

Land Revolution

Mao's Jiangxi Soviet had issued a land law in February 1930; that law now became the Land Law of the Soviet Republic, issued in November 1931. It was at the heart of the revolution for it provided the guidelines for the confiscation and redistribution of land that would result from and constitute class struggle. The law was posited on a hierarchical rural society stretching down from wealthy elites to hired hands. It called for the confiscation of the land of "feudal landlords, village bosses, gentry, militarists, and other big private landowners" and for its redistribution to poor and middle peasants and to "hired farmhands, coolies, and toiling laborers."[10] This prescription for rural revolution sounds quietly objective but masked a fluid indeterminacy and a screaming and bloody violence that ripped apart communities and shattered lives—for this meant the seizure of private property and wealth without compensation, a process that destroyed people's livelihoods, ultimately people's lives. In addition to these confiscations, lands of counter-revolutionaries and of religious institutions or temples were to be confiscated. Rich peasants were a special category that will be discussed later.

What was the configuration of Jiangxi society that would be affected by such radical change? In the period between December 1929 and May 1930, Mao himself conducted a detailed investigation of the economics, society, and culture of Xunwu county to the south of the Jiangxi Soviet's main city of Ruijin. Through this investigation, Mao "wanted to understand both how a revolution could be won through the efforts of peasants and how a mass-based party composed primarily of peasants could be built."[11] The configuration of Xunwu society does not, of course, necessarily fit that of other counties in the province, but it gives us some clue as to possibilities of the numbers of people in the categories constructed for land confiscation and redistribution in this area. As the table below shows, rents were paid in kind, that is, in rice or other grains.[12]

Rural Population in Xunwu County, Jiangxi Province, 1930

Large landlords	0.045%
(receive rent of more than 33.25 tons of rice)	
Middle landlords	0.4%
(receive rent of between 13.3 and 33.25 tons)	
Small landlords	3.0%
(receive rent of less than 13.3 tons of rice)	
Rich peasants	4.0%
(have surplus grain and capital to make loans)	
Middle peasants	18.255%
(have enough to eat and do not receive loans)	
Poor peasants	70.0%
(insufficient grain and receive loans)	
Manual workers	3.0%
(craftsmen, boatmen, porters)	
Loafers	1.0%
(no occupation or property)	
Hired hands	0.3%
(permanent and day laborers)	

As the table indicates, over 92 percent of the population of Xunwu county were to receive land, taken from just over 7 percent of the population, if all the rich peasants had their land confiscated, and from less than 4 percent if rich peasants kept their land. As for landholding, peasants farmed 30 percent of the land in the county; landlords owned 30 percent; and 40 percent was held by corporate owners like temples and lineages.

Land revolution, or as it is more commonly called, land reform was a time-consuming process. At least one estimate suggests that it would take up to half a year for land reform managers to break through peasant passivity and suspicion and have a village population that would be amenable to the revolutionary activity. Implicit in the whole land reform process was that power would flow from the people in what would later be called the "mass line." Already in a late 1929 meeting Mao had drafted resolutions relating to the masses and the Red Army, setting down the principle that the masses had the right to criticize errors and faults in the Red Army and that with the masses would lay the power to carry out party resolutions. Mao believed that in the past too many errors resulted from top-down decisions by arrogant official elites who paid scant heed to the situation of local populations. Populist that he was, Mao deeply believed that the masses had both more practical expertise and moral authority than even party cadres. He believed that party cadres and local soviet leaders had "to be willing pupils of the masses, not just their leaders, and not to regard the masses as clumsy and stupid country bumpkins but as people who deserved trust and must be involved in administration and political campaigns."[13] Thus every step of the land reform process had to be decided on by mass meetings of the people being affected. Given the vast range of human personalities and idiosyncrasies, it is easy to see how the land reform process would stretch into months or longer.

The process, which for the first time brought the rural wretched poor into political participation, went as follows. Once an area was designated for land reform, three committees were formed. Poor peasants and landless laborers served on all three. The first, a confiscation committee, would conduct a census and categorize the population (more on this shortly) and chart the amount and quality of the landholdings. The second, a land committee, made up of the obligatory poor peasants and laborers, party cadres, and representatives of families who had sons in the Red Army, would manage the distribution of land. They would first call a mass meeting to decide the method of land division—either in equal portions according to numbers of consumers or on a mixed method with some in a family, say children under the age of four or those over fifty-five, receiving less than a full share. From the land law:

> the local soviet governments shall on no account carry out this measure [the redistribution] by force or by an order issued by higher authorities, but shall explain this procedure to the peasantry from every angle. This measure may be put into operation only with the direct support and at the desire of the basic masses of the peasantry. Thus, if the majority of the middle peasants so desire, they may [be allowed] not to participate in the redistribution [of land].[14]

Further, since quality of the soil was to be taken into account in the land redistribution, the land reform leaders had to adjust the amount redistributed so that those receiving poorer quality land would receive proportionally more. When redistribution was complete, a third committee came into operation, functioning as an inspection team that investigated complaints and worked at solving attendant problems.

As difficult as these matters were, the trickiest problem was categorizing the "peasants" into their most appropriate social groupings. If a person was fortunate to be placed into the "rich peasant" category rather than the "landlord" classification, he could look forward at least temporarily to less trauma in his economic and personal life. Even better would be to be placed in the "middle peasant" group, for land reform often brought rich peasants severe difficulties also. One can imagine the way landlords would try to use any method—connections, bribes, threats—to be placed in the rich peasant rather than landlord category. One can also imagine the ways that the process would stir up old bitternesses and animosities that existed in the village and how these tensions would flare up into wars of words or fists.

Category "boundaries" especially between landlord and rich peasant, and rich peasant and middle peasant would vary, of course, according to local conditions. In some counties, for example, the rich peasant category would be better off and in some, worse off than the rich peasants in Xunwu; in the former counties they might approximate a small Xunwu landlord, and in the latter they might be closer to the Xunwu middle peasant. No objective standards existed for land reform categories; they were all and always relative—to the locality, its economic situation, and the attitudes and approaches of those managing the whole process. Even more unsettling, they could also be reevaluated at any time with a person being moved from one category to another.

The rich peasant category was especially ambiguous and, because of that, became a major issue and something of a hot potato. While the earlier Jiangxi Soviet land law of February 1930 had called for the confiscation of rich peasant land, in practice in 1930 and early 1931 Mao had held back. He took only the rich peasant land that surpassed the amount of a share of land redistributed to lower categories; and in later redistributions, he took only their "good" land. In part this more lenient policy stemmed from Mao's desire not to antagonize large numbers of very powerful people at the very beginning of his revolutionary effort. This social stratum could throw all sorts of monkey wrenches into land redistribution.

For this approach, Mao was roundly attacked by the 28 Bolsheviks, who were influenced by Stalin's paranoia and treatment of the kulaks, the small stratum of relatively well-to-do peasants, whom Stalin targeted in the late 1920s for no less than physical liquidation. The 28 Bolsheviks argued that since the rich peasants had in the past made loans at usurious interest rates, to have even a hint of a lenient policy toward them would mean watering down class struggle and blurring class lines. Thus, the land law of the Soviet Republic read

> It is a peculiar feature of the Chinese rich peasant that he is at one and the same time a landowner and a usurer; therefore, his land shall also be subject to confiscation. If a rich peasant, after his land has been confiscated, does not participate in any counterrevolutionary activities and works his land by the use of his own labor power, he may be assigned land, but not of the best quality.

Thus, sometimes a rich peasant was dispossessed and then partly repossessed. But in light of the thinking of the 28 Bolsheviks, from this time on rich peasants received only poor land and landlords got nothing.

From June 1933 to October 1934 the Jiangxi Soviet launched a massive land investigation campaign to reclassify peasants. In ordering the investigation, Mao wrote "We should take the working class in the countryside as the leaders, rely on the poor peasants, firmly ally with the middle peasants, and resolutely attack the feudal and semifeudal forces. Weed out all landlords and rich peasants who falsely call themselves 'middle peasants' or 'poor peasants.'"[15] This campaign was really intended to mobilize peasants and bring them closer to the party; Chiang Kai-shek's fourth extermination campaign had failed in early 1933, but there was every likelihood that he would launch another extermination campaign against the Soviet soon. At such a precarious time, this campaign verged on the ridiculous in its policies that lurched first one way and then the opposite, revealing not only the slipperiness of class categories but also an anchorless party.

A major issue here was once again the rich peasant, specifically the demarcation between the rich peasant and the rich middle peasant. Mao's definition of rich peasant was too complex, filled with a range of possible factors that might conceivably go into making a rich peasant classification. The result was mass confusion when investigators attempted to use the definition to make policy. From June to October 1933, many middle peasants were reclassified as landlords. In this context the People's Commissariat stepped in to redefine the rich peasant, specifying that it was one whose total income included no more than 15 percent from exploitation. This definition necessitated yet another investigation (from October to December) and still yet another categorization. This time many of the landlords were reclassified as middle peasants. In one county, for example, out of 3,125 households,

1,512 (48 percent) were reclassified from landlords or rich peasants to middle and even (as incomprehensible as it seems) poor peasants![16] Then suddenly in early 1934, a new more bitter attack was aimed at the rich peasants. With such rapid changes, one might be a middle peasant in June, a landlord in October, and a poor peasant in December—all without changing any economic status whatsoever! The whole land reform process began to antagonize those very people whom the party hoped to attract. The obvious fluidity and continual reassessments of class rankings and the utilization of class struggle which often led to the eruption of violence confused and alienated too many people. At a time when the movement needed the support of larger numbers, it was turning too many of the most powerful people in the communities into enemies. For that reason, the land reform experiment was discontinued, and Mao put into effect the Guomindang land law which placed a rent ceiling for tenants of 37.5 percent.

The Marriage Law of 1931

Mao addressed gender as well as class issues in the Soviet Republic. A purpose of the CCP government as specified in the "Outline of the Constitution of the Chinese Soviet Republic" in November 1931, was "to guarantee the thorough emancipation of women." Announced in December 1931, the new marriage law outlawed arranged marriage, forbade marriage through purchase and sale, and generally made divorce easy. If one's husband was on military service, however, no divorce could be granted.

Already in 1928, the party had noted that one of its main tasks was "to recognize peasant women as extremely active participants in the revolution."[17] In Jiangxi, it should be noted, the motive for the "emancipation" of women was not gender equity but, in line with the 1928 statement, for gaining their support and helping to mobilize them for the national revolution. Unfortunately, Red Army soldiers and party cadres often took advantage of women against their will. Women, for example, were coerced into marrying soldiers whose poverty would have prevented a traditional arranged marriage. Widows were forcibly married to party cadres just after their husbands' deaths. CCP authorities even cooperated secretly in fostering prostitution, sending "teams of laundresses" to Red Army units.

THE OTHER SOVIETS

As we have seen, although the Jiangxi Soviet was the CCP center of power and governance, it was not the only base area and its policies were not necessarily executed in other bases. These soviets and their experiences are the roads that in the end were not taken in the Chinese revolution, but it is still important to remember that at the time no one knew the eventual route and that many Chinese lives were in any case affected by them. The Eyuwan (Hubei-Henan-Anhui) soviet, led by Zhang Guotao, paid less attention to economic work than did Jiangxi, and it also emphasized the emancipation of women more. Zhang Guotao pushed the anti-rich peasant line more wholeheartedly than Mao. In instituting the mass line, Zhang again departed from the Jiangxi Soviet model, relying more on the Red Army to coerce cooperation rather than mobilizing the masses through land reform. The upshot of this approach was that when there were military losses of territory to Chiang Kai-shek's forces and the coercing military was out of the picture, the mass organization and reform efforts that did exist simply collapsed.

Chiang's third extermination campaign against the Jiangxi Soviet (July–October 1931) gave the Eyuwan soviet the opportunity to expand its territory, but, like the Jiangxi Soviet, it was dogged by factional disputes that exploded into a major opposition movement that in turn gave rise to mass arrests and a wide-scale purge. In the end, although Chiang's campaign was shortened by the Japanese aggression in Manchuria, the Eyuwan's Fourth Red Army helped the Jiangxi Soviet in combatting Guomindang attacks. As a prelude to Chiang's fourth campaign against the Jiangxi Soviet, he first undertook action against the Eyuwan and Xiang-exi soviets. Moving against Eyuwan from July to September 1932, Chiang's army forced the abandonment of the base area. As Zhang Guotao and others fled to northern Sichuan, their military losses dropped active forces by half, from thirty thousand to fifteen thousand.

In December 1932, Zhang established the new Sichuan-Shaanxi base area, where over the next two years policies more radical than in the Jiangxi Soviet were set in place. Policies dealing with land confiscation and redistribution were harsher; a military draft of peasants was instituted; and, as in the Jiangxi Soviet, the youth were mobilized in organizations called Red Guards that provided support for the Red Army—all policies formulated for survival against attacks by Sichuan warlords. By the spring of 1935, Zhang and his comrades had been forced to move again to the border of Sichuan and Xikang where they would rendezvous with the evacuees from the Jiangxi Soviet on the Long March (see below).

The Xiang-exi Soviet (west Hubei and Hunan) was even more peripatetic than the original Eyuwan. Controlled by He Long, it developed more rapidly and in different arenas of action from the Jiangxi base. Using better developed mass associations, the base leadership mobilized the population in campaigns for land reclamation and production and against social evils like opium, gambling, and superstition.[18] In an effort to appeal to support as wide as possible, it did not pursue a strong policy against rich peasants. Forced to abandon the base in October 1932, He fled with his three thousand troops to northeastern Guizhou province; but they found it difficult to establish a new base and kept on the move. During this period, they gave up their open advocacy of revolution and appealed to peasant rebels and Miao tribesmen. Late in 1934, they did establish a base area in the border region of Guizhou, Sichuan, Hunan, and Hubei. But in the fall of 1936, they abandoned it to move to the new large Communist base in Shaanxi, the destination of the Long Marchers.

THE LONG MARCH

The Extermination Campaigns

Chiang Kai-shek was extraordinarily fearful of the expansion of Communist power. But there is evidence that he underestimated their fighting ability. In the first two campaigns that Chiang launched against the Jiangxi base (December 1930 and May–June 1931), he used former warlord troops to try to wear down the Red Army. The Red Army's advantages lay in their speed, in their knowledge of the base area, and in their support by the masses, mobilized by land reform and the threat of war. In both these campaigns, the Communists lured Guomindang armies into the base area. Overextended and without proper defensive preparations, the Guomindang forces were then denied intelligence by the base's mobilized masses who, even worse, destroyed bridges to prevent them from retreating and harassed and attacked them from behind. In the third campaign from July to October 1931, Guomindang forces penetrated deeply into the base area, but the Japanese war in Manchuria forced Chiang to retreat. The fourth campaign in early 1933 once again failed, falling victim to the Red Army's speed (that "tired the government troops out in chasing them") and to the mass mobilization (which meant that Chiang's army "had no one to use, thus making [them] both blind and deaf").[19]

The fifth and finally successful campaign was launched in October 1933, with Chiang's forces totaling a million men. This time Guomindang forces moved slowly, building networks of roads to facilitate supply, constructing blockhouses (some built only two-thirds of a mile apart), and undertaking political mobilizational work with masses along the campaign routes. These strategies gradually tightened the noose around the soviet. The Red Army tried to counter by building their own version of blockhouses and by "short, swift [military] thrusts" that would disrupt National Army troops before reinforcements could be brought; but these tactics were to no avail. At an August meeting CCP general secretary Bo Gu, Red Army political commissar Zhou Enlai, and Comintern agent Otto Braun began to plan the evacuation. At the time, Mao was chair of the Soviet Republic's government but not in the party's military decision-making hierarchy.

In mid-October, about 86,000 (including 35 women) broke out of the base to the southwest and began a 368-day forced march of about 6000 miles. This was the fabled Long March, in the words of Edgar Snow, "an Odyssey unequaled in modern times."[20] The marchers faced bombing attacks from Chiang's air force and harassment from Tibetan troops. Snow totes up the statistics, and, in doing so, points to the almost superhuman quality of the trek.

> Out of a total of 368 days *en route,* 235 were consumed in marches by day, and 18 in marches by night. Of the 100 days of halts—many of which were devoted to skirmishes—56 days were spent in northwestern [Sichuan], leaving only 44 days of rest over a distance of about 5,000 miles, or an average of one halt for every 114 miles of marching. The mean daily stage covered was . . . nearly 24 miles—a phenomenal pace for a great army and its transport to *average* over some of the most hazardous terrain on earth.

> Altogether [they] crossed 18 mountain ranges, five of which were perennially snow-capped, and they crossed 24 rivers. They passed through 12 different provinces, occupied 62 cities, and broke through enveloping armies of ten different provincial warlords, besides defeating, eluding, or outmaneuvering the [Nationalist forces]. They entered and successfully crossed six different aboriginal districts. . . .[21]

In the mountains they suffered from altitude sickness and frostbite. In the even worse marshlands, quicksand-like bogs swallowed people alive; they had to sleep standing up lest they sank into the saturated ground. Hunger, exhaustion, and illness were their continual companions. It is not surprising that only eight thousand reached their eventual destination.

One of the most famous military incidents along the march was the crossing of the Dadu River, a raging torrent in western Sichuan province. It had been the site of the 1863 defeat of the army of Taiping leader Shi Dakai. "On moonless nights, local legends ran, 'you can still hear the spirits of our Taiping dead wailing at the Dadu river crossing and over the town where they were slaughtered.'"[22] Crossing the river at any one of the three heavily guarded crossings would have been difficult without other obstacles. But crossing the Luding Bridge was almost made impossible because the planking had been ripped off the chain suspension bridge and because the bridge was targeted by enemy machine guns on the other side of the bridge. To make the task even more treacherous, as Red Army shock troops began to make it across, Chiang's forces set the bridgehead on fire. But twenty soldiers made it across the three-hundred-foot span high over the turbulent water below, crawling across from chain to chain and at the end racing through the flames that burned their clothing and singed their hair. With reinforcements they were able to defeat two regiments defending the bridge.

Which Political Roads to Take?

Along the Long March momentous political happenings occurred. In January 1935 a crucial meeting took place in Zunyi in Guizhou province; by this time, less than half—only about forty thousand—of the original Long March troops remained alive. That high a casualty rate added to the initial fact of the forced evacuation put military policy under the spotlight. Speeches and discussions at the meeting offered a post mortem of the Jiangxi Soviet. Mao, not having been a part of the military decision-making, attacked the losing military strategy of Otto Braun and Bo Gu as too static, as focusing on a "pure positional defense." That line was approved by party resolution. Mao's performance at Zunyi and the party criticism of his factional rivals pointed to the fact that Mao's star was rising. He became one of the five-man Secretariat, thus emerging as one of the five most important party leaders. Perhaps even more important, given the party's factionalism, he was also named to the CCP Central Military Leadership Group, thereby bringing to an end the domination of military affairs by Bo and Braun. Thus, for the first time Mao had defeated the 28 Bolsheviks, now officially blamed for the Soviet's military defeat; and he would lead in the taking of a new or at least different revolutionary road. As one writer has summed up,

> The Zunyi [m]eeting marked the end of the soviet movement in central China. Obsessed with ideological doctrines and basking in revolutionary enthusiasm, Bo Gu and his supporters lacked a profound insight into political relationships within which the CCP found itself enmeshed. Neither could they balance this deficiency with an adequate experience in military command.[23]

Immediately after the Zunyi meeting, the Party asked Zhang Guotao, still based in northern Sichuan, to use his Fourth Front Army to begin offensive actions against Guomindang forces south of his base in order to relieve pressure on the Long March's First Front Army. But instead of complying, Zhang moved north to fight provincial forces in Shaanxi. In part as a consequence, in the late winter and spring of 1935, Mao's First Front Army experienced one defeat after another at the hands of Guomindang forces. By that spring, Mao's troops numbered only fifteen thousand compared to Zhang Guotao's eighty thousand. The two forces met in June in the new base area that Zhang had set up on the Sichuan-Xikang border, and almost immediately a bitter factional struggle erupted between Mao and Zhang. It was a time for another decision on which revolutionary road to take.

Though there was an important policy question at issue—where would they all head?—the real problem was political power. Zhang had over five times as many men, but Mao had the political power as a member of the party Secretariat. Meetings during the summer did involve some give and take on both sides, but in the end the friction and animosity was too great. In September the two groups split up; Zhang was not even present at the Politburo meeting when Mao criticized Zhang for his "opportunism" and "with splitting the Red Army, thus displaying his 'warlord' tendency."[24] Mao then promptly took his Long Marchers to the north (Zhang had originally favored a move east) to Yan'an in Shaanxi province with a view to establishing a new base area on the borders of Shaanxi, Gansu, and Ningxia. Zhang, talking about establishing a base area in the far northwest from which it might be easier to make contact with the Soviet Union, moved his forces first toward Xinjiang before he too eventually trekked to Yan'an. But his going to Yan'an was not out of friendship. Indeed, he pointedly repudiated Mao's leadership. In 1938 he made his break official by defecting to Chiang Kai-shek's side. Although he served the Guomindang in minor roles, he never again played a major political role, moving to Hong Kong in 1949 and eventually to Canada, where he died in 1979.

The Meaning of the Long March

In the chapters of party history the Long March is hailed as a victory; indeed until the late 1990s, the political leadership of the Communist Party and the government of the People's Republic was dominated by veterans of this extraordinary military trek. It must, however, be emphasized that the Long March actually occurred because of a great defeat, probably even proportionally greater than the Communist defeat of 1927. Listen to Mao, writing in late 1936:

> Except for the Shaanxi-Gansu border area, all revolutionary bases were lost, the Red Army was reduced from 300,000 to a few tens of thousands, the membership of the Chinese Communist Party was reduced [by disastrously huge numbers] and the Party organizations in Guomindang areas were almost entirely wiped out. In short, we received an extremely great historical punishment.[25]

Identifying the Long March as a victory then surely comes in part from the survival, if only of less than 10 percent, from such brutal natural and human forces. It is an uplifting tale of the defiance of superhuman odds, of dedication and sacrifice. Most important, it produced among the survivors an unquestionable sense of mission and dedication: while others had died, they had survived. Therefore, to atone for the deaths of their comrades, they had to commit their all to the revolution to assure victory. For Mao who emerged as leader on the march, the experience strengthened his "already deeply ingrained voluntaristic faith that men with the proper will, spirit, and revolutionary consciousness could conquer all material obstacles and mold historical reality. . . ."[26] And it gave him a further sense of destiny, that he and he alone would be the one to lead China out of its miserable past into a future bright with hope. It was thus Mao and his leadership who profited most from the development and perpetuation of the Long March legend for he was able to make it his story and the story of modern China.

The Three-Year War

When the Long Marchers broke out of the Jiangxi base, they left about forty-two thousand troops to make raids on and tie down Chiang's troops and, in the process, to keep a foothold and networks of support in the region. For the next three years they continued sporadic guerrilla activity in eighteen bases primarily along the borders of eight provinces; it is called today the Three-Year War. For many, the hardships of living primitive existences in rugged mountains brought a bonding almost as intense as the trials along the Long March brought its veterans.

The strategies were local. Since each locale was different, the logical approach demanded sensitivity to local realities and willingness to learn from the locals. "Living on society's margins, stretching out tendrils into it, learning its ways, and studying its social arrangements not to change it but to strike deals with it" was the strategy of these guerrilla bands—a sharp contrast to the often-times bureaucratic-centralist style of the Jiangxi Soviet and later policies at Yan'an. Ultimately tailoring one's revolutionary approach flexibly to the locality was a more successful revolutionary strategy.[27] In localities, then, manipulating individuals through local organizations or kinship ties, not mass mobilization, was the key strategy.

Guerrilla political and social policies toward the people in areas they controlled ranged from trying to carry out land reform to working for reductions in rents and interest, from resisting the government's military and labor drafts to confiscating grain and distributing it to peasants. With the exodus of so many males in the Long March, east-central China experienced what one historian has called the "feminization of the party."[28] That meant that women played important roles as intelligence gatherers, fighters, quartermasters, and nurses. In many ways they provided Communist continuity in the area after the Long March. Although there are no direct lines between the Three-Year War and the success of the Communist revolution, the war contributed to the revolution by tying down forces that Chiang could otherwise have used against the main Red Army, by making true the Communist claim that it was a nationwide movement, and by providing bases that the party could use to move into all parts of eastern China during the war against Japan.

BUILDING THE BASE AT YAN'AN

Twice in its fourteen-year history up until 1935 the Chinese Communist Party had been almost wiped out; the blood-letting purge by Chiang in 1927 and 1928 and the military shellacking by Guomindang forces in 1934 and 1935 probably would have led any betting person to predict that it would completely disappear from the scene. Especially this would be the case if one considered where the Long Marchers wound up and where they would try to resuscitate the moribund corpse of the party: Northern Shaanxi province—a remote, barren, backward region, marked by miserable poverty. Listen to Zhou Enlai's evaluation: "Peasants in Shaanxi are extremely poor, their land very unproductive. . . . The population of the Jiangxi Soviet numbered 3,000,000 where here it is at most 600,000. . . . In Jiangxi and Fujian people brought bundles with them when they joined the Red Army; here they do not even bring chopsticks; they are utterly destitute."[29] So much land in the province was given over to growing opium that when drought hit this already arid region there was not enough cultivation of food grains to feed the population. Poverty and malnutrition, even starvation, went hand and hand.

Yan'an to which they moved in late 1936–early 1937 was "an impoverished market town" with a population of maybe ten thousand when it became the Shaan-Gan-Ning base area capital. There was nothing much to distinguish the town; throughout much of its history it had been a military outpost guarding against invasion from regions to the west and north. Life there was hard. Many Long Marchers lived in caves hewn out of the rocky mountains. Yet Yan'an would one day become almost as legendary as the Long March.

In addition to the physical demands of life in Shaanxi, political challenges abounded. When the Long Marchers arrived in northern Shaanxi, they were met by local Communists who had already been active in Communist mobilization since the early 1930s. In the spring of 1935, Liu Zhidan and Gao Gang had established a Shaanxi-Gansu soviet and were directing a vigorous land reform program in the twenty-two counties they controlled. Then the outsider Long Marchers entered the area as if in invasion. The "outsider-local" situation must have seemed reminiscent of the Futian incident of 1930. In the beginning Mao did not seem to handle this situation any more intelligently than he had at Futian. Advance Red Army units in August 1935 arrested Liu, Gao, and other local Communist leaders and imprisoned them for deviating from the party line. But when Mao arrived in late October, the men were released. The arrests were later blamed on party "sectarianism" and personal ambitions. Neither Liu, who was killed in battle in 1936, nor Gao had apparently resisted arrest; and most of those who were involved were absorbed into the party. Over the next decade there continued to be tensions and conflicts between the newcomers and the locals. In the words of one historian, "[i]ndependent local leadership pre-

Communist leaders at Yan'an, from left to right Zhou Enlai, Mao Zedong, and Bo Gu
Source: Courtesy: President & Fellows of Harvard College Peabody Museum, Harvard University. Photo By: Owen Lattimore.

occupied with development of the border region as a revolutionary base was frequently at odds with a party hierarchy dominated by southerners whose concerns were primarily national."[30]

The many revolutionary roads not taken are in the land of history's "might have beens": If the party had continued to focus on the urban proletariat instead of the peasantry, then. . . . If the 28 Bolsheviks had remained in control, then. . . . If the Red Army had adopted a different military strategy during the fifth extermination campaign, then. . . . If the strategies and policies of soviets beyond the Jiangxi Soviet had prevailed, then. . . . If Zhang Guotao had defeated Mao, then. . . . If Zhang had won out in his desire to have the Long Marchers turn west, then. . . . The list is endless, and we can never answer the questions. What we do know is the many roads taken: the focus of the party was now clearly on the peasantry; Mao Zedong was on his way to the top; the experiments of the Jiangxi Soviet, not those of other soviets, were harbingers of the future; the work in fashioning the Jiangxi Soviet went for naught in the disastrous military defeat by Chiang; and the Long March had ended in the barren northwest. There the party would be rebuilt and fashioned into an organization that within little more than a decade would take over the country.

Notes

[1] The phrase is from Jerome Ch'en, "The Communist Movement, 1927–1937," in Fairbank and Feuerwerker, Eds., *The Cambridge History of China, Vol. 13, Republican China, 1912–1949, Part 2*, p. 173.

[2] Simon Leys, "The Art of Interpreting Nonexistent Inscriptions Written in Invisible Ink on a Blank Page," *The New York Review of Books* (October 11, 1990), 12.

[3] Quoted in Ch'en, p. 189.

[4] Mao Zedong, "Report on an Investigation of the Peasant Movement" in Tony Saich, Ed., *The Rise to Power of the Chinese Communist Party* (Armonk, N.Y.: M. E. Sharpe, 1996), p. 198.

[5] Lucien Bianco, *The Origins of the Chinese Revolution, 1915–1949* (Stanford: Stanford University Press, 1971), fn. 10, p. 64.

[6] Mao Zedong, "Letter to Lin Biao (January 5, 1930)" in Saich, p. 485.

[7] Benjamin I. Schwartz, *Chinese Communism and the Rise of Mao* (Cambridge: Harvard University Press, 1951), p. 166.

[8] Saich, p. 511.

[9] The phrase is Saich's, p. 510.

[10] "Land Law of the Soviet Republic (November 1931)" in Saich, p. 556. All subsequent quotations from this law come from this source.

[11] Mao Zedong, *Report from Xunwu,* trans., Roger R. Thompson (Stanford: Stanford University Press, 1990), p. 11.

[12] This table is from ibid., p. 122.

[13] Ch'en, p. 178.

[14] Saich, p. 557.

[15] Saich, p. 604.

[16] Ch'en, p. 195.

[17] Saich, p. 372.

[18] See, for example, Gregor Benton, *Mountain Fires: The Red Army's Three-Year War in South China, 1934–1938* (Berkeley, 1992) and Odoric Y. K. Wou, *Mobilizing the Masses: Building Revolution in Henan* (Stanford, 1994).

[19] Quoted in Ch'en, p. 205.

[20] Edgar Snow, *Red Star over China* (New York: Modern Library, 1938), p. 177.

[21] Ibid., p. 216.

[22] William G. Rosenberg and Marilyn B. Young, *Transforming Russia and China* (New York: Oxford University Press, 1982), p. 144.

[23] Saich, p. 524.

[24] Ibid., p. 658.

[25] Mao Zedong, "Strategic Problems of China's Revolutionary War," in *Selected Works of Mao Tse-tung,* Vol.1 (New York: International Publishers, 1954), p. 193, cited in Maurice Meisner, "Yenan Communism and the Rise of the Chinese People's Republic" in James B. Crowley, Ed., *Modern East Asia: Essays in Interpretation* (New York: Harcourt, Brace & World, 1970), p. 274.

[26] Meisner, p. 271.

[27] This information on the Three Years war comes from Gregor Benton, "Under Arms and Umbrellas: Perspectives on Chinese Communism in Defeat," in Tony Saich and Hans van de Ven, Eds., *New Perspectives on the Chinese Communist Revolution* (Armonk, N.Y.: M. E. Sharpe, 1995), p. 124–126. See also his *Mountain Fires*.

[28] Benton, "Under Arms and Umbrellas," p. 126.

[29] Quoted in Maurice Meisner, *Mao's China and After* (New York: Free Press, 1999), p. 37.

[30] Mark Selden, *The Yenan Way in Revolutionary China* (Cambridge: Harvard University Press, 1971), p.72.

13

A Rising Clash of National Identities: China and Japan, the 1920s and 1930s

_____

_____

___

"China is a society, but she is not a nation. Or rather, it would be fair to say that China is a society of bandits. . . . The Chinese people are bacteria infesting world civilization."[1] The speaker was Major General Sakai Ryu, Chief of Staff of the Japanese forces in North China. The date was 1938, when Japan and China were at war. The judgments expressed reveal several things, the most obvious, a contemptuous attempt to dehumanize the Chinese. Japanese attitudes like this were the foundation for their role in China in the 1930s, years in which modern imperialism reached its greatest height. The first phase of imperialism had been the treaty port system with its various stipulations about foreign "rights." It had been followed, more ominously, by the seizure of Chinese tributary states and, in the scramble for concessions in the late 1890s, the seizure and use of Chinese territory, for a specified period of time. The economic imperialism embodied in the Boxer Protocol and the foreign support of warlords was insidious but dangerous in its impact. In all these phases of imperialism, China seemed almost a limp and passive victim.

But, in the words of one historian, "Japanese imperialism [was one of] the midwives of modern Chinese nationalism."[2] Come the 1930s, when Japan undertook its most flagrant phase of imperialism, China, or at least the Chinese people, had begun to stiffen their resistance. In the end, it was the often-brutal imperialism of the Japanese that gave rise to surging nationalism throughout much of China.

A CASE OF MISTAKEN IDENTITY

One of the most striking aspects of Sakai's assertion is his claim that China is not a nation, but only a society of bandits. For Japanese at least such a belief might be a rationale for Japan, risen to modern nationhood with astounding speed, to whip China into shape and for Japan to take its proper place in the world as East Asian regional leader. But Sakai's statement completely misreads Chinese realities. Nationalism had been a powerful force, at least in Chinese core areas, for thirty years and in many peripheral areas for twenty by the time he made this pronouncement—a vibrant, virile, often violent force. Hundreds of thousands had fought a revolution in the 1920s to establish its national identity. Sakai's misreading points to a more serious reality that dogged Japan's understanding of China: Japan *thought* it knew China better than it really did.

The pattern of Chinese-Japanese relationships in the modern period had been checkered to say the least. Japan had defeated China in war in 1895, had sent troops in with the Allied expedition to quell the Boxers in 1900, had insisted on its Twenty-One Demands in 1915, and had held onto Shandong for three years following the end of the world war. This had been Japan's imperialistic identity. Yet for China, Japan had other identities as well. It also became China's teacher, in that role turning on its head the tributary relationship of long ago when China had been elder brother to Japan's younger brother. In the early years of the century young Chinese flocked to Japan's schools trying to learn the secrets of Japan's rapid modernization. Kang Youwei talked of Japan as a model. Sun Yat-sen lived in Japan in 1897 to 1898, 1900 to 1903, 1905, 1906, 1910, and 1913 to 1916; he became close friends of Japanese liberals who offered him financial and moral support in his revolutionary undertakings. Even Mao Zedong had contacted one of these liberals, Miyazaki Toten, to visit his school in Changsha; Miyazaki complied. Chiang Kai-shek had attended military school in Japan from 1908 to 1911, and, as we will see, strived mightily and foolhardily for some agreement with Japan in the 1930s. Similarly, many Chinese warlords of the 1920s and 1930s had attended schools in Japan and a number had Japanese advisors on their staffs. So for many Chinese, Japan's identity was not all negative in the least.

Japan's Reading of Contemporary China

From Japan's perspectives they shared many commonalities with China. Japan had borrowed heavily from China's traditional culture; and, though they had amended and shaped many of these cultural traditions to Japanese realities, they continued to share many cultural values and roots. Its historical relationship going back for more than a millennium led some Japanese to assume, at least in the face of a possible threat from the West, that cooperation if not friendship was a likely scenario for their relationship. Certainly in comparison to the West or any other nation, Japan knew most about China. It had more China experts and research than any country in the world.

Take, for example, the East Asia Common Culture Academy [Tōa Dōbun Shoin], established with Japanese government support in Shanghai in 1901, primarily to train young Japanese in studies of the Chinese language and contemporary China and also to prepare young Chinese to enter regular schools in Japan. Graduates of the school were often hired on by the Japanese Foreign Ministry for detailed investigations in areas the foreign ministry deemed important. For example, five graduates were assigned from 1905 to 1907 "to major outposts across [Xinjiang] and Mongolia, to report on Russian activities in the wake of the Russo-Japanese War." Or in terms of Chinese domestic developments, in 1909 and

1910, the Foreign Ministry wanted an "[i]nvestigation in thirteen provinces of North, Central and South China, of the workings of China's new provincial assemblies, official/nonofficial relations at the local level, provincial educational systems, the campaign to suppress opium,. . . ."[3] A requirement for graduation from the school was an extensive investigative fieldwork project on an area of contemporary China. Three- to nine-man teams would spend the summer before graduation intensively investigating political, social, and economic aspects of every province in China. Guidelines and instructions for the investigations were drawn up carefully. Confidential reports went to the government, but three series of encyclopedic studies were published: a twelve-volume survey of the Chinese economy (1907–1908), an eighteen-volume gazetteer of the provinces of China (1917–1920); and an eight-volume revised gazetteer of the provinces (1941–1944). The information published in these works was generally dependable. Certainly no other country had studied China in such depth.

But knowledge must be processed through psyches that have their own biases and "takes" on life, others, and the world. Despite the fact that many Chinese had studied and lived in Japan and that many Japanese had lived, worked, and journeyed through all areas of China, the knowledge thereby gained somehow did not establish itself. In the words of one historian,

> How much of this "knowledge" . . . penetrated very deeply into the Japanese psyche? Did not the psychological antibodies of bullying and insensitivity powerfully counteract most cases of possible infection [by knowledge]? Knowledge—in the form of scholarly books and reports and learned specialists—thus coexisted in tension with dark ignorance.[4]

In addition to this psychological predisposition not really to see what there was to see, there was a language problem that also clouded the vision of China among Japan's specialists and that contributed to Japan's drawing wrong conclusions about China's identity. Although the graduates of the Common Culture Academy had to be able to converse in Chinese in order to accomplish their fieldwork, most Japanese experts on China and certainly most Japanese politicians did not know Chinese. The problem stems from the nature of the Japanese language. It is a combination of Japanese phonetic symbols that stand for syllables (called a syllabary), on the one hand, and Chinese characters (called *kanji* in Japanese), on the other. While today most contemporary Japanese is written predominantly in the Japanese syllabary, before the 1950s formal Japanese was written mostly in Chinese characters. Thus, Japanese assumed they could read Chinese newspapers and other publications and understand the Chinese situation, what the Chinese were thinking, and the nature of Chinese attitudes and goals. But this was a faulty assumption for several reasons. First, many Japanese *kanji,* though they look the same, have different meanings or shades of meanings from Chinese characters. Second, to understand the psyche of a contemporary society, the key is knowing the spoken colloquial; but the Japanese experts did not know how to speak Chinese. Third, until the 1920s and in some cases into the 1930s, Chinese publications were written in classical Chinese not the vernacular; so when Japanese experts on China read Chinese, they were reading the traditional classical prose.

Dependence on the classical prose sources that they "read" caused Japanese views of China to be "innocent of the social science approaches of the twentieth century and anchored to the classical tradition in which the Chinese elites had been steeped."[5] This meant that the dominant way Japan's experts conceived of contemporary China was as "unchanging." Listen to Naito Konan, one of Japan's most important scholars of China: "We no longer need to ask when China will collapse. It is already dead, only its corpse is wriggling."[6] Japan's China experts generally knew or understood little about the head-spinning changes and transformations in early twentieth century Chinese society. Warlords? Just like traditional Chinese generals in the interregnum between dynasties. Republican government? Just a surface blip in the ongoing stream of Chinese politics. Since traditional China lay just beneath the surface, information that suggested otherwise was either not analyzed or, as is more likely the case, not even perceived or processed. Such faulty assumptions, perhaps epitomized in Sakai's ignorant evaluations, were the foundation for policies that could not succeed because they were not based in reality.

Contextual Problems

There were two other contemporary contextual situations that contributed to Japan's misreading China's identity and being unable to react to realities. The first was related to Japan's perceived national interests in China. Japanese strategists had located Japan's sphere of interest in the north of China. Japan had swallowed Korea whole in 1910. The Russo-Japanese War had brought her control of the strategically important 650-mile long South Manchurian Railroad that ran from Harbin in central Manchuria to Port Arthur on the tip of the Liaodong peninsula. Japan's role on the continent was predicated on its predominance in Manchuria, with its raw materials, farm land, and living space.

Thus, in the early Republic, Japan had given its special support to "its" warlord in Manchuria, Zhang Zuolin. Japanese had relied on Zhang to work with them to protect their interests. Since Zhang had become involved in the major warlord wars over control of Beijing, Japan's relationship to Zhang as direct patron had great potential benefit if he emerged as the Chinese head of state. In the 1920s Japan was excessively focused on warlords, and it got financially burned in several cases when loans given to warlords were insufficiently secured. The focus on warlords and the north took Japan's vision away from the growing Nationalist revolution in the south. Though some Japanese merchant capitalists had begun to talk of the strategic importance of greater involvement with markets in central and south China, the fixation on the north continued. Lack of flexibility in its policy approach to China (and part of this stemmed from the knowledge problem) made it difficult for policy-makers to change their course.

A second problem was the changing nature of the Japanese political system. While political parties had emerged in the 1920s as the main powerbrokers, the downsides of a more open political system also became visible. Both in election campaigns and the making of policy, "political gamesmanship" that toyed with popular emotion came to play a role. If, for example, a policy needed changing but the reality was that changing it would reflect negatively on Japan's image or past policy or the image of a particular party, then politicians would sit on their hands and change nothing. Given these circumstances, in the late 1920s and the early 1930s a general rising military aggressiveness in Japanese political culture made the support of more moderate approaches less and less possible.

Troubles Emerge

As long as warlords continued to posture and battle, Japan could continue to muddle through on the continent without having to make substantial changes in policy. But relations between Japan and China were far from cordial. Talks over trade and tariffs in 1925 and 1927, though conducted on Japan's side under Foreign Minister Shidehara who was known for his emphasis on international cooperation, were tense and inconclusive. Then several serious factors broke the business-as-usual situation and began to seriously destabilize the relationship.

Out of south China in the mid-1920s came a vibrant and aggressive Chinese nationalism aimed at warlords (like Zhang Zuolin) and imperialists (like Japan). This expansion of a strong nationalism unfortunately came about the same time as difficulties began to shake the Japanese economy and as Japanese began to question the effectiveness and wisdom of civilian party rule. Waiting in the wings was the Japanese military, which had watched political parties slash its budgets and reduce its numbers. The initial military activities were prompted by civilian politics, with the party in charge playing on general fears of Communism and trying to appear hard-nosed in its policies toward revolutionary forces that included Communists. In May 1927, well before Chiang Kai-shek had begun the northern campaigns of his Northern Expedition, the Japanese government transferred Japanese troops from Manchuria to Shandong, the goal being the protection of Japanese living there. Among the Chinese in general, the brief occupation of these troops was hardly noticed amid the crack-up of the united front and the growing White Terror under Chiang Kai-shek.

But then, in April 1928, two thousand Japanese troops were again sent to Shandong to protect Japanese lives. Objective observers note that at this time there was no valid reason for Japan's sending troops; there were no threats to Japanese civilians, and Communists were no longer involved. Though sent to the port of Qingdao, the Japanese troops were moved to Jinan to try to deflect Chinese forces from Japanese interests there. Serious fighting broke out between Japanese and Chinese troops. The Japanese seized that city and held it under martial law until April 1929. This Jinan incident, in which several thousand Chinese were killed, led to substantial bitterness, a variety of protests, and a nation-wide boycott against the Japanese. Anger and distrust were being ratcheted up.

MANCHURIA BECOMES MANCHUKUO: JAPANESE AGGRESSION RUN AMOK

During the Qing dynasty, the reigning Manchus had wanted to maintain Manchuria as the Manchu homeland and so they kept Manchuria closed to Chinese immigration. Because of this policy, in the early twentieth century, it was still relatively sparsely settled. For Japan, Manchuria offered not only space for emigration but also a source for industrial raw materials, an abundance of arable land, and a base for further actions on the mainland. After

1912, Japan encouraged Koreans, now Japanese subjects, to emigrate to Manchuria as a way of making Japan's presence more secure. With a population of about thirty million in 1930, it was home to one million Japanese subjects, about 800,000 being Korean; foreign investment there was 75 percent Japanese, and of all of Japan's trade with China, 40 percent was with Manchuria.

As Chiang Kai-shek's Northern Expedition moved north to Beijing in 1928, his actions seemed more and more threatening to Japan's position on the continent. On May 18, about a week after the end of the fighting in the Jinan incident, the Japanese government sent identical notes to Chiang in Nanjing and Zhang Zuolin in Beijing warning that Japan might have to act if the situation in the north became destabilized. The message read in part, "the Japanese government . . . may possibly be constrained to take appropriate and effective steps for the maintenance of peace and order in Manchuria."[7] The Japanese warned Zhang that he should return to Manchuria while his army was still intact; and stated explicitly that they would not let defeated armies or those pursuing them to cross the border into Manchuria. It is obvious that the Japanese were increasingly wary of what Zhang might do. Since 1925 Zhang had been installed in Beijing sometimes as part of a military coalition, other times as lone de facto head of the government. Now with the Japanese warning, Zhang decided to return to Manchuria. On the way home on June 4, the Japanese blew up his train and killed him; in the brave new world of Chinese nationalism, they simply did not trust him. He was succeeded by his son, Zhang Xueliang, a reputed opium addict, who in negotiations with the Japanese over the course of the next few months agreed to continue to work with the Japanese in friendly fashion. When Zhang raised the flag of the Nanjing government at Shenyang (Mukden) in December 1928, the Japanese issued a mild warning but did nothing to back it up. Japan formally recognized Chiang's government in June 1929.

Once Zhang gave his allegiance to Chiang, he was named commander of the Northeastern Frontier Army. Nanjing then set out to establish a greater Chinese presence in Manchuria. Guomindang party branches were organized everywhere; party publications trumpeting anti-imperialist rhetoric sprang up. The Nanjing government loudly demanded the return of treaty rights claimed by Japan, including extraterritoriality. It tried to undercut the Japanese economic position. For example, it set up competing railroads which, using techniques like rebates and rate wars, began to eat into Japanese railroad profits; Zhang Xueliang refused to negotiate the railroad disputes that resulted. The Nanjing regime constructed port facilities at Yingkou on the eastern coast of the Gulf of Liaodong and planned to do so at Huludao on the gulf's western coast to challenge Japanese facilities at Dairen.

The years from 1928 to 1931 saw increasing tensions over seemingly small things—railroad "wars" and violent incidents between Korean settlers and Chinese over mundane disputes, property boundaries and irrigation rights. At the beginning of July 1931, in the so-called Wanbaoshan incident, Japanese consular police used machine guns fired over the heads of Chinese farmers to disperse them after a confrontation with Korean farmers over the construction of an irrigation ditch. Like other incidents, this was like a pinprick—no serious casualties occurred. Yet Japanese extremists used the right-wing press in both Japan and Korea to intensify the increasingly bitter feelings against China, giving rise to anti-Chinese riots in both Korea and Japan. In Korea Chinese residents were attacked, their shops and homes looted; 127 Chinese were killed and several hundred wounded. In August 1931, there came to light the killing two months earlier of one Captain Nakamura who, traveling as an agricultural expert, was arrested near the Manchurian-Mongolian border. Apparently involved in a secret mission, he was carrying heroin probably to use in transactions with the Mongols. After seizing him, the Chinese shot him as a spy. The Japanese press had a field day with the story, demanding that the murder of an officer of the Imperial Army be avenged and, above all, that Japan put into place a stronger policy with regard to Manchuria.

The Japanese military in the field saw these things close at hand and magnified them into a towering threat to Japan's very position. There are no inevitabilities in history, yet one would have to say that the almost palpable tension that had built between the two countries had to find some way of release, and that it would likely be violent. Thus, field grade officers in Manchuria, without the agreement or even knowledge of the military authorities or the government in Tokyo, plotted to make Japan's position secure by taking over Manchuria. On September 18, 1931, they blew up one length of track on the South Manchurian Railroad, just to the north of Mukden near a large barracks housing Chinese troops. The destruction was not even bad enough to prevent the next train from passing the point successfully. Be that as it may, the Japanese army blamed the bombing on the Chinese, and used it as a pretext to begin a military campaign. Tokyo repeatedly declared that the military action would be halted, only to find that it had to eat its words as the military action continued. Japanese military policy was being made autonomously in the field; there were no controls on it.

The Guomindang military's "resistance" against Japan in the Manchurian fighting amounted in reality to nonresistance; military command in some cases ordered men about to go into battle to lay down their arms and simply surrender. The outrage for patriotic Chinese was that Chiang had established his government under the banner of nationalism but his military decisions seemed cowardly and almost treasonous. Even after all of Manchuria had fallen, Chiang refused to break off relations with Japan, much less to respond with some strong military reaction. What is the explanation for such a seeming anti-nationalistic tack? Partly it was timing. When the Manchurian "incident" occurred, Chiang's military was in the middle of its third extermination campaign against the Jiangxi Soviet. In fact, the "Manchurian incident" (the euphemism the Japanese used to cloak their bloody war) led to Chiang's ending of the third campaign.

But Chiang's appeasement of the Japanese was more than contextual timing. Chiang believed that his army was not strong enough to fight two wars at one time—taking on both Japan and the Chinese Communists. Chiang was relying on German military advisors to help him strengthen his armies. His response to ever more virulent Japanese aggression in north China was that the Communists had be dealt with before the Japanese: The latter he compared to a skin disease while the Communists were a disease of the heart. Obviously a more serious heart problem needed to be treated before turning to a skin disease, unless, of course, the skin disease was melanoma, not a bad comparison given Japan's malevolent actions.

By early 1932, the Japanese conquest of Manchuria was complete. Instead of seizing it outright as they had done with Korea in 1910, the Japanese decided that setting up a puppet state under Manchu leadership might tone down excessively negative foreign reaction. In the fall, the Japanese renamed it and recognized the independent state of Manchukuo (meaning, "land of the Manchus") under the leadership of the last Qing emperor, Henry Puyi. For all Japanese pretense the state was not in the least independent; Puyi was nothing more than a puppet. The League of Nations Lytton commission reported in autumn 1932 that Japan was guilty of military aggression in Manchuria; the League itself adopted the report in early 1933. Japan, thumbing its nose at the world, walked out of the League. International condemnation united Japanese public opinion, creating an even more dangerous chauvinist-charged situation.

For China the turn of events was ominous. In general, "Japan's determination to take Chinese territory as a direct colonial possession, in contrast to the indirect colonial penetration of an earlier era, created a new type of foreign danger for China, one which pressed Chinese leaders to assume national . . . responsibility."[8] Chiang's reaction of nonresistance stimulated many outraged citizens to protest through demonstrations and boycotts; it is no exaggeration to say that the Manchurian incident and the months afterward transformed China's political environment. No small result of the loss of Manchuria was that China lost 15 percent of its revenue that had come into that area through its tariffs. Given the fact that 50 percent of Nanjing's total revenue came from customs duties, this was a substantial reduction.

JAPANESE AGGRESSION ON THE MARCH

The Shanghai Incident

The Chinese people struck back at Japan through a very effective boycott in the autumn of 1931. It slashed the sale of Japanese products in China by two thirds. Tensions were especially high in Shanghai with its population of thirty thousand Japanese citizens; many of them called for the military to come in and end the boycott. The Japanese Manchurian army (the Kwantung army) funneled money to Shanghai to start an "incident" that would take Manchuria out of the spotlight. The military declared the boycott an act of aggression. Skirmishes broke out at the end of January 1932. With the cries of Japanese ultranationalists ringing in military ears—"Teach the Chinese a lesson"—the Japanese navy (wanting to get in on some of the patriotic glory with the Kwantung army) bombed the Chabei sector in northern Shanghai. The Chinese Nineteenth Route Army, against the will of Chiang Kai-shek, resisted forcefully. Fighting was brutal, with the Japanese eventually sending seventy thousand troops to Shanghai and utilizing planes to drop fire bombs and advanced tanks and artillery to shell civilian areas. Over four thousand Chinese soldiers were killed; the Japanese lost not quite 800.

This undeclared war raged around Shanghai for six weeks (January–March, 1932); the fighting stopped when both countries agreed to an armistice. Clearly Japan had decided that it would not push the matter at this time. On the Chinese scene recriminations abounded. Chiang was furious that the Nineteenth Route Army had put up any resistance; he feared that it might ignite a full-scale Japanese war that would have endangered his own position. So he transferred the army, composed largely of men from Guangdong, to out-of-

Captured Chinese who collaborated with the Japanese on his way to death, Shanghai, 1932

the-way Fujian province. Many supporters of the army contended that Chiang had contributed to the army's not being completely successful by withholding both funds and reinforcements. For many Chinese the Nineteenth Route Army became instant heroes, the names of its leaders appearing as brand names for cigarettes and other goods. The reason? As one historian put it, "The Chinese people, who had been gagging on never-ending humiliations and pusillanimous compromises, took the Nineteenth Route Army to their hearts."[9] The Shanghai incident only increased the polarization that was developing between those who called for resistance against this flagrant imperialist threat and the government. Chiang's response to the protesters was to suppress the protests and protesters, a policy that only ratcheted up the level of animosity.

Gobbling Up the North

The years from 1933 to 1937 saw the patterns repeated again and again. Japanese aggression, Chiang's appeasement, mass Chinese reaction, Chiang's brutal suppression of the demonstrating population. During the United States war in Vietnam later in the century, American leaders talked of a domino theory, that if one Southeast Asian country fell to Communism, all would topple like lined-up dominoes; in that particular war that theory was not applicable. But the concept would probably apply here, for what one sees in looking at the three years 1933 through 1935, is the toppling of Chinese property and rights before the Japanese onslaught.

What follows is a summary of the eight major Japanese aggressions in these three years. Japan won every contest but one. But also important in this catalogue of tragedy is the import of each of China's defeats, the reaction of China's people to the defeat, and Chiang's reaction to the people's reaction.

1. January 1–3, 1933

Loss of Shanhaiguan

Import: The name Shanhaiguan literally means the "pass between the mountains and the sea," the site where the Great Wall ends at the Gulf of Liaodong. The Jinzhou (Manchuria)-Tianjin Railroad ran through the pass, linking now Japan-held Manchuria with "China within the Wall." Its fall was of great symbolic value, because it was through this pass almost 289 years earlier that the Manchus had come on their way to taking over China. A shock wave washed over thinking Chinese: could this be a déja vu? Might this be the start of another conquest of China? Many in Chinese society were unnerved.

Chiang's response: No reinforcements were sent to assist the Ninth Brigade which fought well but was no match for the Japanese. Chiang would not act in part because he was in the beginning phase of his fourth extermination campaign against the Jiangxi Soviet.

Popular reaction: There was fear that Chiang would now be willing to abandon Hebei province, where Beiping [the name by which Beijing was known from 1928 to 1949] was located. This perception was stimulated in part because the National Palace Museum, the priceless collection of traditional art masterpieces, as well as Foreign Affairs Ministry Archives began to be sent south. There was considerable clamor for resistance. The Chinese delegation at the League of Nations cabled that Shanhaiguan should be retaken.

Chiang's reaction: Chiang took on a pose of resistance, cabling the League of Nations delegation about Japan's rumored move into the Inner Mongolian province of Rehe, "[Rehe's] territory is the door to north China. If the Japanese invade it, we must resist with all out might."[10]

2. February 23–March 4, 1933

Loss of Rehe Province, Inner Mongolia

Chiang's response: Whatever Chiang had meant by his cable to the League of Nations delegation, he did not resist with "all out might." He ordered the poorest and most politically unreliable troops to fight the battles; they mostly just melted away before the Japanese attacks. He dispatched no planes; he sent no guns. Troops from the national army did not arrive until the battle was over even though the Japanese invasion had been expected for months. Chiang stayed with the anti-Communist campaign in Jiangxi.

Import: In addition to the loss of territory the size of the states of Virginia, Maryland, and West Virginia in just over a week, the conundrum of Chiang's motives grew ever larger.

Popular reaction: Disbelief and chagrin. Longtime party leader Hu Hanmin: "When Shanhaiguan fell and at the time of the Rehe crisis, he used the pretext that the Jiangxi Com-

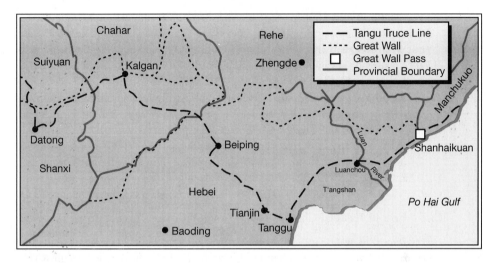

North China, mid-1930s

munists were rampaging. . . . I do not argue that the Communists should not be eliminated, but in today's situation . . . resisting Japan is more important than eliminating Communists." Madame Sun Yat-sen: "The Chinese people want resistance against Japanese . . . imperialism. . . .The time has come when [the Chiang government's] phrases about 'prolonged resistance' can no longer hide the facts of betrayal, cowardice, and non-resistance."[11]

Chiang's reaction: To reiterate his "first internal pacification, then external resistance" policy.

3. May 1933

Tanggu Truce

Import: This negotiated settlement created a demilitarized zone between the Great Wall and Beiping the size of the state of Connecticut. Chiang negotiated it to stop the Japanese advance and the certain takeover of the cities of Beiping (Japanese troops were only thirteen miles from the city) and Tianjin. Chinese troops had to be out of the DMZ, but Japanese troops could remain in the area because of their "right" under the Boxer Protocol. There were a number of secret provisions, one of which allowed the Japanese to have dominant police powers in the DMZ.

Popular reaction: All the most important newspapers used words like "surrender" and "defeat" to describe the truce. Chiang and others in the government were called "traitors." Chiang was compared to Yuan Shikai, as someone "willing to cave into Japanese demands in exchange for their support for his dictatorship."[12] Journalist Zou Taofen in his *Life Weekly* vigorously attacked the agreement.

Chiang's reaction: In the aftermath of the Tanggu Truce, Chiang struck out at his opponents. In June, Yang Quan, the secretary for the League for the Protection of Civil Rights—organized in reaction to Chiang's suppression of the anti-Japanese activity—was assassinated. Zou Taofen, warned that his life was in danger, left China for Europe and America; it was a way of silencing him without ambushing him as they had done Yang. While Zou was away, Nanjing closed his journal. On Chiang's government, Jiang Tingfu, history professor at Qinghua University, wrote

> Assassination is not politics, it is not party struggle, it is killing people, vilely killing people, savagely killing people. Whatever party, whatever faction, uses assassination to overthrow an enemy party or faction exposes its own weakness. It only proclaims to the world, "if we depend on what we advocate, our policies, our achievements, our organization, we cannot support our position. Therefore we must use murder."[13]

4. August 1933

Loss of Eastern Chahar, Inner Mongolia

Import: The territory that was lost was slightly larger than the state of Connecticut. Even more significant was what had led up to the Japanese August seizure. The Japanese had held onto this area before but it had been won back from them with relative ease, not by Chiang but by warlord Feng Yuxiang. The Japanese were able to retake it because Chiang applied all sorts of pressure, including a blockade, to weaken Feng. Two disturbing questions: why would Chiang not fight the Japanese when Feng showed it could be done effectively, and why did Chiang and his generals in essence help the Japanese retake territory that they had earlier lost?

5. April 1934

Japanese Assertion of the Amō Doctrine

Import: While not a formal declaration by the government, the Foreign Ministry asserted this "doctrine." Its import was ominous, for, if carried out, it virtually set up a Japanese protectorate over China. Japan would have control of all aid and development programs that China established with Western nations. The statement read in part, "Any joint operations undertaken by foreign powers even in the name of technical or financial assistance . . . are bound to acquire political significance. . . . Japan therefore must object to such undertakings as a matter of principle."[14]

Popular reaction: While Western governments protested, the Chinese press stridently denounced Japan. Articles worried about whether this was the first move toward the establishment of a Japanese protectorate. There was general agreement that this policy drastically worsened Sino-Japanese relations.

6. June 1935

He-Umezu Agreement

Import: This agreement substantially eroded the power of the Nanjing government in the north. Accompanied by an order that all anti-Japanese activities must stop, this agreement removed all Guomindang and Nanjing government bodies and all army troops from

Hebei province. It removed the mayor of Tianjin and the governor of Hebei. In addition, the agreement threatened to bring Beiping and Tianjin into the earlier-established DMZ, if anti-Japanese actions did not cease.

Qin-Doihara Agreement

Import: This agreement basically gave Japan a free hand in the Inner Mongolian province of Chahar. It stipulated that the Chinese could not interfere with activities undertaken by Japan or Manchukuo in Chahar.

Popular reaction: Though the Nanjing government's censorship of the press grew ever more restrictive, the press response to these agreements generally echoed the ideas from a Tianjin paper that blasted the "traitorous Kuomintang [Guomindang]." "It clears the way for Japanese imperialism, selling the nation's territory and the people's rights. Whatever Japan wants the Kuomintang gives them."[15]

Chiang's reaction: Chiang, constantly pressured by the Japanese, moved to stiffen measures to stifle anti-Japanese activity.

7. September 1935

Demand for Autonomy for Five Northern Provinces

Import: This was the only one of the eight dominoes that did not fall. If Chiang had acceded to this demand, the five northern provinces of China (Hebei, Shandong, Shanxi, Chahar, and Suiyuan) would have been made independent with the Chinese government removed. Japan's motives in north China were not simply military and political but economic as well. Their desire was to make North China a part of an economic bloc composed of Manchukuo, North China, and Japan.

Popular reaction: This demand shocked even Chiang and other government leaders.

8. December 1935

Establishment of the Hebei-Chahar Council

Import: This development really spelled the loss of eastern Hebei province (with its cities of Beiping and Tianjin) to the Japanese.

Popular reaction: This change helped stimulate an anti-Japanese student campaign called the December Ninth Movement. It began in Beiping on December 9 to protest Japan's demands for north China autonomy. Marked by protest demonstrations and rallies, the movement spread to the nation's cities. Students carried the word to rural areas as well. National Salvation Associations, headquartered in Shanghai, were established across the nation; they called for the removal of Japanese troops and puppet regimes in Manchukuo and East Hebei.

Chiang's reaction: Raids on schools, the arrests of student leaders, and the closing of campuses were Chiang's responses to China's students, fervent with nationalism. Chiang and the right wing of the Guomindang attacked them as "tools of the Communists." By March 1936, most students had been silenced, but their ideas would bear some fruit in the months ahead.

Appeasement Begins to Fade

Chiang had initially tried to defuse the December Ninth Movement by co-opting students, inviting student leaders to come to Nanjing for discussions. Some did, but others saw little purpose in meeting. The Beiping Student Union, for example, noted that Chiang had called a similar meeting after Manchuria fell; then he had vowed to win back the territory within three years. The students wrote, "Four years have already elapsed. Not only has no effort been made to recover the lost provinces, but Rehe, and East Hebei, and six counties in northern Chahar have also gone under Japanese control."[16]

By summer 1936, Chiang was well aware of the nation's restiveness. The National Salvation movement, far from being nipped in the bud, was expanding. Chiang also had to deal with a short-lived rebellion of generals from Guangxi and Guangdong provinces who were demanding to be able to fight the Japanese in the north. Following its suppression, Chiang gave the first indication that he might consider some resistance to the Japanese in the future. Specifically, he set forth the idea that appeasement had its limits. Although he still hoped that any future trouble might be handled without recourse to war, he was at least countenancing that possibility. This hint did not mean that Chiang was reacting to nationalistic pressure. In November he had seven of the leaders of the National Salvation Association arrested to the outrage of millions of people across the country. It was a harbinger of what would become known late in the century as "human rights" problems. Even Western intellectuals—Albert Einstein and John Dewey, for examples—cabled Chiang's government asking the leaders' release. At home the arrests only stimulated anti-Japanese activity.

THE XI'AN INCIDENT

Out of this context came one of the most sensational and still mysterious episodes in twentieth century China. Since the Long Marchers had reached Yan'an in late 1935, Chiang had used large numbers of troops to blockade the Communist base. By late 1936 the troop count stood at about 170,000. Its main commander was Zhang Xueliang, the former military leader of Manchuria, who, with many of his troops native to Manchuria, was none too happy to be in northwest China fighting other Chinese. It was the victory of Japan in Manchuria that had ousted Zhang and his fellow Manchurian troops. In part, because of their own "loss" of their homeland, they were very sympathetic to the ideas of the National Salvation movement. Already in April 1936, Zhang had met with Zhou Enlai to discuss a possible united front—between the CCP and the Guomindang to fight the Japanese.

Many Chinese, including Zhang, could simply not understand why Chinese should be fighting Chinese at a time when the Japanese were eating them alive. Chiang's record was a dogged continuous struggle against the Communists: his troops fought five extermination campaigns against the Jiangxi Soviet; they fought the Long March; then once they reached Yan'an, Chiang used his best troops to blockade and quarantine the Communists.

In October Chiang ordered Zhang to begin a campaign against the Communists. Zhang and his fellow commanders just sat on their hands. In early December Chiang flew to Xi'an to determine what was going on. After days of "fruitless exhortations and harangues," Chiang had finally had enough. He relieved Zhang of his command, placed someone more malleable at the head of his forces, and ordered that the army begin an anti-Communist campaign on December 12.

In the pre-dawn hours of December 12, a unit of Zhang's troops, under the direction of Zhang and his fellow officers, attacked Chiang's resort headquarters. While many of Chiang's bodyguards were killed in the attack, Chiang was able to escape to a cave on a nearby mountain. Zhang's men found him still in his pajamas, without his false teeth, cold, and scratched up. They put him in detention—the general having kidnapped his president— and presented him with a group of demands, all dealing with the national crisis with Japan. They included reorganizing the government to include all groups working for national salvation; halting all civil struggle among Chinese; releasing the seven leaders of the National Salvation Association and all political prisoners; guaranteeing people's right to assembly and to organizing to achieve patriotic goals; working to carry out the will of Sun Yat-sen; and convening a National Salvation Conference.

The Nanjing government faced a difficult decision. Should they launch a military effort to free the president now held against his will? Would it be less dangerous for Zhang to try to work things out diplomatically? Action proceeded on both fronts. Nanjing mobilized the air force and army at Luoyang, some two hundred miles east of Xi'an, for a possible strike. On the negotiating front, Nanjing dispatched Chiang's Australian advisor, W. H. Donald, the government's intelligence tsar and Blueshirt leader Dai Li, and Chiang's brother-in-law T. V. Soong. Madame Chiang Kai-shek also flew in, dramatically announcing to Chiang, "I am here to share your fate and to die with you, if God so wills it."[17] Negotiations dragged out as Chiang seemed his usual obstinate self.

Having much earlier opened discussions with Zhang about anti-Japanese resistance, the Communists, headquartered little more than a hundred miles away at Yan'an, also had choices to make. Their chief enemy was now practically in their hands; should he be seized and killed? Or would Chiang be more valuable alive in the present crisis with Japan if he could be persuaded to join a united front? Despite Mao's rise to power apart from help from Moscow, there was still contact between Yan'an and the Soviet capital. When Stalin weighed in on the side of keeping Chiang alive, arguing that Chiang's prestige was still a valuable asset of great potential use in a nation-wide united front, the Communist leadership in Yan'an were either confirmed in or swayed to that position. With this decision, Zhou Enlai on December 16 flew to Xi'an to join the negotiations and push Chiang to accept leadership of a new united front of the CCP and GMD against the Japanese.

Negotiations continued until December 25 when his captors released him after he reportedly gave verbal assurances that he would support a united front. He put nothing in writing, and later declared that he had not agreed to anything. The big question: why would his captors have been satisfied with mere verbal assurances? Was Chiang, with a considerable record of betraying people who had helped him (as at Shanghai in 1927), now deemed that trustworthy? In any event, Chiang flew back to Nanjing, now holding Zhang Xueliang captive. Zhang was court-martialed and then kept in custody under Chiang's control. Moved to Taiwan when the Guomindang lost the civil war in the late 1940s, Zhang remained under house arrest at least until his ninetieth birthday in 1991 and possibly longer. For his part, Chiang emerged from the affair as a national hero. Approximately 400,000 people watched his motorcade from the Nanjing airport on his return; spontaneous celebrations of joy and relief erupted in cities around the country, many people apparently willing to forget Chiang's extended period of appeasement and the harsh repression of many Chinese civilians.

What really happened in Xi'an is unclear. In doing a post-mortem on the episode, there are many questions that are still mysterious. Chiang claimed that he did not agree to anything; he wrote in his diary, "I must maintain the same spirit which led Jesus Christ to the cross." He was released, he claimed, when Zhang Xueliang read Chiang's diary and was converted to see "the greatness of your personality. Your loyalty to the revolutionary cause and your determination to bear the responsibility of saving the country far exceed anything we could have imagined." Though Zhang has never spoken about the event, the language describing this personal "revelation" seems too stilted and hagiographic. Yet that was Chiang's line—"the resolute leader, the conversion of the captors, the unconditional release."[18] But his actions told a different story. Almost immediately the title for Zhang's command, the "Bandit Suppression Headquarters" was dropped; there was a cease-fire between Nanjing's forces and the Red Army; and within little more than eight months a united front was established. It does, in short, seem as though he gave assurances; though it is still a mystery why his captors were so willing simply to accept his words without gaining some more substantial corroboration of his decision, say, even holding hostages until he transformed his words into action.

The Communists would have us believe that it was the superior negotiating power of Zhou Enlai that brought Chiang's conversion. Zhou's December 25 telegram to Yan'an noted that the negotiations had brought Chiang a real change in attitude. Zhou thus became the hero in the affair, described as having undertaken a dangerous and heroic venture in coming to Xi'an. The language and almost superhuman quality of Zhou's contribution seem once again more hagiographic than real.

There are two other significant points in an analysis of the Xi'an incident. Guomindang historians, in addition to hewing to Chiang's line about his refusal to negotiate, often point to the incident as the reason why Chiang was not able to succeed in eliminating the Communists. They argue that "at the time of the [Xi'an] coup, they [only] held four small [counties] in northern [Shaanxi], an area of roughly about 70 sq. kilometers."[19] Once Zhang's army was sent elsewhere, they were simply able to expand and thrive. The implication is that the perfidy of Zhang Xueliang prevented Chiang from succeeding in his long-time goal of exterminating the Communists. Finally, a recent interpretation has seen the whole episode as primarily a "military rebellion" of Zhang and his forces against the central government. Since this scholar believes Chiang was moving away from appeasement in any circumstance, the main import of the episode was military. Just as Chiang was able to defeat the southwest warlords over the issue of resistance against Japan before the Xi'an incident, so the incident allowed Chiang to deal with a northwest military threat by pulling Zhang's military away and breaking up its forces.

MARCO POLO BRIDGE

During night maneuvers of Japanese troops near the Marco Polo Bridge fifteen kilometers west-southwest of Beiping on July 7, 1937, shots were fired at the Japanese soldiers. When one soldier turned up missing, the Japanese demanded the right to search a nearby town.

Although the missing soldier returned less than half an hour after he disappeared, his commanders did not realize that he had returned. In the meantime, when Chinese troops refused to allow the Japanese to search the town, Japanese troops opened fire, and a battle ensued. Though negotiations brought a settlement by July 11, tensions remained high. Fighting broke out again near the end of July, this time with thousands of Chinese casualties. Within days the Japanese held the whole region of Beiping and Tianjin.

It was not only in the field where tensions were exploding in military action. But the position of the two governments was hardening. On July 27, Japanese Prime Minister Konoe had announced that he would seek a "fundamental solution of Sino–Japanese relations." Three days later, Chiang Kai-shek asserted that "the only course open to us now is to lead the masses of the nation, under a single national plan, to struggle to the last."[20]

Was full-scale war inevitable? While nothing in history is inevitable, by late summer 1937 neither country would compromise. National identities had hardened. In Japan's view, it had given too much to the continental struggle to back down. Even though the story of the relationship between the two nations during the 1930s was one long string of Chinese capitulations to Japanese demands, appeasement did not ever satisfy Japan's territorial and political appetites. Japan's attitude was almost that capitulation on every turn was not enough: China also had to show respect to Japan, and cheerfully as well—with a smiling countenance, kowtow and be kicked while they were down. Otherwise China should be taught a lesson. In the summer of 1936, a Japanese merchant was murdered in Shanghai. The Japanese press read a conspiracy into the killing. One newspaper wrote that "the latest incident is a clear instance of China's lack of sincerity and its attitude against Japan and the Japanese. . . . Anti-Japanese feeling in China is spreading like wildfire . . . [and] drastic steps must be taken by Japan in the present situation."[21] Or again, in the summer of 1937, the statement of a Japanese commander in north China that he was going to take "a punitive expedition against Chinese troops, who have been taking acts derogatory to the prestige of the Empire of Japan."[22] It was almost as if Japan wanted China to thank the Japanese for invading them. With such attitudes and with Japan's long history of involvement, Japan would not likely back down or compromise.

On the Chinese side, there could also be no compromise. The tension and drama of the Xi'an incident and Chiang's mysterious "escape" had brought him popularity. The perception, whether it was matched reality or not, was that he had committed himself to resistance against the Japanese. It would have been politically suicidal for Chiang to return to a policy of appeasement. He could not backtrack. Thus, in any crisis he had to avoid even the appearance of caving in to Japanese threats or attacks. This meant, as Chiang himself said, that China had only one route if Japan persisted, and that was "to struggle to the last."

Notes

[1] Quoted in John Hunter Boyle, *Modern Japan, The American Nexus* (Fort Worth: Harcourt, Brace & Jovanovich, 1993), p. 185.

[2] Albert Feuerwerker, "Japanese Imperialism in China: A Commentary" in Peter Duus, et.al., Eds., *The Japanese Informal Empire in China, 1895–1937* (Princeton: Princeton University Press, 1989), p. 435.

[3] These assignments are listed in Douglas R. Reynolds, "Training Young China Hands: Toa Dobun Shoin and Its Precursors, 1886–1945" in Duus, pp. 236–237.

[4] Feuerwerker, p. 437.

[5] Marius Jansen, *Japan and China: From War to Peace, 1894–1972* (Chicago: Rand McNally College Publishing Co., 1975), p. 366.

[6] Quoted in Shumpei Okamoto, "Japanese Response to Chinese Nationalism: Naito (Kónan) Torajiro's Image of China in the 1920s" in F. Gilbert Chan and Thomas H. Etzold, Eds. *China in the 1920s* (New York: New Viewpoints, 1976) p. 164.

[7] The quotations come from Boorman, Vol. 1, p. 121.

[8] Parks Coble, *Facing Japan* (Cambridge: Harvard University Press, 1991), p. 31.

[9] Eastman, *The Abortive Revolution,* p. 91.

[10] Coble, p. 93.

[11] Quoted in Coble, pp. 98–99.

[12] Ibid., p. 114.

[13] Quoted in ibid., p. 87.

[14] Ibid., p. 154.

[15] Ibid., p. 212.

[16] Ibid., p. 288.

[17] Quoted in ibid., p. 347.

[18] Ibid., pp. 346–347.

[19] *Chiang Kai-shek, His Life and Times,* translated by Chun-ming Chang (New York: St. John's University Press, 1981), p. 523, quoted in ibid., p. 348.

[20] James B. Crowley, *Japan's Quest for Autonomy* (Princeton: Princeton University Press, 1966), pp. 338–339.

[21] Coble, p. 309.

[22] Quoted in Lyman Van Slyke, "Nationalist China During the Sino-Japanese War, 1937–1945" in Fairbank and Feuerwerker, p. 550.

14

The Sino–Japanese War, 1937–1945

———
═
—

Items, published in the *Japan Advertiser,* a Tokyo English language newspaper on December 7 and 14, 1937:

> Sub-lieutenant[s] Toshiaki Mukai and . . . Takeshi Noda, . . . in a friendly contest to see which of them will first fell 100 Chinese in individual sword combat before the Japanese forces completely occupy Nanjing, are running neck and neck. On Sunday when their unit was fighting outside Kuyung, the "score" . . . was . . . Mukai, 89 and Noda, 78.
>
> The winner of the competition [over] who would be the first to kill 100 Chinese with his Yamato sword has not been decided. . . . Mukai has a score of 106 and his rival has dispatched 105, but the two . . . found it impossible to determine which passed the 100 mark first. Instead of settling it with a discussion, they are going to extend the goal by 50.
>
> Mukai's blade was slightly damaged in the competition. He explained that this was the result of cutting a Chinese in half, helmet and all. The contest was "fun," he declared. . . .
>
> Early Saturday morning when [he was interviewed] at a point overlooking Dr. Sun Yat-sen's tomb, another Japanese unit set fire to the slopes of Purple Mountain in an attempt to drive out the Chinese troops.[1]

These accounts are of fun and games, Japanese-style—as part of the atrocity now known as the Rape of Nanjing at the beginning of the eight-year long Sino–Japanese War. An estimated twenty million Chinese died in that war. Many more were wounded; more yet

became homeless refugees. The war, coming at the end of a century-long trauma of imperialist depredations, was China's worst nightmare. In the end, it would pave the way for the
Communist party to triumph at last and put in motion the revolution that they hoped would
establish a modern socialist state. But, first the Chinese holocaust.

THE WAR'S GENERAL COURSE: AN OVERVIEW

Central China: The Japanese Go for the Jugular, 1937–1938

Though the fighting had begun in the north and continued there (see below), the main battleground for the first sixteen months of the war developed along the Yangzi river, from
Shanghai to Yichang at the mouth of the Yangzi gorges. Chiang initiated things by station-
ing three divisions in Shanghai, an act that brought Japanese reinforcements and the outbreak of fighting in mid-August. The destruction in the struggle for the city—at least its
Chinese and Japanese sectors—was horrific, with Japanese gunships devastating civilians
and military alike with their point-blank barrage. Chiang lost 60 percent (270,000) of the
modernized core of his army in the three months of fighting; the Japanese, more than
40,000. In early November the Japanese actually put forward an initiative to settle things;
but Chiang did not respond until early December at which point his forces were in full retreat and the Japanese, sensing a rout and a victory, retracted their proposal.

After the defeat at Shanghai, Chiang's policy seemed to be to trade space for time,
that is, to retreat and give up territory to the advancing Japanese, pulling them further inland away from their resources. Chiang believed that pre-industrial western China to which
he was retreating would be able to hold out indefinitely against the Japanese; and that time
would ultimately be on his side.

The Japanese reached Chiang's capital Nanjing in December and unleashed one of
twentieth century's most terrifying war crimes. From the Tokyo War Crimes trial:

> [On December 15], 2,000 of the city's police force, having been captured by the Jap-
> anese army, were marched toward an area . . . where they were systematically ma-
> chine-gunned. Those who were wounded were subsequently buried alive. . . . [On the
> next day], 5,000 refugees who had gathered in the Overseas Chinese Reception Cen-
> ter . . . were systematically machine-gunned and their bodies thrown into the river.

> On December 14, Yao [Jialong], a native of Nanjing, . . . was ordered to watch the
> performance when Japanese soldiers took turns raping his wife. When his eight-year-
> old son and three-year-old daughter pleaded for mercy on behalf of their mother, the
> rapers picked them up with their bayonets and roasted them to death over a camp fire.

> [Between] December 13 [and] 17, a large number of Japanese troops took turns rap-
> ing a young [girl] in the street outside Zhonghua Gate; and when a group of Buddhist
> monks passed by, they were ordered to rape this girl too. After the monks had refused
> to comply with this order, the Japanese cut off their penises, an act which caused the
> monks to bleed to death.[2]

To their families, troops sent photographs of beaming soldiers alongside naked women they were about to rape or had raped and of smiling soldiers holding up severed heads. Altogether an estimated 200,000 to 300,000 Chinese were killed; an estimated 20,000 women were raped.

Historians today believe that this horror came from a number of reasons, foremost of which was Japanese embitterment about Chinese resistance. When the war began, the Japanese predicted a few-months war with the despised Chinese practically rolling over, playing dead. The bloody battle at Shanghai mocked those predictions. The attitude of Japanese officers going in to Nanjing was that the Chinese would pay. Scholars also point to the fact that most Japanese troops were "poor farmers, industrial workers, and criminals" who were physically abused by their officers and filled with propaganda laced with racial slurs about the moral depravity of the Chinese.[3] In other words, many soldiers may have been in a sense "primed" to act. Once they were in Nanjing and their officers gave them orders to revel in crimes against the Chinese, there was little to check their atrocities. Japanese commanders believed that the fall of Nanjing and the subsequent horrors there would bring the collapse of further Chinese resistance. They were wrong.

The Rape of Nanjing: Japanese soldiers bayoneting Chinese, December 1937

Chiang's forces moved upriver, first to Wuhan until it fell in October 1938, then to Chongqing, on the Yangzi river in Sichuan province. Wuhan fell to Japanese forces, clearly superior in artillery, tanks, and planes, four days after Canton had met a similar fate. Thus, by late 1938, most of the major industrialized cities had been taken by Japan; from that point on, though there would be other campaigns, the war in east, central, and south China generally reached a stalemate. New Japanese forecasts after taking Wuhan—that they would win within three years—went the way of earlier wrong predictions. Throughout the stalemated war, Japanese atrocities seemed simply a part of their military repertoire. In east central Zhejiang province in 1940, the Japanese used biological warfare against three cities, dropping bubonic plague-infected material and starting epidemics, and used poison gas against at least one other. Less well-known than the infamous activities of Unit 731 which conducted bacterial warfare research on people in Manchuria, this strategy seems one that the Japanese were very willing to use.[4]

In the North: The Transportation War

In northern China after Marco Polo Bridge, the Japanese quickly built their army up to 200,000. They took Beiping and Tianjin and then moved out along railroad lines heading south. Their dependence on train transportation for moving troops and supplies meant that seizing and protecting 3000 miles of rail lines and occupying urban centers along those

Battle carnage in North China, 1937: Commander of 29th Guomindang army was killed in this bullet-ridden car

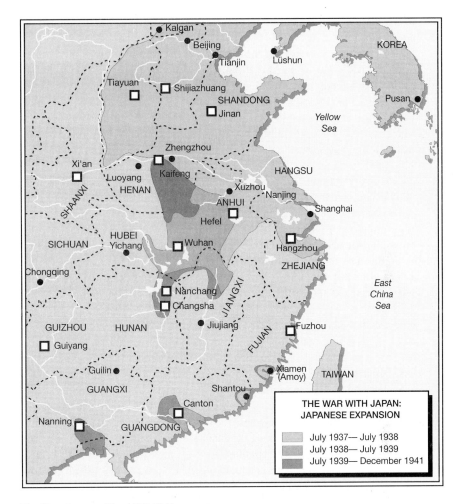

The Sino–Japanese War, 1937–1945

lines became a Japanese focus. Maps of Japanese occupation in the north by mid-1938 show not large chunks of territory held but rather a "network of points and lines."[5] Japan's first major defeat came in April 1938 at Taierzhuang near the Shandong-Jiangsu border, as Japan was moving to take the important railroad center of Xuzhou; Chinese sources assert that 30,000 Japanese were killed. In June 1938 in an effort to slow Japan's march, the Nationalists blasted open the Yellow River dikes. This drastic action stopped the Japanese advance for three months only. But the Chinese people in the flooded area could probably have raised the question, "with friends like these, who needs enemies?" For, it is estimated that at least 300,000 people were drowned; with the inundation of 4,000 to 5,000 villages, over two million were left homeless. Even at the end of the war in 1945, "all that could be seen of some villages was the curving roof of a temple and top branches of leafless trees that poked through many feet of river silt."[6] The flood changed the course of the Yellow river so that now it entered the sea south rather than north of the Shandong peninsula.

The Communists spent the early years of the war establishing base areas across the north. United front or not, by 1939, Chiang, using from 150,000 to 500,000 of his best troops, had already reinstituted a military and economic blockade of the Shaan-Gan-Ning base led by Mao Zedong, in effect, halting its possible expansion. Beginning late that same year the Japanese set out to consolidate its control by clearing areas of anti-Japanese guerrillas, establishing large numbers of linked strong points (similar to the blockhouses in the fifth Guomindang campaign against the Jiangxi Soviet), and forming puppet governments. These policies began to reverse the successes that the Communist party had brought about in organizing peasants. In addition, one of the prime Japanese concerns remained keeping railway and road networks open and protected: the Japanese even had to construct rail lines in Shanxi province to make them consistent with the gauge (the distance between the rails) of surrounding provinces. With its control of the rails, Japan could more effectively exploit economic resources and take away some of the mobility of the Communists.

Because of these policies, in August 1940, the Communists' Eighth Route Army launched its largest campaign of the war, the Hundred Regiments Campaign. Eventually 104 regiments of about 190,000 men militarily challenged the policies of consolidation that the Japanese were attempting. In the first three weeks of the campaign, Communist forces attacked all major rail lines and roads, cutting them in many places; they destroyed bridges, bombed switching yards, and made inoperative the facilities at important coal mines. The second phase of the campaign focused on attacking the blockhouse-like strongpoints, the goal being to get the Japanese to pull back to city garrisons and leave the countryside to the Communists. By December 1940 the campaign came to an end.

Even with their substantial success, the viciousness of the Japanese response led some Communist leaders to second-guess the campaign which came to seem a huge mistake. Responding with a furious revenge, the Japanese launched the "kill all, burn all, loot all" campaign in July 1941; it would continue for over almost three and a half years to November 1944. In effect, the Japanese declared "open season" on any and all Chinese. All of north China became like the later "free fire zones" in the United States war in Vietnam, where anything alive was fair game: simply put, it was the adoption of indiscriminate violence applied to the Chinese population in general. Most small towns and villages in the path of the Japanese troops had their atrocity tales. These "mopping up" campaigns were accompanied by other "pacification" policies, specifically the construction of blockade lines and fortified outposts. By 1942, almost seventy-five hundred miles of blockade lines had been set, and almost eight thousand fortified outposts had been built. In addition, the Japanese attempted to restrict the mobility of Communist guerrillas by digging ditches and moats and setting up palisades. With the exception of the Shaan-Gan-Ning base area, all other Communist base areas were so disrupted that they were reduced essentially to guerrilla bases.

Putting the Heat on Chiang: The Situation in Central China, 1939–1942

When the war in central China stalemated after the fall of Canton and Wuhan in late 1938, the Japanese worked to consolidate their control over the territory they held. (Overall in both north and central China it was only about 10 percent of the land area—mostly cities and rail lines.) The army in central China did not emphasize "pacification" to the degree that the northern army did; "pacification" was consistently utilized as a policy only in the Lower Yangzi region and particularly in the triangle made by connecting the cities of Shanghai, Hangzhou, and Nanjing. The main Japanese strategy was to apply enough pressure on Chiang's government in Chongqing so that it would eventually collapse.

Pressure came from bombing attacks. Though part of the attraction of choosing Chongqing as the wartime capital was that it was frequently fog-enshrouded in fall and winter and thus provided some degree of protection from bombers, many raids were successful. From 1939 through 1941, Chongqing suffered through 268 bombing raids which destroyed much of the city and killed thousands. The air war was an effort to demoralize not only the residents of Chongqing but those of other cities—Xi'an, Kunming, and Guilin— as well.

Pressure came as well from an economic blockade that the Japanese tried to institute throughout central China—but which in most areas leaked like a sieve. The most effective pressure came from various Japanese victories which deprived Chiang's "Free China" (as the territory the Guomindang controlled was called) of the supplies, arms, and ammunition that it needed to carry on any sort of sustained military action. Canton's fall with the Japanese control of the Canton-Hankou Railroad meant that supplies could not reach Sichuan and Yunnan provinces from Hong Kong or Canton. Another route for getting those needed supplies was by rail from Hanoi in northern Vietnam to Kunming in Yunnan. But that route

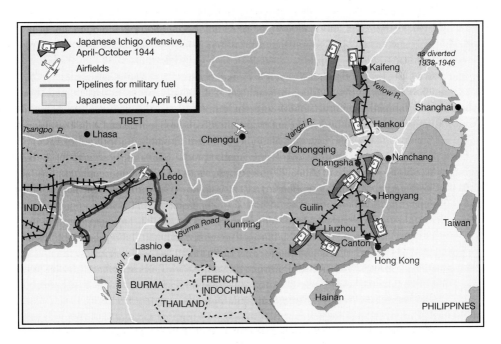

China–Burma–India Theater in World War II

was closed as well when the Japanese took northern Vietnam in September 1940. Then the only route left open to Chiang's China was the Burma Road, a 715-mile mud-surface route connecting Mandalay in Burma with Kunming, which had been completed in late 1938. Despite the fact that a truck convoy might be considered a thrill-a-minute ride, what with slippery roads over high mountain passes, one-lane sections, rickety bridges, and landslides, it was a crucial lifeline for Chiang until it, too, was closed when the Japanese seized Burma in early 1942. Then the only alternative left was an airlift of supplies, a method which would bring in only a fraction of what had come over the Road.

During the stalemate in central China through 1942, the Japanese undertook several campaigns that had limited objectives. As part of an effort to make the economic blockade more effective, in June 1940 the Japanese seized Yichang at the mouth of the Yangzi gorges to stop the hemorrhaging of trade up through the gorges to Chongqing. In the late spring and summer of 1942, the Japanese launched an offensive in Zhejiang and Jiangxi provinces aimed at destroying airbases that might be used for the bombing of the Japanese islands. These bases had been the intended landing site for planes involved in the (James) Doolittle Raid over Tokyo in April 1942, an act that enraged the Japanese military leadership.

The Ichigo Offensive (April–December 1944)

Though most areas in China could not see the impact, the war's face changed dramatically with the Japanese attack on Pearl Harbor on December 7, 1941. Japan's troop strength had to be stretched thinner since from then on it had to deploy troops to Southeast Asia in larger number and to the Pacific—likely part of the reason for the continuation of the military stalemate. The United States (along with the other Allied powers) became an ally of China; the U.S. military role in China (which will be treated more at length below) changed the contours of the China war. A good example is the post-Doolittle campaign of 1942: if U.S. planes had not been involved in the raid and intended to land at bases in southeast China, it is likely that Japan would never have launched the military campaign through Zhejiang and Jiangxi.

One of the objectives of Japan's 1944 Ichigo ("Number One") offensive indeed had similar goals to those of the 1942 Zhejiang–Jiangxi offensive—to destroy air bases in south-central China. These were being used by American pilots under the leadership of General Claire Chennault. In late 1943, Chennault's pilots began to launch punishingly effective bombing attacks on Japanese bases in China and on Japanese shipping along the coast. The U.S. chief of Chiang Kai-shek's allied staff, General Joseph Stilwell had warned that such action might bring Japanese retaliation; and it came in the form of the Ichigo offensive. But the offensive was not only aimed at the south central air bases. It actually began in the north and an additional aim was to create a north-south route from Mukden in Manchuria to Hanoi that could be an alternative to sea routes.

The offensive was a rout; in only one battle, for the city of Hengyang in Hunan province, did the Chinese put up any sustained resistance. The Japanese seized major cities that had to that point been untaken, and they destroyed all the bases that Chennault's men had used. Having successfully opened up a military gash slicing the country apart north to south through central China, the Japanese turned west toward Chongqing. The threat seemed so dire that British and U.S. civilians were evacuated from Chiang's capital. But then the Japanese suddenly stopped. Analysts argue that for Japan at this point, fighting a losing battle against American forces in the Pacific island campaigns, simple survival was their main goal, not delivering a death blow to Chiang. The Ichigo offensive had been blow enough: in it almost half a million soldiers were killed or wounded; property damage was immense; fully one quarter of the factories contributing to Free China's economy were destroyed; and almost the complete grain crop of 1944 (from the province of Henan and large parts of Hunan, Jiangxi, and Guangxi) was lost, making the problem of rice supply for the population nothing short of desperate.

THE EXODUS

When the fighting erupted in and around Shanghai in August 1937, millions of Chinese fled. Leaving one's native place with no specific place to go (except out of the way of the enemy) would be scary in any culture. But for the Chinese for whom personal connections were the defining feature of one's identity and of his or her life in society, becoming a refugee was giving up that known and comfortable world of connections for a new identity sojourning with strangers. Travel itself could be undependable and dangerous, but life would now be lived in a dangerously unpredictable world. It was not a decision to take lightly, but it was often taken out of the sheer panic of being caught in the brutal grip and bloody warfare of the enemy.

Refugees in panic, Shanghai, 1937

There were many different kinds of refugees in the exodus out of the Yangzi valley. Millions were individuals and their families. Though west was the route of most, following the government as it moved up the Yangzi in phases, not all went that direction. Some from the Lower Yangzi went south into Zhejiang or Fujian; others fled to Jiangxi and points southwest. But the greatest number—several million—went up the Yangzi gorges into Sichuan. There they experienced what would best be called culture shock. Many of those accompanying the government were used to wealth and a modern lifestyle. They were moving into an area which the modern world had scarcely touched; it was like moving from the late 1930s back into the Qing dynasty. Sichuan and Yunnan had never even been in Chiang Kai-shek's control. Many refugees tended to look askance at the locals with sneers and condescension; locals reacted with resentment and charged refugees more for the same items that locals could purchase more cheaply. Thus, it was not only that refugees were disconcerted to have to reside in a world of strangers, but the established world of the local residents was disconcerted by these outsiders with their continual pretension and demands.

There were also the institutional refugees. Whole factories were moved. Workers dismantled machines and equipment and packed them up on barges to be sent upstream and reconstructed. After the Marco Polo Bridge incident, military-related industries like arsenals and airplane plants were moved. The government, desperate to be provided with wartime necessities, offered incentives for private industries to move as well, offering low interest loans, free factory sites, and a guaranteed profit of between 5 and 10 percent for five to seven years. In the end, 639 private industries moved, with 75 percent being able to return to production. Though this seems a sizable number, it was only a small portion of the current industrial plant; and they were unable to provide the needed wartime items. Most industries chose to relocate not in China, at risk for wartime damage, but in Hong Kong or the International Settlement in Shanghai. After Pearl Harbor when the International Settlement fell to Japan, that site was also no longer desirable.

In addition to industries, whole schools and colleges also were moved. Laboratory equipment and libraries were, like factory parts, packed up on barges and transported inland. Since educators and students had been in the forefront of the National Salvation Association and anti-Japanese activities during the 1930s, Japanese especially lashed out at them during their military onslaughts. For example, Nankai University in Tianjin was bombed, shelled with artillery, and then set afire with kerosene. Universities in cities like Shanghai, Wuhan, and Nanjing were bombed repeatedly. Over fifty educational institutions fled into the interior with twenty-five retreating to Hong Kong or the foreign concession area of some treaty port. To strengthen their resources in areas which often provided miserable conditions, some universities joined together with others in their wartime exile. The most famous was Southwest Associated University in Kunming, joining together the three famous universities of Beijing, Qinghua (China's equivalent of MIT) and Nankai.

SOLDIERS AND THE MILITARY

The Nationalist army was a coalition of armies, numbering around 3.5 million; most of its units were descendants of warlord armies. The core or Central Army numbered about 300,000 in 1941 and was up to 650,000 by the end of the war. Most of its officers had been trained by German instructors in the 1930s at the Central Military Academy in Nanjing. The Central Army had the best training, equipment, and military expertise of any of the units in the coalition of armies. The military capability, quality of leadership, and even the loyalty of many of the armies to Chiang's regime varied across a wide spectrum. Some armies which had been warlord armies remained more loyal to their former warlord leader than to Chiang Kai-shek. It is probably not surprising that a good number of non–Central Army commanders defected with their troops to the Japanese; between 1941 and 1943, sixty-nine generals defected. Nor is it particularly shocking to learn that in 1944 a coalition of militarists in point of fact plotted a coup against Chiang's government.

Rank and file armies in the early twentieth century were composed of volunteers and those who had been forced to join. Conscription or building an army through a draft was first tried in 1933; the system that was established then was made universal at the outbreak of the war with Japan, but it had for all practical purposes collapsed by 1941. Reorganized that year, the draft system remained, however, seriously flawed. Chongqing determined how many men, ages eighteen to forty-five, it needed and assigned a quota to each province, which, in turn, generally assigned quotas to counties where party cadres were to manage the actual draft. Though there was theoretically to have been one to two months of training for conscription management, barely three thousand men had any training in the decade from 1936 to 1946. Such a situation created a scandalous administration of this important system. Local officials made up or falsified records, sold exemptions, stole money provided by the government to support families of draftees, and drafted those officially exempt: underage children and sole sons of families. The rich were not drafted; but the poor were taken, men who had no money to buy their way out. If local draftees were not enough to fill the quota, passersby were snatched up. An American G.I. reported that in one city, city blocks were roped off and all men of draft age who were caught there were simply sent to the front.

Even the sick were drafted; in fact, in 1942, only 28.9 percent of the draftees from Sichuan province came up to Chinese health standards. Most then were in no shape to face the trials of induction. Draftees were forced to march many, perhaps hundreds, of miles to reach their units. They were, in the words of American journalists Theodore White and Annalee Jacoby, "doomed men."[7]

> Frequently the recruits were tied together with ropes around their necks. At night they might be stripped of their clothing to prevent them from slipping away. For food, they received only small quantities of rice . . . For water, they might have to drink from puddles by the roadside—a common cause of diarrhoea . . . Medical treatment was unavailable, however, because the recruits were not regarded as part of the army until they had joined their assigned units.[8]

It is estimated that over a million men died on the way to their units.

Once with their units, the men were poorly and lightly fed, mostly rice with a few beans or turnips. White and Jacoby note that

> American soldiers used to laugh when they saw Chinese troops carrying dead dogs slung from poles; they cursed when a pet puppy disappeared from their barracks. The

Chinese troops stole dogs and ate them because they were starving and because the fat pets the Americans kept ate more meat in a week than a Chinese soldier saw in a month.[9]

Partly because of diet but also because of appallingly wretched sanitation conditions, contagious diseases—dysentery, tuberculosis, influenza, typhus—frequently raced through units, joining malaria and a host of vitamin-deficiency diseases as killers.

Wounds received in battle would not bring automatic death, but it was a good possibility. If soldiers were lucky, they might make it to a primitive hospital four days to a week after being shot or otherwise injured. "An abdominal or head wound meant certain death; an infected gash meant gangrene."[10] Large numbers, of course, were killed on the battlefield. Even though military stalemate had generally been reached by 1939, many Chinese soldiers were still dying in battle. According to Chinese statistics, in 1940, 340,000 men were killed; in 1941, 145,000; in 1942, 88,000; and in 1943, 43,000. All together in the war, Chinese figures show wartime casualties at 3,211,419 and deaths at 1,319,958.

COLLABORATION

With such horrific statistics coming as a result of actions by the Japanese, it is not surprising that any Chinese who worked with the Japanese would have been viewed as traitors. Millions of people, however, lived in areas controlled by Japan; and Japan, not wanting the burden of governing directly, used Chinese who would collaborate with them. Collaboration may be defined as actions that had the effect of maintaining Japanese power, attaining Japanese ends, or making Japanese control tolerable. Most subsequent Chinese, carrying the torch of Chinese nationalism, have condemned collaborators as morally reprehensible traitors. But a host of reasons can be offered as to why someone would choose to collaborate. Among them may have been a sincere belief that collaboration was the best way to protect the area and its people; previous experience in Japan or connections to the Japanese; previous experience in governing and a desire to serve the people; being forced to do so; a desire to profit economically, politically, or socially from collaboration; or a combination of reasons.

The type and extent of collaboration varied markedly across the occupied territory. A collaborator may have acted under Japanese direction, with Japanese participation, or with tacit Japanese approval. The range of collaborative actions was thus broad. Some collaborators worked directly in Japanese institutions; others worked at the command of the occupiers; some worked for the Japanese for a time and then resisted; others simply assented to Japanese rule by not actively resisting. One writer has noted the types of collaborators seen in Europe during World War II; China had all these types. The unconditional collaborator supports the occupying power in every way; their slogan might be "our enemy is my friend." In occupied areas these were men who served as spies and in different capacities in Japanese military police organs. There were also neutral collaborators—"I conform": those who decided that life must continue, who were determined to survive the war, and who would conform in whatever way was necessary. In occupied zones these were the largest number of citizens and groups like principals and teachers at schools set up under Japanese-controlled regimes; and they often promoted Japanese propaganda.

The actions of two other collaborator types point to the reality that collaboration and resistance "far from being irreconcilable opposites, were as close as two sides of the same coin."[11] There were the conditional collaborators ("I collaborate to a point"). Many collaborationist regimes at the provincial and county levels were of this type. They worked with the Japanese but kept their own institutions, appointed their own subordinates and occasionally stood against the Japanese for a Chinese interest. Finally there were the tactical collaborators ("I do but I don't"), those who performed public service acts whose function was to facilitate the workings of the society or economy under the regime.[12]

In essence, whatever brand of collaborator, they all adopted a new identity. Since motive and intent were crucial aspects of choosing identity as a collaborator, the choice was a complex, even ambiguous phenomenon, involving individual histories, social circumstances, economic self-interest, personal and family safety, and individual inclination. Individual motive and intent are not generally possible to gauge given the nature of the sources; further, even if collaborators had set down their reasons, the issue in retrospect is so emotionally charged that those public reasons would be highly suspect.

There were two main collaborative governments. A "provisional government" in Beiping was established in December 1937 and was headed by Wang Kemin. We have met Wang before: it was his recommendation in 1923 that the Boxer indemnity to France be paid in gold, thus linking the warlord government to the imperialists directly. Wang did this in part because he stood to profit himself. The action led to protesters in Hangzhou destroying his ancestral tablets. Wang had collaborated with the Japanese from 1935 on, serving on a council that oversaw the demilitarized zone established in the Tanggu Truce. The provisional government oversaw the five northern provinces of Hebei, Chahar, Suiyuan, Henan, and Shandong. It issued its own currency starting in early 1938 to finance its operations. In Nanjing in March 1938, the Japanese established the "Reformed Government," headed by Liang Hongzhi, a scholar and longtime fixture in warlord governments. Wang and Liang met in late 1938 in Manchuria where they established a joint committee for the government of China and promised to coordinate and control the postal service, customs, transportation, education, and foreign affairs.

The Japanese were well aware at the time these regimes were being established that former warlord associates did not rank high on the "prestige lists" of most Chinese. Ideally Japan would have liked to find someone with sufficient name and prestige recognition to rival even Chiang Kai-shek and thereby possibly compel Chiang to enter negotiations. In 1939, they hit the jackpot—Wang Jingwei, longtime Guomindang leader, former close ally of Sun Yat-sen, and rival to Chiang Kai-shek. Negotiations in 1939 led to the March 30, 1940 establishment of a new government in Nanjing, recognized both by Wang Kemin and Liang Hongzhi. It was ironical: Wang Jingwei, who had been the golden boy of nationalism following his 1910 attempt to assassinate the Qing regime's prince regent, thirty years later was becoming the betrayer of Chinese nationalism to a foreign power. But Wang had his reasons. He apparently sincerely believed that peaceful accommodation with Japan was the only realistic way to maintain China's national interests and unity. He contended that it was his government, not Chiang's, that was the legitimate national government; further he argued that he was Sun Yat-sen's rightful heir.

Chiang did not bat an eye over Wang's decision, though the Japanese waited until it was clear he would not react before they formally recognized Wang's regime. The Japanese tried to invest Wang's government with a look of some independence and equality. In early 1943, the Japanese gave up their concession areas in China and their "right" of extraterritoriality; Nanjing responded by following Japanese bidding and declaring war on the United States and Great Britain. Nanjing also took over the International Settlement and the French concession in Shanghai. A treaty in October 1943 stipulated that Tokyo and Nanjing would cooperate "as equal and independent neighbors in the establishment of Greater East Asia." Wang thus seemed to have bought into the Japanese idea of a pan-Asian and anti-Western bloc. From this point on, the Japanese made various overtures to Chiang, some through his security and intelligence chief Dai Li, arguing that Chiang's main interest lay in collaborating with Nanjing in order to finally break the back of the Communist movement and that he should thereby break off his relationships with the United States and Great Britain. This was an idea that swayed a number of Chiang's conservative supporters but did not have sufficient appeal for Chiang.

However later Chinese have seen Wang, it is clear that for millions of Chinese in the Nanjing-Shanghai-Hangzhou triangle, Wang was the accepted head of state and that Wang's government, patterned administratively on the Guomindang government in Chongqing, provided some protection for the people. As it turned out, of course, Wang's reason for collaborating—that it was the only way to save China—was faulty. Wang did not live to see the end, however, dying of illness in Japan where he had gone for treatment in late 1944. The other two main collaborators and indeed those who had worked in Wang's government were brought to trial as traitors after the war ended. Wang Kemin died in prison in late 1945; Liang Hongzhi was executed in November 1946; a number of high-ranking officials in Wang Jingwei's administration were executed as well.

WARTIME PROPAGANDA

Those who did not collaborate at all but resisted the Japanese advance were urged on in their actions by propaganda. The Chinese word for *propaganda* (*xuanchuan*) does not carry with it the negative sense of manipulation that the English word contains. It means to inform and to advocate; and it is the word used in Chinese materials for the popularizing of the war so as to build a commitment from the masses for victory. At its most elemental, this involved encouraging a hatred of Japan and its military machine. Japanese troops were commonly depicted as snakes and beasts. Cartoonists made much of their bestiality. Feng Zikai, certainly the most famous of the political cartoonists, for example, drew a picture of a nursing mother in Zhejiang province being graphically killed in a bombing attack. He accompanied the sketch with a short explanatory poem,

> In this aerial raid,
> On whom do the bombs drop?
> A baby is sucking at its mother's breast
> But the loving mother's head has suddenly been severed.
> Blood and milk flow together.

Cartoon by Feng Zikai showing woman decapitated in Japanese bombing
Source: From China Weekly Review 88.6
(8 April 1939): 177.

Side by side with the anti-Japanese coverage in cartoons, newspapers, and street drama came efforts to appeal to heroic Chinese resisters of the past. Two famous women military figures were key models—important in order to inspire women as well as men in the struggle against Japan. Hua Mulan, Tang dynasty woman warrior (and in the 1990s, a Disney film heroine), emerged in cartoons, plays, films, newspaper articles, and *kuaiban* ("rhythmic comic talks to the accompaniment of bamboo clappers").[13] She was joined by another female warrior of the Song who had struggled mightily against invaders from the outside.

The war had the effect of driving the artists and writers out of the eastern cities, most of them captured by the Japanese, into the rural hinterland. The goals: to reach the people where they were and to promote the cause of the war. "Literature must go to the country-side; literature must join the army" was the slogan of the All-China Resistance Association of Writers and Artists. Not only did the slogan point to the arena of action, but it also pro-pelled intellectuals to a self-examination of their roles in the nation's current crisis. Despite their recognition of the horrors of war, many were positive about the role the war could play in helping to remake China. For example, in his poem "Ode to the War of Resistance," written in 1937, Guo Moruo exclaimed (and the context must be Chiang Kai-shek's long record of appeasement):

> When I heard the rumble of guns above Shanghai,
> I felt nothing but happiness.
> They are the auspicious cannons announcing the revival of our people.
> And our nation has determined to resist till the end.[14]

Intellectuals and artists were motivated by the hope of national "revival," by a spirit of individual responsibility for the nation, and by an outrage at the foreign oppression being visited on Chinese society and culture.

Their tools? Cartoons and newspapers were at the heart of things. Cartoons could sum up in a sketch bitter, ironic, even sardonic truths about the war; they could provide impressions about the human side of often horrifying events. Newspapers offered descriptions of Japanese war atrocities and of the courses of battles, interviews with military commanders and government spokesmen, and advocacy pieces and editorials. Political language in newspapers and tracts and flyers has been described as "simple, emotionally charged, and laced with gritty imagery."[15]

But the cultural form that likely had the largest impact was spoken drama. These productions ranged from well-organized civilian and military traveling drama troupes to more impromptu and improvisational newspaper plays and street plays. Newspaper plays were primarily informational, recounting in improvisational ways accounts in the news dealing, among other things, with battles, Japanese atrocities, and heroic Chinese resistance. Street plays, commonly performed by four or five actors and lasting less than half an hour, had more complex plots and stressed audience participation. It was "an improvised piece grounded in simplicity, flexibility, and interaction, unified by the theme of war, and serving as a rallying cry for resistance."[16] For a rural populace accustomed to traveling opera troupes as a part of village festivals, one can imagine that the news and propaganda conveyed in street plays and other dramatic forms swept them up in the issues of the day more easily than newspapers and cartoons. The Communist party was very adept at using all these cultural forms to promote ideas of socialism and the making of a new China.

THE UNITED STATES AND CHINA IN WARTIME: ROUGH SLEDDING

Early in the war, the Soviet Union, driven by the common aim of defeating Japan, was Chiang Kai-shek's biggest supplier of foreign assistance. From 1937 to 1939, it sent one thousand airplanes plus substantial amounts of artillery, munitions, and gasoline. It provided low interest loans, volunteer pilots, and about five hundred military advisors. It is noteworthy that almost no aid was sent to the Communists. Decreased after 1939 when World War II erupted, the aid was stopped with the German invasion of the Soviet Union in 1941.

In contrast, at the Sino-Japanese war's beginning, Great Britain and the United States did very little to assist China out of fear of angering Japan, though the United States, at least, was sympathetic to China's plight. By 1940, the United States began to supply more aid; in 1941, China, like other allies, began to receive assistance under Lend-Lease, a policy that essentially provided free arms and materiel to those fighting the Axis aggressors. That same year the airforce's American Volunteer Group (the "Flying Tigers") under General Claire Chennault became active in Burma.

After Pearl Harbor made them allies, the U.S. goal in China was to build Chiang's forces until they were strong enough to take back eastern China which could then be used as an airbase to attack the Japanese islands. Sufficient arms and supplies were necessary for such a rebuilding program, but, as we have seen, after the Burma Road was cut in 1942, the only way to get the necessary items to Chiang and his forces was the airlift over northern Burma's mountainous "Hump." The tonnage that the United States airlifted into China equaled the Burma Road's 1941 tonnage only in 1944. Only a pittance reached Chiang when what was needed was a profusion of aid. The situation was compounded by the fact that China as part of the CBI (China-Burma-India) theater of the war was low on the totem pole in terms of receiving aid from the United States and other allies. The policy was Europe First; and that priority meant that of the total Lend-Lease aid given by the United States, China received a paltry 1.5 percent in 1941 and 1942, 0.5 percent in 1943 and 1944, and only 4 percent in 1945. U.S. strategic policy and the constraints of the airlift created a situation where the U.S. had in reality little chance of achieving its policy objective of building Chiang's army.

But there were also other problems that bedeviled the relationship between China and the United States. The commander of the CBI theater and the chief of Chiang Kai-shek's allied staff was General Joseph Stilwell. Stilwell on paper looked like the perfect man for the job. He spoke Chinese, having studied it in Beijing during the May Fourth period; he therefore had some knowledge of Chinese society and culture. But he did not get along with Chiang at all; they clashed bitterly in personality. Stilwell, whose appropriate nickname was "Vinegar Joe," was direct, frank, tactless, and unwilling to put up with bureaucratic hassles and ritualistic procedures. He was not a man to stroke other men's egos. Chiang, who often needed his stroked, was indirect, proud, a man of few words, and deeply aware of status and its import. Stilwell did not hide his disdain for Chiang. "The trouble in China," he asserted, "is simple: we are allied to an ignorant, illiterate, superstitious peasant son of a bitch." Stilwell's code name for Chiang in communications was "peanut." He once mused on Chiang: "Why can't sudden death for once strike in the proper place?"

They also had substantive policy differences. Most basic was that Stilwell saw Japan as the enemy against which all military strategy and strength should be brought to bear. In Chiang's estimation the Communists were a more crucial enemy than the Japanese, thus his continuing blockade of the Communist areas using some of his best troops. Given such a basic disagreement, it is not surprising that in looking at particular military strategy they did not see eye to eye. Part of Stilwell's goal was to increase the rate and effectiveness of U.S. supplies and equipment headed to Chiang's army so that the army could be built up to retake eastern China. As long as he had to rely solely on the airlift, this was hardly possible. Stilwell thus wanted to take Burma from the Japanese and reopen the Burma Road. Chiang thought this was asinine: Why send Chinese soldiers who might be fighting to take eastern China to Burma? Instead, Chiang argued, why not use the Flying Tigers (reorganized after 1941 as the China Air Task Force) to bomb Japanese bases and shipping? Claire Chennault had clearly gotten Chiang's ear.

Stilwell warned that the Japanese would retaliate; and, as we have seen, they did retaliate in the Ichigo offensive, a campaign which looked as though it might take Chiang and his government down. In the bloody days of early fall 1944, President Franklin Roosevelt, in order to stanch the bleeding, sent Chiang a demand that he put Stilwell "in unrestricted command of all your forces." Whatever the reality and however Roosevelt perceived his demand, given the long history of China's subordination to foreign imperialism, the demand that Chiang turn his army over to a foreigner was flagrantly imperialistic. Stilwell gleefully described the moment when he turned the demand over to Chiang: "I handed this bundle of paprika to the Peanut and then sat back with a sigh. The harpoon hit the little bugger right in the solar plexus, and went right through him. It was a clean hit, but beyond turning green and losing the power of speech, he did not bat an eye."[17] In the end, instead of getting to run Chiang's army, in October at Chiang's uncompromising insistence Stilwell was recalled from China.

By that time the original goal of using eastern China to bomb Japan had been shelved; for, given the circumstances, that goal seemed impossible. In its place, the United States utilized an "island-hopping" campaign—fighting up from the south Pacific in blood-drenched island confrontations. Once they reached the island of Saipan in the Marianas Islands in July 1944, the Japanese islands were within bombing range. The war would last another year, a period in which both Chiang and Mao were positioning themselves for the war that was to follow the war. When the war suddenly ended in August 1945 after the dropping of the atomic bombs in Japan, the race was on to see who would emerge as rulers of a new China.

FUTURE COMBATANTS: WARTIME ASPECTS OF GUOMINDANG AND COMMUNIST CHINA

The united front established between the two political parties after Chiang's sensational kidnapping in late 1936 had not worked effectively. Though nominally under Guomindang control, the main Red Army, the 8th Route Army in the north was able to maneuver for its own goals. Though it lost tens of thousands of men in bitter fighting with the Japanese, it was able to use the warfare to expand its own power in north China. Chiang reacted to the expansion with the reinstitution of the military and economic blockade of Mao's base. That might be said to have effectively ended cooperation. But a bloodier event ended the united front in reality if not in name.

The New 4th Army was composed of both Guomindang and Communist detachments, the latter of which had been formed from old units involved in the Three-Year War in southeast and central China. Relations between Guomindang and Communist detachments in this army were not good. Communists resented having to take orders from Nationalist leaders; and in late 1939 Communist units clashed with Nationalists. Guomindang leaders, seeing the free rein of the Communists to rove across north China, wanted to keep central China off limits against any possible Communist expansion there. Since the New 4th Army was based in Anhui province, south of the Yangzi river, the Guomindang ordered its Communist detachments to relocate north of the Yangzi. All except the Headquarters detachment did so. In October 1940 bitter fighting between Communist units and Guomindang units ended in the destruction of the Guomindang detachments; this battle really put the lie to the existence of any kind of "united" front.

After this confrontation, negotiations between the Guomindang and the Headquarters detachment went from bad to worse. In early December, Chiang gave the Communists a New Year's Eve deadline to get all New 4th Army units north of the Yangzi and all 8th Route units north of the Yellow River. Once the Headquarters detachment finally started to move, it was harassed by Guomindang units. Attempting to regroup, the Headquarters detachment was encircled by Nationalist troops who conducted a turkey shoot, massacring three thousand and killing many more who were taken to prison camps. Many of those killed were noncombat staff, the high command, and those linked to them. Although bad blood had been increasing in this army and both sides had been guilty of military infractions against the united front, Nationalist actions here were denounced as perfidious. Though the various Communist detachments of this army regrouped once again south of the Yangzi, the incident was, in the words of Theodore White, "one of the major turning points in China's wartime politics."[18]

The war years were also important for the Communists in shaping their party strategy and in developing approaches that would become useful following 1949. The party became more focused on its identity, coherence, even purity. Wartime immigration that poured into Yan'an created these concerns: an estimated 100,000 immigrants—with likely up to 50 percent of them students, teachers, journalists, and intellectuals—from 1937 to 1940. Party membership swelled rapidly, from 40,000 in 1937 to some 800,000 by 1940.[19] The needs of quality control and party cohesion and direction brought the party to draw a firm party "line" and use it to screen out dissenters. Such greater party central control allowed more administrative oversight of the huge variation among and in regions that the party controlled. Its downside, however, was a spiraling civil and military bureaucracy, with its inevitable emphasis on routinization and hierarchy. To deal with that problem, the party devised the "to the villages" (xiaxiang) program—which would remain an important element in its repertoire of state policies. Higher-level party cadres were sent to the countryside to live with and learn from peasants and to help begin to decentralize various party and government functions. Intellectuals were also sent down later to break the barriers between urban elites and peasants. Like the Guomindang regime's dilemma, one of the party's most intractable problems remained deciding what was the most appropriate relationship between the central regime and the localities, between the role of the state and local initiative.

At the level of the localities, mass associations were also a key to the Communist wartime successes. Cadre work teams helped organize peasant associations primarily as bodies for economic assistance. Peasant associations helped lead rent, interest, and tax reduction efforts and were often in charge of the militia. Because peasant associations in the villages carried out Communist economic policies, they directly challenged the village elites. It is no exaggeration to argue that the "rise of the peasant associations fundamentally changed rural power relations."[20] A second wave of mass organizing focused on setting up women's and workers' associations as part of mobilizing the population for war.

At the end of the war, there were nineteen Communist base areas spread across northern China in the provinces of Shaanxi, Shanxi, Shandong, Hebei, Rehe, Liaoning, with Communist units in Anhui and Jiangsu. Communist regimes stretched over a roughly 250,000 square miles area. Mao claimed that there were 1.2 million CCP members by the close of the war. Communist military forces had increased almost ten-fold from the opening of the war, from 92,000 in the 8th and New 4th armies in 1937 to 910,000 in 1945.

With little question, the Communist movement benefited enormously from the war against Japan. One might even suggest that the war saved the Communist movement. One cannot obviously replay history. But if we could, it would be interesting, as in the sciences, to conduct a "CCP viability" experiment. In that historical experiment we would eliminate the variable of Japan—take Japan out of the picture altogether. It seems likely that in that scenario Chiang would have smashed the Communist movement, if not during the Jiangxi Soviet, then most certainly when the bedraggled and decimated Long Marchers reached Yan'an. The war against Japan gave the Communist movement breathing room and the time to expand its support through its nationalistic appeal in fighting the Japanese, its policies of mass mobilization, and the military etiquette ("respect the masses") that it inculcated into and enforced on the 8th Route Army.

While things were looking red and rosy for the CCP, in Guomindang China, there were various cancers eating at the innards of the state. From about 1942 much of the Nationalist army seemed to give up. Though it and the Communist troops tied down a million Japanese troops for eight years, its effectiveness in the last three to four years of the war was practically nil. This was an ominous development for a state whose political power was really built on the army. What did that portend for the state? One thing that increased the military tragedy of the war was that many of the accomplishments of Chiang Kai-shek's Nanjing decade, specifically building the infrastructure of a modern state, were destroyed in the war—highways, railroads, industry, bridges and roads.

The tragedy was ironically intensified because of the scorched earth policies used by Chiang's forces to deny the Japanese use of these facilities. Scorched earth strategies substantially increased the suffering of the Chinese people and were ruinous to the Chinese countryside. The blowing up of the Yellow River dikes is one example. But other examples are depressingly numerous. Two will suffice. In 1933 a bi-level bridge across the wide Qiantang River that flows into Hangzhou Bay began to be constructed; it was a great engineering feat and linked, for the first time, the two sides of the river by both rail and car. It was finished with great fanfare in late September 1937, four years after it had been begun. Three months later, in late December the Chinese blew it up to keep the Japanese from using it.

Later in the post-Doolittle campaign through Zhejiang and Jiangxi provinces, 62,000 workers were requisitioned to destroy railroad tracks, highways, even small mountain and village roads in a frantic and futile effort to stop the Japanese.[21] The logic of such scorched earth efforts seems indeed farfetched. The Japanese had already made the Zhe-Gan railroad inoperable when they blew up its railroad bridges; what was the logic that called for using forced labor to add to the destruction by pulling up the tracks? The governor of the province passed off the highway destruction rather lightly, noting that of the 3717 kilometers of provincial highways before the war *only* 759 kilometers were destroyed under Chinese government order. That figure represents over 20 percent purposefully destroyed. Such questionable imposed self-destruction seems to suggest not only panic, but more importantly, a tragic loss of perspective and sense of reality on the part of military and perhaps civil authorities.

The most virulent cancer attacking the body politic was inflation. While prices rose approximately 40 percent during the war's first year, from the time of Pearl Harbor in 1941, prices increased more than 100 percent each year. The table below reveals the gory details.

Value of Note Issue in Terms of Prewar Prices, 1937–1945[22]

	(amount and value in millions of yuan)		
End of Period	Amt. of note issue of gov't banks	Average price index	Value of issue in terms of prewar notes
1937, July	1,455	1.04	1,390
1938	2,305	1.76	1,310
1939	4,287	3.23	1,325
1940	7,867	7.24	1,085
1941	15,133	19.77	765
1942	34,360	66.2	520
1943	75,379	228.0	330
1944	189,461	755.0	250
1945, August	556,907	2,647.0	210

Thus, a trinket that cost 1.04 yuan at the start of the war would have cost 2,647 yuan at war's end. Nothing guts out the political support of a people for its government faster than inflation, even of the slowly rising kind, much less the marauding strain of inflation seen here. It was produced by simply printing more money when there was an insufficient supply. Its results included hoarding of commodities, creating scarcities and even higher prices; corruption that spiraled out of control; and ravaged standards of living among officials, soldiers, intellectuals, people on fixed incomes, and students. Some, if not all of these, were groups that were dangerous to offend. For sowing inflation through the printing of money, Chiang would reap the whirlwind.

Perhaps the most critical effect of the eight-year-long war and military ineffectiveness, the destruction of scorched earth, and the inflation was a rampant demoralization. Did the government of Chiang Kai-shek really care about the needs of the Chinese people under its control? One answer might be its response to a natural disaster of immense proportions, a famine that ravaged Henan province in 1942 and 1943. Though reports of the serious famine reached Chongqing by October 1942, the government did not send any government representatives out until November. They returned to say the situation was desperate. The government responded by sending $200 million (paper money the value of which had been deeply eroded by inflation) for famine relief; paper money was sent rather than relief grain. By March 1943, fully half a year since the situation had already become tragic, only $80 million had arrived. But worse: "It was left to lie in provincial bank accounts, drawing interest, while government officials debated and bickered as to how it might best be used. In some places, when money was distributed to starving farmsteads, the amount of current taxes the peasants owed was deducted by local authorities from the sums they received; even the national banks took a cut of the relief funds as profit." To the beginning of March 1943, the government had provided money for the equivalent of a pound of rice per person for the "10,000,000 people who had been starving since autumn."[23]

Eyewitness accounts by Theodore White told the horrific story.

> There were corpses on the road. A girl no more than seventeen, slim and pretty, lay on the damp earth, her lips blue with death; her eyes were open and the rain fell on them. People chipped at bark, pounded it by the roadside for food; vendors sold leaves for a dollar a bundle. A dog digging at a mound was exposing a human body. Ghost-like men were skimming the stagnant pools to eat the green slime of the waters. . . .

> The people . . . were tearing up the roots of the new wheat; in other villages people were living on pounded peanut husks or refuse. Refugees on the road had been seen madly cramming soil into their mouths to fill their bellies, and the missionary hospitals were stuffed with people suffering from terrible intestinal obstructions due to the filth they were eating. . . .

> In a fit of frenzy the parents of two little children had murdered them rather than hear them beg for something to eat. Some families sold all they had for one last big meal, then committed suicide.

> By spring . . . the missionaries now reported something worse—cannibalism. A doctor told us of a woman caught boiling her baby: she was not molested, because she insisted that the child had died before she started to cook it. Another woman had been caught cutting off the legs of her dead husband for meat; this, too, was justified on the ground that he was already dead. In the mountain districts there were uglier tales of refugees caught on lonely roads and killed for their flesh . . . we heard the same tales too frequently, in too widely scattered places, to ignore the fact that in Henan human beings were eating their own kind.[24]

An estimated two to three million died of starvation. White perceived "a fury, as cold and relentless as death itself, in the bosom of the peasants of Henan [and] that their loyalty had been hollowed out to nothingness by the [inactions] of their government."[25]

Notes

[1] Quoted in Cheng and Lestz with Spence, pp. 329–330.

2 Quoted in Dun J. Li, pp. 208–209.

[3] Mark Eykholt, "Agression, Victimization, and Chinese Historiography of the Nanjing Massacre" in Joshua Fogel, Ed., *The Nanjing Massacre in History and Historiography* (Berkeley: University of California Press, 2000), p. 16.

[4] For the activities of Unit 731, see Sheldon H. Harris, *Factories of Death: Japanese Biological Warfare, 1932–1945, and the American Cover-Up* (London: Routledge, 1994).

[5] Lyman Van Slyke, "The Chinese Communist Movement during the Sino–Japanese War, 1937–1945" in Fairbank and Feuerwerker, p. 627.

[6] Ibid., p. 555.

[7] Theodore H. White and Annalee Jacoby, *Thunder out of China* (New York: William Sloane Associates, 1946), p. 132.

[8] Lloyd E. Eastman, "Nationalist China during the Sino-Japanese War, 1937–1945" in Fairbank and Feuerwerker, p. 572.

[9] White and Jacoby, p. 133.

[10] Ibid., p. 138.

[11] Werner Rings, *Life with the Enemy: Collaboration and Resistance in Hitler's Europe* (Garden City, N.Y.: Doubleday, 1982), p. 128.

[12] It should be seen, of course, that such acts also underscore the shortcomings of the regime in not providing those services.

[13] The description is from Chang-tai Hung, *War and Popular Culture* (Berkeley: University of California Press, 1994), p. 74.

[14] Quoted in ibid., p. 272.

[15] Ibid., 276.

[16] Ibid., p. 57.

[17] Cited in Eastman, p. 580.

[18] White and Jacoby, p. 75.

[19] John Wilson Lewis, *Leadership in Communist China* (Ithaca: Cornell University Press, 1963), p. 110, cited in Van Slyke, p. 620.

[20] Ch'en Yung-fa, p. 221.

[21] Huang, p. 402, and *Qu xianzhi* (1992), p. 403.

[22] Taken from Eastman, p. 585.

[23] White and Jacoby, pp. 173–174.

[24] Ibid., pp. 169–172.

[25] Ibid., p. 177.

15

Toward Daybreak: Struggling for China's Identity, 1945–1949

On July 15, 1946, in Kunming a memorial service was held for Li Gongpu, a leading member of the Democratic League, a liberal group opposing the government of Chiang Kai-shek. Li had been assassinated six days earlier by Chiang's secret police. Speaking at the service was Wen Yiduo, whose poem "Dead Water" had been marked by hope for a new China on Chiang's ascension to power in 1928. After eschewing political involvement during the Nanjing decade, Wen had become involved in reform politics during the Sino–Japanese War. He was outraged by Li's murder, chalking the killing up to the government's great fear of any opposition.

> The reactionaries believe that they can reduce the number of people participating in the democratic movement and destroy its power through the terror of assassination. But let me tell you, our power is great. . . . The power of the people will win and truth will live forever!
>
> Bright days are coming for us. Look, the light is before us. Just as Mr. Li said as he was dying: "Daybreak is coming!" Now is that darkest moment before dawn. We have the power to break through this darkness and attain the light! To attain democracy and peace, we must pay a price. We are not afraid of making sacrifices. Each of us should be like Mr. Li. When we step through the door, we must be prepared never to return.[1]

That afternoon, as he was walking home, Wen was gunned down on the Kunming streets, a victim of the very terrorist assassins that he had castigated earlier in the day. His murder became a rallying cry for people across China to stand up against the homicidally repressive regime of Chiang Kai-shek.

Wen Yiduo
Source: © ChinaStock/Beijing Office.
All Rights Reserved.

THE COMMUNISTS AT YAN'AN, 1942–1945

As the war was ending it was clear that the struggle between the Guomindang and the Communists, ongoing since 1927, would continue after the war. Did the Communist regime in Yan'an offer a more liberal and tolerant alternative to Chiang's regime, linked as it was to terroristic assassinations? We have seen that the Communists in the Shaan-Gan-Ning base tried to close the gulf between rulers and ruled by instituting the "to the villages" movement. They had tried to encourage the functioning of the "mass line," listening and heeding the voices of the masses in the making of policy, an important aspect of the Jiangxi Soviet land reform.

Yet, the motive force of the revolution during the anti-Japanese war was mass mobilization undertaken by the party. The most important strategy of mass mobilization, class struggle, used both in base areas and in guerrilla zones—not in the form of radical land reform, but in reducing rents, taxes, and interest. The party sent work teams to villages to mobilize against landlords, officials, and the bourgeoisie. Because of the paucity of landlords in the north, there were few problems with tenancy and rent; the key resentment among the masses there was over heavy taxes.

The timing of mobilizational efforts varied from place to place. In some bases of north China these efforts were well under way by 1939 and 1940; in others they were not started until 1943 and 1944. Reforms began in central China bases only in 1941. Rich landlords were more a problem in central and south China, but they were not generally demonized until

1943. Class struggle became almost tangible in the struggle meeting, the "most intense, condensed form of peasant mobilization."[2] These intense, often violent meetings were launched in the north against local despots by 1942 but did not occur in central China until autumn 1943. Party cadres chose the targets and encouraged the expression of latent peasant anger against village bosses and landlords. These staged events became pivotal in shattering mass apathy and passivity and disrupting what former solidarity had existed among targets and community. There were also additional strategies of base-specific mass mobilization.[3]

The secret of Communist revolutionary success varied from place to place, from time to time, and from tactic to tactic. Communist cadres had to understand all aspects of the locale—the natural environment; the social, economic, and political structures; and particular needs and grievances—then build networks and coalitions with local leaders, mobilize local inhabitants, and carry out pragmatic and flexible policies. These efforts were frequently unsuccessful; leftist excesses and rightist betrayal were common; many times contingencies, not strategies, gave the Communists their success. In Henan's Rivereast base, for example, the Communists succeeded only when the Japanese withdrew their troops from the area after the beginning of the war in the Pacific in late 1941.

In contrast to these initiatives two other party efforts emphasized unbending party control. An extraordinarily important strategy to attain party cohesion was the rectification campaign, the first of many in the history of the Communist party and its political regime. By late 1940 and early 1941 the situation at Yan'an had become tense and troubled. The developing military situation provided the greatest threat and seems to have heightened the lack of party coherence. The Nationalists had 400,000 soldiers blockading Shaan-Gan-Ning to its south and west. The New 4th Army incident and Guomindang demands on its remnant units and the 8th Route Army as well put the Communist military on the defensive. In this context, Mao launched the rectification campaign in February 1942. It had several goals. One was to inculcate a uniformity of spirit and a focus on the party's mission into the party's tens of thousands of new members, many of them intellectuals and students who had come from coastal cities.

A second was to challenge Wang Ming, the party's general secretary in 1931 and 1932, and his other returned students from Russia. Though Wang did not have any organizational base in the party, a number of the 28 Bolsheviks did; and they continued to try to speak as the authoritative Marxist-Leninist theoreticians. By this time Mao's party position was strong and secure enough that he wanted to assert his own theoretical vision as the new party orthodoxy, one that emphasized Chinese particularities, not the standard Russian orthodoxy. One such particularity was to make the peasants equal partners with the proletariat in the vanguard of the revolution. Railing against the dogmatic application of Marxist-Leninist thought by Wang Ming and his cohorts, Mao argued that "the arrow of Marxism-Leninism must be used to hit the target of the Chinese revolution." He continued,

> We must tell [those who regard Marxism-Leninism as religious dogma] openly, "Your dogma is of no use," or to use an impolite phrase, "Your dogma is less useful than excrement." We see that dog excrement can fertilize the fields, and man's can feed the dog. And dogmas? They can't fertilize fields; nor can they feed a dog. Of what use are they?[4]

To rectify or reform their thoughts, cadres were to participate in small group sessions studying documents Mao selected; they had to write out detailed self-criticisms; they were often criticized in mass meetings; and they had to confess their errors. If this last step was difficult or impossible for the cadres being rectified, they might be isolated and various psychological pressures might be brought into play against them. In the end, they were often sent to the countryside for menial work and ostracism. Mao believed in the power of human beings to change their thoughts and their lives. At least theoretically such a position meant that, unlike Stalin with his great and bloody purges where many died, Mao would not resort to murderous terror. He once remarked that if you cut off men's heads, they do not grow back like cabbages will. So, the goal should be to change men's minds. Even so, the fact that there is a spectrum of names for what Mao wanted to do, running the gamut from innocuous to scary, reflects the controversy that such a process can engender. From rectification (changing one's ways) to re-education (a goal firmly in line with traditional Chinese moral training) to thought reform (implied authoritarianism) to brain washing (inhuman destroyer of individuality)—whichever view one takes of the process colors its meaning. In the end, the process grew out of the radical logic of those who were certain they possessed the Truth.

For intellectuals, the other target of rectification, Mao expanded his thoughts on the functions of art and literature in a socialist society in May 1942. Art and literature were "powerful weapons for uniting and educating the people . . . , as well as [helping] the people wage the struggle against the enemy with one heart and one mind."[5] Mao's points in this speech and party decisions in spring 1942 foreshadowed the future relationships of state to society, here specifically to intellectuals and artists. Art and literature serve the "people"—defined as workers, peasants, soldiers, not the petty bourgeoisie, students, or intellectuals. Above all, they serve the revolutionary cause. When author Ding Ling criticized Yan'an culture for its sexism and male dominance, she was sent to the countryside. Many writers who had criticized aspects of Yan'an society recanted their criticisms in the rectification effort.

But writer Wang Shiwei did not. He had written two essays that drew attention to the culture of the "new elites" in Yan'an. One, "Wild Lilies," pointed out the inequalities between life styles of the ruling Yan'an elite and non-elites and called for there to be a commonality of life-style for both groups. For this, the party made him an object lesson, putting him on trial as it were in struggle meetings from May 27 to June 11. Author Ai Qing who earlier had said that he had to include the negative realities at Yan'an (in his words, he could not depict "ringworms as flowers") attacked Wang vigorously.

> [Wang] depicts Yan'an as dark and sinister; he pits artists against statesmen, old cadres against the young and stirs them up. His viewpoint is reactionary, and his remedies are poisonous. This "individual" does not deserve to be described as "human" let alone as a "comrade."[6]

Forgetting the adage about cabbage heads, the party executed him in 1947 as they evacuated Yan'an. Historians have noted that Wang was "one of the 'last speakers for the cosmopolitan strain of May Fourth intellectual experimentation'" in the Communist Party.[7] In addition, they have seen the virulence of the campaign against him as a prototype of the style of denunciation that became the rage during the later Cultural Revolution (1966–

1976) when "[i]t was not enough just to attack a person's ideas; it was necessary to show that the person concerned was thoroughly evil and had always been so."[8]

Wen Yiduo . . . Wang Shiwei . . . It is clear that neither side in the coming civil war would let anybody stand in their way. The nation, not individuals, was what mattered, unless, of course, those individuals were the decision-making elites of each party.

THE SITUATION AT WAR'S END

In the last months of the world war, the United States was increasingly concerned about post-war East Asia. A destroyed Japan and a China in civil war seemed open invitations to the Soviet Union to try to take advantage of the situation for its own benefit. Since a united China would be a deterrent, the United States hoped to broker an agreement between the Communists and Nationalists before the end of the war. Franklin Roosevelt appointed Oklahoma Republican Patrick Hurley, a man with no previous knowledge of or acquaintance with China, first to be his personal representative to Chiang and then ambassador to China. Hurley, who stepped off the plane in Chongqing and startled the Chinese with a Choctaw war whoop, was hardly the diplomat to bring the two sides together. He did escort Mao from Yan'an to Chongqing after the war ended. Face-to-face talks between Chiang and Mao extended until October 10, when an agreement on principles was reached. Photographs captured a smiling Chiang and Mao toasting each other. Mao left for Yan'an the next day, but

Mao Zedong and Chiang Kai-shek toasting each other, October 10, 1945
Source: Christopher Liu Collection. © ChinaStock. All Rights Reserved.

Zhou Enlai remained in Chongqing to try to work out the details. Major principles established in the agreement included democratization and recognition that all political parties were legally equal; the unification of military forces; and the convocation of a political consultative conference that would plan the reorganization of the government and ratify a new constitution. Ominously there was no agreement on the legality of the ten remaining Communist base areas and their governments.

While Mao and Chiang were negotiating and agreeing on rather grandiose political principles, a frantic race was on between Communists and Nationalists to reach Japanese-occupied territory as quickly as possible. Whoever could be present to accept the Japanese surrender would have a leg up in controlling that particular territory themselves. The United States, not surprisingly, threw its weight in this race behind wartime ally Chiang Kai-shek. American planes ferried half a million Guomindang soldiers into north China, Taiwan, and Manchuria to try to get them there before the Communist troops. Since the CCP had expanded over north China throughout the war, they had a huge advantage in that region and in reaching Manchuria where 700,000 Japanese troops waited to surrender.

Complicating the situation in Manchuria was the presence of the army of the Soviet Union. Stalin had promised at the wartime allied meeting at Yalta in February 1945 that the Soviet Union would enter the war against Japan within three months after the war in Europe ended. They did so on August 8, three months to the day after VE day, promising Chiang's government that they would withdraw three months after Japan's surrender. Though the Soviet Union did not provide direct military aid to the Chinese Communists, the Soviet army did prevent the United States from landing Nationalist troops at some of the northeastern ports. The 8th Route and New 4th Route armies did exploit the Soviet hold on Manchuria by moving there quickly by junk from Shandong or by foot and by seizing substantial arms and equipment from the surrendering Japanese. When Chiang determined that a Soviet withdrawal by November 15 would in reality leave the Communists holding Manchuria, he persuaded them to delay their pullout. When they left in May 1946, they dismantled many of the former Japanese factories and stole their modern industrial equipment.

In November 1945, Patrick Hurley resigned as U.S. ambassador, attacking the State Department and its Foreign Service officers for undercutting his work and for playing into the hands of the Communists. In December President Truman appointed the highly respected General George Marshall as his special envoy to China, charged with working out a cease-fire and convening the political consultative conference. In the beginning, it seemed as though he would make things happen. A cease-fire was announced on January 10 with a general truce and halt to north China troop movements put in place on January 13. The Political Consultative Conference (PCC), composed of thirty-eight delegates (eight from the Guomindang and seven from the CCP), met from January 11 to 31. There were agreements on almost all substantial civilian and military issues. But from this point, things began to deteriorate. The problem was that there really was no one to enforce the agreements.

The rapidity and sweeping nature of the agreements and then the immediate difficulty in getting them enforced raise questions about the motives of the Guomindang and the CCP. One possibility is that neither party was of one mind on the issues, that some in each party may have wanted the accords while others did not and that the latter sabotaged the effort. Another possibility is that the accords were simply window dressing, put up for the benefit of the United States, who, from the Guomindang perspective, would then continue its aid program. Another possibility, given the rapid turn to military action, is that the accords were simply a way to buy time for working up to military readiness.

Both parties must share some of the blame for the failure of the Marshall mission. The Guomindang reneged on some of its PCC political pledges and the Communists refused to carry out some military pledges. In Manchuria where things got militarily hot very quickly, both sides were guilty of breaking the cease-fire. Fighting there spread slowly beginning already in late January; truce teams sent by Marshall did not get permission to land until April. Marshall was able to engineer a truce in June, but that fell apart also.

But ultimately, the Marshall mission failed because it was an impossibility. That the United States could step into a "rivalry-to-the-death" that had been festering for twenty years and settle it with a few agreements that depended on the good faith of the rivals was idealism with hardly a trace of reality. Further, Marshall was supposed to be an even-handed mediator. Yet the United States continued to funnel huge amounts of aid to the Nationalists while Marshall was trying to get the Communists to agree to a settlement. A huge supply program of arms and equipment was in the works for the Nationalists. In February 1946 the United States established a military advisory group to help Chiang further develop his military; it gave $500 million to the China aid program of the United Nations Relief and Recovery Administration, most of it to go to Chiang; and in June and August, 1946, it gave the Nationalists credits to purchase additional equipment that would be useful in combat. Not surprisingly, the Communists began to attack this relationship in summer 1946. When Marshall tried some even-handedness by pressuring Chiang to undertake some major economic and political reforms to strengthen his regime, his government reacted with bitterness: Prime Minister T. V. Soong saying that "in the old days 'for one government to tell another it should do these things would mean war.'"[9]

When Marshall left China in January 1947, he offered his evaluation of the problem.

> Sincere efforts to achieve settlement have been frustrated time and again by extremist elements of both sides. The agreements reached by the Political Consultative Conference a year ago were a liberal and forward-looking charter which then offered China a basis for peace and reconstruction. However, irreconcilable groups within the Guomindang, interested in the preservation of their own feudal control of China, evidently had no real intention of implementing them. . . .

> The reactionaries in the Government have evidently counted on substantial American support regardless of their actions. The Communists by their unwillingness to compromise in the national interest are evidently counting on an economic collapse to bring about the fall of the Government, accelerated by extensive guerrilla action against the long lines of communication—regardless of the cost of suffering to the Chinese people.[10]

ECONOMIC SUICIDE

China turned quickly to widescale civil war, one of the largest wars of modern times. The actual struggle between the Guomindang and CCP was ultimately decided on the battlefield, but there were underlying problems with Chiang's rule that were probably more significant in understanding the cause of his defeat. Marshall in the statement above points to a crucial reality when he notes that the Communists "are evidently counting on an economic collapse" to bring down the Guomindang.

It was, in the end, Chiang's inability to deal with wrenching economic problems that likely defeated him. We saw in the last chapter how rampant inflation during the Sino-Japanese war eroded people's livelihoods. By 1945 government revenue was covering only one third of its expenditures; to make up what was needed more money was simply printed. It was, on its face, "an easy solution." But the demoralizing outcome was "a government with neither the will nor the ability to do anything but watch over the deterioration of the nation's urban economy."[11] Growing inflation was fueled by shortages of consumer goods, business restrictions, corruption, speculation, and hoarding. The exchange rate for Chinese dollars to U.S. dollars stood 7000 to 1 in January 1947, and 45,000 to 1 in August 1947. Prices in July 1948 were *three million* times higher than in July 1937. And into 1949 it deteriorated even further. Chiang's government tried two major fiscal efforts to stem the disastrous tide. Wage and price controls, introduced in 1947, were not enforced across China in uniform fashion and mostly in the Lower Yangzi region. Then in 1948 the government introduced a new currency. Neither policy worked.

What did this mean to the consumer? In the county of Xiaoshan in Zhejiang province, on the eve of the Communist takeover in April 1949, a picul of rice (about 133 pounds) cost more that 8 billion Chinese dollars, 785,400,000 times more than in 1937. At this rate, each *grain* of rice cost about 2,500 Chinese dollars.[12] At such a rate of inflation, Chiang had lost the city-dwellers—businessmen, salaried classes, intellectuals, workers—and those in the countryside as well. The economic collapse was total.

> By late 1947 and 1948, the very fabric of rural society seemed to be unraveling. Banditry, the traditional sign of feeble political control and deteriorating economic conditions, was pervasive. The inflated currency inspired so little confidence that exchange payments—such as land sales, bride prices, purchases of oxen or furniture, workers' wages, and loans—were being conducted by barter. . . . landlords fled the countryside for the relative security of walled towns. . . . Ordinary peasants, too, abandoned the farms, becoming recruits to the growing ranks of the hungry and destitute, many of whom died in the streets and alleyways of cities. . . . 10 million people were threatened with starvation in 1948; 48 million—about one of every ten Chinese—were refugees. . . . The most desperate reportedly sold their wives and daughters—in 1946, the price of fifteen- and sixteen-year-old girls in [Zhejiang] was said to be 4,000 yuan. . . .[13]

POLITICAL DISASTER

If two words were "worn out" by their continual use to describe Chiang Kai-shek's government, they were "corrupt" and "incompetent." Corruption had been the watchword during the war against Japan as Chongqing government officials and most especially family members and hangers-on in Chiang's circle lived high on the hog. Rumors spread about the extravagant banquets frequented by officials and their women, dressed to the nines, about the luxury items (oranges, butter, perfumes) smuggled in from abroad, about items carried

Panic-struck Chinese desperate to get their money out of a bank before its value depreciates further, December 1948

over the Hump on the airlift for Chiang's favorites. Bitterness among the non-elites who had to put up with shortages and austerity during the war only increased as end-of-war turned into another war. An article in a popular political journal in the spring of 1947 evaluated the political situation in Chiang's China.

> The basis of the present regime's support has been the urban population: government employees and teachers, intellectuals, and business and industrial circles. At present, no one among these people has any positive feelings toward the Nanjing regime. The [GMD's] tyrannical style is causing deep hatred among liberal elements . . . ; the government officials by indulging in corrupt practices and creating every kind of obstruction have caused extreme dissatisfaction in business and industrial circles; and the violent rise in prices . . . and the continuation of civil war is causing sounds of resentment to be heard everywhere. . . .[14]

Repeatedly there had been calls for political liberalization, specifically reforms that might open up the political arena to non-Communist groups to share power to one degree or another with the Guomindang. In 1941 a number of minor political parties joined in a Federation of Democratic Parties, all opposed to the Guomindang monopoly of government power. Already a suspicious development in Chiang's eyes, this federation became involved in 1944 with a group of militarists considering a coup against Chiang. This mix of Western-style political liberals and old-line militarists was a coming together of strange bedfellows, but nothing came of the affair except to heighten Chiang's suspicion and distrust about the federation. In October 1944, the federation became the Democratic League, sometimes referred to as the Third Force, that is, neither Guomindang nor CCP. Chiang might have tried to join with the Democratic League to build a stronger political base, but he never did. The League itself was divided over which main party it should support. In the end Chiang turned to his Guomindang secret police who arrested many and assassinated key League figures like Li Gongpu and Wen Yiduo. Finally, in October 1947, the Nanjing government outlawed the League, with most of its members fleeing to Hong Kong.

As prime example of its ineffectiveness, Chiang's government was never able to win the public over to supporting its war against the CCP. Chiang further antagonized any political dissenters by branding them as Communist tools or dupes. From the end of World War II into 1948, the political landscape was marked by protest even as Chiang's secret police continued to use terror against protesters. Four students were killed in protests in Kunming in December 1945. In December 1946 and January 1947, Beijing exploded in anti-American demonstrations when news spread of an alleged rape of a Beijing University coed by a U.S. marine. In May and June, 1947, by the time the civil war was openly raging, high schools and universities in major cities were swept up in an Anti-Hunger, Anti-Civil War movement. From April to June 1948, a Movement to Protest American Support of Japan sprang up at a time when the United States was moving toward a more conciliatory phase of the occupation of Japan. Then in July 1948, students who had been flown out of Manchuria as a publicity ploy and then not given enough assistance to survive demonstrated against the government. Authorities machine-gunned the marchers, killing fourteen and wounding over one hundred. Basically all these protests were aimed at ending the civil war, ending the close involvement of the United States with the Guomindang, and changing government priorities from military to civilian. They were consistently met by government reactions ranging from disregard to disdain to violent attack.

THE MILITARY STRUGGLE

In the beginning the Guomindang had a huge advantage in numbers of men and amount of war materiel. Forces numbered roughly about three million men with an estimated six thousand artillery pieces compared to about one million Communist troops having about six hundred artillery pieces. Guomindang forces won the initial battles in 1946; they won all the major cities in Manchuria except Harbin, regained control of much of Rehe and Hebei provinces and of key northern railroads, and won Yan'an and many towns in northern Jiangsu.

Initially pushed north of the Sungari River in Manchuria, Communist forces, now called the People's Liberation Army, under the leadership of Lin Biao in late 1946 began hit-and-run raids into southern Manchuria that were the beginning of the turning of the tide. It was not all smooth-sailing for the PLA; in early 1947, Lin lost a major battle for a railway junction against Chiang's forces supported by air power. But Lin quickly regrouped and launched a campaign that began to isolate cities that were held by Nationalist forces. Neither Chiang nor his American advisors foresaw how fast the Communists would be able to transform their anti-Japanese guerrilla units into large regular armies. In the areas they controlled, they recruited soldiers and mobilized support among the local population.

Chiang had made a major strategic blunder when he committed half a million of his best men to Manchuria before he had solidified his control south of the Great Wall. With the Communists in control of the countryside, Lin Biao's campaign quickly turned Nationalist-controlled cities into islands in a Communist sea. To prevent their being completely cut off and forced to surrender, Chiang began costly airlifts to Manchurian cities. It was a self-destructive economic blunder: For example, Chiang used the whole military budget for the last half of 1948 supplying only one city for only two months and four days. That necessitated printing more money and another surge in inflation. When his American advisors suggested that he pull his troops in Manchuria south of the Wall to try to better his position in north China, he refused.

By mid-1948, the Communists had pulled about equal to the Guomindang in numbers of well-armed troops and ahead in numbers of artillery pieces. In the end, the Manchurian campaign ended in a smashing Communist victory in November 1948; it cost Chiang 470,000 of his best troops and countless weapons and pieces of equipment. An American advisor noted that it "spelled the beginning of the end" for the Guomindang war effort.[15] In essence, Chiang lost the civil war even before the battlefields shifted into China proper.

The battle for central China broke out almost at the same time as the Manchurian campaign was ending. Each battle now saw huge numbers of Guomindang soldiers defecting, taking with them more and more materiel. Forsaking their long-time guerrilla action in north China, the Communists now used their Manchurian strategy of deploying large armies against Chiang's troops. Committing 600,000 troops to the battle of Huai-Hai, that centered on the railway center of Xuzhou, the Communists faced the same number of Nationalist troops. The over two-month-long battle began in October 1948 with the prompt defection of two Guomindang divisions. Chiang's army still had a superiority in equipment and was supported by an air force. But the Communist military leaders were clearly better strategists than the former Whampoa commandant. Chiang, who was biased in favor of the officers who had graduated from his academy, refused to listen to superior strategists (former warlords) to make a stand at a more favorable position along the Huai river. He chose instead to stand at Xuzhou where his forces were exposed on three sides. Communist forces simply smashed the Guomindang troops. Chiang lost almost half a million men and almost all his mechanized troops.

Beiping fell on January 31, 1949. By early 1949, Chiang had lost most of China north of the Yangzi; although fighting continued throughout the year, Chiang and his Guomindang national army had been defeated. The capital Nanjing fell in April; Shanghai and Wuhan in May; Xi'an in August; Canton in October; and Chongqing in November. Seeking a site to which to retreat and perhaps regroup, Chiang looked toward his wartime base of Sichuan; but the military commander there refused. Thus, in December the Guomindang government fled to Taiwan.

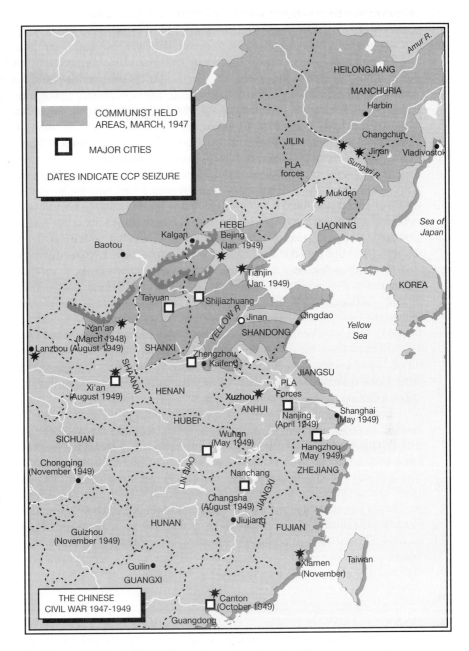

The Chinese Civil War, 1947–1949

DID CHIANG LOSE THE WAR OR DID MAO WIN THE WAR?

The question of whether the Communists won the civil war or whether the Guomindang lost it has frequently been raised. Obviously both alternatives are correct. But on balance which alternative carried more historical weight? On the winning Communists: in the civil war as in the Sino-Japanese War, the secret of Communist success was understanding the particular local situation and acting pragmatically and flexibly. In the military struggle, commanders of the People's Liberation Army "appl[ied] a strategy that elevated flexibility in the field to the highest art of defensive warfare."[16] Certainly the Communists emerged as the superior military strategists. Chiang must be found wanting in the arena of military strategy and execution. Military decision making was to have been Chiang's strong suit, but his record is filled with copious blunders: his unwise troop commitment to the Manchurian campaign, his disasatrous decision to airlift supplies to maintain control of the cities, his blind and narrow primary trust in officers who were personally connected to him in the Whampoa clique, his ridiculously weak strategy at Xuzhou, a battle which he personally insisted on directing even though he was two hundred miles from the fighting.

But only part of the struggle was military. And when one looks at other crucial arenas, it seems clear that Chiang blew it. His political approaches and reactions were counterproductive to his goal of winning the support of the Chinese elites and masses. The Communist 8th Route Army went out to win the hearts and minds of the Chinese peasants and, in many cases, they did; in contrast, the Guomindang secret police goons who assassinated and terrorized those who dissented from the Guomindang line alienated tens of thousands for every victim they shot. A corrupt Guomindang elite, living the "good life" while those around were suffering from the depredations of war, seemed as incongruous and scandalous, as a banquet given during the Henan famine.

Finally, it was the economy that gutted out support for Chiang's government. People watched, disbelieving that the government could do nothing but make the inflation scenario worse—a scenario that made the government seem not only inept but, worse, uncaring. Since people went to the market daily, they never got very far away from the demoralizing reality of inflation: from morning to night prices might rise two or three or more times. When four grains of rice might cost ten thousand cash, the Chinese were, indeed, as the Chinese idiom put it, "eating bitterness," that is, "suffering." It had only been little more than three decades since Chinese political culture had had an active sense of the Mandate of Heaven. Though no one perhaps spoke of it, the collective memory must surely have thought, if only in passing, that for Chiang Kai-shek and his government the mandate was at an end.

JAPAN'S COLONY, TAIWAN

Taiwan and the Penghu Islands (Pescadores) became part of the Japanese empire through the Treaty of Shimonoseki that ended the first Sino-Japanese War in 1895. Originally inhabited by Malayo-Polynesian aborigines, Taiwan saw Han Chinese settlement begin in the late Ming dynasty. It was brought under Chinese control in 1683 when the Manchus finally put to rest the last Ming resistance. It was ruled as a prefecture of Fujian province from that time until 1887 when it became a separate Chinese province. Eight years later, Taiwanese found themselves to be Japanese subjects.

Resistance and Suppression

For many Taiwanese it was an unhappy reality. Initial panic at the exodus of Qing officials was followed by armed resistance across the island, five months of sustained fighting and seven more years of sporadic attacks. Resistance came from some Qing military hangers-on, local volunteers, and even remnants of Black Flag forces who had fought in the Sino-French war of the 1880s. They raided Japanese military installations, police stations, and other public sites. The Japanese reacted brutally. In June 1896, for example, in the so-called Yunlin massacre, six thousand Taiwanese were killed. In the years from 1898 to 1902, twelve thousand more were slain. In the fear and panic of the time, many fled to the central mountainous area, inhabited mostly by the aboriginal peoples, or across the Taiwan Strait to the Chinese mainland; it is said that most of the upper degreed gentry sailed the ninety miles to China.

For all their harshness in trying to snuff out the strong resistance against them, the Japanese actually gave the Taiwanese Chinese two years to make a decision on whether they wanted to go to China and remain subjects of the Qing or stay in Taiwan and become citizens of Japan. From the beginning there was much Japanese discussion and disagreement about the status of Taiwan. Assimilation became a key issue: should Taiwan be brought integrally into the Japanese empire, equal to the residents of the Japanese islands themselves, should they remain subordinate islander inhabitants, or should there be some relationship in between these poles? The answer to the assimilation question varied according to time period and the nature of the rule from Tokyo and of the particular governor-general, the supreme power in the colony. Whatever the stance on assimilation, there was always a strong overlay of the idea that the Japanese were "bearers of a superior culture to be imparted" to the Taiwanese.[17]

The Beginnings of Modernization

From 1898 to 1915 the Japanese moderated their rule: the power of the military was lessened and the governor-general allowed domestic affairs to be carried out by his Chief of Civil Administration, from 1898 to 1906 the rather enlightened Goto Shimpei. During this time he set down the base for substantial economic development. A railroad was built from Taipei in the north to the seaport of Kaohsiung in the south. An important harbor was dredged and prepared at the northern port of Keelung. These years also saw the tripling of the number of miles of primary and secondary roads, the expansion of postal and telegraph facilities, the beginning of telephone service, the construction of a hydroelectric generating plant, the first modern newspaper, the establishment of a banking system, the construction of a public hospital and medical college, and attention paid to public health and sanitation. During this modernizing process, Taiwan became economically tightly connected to Japan, sending exports of rice, sugar, and camphor to the "mother country" and after 1902 importing its largest amount of goods from Japan.

There were six more armed insurrections from 1907 to 1915. Further there was a particularly nasty episode when the Japanese decided to open the mountains, home to the aborigines, to logging. This effort necessitated a subjugation campaign against the aborigines which included attacks from the air and naval bombardment from off the island's east coast. After this spate of revolts and violence abated, the domestic situation calmed down.

A More Liberal Colonialism

From 1915 through the 1920s, the Japanese seemed to tone down their colonial harshness. In part this reflected changes in Japan. The idealism of President Wilson that resonated in many countries around the world did so in Japan as well. The success of democracy or at least party government in Japan from 1918 to the late 1920s suggested a more tolerant attitude from Tokyo. In 1918 and 1919, the Japanese government adopted an assimilation policy that treated Taiwan "as an extension of Japan proper," a change that "moved from highhanded police control and differential treatment of the Taiwanese to a more enlightened self-governance, emphasis on education, and cultivation of a more congenial relationship between Japanese and Taiwanese."[18] Thus, the direct involvement of police in local administrations was decreased; law codes were rewritten to make them less draconian; a governmental reorganization gave rise to considerable decentralization so that local communities had more control; and elements of self-government were introduced.

Perhaps most important, there was a more liberal public climate, a tolerance of ideas that might earlier have been considered subversive. A Taiwanese New Culture movement that paralleled the May Fourth Movement in China began in 1920 when Taiwanese students in Tokyo organized the New People Association and the Taiwanese Youth Association. That same year they began to publish *Taiwan Youth,* like *New Youth* an effort to stir progressive thinking and to discuss the state of affairs on the island; by 1927, its publication site had been relocated to Taiwan. In 1921, a Taipei doctor organized the Taiwan Cultural Association "to advance Taiwanese culture"; though he claimed it had no political goals, it eventually supported such political movements as the establishment of a Taiwan parliament and home rule. The 1920s saw the development of a feminist movement, the organization of the Taiwan Communist Party, and the establishment of a Taiwan Farmers' Union.

Probably most interesting in light of late twentieth century talk of "Taiwan independence" were efforts in the 1920s and 1930s to assert Taiwan separateness. The New People Association rejected both integration with Japan and restoration to China, calling for home rule and a Taiwan parliament. A new organization, the League for the Establishment of a Taiwan Parliament, carried the ball on the latter from its founding in 1923 until its demise in 1934. Through those years it sent a number of petitions to the Japanese Diet, asking for a parliament. The 1926 petition had two thousand signatures, indicating no small support; but the Diet heard none of the petitions. In 1931 and 1932 Taiwan consciousness appeared in debates to create a more Taiwan-centered literature written in Taiwanese. In the words of one scholar, this debate "revealed the anxieties and ambivalent feelings of a colonized people in their attempts to develop a national language. . . . [It also] functioned to sever the Taiwanese intellectuals' emotional ties to China."[19]

Finally, in the first half of the 1930s, some island Taiwanese leaders established the

Taiwan League for Local Self-Government to work for greater power and influence on the island. These men argued that Taiwanese leaders were best prepared to deal with internal developments and problems, that they had the education and experience to do so, and that it was proper that they lead. This effort at home rule was suppressed during the war, but it reemerged after 1945.

Colonial Policies during the War (1937–1945)

As war with China neared, Japan's governor general instituted policies of industrialization and "imperialization" to get Taiwan on a war footing—militarily able and with an industrial base that would help Japan's cause. Japan indeed helped lay modern Taiwan's industrial base. By the late 1930s, in addition to agriculture-related industries like chemical fertilizers and food processing and canning, Taiwan was producing steel, aluminum, cement, chemicals, and petroleum. The number of factory workers rose almost 600 percent from 1914 to 1941—21,800 to 127,700; the number of miners soared over 800 percent—from 6,500 to 53,700. A hydroelectric power plant on the west coast supplied 100,000 megawatts. Several industrial complexes were built, like the Japan Aluminum Company plants in Hualien on the east coast and Kaohsiung on the southwest that by 1940 were supplying Japan with a sixth of the aluminum it imported.

"Imperialization" was an ominous development especially when viewed in the context of the more liberal period of the 1920s and early 1930s. It was an effort to mold Taiwan into the model of Japan as the empire moved to war. In April 1937, for example, newspapers were ordered to stop publishing Chinese language sections and schools were ordered to stop teaching classical Chinese in the elementary education curriculum. Later that year, colonial authorities began to discourage the use of Chinese at all. In the early 1940s, the Japanese overlords ordered all Chinese as well as those of aboriginal stock to change their family and personal names to Japanese names. Given the importance of surnames for cultural identity, this effort was nothing less than an attempt to destroy traditional identity and replace it with a new subordinate colonial identity. Records indicate that only about 7 percent of the Han Chinese had complied with this order by the end of the war, though it is possible that more aborigines had followed through. There were other attempts to destroy elements of Chinese culture and replace them with Japanese culture. The Japanese banned traditional Chinese operas and puppet plays, likely because they could become subversive. Chinese marriage and funeral ceremonies were forbidden, to be replaced by the respective Japanese ceremonies. The Japanese attempted to force Shintoism on the Taiwanese, building public shrines and decreeing that each home should have its own Shinto shrine for household worship. Scholars have judged that on the whole the policy of "imperialization" was not very effective; but the effort itself was something akin to cultural terrorism.

During the war itself, Taiwanese were recruited for military service, a change in Japanese policy, which before 1937 did not allow colonial subjects to serve. Over 200,000 Taiwanese served in the Japanese army or navy during the war, and over 30,000 died. Many more were drafted to labor in military-related industries. Significantly, there were no major Taiwanese resistance or sabotage efforts during the war.

Taiwan itself became an important staging and supply area for the attack on Canton in the fall of 1938 and for the naval seizure of the island of Hainan in late winter 1939. By 1940 the Japanese navy controlled the Taiwan Strait and the coastline of Fujian province. The sudden end of the war brought in large part by the effects of the dropping of the atomic bombs on Hiroshima and Nagasaki surprised all on the island. Controlled for fifty years by a now totally defeated Japan, Taiwan now also had to face a new world. Reportedly enthusiastic crowds welcomed Nationalist troops coming over in the aftermath of the surrender. Taiwan and the Penghu Islands reverted to Chinese control on October 25, celebrated after that as Restoration Day.

GUOMINDANG RELATIONS WITH THE TAIWANESE: FEBRUARY 1947 AND ITS IMPACT

The crowds did not remain enthusiastic for long. Over the next year and a half many Taiwanese would come to believe that Japanese rule, police state though it was, was preferable to control by Chiang Kai-shek's Guomindang. The problems were deep; certainly it was the case, as explained by one scholar, that both Taiwan and China had changed so much since 1895 "that the retrocession was less the restoration of historical ties than the attempt to forge an entirely new relationship."[20] In large part the root of the problems lay in the legacy of the colonial era.

Despite the colonial political controls, Japanese economic and educational policies had helped create a Taiwanese elite who had worked with the Japanese in carrying out day-to-day administration. The level of education had become quite high. While in 1917, 21 percent of Taiwanese males had attended primary school, the number reached 81 percent by 1943; for women in the same time period, the percentage had increased from 4 to 61. There were few in Taiwan who could not read Japanese. For education beyond high school, young Taiwanese went to Japan. In 1922 twenty-four hundred Taiwanese were studying in Japan; in 1942 that number had risen to seven thousand. As part of their educational agenda, the Japanese had set up Taiwan Normal School, which trained most of the island's teachers, and Taipei Imperial University. Many Taiwanese also profited from Japanese industrialization policies, emerging as economic elites in industry and business.

On the whole, after years under Japanese control, Taiwanese enjoyed a higher standard of living and level of education, better public health and sanitation, and more economic advancement than the mainland. The downside was that the Taiwanese were no better than second-class citizens under the Japanese—discriminated against systematically, working always for the benefit of Japan, and frustrated in their political aspirations. Part of the problem that developed under the Nationalists stemmed from the hope of many among the Taiwanese elite that they could turn their educational and economic credentials into greater political participation and control.

From the perspective of the Nationalists, the crucial goal in governing Taiwan was establishing tight central control that would facilitate the reintegration of the island with the mainland as quickly as possible and that would expunge Japan's influence. Chiang appointed Chen Yi, a former chief of Fujian province, to be Commander of the Taiwan Garrison as well as the main administrator of the Taiwan Provincial Administrative Executive

Office. In that capacity, he was in charge of all the governmental organs. In many ways the governmental situation was, then, quite similar to the system of the Japanese governor-general.

In almost all major policy areas, Chen's administration clashed with the Taiwanese elites. His effort to control every aspect of the economy ran head-on into the attempts by wealthy Taiwanese to open or expand businesses in areas that had been dominated by Japanese companies or the colonial regime. What the Taiwanese saw instead was that mainlanders moved into these areas with the connivance of the government. The disposition of Japanese property was also controversial. The Taiwanese, arguing that Japanese property had originally been taken from them, claimed that they should rightfully receive the property; the Chen administration's position was that all Japanese property must revert to the government. More and more it seemed to many Taiwanese that the Nationalist government was just like the Japanese colonial regime in its exploitation of the Taiwanese—except now the Nationalists, they noted, added a few negative qualities: dishonesty, incompetence, inefficiency, and unpredictability. For most Taiwanese inflation, unemployment, and a decline in public sanitation meant a decline in living conditions. In central Taiwan it is said that the masses talked of three "hopes"—the hope after Japan's surrender and before the coming of Nationalist troops that things would improve; the "lost hope" on seeing what the government of Chen Yi was doing; and the hopelessness that things would never improve.

Part of that despair stemmed from the mainlanders' receiving the lion's share of government posts and positions in the state enterprises and monopoly bureaus; the situation in fact was almost a monopoly. Only three of the first twenty-three county magistrate positions went to Taiwanese. Only one of the twenty-one highest provincial government positions went to a Taiwanese. As many as thirty-six thousand Taiwanese lost the posts that they had held in the bureaucracy. Far from having a greater say and role in politics, the Taiwanese were doing far worse than they had done under the Japanese.

Could they protest? No. Chen, like Chiang in the past, interpreted any dissent from his policies as unpatriotic and as tinged with treason. The Nationalists tended to see and treat Taiwan as a conquered territory rather than a part of the motherland being returned after many years. Many Nationalists treated the Taiwanese as disloyal to start with because of their having worked with the Japanese. In response, the Taiwanese were quick to point out that they were also involved in considerable years of resistance and that if they did work with the Japanese, it was because they had no choice since the Qing government had signed them over to the Japanese. Because most Taiwanese spoke Japanese, language became an issue of loyalty to the Nationalist regime: use of Japanese created political problems. Conversely, the speed at which the populace learned the Mandarin dialect, the "national tongue" (which the government promoted beginning in 1946) was a mark of their commitment to "Chinese-ness." The colonial period had indeed created huge identity problems for both the Taiwanese and mainland Chinese alike: In the context of the colonial era, how did each side identify themselves in relation to the other?

Each side viewed the other with disdain. The Nationalist mainlanders talked endlessly about the "Japanization" or, even worse, the "slavization" of the Taiwanese, a condition that left the Taiwanese ignorant of the mainland and its culture. Their lack of fluent Chinese, the Nationalists claimed, made them unready to participate in political decision-making as a part of China. Nationalist hostility and scorn of the Taiwanese would not die quickly; when asked in 1967 how she could tell the difference between mainlanders and Taiwanese, one mainland woman declared that she could smell the difference. The Taiwanese, on the other hand, joked of the five things that all Nationalist officials wanted from their leadership in Taiwan: gold, rank, cars, homes, and women. Rampant corruption, Taiwanese contended were "part of the mainland's defective political culture." Some Taiwanese said that "the dogs (Japanese) had left, but the [greedy and uncultured] pigs (mainland Chinese) had come."[21]

In this context, the Taiwanese began to press for some greater political role, pleading for self-government that would make Taiwan into a model province for the mainland. Representative assemblies were established in 1946, but they had very little power and only proved frustrating to the aspirations of the Taiwanese elites. Men like Wang Tiandeng, newspaper publisher, spoke out about political issues; Wang served on the Provincial Consultative Assembly that was set up in 1946. That same year he was jailed for "undermining public confidence in authority," but the case was dismissed for insufficient evidence.

On February 27, 1947, in the context of rising inflation, open civil war on the mainland, and deteriorating relationships between mainlanders and Taiwanese, an incident occurred that would freeze relationships between the two sides for forty years. A policeman from the Monopoly Bureau in arresting a woman illegally selling cigarettes struck her; a crowd gathered and another officer fired into the crowd, killing one person. This incident brought to a head all the bad feelings that had festered. All over the island Taiwanese began fighting Nationalist forces for control of railroad and police stations and government buildings. In the turmoil there were cases of outright murder of mainlanders by Taiwanese. A February 28 Settlement Committee was hurriedly formed by the Taipei City Council to end the escalating crisis.

At this point the deteriorating situation merged with the desire of Taiwanese elites for greater self-government, already apparent in the Japanese colonial era. Although these elites had played little or no role in the initial uprising, the Settlement Committee was composed of a good many prominent Taiwanese leaders. The committee met with Chen Yi a number of times the first days of March, moving closer and closer to urging Chen to enact political reforms in some form of self-government. For whatever reason, the Committee was emboldened. On March 6, it drew up the Thirty-two Demands, a list of political reforms and requests. The next day, three leaders including Wang Tiandeng presented Chen with the list that included "the election of mayors and [county] magistrates, greater Taiwanese representation in the provincial administration (including government bureaus, courts, and police), abolition of the trade and monopoly bureaus, and that Taiwanese not be drafted to fight in the mainland's civil war. . . . [And finally] the abolition of the Administrator's Office and Garrison Command and greater Taiwanese control over the military forces on the island."[22] Chen was furious. The committee, realizing that it had overreacted, retracted the next day most of the demands that it had made, especially the last two.

But it was too late. Chiang and Chen would not let such a challenge go unanswered. Martial law was declared as more Nationalist troops from the mainland poured ashore in ports north and south. There was little resistance; this had not been planned by the Taiwanese as a military action, but rather as an attempt at reform. The Settlement Committee was declared illegal since it was "part of a revolt." When quiet was returned by March 13, the government announced a campaign to "exterminate traitors"—that is, prominent Taiwanese elites who, in the words of one scholar, "may have offended anyone in the government."[23] Part of the campaign was to sweep through villages to find those leaders who may have fled the cities. Japanese-language materials and other items—flags, uniforms, phonograph records—were confiscated. Terror spread over the island. An estimated ten thousand Taiwanese were killed. Among them was Wang Tiandeng who was burned alive after being doused with gasoline by the policemen who captured him. Another thirty thousand were wounded. In essence, the aftermath of the February 28 incident was the wiping out of a whole generation of potential Taiwanese leaders.

There were a few carrots to go along with the bludgeoning pole. A regular government was established in April 1947, with Chen Yi called back to the mainland. A Provincial Committee was set up to offer the new governor advice on ruling the island; seven of its fifteen members were Taiwanese. But the committee had no power. The government announced its plans to put its own self-government program into practice, but when it was finally announced in 1950 and 1951, it was restricted to city, town, and county—not at the provincial level—and the bodies had no say or control over local governments or budgets.

In the meantime, things only got worse for Taiwan and the Taiwanese. Chiang's impending loss on the mainland stimulated the flow of huge numbers of refugees to Taiwan. In November 1948, for example, thirty-one thousand came each week. This influx made unemployment, housing and food shortages, and crime worse. Then, as Chiang made his decision to retreat to Taiwan, authoritarian control grew ever more severe. Reprising his tragic act of twenty-two years earlier, Chiang in 1949 launched another White Terror. Tens of thousands of people, Taiwanese and mainlander alike, were killed or arrested because they had some sort of alleged link to the Communists. Internecine struggle, like some kind of bacterial contagion, had at last spread to Taiwan.

Wen Yiduo. . . . Wang Shiwei. . . . Wang Tiandeng. . . . Would the day never break?

Notes

[1] "Wen Yiduo: The Poet's Farewell, 1946" in Cheng and Lestz with Spence, p. 338.

[2] The phrase is Chen Yung-fa's, p, 220.

[3] The examples from Henan are in Odoric Wou's magisterial study, *Mobilizing the Masses* (Stanford, 1994).

[4] Saich, pp. 1066–1067.

[5] Saich, p. 1123.

[6] Saich, p. 983 and 1120.

[7] Timothy C. Cheek, "The Fading of the Wild Lilies: Wang Shiwei and Mao Zedong's Yan'an Talks in the First CPC Rectification Movement," *The Australian Journal Of Chinese Affairs,* no. 11 (January 1984), p. 26, cited in Saich, pp. 983–984.

[8] Saich, p. 984.

[9] Suzanne Pepper, "The KMT [GMD]-CCP Conflict 1945–1949" in Fairbank and Feuerwerker, p. 735.

[10] "General Marshall: The Mediator's View, 1947" in Cheng and Lestz with Spence, p. 341.

[11] Pepper, p. 742.

[12] R. Keith Schoppa, *Xiang Lake: Nine Centuries of Chinese Life* (New Haven: Yale University Press, 1989), p. 225

[13] Lloyd E. Eastman, *Seeds of Destruction* (Stanford: Stanford University Press, 1984), pp. 81–82.

[14] Quoted in Pepper, p. 738.

[15] Hsu, p. 730.

[16] Pepper p. 781.

[17] The phrase is in Harry J. Lamley, "Taiwan Under Japanese Rule, 1895–1945: The Vicissitudes of Colonialism," in Murray A. Rubinstein, Ed., *Taiwan: A New History* (Armonk: M. E. Sharpe, N.Y., 1999), p. 204.

[18] Sung-sheng Yvonne Chang, "Taiwanese New Literature and the Colonial Context," in Rubinstein, pp. 262–263.

[19] Ibid., p. 267.

[20] Steven Phillips, "Between Assimilation and Independence: Taiwanese Political Aspirations under Nationalist Chinese Rule, 1945–1948," in Rubinstein, p. 276.

[21] Ibid., p. 291.

[22] Ibid., p. 294.

[23] Ibid., p. 295.

16

Paths to the Future

———
——
—

Mao Zedong stood in triumph on the Gate of Heavenly Peace to announce the establishment of the People's Republic of China (PRC) on October 1, 1949. His vision of the path to the future was the socialist road leading to a Communist utopia. The civil war was not over: Chiang Kai-shek's flight across the Taiwan Strait had prolonged it. But surely the end was near. The battlefield defeats had been clear and decisive; the Guomindang was beaten and demoralized; states around the world were recognizing Mao's regime as the legitimate government of China. The "liberation" of Taiwan was the priority on the PLA's docket for 1950.

But then, into this likely historical scenario, was thrust a contingency, that is, something totally unexpected that changed the whole outlook. The event was the invasion of North Korea into South Korea in June 1950. When that happened, the United States on June 27 ordered the U.S. Seventh Fleet to enter the Taiwan Strait between the PRC and Taiwan to prevent either Mao or Chiang from taking advantage of the crisis to continue the civil war. That United States action has meant that, over half a century later, the civil war was still essentially unfinished. There thus developed two different paths to the Chinese future. This chapter looks at the direction and configuration of these paths.

THE STRUCTURE OF THE COMMUNIST PARTY STATE

Because a revolution is action and movement, tragic and melodramatic, it seems ironic to begin a discussion of the revolution with a sketch of institutional structures plunked down in their stark immovability. But it is necessary to ready the stage for the high drama.

Mao and CCP leaders structured three huge bureaucracies to carry out crucial ruling functions: party, state (or government), and military. At each territorial-administrative level (Center [or nation], province, prefecture, city, county, and township) there was a full range of both party and state organs. A small party committee generally held power at each level. At the Center, the committee was called the Politburo, chaired by the Chair of the Party, and composed of generally fourteen to twenty-four members. Its support staff was the Secretariat. When the Politburo was not meeting, its Standing Committee, made up of five or six of the most powerful leaders in the country, held power. The party had a Central Committee as well (ranging in size from about one hundred until 1966 to almost three hundred in the 1980s and 1990s). It did not always exercise much power; it mainly ratified decisions already made by the Politburo. The Central Committee's full meetings were called plenums, and they were numbered in the order they met following meetings of the Party Congress, a body composed of as many as fifteen hundred people. For example, the 8th Party Congress met in 1956; but the 11th Plenum of the 8th Party Congress met in 1966 and inaugurated the tragedy known as the Cultural Revolution. Finally the party had departments, called Central Committee departments, which, unlike the Central Committee, wielded considerable power. These included the Propaganda Department and the Organization Department, the latter of which was charged with making staff appointments.

The state or government, like the party, had organs at each territorial-administrative level. The most important government body after 1954 was the State Council. Headed by the Premier, it was composed of vice-premiers in charge of specific arenas of responsibility and of those in charge of commissions and ministries. As examples of the nature of the latter, two very important commissions were the State Planning Commission and the State Economic Commission. Theoretically, the party made policy and the state executed it. Because of the complementary nature of party and state, many times the ruling structure in the PRC was referred to as the party–state.

The military (the People's Liberation Army) had bureaucratic rank just like the State Council. It was *outside* the jurisdiction of the state and answered to a *party* body, the Military Affairs Commission. The military's highest priority was protecting the party, not the state. It was the party that propelled the revolution. The party used the military just as it used the state to try to achieve its goals.

To these institutions were brought "an operational set of principles and practices . . . [that might be] labeled the 'Yan'an complex'" because they were developed during the years at Yan'an.[1] For the first decades of the PRC these included the essential nature of ideology in keeping cadres in line with the aims of the party leaders; the importance of the "mass line," and, in the same vein, decentralized rule; a disdain of "specialists" with a preference for officials who could serve in a variety of areas; and, remembering the case of Wang Shiwei, witch hunts, false accusations, and confessions exacted anyway possible from those considered enemies within the Communist movement.

Because Mao Zedong dominated the PRC from its founding until his death in 1976, it is important to survey his thought for those ideas and practices that seemed to have special significance for his approaches and policies. One of his most significant emphases was voluntarism—"that properly motivated people could overcome virtually any material odds to accomplish their goals."[2] It was a strong conviction that the people could exercise willpower to change their world. Traditional Chinese social thought, in contrast, had emphasized that a major force in all lives was fate. One was fated to be born male or female, rich or poor, to be married to this or that individual, to live in this place or that, to be subject to this natural disaster or that physical illness. One must then accept that fate with resignation. It was a world where forces of nature, society, and birth reality dominated humans. Mao's revolutionary romanticism and strong populist faith trumpeted that humans did not have to stand cowed by fate, that they could transcend their fates with willpower and determination. A poem called "Swimming," that he wrote in 1956, puts it this way.

. . . .

Standing at a ford, the Master once said:
"Thus life flows into the past!"

Breeze shakes the masts
While Tortoise and Snake Hills are motionless.
A grand project is being conceived—
A bridge will fly across
And turn a barrier into a path.
To the west, new cliffs will arise;
Mount Wu's clouds and rains will be kept from the countryside.
Calm lakes will spring up in the gorges.
Were the goddess still alive
She would be amazed by the changes on this earth.[3]

Through a number of large-scale construction projects and by a wide variety of forceful and positive changes brought by the Communist regime in its first eight years, Mao had brought this new view of human capabilities into the Chinese social, political, and natural worlds. In terms of practical policies, Mao looked to the mass line and mass campaigns as structures through which to mobilize the willpower of the people. The problem, as it will become apparent, is that sometimes Mao's "revolutionary romanticism" had a way of soaring out of control with little grounding in reality.

If Mao placed great faith in the "people," he had nothing but hatred and loathing for intellectuals. Mao's strong anti-intellectualism was directed against not only scholars, writers, and journalists but scientists, engineers, and doctors as well. He chalked up the problems of late imperial China to intellectuals who were products of the civil service examination and who were in charge of state and society. Further, intellectuals were usually city-based elites who in many cases had been enemies during the revolution. They had none of the practical sense of the "people," yet they gloried in their presumed superiority, putting on airs and demeaning the masses. Mao also thought that they constantly raised nit-picking objections to his programs and policies. His opposition to intellectuals seriously and negatively affected developments in the People's Republic. Although the First Five-Year Plan (see below), shaped and executed with Soviet support, did follow the Soviet model and emphasize technical expertise, Mao subsequently moved away from that practice. In the twenty years from 1957 to 1976, he frequently demonized intellectuals, attacking them viciously and creating, as it were, an intellectual scorched earth policy that undercut China's situa-

Bridging the Yangzi for the first time, Nanjing, 1957

tion more devastatingly than even China's military scorched earth policy had during World War II. Listen to Mao in early 1958, comparing himself to the anti-intellectual first Chinese emperor in the Qin dynasty (221–207 B.C.E.): "He buried only 460 scholars alive; we have buried 46,000 scholars alive. You [intellectuals] revile us for being Qin Shi Huangs. You are wrong. We have surpassed Qin Shi Huang a hundredfold."[4]

Another of Mao's preeminent concerns was the crucial nature of ideology. To be ideologically correct (or in the slang of the time, properly "red" or Communist) was absolutely essential. For only ideological correctness would carry the revolution on to a successful conclusion. What was ideologically correct? From the years at Yan'an, it was "Mao Zedong Thought," an evolving body of thought, often emphasizing practice, not simply theoretical ideas. During his life, Mao was not only the producer but also the interpreter and the keeper of the ideological canon.

Mao's thinking on "class" contributed greatly to Mao Zedong Thought. For many reasons it was quite remarkable for class to become a focus:

> It is hard to imagine a society less subject to class analysis than was China in the 1910s and 1920s [when Marxism-Leninism began to flourish]. Capitalism had barely penetrated the country, and feudalism in its traditional European form had long ceased to exist. Among the key players were regional warlords who had no place in the Marxist analytical scheme. Even Chiang Kai-shek seems to have acted primarily for him-

self and the GMD rather than in the interests of any of the classes . . . at the time. Members of China's urban proletariat were, in most cases, the first generation off the farm and retained strong personal ties to the countryside. In the rural villages, strong ties of kinship cut across supposed class divisions, and clan associations managed the rural rituals.[5]

Be that as it may, Marxism-Leninism seemed to many intellectuals to answer so many questions about China's plight that class automatically became part of the formula of revolution. The core value regarding class was class struggle, which Mao believed would mark society until Communism was attained. Mao further taught in what might be called "ideo-biology" that class status could be determined by political attitudes and that then, unless there were changes in attitude, that class status was passed on almost genetically to succeeding generations. Once a landlord, always a landlord; once a capitalist, always a capitalist. As one scholar suggests, Mao really had created castes—"social orders with permanent, hereditary status that sharply [shaped] one's life experiences and prospects."[6] Even marriage prospects hinged on class status. A person of bad class became a public enemy of the "people," defined primarily as the working class and the peasantry.

THE EAST IS RED: THE HALLMARKS OF
THE COMMUNIST REVOLUTION

The first eight years of the People's Republic are generally seen as being the most successful period of Communist rule under Mao's control. The debilitating inflationary cycle was broken with government policies of price controls, balanced budgets, austerity measures, and currency reform. The new regime began the rigorous task of reconstruction following the years of war and turmoil. The government expelled most foreigners and confiscated their property. The People's Liberation Army in a fashion was able to atone for the wars China had lost in the preceding century by fighting the U.S. army to a standoff in Korea. Most important, Communists were able to launch aspects of their revolution across China.

Land Reform

The heart of the Chinese revolution—land reform—had already begun in the late 1940s, before the Communist military victory. According to Liu Shaoqi, the second-ranking Chinese leader in 1949, the objectives of land reform were "to free the rural productive forces from the shackles of the landlords' feudal land-ownership system, so as to develop agricultural production and open the way for new China's industrialization."[7] The process involved destruction of the old agricultural system through class struggle and construction of a new system based on collective rural production. General application of the concept of class struggle was problematic, given the ecological and social variety of the Chinese countryside. In the north, as we have seen, landlordism was not a major problem; tenancy rates in the 1930s ranged about 10 to 15 percent, as the peasant often tilled the land that he owned. In the south and southwest, however, tenancy rates were much higher (56 percent in

Sichuan); in these regions, absentee landlords exploited tenants. The social and political culture of different regions also differed sharply: for example, lineage groups dominated localities in the south, while secret organizations like the Red Spears were important in the north and the Elder Brothers' Society often held sway in the west. Within regions themselves, there were also stark differences: for example, in the Shaan-Gan-Ning base area, the Yan'an subregion was "sparsely populated, bandit-ridden badlands," while in the subregion directly to its north the population was dense, farming was intensive, tenancy rates were high, and commerce was more developed.[8] To apply one formula for revolution across the board, therefore, proved to be impossible.

The multiplicity of regional wartime experiences also created marked differences in people's attitudes and expectations. The long brutal warfare of much of the north contrasted with the relatively peaceful Shaan-Gan-Ning base, separated as it was by the Guomindang blockade. Parts of central and southern China were controlled by the Japanese for varying lengths of time and parts not at all. Manchuria had experienced a long period of Japanese colonial rule. The southwest had been the Guomindang base, subject to Japanese bombing but not ground invasion. The party had taken control in the north in the midst of war, but in east, central, south, and southwest China the Communist armies seized large amounts of territory with relatively little military action. Land reform in the north thus took place mostly before and during the civil war while in the south it happened after the establishment of the new national government. Therefore the party's approach to land reform varied according to the time it occurred; it was time- and space-specific.

Mobilizing peasants in rural villages through the setting up of mass organizations, which was far easier than land reform, was still usually slow and difficult. The task of organizing peasants was, in the words of Henan province wartime propaganda chief, "a difficult and protracted work. It requires a great deal of patience. One can never organize the peasants by simply issuing a manifesto, holding a meeting, or giving a theatrical performance." The first task in this society, built as it was on personal connections, was to gain access to a village. If organizers and mobilizers were from within the village or had close ties to some resident of the village, the effort would be expedited. Cadres from outside the local community had tougher problems. They had to possess networking skills, and they had to begin their work cultivating social ties in the community. Only by first winning the trust of people in the locality could they begin to build grassroots networks; and only after they had constructed these networks could they begin to undertake their various programs of action.

The other cultural hurdle was breaking down the social-psychological barrier that existed between peasants and local elites. In that traditional relationship, peasants "knew their place" and were extraordinarily careful not to offend or upset their landlords or others in positions of power. They were masters at knowing how to play their social role as subordinates. But now the Communists were mobilizing peasants to be aggressive in attacking those who had held power over them. Peasant Lin in Long Branch village would have felt very leery about attacking Landlord Wu. Though Wu might be under attack now, what would happen if the Communist cadres were ousted or if the Communist cause might go down to defeat and Wu and other landlords returned? Breaking through such concerns was a formidable task.

Land reform in north China was indeed often characterized by a violent settling of old scores against local elites. In the last months of 1945, the scores being settled were often those against elites and even middle and poor peasants who had collaborated with the Japanese. The violence associated with land reform followed a directive of May 1946 that gave free rein to poor peasant leagues and peasant associations to expropriate and redistribute land and property, telling cadres to keep hands-off, a policy that actually encouraged extremism among the masses. This more radical phase of the land reform effort was timed with the Guomindang's unexpectedly strong 1946 military offensive. Party leaders claimed that land reform was an important key for mobilizing the populace against attacks by Guomindang forces. County men formed militia units; local self-defense units transported supplies and ammunition; women's associations managed surveillance posts; youth associations worked in rear areas; cultural teams did propaganda work; and peasant associations spearheaded army recruiting. The connection between land reform, recruitment, and military mobilization was continually stressed.

The years 1948 to 1950 saw a moderation in the land reform effort to turn away from such "leftist excesses" as misclassifying villagers' class status, killing landlords and rich peasants, taking land from middle peasants, and attacking commercial and industrial enterprises. After the party came to power in 1949 and the promulgation of the agrarian reform law in June 1950, land reform began in all areas. The Communist regime faced gigantic challenges; in most areas there had been no advance work and there was therefore little, if any, structural readiness for great social change. There was generally no sense of class sentiments. In many areas of the south and east, tenants rented land from a landlord in their own lineage. Given all-important kin and native place networks, villagers could not easily understand what "feudal" class structures were or what exploitation meant. The pattern of mobilization used in the north was copied elsewhere: target local tyrants, initiate the struggle meeting, and inaugurate a rent reduction campaign. Work teams played a much larger role in land reform after 1949 than in the north in the 1940s. Despite their involvement, there were violent social outbursts, and an estimated one to two million landlords were killed—either in the heat of struggle or in execution. An estimated 88 percent of households in the countryside had completed the "land to the tiller" movement by summer 1952. In the end almost 43 percent of China's arable land was redistributed to about 60 percent of the population in the countryside.

Economists debate what impact land reform had on agricultural productivity. But the main impact was political. Land reform had revolutionized ways of thinking. Ding Ling's novel *The Sun Shines over the Sanggan River* (1948), accorded a 1951 Stalin prize in literature, revealed the changes in the peasant population. In this scene, a local bully called Schemer Qian is being attacked in a struggle meeting.

Peasants surged up to the stage shouting wildly: "Kill him!" "A life for our lives!"

A group of villagers rushed to beat him. It was not clear who started, but one struck the first blow and others fought to get at him. . . .

One feeling animated them all—vengeance! They wanted vengeance. They wanted to give vent to their hatred, the sufferings of the oppressed since their ancestors' times, the hatred of thousands of years; all this resentment they directed against him. They would have liked to tear him with their teeth. . . .

"Bah! Killing's too good for him. Let's make him beg for death. Let's humble him for a few days, how about it?" Old Dong's face was red with excitement. He had started life as a hired laborer. Now that he saw peasants just like himself daring to speak out and act boldly, his heart was racing wildly with happiness.[9]

The social and political horizons of countless poor and middle peasants "had been broadened by the class-oriented perspective of the CCP."[10] Land reform had created new functional associations and social groupings which tended to displace old kinship, religious, and voluntary associations. The common experiences of class struggle gave rise to a stronger social cohesion among those struggling against landlords and village despots and also created a new demarcation of the "us" from the "them." In the old society the "them" for any community was most likely the outsider, the person from a different native place; now the "Other," the "enemy," was inside the community itself, and his status as class alien could be resurrected and used at will.

Landlord under attack at struggle meeting during land reform, early 1950s

Revolution in the Family

One month before the agrarian reform law was announced, the state issued the Marriage Law of 1950. One stipulation of that law allowed single women, divorcees, and widows to own land in their names; land reform thus benefited one group in Chinese society that had never been able to hold land. But the law went well beyond economic rights; it struck at the very heart of the traditional family system and might be seen as a culmination of efforts stretching thirty years back to the May Fourth period to change the system. The Marriage Law abolished the traditional family system "based on arbitrary and compulsory arrangements and the superiority of man over woman." The new system was based "on equal rights for both sexes, and on the protection of the lawful interests of women and children."[11] Arranged marriages, child betrothals, polygamy, and the selling of women into marriage were forbidden. Women, as well as men, could initiate divorce proceedings. Infanticide was prohibited. Equal rights for both sexes: revolutionary indeed in the context of traditional Chinese gender relationships and practices like footbinding.

And yet, as with the marriage law announced during the Jiangxi Soviet, the laws were on the books, but not always put into practice. The right to divorce created considerable confusion and disorder when hundreds of thousands of women in unhappy marriages tried to divorce. Husbands and their mothers who stood to lose wives and daughters-in-law were angry. The local party cadre whose job it was to execute the law was caught in the middle. "If the cadre (usually a man) carried out his duties under the marriage law, he might find himself faced with an angry village and a serious handicap in the 'important' work to come. If he did not, he was returning women, illegally to families who would undoubtedly make them feel their anger for the loss of face they had suffered."[12] In most cases, the local cadres became the major problem that undercut the marriage law; it was not strictly enforced in the countryside. The numbers of murders and suicides stemming from the issue of divorce soared into the tens of thousands.

Urban Revolution

As in land reform, the urban phase of the revolution targeted class enemies. In 1951 and 1952, the party attacked purveyors of what it called non-Communist bourgeois values. Targets of the Three-Anti Campaign were party cadres, government bureaucrats, and factory managers; the goal was to eliminate waste, corruption, and mismanagement. Targets of the Five-Anti Campaign were the national bourgeoisie—industrialists and big businessmen—for corruption including bribery and tax evasion. Like the land reform campaigns, they gave rise to a sense of an enemy presence and a distrust that both mangled old connections and created new commonalities, identities, and networks.

These campaigns had a number of important impacts. They destroyed the self-confidence of the targeted groups and discredited them in the eyes of those, like workers, who had been their traditional subordinates. It removed personnel who had been retained since before Liberation and new cadres whose ideals were not orthodox and thus allowed for the recruitment of new mid- and lower-level personnel in business enterprises and the government. Economically, they brought money from fines and back taxes from large firms to be used for investment in new government enterprises. Heavy fines could be handled by having businesses sell stock to the state, thus creating public-private enterprise. Such arrangements would allow the state to appoint a cadre to take a leading role in management; that would often result in the establishment of party branches in large and medium businesses. Thus, economic involvement led to greater political control.

Like the Guomindang regime in the late 1920s and early 1930s, the Communist regime sought to sink its roots deeply into Chinese society. While the Guomindang attempt was not successful, the Communist *danwei* (unit) was a very effective arm of the state. By the early 1960s, every person was assigned to a "unit": if he was employed, the unit was at his place of work; for students, the unit was at the school; for unemployed or retired people, it was in the neighborhood. The Communist government then used these *danwei* to enforce control, political conformity, surveillance, and ideological correctness at the lowest level of the polity. One had to get permission from his or her danwei to get married, to have a child, to get a divorce, to change a job. The danwei controlled housing, gave out ration coupons, oversaw the birth-control program, mediated disputes, and supplied burial funds. They were also the basic building blocks of mass campaigns.

Providing the balancing social framework for these local units was state-sponsored mass organizations, based on shared interests or sometimes specific objectives. They attempted to enlarge the masses' horizons as they joined together the whole country across provincial and regional lines. By 1953, for example, trade union membership had risen to twelve million; nine million were in the New Democratic Youth League (the pre-1957 name of the Communist Youth League); and as many as seventy-six million women had joined the Women's Federation. They were especially significant forces in the campaigns that became so central a part of the early years of the People's Republic. Both the mass organizations and the mass campaigns provided frameworks for carrying out the party's directives and vehicles for mass mobilization.

AT WAR WITH THE UNITED NATIONS: THE KOREAN WAR

Six months after declaring the Marriage Law and five after the Agrarian Reform Law—that is, generally well before many of the revolutionary programs and campaigns could even get started, China was at war in Korea. It was extraordinarily horrific timing; the PRC was less than fourteen months into its life, struggling with basic tasks of reconstruction and hardly able to commit itself so thoroughly. But it did so, convinced that its actions were necessary. From the beginning Mao had decided that in foreign affairs, China should "lean to one side," that of the Soviet Union. He had traveled to Moscow in early 1950 to sign a Valentine's Day accord with Stalin, though Stalin's treatment of Mao was worse than rude. From the perspective of the United States at the time, such an agreement carried the simple (if wrong) message that the perceived Communist threat was monolithic and that the Cold War was real.

Then in late June 1950, the Cold War suddenly became hot when the Democratic Republic of Korea (North Korea) invaded the Republic of Korea (South Korea). After World War II, the Soviet Union had accepted the surrender of the Japanese north of the 38th parallel, a task that the United States performed south of that parallel. The Soviet and United States occupation of those respective areas had eventually turned into regimes that favored the former occupiers. The Soviet-linked regime of Kim Il-sung and the U.S.-connected regime of Syngman Rhee faced each other with great hostility. After the north's invasion of the south, the United States and other nations fighting under the flag of the United Nations came onto the Korean peninsula at a time when the defeat of the South seemed imminent. North Korean forces, seemingly unstoppable, had driven down the full length of the peninsula to a small perimeter around the southeastern port of Pusan. It was U.N. Commander Douglas MacArthur's decision to execute an amphibious landing at Inchon on the west coast in September that saved the day, turning a North Korean rout of the South into a panicky North Korean retreat. Whereas the original U.N. goal had been to "contain" Communism by pushing North Korean forces north of the 38th parallel and thus restoring it as the boundary between the two Koreas, the United Nations (with the United States calling the shots) changed its policy and decided to "liberate" the north. In the fall U.N. forces invaded North Korea.

By the end of June, the United States had already sent a message of its hostility to the PRC when it sent the U.S. Seventh Fleet into the Taiwan Strait. China saw the United States as the world's foremost imperialist nation, once more intervening in the Chinese civil war; Zhou Enlai called it "armed aggression." By the fall of 1950, that imperialist was now leading the charge up the Korean peninsula toward Chinese territory. Even before the Inchon landing, China had warned that it would intervene if U.N. forces invaded North Korea. The United States passed it off as a meaningless bluff. MacArthur had made increasingly belligerent statements about the artificiality of the border between China and North Korea ("they are all Communists"), about bombing sites in China ("take out all the industrial cities"), and about "unleashing" Chiang Kai-shek against the mainland. The PRC felt its own security was threatened by U.N. actions. Mao explained China's entrance into the war in late November as follows.

> Historical facts teach us that a crisis in Korea has much to do with the security of China. With the lips gone, the teeth would be exposed to the cold; with the door broken, the house itself would be in danger. For the people of China to aid the people of Korea in their struggle against the U.S. is *not merely a moral responsibility but also a matter closely related to the vital interests of our own people, a decision necessitated by a need for self-defense.* Saving our neighbors at once means saving ourselves. To protect our own country, we must help the people of Korea.[13]

Chinese troops in large numbers entered the war, totaling 700,000 very quickly. The Chinese commitment was great. China used 66 percent of its entire field army (the equivalent of twenty-five field corps), 62 percent of its artillery (seventy divisions), 70 percent of its air force (twelve divisions), all three of its tank divisions, 10 railway engineering divisions, and two public security divisions. Commanded by Marshal Peng Dehuai, Chinese forces were noted for their speed and stealth. The early Chinese campaigns were extraordinarily successful, with U.N. forces being driven far south of the 38th parallel in late January 1951. As fighting continued, however, China's primitive logistical supply system and lack of air-

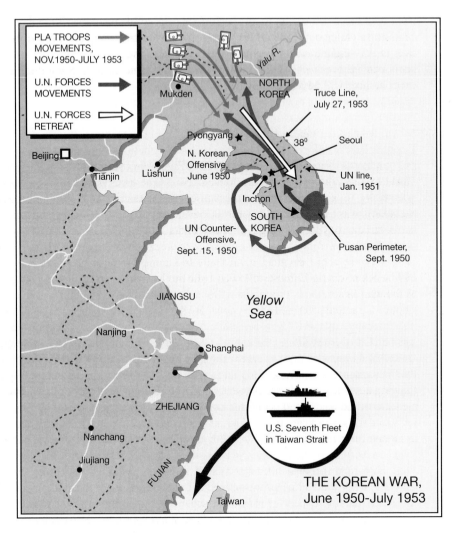

The Korean War

craft and anti-aircraft guns made China's situation desperate. In the end, it was for China a brutally costly war. An armistice was not reached until mid-1953; and many Chinese were killed in the last year of the war by withering U.N. fire power. About one million Chinese soldiers were killed.

    At home, the Chinese government rallied the masses to the war's support; communities, for example, contributed money for the construction of planes and other war materiel. From February 1951 into 1953, the party whipped up hatred for the United States through the campaign of "Resist America, Aid Korea" and its targeting of "counter-revolutionaries." Especially at risk were former Guomindang members or Guomindang military who were now suspected of sabotage. Executions of suspects were the rule rather than the exception. In Guangdong province alone in the period from October 1950 to August 1951, over twenty-eight thousand people were executed. Estimates of those killed nation-wide have reached over half a million with perhaps the same number committing suicide. The exact number will never be known.

THE FIRST FIVE-YEAR PLAN (1953–1957)

In 1953 the government announced its First Five-Year Plan to be structured on the Soviet model of state-controlled economic development. The focus was on heavy industry with the goal being to lay a foundation for subsequent industrial and economic development. Manchuria was a main laboratory for the developing plan: It had many industrial plants that had been held for years by the government (under Japan, then the Nationalists, now the Communists); they were mostly heavy industry; and the area was close to the Soviet Union. Thousands of Soviet engineers and technical advisors came to China to teach Soviet methods during these years. The Chinese followed their Soviet patrons to the letter, and the advances were remarkable: Most of the goals set forth in the plan were substantially exceeded. As examples, the actual production in physical output of coal by 1957 had reached 115 percent of the plan's goal, almost 130 percent of the steel, 220 percent of units of machine tools, and 188 percent of truck units. Economic growth was a high 8.9 percent annual increase, with agricultural output rising 3.8 percent annually and industrial growth climbing an impressive 18.7 percent per year. These solid and impressive statistics are underscored by other data showing how the lives of Chinese were being substantially bettered. Life expectancy, a good measure of the health and economic conditions of a country, rose from thirty-six years in 1950 to fifty-seven years in 1957, an amazing increase. Wages for workers were up by a third; and for peasants income was up by a fifth. It was indeed a stellar beginning.

China's industrialization was to be built on the back of increased agricultural production; land reform was to lead to that higher production. But land reform could not stop with the "land to the tiller" stage where land was broken up into small parcels. What was needed for higher production was large-scale farms on which resources of many farmers could be pooled and that would make possible the use of machines—tractors, seeders, combines, bailers—to bring more efficiency to farming. Policymakers thus saw collectivization—bringing farmers together in cooperative units—as a key to modernizing agriculture and as a way to make collecting tax grain easier. To ease the difficulties of moving into collectives, the government plan set forth a gradual phased process. The first step was mutual aid teams (MAT) where traditional practices of peasant cooperation in sharing labor and farm animals and tools was formalized; in this phase, peasants continued to own their own land, implements, and farm animals. In a typical MAT, there were generally ten or fewer cooperating households. In many areas, they were members of the same lineage. While an estimated 40 percent of all peasant households were MAT members by the end of 1952, the number reached 92 percent in 1956. The date of establishment of these MATs was extremely variable according to area of the country, a reality that had serious impacts on subsequent phases of collectivization.

The next stage of collectivization was the establishment of lower-level agricultural producers' cooperatives (APC). They were made up of approximately three to five MATs or about thirty to fifty households. In the "semisocialist" lower-level APC, the principle of "central management but private ownership" was operative. Members contributed land, draft animals, and equipment as capital shares to the cooperative and received a dividend, after wages were deducted, for what they contributed. The pace of the establishment of lower-level APCs was highly variable. In some areas organized already in 1951, the lower-level APC did not appear in southeast China until 1954 and 1955. By that time, considerable local resistance had begun to rise against the effort; this was especially the case where the "land to the tiller" phase had taken longer than anticipated and MATs had not been developed. In these areas, cadres, in order to keep up the timetable of collectivization, had moved directly from private ownership to the lower-level APC. In Zhejiang province, for example, because of the lateness of the end of the land to the tiller phase, by 1953 only thirty-three hundred APCs had been formed; but by 1954, cadres had established fifty-three thousand. This huge increase in so short a time suggests cadres were forcing the formation of APCs, a clear violation of the government's rule that the formation of APCs should be voluntaristic. It was clear that farmers, many landless for so many years, deeply resented having to contribute their recently acquired land to a cooperative.

Even though it seems commonsensical that if collectivization was to become solidly rooted in the countryside it would take substantial time, the party-state repeatedly showed a great leap mentality and a tendency for this "leapism" to become ever grander. In part that can be laid at Mao's feet, for, as noted earlier, he had a grand, almost romantic belief in the power of people to overcome all odds. In the context of a perceived general success of collectivization through the lower-level APC stage, with Mao forging the path, the leadership decided to push full-steam ahead to the establishment of upper level APCs. This was, somewhat incredibly, at the very time when only 15 percent of peasant households were members of *lower-level* APCs. Frantic organizing in the last months of 1955 led to the skyrocketing membership in lower-level APCs to over 80 percent of peasant households in January 1956. A tragic aspect to these decisions and efforts is that the party leadership abandoned its strategy of pragmatism and flexibility that had brought them political and military victory. As a result, they began to gut out what they had tried to build.

Higher-level APCs were far more revolutionary than their lower level predecessors. They comprised two hundred to three hundred households. Land was owned by the collective; private ownership was ended. Payments for contributions of land and other assets were ended; payment was strictly for labor. By the end of 1956, almost 88 percent of peasant households had become at least nominal members in higher-level APCs. At least one scholar has seen this completion of collectivization as one of the most important developments in the First Five-Year Plan: "it was an enormous achievement of social and institutional transformation to bring the great bulk of the Chinese people under socialist forms of organization. . . ."[14]

Many peasants may have had a different view of the impact of collectivization. Some considered the establishment of the higher-level APC as a negative turning point in their relationship to the party-state and in their day-to-day relationships with the rural cadres who in many cases forced this formation on the people. Further, in the aftermath of the higher-level APC formation, the state attempted to institute direct planning in agriculture. Though they backtracked on this effort, the farmers were still hit with a flurry of marketing restraints, quotas, and rations that increasingly constrained and shaped their actions. As the state daily became more central in decision-making about farming, peasants lost control over their lives to the rural cadres serving as agents of the party-state.

THE TAIWAN MODEL: AUTHORITARIANISM AND REFORM

The development of the Republic of China on Taiwan offers interesting comparisons to development in the PRC. Supposedly in the throes of death in 1950 and on the verge of total extinction (or liberation, depending on one's point of view), the Guomindang regime on Taiwan in the following two decades experienced a miracle of economic resurrection. It would follow a three-phased program of reform, the first which might be called reconstructive or rehabilitative reform and the second and third phase developmental reform.

The Iron Fist

When Chiang Kai-shek was reinaugurated as President of the Republic of China on May 1, 1950, he admitted that he was personally responsible for the loss of the mainland to the Communists. All his important bases had failed—the army disintegrated, the party itself in shambles, the state shrunk to one province. Under the circumstances he had to get what was left of his house in order, aware, as he continually reminded his listeners, that they were still involved in a civil war and that everyone's goal must be retaking the mainland. In a first step to rehabilitate the party, he appointed a Central Reform Committee, composed of former students and confidantes, to overhaul the party. They developed plans to restructure the party's systems of ideological training, organization, and discipline. As had been the fashion in the party since the 1920s, there was another process of party re-registration to be able to weed out undesirables, whether they were politically suspect, corrupt, or just incompetent. These tasks were completed by the 7th Party Congress in October 1952, a meeting which accepted the principle that opposition to Communism and resistance against Russia were basic to all other party missions. There was recognition, however, that in this period of opposition to Communism and Russia, party goals should also include making Taiwan a model province of Sun Yat-sen's Three People's Principles.

Chiang used the ongoing civil war (now cold) as the justification for stringent authoritarian controls. Martial law continued. No one could challenge the Guomindang—which meant no new political parties. There could be no newspapers if they were not sanctioned by the government. The security system was reorganized. A National Security Bureau under the leadership of Chiang's son, Chiang Ching-kuo, was formed to coordinate all security bureaus in the Guomindang, the Ministries of Defense, of Foreign Affairs, of the Interior, the Taiwan Garrison Command, the military police, and the local police. These were tight networks, stringently controlled, and were instrumental in cracking down on any dissent, almost always labeled Communist conspiracies or subversion. The White Terror that Chiang had begun in 1949 continued throughout the 1950s and beyond.

In these years, the government "arrested, imprisoned, and executed thousands on insufficient or circumstantial evidence."[15] Those targeted were sometimes the very famous. The governor of Taiwan province, Wu Kuo-chen, was forced to leave the island in 1953 after he criticized Chiang for his strong-arm tactics against dissenters; once he was off the island, he condemned Chiang's regime as a "police-state." In 1955, Sun Li-jen, Commander of the Army and personal Chief of Staff to Chiang, was obliquely implicated in a plot to overthrow the government; he spent the rest of his life under house arrest. And these had been Chiang's friends. What is obvious is that being based in Taiwan had not changed Chiang's long-time policy of brutally crushing dissent, whether student or otherwise. With the memory of wartime anti-student protests, Chiang appointed his Security Chief son to head the Chinese Anti-Communist National Salvation Youth Corps; it was the only legal intercollegiate organization.

In politics, the Guomindang under Chiang maintained an iron grip. Since the government was still theoretically the government of all China, Chiang and the party declared that the life of representative bodies in the government—the National Assembly, the Legislative Yuan, and the Control Yuan—would be extended indefinitely since nationwide elections could not obviously be held. Eventually in 1969, as men in these bodies began to die, the party allowed for supplementary elections. In any case, in these bodies Taiwan had only a very small representation. For many Taiwanese the absurdity of having little say in the determination of policies that affected only them was more than a little disturbing. In addition to controlling the political situation in Taipei, the Guomindang manipulated local politics. They handed out economic privileges, for example, licenses in lucrative businesses and industries, to cooperative politicians. They also made certain that one group of people did not hold onto local power for a great length of time by encouraging factions and then playing them one off against the other.

Any suggestion of serious opposition or proposals of political alternatives brought a rapid and heavy-handed response. A liberal journal, *Free China Fortnightly,* supported by men like May Fourth period leader Hu Shih, was shut down when in 1960 its editor Lei Chen and a Taiwanese politician organized a China Democratic Party. Lei was arrested and imprisoned for ten years. Four years later, P'eng Meng-min, Chair of the Political Science Department at National Taiwan University, and two students issued a "Self-Rescue Declaration of Taiwan," appealing to both Taiwanese and mainlanders "to work together to establish a democratic country because Taiwan was in reality already independent of China."[16] P'eng received an amnesty after the announcement of an eight-year prison sentence, largely because of pressure from the United States; but the two students spent at least eight years in prison. The government kept very strict control of literature and the arts as well as popular culture, handing out prison sentences as if they were going out of style. Authoritarianism ruled the day.

THE TAIWAN "MIRACLE"

Through currency reform and various measures to take surplus money out of circulation, Chiang's government was able to reduce the 3000 percent inflation in the first half of 1949 to 300 percent in 1950 to 8.8 percent in 1952. Then it was able to turn to more long-term reform.

Rural Reforms

While Chiang had essentially written off the peasants in his Nanjing decade decision to allow land taxes to revert to provinces, one of the first initiatives of his Taiwan government dealt with peasants. Perhaps Chiang had seen the error of his ways. A more likely explanation was that the Guomindang government in Taiwan could act forthrightly in this regard because they had no connections to and thus were unconstrained to local landlords. Already in 1949, the government ordered the reduction of rent to 37.5 percent, the same limits it had set in the Nanjing period. A second step in what should be called land reform—though of a sharply different type than on the mainland—was the sale of public lands to tenant farmers. This land, which had come into government hands from the Japanese colonial administration and from Japanese residents of the island, totaled almost 20 percent of all the arable land in Taiwan. Farmers could buy 1.2 to 4.8 acres of paddy land and 2.4 to 9.6 acres of dry land at a cost of 2.5 times the harvest of the annual main crop per 2.4 acres (known in Taiwan as a *jia*).

In early 1953, the government took the reform one step further with a "land to the tiller" program. Each landlord could keep up to 7.2 acres (3 *jia*) of paddy land and 14.4 acres (6 *jia*) of dry land. If the landlord owned more, the government would buy it and then sell it to tenants for 2.5 times the yield of the main annual crop. The government compensated 70 percent of the payments to landlords in land bonds and 30 percent in the form of stock shares from four government businesses. This latter substantially boosted the government's efforts to spur business. If the landlord was not interested in investment in business and industry, he could sell these stocks to those who were; many became wealthy with such stock from Taiwan Cement, Taiwan Pulp and Paper, Taiwan Industry and Mining; and Taiwan Agricultural and Forestry. In the land reform effort, mostly completed by the end of 1953, 194,823 tenant families had received 345,800 acres (140,000 hectares) of land previously held by landlords. It was a remarkable bloodless effort, obviously helped in part by the relative smallness of the numbers of people and acreage involved. Historians have noted also the important contributions in financial assistance and technical expertise from the Sino-American Joint Commission on Rural Reconstruction, which was established under an act by the United States Congress to set up and oversee Taiwanese rural projects. In the aftermath of land reform, farmers associations were established to provide credit, assistance with marketing and sale of farm commodities, advice and assistance on setting up industries in predominantly rural areas, and aid for the rural establishment of services like clinics and transportation facilities.

The Keys to General Economic Development

From 1960 to 1970, Taiwan was the fastest growing economy in the world with an annual rate of GNP (gross national product, or the total value of all the goods and services in a nation in a year) of 9.7 percent. There are a number of reasons for such rapid economic growth.

Certainly the relatively developed economic infrastructure inherited from the Japanese colonial period was important. Political stability (no major disruptive episodes followed the February 1947 tragedy) was a crucial context for sustained and rising growth. But, in the discussion that follows, the focus is on the role played by the presence of many experienced and well-educated experts in business, industry, and government; on the important contributions of the United States from the early 1950s to the mid-1960s; on the pragmatic responses of the Taiwan government to challenges; and on the importance placed upon education in the development of human resources.

Whereas the Maoist vision emphasized for its leaders ideological correctness and (in the process of destroying those with expertise [see Chapters 17 and 18]), placed its hopes in the common sense of the masses, the Taiwan model exalted the experts. Highly trained and committed professionals, many of whom had been educated abroad, drove the economic juggernaut. Many had majored in economics and engineering. Two of the most famous were Yin Chung-yung (K. Y. Yin), trained as an electrical engineer, and Li Kuo-ting (K. T. Li), a physicist. Yin has been called the "moving spirit" behind the industrial reform of the 1950s: "His goal of an industrialized, independent, and self-sustaining Taiwanese economy combined elements of the *laissez-faire* approach and state planning." Li was the dynamo and "Taiwan's chief economic planner" from 1963 into the late 1980s.[17] They cooperated with U.S. aid officials, accommodating a variety of Western economic theories to Taiwanese realities. A number of men who worked with them in economic planning later became extraordinarily important politically: as examples, Tsiang Yen-shih emerged as Guomindang Secretary-General in the 1980s; Yen Chia-kan became premier in 1969, vice-president of the ROC in 1973, and served as president of the ROC from Chiang Kai-shek's death in 1975 until 1978; and Lee Teng-hui served as vice-president (1984–1988) and then president (1988–2000) of the ROC.

The role of the United States in the Taiwan miracle was crucial. The United States first freed up Taiwan to focus on domestic reform by underwriting Taiwan's military security with the Taiwan-U.S. Mutual Defense Treaty of 1954 and by providing military aid. In the arena of economic development, $100 million of U.S. non-military aid from 1951 to 1965 went to infrastructure-building and -strengthening projects (especially in areas like communications, transportation, and electricity) and to undertakings that fostered human resources. Not only did U.S. economic aid provide about half of the capital formation in Taiwan in these years, but U.S. specialists also played important roles in advising Taiwan policymakers and in training technicians. The United States was Taiwan's chief cheerleader, in the early 1960s urging Taiwan to expand its economy aggressively and promising more economic aid. From the perspective of the Cold War, of course, it was to the advantage of the United States to show how well a "free" Taiwan was doing in contrast to the PRC.

The United States could provide economic aid and advice, but it was the government in Taipei that had to devise and execute policy; and it was generally both pragmatic and creative. In the early 1950s, Taiwan had a huge trade imbalance, exporting primarily sugar and rice and importing almost everything else. To expand business and industry so as to produce manufactured goods for export, the government embarked on a program of tax incentives and rebates. Once industries became productive, high tariffs (a nominal rate of over 40 percent, but going as high as 160 percent) were set in place to provide protection for in-

PATHS TO THE FUTURE

fant industries. The First Four-Year Plan (1953–1956), focused not on heavy industry as in the PRC's First Five-Year Plan, but on light industry in order to produce goods for export and for domestic use. The configuration of development plans in both Chinas developed out of perceived needs and economic realities. In Taiwan, the government provided funds for those establishing textile mills and fertilizer plants. The textile industry developed especially rapidly, and many new jobs were created. By 1956, as the industrial production index soared to about 155 percent, per capita income leaped by 40 percent. The Second Four-Year Plan (1957–1960) continued the important goal of expanding production of electricity, but turned the focus more to heavy industry and national defense industries.

In the late 1950s and early 1960s, the government focused ever more fixedly on strategies to increase exports; above all, that meant expanding industrial production. Setting tax limits, offering tax exemptions, and providing government services in finding industrial plant sites were all part of the strategy to stimulate the establishment of labor intensive industries in textiles, paper and paper products, chemical, and plastic and rubber products. More attention to financial infrastructure—reactivating important banks to assist in promoting industrial production, establishing machinery for investment banking, and setting up a stock market—were efforts to "accelerate economic development," the announced goal of the Third Four-Year Plan (1961–1964). On the whole, the 1950s and 1960s saw Taiwan's economy changing from an agricultural base to an industrial one, as the following chart shows.

Growth of Net Domestic Market

	Agriculture	Industry
1952	35.9%	18.0%
1959	30.4%	25.7%
1970	19.2%	32.5%

One institutional development that points to the creativity and pragmatism of the government with regards to economic development was the establishment of export processing zones. The first was formed at the southern port of Kaohsiung in late 1966; two more were established near Taichung in 1970. They were the "first tax and duty free industrial processing zones" in Asia, set up to encourage exports and attract foreign investments. For the latter, the zones "provided smooth entry, established factory sites, cheap power and utilities, various tax concessions, preferential customs treatment, tariff protection against competition, guarantees against expropriation, easy access to ports, and other incentives."[18] Cheap labor, especially by a skilled female labor force, was one of the big draws that attracted such U.S. firms as General Electric and Singer Sewing Machine Company and such Japanese firms as Hitachi and Canon. Electronics and electrical machinery became the most important exports of these zones. Because of these zones, exports from 1960 to 1970 shot up from U.S. $174 million to U.S. $1.56 billion.

One other significant contextual element for Taiwan's meteoric economic rise was its emphasis on education, which tended to raise the quality of its work force and the literacy of its citizenry. From 1952 to 1960, the numbers of colleges and universities rose from 4 to 15, secondary schools from 148 to 299, and primary schools from 1,248 to 1,982. The percentage of six-year-olds attending school increased from 57.9 percent in 1952 to 72.9 percent in 1960 to 85.3 percent in 1970. In the years between 1954 and 1968, fully 13 percent of Taiwan's budget was spent on education. In 1968, as further evidence of ongoing commitment to education, compulsory school attendance was raised from six years to nine.

The paths to the future for the two Chinas cannot have been more different. They shared only one thing: the authoritarianism of their governments. The White Terror in Taiwan and the Red Terror in the People's Republic under governments that were essentially police-states left no room for dissenters. But on the development road, Taiwan emphasized scientific and economic expertise, a literate and educated populace, land reform where landlords were reimbursed for the land they lost, openness to the international community for investment and trade, and a strong relationship to the United States which helped relieve some of the military expenditures that otherwise would have slowed domestic economic development. In contrast, the PRC leadership stressed the innate moral power of the people (downplaying expertise), the power of ideology to shape human lives, the importance of struggle in moving forward, self-reliance (remaining relatively closed to the outside world), land reform that featured violence and the deaths of hundreds of thousands of people, and a relationship, rocky from the start, with the Soviet Union. Despite these differences, both the PRC (1949–1957) and Taiwan (1949–1970) had made relatively good beginnings on the road to development. Unfortunately for the PRC, the situation would soon begin to go very, very bad.

Notes

[1] Kenneth Lieberthal, *Governing China* (New York: W. W. Norton, 1995), p. 51.

[2] Ibid., p. 63.

[3] Cited in Chen, *Mao and the Chinese Revolution,* p. 346.

[4] Lieberthal, p. 71.

[5] Ibid., p. 74.

[6] Ibid., p. 75.

[7] Quoted in Edwin E. Moise, *Land Reform in China and North Vietnam* (Chapel Hill: University of North Carolina Press, 1983), p. 106.

[8] Pauliine Keating, "The Yan'an Way of Co-operativization," *China Quarterly* 104 (December 1994), pp. 1029–1031.

[9] Ding Ling, *The Sun Shines over the Sanggan River,* selection cited in Cheng and Lestz with Spence, pp. 369–371.

[10] The phrase is Frederick C. Teiwes, "Establishment and Consolidation of the New Regime," in Roderick MacFarquhar and John K. Fairbank, Eds., *The Cambridge History of China, Vol. 14, The People's Republic, Part 1: The Emergence of Revolutionary China, 1949–1965* (Cambridge: Cambridge University Press, 1987), p. 87.

[11] "The Marriage Law of the People's Republic of China, May 1, 1950," reprinted in Gentzler, *Changing China,* p. 268.

[12] Margery Wolf, *Revolution Postponed: Women in Contemporary China* (Stanford: Stanford University Press, 1985), p. 18.

[13] Quoted in Mineo Nakajima, "Foreign Relations: from the Korean War to the Bandung Line," in MacFarquhar and Fairbank, p. 275.

[14] Teiwes, p. 110.

[15] Peter Chen-main Wang, "A Bastion Created, A Regime Reformed, An Economy Re-engineered, 1949–1970," in Rubinstein, p. 330.

[16] Ibid., p. 335.

[17] Gary Klintworth, *New Taiwan, New China: Taiwan's Changing Role in the Asia-Pacific Region* (New York: St. Martin's Press, 1995), p. 117.

[18] Ibid., p. 123.

17

Coming Unglued

———————

———

—

Amid the considerable economic success it experienced in the first years of the 1950s stood two harbingers of the bad times ahead for the Communist leadership. Harbinger One: the purge in early 1954 of Gao Gang, Politburo member, head of the State Planning Commission, and key party-state-military figure in Manchuria, and Rao Shushi, key party and state leader in Eastern China as well as head of the Central Committee's Organization Department. The reason: an apparent power play to replace Liu Shaoqi and Zhou Enlai among the top leadership. Although the dynamics here were apparently strictly politically personal, the episode was an indicator that the leadership at the top, a ruling coalition put together during the Yan'an years (and Gao had helped build the Shaan-Gan-Ning base) was not necessarily permanent. Factionalism, so much a part of the early Communist party years, would rear its increasingly destructive head in the years ahead.

Harbinger Two: the 1955 campaign against intellectual-author Hu Feng. A professional editor and writer, Hu had struggled since the 1930s with orthodox Communist literary critics who contended that politics and ideology, not artistic values, should dominate art and literature. Hu's position was that artistic standards and the autonomy of the artist were crucial. For orthodox Maoists, this position was anathema; the Yan'an legacy of party control of thought, art, and literature had to be maintained. Therefore in mid-1955, the party launched a vitriolic nation-wide campaign against Hu Feng and "Hu Fengism." Hu was arrested and imprisoned, and one of his closest disciples was committed to a mental hospital. The hysteria of the campaign further intimidated intellectuals, writers, and artists and even led to some suicides in these circles. The relationship between the state and its intellectuals, long demoralized and generally cowed into silence, deteriorated even further and set the stage for greater tragedies.

"LET A HUNDRED FLOWERS BLOOM!" (THEN CUT THEM DOWN)

In apparent sharp contrast to the anti-Hu Feng campaign, Mao and a rather reluctant party began to make overtures to those very intellectuals they had mired in alienation. Perhaps the motive was a keen awareness that the anti-Hu Feng campaign's getting out of hand had so browbeaten intellectuals that, if things continued as they were, they would never again contribute to or facilitate China's national progress. Perhaps the motive was a sense that developments under their leadership had gone so swimmingly that it was the opportune time for overtures to those intellectuals they had helped to alienate. Indeed some historians have detected by early 1956 what might be called a relaxed moderation in party-state policies regarding the outside world.

In foreign policy, the watchword—after war in Korea and assistance in the anti-French struggle in Vietnam—became "peaceful coexistence." It was a policy facilitated by Zhou Enlai who emerged as foreign minister and who played an important role at the April 1955 meeting of the representatives of twenty-nine independent Asian and African states in Bandung, Indonesia. In what might be called the Bandung line, Zhou argued "What our nations in Africa and Asia need is . . . to establish peaceful, cooperative relations with [developing] countries of other regions as well."[1] Zhou's leadership in Bandung helped pave the way for his successful tour of Asian countries a year and a half later and visits of Asian leaders to Beijing. It was this moderate policy that allowed the beginning of ambassadorial talks with United States diplomats first in Geneva in late 1955, then later in Warsaw. Beijing's stature in the Communist world was also raised by the general loss of face the Soviet Union experienced in that world from Premier Nikita Khrushchev's criticism of Stalin (dead in 1953) and from the Soviet Union's invasion of Hungary in October 1956.

The international initiatives perhaps raised the confidence of the leadership that they could deal constructively with Chinese intellectuals. In a policy first set forth by Zhou Enlai in January 1956, confirmed by Mao in May, and announced in late May by Lu Dingyi, the director of the Propaganda Department of the Central Committee, the party called for the input, suggestions, and reactions of intellectuals to current conditions in state and society. Lu said

> If we want our country to be prosperous and strong, we must, besides consolidating the people's state power, developing our economy and education and strengthening our national defense, have a flourishing art, literature, and science. That is essential.[2]

"Let a hundred flowers bloom; let a hundred schools of thought contend." Perhaps what was most striking in Lu's speech, which on its face seemed to be a call for tolerance, or at least openness, were the frequent intimations of Mao's restrictions on art and literature given at the 1942 Yan'an forum. One wonders how many of the hundred flowers heard these lines?

> . . . in the case of art and literature . . . we can see things that are obviously pernicious. The stuff written by Hu Feng is one such example. Pornographic and gutter

literature that debauches people and turns them into gangsters is another. Still another example is the so-called literature summed up in phrases like "let's play mahjongg and to hell with state affairs" and "the moon in America is rounder that the moon in China," etc. It is perfectly right and proper for us to look on literature of this pernicious kind as a par with flies, mosquitoes, rats, and sparrows and rid ourselves of it all.[3]

It is probably not surprising that writers at first hesitated to speak out after the calls for blooming and contending. Scientists and engineers first came forward with calls for less interference in their work by generally ignorant party cadres, for fewer time-consuming political sessions, and for more accessibility to Western as opposed to Soviet publications. When writers, many of the May Fourth generation of intellectuals, did begin to speak out, their criticisms were leveled against party and bureaucratic dogmatism and against areas where the party had failed to live up to its principles. There was obvious immense dissatisfaction with an increasingly bureaucratized party-state.

Two journals, *People's Literature* and *Literary Studies,* became the vehicles for critiques by intellectuals. They published short stories by journalist Liu Binyan who wrote of the discrepancy between Communist ideals and PRC reality. In the fall of 1956, a new literary voice, Wang Meng, published a short novel, *The Young Man Who Has Just Arrived at the Organization Department,* which pointed to the unresponsive and arbitrary nature of party leaders. On the whole, though there were sporadic criticisms of the party-state, the campaign seemed in late 1956 and early 1957 quite moribund. Intellectuals were still somewhat fearful to put themselves on the line, and party leaders seemed uncertain about whether they wanted this campaign and how to handle criticism they received.

Then in February 1957, Mao tried to breathe new life into the effort, seeming to praise those who had criticized the bureaucracy; the goal was to achieve a greater unity for the challenges ahead. For five weeks in May and June the flowers bloomed, intellectuals apparently convinced that the Yan'an restrictiveness had been lifted. Criticisms of basic party policy and of the party itself were brutally frank. Moreover, the criticism spread quickly to other groups, including farmers and urban workers. By mid-May students on campuses around the country were putting up critical wall posters. At Beijing University they were attached to what became known as Democracy Wall. The criticism was sharp. Lines from a poster at Qinghua University in Beijing:

What does it mean when the Communists say . . . they let the people enjoy things before they do the same? . . . In Yan'an was Chairman Mao, who had two dishes plus soup for every meal, having a hard time? Were the peasants who had nothing to eat but bitter vegetables, enjoying the good life? Everyone was told that Chairman Mao was leading a hard and simple life. That son of a bitch! A million shames on him! . . . Our pens can never defeat Mao Zedong's Party guards and his imperial army. When he wants to kill you, he doesn't have to do it himself. He can mobilize your wife and children to denounce you and then kill you with their own hands! Is this a rational society? This is class struggle, Mao Zedong style! This is the spiritual side of our age.[4]

By June 8 the party moved to tear out the blooming flowers by their roots, stopping the movement it had started. Noisily proclaiming a nation-wide "anti-Communist plot," it announced a campaign against "rightists." It was a bitter harvest for intellectuals and artists. The execution of the campaign was itself an object lesson in party arbitrariness: a statement by the party center that at least 5 percent of the leaders in any area were likely "rightist" was taken to mean that local party branches had to find a quota of 5 percent who would be tagged as "rightist." Many were attacked; sometimes accusers denounced people with their primary objective being the taking of the positions of those they denounced. Within the next few months, between 400,000 and 700,000 intellectuals lost careers and titles, were jailed, sent to labor camps or to do heavy labor in the countryside. Some committed suicide. Most were not rehabilitated until 1979, many of those posthumously. Mao in a real sense had burned his bridges to China's intellectuals, in effect discarding them as of no use in the development of a modern socialist China; the chasm between the party and intellectuals was both deep and gaping.

THE GREAT LEAP FORWARD (AND BACKWARD)

Mao's disdain for the intellectual elites pointed all the more to his infatuation with people power, specifically the power of the mobilized masses to remake China. A mobilized populace was the key both to leaping over the mistakes that other developing states had made and leaping forward into the developed future. We have seen that by late 1956 almost 90 percent

Revising History: Peng Zhen (holding shovel with Mao) is airbrushed out of 1958 photograph when he fell out of favor in 1966

of the rural populace were members (some quite unwillingly) of higher-level agricultural producers' cooperatives. The relative ease with which this had been accomplished gave PRC leaders—and especially Mao—a sense that collectivization could now be carried to its logical conclusion. Attempting to turn what was a fairly consistent twentieth century "great leap" mindset into a reality, in 1958 the party launched the Great Leap Forward, a utopian campaign, part of which was to establish communes on which Chinese life and labor would be militarized. A Politburo resolution in August 1958 called the people's communes "the basic social units of Communist society" and called for "actively us[ing] the form of people's communes to explore the practical . . . transition to communism."[5] Mao and the party-state hierarchy assumed that larger agricultural production units would bring more efficiency and productivity. The commune on average was made up of about fifty-five hundred households—approximately twenty-five times bigger than higher-level APCs. It became the locality's main governmental unit and socioeconomic organization, charged with agricultural production; the development and fostering of industry and commerce; the provision of health care, police and social services, and education; and the collection of taxes. With astonishing speed, by the end of December 1958, 99.1 percent of all rural families were members of communes. On communes, private garden plots and private ownership of livestock were forbidden; the numbers of rural periodic markets where peasants had in the past sold vegetables, eggs, and perhaps pigs were consequently cut back. Authorities adopted a communist distribution system where earnings were paid on a per capita basis—not on their labor contributions. Thus, differences between incomes on communes were greatly reduced.

There were perhaps two commune structures that best epitomized the Great Leap, the backyard steel furnace and the commune mess hall. Rooted in Mao's idealistic populism was the sense that if the people had a participatory stake in production, their energies would be released and production would increase dramatically. While industry had generally not been located in the countryside, Mao believed that communes should develop local industries in which people could participate and thereby contribute their productive capacities.

Steel making was one such area. Communes built their own steel furnaces—at least one million dotted the Chinese landscape. Fueling them led to wide-scale deforestation; any wood, including that of used coffins, was gathered to stoke the flames to keep them as hot as possible. All over China furnace fires studded the blackness of night. For the cause, peo-

Backyard smelters during the Great Leap Forward

ple contributed iron tools and implements, window frames, pots and pans all to go into the making of pig iron. But because the manufacturing techniques were faulty, what was produced cracked easily. Useful iron implements, tools, and utensils, in many cases necessary for daily tasks, had been turned into something totally useless. Not only that, but in its useless state, it filled railroad car after railroad car that then clogged trainyards and snarled train tracks around the country. In terms of economic development, it was ridiculous: the expense of setting up the furnaces and the use of huge numbers of people to operate them surpassed by far any contribution to China's steel industry. Yet the primary and ultimate goal was political: to marshal the people's energy and give them a stake in the making of the new China. For example, there is this view of steel making in Hunan province:

> Iron and steel production is not simply a technical job; it is also a political task that has an important bearing on all other activities. . . . [After the introduction of the idea of commune steel-making], more than half a million pledges were sent to the party [in the Shaoyang region] in support of the campaign. The people felt elated and stimulated; millions of hearts had only one wish—to fight hard to achieve and surpass the goal of producing 300,000 tons of iron in 1958. . . . The people composed a song describing [the construction of large numbers of furnaces]:
>
>> The Communist Party is really wonderful.
>> In three days more than a thousand furnaces were built.
>> The masses' strength is really tremendous.
>> The American imperialists will run off, tails between legs.
>> The Chinese people will now surpass Britain.
>> The East wind will always prevail over the West wind.[6]

Perhaps no change made a starker difference in people's daily lives than commune mess halls. A traditional centerpiece of farm life—the daily coming together of family for shared meals—was now gone. Though not meant to be a direct blow against family cohesion, it probably undermined to a degree the closeness of the family unit. From the standpoint of agricultural production, mess halls "meant that each commune member had three extra hours for work or study, labor productivity had been raised by about 30 percent, and six million units of female labor power had been released from domestic chores."[7] The construction of mess halls was a major undertaking. In the average-sized county of Xiaoshan in Zhejiang province, 2,726 mess halls were constructed between 1958 and 1962. It is said that such construction was yet another cause of deforestation in the county.

Other commune institutions like nurseries and kindergartens also tended to erode familial cohesion. Grandparents, freed from the responsibility of babysitting their grandchildren, could spend their time at "happiness homes" for the elderly. Some children boarded at primary schools and even kindergartens away from home, thus removing them from their parents' control at an early age. The state thus impinged far more deeply into people's lives than ever before, for the first time ever penetrating directly into family life by beginning to replace traditional family practices with governmental services.

From one viewpoint, these revolutionary changes advanced the social and economic position of women. Changes in commune-living freed women from the daily responsibilities of cooking and child care; now they were free to labor on the land with the men. From one perspective this helped equalize the status of men and women. More significant, for the first time rural women achieved their own economic identity; an estimated 90 percent performed farm labor in 1958 and 1959. From another perspective, however, this shift simply redefined women primarily as workers who labored with men outside the home. The sense of the Communist party was that *proper* women served the state, not simply the family. This policy perpetuated the Yan'an period's talk of the "national woman," identified as a new unit for purposes of the party-state, not for purposes of gender equity.[8]

Life in the people's communes also saw the culmination of the militarization of Chinese society, a trend that had been gradually developing since the first years of the twentieth century. The commune work force was organized into military units named "brigades" (sometimes, "companies") and were further divided into "production teams" or "platoons." Overseeing brigades were management districts, usually denoted as "battalions." The use of military terminology points to the militarization of labor even as it suggests the degree of regimentation imposed on the people by the party-state. In some areas at least the military ethos was conveyed by the rhetoric of competition in the massive production campaigns. Cadres in a Guangdong commune, for example, asserted that in their competition with other areas, "Our soldiers and horses are strong, our generals brave and numerous. . . . Clad in our armor and ready in our formations, we await the battle cry."[9] Peasants were referred to as "fighters" on the "agricultural front"; the countryside became the "battlefield"; and nature itself became an "enemy" to be overcome.[10]

The establishment of the commune militia further enhanced militarization on the commune. Able-bodied citizens between the ages of 15 and 50 were in the ordinary militia and 16 to 30 year olds were in the so-called "hard-core" militia. By January 1959, 220 million men and women were serving as militia members. Most members of the hard-core militia never fired a gun, but they trained two to three hours each day and were thus "psychologically mobilized." Militia members were required to adhere to "rising, eating, sleeping, setting out to work, and returning from work" at the same times: "This greatly strengthened the collectivization of life and organizational discipline, and nurtured the fighting style in production and work."

In some areas the Great Leap Forward was marked by the massive mobilization of labor for water control and irrigation projects undertaken with the goal of increasing agricultural production. Some have seen the cooperation between a number of higher-level APCs in these projects as the forerunner of the communes. Upwards of a million workers might be mobilized for a particular project: it was images such as this that gave rise in the Communist-paranoid and racist West to using metaphors like "blue ants" for Chinese workers. By early 1958 some 100 million peasants had worked on projects that enabled over 19 million acres to be irrigated for the first time. But such works were common throughout the 1950s. In Xiaoshan county, Zhejiang, for example, from February to May 1952, 840,000 workers from six districts widened a river southeast of the provincial capital of Hangzhou.

Despite the capability of the authorities to mobilize hundreds of thousands of workers on worthwhile public projects, it was clear by the end of 1958 that the Great Leap had fallen flat on its face. The utter failure of the steel-making experiment and its ripple effect on the economy at large was compounded by a deepening agricultural tragedy. Though the 1958 harvest was dismal, grain production estimates had been extremely overinflated. In large measure such exaggeration of production grew directly out of the dynamics of the Great Leap campaign; the battle rhetoric often associated with the competition between communes to produce more than others created a mentality that the sky was the limit in terms of production. Inflated statistics were passed up the chain of command and inflated even more; and, more crucial, there were few attempts, if any, to verify the validity of the reports. In August 1958 projections had posited a minimal harvest of 240 million metric tons of grain, with a maximum perhaps up to 300 million tons. But by December the reported harvest had soared, according to the party, to 375 million metric tons—double the harvest of 1957, and clearly an impossibility. And yet the State Statistical Bureau confirmed that figure in the spring of 1959. The figures were very satisfying to Mao because they confirmed his own assessment of the production benefits of the commune system.

The tragic problem developed when the state assessed taxes, which were collected in the form of grain: It based the amount of tax upon the estimates of the harvest. Since the estimates were so high compared to how much was really produced, the state ended up taking most of the grain that was produced. The upshot was that little grain was left for the masses. People in the countryside were beginning to go hungry. The situation was compounded by widespread mismanagement of communes which had been so hastily put together that there was insufficient time for effective organization. Some crops were not harvested or harvested incompletely or harvested too late because too many people had been assigned to backyard steel furnaces or had left for cities. Party leaders touring the provinces in the fall saw evidence of serious problems. Even Mao saw that communization, as it had been attempted, was going too far too fast, and that adjustments in the Great Leap had to come. For example, the steel production goal for 1959 had been set at 30 million tons, a nearly 600 percent increase over 1957—clearly another impossibility. Mao in his infinite rationality wanted the goal to be dropped to 20 million tons, so that the increase would be only about 400 percent! Indeed, it was Mao's positions regarding the Great Leap and the sense on the part of some leaders that a disaster might be approaching that led them to compel Mao to relinquish the post of president of the PRC to Liu Shaoqi at a party central committee meeting in December 1958.

At first glance, studying the decision making of the Chinese leadership during the Great Leap causes one to ask if they had all taken leave of their senses. Projections of harvests, reports on harvests, and decisions made on the basis of those reports all had little relation to reality. For example, on the basis of the reported huge 1958 harvests, leaders decided that since so much grain had allegedly been produced, the amount of land to be sown in grain in 1959 should be reduced, with more land devoted to cotton and non-grain crops. Thus, in 1959 with a worsening problem of insufficient grain in the country as a whole, government decisions meant that the grain harvest fell by another 25 million metric tons. Further in some areas, there was the failure or misfunctioning of water control and irrigation projects that had been constructed so rapidly by so many workers whose work could not possibly been overseen properly; especially in north China, these flawed projects harmed rather than helped production.

The answer to what was going on was not, of course, that people had lost their rationality. The answer was that people, including those in the leadership circles, were fearful of punishment. Comrade Li asked whether production projections are too high. He must be a rightist! Mr. Zhang questioned the validity of impossibly high harvest reports. He is surely a weak-kneed rightist! Comrade Shen asked whether water projects carried out so swiftly and constructed with untrained workers would function properly? He dares to question the will and power of the people? He is clearly an elitist, a rightist, and a counterrevolutionary. In other words, building on a series of political campaigns and terror related to those campaigns, Mao had created an ongoing situation that saw honest questioning and honest disagreement as evidence that questioners and those who disagreed were the enemy, traitors to the revolution. Only Mao understood and could properly interpret what was revolutionary and what was not. Even before the formal Mao cult of the 1960s, Mao had so traumatized the Chinese polity that few people would raise questions or speak against him or his positions.

The Lushan Conference

In July 1959, in a month-long conference of Chinese leaders at the resort of Lushan in Jiangxi province, rancor over the Great Leap began to tear apart the "political consensus" of the leadership group that had formed at Yan'an.[11] Called "one of the most fateful in the history of the PRC," this meeting set the stage for the national tragedy of the so-called Cultural Revolution that would dominate the 1960s and 1970s.[12] The major clash pitted Mao against his Defense Minister Peng Dehuai. Undoubtedly personal issues and motives, such as ambition, animus, and jealousy, were involved in this confrontation. But the policy issues were crucial. In a letter to Mao that the Chairman made public, Peng charged that the Leap was not working, that the huge grain harvest figures were not credible, and that he was concerned about the direction of policies. In an earlier written poem he had set forth his concerns:

> Millet is scattered all over the ground.
> The leaves of the sweet potatoes are withered.
> The young and the strong have gone to smelt iron,
> To harvest the grain there are children and old women.
> How shall we get through next year?
> I shall agitate and speak out on behalf of the people.[13]

On July 23, in response to Peng's criticism, Mao went for the jugular. He was visibly agitated. "Now that you have said so much, let me say something, will you? I have taken sleeping-pills three times, but I can't get to sleep." He then proceeded to attack Peng for going beyond the pale of permissible criticism. Peng's position amounted to what Mao called his "right opportunism." There it was: Peng was a counter-revolutionary rightist! Only one leader at the meeting, attended by luminaries like Liu Shaoqi and Zhou Enlai, stood up for Peng and obliquely challenged Mao. That was Zhu De, founder of the Red Army in the late 1920s, and chess partner of Peng. But no one followed up, and for his audacity Zhu had to write his own self-criticism. But Mao was not finished: He accused Peng of complaining to Khrushchev about Great Leap policies on a June trip to Warsaw Pact countries. He made that accusation based on Khrushchev's July 18 open criticism of the Chinese communes and Great Leap policies in a speech in Eastern Europe. Then Mao made a threat. If criticisms continued, "I will go to the countryside to lead the peasants to overthrow the government. If those of you in the Liberation Army won't follow me, then I will go and find a Red Army, and organize another Liberation Army."[14] After this confrontation Peng, the heroic Chinese commander during the Korean War, was dismissed at a September meeting of the Enlarged Military Affairs Committee. Lin Biao, a strong supporter of Mao, was named new defense minister.

There were other more long-lasting consequences of the Lushan showdown. Mao had poisoned the air among China's leaders. Labeling Peng's critique as "unprincipled factional activity," Mao made it less likely than ever for oppositional viewpoints to be taken as anything but treachery and, worse, counterrevolutionary activity. How could free discussion ever occur again among the handful of decision-makers in the Politburo? More tragic for the nation, the confrontation seemed to make Mao more obstinate in supporting and even expanding the Great Leap. Before Lushan Mao, both in late 1958 and early 1959, had spoken of slowing down the Leap and adjusting policies to fit changing circumstances. But after Lushan, as if in defensive response to criticism, Mao's attitude changed to one that signaled "full steam ahead." In early 1960 Mao led the charge for a new Great Leap, advocating the establishment of urban communes, the sending down of party cadres to the countryside to learn from the peasants, and maintaining the impossible agricultural goals and the far too high tax levies. As another indication of Mao's turn farther to the left was his support of a revised "constitution" for the major Manchurian Anshan Iron and Steel Works that would do away with the management approach modeled on the Soviet system and replace it with one that would emphasize political orthodoxy and correctness.

This second Great Leap failed spectacularly. Output in heavy industry in 1961 dropped precipitously, down about 47 percent compared to 1960, and in 1962 down another 22 percent. Light industry production in 1960 fell about 10 percent from 1959, another 22 percent in 1961, and another over 8 percent in 1962. But it was in agriculture that the bottom fell out and helped produce one of the world's worst twentieth-century tragedies. Grain output had been at 200 million tons in 1958; it dropped to 170 million tons in 1959 and to 144 million in 1960—a 28 percent decline from two years earlier.

THE WORST FAMINE IN HISTORY

The crisis of declining grain harvests was exacerbated in 1960 by natural disasters. Typhoons caused devastating flooding in parts of south China and in Manchuria; drought was so severe along the Yellow River that its water level was decreased by two-thirds; insect pests affected vast areas. Over 60 percent of farmed land was affected, resulting in paltry harvests. The depth of the tragedy is revealed by the fact that per capita food production would not again reach its pre-1957 level until the early 1970s.

Rural areas were more affected than cities, though all suffered. Overall Chinese mortality rates, averaging 11.1 per thousand in 1956 and 1957 climbed to 14.6 per thousand in 1959 and shot up to 25.4 per thousand in 1960. But particular regions suffered more than others. The following table shows the number of deaths in particularly hard-hit provinces, using 1957 as the pre-famine baseline.[15]

**Numbers of Deaths in Particular Provinces,
1957 and 1960**

Province	1957	1960
Anhui	c. 250,000	2,200,000
Gansu	142,041	538,479
Guangxi	261,785	644,700
Henan	572,000	1,908,000
Hubei	290,600	670,300
Hunan	370,059	1,068,118
Jiangsu	424,500	785,900

Best estimates are that thirty million people died because of the famine that was worsened by nature but stemmed basically from human policies that bordered on sheer lunacy.

Such statistics can only suggest the nightmare of these years for the masses. People were not allowed to become refugees and move to other areas in search of food. Most knew only what was happening in their areas and did not know the extent of the famine. Starving people ate rice husks, corncobs, weeds, grass, tree bark, even earth itself in an effort to remain alive. The situation was so severe in Anhui province that in at least one county "boiled water was a luxury because fuel was scarce"—until as late as 1969! [16] Malnutrition was rampant.

> In Chengdu [capital of Sichuan province], the monthly food ration was reduced to 19 pounds of rice, a third of an ounce of cooking oil, and 3.5 ounces of meat when there was any. Scarcely anything else was available, not even cabbage. Many people were afflicted by edema, a condition in which fluid accumulates under the skin because of malnutrition. The patient turns yellow and swells up. The most popular remedy was eating chlorella, which was supposed to be rich in protein. Chlorella fed on human urine, so people stopped going to the toilet and peed into spittoons instead, then dropped the chlorella seed in; they grew into something looking like green fish roe in a couple of days, and were scooped out of the urine, washed, and cooked with rice. They were truly disgusting to eat, but did reduce the swelling. [17]

It is little wonder that the per capita consumption of food items in these years fell to shocking levels as the table shows. [18]

Even in provinces like Hebei where the famine was not so severe, social problems stemming from the tragic conditions abounded. Wives were sold. Wives left their families and, in a survival strategy, started living with better-off men. The number of divorces shot up. Bandits attacked trains and grain storage facilities. And as with the great Henan famine during World War II and other famines in the Chinese past, cannibalism reared its ugly head. A Sichuan official reported that "one day a peasant burst into his room and threw himself on the floor, screaming that he had committed a terrible crime and begging to be punished. Eventually it came out that he had killed his own baby and eaten it. . . . With tears rolling

Per Capita Consumption of Major Food Items, 1957 and 1960

(in catties, with a catty approximately equivalent to a pound)

	1957	1960
Grain	406.0	327.0
Urban	392.0	385.0
Rural	409.0	312.0
Vegetable Oil	4.8	3.7
Urban	10.3	7.1
Rural	3.7	2.9
Pork	10.2	3.1
Urban	18.0	5.4
Rural	8.7	2.4

down his cheeks, the official ordered the peasant to be arrested. Later he was shot as a warning to baby killers."[19]

But there were greater criminals. Though it is said that Mao even denied himself meat for seven months in 1960, he was not in the least contrite for his role in the catastrophe, in early 1961 denying categorically to future French president Mitterand that there was any famine at all in the country. The truth, as a Chinese economist noted, was that "the Great Leap exacted a 'high price in blood.'"[20]

As scandalous as getting the country into such a state was the fact that the government did very little to respond to the crisis, called by one scholar "the most severe challenge the Party had faced since coming to power in 1949."[21] The party seemed paralyzed. The state gave out relief funds on an almost infinitesimal level. From 1958 to 1962, years which include the height of the famine, relief for rural areas totaled about 450 million yuan per year—or a total of about 0.8 yuan per person on the communes. This was at a time when a kilogram of rice cost between 2 and 4 yuan! In 1960 band-aids were applied to try to stanch the massive bleeding: The assessed tax was scaled back slightly; export of grain was cut back; and wheat imports were arranged—though mainly for urban consumption. If this had been imperial China, people would most certainly have been asserting that the Mandate of Heaven was sliding away from the regime in power.

THE SINO–SOVIET SPLIT

Even though Mao had risen to power more in opposition to Moscow than with its support, Mao and the Communist leadership had decided in the first months of the PRC to lean to the side of the Soviet Union in foreign relations. The Sino-Soviet security treaty of 1950 and the presence of thousands of Soviet technical and industrial advisors coming to assist in the Soviet-modeled First Five-Year Plan underscored this foreign policy choice. China continued to see the United States as the chief imperialist power in the world, and the reality was that the Soviet Union was the sole Chinese shield against any possible U.S. nuclear missile attack. That uncomfortable reality hit home in 1957 when the United States announced that it would be sending Taiwan Matador missiles that were capable of carrying nuclear warheads. In light of that threat, that fall when Mao traveled to Moscow for the fortieth anniversary celebration of the Bolshevik revolution, Khrushchev promised Mao "a sample of an atomic bomb" and the information needed to complete its manufacture. In 1958 and 1959, the Soviet Union did help China develop, among other nuclear-related facilities, uranium mines and a nuclear testing site. China thus looked to the Soviet Union for protection, guidance, training, and aid.

But even so, from the beginning this had not been the rosiest of relationships. Stalin had been downright rude to Mao when he had traveled to Moscow in early 1950. One might have thought, given the rocky relationship between Mao and Stalin since the late 1920s, that Mao would have taken a certain glee over Khrushchev's de-Stalinization campaign in 1956. But instead, for the Chinese leadership, the Soviet premier's criticism of Stalin stirred up considerable consternation about what the campaign meant in terms of trends in the Soviet Union and the leadership situation in China.

Then came the Great Leap. In it the Chinese had chosen to break with the Soviet model that it had adopted so thoroughly earlier in the decade. The bad blood that became evident developed from different arenas, including practical policy and ideology. From the Soviet perspective, they had spent much and given huge amounts of development aid and assistance to the Chinese; they had tutored the Chinese in their technocratic model of development; they had done what they could to help protect and nurture Chinese progress. To witness the Chinese embark now on the radically different developmental route of mass mobilization was upsetting, especially because things in China seemed to be going so drastically awry. Furthermore the Soviet Union saw itself as world Communist leader and patron for developing Communist states. Chinese actions were like a slap in the face. From the perspective of the Soviet Union, Khrushchev's criticism in the summer of 1959 was understandable. From the Chinese perspective, the criticism was unjustifiable intervention in China's domestic affairs.

The Taiwan Strait Crisis

There were other sources of the uneasy, almost queasy relationship between the Soviet Union and China. Most came from the reality that the two countries had their own national perspectives in mind and national interests to protect and nurture; two Communist states they were, but when national push came to national shove, ideology played a markedly subsidiary role. Mao and the Chinese leadership were often put off by what they considered Khrushchev's weakness in the face of the actions of Western states. In 1956, he had announced that the policy of the Soviet Union was "peaceful coexistence" with the non-Communist world.

The summer of 1958 presented several object lessons in this regard. When a pro-Western regime in Iraq was overthrown, the United States sent forces to Lebanon and Great Britain sent forces to Jordan to prop up those Western-leaning regimes. Khrushchev did not respond strongly, insisting on trying to work out the issues diplomatically. The Chinese considered him overly cautious. As a sign of Mao's displeasure with and disdain over the Soviet premier's action, when Khrushchev flew to Beijing for a summit with Mao (July 31–August 3), Mao greeted him in not very diplomatically correct circumstances—at a swimming pool, where "the two leaders [sunned] themselves on their towels 'like seals on the warm sand.'"[22] At this meeting, Mao was offended by three requests from Khrushchev that had military overtones: that the Soviet Union be allowed to build a radio station on Chinese territory to be able to communicate with Soviet submarines in the Pacific; that Soviet submarines be allowed to refuel at Chinese ports and that their crews be allowed short leaves at the ports; and that for China's protection the Soviets be allowed to station interceptor planes in China. Mao considered them all encroachments on Chinese sovereignty. The meeting ended without Mao telling Khrushchev that he had plans up his sleeve to try to change the current stalemate with Taiwan through the use of force, an action that would challenge the United States.

The United States, as we saw in the last chapter, became rather quickly a close supporter of the Taipei regime. In mid-1954 Beijing declared that it was about to "liberate" Taiwan. In September they began to bombard two small islands very near to the coast, but still held by the Nationalists on Taiwan—Quemoy off the coast at Amoy and Matsu near Fuzhou. In December the United States and Taiwan, in clear response to Beijing's challenge, signed a mutual security treaty. In 1955, with hardly any dissent in the U.S. Congress (the vote in the Senate was 83–3, in the House, 410–3), the president was given the authorization to use American combat forces to defend Taiwan and the islands it controlled in the Taiwan Strait. Step by step the United States was being drawn militarily closer into the Chinese civil war. The Eisenhower administration opted to take such a stance as a clear symbol of its ability to be tough in the face of Communist threats. Vice-President Richard Nixon laid it on the line, evidencing U.S. beliefs at the time that there was a monolithic Communist threat endangering the world: "If we let them know that we will defend freedom when the stakes are small, the Soviets are not encouraged to threaten freedom where the stakes are higher . . . that is why the two small islands . . . are so important in the poker game of world politics."[23] China, without assurance of Soviet support, pulled back and agreed to the ambassadorial talks that began with the United States in 1955. These talks, however, came to a sudden end in December 1957, as relations between the two countries deteriorated.

On August 23, 1958, the PRC launched a massive bombardment of Quemoy, just less than three weeks after the Mao-Khrushchev summit. At least one scholar thinks that among Mao's motives was to show Khrushchev that if a nation stood up to the United States, the United States would back down. But Mao clearly miscalculated the U.S. response, which was quick and extensive. President Eisenhower ordered the U.S. Seventh Fleet to convoy Nationalist supply ships to the island and for U.S. planes to airlift Nationalist troops to the island, announcing in a World War II mentality that to abandon the offshore islands would be a "Western Pacific Munich." It was not until September 5 that Soviet Foreign Minister Gromyko made it to Beijing for consultations; Soviet support for the PRC's position did not come until September 7, fully fifteen days after the crisis had begun. The day before, Zhou Enlai had called on the United States to reopen the ambassadorial level talks that had been halted nine months earlier. The U.S. government suggested to the PRC that "mutual de-escalation" would be best for all concerned. Beijing responded by stopping the shelling for a week; and when they resumed it, they shelled the island only on even-numbered days.

The best evidence suggests that the PRC was trying to force a Nationalist withdrawal from the island, not that this was preliminary to an invasion. Whatever the case, the episode was a disaster for Sino–Soviet relations. Khrushchev was bitter that he had not been informed of Mao's plans; under the 1950 security treaty, Mao had that obligation. More important, Mao's actions might have precipitated a war between China and the United States into which the Soviet Union would have been pulled—at a time when it was trying to maneuver its own summit with the United States. By late 1959 through the eyes of Moscow, in initiating the Taiwan Strait crisis and undertaking the Great Leap Forward, Mao had been guilty of huge miscalculations; indeed the "magnitude of miscalculation in both instances suggested megalomania."[24] As a direct result of the Taiwan Strait crisis, Khrushchev decided to cancel the nuclear weapons technology offer that he had made to Mao in the fall of 1957 in Moscow—a cancellation that in turn embittered Mao and the Chinese government.

China in Tibet

China's relationship with the Soviet Union was also affected by Chinese actions in Tibet, specifically as they related to India. To understand the situation, a brief look at China's history in Tibet is important. The protectorate that China had established over Tibet in the eighteenth century remained into the twentieth century. By the late nineteenth century, however, given the weight of China's domestic and foreign-related burdens, Chinese hegemony over Tibet remained in theory but in actuality was a dead letter. In the 1880s and 1890s Great Britain, strongly entrenched in the Indian subcontinent and intent on seizing small principalities in the Himalayas, was beginning to knock on Tibet's door. In 1893, the British got trading rights at a post just inside the Tibetan border with the stipulation that a British official could be stationed there to oversee the trade. When the Tibetan religious and political leader, the Dalai Lama, refused to answer British requests for the further opening up of relations, the British invaded to force negotiations. In August 1904, British troops led by the British viceroy in India, Lord Curzon, seized the Tibetan capital, Lhasa. In the Anglo-Tibet convention of 1904, Britain opened up three Tibetan towns for trading, levied a huge indemnity, and sent forces to occupy Tibetan territory contiguous to Sikkim (which Britain held) until the indemnity could be paid. In a real sense, the British were making Tibet their protectorate. China had not been a party to the convention; its Manchu official in Lhasa had refused to participate.

The situation was complicated by the fact that the British government had not given Curzon orders to invade Tibet. They were aware of the historical relationship between China and Tibet and also did not want to have the Tibetan situation affect negatively their relationship to China. Therefore in 1906, the Anglo–Chinese convention modified the 1904 convention by recognizing "China's legitimate authority over its dependency Tibet."[25] British actions in Tibet were a wake-up call for the Chinese, who, though they could hardly afford to act as they were inching toward revolution, decided that they had to act more aggressively in their Tibetan protectorate. In 1910, Chinese troops entered Lhasa, deposed the

Dalai Lama (a practice begun already in the eighteenth century), and moved to take more direct control of day-to-day rule. A betting person would have wagered that soon Tibet would become a part of China proper. But then the Qing dynasty was overthrown in 1912. With the political and military weakness of the early Republic, the Dalai Lama, in exile in India, returned to Lhasa in 1913 and ruled until his death in 1933. British efforts to resolve the question of Tibet's political status at a conference in Simla, India in 1913–1914 ended only in fuzziness: Tibet, the Simla Convention said, would maintain its autonomy from China, but it would also have to recognize that China had suzerainty over Tibet. With all Chinese leaders from Sun Yat-sen to Chiang Kai-shek to Mao Zedong claiming that Tibet was part of the Chinese nation, it was only a matter of time before the Tibetan question would be re-opened.

At the time of the Simla meeting in 1913–1914, Britain had an interest in settling the Tibetan problem because of its control of India. But by the time that the PRC was established in 1949, India had been independent from Britain for two years, and Britain no longer had an interest in Tibet's political status. Thus, in 1950 when it looked like the PRC would move to establish direct control, Great Britain and the United States, when contacted by Lhasa, did not respond with any support. Though the Chinese government tried to negotiate a "peaceful liberation," the Tibetan government put them off. Thus, in October 1950, PLA forces invaded Tibet. The Tibetan military, weak and poorly organized, was quickly captured by the PLA. Tibetan appeals to the United Nations were turned aside mainly at the urgings of India, backed by Great Britain. Tibet had no choice but to negotiate with Beijing; an agreement, the "Seventeen-Point Agreement for the Peaceful Liberation of Tibet," was signed in May 1951. Point One states in no uncertain terms: "the Tibet people shall return to the big family of the Motherland—the People's Republic of China."[26] In this formal agreement, Tibet thus recognized China's sovereignty—in exchange for which China agreed to maintain the traditional political and economic system, including the Dalai Lama. The Dalai Lama telegraphed Mao his acceptance of the arrangement in October 1951.

Scholars point out that the period 1951 to 1959 saw a moderate Chinese policy in Tibet. Mao's policy was one of gradual change, believing that the cooperation of the Dalai Lama was the key. Mao's "Tibet strategy sought to create cordial relations between Han (ethnic Chinese) and Tibetans, and allay Tibetan anxieties so that Tibet's elite would over time genuinely accept 'reintegration' with China and agree to a social transformation." [27] The Indian representative in Lhasa noted indeed that

> there is everywhere a keenness to imitate the Chinese . . . and this is particularly noticeable among the respectable bunch of official families in Lhasa . . . The inroad of neo-Chinese culture into Tibetan society . . . is truly remarkable for what was static in this land has become alive and dynamic. There is not a home in Lhasa where portraits of Mao and his colleagues have not found a place in the domestic shrine.[28]

But by the mid-1950s things had begun to deteriorate. While Mao had been willing in Tibet to slow the social revolution that was remaking China, others in the Chinese leadership saw no reason to make Tibet an exception in the revolution. The United States, fueling the unstable situation had by 1957 actually started to train and arm anti-Chinese Tibetan guerrillas. Further there were many dissatisfied ethnic Tibetans living in China proper, especially in Sichuan, Qinghai, and Xikang. When authorities in Sichuan tried to move toward agricultural collectivization, riots erupted among ethnic Tibetans and quickly turned into outright rebellion. In 1959, rebels and refugees moved toward the political unit of Tibet, crossing its borders and spreading rebellion toward Lhasa. In the wake of a mass demonstration in Lhasa, the PLA opened fire and bloody fighting erupted; the Dalai Lama fled to India, which welcomed him with open arms—a welcome the Chinese bitterly denounced as "interference in China's internal affairs."

China's relations with India were yet another sore point in the relationship between China and the Soviet Union. The year before the Dalai Lama's flight, relations between India and China had turned sour, a reality that played into the Tibetan crisis. The initial disputes concerned borders. China had constructed a road to link Xinjiang and Tibet, but the road ran across the Aksai Chin plateau, an area claimed by India. When India sent patrols to ascertain the situation, the Chinese detained them for several weeks. When India protested this action, Zhou Enlai argued that the borders had never been firmly set and that the road ran through Chinese territory. Prime Minister Nehru was firm in his demand that China must pull back behind its borders. Then came the Tibet crisis. India was openly sympathetic with Tibet, granting the Dalai Lama and thousands of Tibetan refugees asylum. Clashes between Chinese and Indian troops occurred in high Himalaya mountain passes which the Chinese tried to occupy in order to stop the flow of Tibetan refugees. In clashes in August and October 1959, over ten Indian soldiers were killed and more taken prisoner.

The Soviet Union, who saw India as an ally, never took China's side in any of these affairs. Indeed, the Soviets explicitly rejected the Chinese claims that India was at fault both in the Xinjiang–Tibet road controversy and later in the bloody clashes in the passes. Their rejection of September 10 was followed three days later with the announcement that Moscow was extending aid to New Delhi in the form of $375 million for India's current Five-Year Plan. From the Chinese perspective it was like adding insult to injury.

With the deterioration of relations between China and India and China and the Soviet Union came the end of Mao's period of moderation in dealing with Tibet. In the view of the PRC, government efforts to nurse Tibet along to the Chinese point of view had failed. Beijing believed that the only alternative remaining was brute force. One scholar has described the years for Tibetans after 1959 succinctly and with a sense of the incredible Tibetan loss.

> Buddhism was destroyed and Tibetans were forced to abandon deeply held values and customs that went to the core of their cultural identity. The class struggle sessions and the constant barrage of propaganda contradicting and ridiculing everything they understood and felt, sought to destroy the social and cultural fabric of the Tibetans' traditional way of life. These were terrible times for Tibetans in Tibet.[29]

CRACK-UP

Everywhere China and the Soviet Union turned they found more to distrust about the other. Mao and his colleagues could not abide Khrushchev's criticism of Stalin, his support of peaceful coexistence, his apparent cozying up to the Eisenhower administration, his silence and anger about the Taiwan Strait crisis, his support of India and outspokenness about Chinese blame in that crisis, and his military requests from China that seemed from their perspective to smack of old-time imperialist demands. Khrushchev could not abide the apparent blitheness with which the Chinese leaders played with war in a nuclear age—whether in the Taiwan Strait or the Himalayan passes. Even more he could not tolerate Mao's cavalier attitude toward nuclear war, stated in May 1958 at the Eighth Party Congress:

> If [nuclear] war breaks out it is unavoidable that people will die. We have seen wars kill people. Many times in China's past half of the population has been wiped out. . . . We have at present no experience with atomic war. We do not know how many must die. It is better if one-half are left, the second best is one-third. . . . After several five-year plans [China] will then develop and rise up. In place of the totally destroyed capitalism we will obtain perpetual peace. This will not be a bad thing.[30]

He found the Great Leap Forward abhorrent; not only was it a radical departure from the Soviet model, but it was leading to chaos and confusion, to economic loss and deprivation, not to development. All the Soviet expense and work in trying to help build China was going up in the smoke of backyard steel furnaces. Khrushchev looked at Mao and saw, if not a dangerous madman, then a dangerous megalomaniac.

Khrushchev and other Soviet leaders flew to Beijing in October 1959, one month after the Soviets had sided so strongly with India. The meetings were cold and hostile: Khrushchev did not change his position. In the months that followed into February 1960, the Chinese sent a string of protest notes to the Soviet Union about its foreign policy "neutralism" in the Sino-Indian dispute. Chinese leaders celebrated the ninetieth anniversary of Lenin's birth in April 1960 by lambasting Soviet foreign policy. For the first time Beijing stated openly that the Soviet Union had lost the qualities that the leader of the Communist world must display and argued that China was now the center of Leninist orthodoxy which could lead the world Communist movement. It was in the words of one scholar "a public declaration of independence from the Soviet Union."[31]

In mid-July 1960, as starvation was spreading in China, Khrushchev suddenly called back to the Soviet Union all the scientists, engineers, and industrial advisors that had been working in several hundred Chinese firms. In a June meeting in Bucharest, the Sino-Soviet split had erupted in the open with Khrushchev and Peng Zhen, the Chinese delegate, attacking each other in scathing personal, national, and ideological denunciations. It must have been the proverbial straw that broke the camel's back. When Soviet advisors were called back, they were to take with them all their blueprints and materials; no fewer than 257 scientific and technical projects were cancelled. By early September no Russian technical and scientific advisors were left. The short-term effects on China were severe, especially in light of the economic crisis and the institutional turmoil into which the Great Leap had thrown party and state.

> The abruptness of the withdrawal meant that construction stopped at the sites of scores of new plants and factories while work at many existing ones was thrown into

confusion. Spare parts were no longer available for plants built according to Russian design and mines and electric power stations developed with Russian help were closed down. Planning on new undertakings was abandoned because the Russians simultaneously canceled contracts for the delivery of plans and equipment."[32]

As divorces go, this was a particularly hostile and bitter crack-up. No reconciliation would take place for almost thirty years; and when it did come the world would be completely changed. For the time being, China had to cope with the largest famine in history, the economic shambles of the Great Leap Forward, an alienated intelligentsia, a splintering leadership, and humiliation in foreign affairs. China was entering a new dark age.

Notes

[1] Mineo Nakajima, "Foreign Relations: From the Korean War to the Bandung Line," in MacFarquhar and Fairbank, p. 283.

[2] Lu Dingyi, "Let Flowers of Many Kinds Blossom, Diverse Schools of Thought Contend" in Cheng and Lestz with Spence, p. 387.

[3] Ibid., p. 387–388.

[4] Gregor Benton and Alan Hunter, Eds., *Wild Lily, Prairie Fire* (Princeton: Princeton University Press, 1995), pp. 100–101.

[5] Quoted in Allen S. Whiting, "The Sino–Soviet Split," in MacFarquhar and Fairbank, p. 500.

[6] Yin Zeming, "The Strength of the Masses is Limitless," in Cheng, Lestz, and Spence, pp. 405–406.

[7] Issue of October 25, 1958 cited in Roderick MacFarquhar, *The Origins of the Cultural Revolution, Vol. 2: The Great Leap Forward, 1958–1960* (New York: Columbia University Press, 1983), p. 103. This was the situation specifically in Henan province.

[8] See the discussions in Christina K. Gilmartin, Gail Hershatter, Lisa Rofel, and Tyrene White, Eds., *Engendering China* (Cambridge: Harvard University Press, 1994). Especially helpful are Gao Xiaoxian, "China's Modernization and Changes in the Social Status of Rural Women" and Lisa Rofel, "Liberation, Nostalgia, and a Yearning for Modernity." The term "national woman" is Tani Barlow's.

[9] Helen F. Siu, *Agents and Victims* (New Haven: Yale University Press), p. 176.

[10] Quoted in MacFarquhar, pp. 101–102.

[11] Kenneth Lieberthal, "The Great Leap Forward and the Split in the Yan'an Leadership, 1958–1965" in Roderick MacFarquhar, Ed. *The Politics of China, 1949–1989* (Cambridge: Cambridge University Press, 1993), p. 111.

[12] The phrase is from Lieberthal, "The Great Leap Forward and the Split in the Yan'an Leadership, 1958–1965" in MacFarquhar and Fairbank, p. 311.

[13] Cited in MacFarquhar, *The Origins of the Cultural Revolution, Vol. 2: The Great Leap Forward, 1958–1960,* p. 200.

[14] Mao Zedong, "Speech at the Lushan Conference, July 23, 1959" in Stuart Schram, Ed., *Chairman Mao Talks to the People* (New York: Pantheon Books, 1974), p. 139. Earlier quotation is on p. 131.

[15] Roderick MacFarquhar, *The Origins of the Cultural Revolution, Vol. 3: The Coming of the Cataclysm, 1961–1966* (New York: Columbia University Press, 1997), pp. 2–3.

[16] Ibid., p. 1.

[17] Jung Chang, *Wild Swans* (New York: Simon and Schuster, 1991), pp. 231–232.

[18] MacFarquhar, *The Origins of the Cultural Revolution, Vol. 3: The Coming of the Cataclysm, 1961–1966,* p. 14.

[19] Ibid., p. 234.

[20] The economist was Sun Yefang. Cited in Thomas P .Bernstein, "Stalinism, Famine, and Chinese Peasants," *Theory and Society,* 13, no. 3 (May 1984), p. 343.

[21] Nicholas R. Lardy, "The Chinese Economy under Stress, 1958–1965" in MacFarquhar and Fairbank, p. 378.

[22] MacFarquhar, *The Origins of the Cultural Revolution, Vol. 3: The Coming of the Cataclysm, 1961–1966,* p. 95.

[23] Cited in Thomas G. Paterson, J. Garry Clifford, and Kenneth J. Hagan, *American Foreign Policy, A History* (Lexington, Mass.: D.C. Heath and Co., 1977) p. 501.

[24] Allen S. Whiting, "The Sino–Soviet Split," in MacFarquhar and Fairbank, p. 501.

[25] Melvyn C. Goldstein, *The Snow Lion and the Dragon* (Berkeley: University of California Press, 1997), p. 25.

[26] Melvyn C. Goldstein, *A History of Modern Tibet, 1913–1951* (Berkeley: University of California Press, 1989), p. 765.

[27] Goldstein, *The Snow Lion and the Dragon,* p. 52.

[28] Quoted in Tsering Shakya, *The Dragon in the Land of Snows* (New York: Columbia University Press, 1999, p. 117.

[29] Goldstein, *The Snow Lion and the Dragon,* p. 60.

[30] Cited in Whiting, pp. 488–489.

[31] Maurice Meisner, *Mao's China and After* (New York, 1999), p. 235.

[32] "The Sino-Soviet Split—The Withdrawal of the Specialists," *International Journal* (Toronto), Vol. XXVI, no. 3 (Summer 1971, p. 559), cited in Meisner, p. 249.

18

Death Dance: The Great Proletarian Cultural Revolution

They lured her from her home, telling her that her child had been injured in an accident. They dressed her as a whore and dragged her before tens of thousands of people at Qinghua University where she was taunted and jeered and humiliated. Afterwards, under the orders of Chairman Mao, they threw her into prison where she lived in solitary confinement for over a decade. With the express permission of Chairman Mao, they publicly tortured and beat her husband. In the end, mortally ill and the target of frequent beatings, he was put in a darkened room, naked and untreated; there in 1969, he died alone. The man? He was, until late 1967, the President of the People's Republic of China, Liu Shaoqi. His wife, Wang Guangmei, had been an important political figure in her own right. Both had allegedly become enemies of the revolution—like countless "cows, ghosts, snakes, and monsters" who would be attacked during this phase of the Chinese revolution, the last insane act of Mao Zedong's career, the Great Proletarian Cultural Revolution.

During the height of the Cultural Revolution, the adulation of Mao whose cult had transmuted him almost into a deity reached such a point that at certain times every day people had to perform a "loyalty dance" to Mao, "the Reddest Sun that Shines in our Hearts." Stewardesses on airlines reported that in flight they had to do the "loyalty dance." In places around the country villagers began meetings performing the "loyalty dance" to tunes like "Sailing the Seas Depends on the Great Helmsman, Making Revolution Depends on Mao Zedong's Thoughts." In truth, what was being performed in China during these years was a death dance. In this macabre performance each step led to higher and higher human costs, to deeper and deeper chaos, to greater and greater destruction. Once begun, the dizzying tempo of this dance inexorably picked up speed until the relentless pace threatened to spin China apart and once again toward civil war. Insanity might indeed be an understatement.

WHY?

The cataclysm of the Great Leap Forward had created a bitter split in the party leadership. Following Mao's ouster of Peng Dehuai at Lushan and the Great Leap with its deadly aftermath, a number of leaders, including President Liu Shaoqi and CCP General Secretary Deng Xiaoping, began to see Mao's whole approach as antithetical to the goal of building a modern socialist state. As the state began a slow recovery from the disasters of the late 1950s, a dispute between the Maoist line with its fundamentalist approach and the Liu-Deng line with its pragmatic approach began to fester. Scholars have suggested that the two-line approach is too simplistic and covers a more complex reality; for purposes here, however, drawing the line starkly highlights the most essential differences in understanding subsequent developments.[1]

Though Mao clearly saw that the Great Leap had failed, he was not particularly upset. He still trusted his Communist goals and believed in motivating people through moral incentives. If people were properly motivated by revolutionary goals, he did not doubt that they would use all their energies unstintingly and give "their all" to achieve those goals. Peasants, whom Mao had called "blank sheets," would build a strong China simply because Mao would write on them the words to inspire them to superhuman effort if need be. Mao obviously thought that people (as opposed to "enemies of the people") were by nature good. They also had more innate abilities, more common sense than did intellectuals. Thus, Mao was ready to rely completely on them. He was, as we have seen, hostile to the established, bureaucratized party cadres and to "experts" of any variety. It was much better to be ideologically correct than to have the correct factual knowledge, better, in other words, to be "red" than "expert." Perpetual revolution through perpetual class struggle was a necessity because enemies of the people—intellectuals, capitalists, former Guomindang adherents, reactionaries—would rear their ugly class heads to challenge the people. Indeed, Mao had called his clash with Peng Dehuai at Lushan "class struggle"—with Peng, the long-time Communist military hero, tagged a "bourgeois element."

In contrast, Liu Shaoqi and Deng Xiaoping believed that the failure of the Great Leap was an unmitigated disaster that simply could not be repeated. They argued that people were most motivated by material incentives, that is, by rewards, bonuses, and higher wages when they excelled or when they worked harder than others. Human nature being what it is, they were convinced that these incentives would be stronger than moral encouragement, suasion, and propaganda. Mao reviled such policies because they had the smell of "revisionism," a revising of Marxism by sneaking in capitalistic elements and methods—a practice Mao associated with the despised Khrushchev. In the debate over "redness" or "expertise," Liu and Deng championed expertise. Getting the job done right was the main criterion of whether something was the right or wrong method of doing it. If a person was ideologically correct, that is, properly red, but did not know the first thing about a crucial manufacturing procedure, then, this line would argue, he should not attempt the job because he would likely mess it up. Get someone instead who knew how to do the job. Deng put it simply: "It doesn't matter if the cat is white or black, so long as it catches rats."[2] More pragmatic than Mao's approach, the Liu-Deng line valued knowledge of technology and science and organizational and procedural approaches that emphasized logical and efficient routines. In the same vein, it also valued political stability that was a prerequisite for the successful building of a modern socialist nation.

In the late 1950s Mao had shown increasing tendencies to manage and control the party in what might be called "guerrilla" fashion, that is, he depended on small informal, usually ad hoc meetings for major decision making. Sometimes that meant making decisions himself and then bouncing them off several of his closest supporters. In the aftermath of the Great Leap, Mao's comrades restored collective decision making in an effort to restrain him, relying on larger more formal central work conferences to which experts were invited. Both Liu and Deng spoke of serious shortcomings in the party leadership. Mao resented their approach; as party chairman, he still had a commanding presence in the party and thus still had the power to intervene directly in any situation. He was especially annoyed by Deng who in his role as party general-secretary tended to ignore Mao and make decisions on his own.

In 1962 Mao began a "Socialist Education Campaign" to deal with the quality of local cadres and to refocus the party on the value of class struggle. Only about 2 percent of the rural population belonged to the party in 1960; local party cadres thus had no choice other than to work effectively with local officials and their local communities. Since many had become local party leaders in the halcyon days of the early 1950s, the turmoil of the Leap and the famine might have made them less eager to do the party's bidding; they could indeed become obstructionist. Thus, need for the Socialist Education campaign. But the campaign almost immediately became an issue in the struggle between the two lines. The party decided that the campaign work was to be undertaken by large work teams made up of party cadres; as we have seen, Mao distrusted party cadres and would have much preferred to use the masses more directly.

The campaign did reintroduce class struggle into local communities once again. Class labels which had been ascribed either at the time of land reform or were inherited had become fixed by this time. There was no way to escape one's label; the families of the four bad types—landlords, rich peasants, counterrevolutionaries, and "bad elements"—would always remain the four bad types. As might be expected, these class labels could quickly become "deadly weapons" in local political struggles. For this reason, Liu and Deng rewrote directives for the work teams that deemphasized class struggle. Mao was scandalized: He saw his program for rectification changing into a tool for "revisionists" to reassert party control in the countryside. He became convinced that the Chinese revolution was in danger. Seeing himself and the revolution as one and the same, he felt compelled to destroy the party that he had spent his life building, but that now, in his estimation, had gone so wrong. The phrase "one divides into two" was heard increasingly in the years after 1962. Though originally meant to describe the Sino-Soviet split, it came to signify the necessity of struggling against "capitalist roaders" within the CCP.

THE VIOLENTLY RADICAL RED GUARD PHASE, 1966–1969

Between 1964 and 1966, Mao set out to forge a coalition that could help him take on the party. It was composed ultimately of three components. Most important was the PLA under strong Mao-supporter Lin Biao; the PLA probably did more than any other group or institution to build the Mao cult. Second was a group of what has been called radical intellectuals. Key here was Mao's wife Jiang Qing. In the 1930s Jiang had been a second-rate Shanghai actress; she had journeyed to Yan'an where she linked up with Mao; until the early 1960s she stayed out of the political arena. Beginning in 1963 she emerged as leader of an effort to reform the world of culture and the performing arts. Her associates were men from the Chinese Academy of Sciences in Beijing and the Municipal Propaganda Department in Shanghai. The third component in Mao's base was groups of the mass population mostly from cities who saw themselves as increasingly disadvantaged. One such group was high school and college students who faced shrinking opportunities for upward mobility. Another group was workers who were negatively affected by a system of employment that brought workers in on a temporary or part-time basis so that enterprises could pay them lower wages without pension or medical benefits. Mao cultivated these groups and bided his time.

In late 1965, Mao made a first step toward beginning his battle against revisionism. He became very upset about a play, *Hai Rui Dismissed from Office,* written by the deputy mayor of Beijing, Wu Han. Hai Rui was a morally upright and caring Ming dynasty official who was wrongly dismissed from office by the emperor. Mao chose to believe that Wu Han really meant the play to be an allegorical critique of Mao's dismissal of Peng Dehuai at Lushan. He asked a Five-Man Group on cultural revolution, formed in 1964, to look into the matter. The Group was headed by Peng Zhen, mayor of Beijing, who made clear very quickly that the Group would take the play at its historical face value and not as an allegory. Suspecting such a tack, Mao had also asked one of Jiang Qing's Shanghai colleagues, Yao Wenyuan, to write a harshly critical piece on the play; it was published in early November 1965 and is often considered the opening salvo of the Cultural Revolution. When Peng Zhen and the Five-Man Group persisted in defense of Wu Han, Mao and his allies pilloried them at an April meeting; at a Politburo meeting in May, the Five-Man Group was abolished, and Peng and others lost their official positions. Mao then established a new Cultural Revolution Group composed of his strong personal supporters, headed by his long-time personal secretary Chen Boda, and including Jiang Qing; her ally, sinister security apparatchik Kang Sheng; and two men from among Jiang's Shanghai allies, Yao Wenyuan and Zhang Chunqiao, director of the Shanghai Propaganda Department.

Between mid-May and mid-July, Mao stayed out of sight leaving it up to Liu Shaoqi to carry out the Politburo's May decision to continue the war against revisionism and the "people of the Khrushchev brand still nestling in our midst."[3] By late May unrest had broken out at several Beijing colleges, stirred up by allies of the new Cultural Revolution Group. A big-character wall poster by a teaching assistant in the philosophy department at Beijing University drew much attention when Mao had it broadcast and published all over the nation; it attacked the university's administration for having supported the original Five-Man Group over the *Hai Rui* issue. Liu's answer to handling increasingly restive college campuses where students were beginning to challenge the authority of those in power was to send large work teams made up of Party cadres. These work teams attempted to restore the authority of university officials and rein in more fire-eating radical students. Mao and his allies were furious; they saw Liu Shaoqi as doing the same thing he had done in the Socialist Education Campaign—undercutting the effort to realize class struggle. More and more they saw Liu as a person "of the Khrushchev brand."

In mid-July on his way to Beijing, Mao stopped for a swim in the Yangzi. Aimed to show that he was fit for battle (after years of rumored illness and even death), the swim garnered huge media coverage. The tone of the articles was like a political weather vane: Mao was going to take Beijing like a typhoon.

> The official report . . . carried by the New China News Agency began . . . "The water of the river seemed to be smiling that day" and went on to tell of a militiaman . . . who "became so excited when he saw Chairman Mao that he forgot he was in the water. Raising both hands, he shouted: 'Long live Chairman Mao! Long live Chairman Mao!' He leapt into the air. But soon sank into the river again. He gulped several mouthfuls, but the water tasted especially sweet.[4]

Though we can wonder what kind of pollutant tasted sweet, the fact was that all over China people began to throw themselves in rivers to emulate Mao's swim. It was doubtful, how-

Mao swims the Yangzi as a sign that he's a force to be reckoned with at the beginning of the Cultural Revolution, summer 1966

ever, that they could outdo the seventy-two year old Chairman: His speed reported by official sources turned out to be "four times the world record"!

On August 5, 1966, during a Central Committee meeting attended by only about half of the members, Mao wrote a big-character poster of his own. Its title says it all: "Bombard the Headquarters," by which he meant the Communist Party itself. Thus he launched a ten-year experiment in madness, one of the most bizarre and spectacular events of the twentieth century. It was a struggle over the direction of the revolution—pragmatic reform undertaken gradually by experts and regularized bureaucrats or revolutionary turmoil brought by young Red Guards in a never-ending revolution fueled by class struggle. It was also in part a personal power struggle—Mao had reportedly felt so out of power, so ignored by other leaders of the party–state that he had to restructure his own power base and claw his way back to power. It was, in addition, Mao's quest for "revolutionary immortality."

In August rebellious student groups reorganized themselves as Red Guards; soon most colleges and middle schools had their own Red Guard units. Shouting slogans like "it is justified to rebel," a million young people assembled on August 18 in Tian'anmen Square to see Mao at sunrise on top of the Gate of Heavenly Peace. Eight such rallies were held between then and the last, on November 26; a total of thirteen million students came as if on a pilgrimage (or, as it was more commonly said, on their own "Long March") to see their "Great Helmsman," their "Red Sun," their "Supreme Commander." Mao directed them to destroy the four "olds": old ideas, habits, customs, culture. They were to be the soldiers in the war against party and state leadership; they were to be the vanguard in class struggle. Mao announced that his successor would be Lin Biao. He made no secret of the fact that the two targets of the Cultural Revolution artillery were Liu Shaoqi and Deng Xiaoping.

The last months of 1966 saw utter confusion. Red Guard units rampaged throughout China, seeking out anything representative of the feudal past and the bourgeois present in order to destroy it. Their actions ranged from somewhat amusing to criminal. Shop names and street names were changed to make them more revolutionary. People with long hair were seized and had it cut off. "Women wearing tight slacks were subjected to the 'ink bottle test': If a bottle of ink placed inside the waistband could not slip freely to the ground, the pants would be slashed to shreds."[5] More destructively, Red Guards ransacked homes and pillaged museums and libraries. They indiscriminately trashed books and newspapers, the notes and writings of scholars, religious art, and recordings of Western music.

But their "revolutionary action" went well beyond things. As the tempo of the death dance sped up, mindless violence and brutality became the beat. Red Guard youths tortured and beat people, especially teachers, principals, intellectuals, and those with bourgeois backgrounds—sometimes to death. A woman Red Guard reported how her middle-school classmates participated in the beating death of an elderly former businessman—and one of those who joined in the murder was the victim's own granddaughter. The humiliation and degradation that Red Guards inflicted drove many to suicide. The most well known likely such victim was Lao She, author of the important novels *Rickshaw* and *Cat Country* and a number of important plays. Middle-school Red Guards repeatedly ordered him to struggle meetings; they ransacked his house and burned his books. His body was discovered in a lake in late August, a victim of suicide by drowning or perhaps even of murder.

In the face of the aimless violence in the fall of 1966 Mao and the Cultural Revolution Group further radicalized the movement. They informed Red Guard organizations that Liu Shaoqi and Deng Xiaoping had to be struggled against. In speaking of Liu and Deng, one of the Cultural Revolution Group ordered demonstrators to "flog the curs which have fallen in the water" and to "make their very names stink."[6] Liu and Deng began to be strongly criticized and subjected to humiliating and often physically painful struggle meetings. In the summer of 1967 they were put under house arrest.

As this drama played itself out at the capital, Red Guard units around the country often engaged in violent fighting, not always with conservatives but with rival groups of Red Guards. Factionalism was a serious problem. Sometimes the source was strategy; as time wore on, the source increasingly became disputes over who were more grandly red, over who were the most committed and vigorous supporters of Chairman Mao. Fighting also erupted between Red Guards and groups of farmers and workers who resented the youths inserting themselves forcibly into local situations they knew nothing about. Local cadres began to form conservative mass organizations among workers ("Scarlet Guards") to fend off attacks of Red Guards. The situation in many places was becoming dangerously polarized. One of the most polarized by the end of the year was Shanghai where the government became immobilized by the demands and struggles of Red Guards and Scarlet Guards. All over the country in provinces and in cities in similar situations, governments were collapsing; China was descending into chaos.

Destruction of many of these institutions had been Mao's purpose; the question was what would replace them. The Shanghai political and economic paralysis was ended only when the PLA was brought into the city to maintain order and when Zhang Chunqiao of the Cultural Revolution Group went to the city in January 1967 and with the support of radical organizations destroyed the existing party and government structures. In February he announced the establishment of the Shanghai People's Commune, a name reminiscent of the Paris Commune of 1871, a model to which the Chinese radicals had been attracted. But the institution of this model promised complete and immediate democracy, and Mao feared that attempting to follow that model would only lead to more chaos. What emerged instead out of the Shanghai experience and developments in several provinces was the revolutionary committee. Composed of revolutionary masses (Red Guards and the workers' "Revolutionary Rebels"), party cadres, and the PLA, the revolutionary committee became the new governmental structure promoted by Mao and his colleagues. The presence of the army in the local and provincial leadership structures was important. Because regular party structures were weak, if functioning at all, and because often violent factionalism made any constructive action impossible, the army emerged as key power broker and dominant player in both political and economic matters. Mao increasingly depended on the military for maintaining some degree of stability.

The most dangerous situations in the months that followed developed where mass organizations formed factional ties with military commanders. The Wuhan Incident of July 20, 1967, is a case in point. There, as in many areas, the PLA had a natural predisposition for siding with conservative mass organizations, first because many of the organization's leaders were party officials whom the PLA commanders knew before the chaos had started; and second, because the conservative bodies, like the PLA, favored order and stability. In many areas, then, the PLA had moved to quash radical organizations. In early 1967, to halt such actions, the Maoists decreed that in the future only the central government could decide what organizations could be suppressed. The upshot of this decision was that conflicts between conservative and radical mass organizations increased because the PLA was not able to intervene. As radicals seized trains loaded with arms intended for export to North Vietnam, the PLA supplied conservative groups with arms for defense against the radicals. Because of the increasingly dangerous situation, the commander of the Wuhan Military Region had two meetings with Zhou Enlai and two representatives of the Cultural Revolution Group. After the second, a large conservative organization known as the Million Heroes stormed the hotel where the representatives of the Cultural Revolution Group were staying, detained them, and probably beat one of them. Zhou Enlai who had already returned to Beijing had to come back to Wuhan to gain the release of the detained man. Beijing then sent air and naval forces to seize Wuhan and restore order.

Bloody and destructive battles erupted all over the country between the PLA and revolutionary rebel groups who were seizing weapons from military bases. By late summer 1967, China tottered on the edge of anarchy. The domestic turmoil spread briefly into the

Zhou Enlai
Source: © Marc Riboud/Magnum Photos

international arena when rebels took over the Foreign Ministry in Beijing for two weeks. The "proletarian internationalism" that they attempted to put into practice was perhaps best symbolized by their seizure and burning of the British diplomatic compound in the capital. By early September even Mao saw that if the anarchy continued China's political and economic systems might simply collapse. He thus gave the PLA orders to restore order. It was not quickly accomplished.

In the spring and summer of 1968 another wave of violence erupted between competing rebel groups, purportedly encouraged by Mao's wife, Jiang Qing, who had emerged as the cultural dictator of the revolution. Struggles were especially bitter in Shanxi, Shandong, Hebei, Guangdong, and Guangxi provinces. It was the battles at Qinghua University in Beijing, however, that led finally to the end of the radical mass organizations that had wreaked such havoc. There struggles between Red Guard groups, each claiming to be more Maoist that the other, had begun with "cold" weapons—stones, bricks and concrete chunks catapulted by each side—but had quickly escalated to hot weapons—rockets and projectile missiles carrying fire bomb warheads—launched against rivals' dormitories. In this "war," a number of students were burned alive. In the summer of 1968, workers from the area were sent onto the campus to try to restore order; five of them were killed in the continuing fighting. The conflict finally was extinguished when Mao visited the campus in late July and scolded the student radicals. To the more moderate faction he presented mangos, which, being a gift from the Red Sun, were put under glass for people to file past and admire in adoration.

This violent phase of the Cultural Revolution came to an end with the meeting of the Ninth Party Congress in April 1969. Fought to destroy the party, the revolution ended up reasserting party power. But there was a significant change: military officers were represented in important positions as never before. In many ways the twentieth century trend of the militarization of Chinese politics and society was seen in this new face of the party. Of the 279 members and alternates of the new party central committee, 45 percent was from the PLA, 28 percent from revolutionary party cadres, and 27 percent from revolutionary masses. With the rise of the military, the commander of the PLA and Defense Minister Lin Biao, often linked with the Cultural Revolution radicals, gained considerable stature.

A post mortem of this phase of the Cultural Revolution would need to consider both the short-term and long-term results. An estimated 400,000 to 500,000 Chinese were killed in these three years. The harassment, persecution, and torture of intellectuals and writers was commonplace all over the country. The indictment against the Gang of Four (the extreme leftists in control during much of the Cultural Revolution, that is, Jiang Qing and cronies) at their trial in 1980–1981 specified that "2,600 people in literary and art circles, 142,000 cadres and teachers in units under the Ministry of Education, 53,000 scientists and technicians in research institutes, and 500 professors and associate professors in medical colleges and institutes" were persecuted and that "an unspecified number" of them died.[7]

Mistreatment of party cadres and government officials was widespread. The purge rate of provincial and regional officials was 70 to 80 percent; altogether about three million people were purged, with most rehabilitated only in the late 1970s. Others met beatings, torture, and even death. The best known was Liu Shaoqi, the former president of the government and leader in the Communist party since 1923. He was denounced as a "renegade, traitor, and scab hiding in the Party, a lackey of imperialism, modern revisionism, and the

Guomindang reactionaries."[8] He was expelled from the party in October 1968. Tortured and beaten by Red Guards, he died in 1969 of pneumonia, naked on a prison floor, denied medicine or medical care. Deng Xiaoping, Mao's other main target, fared some better. Like Liu, humiliated at struggle meetings, he was sent to Jiangxi province in an exile of sorts where he remained under house arrest and worked part-time as a fitter in a tractor plant. His son, Deng Pufang, was permanently paralyzed below the waist when he fell from a building at Beijing University after being pursued by Red Guards.

Among long-term consequences was a weakening of the party–state; these years shattered the party, fragmented its leadership, and in its place established weak and untried institutions. Further, the struggle between two lines had not in the end been decisive. Mao and the radicals had to pull back in order to stop the Cultural Revolution's death dance from ending in death for the national polity. So the struggle would continue, though not against a backdrop of national anarchy. With the conclusion of this violent phase, there was in the nation as a whole a substantial migration of peoples from cities to the countryside. Over four million high school and university students (many former Red Guards) were sent to the countryside to live with farmers and undergo a period of re-education, an experience that left many without college opportunities and that helped create a "lost generation" of disillusioned, cynical, and even anti-social adults. They had lost faith in the moralistic rhetoric of Mao and above all in the value and validity of the Communist political system; it is not surprising that they would be open to the rampant materialism that would shape the 1980s and 1990s.

One other group finding its way to the greater poverty and inconvenience of farm life

A victim of the Cultural Revolution in dunce cap

were party cadres and bureaucrats, sent for productive labor and political study—more realistically, hard labor and indoctrination—at so-called May Seventh Cadre Schools. Up to three million bureaucrats and party cadres spent varying lengths of time in the countryside.

THE MYSTERY OF LIN BIAO

The first phase of the Cultural Revolution stimulated the rise of a kind of malignant factionalism. The second phase (1969–1976) was marked by continual factional disunity, tension, and struggle. At least four factions tried to take the leadership of the Cultural Revolution in particular ideological directions: Lin Biao, ultra-left military; Mao and the Gang of Four, ultraleft; Zhou Enlai, centrist; Deng Xiaoping, pragmatist. Rumbling beneath the surface as an increasingly pressing concern was the question of Mao's successor.

The most mysterious of the factional struggles concerned Lin Biao, the hero of the Manchurian campaign in the civil war, who had been named Defense Minister after the ouster of Peng Dehuai in 1959. He had been one of Mao's strongest supporters during the Cultural Revolution and had been perhaps the central figure in building up the cult of Mao. With the military dominance at the Ninth Party Congress in 1969, his power had increased substantially. It is at this point that the story of Lin becomes murky: historical sources go all over the map in describing the man and his motives. The original source of tension between Lin and Mao, who in 1966 had named him his successor, remains unclear to this day. Lin may well have thought that Mao's pulling back from the radicalism of the Cultural Revolution was giving up any gains that had been made in the movement. With this in mind, some have contended that Lin in his radicalism was pushing a new great leap to get the Cultural Revolution back on track, but others have pointed out that Lin had never taken any interest in economic matters and would not have pushed a policy like this. One scholar contends that "[w]here broad issues of domestic and foreign policy were concerned, e.g., economic strategy or diplomatic initiatives, he was basically passive to the point of being virtually invisible; the attitude was truly one of 'Do whatever the Chairman says.'"[9]

Some contend that ill feelings sprang up over issues of foreign policy. Fighting with the Soviet Union had erupted on an island in the Ussuri River in March 1969, and in late summer there was a serious outbreak of fighting in Xinjiang. Ominously word had also gotten out from Eastern Europe that the Soviet Union was talking "about a 'surgical strike' against Chinese nuclear weapons installations."[10] The tense relationship with the Soviet Union had stimulated some Chinese leaders into thinking about a possible rapprochement with the United States. Bringing the U.S. "card" into play might make the Soviet Union a little less aggressive and thereby help attain greater national security. Some sources indicate that ideologically Lin opposed such a rapprochement. Others contend that such opposition was fictional, that Lin took no position, indeed had no interest in foreign policy directions apart from specific military issues.

Much has been made of Lin's personal ambition. Beginning in mid-1970, Lin pressed Mao to have the post of the presidency of the PRC written into the new constitution; Lin repeatedly pressed Mao to reassume that post. Mao resisted these demands and was irritated at Lin's persistence. Mao believed that Lin wanted the post himself and that he was trying to manipulate the political situation to his own ends. At another ill-starred meeting at Lushan in August and September 1970, Mao had turned quite hostile over the issue and had had Chen Boda, who had taken Lin's line, purged from the party. Everything between Lin and Mao, scholars have generally agreed, was all downhill after this.

Some scholars, however, have challenged the thesis about Lin's ambition. Lin, they claim, did not want the chairmanship himself. He was a shy man, who was bothered by a sometimes incapacitating chronic illness. The heavy public duties of the position were not attractive to him, especially meeting foreign visitors—a duty he hated. These scholars do admit that Lin's wife, Ye Qun, was ambitious and pushed him in directions that he might not normally have gone; he was reportedly quite dependent on her even to the point of asking her "whether he should swallow or spit out phlegm in his throat."[11] But these scholars contend that Lin's continual bringing up the chairmanship to Mao stemmed from the general desire on the part of all the leadership to constantly bring to the fore the genius of Mao and how this position would only underscore further his greatness and brilliance. This version points to how the Mao cult had changed Chinese politics. Mao now expected that he would be treated as indispensable: "[n]ow there was an extreme concern with slogans and the Mao cult, a game that was de rigueur for all actors, not just Lin Biao and the [radical intellectuals]."[12]

Whatever the reasons, after Lushan, Mao and Lin were on a collision course. Mao verbally targeted those closest to Lin, almost goading him to act. The official story of what happened was first supplied by Zhou Enlai. Lin began planning a coup attempt in early 1971. The objective of Plot 571 was to arrest two men from the Gang of Four and precipitate a crisis which Lin could use the military to handle. In the end, the plot was changed to try to assassinate Mao by blowing up his train. When the plot did not evolve as it had been devised, Mao escaped. On September 13, Lin and his entourage attempted to flee, apparently to the Soviet Union, but their plane crashed in Mongolia, killing all on board, including Lin's wife Ye Qun and his son Lin Liguo.

Many today believe that the chief conspirator was twenty-four-year old Lin Liguo who through the obvious help of his father had been made the deputy director of the General Office and the deputy chief of operations for the Chinese Air Force. Some scholars even question whether Lin Biao knew about the plot before it went awry. Whatever the case, in this extraordinary still-mysterious episode, Mao's chosen successor or those closest to him had attempted to assassinate the Great Helmsman. Questions about Mao's judgment of his comrades-in-arms arise from Lin's actions, but Mao's treatment of Liu Shaoqi had already raised them. Even more, the in-house machinations and treachery in this episode raise questions about any supposed salutary impacts of the Cultural Revolution on political culture; it seems instead to have created a climate where palace intrigues as bizarre as any in imperial days seemed the norm.

THE GANG OF FOUR

The years after Lin's demise saw increasing focus on who would emerge as Mao's successor. There was an even greater sense of urgency in doing so because Premier Zhou Enlai had cancer and because the health of Mao, ill with amyotrophic lateral sclerosis ("Lou Gehrig's disease"), was failing rapidly. In this context, the manipulation of the political scene by the so-called radical intellectuals to try to establish their position as Mao's successor became intense. Until the fall of 1972, the core of the group was Mao's wife, Jiang Qing, and her two Shanghai-based allies Zhang Chunqiao and Yao Wenyuan. In that fall, Mao brought to Beijing a handsome young (thirty-seven years old) Shanghai radical, Wang Hongwen, to be groomed for top leadership. Wang, a former factory security chief who had risen since January 1967 to Shanghai's leader and political commissar of Shanghai's PLA garrison, became the fourth radical in the Jiang Qing group, subsequently known as the Gang of Four. Wang's unusual rise stemmed from the fact that when Mao surveyed the political scene there was no one who looked like a potential successor. Zhou was ill; and he was bitterly opposed by the Gang of Four in any case. The Gang of Four and the PLA were bitter enemies; choosing someone from either camp would bring the other out screaming in opposition. Even if Mao had wanted to name a radical who had been on the scene during the first phase of the Cultural Revolution, there was no one he would choose. Given the traditional Chinese views of woman rulers, Mao could not consider grooming his wife for the job. He also felt that Zhang Chunqiao, the most accomplished of the radicals, would create such a backlash with insistence on radical policies, that all the gains (?) of the Cultural Revolution would be lost. Thus, he decided to give Wang a shot; Wang's personable presence might also help give the image of the radicals a boost.

It was the radicals who in early 1974 promoted the rather mysterious "Anti-Lin [Biao], Anti-Confucius campaign." This movement coupled as targets the radical Lin and the reactionary Confucius, but it was actually aimed at Zhou Enlai in an attempt to discredit the man who was most often seen as a moderating and pragmatic influence in policy. Though the linking of the two seemed far-fetched, the Gang explained that though Lin had appeared far-left, he was actually far-right. Any results of the campaign are hard to determine; its importance rests in its revelation of the Gang of Four's determination to beat back anyone who might emerge as Mao's successor. Then in mid-1974 Zhou's permanent move to the hospital made it essential that Mao choose someone to serve for Zhou in running the daily business of the country. In the less than two years since his presence in Beijing on the Politburo, Wang Hongwen had not distinguished himself and had become mostly a pawn of Jiang Qing. So Mao looked elsewhere. His surprise choice, and an outrage to the Gang of Four, was Deng Xiaoping, the Number 2 target during the Cultural Revolution. He was pulled from his Jiangxi exile and brought back to Beijing as first vice-premier. Mao made this astonishing decision because of his considerable uncertainty about the military and the role that it might play in politics; the taste of the Lin Biao affair was still strong in his mouth. He wanted some reliable and respected old comrade who key generals could trust and who could take over the Military Affairs Commission and maneuver military leaders out of constant participation in politics.

Policy documents produced under Deng's direction during his year in power foreshadow the direction he would take China during the 1980s and 1990s; they are a good indication why the Gang of Four would oppose him. Deng called for speeded up industrialization by introducing foreign technology, putting quality first, and restoring material incentives. Deng also called for more expert leadership based upon an education with higher standards. At Politburo meetings Deng criticized the Gang of Four; Jiang Qing, the main spokesperson for the Gang, repeatedly battled with Deng. Mao seemed ambivalent; he publicly backed Deng, but he also encouraged the radicals to set forth their own views. For whatever reasons, Jiang had apparently become estranged from Mao, having moved away from the government compound of Zhongnanhai. Mao's health was deteriorating quickly. By 1975, "[h]aving trouble speaking, he could only utter some mumbled words and phrases. . . . When his speech was at its worst, he could only write down his thoughts with a pen. Later . . . he could not walk on his own; he could not even move a step without help."[13] Jiang was increasingly strident in her determination either to succeed Mao herself or at least to have someone from the Gang do so.

THE YEAR OF THE DRAGON

The year 1976 was traumatic for the Chinese nation. When Zhou Enlai died on January 8, the logical choice to replace him was Deng Xiaoping. But Mao, perhaps fearing that ensconcing him in power would lead to the inevitable undoing of Cultural Revolution values, replaced him with a dark horse, Hua Guofeng. During the Cultural Revolution, Hua had been secretary of the CCP provincial committee in Hunan and had been a member of the Politburo since the Tenth Party Congress in 1973; now he became acting premier. The Gang of Four was infuriated by this appointment; the early months of 1976 saw them increasingly hell-bent in their drive to seize power. In their obsession and with a good deal of hubris about their very closeness to power (Mao *was* Jiang's husband, estranged or not; and Mao generally shared *their* radical views, not those of others), the Gang made no allies among other groups that might have enlarged their potential. It seems apparent that public policies and the country as a whole were at most in the peripheral vision of the Beijing players in 1976: the Cultural Revolution had come down to one thing and one thing only—seizing the helm from the Great Helmsman.

In mid-March small groups began to leave wreaths in memory of Zhou Enlai at the Heroes Monument in Tian'anmen Square. This happened at a time when the Gang of Four was continuing to work to discredit Zhou—and by extension that other pragmatist Deng Xiaoping. On March 25, a Shanghai newspaper controlled by the Gang called Zhou a "capitalist-roader"; students in Nanjing demonstrated in protest, writing anti-Gang of Four slogans in tar on railroad cars. In Beijing the parade of wreath-bearers continued to come to Tian'anmen Square with the numbers escalating daily. On April 4 on the Qing Ming festival, the day Chinese traditionally tend the graves of their family dead, an estimated two million flocked to the square with wreaths. Some eulogies praised Zhou: "He left no inheritance, he had no children, he has no grave, he left no remains. His ashes were scattered over the mountains and rivers of our land. It seems he left us nothing, but he will live forever in our hearts." Others attacked the Gang of Four; here specifically Jiang Qing.

> You must be mad
> To want to be an empress!
> Here's a mirror to look at yourself

And see what you really are.
You've got together a little gang
To stir up trouble all the time,
Hoodwinking the people, capering about.
But your days are numbered. . . .[14]

The Gang was convinced that the masses in remembering Zhou were really saying that Deng should be his legitimate successor. Obviously fearing the people (whom they always claimed they championed), they worked with other like-minded government leaders to declare what was happening a "counter-revolutionary incident." The next day when many people returned to the Square, police had already taken away all the wreaths. Violence broke out; outraged citizens burned police vehicles and a police command post. Eventually public security and Beijing garrison forces appeared; they attacked and beat people who remained on the Square. This Tian'anmen incident was a new breed of demonstration in the People's Republic, an apparently spontaneous outpouring of grief and admiration for a man truly revered and a public action undirected by government or other authority. Perhaps the Gang had reason to fear. In any case, two days later Mao ordered that Deng Xiaoping be stripped of all his posts and that Hua Guofeng be named premier and first deputy chairman of the CCP. Mao had named yet another successor.

But there were more shocks to come. On July 6, Zhu De, the founder of the Red Army during the days of the Jiangxi Soviet and one of Mao's earliest allies after Chiang Kai-shek's White Terror of 1927, died. Then in predawn hours on July 28 a devastating earthquake with a magnitude on the Richter scale of 7.8 leveled the city of Tangshan near Tianjin. At least a quarter of a million people were killed with some estimates going as high as two-thirds of a million.

Nature's evil drama had changed the face of Tangshan beyond recognition. Scattered concrete beams and pillars, . . . tilting utility poles, water towers cut in half . . . Floorslabs hanging in mid-air, twisted reinforcing bars. . . . In that dismal fog, the most heart-rending of all were the corpses hanging from tall buildings. Some were pinned only at the hands by floorslabs, their split skulls flopped to one side; some had their feet smashed as they tried to jump, and they hung upside down in mid-air. They were the victims with the quickest reflexes; they had already been startled awake from their dreams, they had already jumped out of bed, and run to the porch or window, but their escapes were cut short by death. There was a young mother, with half her body already out a third-storey window, but a heavy floorslab had fallen and crushed her there on the windowsill. She died in mid-air, with a child in her arms. Rocking with the building in the aftershock, her hanging hair swung in the fog.[15]

As horrifying as the experience was the life of the survivors was also tragic. About ten thousand people lost their spouses in the earthquake; over four thousand children were orphaned; at least thirty-eight hundred were made paraplegics or amputees. In traditional China such disasters were interpreted as the natural world's reflection of similar traumas in the world of humans. The Gang of Four in Beijing, not wanting people to think about what kind of portent this might be, ordered a movement to criticize the Mandate of Heaven idea and associated superstitions—and to continue the attacks on Deng Xiaoping, the "unrepentant capitalist-roader."

Then on September 9, Mao himself died. He had had major heart attacks on May 11, June 26, and September 2. The national mourning period continued into early October. People, especially party officials, had to take great care in how they mourned. The Cultural Revolution had so politicized every action that mourning that was in some way "out of the ordinary"—that is, with too much grief (which might raise questions about sincerity) or too little (which might evidence anti-Mao feelings)—could be suspect and therefore dangerous. Officially the Central Committee's obituary of Mao read in part,

> The passing away of Chairman Mao Zedong is an inestimable loss to our Party, our army and the people of all nationalities in our country. . . . His passing away is bound to evoke immense grief in the hearts of the people of our country and the revolutionary people of all countries. The Central Committee of the Communist Party of China calls on the whole Party, the whole army, and the people of all nationalities in the country to resolutely turn their grief to strength: We must carry on the cause left behind by Chairman Mao . . .

The statement also noted as an accomplishment Mao's many factional victories over party rivals: "during the Great Proletarian Cultural Revolution [he triumphed] over the counter-revolutionary revisionist line of Liu Shaoqi, Lin Biao, and Deng Xiaoping. . . ."[16] Little, of course, did the writers of this document know that within less than two years, Deng would be resurrected and forthrightly set out to bury Mao and Mao's form of revolution.

But Mao's corpse was not buried. While Mao had pledged in the 1950s to be cremated, the Politburo after his death decided that Mao's body, like Lenin's in the Kremlin, must be preserved and maintained in a mausoleum built on the axis running through the center of Tian'anmen Square to the Gate of Heavenly Peace to the Forbidden City. It was as if Mao's commemorators envisioned him as equivalent to an emperor from days long gone. But the preservation of the corpse did not properly fit the dignity of a departed emperor, for attending doctors did not know exactly how to do the heavy-duty embalming. When they injected too much formaldehyde into his body, "The results were shocking. Mao's face was bloated, as round as a ball, and his neck was now the width of his head. His skin was shiny, and the formaldehyde oozed from his pores like perspiration. His ears were swollen, too, sticking out from his head at right angles. The corpse was grotesque."[17] Though they were able to right the damage, the scene points to a reality that Mao appears to have forgotten amid the adulation in his last decades as the Great Helmsman—that he too was one of the people, not a god, and that he too would die—like so many who died because of his policies.

For those who survived Mao, the moment for which all the maneuvering in the last years of the Cultural Revolution had taken place had now come. The Gang of Four was too sure of themselves and not as prepared for eventualities as their opponents. With word being bandied about that the Gang was prepared for a military coup and that they had 100,000 armed Shanghai militia ready to take up their cause, others in the government, including

Hua Guofeng, were increasingly on guard. In early October after some fire-eating speeches by Jiang Qing and Wang Hongwen and word that the Gang had told their followers that good news would be coming by October 9, Hua and his allies decided they had to act. They arrested the Gang of Four on October 6. A Chinese scholar put it tersely: "When Jiang Qing was arrested at her residence, her servant spat on her. The Cultural Revolution was over."[18]

There were two codas to the story of the Cultural Revolution. The first was the political trial of the Gang of Four (November 1980 to January 1981). This trial followed the years of the late 1970s when every conceivable difficulty and problem in Chinese society— from weak schools to bad harvests to infertility—were blamed on the Gang of Four, often referred to with five fingers, not four, held up; the fifth, of course, represented Mao. Among charges at the trial were that the Gang had persecuted 729,511 party cadres and citizens and killed 34,800 of them. All were found guilty; everyone but Jiang Qing confessed. Jiang and Zhang Chunqiao were sentenced to death, but after the trial, their sentences were commuted to life imprisonment; the others received prison terms of varying length. In May 1991, Jiang committed suicide in prison.

The four were blamed; the four were found guilty, and the slate was apparently wiped clean. But no one asked the million-dollar question: Why did hundreds of millions of Chinese permit themselves to be so led astray into such disastrous policies by a mere handful of plotters? Was there something about Chinese political culture or national personality that would allow a response that seems so unthinking, so lemming-like? On this level, the more likely answer is the same as that of the earlier question regarding why no one questioned the policies of the Great Leap Forward—fear of those in authority, a quaking before the infallibility of Chairman Mao and the power of his minions.

But, more troubling, for many it was not simply a passive following of authority. Many joined willingly in violence, engaging in wanton destruction, rape, murder, allegedly even cannibalism. The historical record of the Cultural Revolution is filled with voluntary criminal acts on the part of many civilians—as in the earlier described school-age granddaughter who willingly participated in the murder of her grandfather or the writer Ma Bo who described how much he enjoyed beating people. Some suggest such acts and anti-social outbursts were an explosion of anger against party and state bureaucrats that had been building since 1949. A Shanghai journalist explained, "Once the labels were available, once you could attack someone by calling him a 'revisionist' or a 'capitalist-roader,' the labels were used like cannon, just to attack anyone against whom you felt any grievance of any kind, whether public or private." A young Chinese writer suggested, "It is more plausible to say, but difficult to admit, that almost everyone was at fault. We might better say we all turned abnormal for a while. But then, how do we explain *that?*" He concluded soberly, "We won't be done with the history of the Cultural Revolution until we can answer that question. The trouble is, few want to try. It requires self-dissection of a painful kind."[19]

MAO IN RETROSPECT

The second coda to the Cultural Revolution was the summer 1981 adoption of the "Resolution on Certain Questions in the History of Our Party since the Founding of the PRC."

Before looking at the party's official handling of Mao's record, it is interesting to note what Mao himself thought. At a meeting with Politburo colleagues less than three months before his death, in June 1976, Mao mentioned two things that he had accomplished of great consequence: his defeat of Chiang Kai-shek and his fighting to defeat the Japanese. Curiously, he did not mention any of his record after the establishment of the People's Republic. When asked about the Cultural Revolution, he replied that "[t]hat revolution remained unfinished . . . and all he could do was pass the task on to the next generation. If he could not pass it on peacefully, then he would have to pass it on in turmoil."[20]

Reportedly four thousand party leaders participated in some fashion in drawing up the 1981 party resolution. Deng Xiaoping played a key role; like most other party leaders who had been purged during the Cultural Revolution, he was "eager to avenge [himself] on Mao's ghost, [but he] appreciated the political need to preserve Mao as a symbol of both revolutionary and nationalist legitimacy."[21] The resolution noted that Mao's contributions far transcended his mistakes. Specifically it pointed to his success in the revolutionary struggle against the Guomindang (as Mao also had noted) and in the economic successes in the socialist transformation in the first years of the PRC. But it criticized Mao strongly for the extent of the 1957 anti-rightist campaign (interestingly enough, a campaign headed by Deng Xiaoping); for his "leftist" proclivities and mistakes in the Great Leap Forward; for his disregard for Leninist principles through his sponsoring a personality cult and his "personal arbitrariness," and for his leftist error in planning and conducting the Cultural Revolution. In the end, it said that "chief responsibility for the grave left error of the Cultural Revolution, an error comprehensive in magnitude and protracted in duration, does indeed lie with Comrade Mao Zedong."[22]

Perhaps it was economic expert Chen Yun who best captured Mao's historical role: "Had Chairman Mao died in 1956, there would have been no doubt that he was a great leader of the Chinese people . . . Had he died in 1966, his meritorious achievements would have been somewhat tarnished, but his overall record was still very good. Since he actually died in 1976, there is nothing we can do about it."[23]

Notes

[1] Lieberthal, *Governing China,* p. 125.

[2] Richard Baum, *Burying Mao: Chinese Politics in the Age of Deng Xiaoping* (Princeton: Princeton University Press, 1994), p. 29.

[3] Cited in Harry Harding, "The Chinese State in Crisis," in MacFarquhar and Fairbank, p. 133.

[4] Ibid., p. 138.

[5] Ibid., p. 144.

[6] Cited in Richard Evans, *Deng Xiaoping and the Making of Modern China* (London: Hamish Hamilton, 1993), p. 183.

[7] Harding, pp. 211–212.

[8] Ibid., p. 226.

[9] Frederick C. Teiwes and Warren Sun, *The Tragedy of Lin Biao* (Honolulu: University of Hawaii Press, 1996), p. 161.

[10] Roderick MacFarquhar, "The Succession to Mao and the End of Maoism," in MacFarquhar, Ed. *The Politics of China, 1949–1989*, p. 263.

[11] Teiwes and Sun, p. 14.

[12] Ibid., p. 163.

[13] Cited in Roderick MacFarquhar, "The Succession to Mao and the End of Maoism," in MacFarquhar and Fairbank, p. 355.

[14] Both of these are cited in Ibid., p. 362.

[15] Qian Gang, *The Great China Earthquake* (Beijing: Foreign Languages Press, 1989), pp. 41–42.

[16] "Central Committee 'Obituary' on the Death of Mao Zedong, October 1976" in Cheng and Lestz with Spence, pp. 444–445.

[17] Li Zhisui, *The Private Life of Chairman Mao* (New York: Random House, 1994), p. 20.

[18] MacFarquhar, p. 370.

[19] Perry Link, *Evening Chats in Beijing* (New York: W. W. Norton, 1992), p. 153.

[20] Jonathan D. Spence, *Mao Zedong* (New York: Lipper/Viking, 1999), p. 178.

[21] Maurice Meisner, *Mao's China and After* (New York: Free Press, 1999), p. 444.

[22] Meisner, pp. 463–464.

[23] *Ming Bao*, January 15, 1979, p. 1. Cited in Roger Garside, *Coming Alive: China after Mao* (New York: McGraw-Hill, 1982), p. 190.

19

The End of Communism: "Tomorrow is the Children's"

────────

────

──

The succession crisis following Mao's death lasted until 1979. On his own behalf, Hua Guofeng, chosen by Mao in the last year of his life as his successor, was able to brandish repeatedly the note Mao allegedly had penned shortly before his death: "With you in charge, I'm at ease." In many ways, Hua tried to pick up where Mao dropped off, saying that he would "support *whatever* policy decisions were made by Chairman Mao" and "unswervingly follow *whatever* instructions were given by Chairman Mao."[1] Because of these assertions, opponents immediately branded Hua and his allies as the "Whatever" faction. Hua was more tolerant of intellectuals and artists than Mao had been. He also had ambitious plans to develop the Chinese economy, setting forth a Ten-Year Plan which would lead, he claimed, to industrial output near that of the world's most developed countries by 2000. But his plans were too grandiose, little more grounded in economic reality than Mao's were. He also was a newcomer to national politics and leadership, still surrounded by many veterans of the Long March. He was thus thin on credentials, and his bland personality did nothing to help his standing.

But his chief difficulty was that waiting in the wings for his second resurrection on China center-stage was Deng Xiaoping. In April 1976 in the aftermath of the Tian'anmen incident, Deng had been summarily dismissed from all his posts in the party-state. He had gone into hiding immediately since the Politburo had made his case an "antagonistic contradiction"—a situation that essentially made him a fugitive. We are unsure of how or where he spent the next year or so, because there are a number of contradictory accounts. By mid-1977 with the help of colleagues, specifically PLA commanders and high-level party-state bureaucrats, Deng Xiaoping had been reappointed to his old governmental positions. Though he was still subordinated to Hua Guofeng, he was determined to attain complete rehabilitation, to edge Hua out, and to take the top leadership spot in the nation. Deng and his allies became known as the "Practice" faction from their slogan, "Practice is the sole criterion of truth; and they now did battle with Hua's "Whateverists." In 1978, the reha-bilitation of 100,000 cadres and intellectuals who had been held as political prisoners since the 1957 anti-rightist movement swelled the ranks of Deng's supporters (extremely ironic given the fact that it was Deng who masterminded and managed that very anti-rightist movement).

In 1978, there was another sign of the direction the wind was blowing in leadership circles (toward Deng, away from Hua) when the party announced a reassessment of the 1976 Tian'anmen incident. Even after Deng was rehabilitated, Hua had continued to sup-port the Gang of Four's pronouncement that the incident was a counter-revolutionary event—not very politically astute on Hua's part. The party's new rendering of the event called it "revolutionary." That was a sign that Hua was on the way out. At the Third Plenum of the Eleventh Central Committee in December 1978, Hua's exit and Deng's triumph be-came reality. From this time on, Hua, though he retained his titles, did little but perform cer-emonial duties under Deng's direction. In 1981, he had to give up his titles as well.

Deng Xiaoping

SOCIALISM WITH A CHINESE FACE

Deng would have a little over eighteen years to remake China according to his vision—and remake it he certainly did. Deng's policies were based on two wheels, economic reform and political authoritarianism; or, more directly put, open up the door to market capitalism but slam the door shut on any effort to liberalize the political system. First, the remarkable economic reforms. The goal was to bring into being what became known as the "Four Modernizations" in the arenas of agriculture, industry, national defense, and science and technology. Even while Deng was still sharing the stage with Hua, he moved toward modernization in national defense by favoring programs to develop a nuclear arsenal and an ICBM warhead delivery system.

At the Third Plenum in December 1978, where Deng's power was officially solidified, the question of how to realize the Four Modernizations was clarified.

> Carrying out the Four Modernizations requires great growth in the productive forces[;]and . . . changes in all methods of management, actions, and thinking that stand in the way of such growth. Socialist modernization is therefore a profound and extensive revolution.[2]

In sum, nothing less than a revolution—in economic structures, methods, actions, and thought—was needed to bring about China's modernization. Such a revolution had to involve both the internal or domestic situation and the relationship to the outside world.

Reform of the domestic economy using capitalist techniques (or in Chinese governmental euphemism, "socialism with Chinese characteristics") has been the most important shaping feature of Chinese life since Deng's reforms began. Deng first looked to the countryside. Between 1979 and 1984, the people's communes were abolished, and there was a return to family farming. Under the "responsibility system," a family leased land from the collective for a fifty-year period; even though this was not a reversion to private ownership, the land nevertheless could be bought, sold, and inherited. Beginning in late 1980, this new system allowed farmers to keep the profits after remitting their financial obligations to the state; by the end of 1983, a quarter century after the establishment of communes, 98 percent of farm households were participating in the responsibility system.

Its impact was enormous. Being able to keep profits helped serve as the crucial incentive that prompted the rapid development of family farming and stimulated a striking surge in agricultural production. In the period from 1978 to 1984 the annual average gross value of agricultural output was an impressive 9 percent. The new possibility of attaining some wealth motivated farmers to move resources into cash crops that would bring higher prices; some farmers used capital to move into food-processing and other small-scale enterprises. After the mid-1980s, prosperity in the countryside was indeed maintained because of the expansion of such township and village enterprises, which by 1995 employed over 125 million workers.

With these changes, per capita income in rural areas almost doubled from 1978 to 1984. With the sudden infusion of capitalism a growing differentiation quickly developed between rich and poor. Many farmers' living standards greatly improved as evidenced by the construction of new homes, a better diet, and increased purchase of consumer goods. Stories spread of newly affluent farmers buying not only modern conveniences and luxuries but a few even their own airplanes. In many cases, not surprisingly, local CCP cadres have fared very well, using their political power to make it possible for them and their family to get the best land and buy into the most profitable businesses. Some, in contrast, did not do so well. The new system allowed farmers to rent out their land and to hire wage laborers for help on the farm. Those who worked essentially as sub-tenants and hired hands were among the poor. Most towns and villages in the countryside were marked by greater inequality; and the reappearance of class divisions was usually rationalized by Deng's saying that "some must get rich first."

In urban business and industry, the "market model"—allowing the production and distribution of goods to be determined by the market rather than by central government planners—was adopted in late 1979. It called for individual enterprises to operate generally autonomously (within broad state guidelines) and for profit. Decisions were to be made by factory managers who could also hire and *fire* their employees. The key word here is "fire," for until this point in the PRC, workers in state enterprises (read: all enterprises) could never be fired. They held "the iron rice bowl," the term that described lifetime job security. Though the numbers of state enterprises committed to the market model were increased in 1980, the early 1980s saw declining industrial production, rising inflation, and rising government budget deficits—realities that led the government to shelve the market model temporarily. It was taken off the shelf and dusted off in 1984, in the midst of genuine euphoria about the success of the rural reforms.

The late 1980s saw a booming industrial production as well as higher inflation (up to 25 percent in early 1989). When the state encouraged the creation of private and collective enterprises outside the state sector, such enterprises quickly began to compete with and challenge state sector business and industry. An industrial "responsibility system" replaced the old pattern where the state received all the profits. According to the new system, after an enterprise paid the state a 55 percent tax on revenues, it could keep half the profits after production costs were deducted (the state received the other half). Controls on prices of small consumer items were lifted, with the prices allowed to float according to market level. As the private sector grew, the urban economies of many cities were invigorated. Urban workers saw their average real wages more than double in the decade from 1979 to 1989. With improving living standards, people ate better, especially more meat; wore better and more varied clothing; and bought the consumer items that became all the rage: television sets, refrigerators, sewing machines. New factories and businesses created in the capitalist expansion offered jobs to thousands of people migrating to urban centers from the countryside.

Farmers, freed from restrictions binding them to their land, traveled in large numbers to urban centers, in the mid-1980s an estimated 100 million people. Many of them did not have jobs. Unattached to work or neighborhood units, which during the Maoist period constituted the major local controlling institution for individuals, this so-called floating population represented a degree of social mobility that some government leaders saw as potentially disruptive. They were joined by migrant day laborers who came into towns and cities from surrounding areas. Many in the floating population rather quickly became the wretched poor. The lucky found lodging in bleak shantytowns that grew up at city's edge; the others lived on the streets, in parks, in train stations. They created a serious social and economic problem that would only get worse. In Beijing, for example, the floating population was 0.3 million in 1982, but it had skyrocketed up to 1.3 million by 1989. While in the latter year, over 70 percent of these people had some job "in the trades or in business," police noted the increase in crime from those in the floating population.[3] In sum, just as in the countryside where the reforms had brought a rapidly increasing economic and social inequality, so also in the cities, where shanty and luxury boutiques grew up side by side. In both rural and urban China, the pretty face of economic reform had ugly warts and blemishes.

As in the countryside where party cadres were able to parlay their official positions into personal economic gains, so too in cities party leaders and their families were able to use their positions and influence to gain for themselves affluence and even great wealth. Often corruption and nepotism were partners in the drive toward riches. The son of party senior leader Hu Qiaomu, Hu Shiying by name, was reportedly involved in "illicit activities, including providing pornographic videotapes for PLA sex parties and skimming off 3 million [yuan] in tuition fees to his privately operated correspondence law school."[4] When he was arrested, his father tearfully appealed to Deng Xiaoping to show mercy to his son; Hu Shiying got off with a slap on the wrist—as all charges against him were dropped.

Indeed, one of the hallmarks of the reform period was the exaltation of material incentives over ideology. Deng's pragmatic openness to capitalistic innovations in order to build a modern socialist state is undoubtedly best symbolized by his "It doesn't matter if the cat is white or black, so long as it catches rats." To Mao Zedong the color of the cat mattered desperately (it had to be red); but with Deng in charge his second most famous dictum—"To get rich is glorious"—carried the day. The title of a book analyzing the Deng years has it right: *Burying Mao;* surely at the very least Mao was turning over in his glass casket.

OPENING THE WINDOW TO THE WORLD

Until the mid-1960s the border between China and the Soviet Union had been lightly guarded. However, their bad relations since the early 1960s, China's first successful detonation of an atomic bomb in 1964, and Mao's ominous references to the two countries' outstanding territorial disputes led the Soviet Union to begin to increase its military strength along the border. Fairly serious border incidents occurred in 1967 and 1968, some caused by Cultural Revolution violence. Then on March 2 and 15, 1969, Chinese and Soviet troops fought several engagements on Zhenbao Island in the Ussuri River separating Manchuria and the Soviet Union's Maritime Provinces. The Chinese initiated the first incident, though the rationale for their action is not clear. Perhaps the most likely was that this attack was meant to warn the Soviets off from undertaking aggressive military action. The 1968 Soviet invasion of Czechoslovakia, the announcement of the [Soviet premier] Brezhnev doctrine ("the Soviet Union had the unilateral duty to make sure that a country once communist would stay that way"), and the build-up of Soviet forces along the border had made the

Chinese apprehensive about Soviet intentions. In the first incident at least twenty-five Russians were killed, nineteen of them summarily shot after they were taken prisoner. In the second incident, there were about sixty Russian casualties and some eight hundred Chinese. Another serious clash came in August on the Xinjiang-Kazakhstan border in central Asia. Although talks defused the crisis, tensions remained high.

In this context, Beijing began rethinking its relationship with the United States. In late 1968, Beijing had suggested to Washington that they resume the sporadically held ambassadorial level talks in Warsaw. The talks did not resume until January 1970 primarily because of a lukewarm U.S. response. The United States was still deeply mired in its war in Vietnam, and only slowly did Washington become aware of the depth of the Beijing-Moscow split. After an exchange of letters between Zhou Enlai and President Richard Nixon in late 1970 and early 1971, Zhou invited Nixon's National Security Advisor Henry Kissinger for a secret visit to Beijing to plan a visit by the President. Kissinger went in July and again in October. In the midst of the planning China won a huge victory: On October 25, 1971, it was admitted to the United Nations, replacing Taiwan in that body, and taking its place as one of the five permanent Security Council members. China was stepping out on the world stage more visibly than at any time since World War II. Four months later, in February 1972, Nixon made his historic visit. For China, "[m]ore than any other event, the opening to America had unhinged a decade of ideological rigidity at home and abroad. The Nixon visit was the crucial opening move in this process; foreign policy had been released from its doctrinaire moorings. . . ."[5]

The huge question that loomed over any bettering of relationships between the two countries was Taiwan, with which the United States had developed close economic and political ties. Amid all the hoopla—visits to the Great Wall and Hangzhou's West Lake and being hosted by Jiang Qing for a revolutionary ballet—was serious talk. The February 28, 1972 Shanghai Communiqué set down the general framework in which to guide future relations between China and the United States. From the Chinese perspective, the most important points in the communiqué were the general foreign policy pledges and the U.S. statement on Taiwan. Both countries pledged not to "seek hegemony" in the region, to oppose other countries doing so, and to oppose as well efforts of major countries to divvy up the world into spheres of interest. The U.S. statement on Taiwan follows.

> The United States acknowledges that all Chinese on either side of the Taiwan Strait maintain there is but one China and that Taiwan is a part of China. The United States does not challenge that position. It reaffirms its interest in a peaceful settlement of the Taiwan question by the Chinese themselves. With this prospect in mind, it affirms the ultimate objective of the withdrawal of all U.S. forces and military installations from Taiwan. In the meantime, it will progressively reduce its forces and military installations on Taiwan as the tension in the area diminishes.[6]

The two agreed that trade, cultural, and scientific exchanges should be emphasized and increased and that they should work to establish full diplomatic relations.

But domestic problems in both countries interrupted that work and delayed the opening of full diplomatic relations until January 1, 1979. By that time Mao and Zhou, the most important advocates of rapprochement with the United States, were dead; and Deng Xiaoping had been able to vanquish the Gang of Four and Hua Guofeng. In the United States, Richard Nixon had resigned, and the Democratic Party swept into power in 1976 under President Jimmy Carter. On December 15, 1978, three days before the opening of the pivotal Third Plenum of the Eleventh Central Committee where Deng emerged as top leader, a joint communiqué establishing diplomatic relations was released. In it the United States also restated its position on Taiwan in the Shanghai Communiqué: "The United States recognizes the Government of the People's Republic of China [and] acknowledges the Chinese position that there is but one China and Taiwan is a part of China." Contact with Taiwan would continue "through nongovernmental means."[7]

To nurture the burgeoning U.S.–China relationship, Deng Xiaoping visited the United States for a week in late January–early February 1979. The diminutive (4' 9") leader was serenaded at the Kennedy Center in Washington, D.C. with the strains of "Getting to Know You." He donned a ten-gallon hat and ate barbecue at a Texas rodeo. At the Johnson Space Center in Houston, he took the controls of a space-shuttle simulator. It was a public relations coup.

The United States was not alone, of course. The number of countries that established diplomatic relations with China rose from 57 in 1970 to 119 in 1979, the greatest number of international ties since the 1949 establishment of the regime. A decade later, by May 1989, those nations that had diplomatic relations with China increased to 137. As China stepped ever more firmly into the international arena, people to people contact increased. In the 1980s an increasingly large number of foreign tourists stimulated the rapid growth of the tourist industry; at the same time ever-greater numbers of Chinese were traveling abroad. The numbers of students going overseas to study rapidly increased, as did the number of foreign students coming to China. From 1979 to 1989 approximately 80,000 students and scholars came to the United States alone, and the total number of student visas from 1983 to 1988 reached 150,000. Coming to China in 1987–1988, were 6,000 foreign students and 36,000 foreign experts and staff. The goals of the Chinese government in sending students abroad was to provide advanced training so that they might return to help realize the Four Modernizations. This goal was especially crucial in light of the essential destruction of the Chinese educational system during the Cultural Revolution. One problem that developed in this regard already by the mid-1980s was that students stayed much longer in their programs than the government had anticipated and that many faded into the American woodwork and simply chose to remain in the United States. By 1989, 11,000 students had become permanent residents.

"Opening" also applied to encouraging foreigners' involvement in the Chinese economy through an expansion of foreign trade and, something new, of foreign investment. Beginning with a handful of loans, credits, and joint ventures, the opening eventually led to full foreign ownership and operation of enterprises. In many ways this was a shocking development. For much of the nineteenth century to 1949, Western business and industry had dominated Chinese treaty port cities. This Western involvement was made even more serious by the numerous and sizable foreign loans and by foreign control even of nominally Chinese firms and industrial concerns. The Communist revolution had ended that Sino-foreign system; nationalism and self-reliance became the watchwords of the day. Now with the drive toward modernization, foreign investment and know-how were seen to be the engines that could rev up that drive.

In 1979 four special economic zones (SEZs) were opened on the southeast coast to offer special concessions to foreign investors. They were Shenzhen, across the border from Hong Kong; Zhuhai, near Macao; and Shantou and Xiamen, across the Taiwan Straits from Taiwan. Fourteen more were added in 1986; in the latter year, Hainan Island was also so designated. To lure foreign investment they provided many incentives: low tax rates, the establishment of transportation networks, the construction of industrial plants, and a well trained but cheap labor force. In many ways, these zones were reminiscent of old treaty ports. They provided the foreigners amenities for a privileged life-style that featured Chinese servants. They created a situation where foreigners once again exploited Chinese labor. They created a world that was, in the words of one critic, "savagely capitalist." But the zones took off and brought substantial economic benefits: "the influx of foreign capital to finance industrial enterprises and various other modernization projects, the alleviation of chronic shortages of foreign exchange, greater access to the advanced scientific and industrial technology of Japan and the Western countries, and employment for Chinese workers who would otherwise be unemployed."[8] Joint ventures in these and other cities also helped create a flourishing private sector.

The SEZs and the desire to attract foreign investors had a cascading effect that went far beyond the delimited zones. If foreigners expected to do business in China, they needed predictable and regularized economic conditions in which to work. Predictability came with laws that protected property, that specified taxes, that governed contracts. But China essentially had no such laws as of 1977. It was "governed by decrees, by bureaucratic regulations, and by personal orders of various officials."[9] In the decade of the 1980s, then, China began to develop a legal system that included laws, a court system, and lawyers knowledgeable about the new laws and procedures. In 1980 China had only about 3000 lawyers. Goals announced in 1993 had called for the training and establishment of 150,000 lawyers by the year 2000.

Becoming part of the international economic system meant that China wanted to join international economic organizations like the World Bank, the International Monetary Fund, and the Asian Development Bank. These provided low interest loans and various kinds of technical and economic advice. In 1980, China replaced Taiwan in the World Bank and the International Monetary Fund. Membership was a two-way street: it could obviously bring China great benefit, but it also could provide international pressure on Chinese developments. For example, economic reporting requirements from member countries to these organizations were strict and had to be done according to internationally acceptable guidelines. Joining these organizations thus meant that China had to be more open about its economic realities.

Perhaps, above all, as in this last shift to a required greater openness, the changes brought about by "opening" meant that the Chinese leadership had to end its monopoly over vast amounts of information that the nation's elites at least should have been privy to. "Opening" meant more porous borders with Chinese returning from overseas with new outlooks and information; foreigners traveling in China talking with Chinese about ideas and concerns; increasing numbers of foreign books and journals available; and the presence of computers and electronic media. What about Western "bourgeois" ideas? Policymakers understood that an opened window might let in some mosquitoes and flies, but self-assuredly noted that they could be quickly swatted down and killed.

POLITICAL AUTHORITARIANISM

If, in the 1980s, there began to be greater economic freedom and various ripple effects from the policy of "opening," the political realm in its repressiveness remained as bitterly cold as an Arctic night. There was an occasional warm-up or two, but they were followed by a return to even more frigid conditions. It is important to see that the government leadership was not monolithic in its attitude toward political liberalization; some favored greater political tolerance while others championed repression to keep order and stability. Factional struggle was as much a reality as struggle between the government and those in society pushing for greater political change.

Brief thumbnail sketches of these key figures will provide important information for understanding the episodes of slight thaws and deep freezes. Among those who were primarily economic reformers, the key figure was Zhao Ziyang, provincial reformer in Sichuan and protégé of Deng Xiaoping, who became premier in the early 1980s. The second of Deng's protégés, Hu Yaobang, was a political liberal. He had served many years as head of the Communist Youth League and the Chinese Academy of Social Sciences; he became party general-secretary in the early 1980s. Each was opposed by more conservative leaders. It is important to see that in the reform context of the 1980s, those opposed to capitalistic reform were the old Maoists. In the context of the 1960s and 1970s, they would have been called leftists or radicals. Thus, political labels are relative to the context in which they are being used. Chen Yun, a man who had built a record as most important economic planner in the PRC, was not in favor of rapid economic reform, calling instead for what one analyst has called economic neotraditionalism.[10] At least three key figures, Hu Qiaomu, Deng Liqun, and Wang Zhen were ideological conservatives bordering on being political reactionaries. There were others, former military men Ye Jianying and Li Xiannian, who served as "balancers" between the factional poles. The names to remember, in addition to Deng Xiaoping, of course, are those of Hu Yaobang and Zhao Ziyang.

Democracy Wall (1978–1979)

A day after the publication of the party's reassessment of the 1976 Tian'anmen Incident in November 1978, posters began to go up on a stretch of wall along Chang'an Boulevard which runs across the north end of Tian'anmen Square. Featuring essays and poetry, they offered general support for Deng and criticism of Hua Guofeng and Mao Zedong; they were soon joined by papers, pamphlets, and mimeographed magazines with titles like *Explorations, April 5 Forum,* and *Beijing Spring.* At the wall itself debates sprang up about a host of political and social issues. Many of the participants were blue-collar workers with high school education or less. Deng first seemed to give the wall his blessing ("The masses should be allowed to vent their grievances").

But many in the leadership perceived the combustible potential of the situation. At the same time that Democracy Wall began to flourish, hundreds of thousands of those who had been sent to the countryside during the Cultural Revolution were returning to the cities with petitions of grievances about their unjust sufferings. The party under its general-secretary Hu Yaobang came out strongly in calling for the reexamination of cases of "unjust persecution." Over 100,000 came to Beijing and Shanghai alone. In Beijing in front of the residence compound for Chinese leaders, Zhongnanhai, rural petitioners sat down and refused to leave until their petitions were received. Given the potential for social turmoil from this source, Democracy Wall's widening criticism of existing conditions became yet another potentially disruptive element beyond the control of the party. The memory of Cultural Revolution social violence and its horrible impact on Chinese life was all too fresh; unleashing a new round, some leaders thought, would undercut any hope of achieving the Four Modernizations.

Then there came a call at the wall for the Fifth Modernization. Wei Jingsheng, a twenty-eight-year-old electrician who had been arrested and jailed after his elite Beijing Red Guard unit clashed with units loyal to Jiang Qing and had subsequently served four years with the PLA, wrote a poster by that name in early December. The Fifth Modernization was, he said, democracy, the "holding of power by the laboring masses themselves. . . . [In democracy] the people must also have the power to replace their representatives any time so that these representatives cannot go on deceiving others in the name of the people."[11]

There was support in the networks of Hu Yaobang for political toleration and for moves toward major democratic reform. In Hu's corner were men like the editor and associate editor of *People's Daily,* the main government organ, and an important vice-president at the Chinese Academy of Social Sciences. This faction, however, was clearly in the minority, with most of the party leaders opposing calls for political liberalization. Deng Xiaoping was still open to the minority. In a speech to senior leaders on March 16, he stated that if "the old road of suppressing differing opinion and not listening to criticism" were followed, "the result will . . . make the trust and support of the masses disappear."[12] Yet he was willing to go along with the majority.

In essays published in the journal *Explorations* on March 25, editor Wei Jingsheng challenged Deng with blistering criticism.

> Does Deng Xiaoping want democracy? No, he does not. He is unwilling to comprehend the misery of the common people. He is unwilling to allow the people to regain those powers usurped by ambitious careerists. He describes the struggle for democratic rights—a movement launched spontaneously by the people—as the actions of troublemakers who must be repressed. . . . If his idea of democracy is one that does not allow others to criticize those in power, then how is such a democracy different from Mao Zedong's tyranny concealed behind the slogan "The Democracy of the Dictatorship of the Proletariat"?[13]

With the movement beginning to spread across China, Deng was convinced by the majority that the effort could not be allowed to continue. Thus, on March 29, the Beijing municipal government issued strict new regulations limiting mass meetings and demonstrations. On that day the "four cardinal principles" were issued, shoving out of sight the "four big freedoms" that had been set down in the revised constitution early in 1978 (the freedoms to "speak out freely, air their views fully, engage in great debates, and write big-character posters"). The new four cardinal principles set the boundaries of free speech, fully aired views, great debates and big-character posters: "All activities in opposition to social-ism, in opposition to the proletarian dictatorship, in opposition to leadership by the party, or in opposition to Marxism-Leninism-Mao Zedong Thought . . . are prohibited by law and will be prosecuted."[14] In January 1980, Deng proposed the permanent elimination from the constitution of the "four big freedoms."

Democracy Wall under Deng Xiaoping was apparently no more viable than the Hun-dred Flowers were under Mao Zedong. It should not, of course, have been terribly surpris-ing given the fact that Deng over two decades earlier had been in charge of trampling the flowers. The upshot was that Wei Jingsheng, along with other activists and journal editors, were arrested. Wei was charged with "counterrevolutionary incitement" and spying—specifically that he had turned over information on the just-finished debacle of China's in-vasion of Vietnam (see Chapter 20) to a foreign journalist. Tried in October 1979, Wei was sentenced to fifteen years in prison; most of his arrested colleagues received from ten to fif-teen years, often in solitary confinement. By the end of 1979 Democracy Wall was moved to an out-of-the-way location two miles from its former location. The closing of Democ-racy Wall in 1979 at the beginning of the economic reforms was symbolically indicative of the repressive political policies that continually won out over more progressive policies in both the regimes of Deng Xiaoping and his successor Jiang Zemin.

Wei Jingsheng

Campaign against Bourgeois Liberalization (1981)

From the 1942 Yan'an Forum on Arts and Literature into the 1980s intellectuals and writers had been the political and ideological lightning rods for the party. Again and again mass campaigns were kicked off by angry and belligerent attacks on individual artists. In the campaign against "bourgeois liberalization" in 1981, the party targeted several writers, criticizing them for forsaking the "four cardinal rules" and glorifying bourgeois values. It was the handiwork of the conservatives, fearful of what the economic reforms and "opening" might bring. They were not so afraid of mosquitoes and flies as of the snakes and monsters of Western liberal political thought and that continually-talked-about bugaboo of "pornography." No, what they were most afraid of was being deposed by the people.

Probably the most famous target of the campaign was long-time PLA writer Bai Hua, who had published in September 1979 a screenplay for a film called *Unrequited Love* (*Kulian*). It recounts the tale of a young Chinese who studied painting in the United States in the 1940s but returns to China after Liberation to serve the nation. Attacked during the Cultural Revolution for being a "bourgeois revisionist" and embittered by the cruel violence of the state, he wrote a big-character poster condemning the dictators in Beijing and he placed it in Tian'anmen Square on the day of the April 1976 Tian'anmen Incident. Named a criminal and made a fugitive by the government, he is hunted down. In death, his body forms a question mark in the snow. Saying that Bai Hua's work had called into question patriotism, the *Liberation Army Daily,* attacked it as a sign of the times, calling it "anarchistic, ultra-individualistic, bourgeois liberalistic, anti-four cardinals principles thinking" and arguing that "if this erroneous type of thinking is allowed to spread freely, it will inevitably become a threat to our political stability and unity."[15] Deng Xiaoping explicitly called for the work to be heavily criticized; even liberal Hu Yaobang caved into conservative pressure and denounced Bai Hua's screenplay as a "counterrevolutionary crime." Bai Hua wrote a self-criticism and addressed it to Hu, publicly apologizing for his "erroneous trend of thought." When Deng Xiaoping declared the affair over in December 1981, Bai Hua retained his party membership and was allowed to return to writing. The main purpose of the government attacks was to cow Bai and other writers and intellectuals to keep them from challenging the party-state.

Others were not so ready to back down as Bai Hua. In the dark days of 1974 during the factional struggle for determining Mao's successor, three men from Canton formed a collective writing group called Li Yizhe (their names were *Li* Zhengtian, Chen *Yi*gang, and Wang Xi*zhe*). In a busy street in the city, they put up a big-character poster bitterly attacking the Cultural Revolution and the "feudal-autocracy" that was the Chinese state. They were imprisoned without a trial. In December 1978 amid the rehabilitation of those who had been purged in the past, Deng Xiaoping had them released and exonerated. Now in the campaign against bourgeois liberalization, Wang Xizhe, the most aggressively direct in his continuing criticisms, was again detained without trial and sentenced to labor reeducation for a period from ten to fifteen years.

Finally there was the case of Ye Wenfu, publicly attacked by Deng Xiaoping and others for his poem "General, You Can't Do This!" Published in 1979, the poem was a reaction to the allegedly true account of an older general with prime revolutionary credentials who ordered the demolition of a kindergarten so that he could use its site for his new lavish mansion. Ye wrote about the perversion of revolutionary goals for self-interest, painting a scathing portrait of what revolutionary leadership had become.

> My high and mighty General,
> You rode in battle for decades,
> What was it ultimately for?
> Ignoring people's sufferings,
> You!
> Is not the conscience of a Communist
> Rebuked by truth?
> Could it be that you firmly believe
> That the law
> Is but a card in your hand,
> Or at most
> A gentle breeze on a summer night?
> Could it be that
> All the pores of your body
> Are now impermeable to even a drop
> Of Premier Zhou's virtue?
> For your own Modernization
> The kindergarten was torn down
> The children forsaken!
> Snowy-haired one
> How many more years of comfort can you have?
> Tomorrow is the children's.
>
> What right do you have
> To brazenly squander
> The blood of martyrs
> The people's faith in the party
> The hardworking sweat of the laborers?!
> Must the Four Modernizations,
> Solemnly proclaimed
> By Premier Zhou,
> The Four Modernizations for which
> The party and the people,
> Enduring ten years' wounds,
> Are sweating and bleeding
> In front of furnaces,
> In the fields,
> Be the greasy crumbs
> And
> Spittle,

That you,
Belching,
Casually toss to us?[16]

One can imagine how livid such lines made the party leadership. Ye refused to give a self-criticism. The government banned him from publishing and imprisoned him in a room that in winter reached five degrees below zero. But he was not isolated and ostracized as he would most certainly have been in the days of Mao.

The Campaign against Spiritual Pollution (1983)

The anti-spiritual pollution campaign began as part of the factional struggle between reformers and conservatives among the party leadership. At the Second Plenum of the Twelfth Party Congress, Deng gave an address that struck out both at those who participated in or profited career-wise from the Cultural Revolution, on the one hand, and those who fostered "spiritual pollution"—an "attitude of doing anything for money," on the other. He especially decried writers and artists who use "low and vulgar form and content to turn an easy profit." Signs of spiritual pollution were "weakness, laxity, and liberal attitudes"—problems to be taken seriously. "If we do not immediately . . . curb these phenomena . . . the consequences could be extremely serious."[17] Though Deng was even more negative about the Cultural Revolution group (and he clearly felt that position was the more serious of the two), his spiritual pollution remarks presented the conservatives with an issue they could use to hammer their factional rivals, the reformers. "Look," said men like Deng Liqun and Hu Qiaomu, "the reforms are leading to pornography and box office values in literature and art. This must be stopped. The people must be trained in the four cardinal principles." They were the heirs of Mao, concerned more about the proper thought than about what the economic reforms were doing for the country.

Thus, during autumn 1983 the anti-reformers went out to purify the pollution. Several people of the reform faction lost their jobs, not so much in the government as those in government related positions at organs like *People's Daily;* but on the whole not many were purged. The attack mostly focused on specific elements of the pollution. They leveled harsh criticism against Western style individualism, clothing, hair-dos, and facial hair (mustaches and beards); pornographic (called "yellow" in Chinese) films and videotapes; "decadent" music; and the reappearance of "feudal" superstitions and religion. In addition to editorial rantings and haranguing speeches, in places anti-pollution vigilantes conducted searches for "yellow" films and books and harassed those sporting "polluted" styles. The Beijing Municipal Party Committee put up a sign in its entryway: "No admittance to persons with hair too long, skirts too short, slacks too tight, or face powdered and rouged." It was almost reminiscent of Chiang Kai-shek's New Life Movement of the 1930s. All of these evils allegedly were a spin-off of capitalism, about which Deng Liqun screeched in surveying the biggest SEZ of them all: "Nothing in Shenzhen is socialist except for its five-starred flag. [It is] practically like Hong Kong."[18]

The campaign came to an abrupt end when Hu Yaobang and Zhao Ziyang fought back—and Deng Xiaoping backed them up. Zhao especially put the spiritual pollution police in their place. At a party leaders' meeting Deng Liqun yelled that "spiritual pollution threatens the life of the party." Zhao retorted that foreign countries who wanted to invest in China were beginning to have second thoughts in light of the spiritual pollution campaign, and that, if China were going to continue to modernize, it had better stop this sideshow. As if to taunt the conservatives, Hu and Zhao both began to wear Western style suits and ties for meetings and public functions—rather than the old Mao jacket.

Exit Hu Yaobang (1986–1987)

More serious problems for the reformers erupted in late 1986. The year before had seen a flurry of campus unrest across the country over a wide range of issues: poor campus living conditions, racial tensions and relations, outrage at the Japanese Prime Minister's visit to a Shinto shrine where some war criminals were buried, and continued Chinese weapons testing in central Asia. In addition, there had been some flagging of the economic reforms; many people were experiencing a malaise from a sense of unequal opportunity in the new economy; and inflation was rising. With regard to these changes, in the summer party leaders had begun to debate the advisability of instituting greater political reforms. The debate only sharpened the antagonism between the factions.

Although several liberal social theorists and critics began to call for basic political change, including a multi-party parliamentary system, the most influential was astrophysicist Fang Lizhi, one of China's leading scientists. Fang was no shrinking violet when it came to letting his political views be known. In an open session with students in November 1986, he trumpeted, "I am here to tell you that the socialist movement, from Marx and Lenin to Stalin and Mao Zedong, has been a failure. I think that complete Westernization is the only way to modernize."[19] Speaking on various campuses, he encouraged students to take the struggle for democracy in their own hands. Not surprisingly, when students took to the streets in December to protest the fact that slates of candidates for the provincial People's Congress were put up solely by the party, it was in Fang Lizhi's home city of Hefei in Anhui province. Within the month the demonstrations spread to 150 campuses in 17 cities; demonstrators numbered in the tens of thousands. Students called for greater freedom, an end to party nepotism, and better university dormitories and cafeterias. They were met by a stone wall. In Shanghai, Mayor Jiang Zemin tried to reason with the students, reminded them that the "four big freedoms" were no longer in the constitution, and then sent in police to forcibly remove students encamped around city hall. Demonstrations quickly died down. In Beijing Deng Xiaoping ordered students to get back to class; they did.

The major casualty of the affair was Party General Secretary Hu Yaobang, one of Deng Xiaoping's chosen successors. In line with his more liberal political views, he had called for conciliation with the students. Faced with a barrage of panicked shrieks from the conservatives about the dangers of bourgeois democracy, Deng decided Hu had to go. The party line was that he had not been tough enough in his efforts against spiritual pollution and that he had not provided the proper kind of leadership for the party. Hu resigned from his post in January 1987. Several prominent intellectuals, including Fang Lizhi, were expelled from the party; and in the wave of anti-bourgeois liberalization that swept over the country in 1987 other liberal intellectuals were asked to resign from the CCP.

The Democracy Movement ("Beijing Spring") (1989)

The late-1986 to early-1987 demonstrations were but the precursor for the so-called Democracy Movement in the spring of 1989. Between the two movements, the liberal reformers had held sway, with many of the older conservative members of the Politburo retiring at the Thirteenth Party Congress in the fall of 1987; at the congress, Zhao Ziyang was confirmed as Hu's successor as general secretary. In 1988, the economy started overheating with rising inflation, declining wages for workers, and rising unemployment. To complicate the economic picture, in the spring of 1988, the government began to deregulate prices of specific retail items—eggs, meat, vegetables, and sugar; in July cigarettes and alcoholic beverages joined the list. Before each deregulation occurred, consumers tended to panic, going on buying sprees out of fear that once price controls were gone inflation would go through the roof. People began to use all their savings and regular checking accounts to buy up items rumored to be next. For example, in the city of Harbin in Manchuria in July 1988, the biggest department store sold two hundred times its usual monthly average of electrical appliances; in a three-day period late in the month account-holders withdrew twelve million yuan from their bank accounts. Both Zhao and Deng had been proponents of price deregulation, but that summer Deng moved away from that position, leaving Zhao suddenly quite vulnerable.

Coupled with the economic woes were social problems. Some grew out of the economic difficulties. Labor unrest increased; it was said that between twenty and thirty million workers in state enterprises were laid off. Urban unemployment in August 1988 was over four million. The situation was not helped by the ever greater influx of the floating population which reached 1.1 million in Beijing alone. Crime was on the increase, not the least of which was the white-collar corruption of party bigwigs and cadres. College campuses continued to be unsettled with several racial incidents, with demonstrations following the murders of fellow-students, with complaints about living conditions. There were calls for demonstrations against party cadre corruption and nepotism and for human rights.

The party took it on the chin in public opinion polls as cynicism and even defiance of the party became common. Just 7 percent of 600,000 workers thought that the party had changed for the better in the last three years. Among students especially the party fared poorly. In Gansu province only 6.1 percent of 2,000 educated rural young people wanted to join the party. In one poll, 62 percent of undergraduates and 92 percent of graduate students contended that the main causes of student unrest were "corrupt party work styles and/or lack of democracy." Among the party leadership was a growing dissatisfaction with the economic policies carried out by Zhao. Premier Li Peng for one wanted to pour ice water on the overheated economy by slowing down the pace of development. Li and others seemed to be winning out: at the end of the year price controls were put back in place on items ranging from eggs to shoes to washing machines. Zhao began to be hammered by some of the older conservatives who had left the Politburo but stood carping in the wings; Chen Yun, former economic czar, for one, launched a diatribe against Zhao's favoring bourgeois ideologies. Many of the old guard began pressing Deng to get rid of Zhao.

In the midst of troubles all around, liberal intellectuals including Fang Lizhi and others active in 1985 and 1986 continued to write and speak about the necessity of democratic reforms. Some became very bold, attacking the campaigns against bourgeois liberalization and spiritual pollution. On January 6, 1989, Fang sent an open letter to Deng Xiaoping that asked for the release of all political prisoners, including Democracy Wall victim/hero Wei Jingsheng. Within two months two other letters supporting Fang had been sent by seventy-five scholars and writers.

A contingent event coalesced many of the strands in the increasingly uneasy national situation: On April 15, Hu Yaobang died. He had been the student's supporter in 1986 and the strongest voice in the government for political reform. As in the case of Zhou Enlai in 1976, commemoration of Hu became a pretext for action. Students flocked to Tian'anmen Square and took to the streets of cities all over the country; they organized autonomous student organizations. They called for the same reforms that had been their cry over two years earlier—a general call for "democracy," an end to nepotism and corruption within the party, increased salaries and budgets for education, plus three new demands: a reevaluation of the role of Hu Yaobang, rehabilitation of those persecuted in the anti-bourgeois liberalization and anti-spiritual pollution campaigns, and publication of incomes of top leaders and their children.

Party leaders immediately used combative language to denounce the demonstrations. Deng Xiaoping believed that the government should not give an inch, for if one thing were gained, the demands would keep coming; he and the party called student actions "turmoil," a particularly strong condemnation. Zhao Ziyang, already in serious trouble among the party leaders because of the economy, further alienated conservatives by his efforts to try to defuse the situation with the students in a more conciliatory way. The party's judgment that student actions constituted "turmoil" only stiffened the backs of student leaders who seemed filled with a sense of destiny. They organized huge demonstrations, one of the largest to commemorate the seventieth anniversary of the May Fourth Incident. Between that day and May 19, over 1.5 million students in 500 colleges and universities from around the country demonstrated in support of student actions in Beijing; by the end of May that number had risen to 3 million.

Some flagging of student commitment in Beijing in early May was revived by a hunger strike staged at Tian'anmen Square, the destination of the demonstration marches. The hunger strike changed the whole situation dramatically. First, it turned the student effort into a moral crusade against an evil government, a crusade that was based on the possibility of martyrdom. This meant that for hunger strikers compromise was less possible and that the rhetoric of moral superiority and outrage was heightened.

The new reality created by the hunger strategy split the student demonstrators into two camps, mirroring the division in the government leadership. There were those student leaders like Wu'er Kaixi and Wang Dan who were willing to seek some conciliatory compromise, and there were leaders like female student Chai Ling who were moral zealots unwilling to budge an inch. The position of the zealots is best put forward by Chai herself: ". . . how can I tell them [her fellow students] that what we are actually hoping for is bloodshed, the moment when the government is ready to butcher the people brazenly? Only when the square is awash with blood will the people of China open their eyes. Only then will they really be united."[20] Several government initiatives tried to deal with the students but went wanting because student radicals refused. The second change brought by the hunger strike was that more than any strategy or tactic, it stimulated support from Beijing society at large. By mid-May demonstrators were being supported and joined by workers, teachers, police, doctors, nurses, and journalists.

Student occupation of the square which was increasingly awash in trash and festering with unsanitary conditions was a huge embarrassment to the Chinese government when Mikhail Gorbachev arrived on May 15 to normalize relations between China and the Soviet Union. What was to have been a crowning glory for the aged Deng turned into humiliation. Shortly after Gorbachev's departure on May 18, party hard-liners led by Premier Li Peng eliminated any remaining power of party general-secretary Zhao Ziyang, one of the few supporters of the students in the government. Zhao was formally ousted from the Politburo on May 24.

On May 20 Premier Li announced the imposition of martial law: "The situation in [Beijing] is still worsening, and has already affected many other cities in the country. . . . This will lead to nationwide turmoil if no quick action is taken to turn and stabilize the situation. The nation's reform and opening to the outside world, and the fate and future of the People's Republic, are facing serious threat."[21] Units of the PLA were ordered to clear the streets of demonstrators. But an estimated one to two million people in Beijing took to the streets to block the advancing soldiers and to dissuade them from taking action against the demonstrators. The government ordered the troops pulled back temporarily.

This massive and unprecedented display of people power brought in a new group to the demonstrations that had been participating since early May but somewhat on the periphery—industrial workers. On April 20 the Beijing Workers Autonomous Federation had been formed. Concerned more with bread and butter issues ("The bureaucratic cats get fat, while the people starve") than abstract issues of democracy, the federation nevertheless had thrown its support behind the students. With only two thousand members at the beginning of May, membership shot up to twenty thousand after the declaration of martial law. Students in the Square had little contact with the federation until, with student ranks beginning to thin at the end of May, they invited the federation to set up their headquarters at the Square.

For two weeks the stalemate between the people and the PLA continued. On May 30 the demonstrators unveiled a styrofoam and plaster statue, the "Goddess of Democracy," ironically the last major effort of the movement. In the early morning hours of June 4 came the crackdown. Many citizens died along the western reaches of Chang'an Boulevard that ran along the north side of the square; in the square itself there were few, if any, casualties. Estimates of those killed have varied from the hundreds to the thousands. The PLA also had losses. On one stretch of Chang'an Boulevard, 65 PLA trucks and 47 APCs were reportedly totally destroyed with another 485 being damaged; government sources reported that in this battle alone, 6 PLA soldiers were killed and 1114 wounded.

The government's rationale for the crackdown was fear of anarchy and "counterrevolution." Conservatives in the leadership, epitomized most clearly by Premier Li Peng, became convinced that the movement had to be stopped. Most threatening to the leadership were the formation of independent workers unions, the large numbers of citizens from many walks of life who had supported the movement, the actions of the people of Beijing in immobilizing the PLA, and the rhetoric of the students. From the perspective of the people, the *People's* Liberation Army had been mobilized for the first time against the people. Around the world there was shock, dismay, and condemnation that the government had not been willing to seek a compromise and had resorted instead to brute force. Only later did we learn that the students were also to blame, that the tragic stalemate was kept alive because a handful of student radicals refused to consider compromising.

The unveiling of the Goddess of Democracy

Protest demonstrations over the government's bloody handling of the crisis erupted in at least a dozen places around the country. The bloodiest was in Chengdu, the capital of Sichuan province, where rioting led to martial law which led, in turn, to the killing of from thirty to three hundred people. In Shanghai six people were killed and as many injured when a train plowed into a group of demonstrators; the protestors then set the train on fire.

With mass arrests, the government once again enforced at least outward conformity to its rule. The aftermath of the "Beijing Spring" was harsh repression. The numbers of party cadres expelled from the party because they had participated in or sympathized with the Democracy Movement numbered in the thousands. Intellectuals again became targets. Along with newspapers and journals, intellectuals lost the small gains in autonomy that they had won in the movement. Political heretics and dissenters were sought out and imprisoned. In the end, after trials for counterrevolutionary crimes in early 1991, thirty-one dissidents were convicted and sentenced to from two to thirteen years in prison. Fang Lizhi and his wife, who had taken refuge in the U.S. embassy following the episode, were allowed to leave the country in June 1990.

THE CHILDREN

"Save the children" is the last plaintive line of Lu Xun's short story, "The Diary of a Madman." Perhaps there were children who had not yet participated in the peculiar cannibalis-

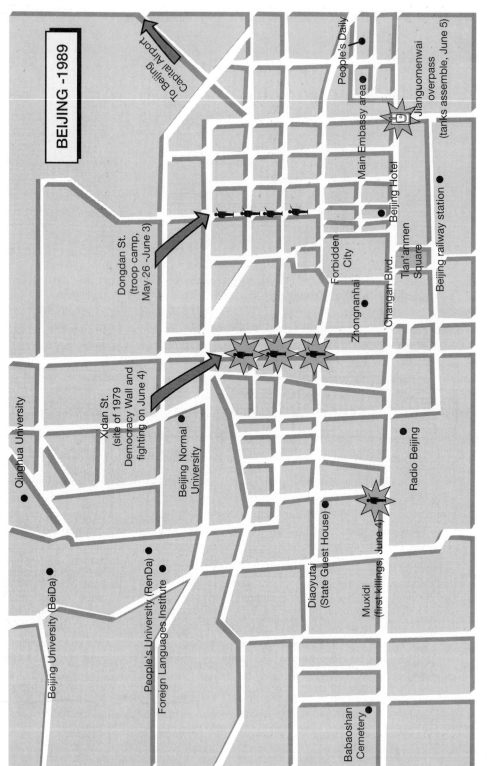

BEIJING - 1989

To Beijing
Capital Airport

Dongdan St.
(troop camp,
May 26 - June 3)

Xidan St.
(site of 1979
Democracy Wall and
fighting on June 4)

Qinghua University

Beijing Normal
University

Beijing University (BeiDa)

People's University (RenDa)

Foreign Languages Institute

Diaoyutai
(State Guest House)

Muxidi
(first killings, June 4)

Babaoshan
Cemetery

Radio Beijing

Zhongnanhai

Forbidden
City

Changan Blvd.

Tian'anmen
Square

Beijing railway station

Beijing Hotel

Main Embassy area

People's Daily

Jianguomenwai
overpass
(tanks assemble, June 5)

Beijing, 1989

tic Confucian tradition of eating of people, that is, of destroying others in the name of morality. These children were innocent, not yet infected by the bacillus of egoism. The future belonged to the children. It is the same idea put forth six decades later by Ye Wenfu in his poem "General, You Can't Do This!" In it Ye asserted that "tomorrow" was no longer the day for the storied general to bulldoze the children's kindergarten, but for the children to learn and develop and grow.

Yet the image of children that emerged from demonstrators in the 1989 Democracy movement was strikingly different. From the declaration of the hunger strikers, May 13, 1989:

> Democracy is the most noble feeling of human existence and liberty is a natural human right bestowed at birth. Can the Chinese people feel proud that here we must exchange our young lives for such things? A hunger strike is a last resort but at last it must be done. We use the willingness to die to fight for life.

> But we are still children! We are still children! Mother China, please cast a serious eye on your children. Hunger is ruthlessly destroying our youth. Can you fail to be moved as death approaches us?[22]

"We are still children!" But the tomorrow that they envisioned here was death—death brought by their own government and by their own choice. There was a bleakness about the

A single man blocks a tank column, June 5, 1989

political situation near century's end that, as so many times in the twentieth century, contradicted earlier hopes. Perhaps the bleakness was magnified because of the dashing of hope that things were finally changing after the bleakest of times, the Mao years. As China entered the last decade of the century questions about its children, its people, its government abounded. But the main question that had echoed throughout the century and was still the central question for the nation was "where was China headed?"

Notes

[1] Cited in Meisner, *Mao's China and After,* p. 428.

[2] "Quarterly Documentation," *China Quarterly* 77 (March 1979): p. 168.

[3] Yang Wenzhong and Wang Gongfan, "The Influence of the Floating Population Upon Social Order," *Police Research,* 2 (1989), cited in Michael Dutton, *Streetlife China* (Cambridge: Cambridge University Press, 1998), pp. 89–92.

[4] Baum, p. 176.

[5] Jonathan D. Pollack, "The Opening to America" in Roderick MacFarquhar and John K. Fairbank, Eds., *The Cambridge History of China, Vol., 15, The People's Republic, Part 2: Revolutions within the Chinese Revolution, 1966–1982* (Cambridge 1991), pp. 418–419.

[6] Ibid., pp. 423–424.

[7] Cited in Pollack, p. 442.

[8] Meisner, pp. 457–458.

[9] Lieberthal, *Governing China,* p. 151.

[10] This description and categorization is from Baum, p. 9.

[11] Quoted in Spence, *The Search for Modern China,* pp. 626–627.

[12] Quoted in Baum, p. 78.

[13] Wei Jingsheng, "Democracy or a New Dictatorship?" *Explorations* (March 1979) reprinted in Gregor Benton and Alan Hunter, Eds., *Wild Lily, Prairie Fire* (Princeton: Princeton University Press, 1995), p. 182.

[14] Quoted in Baum, p. 79.

[15] Quoted in Baum, p. 127.

[16] Ye Wenfu, "General, You Can't Do This!" reprinted in Helen F. Siu and Zelda Stern, Eds., *Mao's Harvest* (New York: Oxford University Press, 1983), pp. 163–164.

[17] Quoted in Baum, pp. 157–158.

[18] Quoted in Baum, p. 160.

[19] Quoted in Baum, p. 201.

[20] Quoted in Geremie Barmé, *In the Red* (New York: Columbia University Press, 1999), p. 329.

[21] "Li Peng's Announcement of Martial Law, May 20, 1989," in Cheng and Lestz with Spence, p. 497.

[22] "Open Declaration of a Hunger Strike" in Cheng, Lestz and Spence, p. 494.

20

Successes and Problems
at Century's End

——————
————
——

In the summer of 1988 a six-part television documentary, *River Elegy* (*Heshang*) raised the question of where China was headed as it neared the twenty-first century. Using vivid imagery, especially that of the Yellow River, the film was caustically critical of the "dogmatic chauvinism inherent in classical Confucianism and revolutionary Maoism alike" and highly enthusiastic about modern Western ideas, values, and institutions.[1] It advocated leaving behind the "Yellow River civilization" and moving into the "Azure Ocean civilization."

> Today . . . the Chinese sigh yet another sigh . . . why is it that our feudal era never ends, why is it as endless as the ceaseless flow of the Yellow River? . . . history grinds on, slowly and heavily, in the riverbed which has accumulated silt and sand of the ages. . . . It needs a great flood to wash it away. This great flood is already upon us. It is none other than industrialized civilization.[2]

Shown well before the events of 1989, the film's script might well have been reflecting on those events with its "sigh yet another sigh" characterization of the Chinese. Not surprisingly, the party's central propaganda department banned the film, and in the summer of 1989 "rooted out copies to crush beneath steamrollers."[3] The period since 1949 had seen first the state's championing of ideology above all else; then the 1980s and 1990s saw the glorification of money and wealth above all else. Where was China's soul? Where was China going?

ECONOMICS IN COMMAND

The Political Context

To succeed Zhao Ziyang as the party general secretary, Deng chose his "third" successor (indeed, three times was the charm) in centrist Jiang Zemin, former mayor of Shanghai; Jiang supported reforms yet he also stressed the four cardinal principles. In addition, as mayor, Jiang had handled Shanghai students firmly both in 1986 and in May 1989.

The crisis in the spring of 1989 did not end the wrangling between avid reformers and embittered conservatives who initially spent much time trying to demonize Zhao and then, focusing again on bourgeois liberalism, threw every roadblock in the path of the reformers that they could erect. The compromise: reform but go slowly. Deng seemed always to be championing speedier approaches, however. In April 1991, much to the chagrin of the conservatives, he selected another former mayor of Shanghai, Zhu Rongji, well known for his commitment to reform, to head economic restructuring efforts as governor of the People's Bank of China. The following fall, the cries of the conservatives became ever more strident, asserting that the "'reformist road' was actually the 'capitalist road.'"[4] Some, like firebrand Deng Liqun, actually sought to resurrect Mao Zedong Thought. Deng Xiaoping, eighty-seven years old, who now walked and talked with difficulty, grew increasingly angry. When a group of retired conservatives fired off a letter to the Central Committee in December and called for the restructuring of the SEZs because they "were capitalist in nature and had become hotbeds of peaceful evolution [rather than revolution through class struggle]," Deng knew he had to act dramatically to save his reform program.

From January 18 to February 21, 1992, Deng traveled to the south to inspect two SEZs, Shenzhen and Zhuhai, and visit three cities—Wuhan, Canton, and Shanghai. His goal was to point to the progress brought by reform and "opening," thereby justifying his policies. Deng himself was amazed at the progress and used the tour as an occasion for calling for even faster progress.

> We should be bolder in carrying out reforms and opening up to the outside world and in making experimentations; we should not act like a woman with bound feet. For what we regard as correct, just try it and go ahead daringly. Shenzhen's experience means daring to break through. One just cannot blaze a trail, a new trail, and accomplish a new undertaking without the spirit of daring to break through, the spirit of taking a risk, and without some spirit and vigor.[5]

Though Deng's description and prescriptions on the southern tour angered the conservatives and got them to vow to fight to the end, the Fourteenth Party Congress, which met in October 1992, confirmed Deng's directions for rapid economic market reforms. It also swept into the Politburo seven strong supporters of the Deng program. The deaths of Wang Zhen (1993) and Chen Yun (1995) took off the public stage two of the most outspoken opponents of reform.

Deng himself died on February 19, 1997. Perhaps an American scholar said it best: "Although Deng Xiaoping could claim a long revolutionary lineage, he will best be remembered as the father of Chinese capitalism."[6] Even his lingering death (his last public appearance came in February 1994) helped perpetuate his program, for it allowed Jiang Zemin and the reformers to get firm control of the policy-making apparatus. Indeed, the Fifteenth Party Congress held seven months after his death, in September 1997, reconfirmed the party's commitment to Deng's vision. Further, in March 1998, the reformer Zhu Rongji replaced conservative Li Peng as premier.

By 2000, as Jiang, Zhu, and Li Peng were all in their seventies, a new generation of leaders in their forties and fifties was emerging. Jiang was apparently grooming Hu Jintao, head of the Communist Youth League in the 1980s and member of the Politburo Standing Committee since 1992. Hu has been an activist reformer. If he did succeed Jiang, it seemed that economic reform would remain the major governmental objective. In this regard, the new emerging generation of leaders contained more experts in economics and finance than any in the past.

Economic Policies

In the 1990s China experienced an economic boom unprecedented in China or perhaps the world. From 1991 to 1997 the gross domestic product (GDP) rose at an annual average rate of 11 percent. Between 1980 and 2000, the size of the Chinese economy quadrupled. Indeed, as one journalist put it, "The explosion of wealth in China may prove to be the most important trend in the world during this age."[7]

The engine fueling this growth was an ever-more-rapid move toward capitalism and capitalist techniques. After Deng's southern tour, state enterprises were given greater autonomy to deal with capitalist markets at home and abroad and to issue stocks that could be bought and sold on stock exchanges that were set up in Shenzhen and Shanghai. In the middle of the decade, economic czar Zhu Rongji was able to slow a soaring inflation—24 percent in 1994—to a respectable rate of 6 percent in 1996 and still maintain the charging economic growth. While in the beginning of the 1990s, most of the soaring foreign investment had come from overseas Chinese via Hong Kong and Taiwan, by late in the decade multinational groups, including Japanese and United States corporations, had begun to surpass the earlier investors.

The most daring of Jiang Zemin's economic proposals was partially privatizing state enterprises. These made up 40 percent of industrial output in 1997 and were critical in the area of high technology and heavy industry (steel, mining, machine building, petrochemicals). Almost 70 percent of these state industries were losing money and had to be subsidized by the state, a policy which depleted the state budget and did nothing to spur development and modernization. The "daring" quality of the proposal came primarily from two reasons. First, by conventional definition, "socialism" (which all the reformers still claimed was the Chinese system) is a system where the state owns and controls industry. If the state was now giving most industry ("key" industries were to be excepted) over to private hands, where was the socialism that was supposed to be the hallmark of the system? But more important from a practical sense was that these state enterprises employed over 120 million workers. When enterprises were privatized and profit became the bottom line, many of these workers would have to be let go (estimates were up to one third). Given the huge problems at decade's end with unemployment and the floating population, the impact of large numbers of new unemployed could indeed pose serious social problems. Be that as it may, the Fifteenth Party Congress in September 1997 gave the go-ahead to privatization, a process that could take a decade or longer to complete.

THE IMPACTS OF ECONOMIC REFORMS

The Consumer Revolution

The economic reforms gave rise to nothing less than a "consumer revolution" in China of the 1990s and beyond, a Second Liberation after that of 1949.[8] In 1980 the shelves on the upper floors of the Nanfang Department Store in the city of Canton (Guangzhou), the premier department store in south China, were stocked with canned food, thermos flasks (to keep water hot), and plastic inflatable toys for children. Would-be buyers of table lamps had a selection of exactly one lamp at the lighting fixtures counter. By the end of the decade the Nanfang Department Store had an entire section given over to video games and videocassettes.[9] Canton, the capital of Guangdong province, now the richest in China, was not alone. The rampant consumerism in most areas of the country seemed to bear out such findings. Purchases of electric fans, sewing machines, color televisions, stereo tape recorders, washing machines, and refrigerators abounded; in the 1990s the list was lengthened to include air conditioners, high-tech sound systems, videocassette recorders, and even motorcycles. The following chart reveals the reality of consumer changes and reflects the fact that per capita income doubled between 1978 and 1990 and went up another 50 percent from 1990 to 1994.

A 1994 Guangzhou poll on reactions to the reforms showed that close to 80 percent of the 461 participants in the poll were pleased by the availability of goods and something over 60 percent were positive in their evaluation of the overall economic results of the reforms. The positive reactions to greater availability of consumer goods and the ability to

Consumer Items Owned per 100 Households in Selected Cites, 1986 and 1995[10]

	Refrigerators		Washing Machines		Color T.V.	
	1986	1995	1986	1995	1986	1995
National						
Average	18	66	65	89	29	90
Beijing	62	98	76	100	51	102
Guangzhou	52	102	68	105	46	111
Shanghai	47	98	39	78	36	109
Shenzhen	77	102	73	97	83	125
Wuhan	29	96	24	91	17	94
Xi'an	14	83	72	96	33	101

purchase them notwithstanding, over 50 percent of those polled were dissatisfied with other economic issues. These included level of personal income and opportunities to make money, housing conditions, ability to change jobs, and ability to obtain medical care. The dissatisfactions also included a host of social and political issues that the reforms stimulated or made worse: educational conditions, corruption, crime, traffic, the social atmosphere, and the environment.

Income Disparity and Growing Economic Inequality

Personal income and opportunities to make money seemed paramount concerns for individuals looking at themselves and at society in general. The name of the American board game "Monopoly" was translated into Chinese as "Entrepreneur," an intimation that all entrepreneurs could become fabulously and monopolistically wealthy. The amassing of money and material goods seemed to have become an increasingly legitimate value in itself along with the thought that the end (making money) justified any means. Individual attitudes seemed to be "I'll take whatever I can get; everyone else, be damned." In Beijing, the slang expression *sha ci* ("to kill the closest") became common in the mid-1990s among "money-hungry" men and women. "To *sha ci* was to take advantage of those close at hand, one's confidants and friends, to get a foot in the door of the marketplace and steal a march on the competition. If in the process, a former comrade-in-arms, a childhood friend, or long-term associate had to be sacrificed for the sale of a business deal, then so be it."[11]

The crucial issue in the drive for wealth was the growing income discrepancy and inequality among people within cities, between cities and rural areas, between coastal regions and the interior, and between state and private workers. Already by the mid-1980s came reports of a growing social dissatisfaction among city-dwellers that other city-dwellers were outpacing them in the race for riches; this tendency only increased in the 1990s. Newspapers noted that constant complaining about this inequality was a key symptom of the "red-eye" disease (open jealousy).[12] It was common for workers in state sector enterprises to complain about their less lucrative situation than that of private sector workers. All people tended to rail against the advantages of party cadres, who were often (and with just cause) accused of corruption and greed.

Personal discontent with one's economic plight was not helped by the increasing amount of conspicuous consumption; the wealthy bought not only one car but three or four, among them often a Lexus or a BMW. A 1998 study by Chinese economists revealed that 0.1 percent of the Chinese people had one-third of the nation's private savings. Two of the most discontented and even embittered groups among the new social and economic "have-nots" were intellectuals and educators. Some professors were paid half as much as or less than waitresses in joint venture hotels; some began to moonlight by setting up their own noodle stands or shoe stalls.

It was not only jealousy about others' success relative to one's own, but there were other reasons that the income gap and consequent difference in living standards were upsetting. Still-believing Communist Party members saw the return of capitalism and its evils as anathema; that is why the party continued to try to cover it up by calling it the particular face of Chinese socialism. Among authorities and the masses alike there were concerns that

Symbols of the growing gap between rich and poor: In Shenzhen, shantytown with the backdrop of a castle at an amusement park

the widening disparity had the potential for unleashing social disruption and chaos. The disparity created new social tensions: those who saw their incomes and living standards as lower than other groups tended to believe that better-off groups were unfairly advantaged. Social perceptions thus gave rise to various social rifts that had the potential to undermine social harmony.

Income Disparity: City Versus Countryside

The reforms first began in rural areas; at least in certain regions the countryside got off to an early start in making and saving more money. Thus, early in the reform period urban workers watched enviously as farmers turned entrepreneurs in the countryside. Farmers continued to make progress. The average annual savings of a farm household in 1979 was little more than 10 yuan; but by 1994, it was almost 600 yuan. But in the 1990s cities became the far more advantageous place to be located. In the mid-1990s, the average annual income for city-dwellers was 3855 yuan, while in the countryside it was less than 1550 yuan.

Two facts make these already appallingly low incomes for people in the countryside even more depressing, for they suggest that for huge numbers of people in rural areas, the reality is much worse. First is that the category rural incomes includes the incomes of people involved in what are called "township and village enterprises." Their incomes were substantially higher than farmers who did not play any role in these rural industries which were seen as the "most rapidly growing sector" of the Chinese economy. The second reason why the 1550 yuan annual average income in the countryside hid reality was that farmers in the most developed regions made more than those in the least; thus farmers in the poorer interior made far less than the average amount. Much indeed depended on the region (see below).

In the past a rural-urban "split" may not have been noticed when there was far less mobility in China than at the turn of the twenty-first century. But in the 1990s, farmers could see urban realities and lifestyles on television and thus be reminded of just how much of a gap there was. Many rural families also had members who became part of the floating population, who would have sent back or brought back news of the vastly different situation in cities.

In a sense, the tensions between urban and rural were a revival of the clash that had long marked Chinese society, a clash in which authorities had generally taken the side of the cities. In severe floods in the summers of 1990 and 1998, for example, the state blew up dikes and levees protecting farmland along the Yangzi River in order to save cities downstream. Farmers lost their homes, their crops, their farm animals—all to save the cities, a stark example of what seems an obvious second-class citizenship. Another example of pro-city bias was in the system of state subsidies. In the late 1980s, for example, city-dwellers received average overall subsidies (including items like grain subsidies and subsidies to state enterprises) that came to almost 40 percent of their total income; while taxes in the countryside were so high that they exceeded state subsidies by 2 percent.

High taxes were a continuous problem in the countryside. Though the national government's tax on rural household income was set at 5 percent, local government officials collected other special levies, tolls, and fees that jacked up the total tax bill for the rural dweller of from 15 to even 50 percent of a household's income. When much of the added tax money ended up in local officials' pockets and reappeared in luxurious life styles, farmers became embittered. The period saw farmers asserting themselves in violent outbursts. In January 1993, for example, about ten thousand farmers in Renshou county, Sichuan province reacted to their crushing burden of about 115 separate taxes. They attacked township government offices, burning a police car and destroying the homes of township elites. Temporarily soothed by government promises, the farmers exploded again in late spring when the county government persisted in demanding new taxes. Thousands launched attacks on office buildings, setting fires, burning vehicles, and taking a policeman hostage. Eventually the government backed down. In August 2000 in the area of the old Jiangxi Soviet, twenty thousand farmers, armed with sticks and clubs, revolted against harsh taxes; hundreds of farmers were arrested. Such mini-rebellions raised questions not only about the future of the Communist regime but also about the future relations of urban-rural areas and of developed coastal and less developed interior regions.

Regionalism: Eastern vs. Western China

The reforms promoted a pattern of regional growth with southeastern coastal areas from Hong Kong and Canton to Shanghai the most dynamic primarily because of the SEZs established there from 1979 to 1986. That has produced a situation such as exists in Zhejiang province where by 1997, farmers near Hangzhou Bay were living in attractive modern two-story homes with garages, satellite dishes, and all the modern conveniences, quite similar in appearance inside and out to homes that might be found in any U.S. suburb.

Numerous incentives, including low tax rates, attracted investors as did the resource advantages of the coastal regions: higher skill levels of workers, better infrastructure, and easy accessibility. From 1990 to 1995, though only making up 15 percent of Chinese territory, the coastal areas received 67.4 percent of investments. Not surprisingly, the interior areas lagged far behind in economic development. In the first half of the 1990s, the GNP of eastern China increased by 16 percent each year, compared to 9 percent in central and western China; there was a predictable large gap in per capita wealth. The following table shows the 1994 per capita gross domestic product (GDP) and amount of foreign direct investment for regions and province/city. The GDP includes agricultural, commercial, industrial, and service outputs; the foreign investment figures are in billions of dollars.[13]

Obviously the coastal regions were far wealthier with a tremendous advantage over

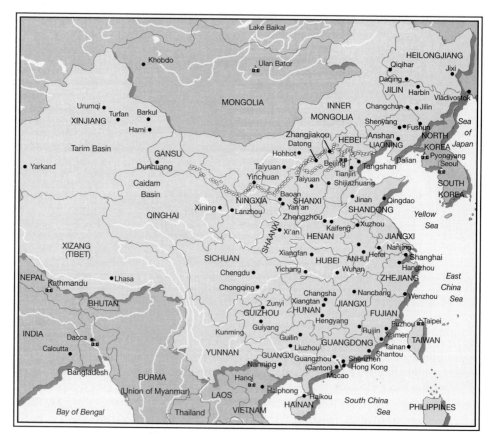

The People's Republic, 2000

	Per capita GDP	Rank	Foreign Investment	Rank
Coastal China				
Beijing	261	2	1.37	7
Fujian	137	8	3.71	3
Guangdong	162	4	9.46	1
Hainan	123	9	0.92	11
Hebei	86	14	0.52	14
Heilongjiang	113	11	0.35	17
Jiangsu	148	7	3.76	2
Jilin	95	13	0.24	20
Liaoning	156	6	1.44	6
Shandong	114	10	2.55	4
Shanghai	388	1	2.47	5
Tianjin	208	3	1.02	9
Zhejiang	157	5	1.15	8
Average	165		2.23	
Central China				
Anhui	64	24	0.37	16
Henan	63	25	0.39	15
Hubei	85	15	0.60	13
Hunan	69	21	0.33	18
Jiangxi	61	26	0.26	19
Shaanxi	60	27	0.24	21
Shanxi	72	18	0.03	28
Sichuan	64	22	0.92	10
Average	67		0.39	
Western China				
Gansu	49	29	0.09	22
Guangxi	71	19	0.84	12
Guizhou	40	30	0.06	25
IMAR*	77	16	0.04	27
Ningxia	69	20	0.07	23
Qinghai	74	17	0.02	29
Tibet	51	28	n.a.	n.a.
Xinjiang	101	12	0.05	26
Yunnan	64	22	0.07	24
Average	66		0.14	

*Inner Mongolian Autonomous Region

the interior in foreign investment attraction. While central and western China were about equal in per capita GDP, the central provinces were attracting substantially more foreign investment—a fact that would likely put this region on a faster track to development.

The 1990s saw the development of considerable bitterness in the central and western regions over Beijing economic policies that favored the coast. In 1995 and 1996, a number of provinces—Shaanxi, Sichuan, Guizhou, Gansu, and Xinjiang—asked to start their own SEZs; Beijing said no, pointing to the poor transport networks and the fact that profit realities would not attract foreign investment. Also in 1995 party secretaries of seven interior provinces petitioned Beijing to put in place for their provinces a system of "Hong Kong-style autonomy." Again the answer was "No." The rationale of the national government was, in a sense, a "trickle-down theory." Beijing leaders had made the decision that Guangdong, the southeast coast, and Shanghai and Pudong (the territory of Shanghai east of the Huangpu river) would be the engine to drive the national economy. As they forged ahead, other areas would begin to benefit also. Li Peng explained it: "If areas with the necessary qualifications go faster, this will be beneficial towards strengthening the national economy and supporting the development of backward areas."[14]

The trick, of course, was keeping the central and western regions satisfied enough to keep them loyal to the national government. In the late 1990s provincial party chiefs in these areas became quite demanding that the government provide more funds in their areas for industrial development and electricity-generation. Beijing committed itself to doing these things. In addition, to "jumpstart" the development of the interior provinces, Beijing initiated a "help the poor" program where wealthy cities and provinces along the coast would be assigned an interior province to help it become economically self-sufficient. Thus Shanghai was assigned to stimulate Xinjiang, and three booming cities—Shenzhen, Ningbo, and Qingdao—were to take on the job for Guizhou province. But this solution made no one happy. The west and center saw it as a way Beijing could duck its responsibilities. Wealthy eastern cities were not eager to shell out their money for the interior. Those in the interior saw coastal economic involvement in their region as exploitation, simply a way for the east to get hold of their mineral resources and cheap labor.

It was a difficult problem for the future of the nation. Intra-province differences were also substantial, especially given the fact that some provinces were as large as European nations. These differences, like those between large regions, were mirrored in the competition between localities themselves and in what would be seen as local protectionism regarding economic resources.

Decentralization

The problem of regionalism was not made any easier by another result of the economic reforms—decentralization. The economic reforms brought a shift in economic decision making to the lower levels of the Chinese state. From the beginning, central policymakers decided that local communities had to have the capability to use local resources to try to spur economic growth and stability. Beijing and localities cut an implicit deal that localities could initiate economic policies different from those promoted in Beijing as long as they maintained the desired stability. Such an exchange provided localities with a weapon to fend off Beijing's unwanted intrusion into the economy—the threat that such an intrusion might bring on local instability. During the 1980s and through the mid-1990s, authority in the political system fragmented. Governing bodies at the provincial, city, county, and township levels gained immense political and economic initiative and became forcefully powerful in the economy. They did so at the expense of the central state bureaucracies stretching from Beijing to those same localities.

Gone were the days when party cadres promoted struggle meetings and egalitarianism; in the 1990s, their focus was on working to realize and sustain economic growth. In many cases much of the local government's budget came to be funded by profits from collective and private enterprises. An example is one Su Zhiming, party official and mayor of a town near Canton. In 1993, he disregarded Beijing's order to stop importing new cars, instead ordering over forty more, including a Rolls Royce. The cash came from the profits of over thirty local companies that the town government managed, monies that also paid the incomes of town officials. Because of the prosperity in that year officials received bonuses six times their salaries; Su's income was higher than CCP Chairman Jiang Zemin's.[15]

The Center did not give up all its power. It continued to appoint all provincial leaders (city, county, and township leaders are appointed by the next higher level). It maintained substantial coercive powers, controlling, for example, crack units of the People's Liberation Army and civilian security agencies. Despite allowing immense local flexibility in economic matters, it maintained considerable economic power; as examples, it continued to allocate scarce resources like petroleum and electric power; it served as source of expertise in matters of economic development; and it controlled the money supply. Its degree of authority varied according to issue arena, population control being one where it was especially strong.

Given the risky political nature of such a decentralized system where more and more power tends to slip away, in the late 1990s, Jiang Zemin and Zhu Rongji attempted to initiate a recentralization effort. The central government's power of appointment was an important weapon against provincial chiefs who were seen to be becoming too powerful; they were transferred to other posts or forced to retire. Important leaders were shuffled off to other positions. In 1996 the government ordered that local cadres were duty-bound to "remain in unison with the central authorities with Jiang Zemin as their core" and that they "must resolutely counter and suppress opinions that are opposed to the party's basic lines."[16] Beijing also tried to assert greater control of localities by setting quotas that local officials had to meet—from grain production to the numbers of corrupt officials who must be arrested.

From 1995 to 1998 the Beijing regime also tried to rein in some of the freewheeling economic activity of localities. They forbade deficit budgets in an effort to stop provinces and localities from over-spending. As part of national bank restructuring in 1998 and 1999, they took away the power that provincial governors and city mayors had over banks located in their areas. They tried to check what appeared in the mid-1990s as mindless overbuilding and overdevelopment in some cities—such as in Pudong where in 1997 the occupancy rate of 250 skyscrapers was less than 50 percent. The main question as always in these economic issues was how much the Center's interference would damage the local economy. At the turn of the century, the problem of the relationship between the center and the localities remained very much unsolved.

The Increase of Individual Responsibility

For individuals and other units in Chinese society decentralization also had a profound impact. The agricultural and industrial responsibility systems gave individual farm family and individual factory or firm much choice in what, how, and how much to produce, and then what to do with that produce. It thus took away control and decision-making power from higher levels of the system. As the state lessened its degree of central economic planning and as it decentralized its administrative powers, it in turn helped increase the power of factory managers and directors. When the government cut back on financial support that it once gave to institutions like schools and the media, they were forced to raise the money they needed. That meant a new world for some, with implications far beyond finance. The print and broadcast media, for example, raise funds primarily by selling advertising. But advertisers could pressure the media about what it published or broadcast, so the new funding reality had an impact on what was printed and broadcast.

On the level of the individual, until the reforms, workers did not have to contribute to their pensions or for their medical care. But, given the growing numbers receiving pensions and the escalating per capita costs of health care, decentralizing the social welfare system was the only fiscally sound option from the state's perspective. Beginning in the mid-1990s co-payments began to be required for insurance coverage, and contributions toward pension funds also became standard. In political terms, the state began to lose some of the control that it had exercised in these socially critical areas. But more importantly, many people could not afford payments to retain comparable benefits. A 1998 study showed that 100 million retirees received "only a partial pension or none at all" and that "only 34 percent of the Chinese population [was] covered by any sort of social safety net."[17]

THE REFORMS AND COLLATERAL SOCIAL CHANGES

Corruption: "The Kudzu of Contemporary China"[18]

Kudzu is a Asian vine that creeps and crawls and eventually grows over everything in its environs. Today if you travel to the American South where it was brought to check erosion during the Great Depression, you will see fences, electric poles, trees, the ground for miles around covered with the leafy plant. It is an excellent metaphor for corruption in contemporary China, corruption that is present everywhere and that covers the political, social, and economic landscape. Clearly corruption long predates the economic reforms installed in the 1980s. But, the reforms, coupled with a social system based on personal connections, opened up new possibilities for corruption that were too enticing for many to resist. If the goal was getting rich, the thinking went, do whatever it takes. The foundation for corrupt actions was connections; it was always difficult to draw the line between legitimate *guanxi*-making, which always entailed gift giving and bribery. Bribery was, however, only one of the tools of corruption; they also included embezzlement, nepotism, smuggling, extortion, cronyism, kick-backs, deception, fraud, squandering public monies, illegal business transactions, stock manipulation, real estate fraud.

The historical context also promoted corruption. Five decades of socialist rule had brought new kinds of bureaucrats into power: party cadres and managers of state enterprises who monopolized means of production, resources, education, and recruitment into the system. Thus they could use the enterprise and its resources for their own personal betterment; and they could manipulate recruitment so that family and connections could profit as well. Add to that the conditions under the reform movement of an economic system partially controlled by the party-state and partially by market forces.

Most decisions about allocating resources are made by the market, but decisions about allocating certain critical resources are still made by Party and state officials. The sharp competition among the state, the collective, and the private sector has raised the ante in decisions about who gets what quantity or critical items in short supply, a situation rife with opportunities for corruption.[19]

Ironically, if the reforms gave rise to corruption, in many ways corruption made the reforms more possible. In order to get and maintain support for the reforms, Deng Xiaoping allowed party figures (and their families), whose support he needed for the reform efforts, to profit from opportunities provided by the reforms. Sons and daughters of these men took positions from which they could gain spectacular windfalls. Utilizing their personal and family connections, they were able to manipulate lucrative stock and real estate deals, gain inside information, receive hard-to-get licenses, and avoid prosecution. Many of them became fabulously wealthy through what amounted to an abuse of power, often milking gray areas of business activity.

One of the most infamous was the Beijing municipal government's involvement in taking bribes for the issuance of construction permits. Mayor (and Politburo member) Chen Xitong and many others made huge fortunes. In April 1995 the vice-mayor committed suicide over the affair. Chen's fate points to a major problem in getting corruption under control. After a brief secret trial in July 1998, he was sentenced to sixteen years in prison; but authorities took no further action against a rumored large number of other officials who were involved in the huge corruption scheme. The reason for the inaction? Fear on the part of Chairman Jiang Zemin about loss of support in the government if Chen implicated large numbers of them in the scandal. The words of Chen on his arrest must have echoed menacingly in the halls of party and state power: "It is true that I may have to take moral responsibility in the Beijing municipality. But who is to take responsibility for corruption in the entire CCP?"[20]

To help control corruption, hundreds of regulations were sent down from Beijing; anti-corruption bureaus were set up; hotlines were established so that people could report corruption; cadres in official positions were regularly rotated. Why could these mechanisms not do the job? Because they were all under the control of the party and the party was covered by the kudzu of corruption. Any strong continuous action against corrupt party members would have had serious political consequences for those in power. Thus, early on, Jiang Zemin decided that he would not touch families of "first-generation revolutionaries," no matter how much they were involved in corrupt activities. It was clearly politics, not morality, in command. Those few cadres brought to justice were usually on the outs anyway; those cadres who were accused but on the rise in the party generally got off scot-free.

Many times corruption flourished because of the blurred lines between what was public and what was private, an issue in Chinese culture for centuries. Institutional realms like government and the market could also be made indistinct for manipulation. Despite the fact that a wide range of cultural and institutional bases promoted corruption, in the late 1980s and 1990s the public became increasingly indignant over the situation, even as they joined in. While a government official might earn three hundred yuan per month, a waitress in a joint venture hotel could earn nine hundred or one thousand yuan. In such circumstances,

Communist party cadres and *danwei* heads who gave permission for marriage, renting an apartment, even having a baby frequently demanded bribes. Petty graft and bribery became common inside the party and government and without.

The Floating Population and Unemployment

Another social problem spawned by the reforms was the estimated 100 to 130 million floating population, people who migrated from the less-developed interior and rural areas to urban centers attracted by the possibilities of getting rich, or at least having a better life. Without housing, job, or connections, they traveled to cities with no return tickets. They slept in railroad stations, under highway overpasses, in parks, or on the streets. If they found jobs, "floaters" usually took low-paying jobs that other workers refused to do: street vendors, prostitutes, hawkers, or simply panhandlers. They were not entitled to the regular welfare safety-net subsidies of people who had urban residence certificates. Commentators pointed to a substantial rise in street crime, especially petty theft. Generally government authorities, police, and permanent city residents viewed the floating population with repugnance. On the whole, the floaters remained peaceful, but the possibility of trouble always seemed just around the corner.

A potentially more serious political problem for Chinese authorities was that the float-

Migrant workers camped out at the Beijing railroad station

ing population, having left their places of residence and without work, was not attached to any work or residence unit. Created in the early days of the People's Republic, these units were crucial multi-purpose bodies. In charge of such mundane but essential things as administering housing and medical care facilities, dispersing ration coupons, managing birth control programs, and mediating marriage disputes, they had also been charged with political tasks. From the 1950s into the 1980s, they had played crucial roles in mobilizing people in political campaigns, and they had exercised important surveillance and control functions. Before the reform movement, it had been rare to be able to transfer from one's unit. By the 1990s that had changed. As political scientist Kenneth Leiberthal noted, "The reforms [have] thus eroded the fundamental link the Maoist system created to handle the relationship between the state and society. . . ."[21]

If workers liked the reform in part because it gave them the opportunity to choose their jobs and their locations, the other side of the coin was that the state no longer guaranteed a job. Given the realities of population, the problem of unemployment began to reach staggering proportions. In the mid-1990s there were approximately 580 million people in the work force: 160 million in urban areas and the rest, about 420 million in the countryside. It was estimated that fewer than 200 million were actually needed in the rural work force; of the remaining 200 million, an estimated 100 million found work in the 1980s in township and village industries. That still left a surplus of 100 million people without employment who became the floating population. But that was not even the whole picture, because the population in the countryside was growing by roughly 15 million a year.

Unemployment with its possible social and political implications became a serious problem. The *urban* unemployment figures (not even counting the floaters) at the end of 1998 had risen to from 8 to 8.5 percent (16.4 million). Exacerbating these demographic realities was the late 1990s announcement of plans to close state-owned enterprises (SOEs) that were operating in the red, thereby increasing the number of unemployed. Tens of millions of people were to be added to the ranks of the unemployed. As if that were not bad enough, at century's end, 4 million new unemployed were added because of the government's policy of downsizing the bureaucracy; 10 million new unemployed were added after being displaced by technology in rural industries; and half a million soldiers were dismissed as part of the PLA's efforts to professionalize their forces. The government began to set up a rudimentary welfare safety-net system that covered some workers with unemployment insurance, a minimum wage, pensions, health insurance, and disability payments. But it was projected to take years, if not decades to have it cover most workers.

There is thus little surprise that the 1990s saw increasing labor agitation and turmoil. Unemployment with no economic back-ups meant disaster for millions of workers and what seemed like a powder keg for government and society. As an example, take Sichuan in the last half of 1997, when there were 500,000 unemployed in the province. In July, 10,000 workers marched in the city of Mianyang after losing their jobs when textile factories closed; the police arrested the leaders of the protest. In August, 500 retirees rallied outside government offices in another town to protest declining amounts in pension payments. The same week in the same town over 1000 unemployed pedicab drivers fought with police. In October in the city of Zigong, 300 workers who had not been paid by their radio factory employer for over a year found themselves confronted by riot police when they marched in protest. If one keeps in mind the strong security apparatus in the country, these kinds of incidents that nevertheless occurred point to the seriousness of the problem of rising labor unrest.

One last episode points to the desperation (and therefore gullibility) of the unemployed and the kinds of unscrupulous corruption that can take advantage of the desperation. In the central city of Wuhan in the fall of 1997, the Hubei Changrui Technology Company announced the opening of a "hi-tech agri-business": raising super-ants for medical research. People were asked to shell out a deposit of 550 yuan for which they would get 100 of these super-insects which would bring in a profit of at least 1000 yuan each month. Thousands of unemployed workers put the money down; the fly-by-night "agri-business" entrepreneurs absconded with all the money. Protests by those workers who lost their money in this scam were of no use.

The Population Problem

While the important issue of limiting population growth was mentioned in passing in the 1950s, nothing was done to put in place any restrictive policy until the late 1970s. Indeed, in the 1960s and early 1970s, families often produced five or six children. In the mid-1970s the government began to disperse birth control devices and ratchet up population control propaganda. The reality was that population had to be controlled for there to be even a chance of China's modernizing and raising its people's living standards. In 1980 Hua Guofeng, exiting as party chairman, pushed for a one child per family policy except among minority peoples. This call prompted a new marriage law that raised the marriage age for men to twenty-two (up from twenty) and for women to twenty (from eighteen).

When 1981 statistics revealed that about six million one-child families had another baby and that over 1.5 million families with five children or more had another baby, the government decreed a more draconian population control effort. If a woman had one child, she had to have an IUD implanted; and if a couple had more than one child, the wife or husband had to be sterilized. Birth-control cadres had to carry out sterilization quotas and, if necessary, force even late term abortions. Families who had more than one child lost various welfare and medical benefits and might be fined; in the rural areas, they might even lose their land. Such policies enforced the international image of a totalitarian state intruding into the most personal decisions.

Despite this rigorous birth control program, a rapid population growth continued. In part this came from the difficulties of enforcing the program. As a gesture to farmers, who under the economic reforms could likely increase their profits with more children working in the fields, rural couples were permitted to have more than one child. Even in urban areas, however, the one-child rule was difficult to carry out effectively. In the early 1990s, about one third of all births were second children and close to one sixth were third children.[22] This situation was worsened by the freedom of movement brought by the reforms, for that has taken away many from the controls of *danwei*. Outlooks for the future were grim. In the 1990s, China added 125 million people to its population, the equivalent of adding a contemporary Japan. If the 1995 population growth rate continued, China's population by 2015 would top 1.5 billion. The population would then be three times what it had been at the time of the PRC's establishment in 1949. But the grimmest figures showed that in 2015 the total grain required to feed China's populace would be almost 50 percent more than the total 1994 harvest at a time (see below) when the amount of land under cultivation in the country is shrinking.[23]

Scholars have noted other social and cultural issues raised by the population control policies. The one child per family policy played havoc with the traditional custom of the son's caring for aging parents. If that one child happened to be female, she would be married off, leaving no one to carry out that traditional role and perhaps leaving the parents in a precarious social and economic position. For this reason, reports of female infanticide surfaced in some areas. With ultrasound technology available for checking the fetus, a rash of post-ultrasound abortions of female fetuses occurred. The government quickly stepped in and forbade the procedure for gender control. Nevertheless, statistics showed that the number of births of males was significantly greater than the number of births of females (114 to 100), a statistic that pointed to future social problems that would likely be produced by a surplus of males once they attained the marriage age.

Perhaps most significant, if the one child per family policy would be generally successful, it would ultimately create a cultural revolution. It changed the concept of the family. Gone with the family planning clinic was the old ideal (however different in reality) of the extended family. There would be no siblings, no aunts, no uncles, and no cousins. Parents doted on their single child. If the child were a son, he became the only way that the family line could be extended. Some commentators noted that this pampering had produced a generation of so-called "little emperors" or, perhaps more appropriately, "little meatballs," the first generation of fat children that China had ever seen.

Environmental Crisis

Environmental concerns, like corruption, predated the reforms. In part they came from the huge increase in population from the eighteenth century on. In part they came from the general industrialization of the country, mostly in the twentieth century. But as at least one commentator has pointed out, part of the environmental degradation came because industrialization occurred under a socialist regime—for these reasons. "For one thing with the land and its resources publicly owned, no one takes responsibility for the land or represents its interests. For another, water and energy are supplied to consumers at no cost or at a heavily subsidized cost, and there is no incentive to conserve their use." [24]

But the reforms made the situation worse. Most obvious were the consequences of the emergence of a consumer society. Their impact on the crucial triumvirate of the environment—air, water, and land—was ominous. The burgeoning numbers of cars, motorcycles, and trucks intensified both noise and air pollution. Industrial smokestack emissions, vehicle emissions, and the pollution caused by the major source of cheap fuel, soft coal, choked cities. As rural industries proliferated, the noxious pollution of rural chemical and fertilizer factories obscured the sky in many areas of the country with its yellow-brown haze. The air in Beijing was already polluted sixteen times over that in New York City. China's government mandated clean air standards, but the air quality in 90 percent of

China's cities did not meet them. The government's decision to make the automobile industry a central feature of the next stage of development could have a disastrous environmental impact. The prediction: "A quarter of a billion of automobiles would pollute the air, require paving over still more acres of scarce farmland, exhaust the country's oil reserves, and render China's already congested cities unnavigable."[25]

The situation with water was no better. The amount of sewage and industrial wastes flushed into the country's streams and coastal waters in 1995 totaled 37.3 billion tons. 90 percent of the water flowing through the cites was not drinkable. In addition, there was a paucity of water. In 1997 half of all of China's cities had a water shortage; indeed the volume of tapwater consumed in China's urban centers increased five times from 1982 to 1997. One basic problem was the distribution of water supplies. Southern China had 75 percent of the water supply for about a third percent of the land; northern China had comparatively little water. Estimates made in 1997 were that by 2010 Beijing would be short as many as 250 billion gallons of water per year.

Another environmental area of concern was land usage. In the economic reforms, some farmers began abandoning their land for what they considered more profitable pursuits. The conversion of cropland into various uses that might bring more money led to a significant decline in cultivated land itself and raised deadly serious questions about where the supply of grain to feed China's billions would come in the twenty-first century. Fishponds, forests, grazing lands, rural enterprise sites, and even golf courses (forty reportedly were constructed in Guangdong's Pearl River region) appeared where there was once productive cropland. During the last thirty years, the net loss of arable land equaled almost a million acres each year, cutting China's already tiny total by almost 10 percent.[26] That bleak picture meant that while in 1973, arable land per capita had been 1.6 mu, it had fallen to 1.2 mu by 1993 and was projected to fall to .83 mu by 2030 (a mu is about ⅙ acre).

It is not that China was sitting on its hands. There were a good number of regulations and agencies to monitor and deal with the problems. The problem was that many environmental issues touched on the interests of many people, groups, and institutions, and that decision making became very political. Negotiations about the construction of the controversial Three Gorges Dam on the Yangzi River revealed the kind of deal making that became a central attribute of environmental decision making, as well as under the reforms in general. Supporters of the dam argued that it would provide flood protection and electricity for Middle Yangzi provinces like Hubei and Hunan. Severe floods in 1990 and 1998 gave credence to their arguments. On the other hand, opponents argued that over a million people who lived west of the dam site—mostly in Sichuan province—would have their homes, cities, and cropland inundated and would be forced to resettle. From the dam, Sichuan would obviously receive no flood benefits and would not obtain much of the generated electrical power.

Deal making became necessary because the main political actors—the provinces of Sichuan, Hunan, and Hubei, and the pertinent central government ministries—had no decision-making authority over the others. Thus, the chief institutional proponent of the dam, the Ministry of Water Resources, was compelled to lead negotiations among parties who for various reasons were opposed. Among the deals was agreement to reduce the height of the dam from the original design, a plan that, had it been implemented, would have flooded the city of Chongqing. The height limit would also make the city a major port since the reservoir behind the dam would end at the city. Oceangoing ships of up to ten thousand tons displacement would, once the dam was constructed, be able to sail to the city. Further, to allay fears that the dam might harm Yangzi river shipping, the parties involved decided to build the dam with an intricate system of ship lifts. To help in the cost of resettling the estimated 250,000 displaced residents, Sichuan received special funds from the State Planning Commission. But resettlement was a very expensive proposition. When the city of Wanxian submitted its estimate of the cost of resettlement for its people, it was $2.9 billion, a figure that shocked the Beijing decision-makers who had budgeted only $3.5 billion for all resettlement expenditures. The whole project was controversial from the start and there were skeptics who believed it would never be completed.

The Search for China's Soul

Chinese reacted negatively to some of the offshoots of reform, especially the apparent turn on the part of many to wealth and consumerism as the only seeming goal and value. It is noteworthy that television advertising's main pitch was to making life more comfortable and enjoyable and to making oneself healthy and attractive; "not a single advertisement uses patriotism, revolutionary spirit, or socialism to sell its product."[27]

To many, putting a price on everything and the commodification of essential aspects of social life under the beacon of "to get rich is glorious" sounded tawdry and immoral compared to the self-giving, patriotic language of Maoism. Indeed by the middle 1990s, there was a marked resurgence of nostalgic enthusiasm for Mao. Yet it was of Mao as commodity. The "Chairman Mao craze" included an album, "Red Sun," a collection of rock renditions of revolutionary songs which set "an all-time record for monthly sales of a pop music album," photographs of Mao that truckers and taxi drivers hung for good luck on their rear view mirrors, and lighters that played "The East is Red."[28] In 1994 a fifty-acre "Mao Theme Park" was built near Mao's boyhood home in Shaoshan, Hunan, at a cost of about $6 million U.S. As one commentator noted, "Mao is once again valuable, but now he has a price on his head!"[29]

This focus solely on money especially seemed negative when it was linked with the omnipresent corruption which reared its ugly head continually. An American journalist raises two examples. A young Beijing judge, making about $500 per year, spent $500 per year on a health club membership alone, owned his own motorcycle, frequented fine restaurants, and owned an extensive wardrobe of expensive Western clothes. This may have been a case of a bribery judge profiting by the very crime he was judging. A story of one twenty-four year-old woman in north China involved a more repugnant case of ends and means. Leili's mother was dying of stomach cancer. To insure that her mother got the best treatment possible, Leili and her father had to present cash and gifts (television sets, jewelry, radios) to the government doctors as bribes, who, reportedly, "took it without embarrassment."[30]

About the question of whither China's "soul," one cadre, who had once supported widespread reform, mused in 1993,

Whither China's soul? Poverty and modern
advertising, Shenzhen, 1993
Source: © Marc Riboud/Magnum Photos

the level of morality has dropped drastically. Girls think nothing of coming from villages for a short stint as a prostitute and then going home proud of the money they
take back. *Nothing* is guiding people—not Marxism, not Confucianism, not religion.
At least religion put the fear of hell into one, but now people don't believe in those
things.[31]

The sense that even a higher standard of living could not substitute for lives empty of more
substantive values led to some widespread disillusionment. No consensus developed on
what values should be upheld as the guiding principles. For many as the world entered the
twenty-first century, China seemed culturally and morally adrift.

Notes

[1] Baum, pp. 231–232.

[2] Cited in Craig Dietrich, *People's China* (New York: Oxford University Press, 1994), p. 277.

[3] Link, *Evening Chats in Beijing,* p. 157.

[4] Baum, p. 339.

[5] "Main Points of Deng Xiaoping's Talks in Wuchang, Shenzhen, Zhuhai, and Shanghai from January 18 to February 21, 1992" in Lawrence R, Sullivan, Ed., *China Since Tiananmen* (Armonk, N.Y.: M. E. Sharpe, 1995), p. 151.

[6] Meisner, *Mao's China and After,* p. 521.

[7] Nicholas D. Kristof and Sheryl Wudunn, *China Wakes* (New York: Times Books, 1994), p. 14.

[8] The term is from Richard Madsen, "Epilogue: The Second Liberation," in Deborah S. Davis, Ed., *The Consumer Revolution in Urban China* (Berkeley: University of California Press, 2000).

[9] Charlotte Ikels, *The Return of the God of Wealth* (Stanford: Stanford University Press, 1996), p. 55.

[10] Taken from Deborah S. Davis, "Introduction: A Revolution in Consumption" in Davis, *The Consumer Revolution in Urban China.,* p. 4.

[11] Geremie R. Barmé, *In the Red: On Contemporary Chinese Culture* (New York: Columbia University Press, 1999), p. 98.

[12] Lieberthal, *Governing China,* p. 308.

[13] The source of these figures is John Bryan Starr, *Understanding China* (New York: Hill and Wang, 1997), p. 39.

[14] Quoted in Willy Wo-lap Lam, *The Era of Jiang Zemin* (Singapore: Prentice Hall, 1999), p. 232.

[15] Lieberthal, pp. 300–301.

[16] Lam, p. 218.

[17] Li Cheng, "China in 1999: Seeking Common Ground at a Time of Tension and Conflict," *Asian Survey,* 40:1 (January/February 2000), p. 122.

[18] This delightfully accurate metaphor is from Starr, p. 129.

[19] Ibid.

[20] Lam, p. 77.

[21] Lieberthal, p. 168.

[22] Data comes from Spence, *The Search for Modern China,* p. 736.

[23] Data is cited in Starr, p. 17.

[24] Ibid., pp. 168–169.

[25] Ibid., p. 170.

[26] Starr, p. 17.

[27] Ikels, p. 66.

[28] Elizabeth J. Perry, "China in 1992: An Experiment in New-Authoritarianism," *Asian Survey,* 33, 1, (January 1993), p. 18.

[29] Dutton, p. 237.

[30] Kristof and Wudunn, p. 193. The story of the bribery judge is on p. 197.

[31] Cited in Ikels, p. 269.

21

Nation and Identity: The Place of China in the World and of the Chinese in China

_____
_____
__

Flanking the highway from Beijing's international airport into the city in the summer of 1993 were poles with pennants sporting drawings of the rings of the Olympic Games, touting Beijing to be the host of the 2000 Summer Games. The government was on its best behavior, even releasing some of its key political prisoners, as a gesture to Western countries that constantly criticized China on the issue of human rights. Chinese newspapers asked the world to "give China a chance." When the International Olympic Committee finally chose Sydney instead, the Chinese blamed this "affront to Chinese national sentiment" on "Western bullies," especially the United States.[1] The episode highlighted issues involving the identity and place of the Chinese nation among the nations of the world and about the place of Chinese, especially dissidents and ethnic minorities, in a China striving to be completely accepted by the world. This chapter probes those issues of identity.

In Beijing there are a number of "ring roads" that encircle the city. In China's dealings with the "Other" both at home and on the world stage there were also various concentric "rings" or categories of key relationships. The first ring was *within* China, made up of non-Han ethnic groups living in what has been called "autonomous regions"; these include Tibet and Xinjiang among others. The second ring was what might be called "greater China"; it included Hong Kong, Macao, and Taiwan. Moving beyond "China" was the third ring of relationships, its East Asian neighbors, Japan, Korea, and Vietnam. Powers beyond composed the outer ring; here we focus on China's key relationships with the United States and Russia. An overview of these relationships reveals China's importance as an international player by the late 1990s.

AUTONOMOUS REGIONS

Tibet Autonomous Region

Both the PRC and the Guomindang government on Taiwan believe that Tibet is an integral part of China. First made a Chinese protectorate in the middle of the eighteenth century, Tibet fell out of the Chinese orbit with the collapse of the empire in 1912. Even though Chiang Kai-shek's regime did not control the government in Lhasa, it still interfered in Tibetan religion and politics; in 1937, for example, it threw its support behind a young boy as the tenth Panchen Lama, the second in authority after the Dalai Lama, Tibet's spiritual leader. In October 1950, China invaded the country and forced the Dalai Lama to sign an agreement giving Beijing control in 1951. The tenth Panchen Lama, seen by many Tibetans as under Beijing's thumb, was installed in 1952. In 1959, as we have seen (Chapter 17), armed rebellion against Chinese control was forcefully put down, and the Dalai Lama fled to India for sanctuary.

Tibet experienced the same brutal chaos as China proper during the Cultural Revolution. Traditional Tibetan culture was trashed just as traditional Chinese culture was attacked. At revolution's end, all "expression of Tibetan identity and culture was forbidden with the single exception of the language." Tibetans described it as the period when "the sky fell to the earth."[2] Under Deng Xiaoping's reforms, however, China's policy was more conciliatory; there were negotiations to try to get the Dalai Lama to return to Tibet, on China's terms, of course. Hu Yaobang himself went to Lhasa to announce the economic reforms. When they were instituted, they were immediately successful: from 1979 to 1981, the per capita income of Tibetan peasants rose 73 percent. Perhaps even more important, traditional customs and cultural practices emerged from the dustbin into which they had been discarded during the Cultural Revolution. Indeed, the years 1979 to 1987 saw a general relaxation of Chinese controls

In 1986 a new First Party Secretary liberalized the party's policy toward religion, allowing a certain religious ceremony for the first time since its cancellation in 1967. Many Tibetans took advantage of the loosening of restrictions by putting up photographs of the Dalai Lama and defying Chinese regulatory laws restricting numbers of monasteries and numbers of men and women entering them. In the midst of this Tibetan assertiveness, a new destabilizing force emerged in a large influx of Han Chinese, ranging from laborers to professionals to demobilized troops, encouraged by the Chinese government to settle in the country. In late September 1987, having tasted some greater freedom but wary about the immigration of Chinese, Tibetan monks demonstrated for independence. Their arrests and beatings brought further demonstrations, confrontations between demonstrators and Chinese police, and eventually police firing into crowds of protestors. Continuing demonstrations, led by monks and nuns, caused the Chinese to declare martial law for a period and institute a news blackout. But demonstrations continued. The largest anti-Chinese demonstration since the 1959 flight of the Dalai Lama erupted on March 5, 1989, and was followed by three days of street battles in which hundreds of Tibetans were killed or wounded. The Chinese again declared martial law, in place this time for a year. Social outbursts continued through the early 1990s. By this time, the Dalai Lama who earlier had endorsed the notion of Tibetan self-governance under Chinese sovereignty had come to support complete independence for his country. Through the 1980s, he traveled all over the world seeking support for Tibetan's indigenous Buddhist culture, was received by world leaders, and won the Nobel Peace Prize (1989). Beijing feared that his visibility and considerable respect on the world stage might cause Tibetans to become more determined to win their independence and might cause more countries to become supporters of the Tibetan cause.

In order to maintain political control, the Chinese also had to assert strong control over religion and religious institutions. When the tenth Panchen Lama died unexpectedly in January 1989, the Chinese tried to control the naming of his successor. Traditionally the Dalai Lama selected the Panchen Lama; but with the Dalai Lama a strong antagonist of the Beijing government, it could not allow Tibet's spiritual leader to play such a role. When the Dalai Lama announced from exile in May 1995 the selection of a boy from northwest Tibet as the reincarnation of the tenth Panchen Lama, the Chinese government denounced the action as "illegal and a political plot by the Dalai clique to split the Motherland."[3] Asserting its own control with the support of some Tibetan monks, the Chinese announced in November 1995 the selection of the eleventh Panchen Lama, pointedly refusing to consider the boy named by the Dalai Lama. Indeed, that boy disappeared shortly after the exiled leader had named him; the Chinese authorities would not disclose his whereabouts. Chinese actions, however reprehensible, were simply a continuation of the same interference in Tibetan religious practices that were seen during the Qing dynasty and during the days of the Republic. In the spring of 1996 the Chinese launched a new campaign against the Dalai Lama, whom they described as "not a religious leader," but a "political fugitive."

At the turn of the century, what the future held for Tibet in the grip of China was unclear. The religious impasse clearly would not be broken easily. The most disequilibrating element in future China-Tibet relations will likely be economic development. A 1994 CCP Central Committee planning meeting for Tibet's modernization called for speeded-up economic development with an emphasis on stimulating light industry and energy resources, the latter since there was not enough electric power even for domestic uses. That same year the Chinese opened the Lhasa Stock Exchange in order to build a foundation for a market economy. Capital began to pour into the country and into enterprises, often headed by Chinese. Development continued apace throughout the 1990s, with an urban rate of growth (mostly benefiting Chinese) of 10 percent and a rural growth rate of 3 percent. Some commentators believed future troubles might stem from the conflict between the economic haves and the have-nots in Tibetan society.

Xinjiang Autonomous Region

At the turn of the twenty-first century, the most potentially explosive of the autonomous regions was Xinjiang. Oil and mineral rich with the sparsest population density in the country, Xinjiang's population has millions of Muslims, many of whom have only feeble allegiance to Beijing. Tensions and animosities between Chinese authorities and local ethnic groups festered for decades. The great fear of Beijing was that Islamic fundamentalism might take root in former Soviet Central Asia and spread across the border. That did not happen, but the threat of Muslim separatists remained very real. In 1981 Uighur (Turkic

Muslims) guerrillas attacked a PLA armory near Kashgar to get arms for an anti-Chinese uprising; they were fired on by Chinese troops with some loss of life. A confrontation that ushered in a much more violent decade than the 1980s came in April 1990. At that time, trouble broke out when Chinese troops tried to break up a rally of some two thousand Uighur separatists at a town near Kashgar. The Uighurs were rumored to have smuggled in weapons from Afghanistan to use in a Jihad or "holy war" to free Xinjiang from China. Dozens were killed and hundreds injured in the clash. Following this incident, the Chinese substantially upped the numbers of troops they had in Kashgar, Urumqi (the provincial capital) and elsewhere in Xinjiang. Rumors abounded that secessionists were aiming at the establishment of an East Turkistani Republic that would incorporate Uighurs from China and Russia. In early 1992, Muslim separatists in Urumqi bombed a Chinese bus causing twenty-six casualties.

In the mid-1990s, Xinjiang leaders asked Beijing for more autonomy, but Jiang Zemin was determined not to give an inch to what were called "splittists." In March 1997, the separatists (or, if seen from their point of view, the freedom fighters) answered that hard line, reaching into Beijing itself in a series of bombing attacks. The late 1990s saw a sporadic campaign of bombings and assassinations carried out by separatists. In July 2000, executions of Muslims were carried out, charged as they were with murder, bomb plots, and establishing a "Party of God" to move toward the formation of an independent Islamic government. The future of Chinese-Muslim relations in Xinjiang seemed fraught with considerable peril.

GREATER CHINA

Hong Kong

In its relationship to "greater China," China's most important objectives were regaining control over units that had been separated from it (Hong Kong, Macao, and Taiwan) and retaining control of Tibet which China saw as part of itself. Hong Kong had historically been made up of three parts: Hong Kong island, ceded to Britain in 1842 following the Opium War; the Kowloon peninsula, ceded to Britain in 1860 after the Arrow War; and the New Territories, leased by Britain for ninety-nine years in 1898. In the early 1980s China made it known not only that it would not allow Britain to renew the leasehold over the New Territories when it ended in 1997 but that it also wanted to negotiate the return of the other two parts of Hong Kong. Aware that it could not militarily defend Hong Kong in the face of Chinese determination to take it, the British agreed to negotiations that led to an agreement in September 1984. Britain agreed to return Hong Kong on July 1, 1997; for their part the Chinese stipulated that for fifty years after that date, Hong Kong would retain a capitalist economy, becoming a "special administrative region" under the formula of "one country, two systems." During that period, until 2047, English would remain the official language; Hong Kong residents would pay no taxes to China; and the city's economy would remain generally autonomous. Hong Kong's defense and foreign policy would fall under China's control. Although Hong Kong residents were very nervous about this agreement, especially after the events of 1989 in Beijing, the transfer of the former crown colony went off without a hitch in July 1997.

While there had been much talk about the meaning of China's "taking over Hong Kong," some commentators talked instead of the reverse phenomenon—of "Hong Kong's taking over China." As the reforms took off in the 1980s, Hong Kong investors became prime movers in China's economic development. By the time of Beijing Spring in 1989, Hong Kong entrepreneurs had ownership interests in over 2000 factories in Guangdong province. Indeed, in 1992, the vast majority of direct foreign investments contracted in China came from Hong Kong, some $40 million U.S., as compared to a little over $3 million from the United States and $2 million from Japan. It should be noted that substantial amounts of the $40 million investment in 1992 came from Taiwanese interests who, because of the absence of relations between Taiwan and China, had to route their investments through Hong Kong firms and agents. In any case, the economic interdependence of Hong Kong and the two provinces where much of the investing has gone—Guangdong and Fujian—has played a huge role in the success and expansion of the Chinese economic reforms.

Macao

Negotiations with Portugal over the return of Macao occurred in 1985. The small peninsula had been occupied in 1557 and controlled since then with tacit Chinese consent. It was the Chinese territory held the longest by a foreign state, almost four and a half centuries. Not as significant economically and strategically as Hong Kong, it was nevertheless of great symbolic importance. The eagerness of the Chinese government to re-incorporate Macao was shown by the clock put up on the east side of Tian'anmen Square that ticked off the seconds until Macao's transfer. The territory reverted to Chinese control in December 1999.

Taiwan

In his speech marking the reversion of Macao to China, Jiang Zemin indicated that it was now time to deal with the Taiwan question; he suggested the "one country, two systems" model as the answer to the question. But in its emotionally charged complexity, the case of Taiwan was much more difficult. Born out of Chiang Kai-shek's loss in the 1940s' civil war, the island regime took the position during Chiang's rule (1949–1975) that the Beijing government was illegitimate, run, they said, by "communist bandits." Chiang's foremost goal was to retake the mainland. The Taiwan Strait crisis of 1958 underscored the reality that the civil war was still very much alive. Taiwan agreed with the Beijing argument, as had the United States in the 1972 Shanghai Communiqué, that "there is one China and that Taiwan is a part of China"; they just could not agree on the more basic—what "China" was in the formula. In its recognition of the Beijing government in 1979, the United States noted that "the Government of the PRC [w]as the sole legal government of China" and expected that the PRC's relationship with Taiwan "w[ould] be settled peacefully by the Chinese themselves."[4]

In 1949, 90 percent of the people of Taiwan had been native Taiwanese, not mainland Guomindang refugees. One could expect that their children and grandchildren, submerged politically for so long to the minority mainlanders, might espouse an independent Taiwan if given a voice to speak. Political changes in Taiwan (see Chapter 23) during the governments of Chiang's son, Chiang Ching-kuo (1978–1988), and Taiwan-born Lee Teng-hui (1988–2000) did indeed bring greater democratization to the island and thus a greater threat to the mainland. For, the thinking went in Beijing, if native Taiwanese had a chance to speak out, the long-outlawed Taiwan independence movement would surely be openly resurrected. Lee's own Taiwanese identity made the Beijing regime instinctively suspicious about all of his actions. He stressed that he did not sympathize with the Taiwan independence movement; but during his second term as president, his actions began to suggest that he increasingly saw Taiwan as an independent nation state.

In part to soften the impact such a direct policy might take, he set out to strengthen ties to the mainland. He lifted all restrictions for Taiwanese to travel to the PRC; within several months, the numbers of Taiwanese traveling to the mainland reached ten thousand per month. Taiwan businessmen now participated directly in PRC economic development, not having any longer to work through their former Hong Kong agents. Representatives from both governments held talks on emigration, fishing rights, and establishing direct air links between Taiwan and the mainland. As for Taiwan's relationship to China, Lee continued to acknowledge that there was only one China.

Anything that suggested a tilt toward greater independence for the Taiwan regime reverberated loudly in Beijing. Lee's policy of "flexible" or "pragmatic" diplomacy—that is, seeking international recognition for the Taiwan government through various means—antagonized Beijing leaders. Lee worked to establish various economic ties around the world, set out to gain formal or quasi-formal diplomatic recognition from some countries, and established air links with some countries—all with a view to breaking down Taiwan's international isolation. And he was strikingly successful in many of his initiatives.

In June 1995, Lee, a graduate of Cornell University, received a visa to come to an alumni reunion in the United States. Since the 1972 Shanghai Communiqué and the statement of the "one China" policy, it had been the practice that no top Taiwan government official was allowed to visit the United States in a public capacity. But the U.S. Congress and President buckled under political pressure. Though Lee came for his own private purpose, the trip was "very public and highly publicized."[5] PRC editorials portrayed Lee as "traitorous to the cause of Chinese nationalism and putting personal ambition above the safety and security of the Chinese citizenry."[6] Jiang Zemin suspended the heretofore-promising talks with Lee on various issues. In July and August, the PRC used the area off the northern coast of Taiwan for missile tests as a way of showing their displeasure with Lee's actions.

In the middle of the 1990s the main opposition to the Guomindang was the Democratic Progressive Party which had a strong Taiwanese identification. Beijing thus watched March 1996 presidential elections closely and crudely used military games off the northern Taiwan coast in March 1996 to try to intimidate Taiwan voters. This brought the unpredictable reality of the Beijing-Taipei-Washington triangle into play: The United States re-

Lee Teng-hui, president of the Republic of China, 1988–2000

sponded by sending two nuclear-armed aircraft carrier fleets into waters in the western Pacific. Though both Beijing and Washington pulled back, the volatility of the continued face-off between Taiwan and the mainland was again evident.

Lee kicked open another hornets' nest in July 1999 with a statement that "Taiwan would treat contacts with the PRC as special state to state relations."[7] Beijing saw the statement as another indication of Lee's goal to establish Taiwan's national independence. It responded with more bellicose statements threatening force to reunify the island with the mainland. Mainland-island relations regarding the presidential elections in March 2000 were especially tense, with Beijing once again threatening to hold war games to remind Taiwanese voters of the dangers of voting for anyone who might move toward independence. When the Democratic Progressive Party candidate Chen Shui-bian, who had spoken in the past of independence for the island, won the election, tensions were high. Despite its almost rabid pre-election rhetoric, Beijing adopted a wait-and-see attitude; and Chen immediately waved olive branches in the direction of the mainland. Tensions again were lessened. In July 2000, PRC Defense Minister Chi Haotian told the U.S. Defense Secretary that "although China reserves the right to use force against Taiwan, that does not mean it intends to do so." The future between the PRC and the ROC remained unsettled and possibly dangerous, not only for the two principal players but for world peace.

ON THE INTERNATIONAL STAGE: EAST ASIA

Japan

Relations with the economic giant in East Asia, Japan, have been mostly economic. In 1978, the two countries signed both a peace treaty and long-term trade agreements that paved the way for Japan's assistance in China's economic development. In the early 1980s this assistance began to become specific with a $10 billion industrial aid agreement. China and Japan jointly explored for oil in the North China Sea, and Japan invested heavily in the Liaodong peninsula in southern Manchuria. Japan's involvement in this area where it had been deeply involved before World War II coupled with memories of the nightmarish war experience stimulated an almost tangible sense of unease about Japan's new role. Japan's seeming inability to accept full responsibility for its actions in the war made the situation worse. In 1985 the Japanese prime minister poured gasoline on the live coals of wartime memory by visiting the Shinto shrine where some Japanese war criminals were buried. Outraged students in Beijing took to the streets to protest the visit. The Japanese government's sponsorship of textbook revisions that downplayed and rationalized Japan's wartime roles also contributed to a political relationship between the two countries that was polite but less than cordial.

State visits, however, continued. The 1991 visit of the Japanese prime minister to Beijing was followed in 1992 by one from the Heisei Emperor, the first ever by a Japanese emperor to China. The firing of Chinese missiles north of Taiwan in 1996, however, brought their relations to a low point. In 1998 to repair those ties if possible, Party Chairman and President of the PRC Jiang Zemin visited Japan, the first visit ever by a Chinese head of state. China hoped for a strong apology from Japan for its wartime aggression. Jiang also sought Japan's unambiguous support for what China referred to as the "three no's": no support for Taiwan's independence, no support for "one China, one Taiwan" or for "two Chinas," and no support for Taiwan's membership in international organizations that were made up of independent states. In the end, China got nothing. Japan did not come out explicitly for the "three no's," and the two failed to agree on the wording for a formal apology for Japan's brutal role in World War II. To end the unsatisfying visit, Jiang turned down the offer of an honorary degree from Waseda University where he lectured, and (rather curiously) wore a Mao jacket to the imperial banquet.

The Koreas

China remained an ally of North Korea, though it made it clear it would not step in to take up the slack when the Soviet Union fell in 1991. Its relationship with the North Korean regime allowed it to become something of a broker with other nations, like the United States, that have limited contact with the regime in Pyongyang.

Ironically, its relationship with South Korea in the 1990s became closer than that with the north. Attracted by possibilities of technical assistance, given South Korea's level of economic development, China and the Seoul regime established diplomatic relations in 1992. Trade grew rapidly, as South Korea poured much of its substantial China investment into Shandong province. Chinese leaders were also attracted by the South Korean industrial model that substantially wedded industry and government, a model that was seen as crucial for South Korea's 1960s' economic take-off. Jiang Zemin's tour of South Korea in 1995 convinced him that this was a model useful for developing China's state-owned enterprises. Chinese delegations were sent to South Korea in 1996 and 1997 to study the full range of economic issues relating to the South Korean approach. Although the 1997–1998 Asian financial crisis that seriously damaged South Korea's economy gave the Chinese second thoughts, the Chinese leadership still considered the model worth emulating.

Vietnam

China's relationship with Vietnam in the last quarter of the twentieth century was not a happy one. In the years before the Cultural Revolution, China had given advice and assistance to North Vietnam in its anti-U.S. war. But in the 1970s relations turned frigid over the issue of Cambodia. In that decade China had established an alliance with Cambodia's Communist Khmer Rouge. When the Khmer Rouge took power in 1975, they unleashed a reign of terror, now often referred to as a holocaust, that led to killings of ethnic Vietnamese living in Cambodia and to increasingly bad relations between Cambodia and Vietnam. Vietnam consequently invaded Cambodia in late 1978, establishing a regime that it could control. This takeover and especially the brutality of the Vietnamese regime toward ethnic Chinese enraged the Beijing leadership. In 1978, China cut off all its aid from Vietnam; and in February 1979, it invaded Vietnam "to teach it a lesson." The campaign was over in a month with China's turning out to be the combatant having been taught a lesson. It had nothing to show for the effort except high Chinese casualties and evidence that the PLA was, as one critic put it, "deficient in modern warfare."[8] The military action poisoned relations between China and Vietnam into the twenty-first century.

The South China Sea

Of increasing concern in the mid- to late-1990s was China's aggressive stance regarding the Spratly Islands in the South China Sea. Under a loose interpretation of the 1982 Law of the Sea Convention, it claimed that almost all of the South China Sea falls under its sovereignty and specifically that it has a two hundred mile "exclusive economic zone" around each of the Spratly Islands. Thus, the reportedly rich oil reserves off the Spratly Islands belong to China. The difficulty here is that the islands are also claimed by Taiwan, the Philippines, Malaysia, Brunei, and Vietnam. China was quite aggressive in making its claims, seizing six atolls from Vietnam in 1988 and establishing outposts on many of the islands.

In this instance, at least, China showed itself to be somewhat expansionist. Commentators have wondered if a strong and even strident nationalism might replace the now defunct ideology of Marxism-Leninism-Mao Zedong Thought as the motivating force in China's policies both at home and abroad. A New China News Agency editorial in 1996 set forth a prescription for the future. "At present, patriotism is both a great driving force to en-

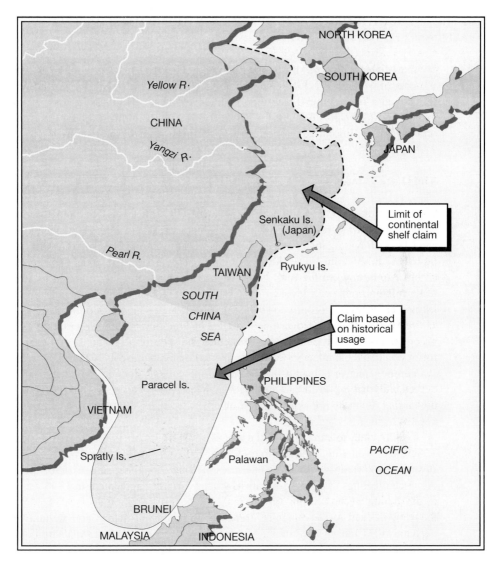

China's Maritime Territorial Claims in Regional East Asia

courage the Chinese people to revitalize the nation and a banner to unify the whole nation. In the face of attempts to 'Westernize' and 'split' China by US-led countries, it is highly necessary that the Chinese people become more closely united and move vigorously to promote patriotism."[9] It specifically demonized the United States as the neo-imperialist bogeyman behind its problems with Taiwan and Tibet and its not being awarded the host city site for the 2000 Olympic Games.

ON THE INTERNATIONAL STAGE: DEALING WITH THE UNITED STATES AND THE SOVIET UNION

By the 1990s the People's Republic had important global credentials. It was a permanent member of the United Nations Security Council; it participated in the World Bank, the International Monetary Fund, and the Asian Development Bank; and it possessed a nuclear arsenal and its means of delivery.[10] Its relations with the global powers, the United States and the Soviet Union until its collapse in 1991, ran from warm to chilly in the 1980s and 1990s.

The United States

After the first corporate agreements in late 1978 with Coca-Cola and Boeing, United States-based firms greatly expanded their China operations in investments and trade. But the 1989 Beijing tragedy poisoned relations with the United States. It threw the trading relationship throughout the 1990s into jeopardy as the U.S. Congress debated every year whether to bestow on the PRC "most favored nation status," that would permit them to trade at the normal tariff level enjoyed by U.S. trading partners. As memories of the 1989 turmoil and repression continued to be the lens through which U.S. politicians and the press viewed China, the U.S. government carped about China's record on human rights, technology transfers, trade, and various strategic issues. Beijing's response to the frequent criticism was that the United States was trying to contain and isolate China as it tried to assert its own hegemony; indeed a mid-1996 poll of college students found that 95.7 percent agreed with that proposition. During 1996 an anti-American book *China Can Say No* reiterated that point; its popularity was shown by the selling out of its first printing (130,000 copies) in several weeks.

U.S. policy toward Taiwan, the touchiest of all Chinese issues, was a constant irritant. U.S. sale of planes and other military hardware to Taiwan and especially U.S. deployment of ships in the vicinity of military exercises off Taiwan in the spring of 1996 stirred up anti-American feelings. The United States-Japanese security agreement in 1996 was also seen as threatening because it put Taiwan in the "sphere of common defence [sic] interests" of the two countries. A spokesman for Jiang Zemin stated that "[t]his can absolutely not be accepted by the Chinese government and the Chinese people."[11] State visits by Jiang in 1997 and President Clinton in 1998 seemed to warm up the oftentimes-chilly relationship.

But in 1999 that thaw was overcome by a freeze, taking the relationship to its iciest since the establishment of diplomatic relations two decades earlier. Charges in the United States of alleged Chinese spying at U.S. nuclear facilities and of alleged Chinese attempts to buy influence through contributions to President Clinton's 1996 reelection campaign led to frequent China-bashing in the U.S. Congress and in some media. In May 1999, during the war in Kosovo, NATO planes bombed the Chinese embassy in Belgrade, destroying the building and killing several Chinese journalists. The United States called the bombing a mistake, attributing it to faulty maps. The Chinese sneered at what seemed to them like a lame excuse. They argued that the bombing was intentional and that the U.S.-led West was trying to send a message to China: Don't try to deal with ethnic problems in Taiwan and Tibet like Serbia's leader had done against ethnic Albanians, that is, by using force. Or else, there will be more bombs raining down. Chinese students reacted violently to the bombing, taking to the streets and attacking the U.S. embassy. The bombing seemed to crystallize the surging anti-American feelings that the United States would not allow China to take its rightful place among the nations of the world. Oscillating between warm and freezing in the last decade of the century, Sino-U.S. relations were anything but predictable for the foreseeable future.

The Soviet Union

The hostility with the Soviet Union that had produced the Sino–Soviet split in 1960 and outright war in early 1969 did not begin to subside until the presidency of Mikhail Gorbachev. In 1985, as expanded trade and cultural contacts began to relieve tensions, consulates were reopened in Shanghai and St. Petersburg; China also purchased Soviet aircraft. Gorbachev's trip to Beijing in May 1989, at the time of the democracy demonstrations, formally healed the rupture that had existed between the two countries for three decades. The Soviet Union's collapse in 1991 left an impotent Russia with whom China midway through the decade was undertaking some exchanges. Russia's President Yeltsin visited China three times between 1992 and 1996; at the last visit, he and Jiang signed agreements that put to rest long-simmering border disputes. The Russians offered assistance in the Three Gorges Dam project and were eager to sell excess military equipment to China. Though Russia was not a strong antagonist like the Soviet Union had been and was therefore no immediate threat to China, the long border they shared made Russia an important player in Chinese strategic considerations.

THE ROLE OF THE PEOPLE'S LIBERATION ARMY

It is, of course, up to China's military to defend the country's interests abroad and to keep order at home. The history of the military is in itself an interesting and important part of modern Chinese history. One of the major trends in China's twentieth century was the increasing role of the military in the life of the nation. Warlordism in the 1910s and 1920s had forced major political parties—the Guomindang and the CCP—to recognize the essential need for having their own armies. By the 1940s these armies squared off against each other in civil war. The victorious People's Liberation Army, apart from its huge commitment in the Korean War, was generally a quiet force in Chinese domestic affairs until the tumultuous years of the Cultural Revolution. Then, Mao had to rely on it to bring order out of the Red Guard chaos that threatened all-out civil war. Since that time, however, it has played an on-again, off-again player on the national stage. It dominated the party from the Ninth Party Congress in 1969 until 1973. But then in the early days of Deng Xiaoping's reforms, it was reined in: during the 1980s, the military budget, for example, actually shrank in real terms. Morale declined and recruitment was a problem (in 1988 a PLA officer was earning only half the salary of an average urban worker).

Nevertheless, it was the institution on which the party had to rely to deal with the events in the spring of 1989. Reformers liked to point out that the PLA had ridden into Beijing in 1949 as the champions of the people, but that in 1989 their tanks drove into the streets of the capital to crush the people. From the perspective of the PLA and the party-state, the PLA was simply reprising its late 1960s role in bringing order to the state. For many in China, however, the actions cost the army a huge amount of respect.

In the early 1990s, the military budget expanded. The budget was four times larger in 1997 than it was when Deng began his reforms in the late 1970s, yet government leaders liked to point out that its military expenditures were rising relatively little in relative terms. Using expenditures in 1978 as a base of 100, the real growth in military expenses after the largest increase in the military budget in 1995 was only 100.28. All this was misleading, however, because two sources of PLA income were not included in the formal budget. First was the sale of military equipment and technologies abroad, profits from which reached $2 billion per year in the late 1980s. These sales were totally controlled by the PLA; they were not monitored or approved by the Ministry of Foreign Affairs. Second was the sale of civilian products (air conditioners, for example) manufactured in over 10,000 PLA factories, and the proceeds from investments in some 10,000 other commercial and service enterprises (among them, nightclubs, restaurants, and joint venture hotels and resorts). Indeed its investments, including large chunks of real estate in Hong Kong, have made the PLA, in the words of one scholar, "a major power in international trade and finance."[12]

As its economic empire grew, the party became aware that, in certain circumstances, the PLA might be tempted to act on its own. In the early 1990s the party worked to have the principle of army allegiance to the party firmly etched into the thinking of military leaders. Institutionally at least, the party controlled the army. In 1991, Deng Xiaoping appointed Jiang Zemin chair of the Central Military Affairs Commission, which exercised leadership for the military. Jiang wanted the PLA to be the "point man" in leading a campaign for "spiritual civilization." Indeed, the military leadership in the mid-1990s returned to the rhetoric of Maoist-style indoctrination. In 1996 Defense Minister Chi Haotian remarked that "ideological and political work should be put at the top of the army's agenda."

Above all, as the country threw itself into the race for rapid riches, the army, Chi contended, would be "an ideological Great Wall against corruption and [bourgeois-liberal] changes."[13] Units of the PLA that were seen as especially admirable were touted in the national media as models to be emulated. One example was (as it was called in the media) the Wonderful 6th Company of the Spiritually Civilized Shenzhen Special Economic Zone. This unit was so great because it could "withstand the sugar-coated bullets of capitalism. . . . After all, there were 150-odd karaoke bars, massage parlors, sauna baths and assorted clubs within a 500-metre radius of platoon headquarters. Members of this saintly company did not smoke, drink, swear, or gawk at women. They also spurned the favorite national pastime: dabbling in the stock market."[14] Since this description of the 6th Company flew in the face of accounts of most units in the developing southeast coast who were enthusiastic participants in the economic free-for-all, the public only grew more cynical about the PLA and what it was really up to.

Reports have suggested that the high point of PLA influence in the 1990s came with the Taiwan crisis in 1995 and 1996. The military was apparently livid over Jiang Zemin's "weak" handling of the crisis precipitated by the visit of Taiwan's president Lee to the United States in summer 1995. Indeed, the military men on the Military Affairs Commission eventually forced Jiang and his closest advisors to make self-criticisms over their action which had initially been conciliatory about Lee's action. For a period, the military, seeing itself as the first line of defense against the "neo-imperialism" of the United States, took over the day-to-day policy regarding Taiwan. There was a good deal of saber rattling with talks of "teaching Taiwan a lesson"; they actually turned the Nanjing and Guangzhou military regions into "war zones" before conducting war games north of the island. But in the end, their efforts appeared counter-productive: They did not intimidate the Taiwanese, and Lee won reelection by a large margin. Furthermore, countries throughout the Asian-Pacific region, already wondering about China's hard line regarding the Spratly Islands, were unnerved by the aggressive actions of the Chinese military. Jiang was able to hold his own in his position as chair of the Military Affairs Commission, but commentators noted that he did so only by assenting to continuing PLA clout.

At the turn of the twenty-first century, it seemed that the party and the army were unmistakably separating. Since the army was formed in the early 1930s as the Jiangxi Soviet Red Army, it had been the party's creation and handmaiden. Leaders of the party had been leaders of the army; many of the key party and state leaders into the 1990s had been military leaders on the Long March and during the Sino-Japanese War and Civil War. There had indeed been an interlinking or perhaps a marriage of the two. But a divorce was in the offing. In 2000, none of the senior party leaders had any military background, and none of the leading military men had any political experience. To make the separation more likely was the fact that the 3.2 million strong PLA was increasingly emphasizing professionalism and a sense of itself as a corporate unit. Thus, the party-state leadership

> will command a military establishment that is becoming more complex, specialized, and professional—which constitutes another limit on its political influence. This is because, as its modernization advances, it will become more inward-looking and separated from the party in interests, function, and outlook. Separation will strengthen its inclination to avoid political entanglement, which can only be inimical to its corporate well-being. . . . This means . . . that if the Chinese Communist Party is to stay in power . . . the CCP cannot necessarily rely on the PLA to rescue it again and keep it in power. The military's interests are diverging from the party's.[15]

The crucial question at century's beginning was how the PLA would understand its role and respond to future crises. Some in East Asia and beyond were concerned about an aggressive Chinese military that might turn adventuristic. They pointed out that in the early 1990s, the stated main PLA goal was the "protection of territorial integrity." But by the mid-1990s, there was a longer list of goals, including "defending the nation's sovereignty over its land, sea, and air space as well as its maritime rights and interests." The latter rights and interests were spelled out in late 1996 as including "three million square kilometers of 'economic zone' which fell within 200 nautical miles of China's lengthy coastline."[16]

THE PLACE OF CHINESE IN CHINA: THE HUMAN RIGHTS ISSUE

At first thought, it seems absurd to talk about the Chinese "place" in China, yet the government of the People's Republic has continually differentiated some Chinese from others. From the very beginning in the 1950s, the constitution guaranteed the "people" certain rights, but then specified who the "people" were and noted that some of the people (capitalists, intellectuals, Guomindang supporters) were not really "people." During the Cultural Revolution, some were of the color red and some were of the color black; the red were obviously preferred to the black. The many minorities have been consistently handled differently from the Han Chinese. And it has been repeatedly made clear that those opting to dissent politically have their own place in China—usually prison or labor camps.

The issue of human rights is not only a domestic Chinese issue, but one that has been increasingly raised in the context of global interdependence and citizenship. Thus, it has almost as much to do with China's place in the world as it has to do with the Chinese place in China. "China's compliance or noncompliance with the norms of the human rights regime constitutes the most rigorous test of international citizenship, for human rights present an immediate challenge to the principle of state sovereignty."[17]

Human rights have been defined as "claims which, it is agreed, every individual has, or should have, upon the society [as represented by government and its official] in which he/she lives."[18] It applies, or should, to all human beings in every society. The concept grew out of the Western concept of an individual's natural rights and has been set down in various U.N. covenants, the most basic being the Universal Declaration of Human Rights, adopted in 1948. Rights guaranteed there include

> every person's right to life, free from arbitrary killing, and to physical and psychological integrity, free from torture or mistreatment; to freedom from slavery, and from arbitrary arrest, detention, or other physical restraint; to fair trial in the criminal process; to freedom of residence and movement within one's country, including the right to leave any country, as well as the right to return to one's own country; to freedom of conscience and religion, expression, and association; to participation in government; to the equal protection of the law; as well as, and not least, a claim to have basic human needs satisfied—food, shelter, health care, an adequate standard of living for oneself and one's family, education, work, and leisure.[19]

As a U.N. member since 1971, China was required to respect these principles. The PRC has had four constitutions (1954, 1975, 1978, and 1982). All four guaranteed economic, social, cultural, political, and civil rights: freedom "of speech, correspondence, press, assembly, association, procession and demonstration, and for freedom of person, freedom of religious belief, the right of appeal against state functionaries, and the autonomy of national minorities."[20] Other civil rights included in the Universal Declaration, however, were not included in the Chinese constitutions: "freedom of residence or movement, the right to choose one's work, freedom from forced labor, freedom from torture, and the right to the presumption of innocence." While the right to strike was included in the two 1970s constitutions, that right was eliminated in the 1982 document. The "crucial limitation" about rights enunciated in the Chinese constitutions was that law in China was based on the "will of the state . . . [and] [s]ince the Constitution was not judicially actionable, the state was not obliged to put the guaranteed right into action."[21]

Over the years, in its treatment of dissidents and Tibetans, for example, it has been accused of violating many of the rights specified in the Universal Declaration through countenancing torture, arbitrary arrest, unfair trials, and the selective protection of the law and through trampling on freedom of religion, expression, and association. Look at its record in the decade of the 1990s, which saw a continuing on-again, off-again policy, with periodic roundups of dissidents and periodic releases of dissidents from prison. In part this seemed to reflect the government's effort to respond to foreign criticism about its human rights policy so as to avoid various kinds of penalties that foreign nations might apply. On the other hand, the erratic policy reflected the continuing distrust and fear among the leadership about the potential for political trouble if a more liberal policy were adopted. Thus, for example, one of the 1989 student leaders, Wang Dan was sentenced to four years in prison in 1991, but he was released in 1993. Later he was reimprisoned before his being allowed to leave China in 1997. Similarly, the most famous dissident, Wei Jingsheng, imprisoned since the Democracy Wall episode of 1979, was freed in 1993, reimprisoned in 1995, and in 1998 released and allowed to leave China. A remarkable nationally televised debate between Chairman Jiang Zemin and President Bill Clinton in June 1998 that dealt with human rights issues among others raised hopes that the government might be beginning to change its views.

Presidents Jiang Zemin and Bill Clinton, Beijing, 1998

But late in 1998 a series of arrests of dissidents trying to form an alternative political party once again dashed hopes that any such change was occurring; 1999 saw widespread religious persecution of the Falun Gong or Buddhist Law Sect (see Epilogue).

For this record, China was pilloried in the West, especially in the United States where the issue gave rise to much China-bashing and held up trade status and agreements as well as China's entrance into international organizations like the World Trade Organization. China's (and much of Asia's) response was that many of the individual rights laid down by Western nations in the Universal Declaration were culture-specific and did not apply in the same way in all cultures and countries. In China traditionally the individual did not have *rights* but *responsibilities* to the collective (the family or larger society or the state). In such a culture, the Chinese asserted, the rights of the collective were what were properly called human rights. Further, they argued that when the West talked about human rights, the West focused on rather narrow political and civil rights. China argued that economic and social rights had to precede political rights: What good is the right to assemble when one is too poor to have food to eat? Finally they emphasized state sovereignty whenever they were attacked for their "human rights record." States signed the U.N. charter; thus the human rights entailed in being a U.N. member were granted in sovereign states.

Before a U.N. World Conference on Human Rights in Vienna in 1993, Asian states met in Bangkok (March 29–April 2, 1993) to clarify their position on human rights and to assert their way of looking at the problem. The Bangkok Declaration issued at the end of the meeting was Asia's official view of human rights (not the view of the many non-governmental Asia groups who attended). Its crucial ideas were set forth at Vienna by the Chinese delegate to that meeting. Although it is lengthy, it bears careful reading for it makes the Chinese point of view very clear.

> The concept of human rights is a product of historical development. It is closely associated with specific social, political, and economic conditions and the specific history, culture and values of a particular country. Different historical development stages have different human rights requirements. . . . Thus, one should not and cannot think the human rights standards and models of certain countries as the only proper ones and demand all other countries to comply with them. . . . For the vast number of developing countries, to respect and protect human rights is first and foremost to ensure the full realization of the rights to subsistence and development. . . . To wantonly accuse another country of abuse of human rights and impose the human rights criteria of one's own country or region on other countries or regions are tantamount to an infringement upon the sovereignty of other countries and interference in the latter's internal affairs. . . . State sovereignty is the basis for the realization of citizens' human rights. If the sovereignty of a state is not safeguarded, the human rights of its citizens are out of the question, like a castle in the air.[22]

Many scholars, legal experts, and human rights specialists attacked outright the cultural relativist arguments that Western law traditions infusing the "human rights regime" made them inappropriate for non-Western countries. They argued that the "regime" has truly become universal. "Human rights is the idea of our times. . . . The principal covenants and conventions . . . have been subscribed to by many nations, of every ideological complexion and political or economic commitment—Western and Eastern, developed and developing, democratic, authoritarian, and totalitarian, rich and poor, free enterprise and socialist."[23] Others have argued that Confucianism itself holds values that are much in harmony with many of the human rights, so that the cultural relativist arguments hardly apply.

It is interesting that Deng's reforms placed much more emphasis on the individual; it is individuals, after all, who were getting rich; the role of the state has been lessened. And yet there have developed no new legal protections for the individual; the right of due process, for example, was still frequently violated. In the 1980s and 1990s there were frequent anti-crime campaigns with executions widespread: between August and October 1983, for example, there were 600 executions; and in 1990, 750 of 960 death sentences were carried out—totaling a third of the world's executions that year. (When judging such things, one must take care: in 1999, the United States was incarcerating two million people, fully one quarter of the world's prison population.)

One of China's practices was to talk the human rights game but continue to walk according to its old standards. A look at torture cases reveals the pattern. Torture had traditionally been a common method to extract confessions from persons accused of or charged with a crime. Thus in the anti-crime campaign of 1983, torture was widespread. From 1985 to 1989 the state conducted an anti-torture campaign in which torture cases actually increased; and it was during this very time period that "China signed (12 December 1986), ratified (4 October 1988), and enforced (3 November 1988) the Convention Against Torture. . . ."[24] Indeed China claimed to have been a leader in drafting the convention. Yet report after report of conditions relating to torture in China showed nothing much improving. In April 1990, the International League for Human Rights claimed that torture is a "routine part of the modus operandi of [China's] law enforcement officials."[25] A 1995 Amnesty International report stated that "seven years after it ratified the Convention against Torture, the government still has not taken measures to prohibit all acts of torture by law. . . . The ineffectiveness of the measures taken by the government is demonstrated by the continuing high incidence of torture in China."[26]

Hundreds of such complaints continued to come from China. In May 1996, the U.N.'s Committee against Torture (CAT) made nine recommendations to China about its torture record. Basically, the committee told Beijing to clean up its act. But China's defensive response came straight from the substance of the Bangkok Declaration. "[A]s the proceedings before the CAT ended, the Chinese Ambassador excoriated the Committee for failing to understand China's cultural conditions and the problems faced by the Chinese government."[27] More government decrees in January 1998 calling for the end of torture by police indicated that the problem continued.

China continued to sign human rights documents. Near century's end it signed two covenants, expansions of the Universal Declaration—the three are now often referred to as the International Bill of Rights. In October 1997, China signed the International Covenant on Economic, Social, and Cultural Rights; and in October 1998, it inked the Covenant on Civil and Political Rights. It had not yet ratified them by summer 2000, meaning that it is not yet subject to the committees that will monitor compliance with the covenants. What meaning they will have for the people of China is problematical, but the human rights issue had substantial impact on China in the world. It "has changed China's international relations by causing it to lose control of its own foreign policy battles," that is, involvement in the human rights regime allowed other countries in some ways to channel foreign policy issues and discussions in certain ways. The ultimate impact was that China had to adjust to the international community if it wanted acceptance; then and then only would China find its place in the world and, if the human rights regime was adhered to, would the Chinese find their human rights protected in China.

Notes

[1] Barmé, *In the Red,* p. 258.

[2] Shakya, pp. 347–348.

[3] Ibid., p. 440.

[4] Quoted in Spence, *The Search for Modern China,* p. 667.

[5] Meisner, *Mao's China and After,* p. 530.

[6] John Bryan Starr, "China in 1995: Mounting Problems, Waning Capacity," *Asian Survey,* XXXVI, 1 (January 1996), p. 23.

[7] Li Cheng, "China in 1999: Seeking Common Ground at a Time of Tension and Conflict," *Asian Survey,* XL, 1 (January/February 2000), p. 127.

[8] Dietrich, p. 265.

[9] New China News Agency, November 6, 1996, quoted in Lam, p. 267.

[10] Lieberthal, p. 332.

[11] Lam, p. 388.

[12] Meisner, p. 478.

[13] Lam, pp. 157 and 160.

[14] Ibid., p. 161.

[15] The part of the quotation to "its corporate well-being" is from Ellis Joffe, "Ruling China after Deng," *The Journal of East Asian Affairs,* Vol. 11, No. 1 (Winter/Spring 1997), 219 as cited in David Shambaugh, "China's Post-Deng Military Leadership" in James R. Lilley and David Shambaugh, Eds., *China's Military Faces the Future* (Armonk, N.Y.: M. E. Sharpe, 1999), p. 32. The last part of the quotation is Shambaugh, p. 32.

[16] Lam, p. 163.

[17] Ann Kent, *China, the United Nations, and Human Rights* (Philadelphia: University of Pennsylvania Press, 1999), p. 2.

[18] Louis Henkin, "The Human Rights Idea in Contemporary China: A Comparative Perspective," in R. Randle Edwards, Louis Henkin, and Andrew Nathan, Eds., *Human Rights in Contemporary China* (New York: Columbia University Press, 1986), p. 8.

[19] Ibid., p. 9.

[20] Kent, p. 29.

[21] Ibid., p. 30.

[22] Speech by Li Huaqiu (Vienna: Permanent Mission of the PRC to the United Nations in Vienna, June 15, 1993), quoted in Michael Davis, "Chinese Perspectives on Human Rights," in Michael C. Davis, Ed., *Human Rights and Chinese Values* (Hong Kong: Oxford University Press, 1995), p. 17.

[23] "Preface" in Edwards, Henkin, and Nathan, p. 1.

[24] Kent, p. 85.

[25] Ibid., p. 94.

[26] Ibid., p. 101.

[27] Ibid., pp. 104–105.

22

Riding the Political Waves:
Literature, Art, Cinema,
and Popular Culture

_____
_____
___

A poem for the times: 1963.

> This land slumbers on, as in an immense dream.
> No voice of man to be heard, only howling wolves, bears, and tigers;
> This land, always covered in tall grass.
> For days on end, no man casts any shadow on it, only the sky, and the
> water, and the red sun large as a cartwheel . . .
> No tractors, no motor caravans, no pack horses,
> But here is the land, tens of thousands of acres, turning over in the warm
> spring breeze.
> No houses, no inns, no hamlets sending up wafts of smoke of evening cooking.
> But here are several state farms, taking root among a forest of tents. . . .[1]

> _Guo Xiaoquan, "Carved on the Northern Wasteland"_

A song for the times: 1987.

> It's ages now I've been asking you:
> When will you come away with me?
> But all you ever do is laugh at me, 'cause
> I've got nothing to my name.
>
> I want to give you my hope
> I want to help make you free

But all you ever do is laugh at me, 'cause
I've got nothing to my name.
Cui Jian, "Nothing to My Name"[2]

The very different values set forth in these poems point not only to the sharply different spirit of Mao's China and the China of Deng's reforms, but to a basic and ongoing conflict in the world of literature and the arts. At the heart of the conflict is the question, "What is the purpose of art and literature?" The state and most artists have had markedly different answers to this question.

The first poem focuses on a world that waits to be developed, for it is an immense land largely without "things"—tractors, motor caravans, pack horses, houses, inns, or hamlets. But change was coming, brought by the *state* in the form of state farms or communes. That was the essential fact, the "big picture." Those with concerns about state and national development and the march toward Communism—really the subject of this poem—would argue, like Mao did at the 1942 Yan'an Forum on Literature and the Arts, that art and literature are to serve the state, especially the peasantry and the proletariat.

The second poem, a song by rock star Cui Jian, focuses on one individual, romantic love, and "things." As such, it represents those "bourgeois" values that the government leaders saw as inimical to the development of the Communist state. Even more, in this poem, the "I" has high-minded reasons to show his love to his girlfriend—to bring hope and to liberate; but in the new capitalist age of the 1980s and 1990s, she only laughs at him for these high-minded reasons because he is poor. In any event, many writers and artists claimed that dealing with such material was surely in the domain of the creative artist, but carrying forward that view they ran smack-dab into the contrary viewpoint of the state, persecution, prison, and sometimes death. This chapter looks at the often bitter and unhappy history of the relationship between the party-state and artists in general in the People's Republic; it also surveys that relationship in Taiwan. In focus here are literature, the performing arts, cinema, and rock music and popular culture.

> To highlight the relationship between the state and the artist in twentieth century China, the persecutions suffered by artists and writers are listed (in this font) after pertinent sections.

THE BASE: REPUBLICAN LITERATURE AND ART

The basic issue that has become so politicized during the PRC—the function of art and artists in a developing state—was already an issue during the Republic. Then it was framed as a disagreement between those who championed "art for art's sake" and those who supported "art for life's sake." These are, of course, polar views: many artists would have opted for something in between, that is, art carried out with exacting artistic values but relating in some way to the context in which they lived.

Perhaps the best example of "art for art's sake" during the Republic was the so-called "mandarin duck and butterfly school" in the period 1910 into the 1930s. This was escapist and sensationalistic literature—novels and short stories—that appealed to middle- and lower-class tastes in urban settings. Composed mainly of love stories, detective tales, and knight-errant novels, this huge body of work (in these years, output totaled 2215 novels and filled 113 magazines and 49 newspapers) can best be described as lowbrow urban popular fiction.

The concerns of the New Culture movement in the May Fourth period played a role in shifting the concerns of committed and gifted writers to the serious problems in Chinese state and society. Some reflected concerns of the New Culture movement itself; others probed the realities of Chinese society. An example of the first looks initially like a love story specimen from the mandarin ducks genre. It is the most well-known story by China's most famous twentieth century woman author Ding Ling, "Miss Sophie's Diary," an account of a "modern girl" who was torn in her affections between two men. Of the two, Sophie was more attracted to the handsome, rakish Singapore playboy, but she felt guilty about her feelings. The story raised issues about the role that women were to play in the new culture (Sophie was quite sexually aggressive) and the effects that such actions had on women's psyches. Hear her out:

> I shouldn't be so open with so handsome a man and make myself look cheap. But I love him. . . . It seems to me no reason why I shouldn't be allowed to give him a hundred kisses provided nobody else is harmed. . . . Tonight I've gone completely crazy. . . . My heart feels as if it's being gnawed by hordes of mice, or as if a brazier were burning inside it. If only I could smash everything or rush wildly out into the night. I can't control the surges of wild emotion. . . .[3]

Several other writers depict in stark relief the issues in the New Culture movement. Ba Jin's novel *Family* (see Chapter 9) also spotlights the importance of relationships between fathers and sons, husbands and wives, and brothers that were at the heart of so much May Fourth discussion and change. In his longest story, "The True Story of Ah Q," Lu Xun describes a social loser and the society he inhabits at the time of the 1911 revolution. Besides painting a scathing portrait of that revolution as empty and meaningless, Lu sketches a bleakly dark Chinese political culture that is marked by self-delusion, mean-spiritedness, crassness, and a slave mentality.

An important development in literature and the arts in the Republican period was the formation of professional associations that helped artists to find commonalities with and support among the community of artists. An Association for Literary Studies, for example, was established in 1921, "dedicated to the practice of literature as an independent and honorable profession."[4] It published journals and offered support to young writers trying to get started. But as more associations begin to form, they tended, in the increasingly politicized atmosphere of the 1920s, to take as their mission the promotion either of "art for art's sake" or "art for political purpose." The Creation Society (1921) was established by three men who had been fellow students at Tokyo Imperial University. During its first three years, it emphasized art for art's sake and, with it, a romanticism that infused the writings of its members. This vision was shared by the later Crescent Moon Society, established in 1928 by Anglo-American scholars, who stressed the autonomy of literature. One of its leaders argued that "[t]rue literature was above class; its right domain was the 'fundamental human nature'—love, hate, pity, terror, death—that could not be confined to any class."[5]

But the opposing position—that literature and the arts were intimately tied to class and politics—came to be espoused by even more powerful groups. In 1924 the old guard leadership of the Creation Society was overthrown, and young men, radicalized by the revolutionary forces then erupting all over China, seized control. From that point on, the organization championed Marxist values. In 1930 a CCP-inspired organization, the League of Left-Wing Writers, came into being with Lu Xun as a kind of godfatherly figurehead. As the 1930s proceeded bitter debates erupted between writers and artists about the extent to which art should be controlled by politics and political considerations; the battlelines were drawn, not surprisingly, between Communists and non-Communists. On the Communist side, the spokesman, more often than not, was the fire-eating secretary-general of the League from 1931 to 1936, Zhou Yang.

Under his leadership, the League was dissolved in the spring of 1936 to make way for a larger coalition, the Association of Chinese Writers and Artists, of which he became the leading figure. It was at this time when the CCP was pushing for a united front against Japan. Zhou became quite dictatorial in demanding that writers focus on producing "national defense literature": He declared that "national defence [sic] should become the central theme in the works of *all* writers except traitors," and he even prescribed what the literature should include. He argued that "the party policy of the united front took precedence over everything else, including artistic creation."[6] Zhou's demands stirred up great anger among writers like Lu Xun (then in the last months of his life) and novelist Mao Dun, who argued that the standard for writers must remain creative freedom in the context of political commitment. What was really at stake in these battles was the effort to transform an "elitist, author-centered culture (i.e., one designed by authors) into a mass, audience-centered culture (i.e., one designed by or for the audience)."[7]

Scholars have pointed out that despite Zhou and others' efforts to put literature and the arts into a straitjacket that they would design, the mid-1930s saw a great outpouring of creatively impressive work, especially in the novel, poetry, and drama. This is not a literary history text, so only the crème de la crème of these important works will be touched on. The giants in the world of the novel in this period were Mao Dun and Lao She. Mao's masterpiece, *Midnight,* was published in 1933; it depicted the crisis brought to Shanghai's commerce and industry by the forces of international capitalism. Lao She, an ethnic Manchu, parodied the wretched state of China in his 1932 *Cat Country;* but his greatest work was *Camel Xiangzi* (1936), translated into English as *Rickshaw.* It is the unhappy story of a young Beijing rickshaw puller that gives a biting look at lower-class life in the northern capital. In the genre of poetry, Wen Yiduo of *Dead Water* fame (see Chapter 11) was a major figure.

The major new genre of literature was the spoken drama. Traditional Chinese theater was opera, a dramatic form incorporating singing, dance, and balletic gymnastics. Spoken drama began only in the twentieth century as a "Western-inspired new [form] in conscious reaction against tradition."[8] The foremost dramatist of the day was Cao Yu, who, in his last year as an undergraduate at Qinghua University, wrote *Thunderstorm,* "the most famous dramatic work of the pre-war period and possibly the most performed play in the modern Chinese theatre."[9] Its themes include the May Fourth struggle for emancipation from the constraints of family and the effects of capitalism on labor, but it is at once made both more powerful and more modern by Cao's exploration of the theme of incest. From the 1930s into the 1950s, Cao wrote five other major plays. A secret to his success was that he envisioned each play as both literature and *performance* while most playwrights considered their works primarily as literature. As we have seen (Chapter 14), various types of spoken drama played an important role in popularizing the war against Japan in the late 1930s and 1940s.

Ba Jin was brutally persecuted during the Cultural Revolution, rehabilitated in 1979.

Cao Yu was targeted during the Cultural Revolution, rehabilitated in 1979.

Ding Ling was exiled to northern Manchuria, 1957–1978.

Lao She was criticized, beaten, and either committed suicide or was killed in 1966. He was rehabilitated posthumously.

Wen Yiduo was gunned down by Chiang Kai-shek's secret police in 1946.

THE YAN'AN FORUM

The 1942 Yan'an Forum on Literature and Art took the semi-official position of critics like Zhou Yang—that literature and art existed only for purposes extraneous to that literature and art—and made it the official line of the Communist Party.

> In the world today all culture, all art and literature belong to definite classes and follow definite political lines. There is in fact no such thing as art for art's sake, art which stands above classes or art which runs parallel to or remains independent of politics. Proletarian art and literature are part of the whole cause of the proletarian revolution. . . . Therefore, the Party's artistic and literary activity occupies a definite and assigned position in the Party's total revolutionary work and is subordinated to the prescribed revolutionary task of the Party in any given revolutionary period.[10]

The phrase most destructive to writers and artists comes at the end: "subordinated to the prescribed revolutionary task of the Party in any given revolutionary period." It meant that they would have to tailor their work to be politically correct by fitting with every shift in direction of the party's policies; it meant that their creativity had to be straitjacketed. They must give up their own consciousness and take on the consciousness of the masses. It was the worse than the old eight-legged essay prescribed for the traditional civil service examination.

To insure compliance with the party's rigorous requirements for writers and artists, the party had various "control mechanisms." Most simply they could be co-opted into the party where close surveillance would likely keep them following the party line. Professional associations, like the Chinese Writers' Association, could keep its members walking that party line. Finally public campaigns, often aimed at a writer or artist who the party thought guilty of egregious doings, might be unleashed to intimidate or terrorize others who would think not twice but twenty times before engaging in questionable creative endeavors.

LITERATURE IN THE PRC: BEFORE THE CULTURAL REVOLUTION

The years between Liberation and the holocaust known as the Cultural Revolution saw heated debates and campaigns erupt between those who contended that art was for the state and those who demanded that the artist was autonomous in choosing his subject and approach. The first I will call "reflectors," for their primary purpose was to reflect the masses and their party-perceived needs; the second, I will call "creators," for artistic creation was their primary purpose. Not surprisingly it was the reflectors, men like Zhou Yang and the poet Guo Moruo, who emerged as leaders of the All China Federation of Literary and Art Circles, Guo serving as president from 1949 to his death in 1978 and Zhou serving as a vice-president from 1949 until he took over as president in 1981. The Federation was an umbrella organization overseeing more specialized "unions," for example, the Writers' Union and the Dramatists' Union. Mao Dun, who championed something of a middle position between reflectors and creators, served as head of the Writers' Union and as Minister of Culture from 1949 to 1965.

None of these three had creative achievements after 1949. Guo, one of the more eminent poets around, took to writing poems on all things political and on such inspiring topics as bridges and reservoirs; most were shallow and unimaginative. Mao Dun, taking on administrative functions, simply stopped writing. Zhou, as far as that goes, had never been creative. But to clash with him meant big trouble. It was Zhou who had been the foremost critic and assailer of Hu Feng who had spoken out for artistic autonomy (see Chapter 17). Woman writer and Stalin Prizewinner, Ding Ling was another bitter enemy of Zhou Yang. According to some critics, she apparently dissipated her talent in various political schemes in the 1950s, some aimed at Zhou. In the end, she antagonized so many in the party-state that she was kicked out of the Writers' Union and exiled in far northern Manchuria.

Crunch time in the conflict between the party-state and reflectors, on the one hand, and the creators, on the other, was the Hundred Flowers movement and its segue into the Anti-Rightist movement. We will not here reprise the distressing events (see Chapter 17). Suffice it to say, the experience of many writers and artists at the time (ostracism, imprisonment, forced labor, and exile) made it less and less likely that creators would want to create. It is not surprising that in the Great Leap Forward period, the published literature hewed tightly to the political line. Common themes of stories and poems were the bad old days and the wonderful present, Joe Peasant learns the value of cooperation with his fellow peasants, and utilizing wartime fervor for installing the Great Leap policies.

There were some major novels, all dealing with peasants and revolution. Zhao Shuli, the most praised writer on peasant life, began writing in the 1940s and produced several major novels. In 1955, he wrote *Three Mile Bend* about the completion of an irrigation project. But his historical novel, *Magic Spring Caves* (1959), about the anti-Japanese resistance of villagers in Shanxi province, struck most critics as much better. In the same genre, though considered much richer was *Red Crag* (1961) by Luo Guangbin and Yang Yiyan. A complex, long (about four hundred thousand words) work about the civil war period, it "furnishes a gallery of portraits of disciplined revolutionaries both male and female, of waverers and turncoats, and of guileful but despairing functionaries of the Nationalist secret service." A scholar has called it "an impressive monument to the many dedicated Communists who died in the underground struggles of two decades."[11] *Red Crag* has likely had more readers than any other Communist work, and it has been made into a play and film.

Hu Feng was imprisoned, 1955–1981.

Luo Guangbin was criticized, beaten, and then either committed suicide or was killed in 1967. He was rehabilitated posthumously.

Mao Dun was targeted briefly during the Cultural Revolution.

Zhao Shuli was criticized, tortured, and died in prison in 1970. He was rehabilitated posthumously.

Zhou Yang was imprisoned, 1966–1976.

THE PLAY'S THE THING

The relatively new spoken drama continued to be written. In 1957, for example, Lao She wrote *Teahouse,* an intriguing play that depicted actions in a teahouse during three different times of the past, during the 1898 reform movement, during the early warlord era in 1916, and right before the civil war in 1946. It depicted the evils of the old society, but also cast questions about the roles of the governments that had existed at those times.

But traditional Chinese theater or opera still held sway. Modern operas with revolutionary themes began to be written in the 1940s and 1950s. *The White-Haired Girl* was one of the most famous, winning a Stalin Prize in 1951. It told the story of a girl turned into a demon by the actions of a vicious landlord; in the end she was rescued by the Eighth Route Army and turned back into a girl. One of the most prolific dramatists of the twentieth century was Tian Han, in the 1950s head of the Dramatists' Union; he was also one of the bravest. In two plays, *Guan Hanjing* (1958) and *Xie Yaohuan* (1961), he made strong statements for the autonomy of the artist and against the government. He paid for it with his life. *Xie Yaohuan,* an account of a Tang dynasty ruler and her ultimate failure at leadership, was attacked by Mao as one of the "three most poisonous weeds" among plays of the time. One of the other weeds was Wu Han's *Hai Rui Dismissed from Office,* the attack on which was the opening salvo of the Cultural Revolution.

During the Cultural Revolution, Mao's wife Jiang Qing emerged as cultural czarina. She condemned traditional operas as "feudal" for they dealt with the old society, and she led the way to developing a politically and ideologically correct repertoire of "revolutionary model operas." Five revolutionary operas comprised the repertoire—"blueprint works," as they were called. All but one were military in theme. Set during the war against Japan were *Red Lantern* and *Shajiabang,* each one focusing on a war hero, in the first a railroad worker and in the second a teahouse owner. *Taking Tiger Mountain by Strategy* dealt with the successful seizure of a bandit hideout by the PLA in 1946. *Raid on the White Tiger Regiment* was a story in the Korean War. The non-military opera, which was also the only one with a contemporary theme, was *On the Docks;* it told the story of a battle against a saboteur. Reportedly these revolutionary operas were popular and at times spectacular in music, dance, and presentation, but with such a small repertoire, they did not offer return-goers much variety.

Apart from model revolutionary operas, the Cultural Revolution creativity came from novelist Hao Ran, a former peasant turned writer who focused in his work, not surprisingly, on peasants. As one would expect at such a time, the novels are all perfectly ideologically correct. In one of his best known, *Bright Sunny Skies,* progressive poor peasants battle rich and middle peasants who are trying to take advantage of them. One scholar said of Hao that he could "make a story out of the salvaging of a sick horse or the repairing of a wheelbarrow."[12] On the whole the Cultural Revolution years were the bleakest of the bleak; many writers and artists suffered desperately. Even if there had been more people writing, they would have been up against a leadership that went so far as to set down this formula for "artistic creation": "Among all characters emphasize the positive; among the positive, emphasize the main heroic character; and among the main characters, emphasize the primary central character."[13]

> Tian Han was struggled against and died in prison in 1968.
> Wu Han was struggled against, beaten, imprisoned, and committed suicide in 1967.

WRITERS AND ARTISTS UNDER THE REFORMS

With Mao's death in 1976 a very slow thaw began in the state's thirty-four-year icy grip over intellectuals and the arts. Bitter memories of the suffering of the Anti-Rightist Movement of 1957 and the Cultural Revolution when intellectuals had been murdered and committed suicide led to the production in the late 1970s of mildly dissident writings that were called "scar literature" or "literature of the wounded." But shades of the Maoist period persisted. Although the Third Plenum of the Eleventh Party Congress in December 1978 called on intellectuals "to liberate their thoughts, to break into previously forbidden zones, and not to fear a return of repressive policies,"[14] the Democracy Wall repression began only a few months later. As we have seen (Chapter 19), the 1980s brought wave after wave of repressive campaigns, indicating the vacillating policies of the party-state. In the early years of the decade there was a return to a colder climate for intellectuals and artists; conservatives set in motion the campaign against bourgeois liberalization that targeted screenwriter Bai Hua and his script for *Unrequited Love*. But Bai Hua was not alone: the party-state put pressure on all unofficial publications.

Appearing at the same time as scar literature and extending into the 1980s was a literature of exposure of government misdeeds and corruption. These appeared as poetry, drama, and prose. One of the more famous exposure poems was Ye Wenfu's "General, You Can't Do This!" (see Chapter 19). Some exposure poems, like this one by Feng Yu, were quite blunt.[15]

Two Cents

Bureau head, factory manager, Party secretary,
When you meet the
Withered, begging hands
Of an old man, a woman, or a child.

Please don't bring out
Two cents.
That won't quiet your conscience.
For in your hands

Is the power
They gave you.

Others are more symbolic. Two of these leading poets, Gu Cheng and Bei Dao, were criticized for their "obscurity." Here Gu uses darkness for the Cultural Revolution and its aftermath and light for hope in the future.[16]

One Generation

The black night has given me black eyes,
Yet I use them to search for the light.

Bei Dao's "Reply" reflects on the same time period using different imagery, but it has a more assertively aggressive tone than Gu Cheng's. Included here is only a section of the poem.[17]

Reply

Baseness is the safe-conduct of the base;
Nobleness is the epitaph of the noble.
Behold, in the gold-plated sky
Flutters a host of snarled reflections of the dead.

The Ice Age is passed,
Why are icicles still covering the earth?
The Cape of Good Hope has been found,
Why are sails still jostling in the Dead Sea?

I came to this world with nothing
But paper, rope, and a shadow
In order to declare the voiced of the sentenced
Before judgment.

Let me tell you world,
I—don't—believe!
Even if a thousand challengers are at your feet,
Count me as the thousand-and-first.

Dramas of exposure in this period were successful especially in dealing with people of power in party and state. In Wang Jing's *In Society's Archives,* the army covers up murder and rape in order to protect elite officers. Occasionally a play cut too close to home for party cadres. *If I Were Genuine* was closed after several performances. It told the story of a young man who impersonates the son of a powerful party cadre. Fawning bureaucratic subordinates think that by carrying out his schemes they might be able to get something out of his father. He loses all when his impersonation is made known, but it is clear that in this political culture, if he had been the cadre's son, he would have been able to keep all he had gained. He says, "I was wrong to be a fake. If I really were the son of Zhang Senior or another leader, then everything I've done would be completely legal." And in the end Zhang Senior berates high party cadres:

> In the past the masses gave us their unbounded sympathy and devotion. They thought we could save the nation. They hoped we would benefit the people. But today you have forgotten all that! . . . . You tell everybody else's children to "put down roots on the farm," while you use every means at your disposal to have your own sons and daughters transferred back to the city. And you want the masses to suffer privation and live simply while you yourselves crave a life of even greater luxury. . . . I am really afraid for our cadre system, which may be brought to ruin by its own corruption.[18]

The two key prose writers who produced their own versions of exposure literature had had trouble with party-state guidelines on creative work since the 1950s. In his role as *People's Daily* correspondent, journalist Liu Binyan continued the type of "reportage" that he had become noted for in the 1950s. For example, his 1979 "People or monsters" exposed a female party cadre in Manchuria who built her own empire of power and money in her position as manager and party secretary of a coal company. As the 1980s progressed, his tone became increasingly strident; and in 1987 he lost his party membership. He went to the United States in 1988 where he remained.

The execution of "the monster," a corrupt female party cadre exposed by journalist Liu Binyan

The other "exposer" of party misdeeds was short story writer Wang Meng. Wang produced stories of party corruption, arrogant cadres, and party factionalism. He often avoided strong criticism by giving his stories upbeat endings. Through the 1980s and 1990s, Wang remained what one analyst called "a liberal moral guide and cultural mentor."[19] From 1986 to 1989 he served as Minister of Culture: the fact that the party leaders would name him to that post indicates indeed how much more liberal and tolerant the party was in the late 1980s. Writing under the pen name of Yang Yu in the late 1980s, he addressed such issues as cultural pluralism and diversity. After the June 1989 crackdown, Wang asked to resign, when the post-crackdown purge made his remaining in the government position no longer realistic or logical.

But Wang continued into the late 1990s as a liberal gadfly. He attacked authoritarianism; and he championed humanism. As the focus of society turned more and more to making money, he wrote essays that praised cultural pluralism and market reforms. In the mid-1990s he was criticized not so much by party-state leaders as by younger scholars and writers who argued that Wang had sold out to the market and to commercial culture. The new culture wars in the 1990s took the form of writers who supported the new monied culture and those who felt that China had moved away from any bedrock principles, either moral or artistic. The party-state seemed uncertain of which point of view it should take, vacillating between wholehearted support of thoroughgoing marketization of society and fear of what impact that would have on the culture. Wang Meng was especially condemned for his support of one of the most popular writers in China from the mid-1980s to the mid-1990s, Wang Shuo.

Wang Shuo, whose writing was often called flippant, was the epitome of the individualist in China amid the glories of getting rich. In his novels, written between 1986 and 1993, "Wang capture[d] the crude vitality of the entrepreneur unbound, the loose world of the modern criminal, and the boredom and amorality that occasionally [led] good girls into the arms of bad men."[20] Wang's stories were peopled by so-called *liumang,* roughly translated as hoodlums, hooligans, or punks—a group that proliferated in the glory days of reforms. At focus in many of his stories was a splashily colorful, raucous, and profane street culture. An ethnic Manchu, he was sometimes compared (to the chagrin of more conservative critics) to the Manchu writer Lao She who also described street life in Beijing. In many ways the subject matter of Wang's stories was a natural for being transformed into appealing films. Many were; in 1988, for example, no fewer than four of his stories were showing simultaneously as feature films.

A brief description of one of these stories, "Hot and Cold, Measure for Measure," gives a sense of the nature of Wang's work. Zhang Ming is an ex-convict who extorts money from wealthy Hong Kong travelers who provide women whom Zhang makes into prostitutes. A naïve university student, Wu Di, falls in love with Zhang; to be with him, she herself becomes a prostitute. It is unclear whether Zhang ever loves Wu. In the end, after she and Zhang are both taken into custody by the police, Wu kills herself; Zhang is returned to prison. Released at the end of the story, he becomes involved with another girl who is much like Wu. A critic attacked the story as "a primer for sexual crime."[21]

In the early 1990s, Wang continued to write novels and for television. He had clearly become a pop cultural figure. As an indication of the interrelated nature of the market culture, phrases from Wang's novels came to be printed on so-called cultural T-shirts, the production of which had begun in the heady days of demonstrations in 1989. In the end, Wang had skated on thin ice for too long. In 1995 and 1996 during a new wave of cultural conservatism in the party Wang was attacked; and in mid-1996 his works were banned. He went to the United States but stayed only a few months. On his return to China in 1998, he put together a collection of his work, which became a best-seller, and announced in the process that he had become an intellectual!

In the money-crazed 1990s, the literary bombshell was not one of Wang's works or a work of political dissent but a popular novel focusing on the once-forbidden topic of sex. The 1993 publication of *The Abandoned Capital* by Jia Pingwa was a sensation, selling half a million copies within a few months of its publication. This soft-porn novel recounts the sexual exploits of a middle-aged writer; for many, even toned-down descriptions of sex seemed shocking, but apparently, based upon sales, appealing. Some critics saw the import of the book as more profound. Young critic Xiao Xialin wrote that the various opinions about the book

> make us confront the image of a place that, in the present age of transformation, can be claimed to be nothing less than an "abandoned capital society." Ours is the world of the abandoned capital. Everywhere you look, the basic values of civilization—justice, truth, ideals, and the sublime—are in a state of alienation. Morality itself has nothing more that a utilitarian value. All we dream of now and hope for in the future are money and sex. The unprincipled process of moneymaking and sexual gratification has gravely undermined the pillars of civilized society.[22]

ROCK AND POP CULTURE

In most cultures since the mid-twentieth century, rock music has been a weather vane of sorts for popular culture and a vehicle for expressing anti-establishment messages. In China of the 1980s and 1990s, rock emerged to offer challenges to the party-state and alternative visions of Chinese culture and society. It has been linked in many people's minds with *liumang*—as punk rock stars with long hair, leather, and outrageous costume shout lyrics about the end of Communism and the revolutionary power of romantic love.

Some have taken the young generation of the 1990s, most affected by rock, to be the "*liumang* generation." To one Western critic, the *liumang* generation

> is a wider concept [than simply the young hoodlum]. Rapist, whore, black-marketeer, unemployed youth, alienated intellectual, frustrated artist or poet—the spectrum has its dark satanic end, its long middle band of relentless gray, and shining at the other end, a patch of visionary light. It is an embryonic alternative culture, similar in certain striking ways to that of the 1960s in the United States and Europe. In one sense these are the lost generation.[23]

The rock star who most symbolizes this generation is Cui Jian, whose music, in the words of one entertainment publication, combines "buzz-saw guitars with intense lyrics."[24] Cui had a checkered relationship with the party-state, more an indication of the vacillation of Communist party officials than of Cui's actions. Repeatedly since 1987 he was forbidden to perform in Beijing, yet at times he was treated well by those in power—as when he performed benefit concerts for the eleventh Asian Games in 1990. He was praised by Wang Meng in March 1989 as an "example of the mainland's cultural liberalism." Despite his being frequently banned in Beijing, his albums continued to be sold in official outlets. In the late 1980s and through the 1990s, he gave concerts around the country as well as in Hong Kong and the United States.

The party-state's wary reaction to Cui generally reflects its reaction to rock and protest music and their potential destabilizing power in Chinese culture. Protest music in the form of prison or labor camp songs of suffering and "*liumang*" songs joined rock as music that could pose problems for those in authority. Here's an example of a *liumang* song that might do more than rankle a party bigwig.

The Official Banquet Song

I'm a Big Official, so I eat and drink, eat and drink,
Everyone says I'm a Big Official, so I eat and drink.
I can really eat, in I shove it,
And I've got the potbelly to prove it.
I can really drink, and boy do I love it:
Beer, spirits, rice wine, love potions, medicinal grog—
I drink it all.

Mongolian hot pot? Off to the Mongolian restaurant we go!
Peking duck? To Quanjude with all in tow!
It's not my money we're spending, after all,
So eat and be merry and let's have a ball! . . . .

Want to eat chicken, let's go to Kentucky,
A Western meal, Maxim's if we're lucky.
Or to Fangshantang to eat like Empress Cixi.
Or Renren Restaurant for Cantonese,
So let's book a table for two or three.

I'm a Big Official, so I eat and drink, eat and drink,
I'm a Big Official, so I eat and drink, that's me.

When I eat and drink on your expense
Don't get worried, don't get tense,
When you want something done and don't know where to go,
I'm a useful chap to know.[25]

In a sense, rock "took off" around the country in the early 1990s with the widespread screening of music videos and the huge popularity of karaoke. Because of the government's hesitance about allowing the rise and expansion of rock in the PRC itself, most rock music in the early 1990s came from Hong Kong and Taiwan. All of the ten pieces at the top of the charts in 1991 and seven of the top ten in 1992 came from Hong Kong and Taiwan. Government repression forced stars like Cui and others—Chang Kuan and female vocalist Ai Jing—to seek contracts for production and distribution abroad, primarily in Hong Kong and Taiwan.

One of Cui's East Asian competitors was Taiwan's Hou Te-chien. Hou was a hot star in the early 1980s. He left Taiwan for the mainland in 1983 and became known as a strong critic of the party-state. In the closing days of the drama of Beijing spring in 1989, Hou participated in the events in Tian'anmen Square. Because of his outspoken critiques of the government, he was forced back to Taiwan in mid-1990. Hou's more overt political stance was underlined again in a conversation he had with Cui in a Hong Kong television dis-

Hou Dejian, the biggest rock star in Taiwan, who wrote the song that almost became an anthem for many Chinese in the 1980s

cussion: he noted that rock was a "significant mouthpiece" for the frustrations of young people.

As the decade rocked on, more and more PRC rock music (as opposed to that from Taiwan and Hong Kong) was played. The rock scene became more home based.

> A sign of the times was the debut, in late 1995, of the fashion shop Heavy Metal Heaven . . . in central Beijing. HMH, one of a number of such stores, catered to heavy metal groups, fans, and fashion victims given to decking themselves out in leather and chains for gigs at the hot nightspots like Poachers' Inn . . . , NASA with its Russian dancing girls, or Hot Spot, a disco in the 3581 Military Compound staffed by tall, demobilized PLA soldiers dressed in black and carrying small electric truncheons.[26]

On the less "heavy" end of rock fashion, Cui Jian and others were celebrated with their faces or their lyrics on the T-shirts that were sported by the young. Rock, however, still scared many because of its perceived revolutionary potential. At a seminar on culture in 1990, a spokesman of the Shanghai Philharmonic Orchestra put it this way: "The bourgeoisie of the West use pop songs to propagate their view of life and their value system. We should never underestimate [the danger] of this. Our foreign enemies have not for an instant forgotten that music can change the way people think."[27]

Though many critics thought that Cui's musical quality declined as he advanced toward middle age and though there were many younger rockers waiting to take his place, Cui's often discordant duet that he played with the government kept him in the limelight. In May 1998, he released a new album, *The Power of the Powerless,* which was a great success. Never far hidden in Cui's work was political suggestion or comment: the cover of the album showed a "blob-like infant nursing a baby bottle as if it were a rifle."[28] Indeed, in looking back at the 1990s, the judgment of two journalists may ring true: "Literature, music, and the popular press have largely wriggled free from the commissars' grip, so that these days almost anything is permitted if it does not directly challenge the party."[29] Only time would tell whether the commissars would once more tighten their grip.

THE CINEMA

In the late 1980s, the so-called "Fifth Generation" of directors (filmmakers who came of age after Mao) emerged to lead a motion picture revolution with a series of films praised and given prizes around the world. Most were banned in China for their political overtones. Though a number of important directors have emerged, here only two giants will be treated. Born in Shaanxi, Zhang Yimou had to overcome the stigma of a father who was a Guomindang army officer. Because of his class background, during the Cultural Revolution, he labored on a farm and in a textile mill. After taking up painting and photography, he applied to the Beijing Film Institute but was rejected as too old (twenty-nine); he was admitted upon appeal to the minister of culture. He first came to prominence with *Red Sorghum* (1987), an earthy and violent tale of rural life that ends as a heroic drama of guerrilla resistance during the war against Japan. It won the Golden Bear at the 1988 Berlin Film Festival. His 1990 film *Judou*, a story of doomed love set as a struggle between generations was the first Chinese film to be nominated for an Academy Award for Best Foreign Film. That was followed by another Academy Award nomination for *Raise the Red Lantern* (1991), a film with striking cinematography that explores the often-tragic situations of women in traditional times. Indeed, many of Zhang's films focused on conflicts between strong-willed women and the intransigence of Chinese traditions and the brutality of Chinese patriarchal repression. It was little wonder that the films were first banned in China.

Zhang's *The Story of Qiu Ju* (1992) was set in contemporary China and filmed in almost documentary style; it recounts a wife's search for justice for her husband who has been kicked in the groin by a party cadre. His 1994 film, *To Live,* was the winner of the Jury Prize at the Cannes Film Festival; it was a melodramatic tale of the impacts of China's revolutionary political roller coaster on the life of one family. *Shanghai Triad* (1995) is a bloody story of gangster power in Shanghai.

Son of a filmmaker and also a graduate of the Beijing Film Institute is the other giant in directing, Chen Kaige. His first picture, *Yellow Earth* (1984) told the story of a poor

Actress Gong Li, star in many films of Zhang Yimou
Source: © Marc Riboud/Magnum Photos

peasant girl who falls in love with a Communist soldier; but her efforts to escape her arranged marriage end tragically. His major success *Farewell, My Concubine* (1993) won the Palme D'or, the top award at the Cannes Film Festival as well as prizes in Berlin and in Tokyo. This rich but frequently violent film looks at China from the warlord period to the Cultural Revolution through the relationship of two actors in the Beijing opera and the woman who comes between them. In the film, Chen touched on important and controversial themes, including the role of tradition, friendship, homosexuality, betrayal, and the relation between politics and art. Chen's 1998 film, *The Emperor and the Assassin,* won a prize for technique at the 1999 Cannes festival.

LITERATURE, MUSIC, AND CINEMA IN TAIWAN: AN OVERVIEW

Literature in Taiwan since 1949 has been marked by three groups; the so-called modernists, affected by European trends; the "native soil movement," stressing Taiwanese locales and themes; and non-resident writers who nevertheless publish on the island. The modernists, known for their avant-garde approaches in plot, characterization, and language are perhaps best represented by the two men who in 1960 founded the very important journal, *Modern Literature*—Pai Hsien-yung and Wang Wen-hsing. Pai, the son of important Kuomintang general Pai Ch'ung-hsi, in 1971 produced a collection called *Taipei Characters.* One of those stories, "The Eternal 'Snow Beauty'" was the first Taiwan work of literature to be reprinted in the PRC. His *Crystal Boys* (1983) was a novel about the homosexual community of Taipei's New Park; Pai infuses it with an "anarchic assertion of the emancipatory power of the Dionysian impulse, [a] celebration of youth and beauty in their ephemeral physical forms, and [a] romantic affirmation of the redeeming virtue of love."[30] It shares a "father-quest" motif with Wang Wen-hsing's *Family Catastrophe.* That work is highly innovative in form: Wang plays with words and sentence order, makes up new words, and forms the work into over 150 sections, some very short. It focuses on the changing relations between father and son, from reverence to contempt to cruelty to remorse. Wang's second book, *The Man with His Back to the Sea* (1981), was as much a *cause celebre* as his first. It begins with a long paragraph of nothing but obscenities and continues to depict "a world even more nihilistic yet morally anxious than that" of *Family Catastrophe.*[31]

The "native soil" literary movement began in the 1970s, in part as a backlash against modernism and its allegiance to the world beyond, and in part as an expression of Taiwanese seeking to explore their identity. Most famous here is Ch'en Ying-chen, a native Taiwanese writer. He has explored some of the most important issues in contemporary Taiwanese life. With an almost austere style, he depicts in many of his stories "an unfortunate or an outcast [who] confronts failure, bitter suffering, or death and attempts to wring some kind of understanding of the truths of existence." One critic has argued that "few stories written in Chinese in [the twentieth] century have achieved the power of Ch'en Ying-chen's best work."[32] An example is "Roses in June" (1967), a story of the despairing relationship of a black G.I. on R&R leave from Vietnam and the bar girl whom he takes up with.

One of the spokesmen of the native soil movement in poetry was Wu Sheng who relied upon the memory of his native village to deal with modern urban challenges. Here is his "The Earth" (1974).

Day after day, from sunrise to sunset
Mother who is blind to fatigue says—
The fresh breeze is the best electric fan
The rice field is the best scenery
Water and bird songs are the sweetest music.

Undisturbed by the taunts of
The civilization of distant cities, my mother
On this our family's land
Waters her dreams with a lifetime of sweat.[33]

A third group of writers set apart more by their non-resident relations with Taiwan than by any stylistic method or approach have published primarily in Taiwan. The earliest, Chang Ai-ling (Eileen Chang), never lived in Taiwan. Born on the mainland, she left for Hong Kong in 1952 and for the United States in 1955. She wrote powerful anti-Communist novels in the 1950s stemming from her disillusionment about what was happening on the mainland; but her most famous work, *The Golden Cangue,* was written in 1943. It tells a depressing story, though one "rich with sensuous imagery," of a girl married off to a wealthy crippled opium addict who grows increasingly bitter and takes this bitterness out on her own children. Several women writers were born or lived in Taiwan, but at the turn of the twenty-first century lived in the United States. Ch'en Jo-hsi returned to the PRC in 1967 to "serve her motherland," but the experience of the Cultural Revolution so embittered her that she left in 1974. Many of her stories have depicted the insanity of China during those years. Nieh Hua-ling, at the University of Iowa for many years, has written a number of novels. Her most innovative, according to critics, was *Mulberry Green and Peach Red* (1976), which interweaves a story of a Chinese woman whose life seems to be spinning apart because of the national turmoil with the trials and suffering of the doomed Donner party in the Sierra blizzards of the 1840s.

If the PRC has given the world noted filmmakers, Taiwan has also provided a cinematic artist, Hou Hsiao-hsien, who has become world renowned. Whereas Zhang Yimou's and Chen Kaige's films have generally featured larger-than-life grand scenarios, Hou has instead focused on the more human dimension, "the commonplace, ordinary people, the dross of daily life . . . memory and the past." Indeed, once Zhang and Chen became familiar with Hou's work they were both, according to a critic, "unsettled" and "inspired" by it.[34] Hou's masterpiece was a trilogy. *City of Sadness* (1989) looked at a Taiwan family's experiences in the period 1945 to 1949 from the collapse of Japanese rule to Kuomintang rule to the February "incident" (1947). Indeed, this movie broke the long-held public silence about the 1947 episode. *The Puppetmaster* (1993) depicted the Japanese occupation of the island through an "anecdotal biography" of Taiwan "living national treasure," master puppeteer Li T'ien-lu. The third film in the trilogy, *Good Men, Good Women* (1995), uses the

Kuomintang government's White Terror in the 1950s as a backdrop and a force in the life of a contemporary actress starring in a movie based on the lives of leftists targeted in the Terror.

As implied above, movies, music, and styles from Taiwan have played a pivotal role in "helping to define modernity for the PRC."[35] Tapes of a wide range of Taiwan singers have become immensely popular in the mainland. Still the best-known star was Hou Te-chien (Hou Dejian), discussed briefly above. He was born in Taiwan and soared to stardom with his 1979 hit "Heirs of the Dragon." He became the first important cultural figure to defect from Taiwan to the mainland—on June 4, 1983. Six years later to the day, he would become a key figure at Tian'anmen Square negotiating the departure of students from the Square with the PLA. With his music banned but with his continuing to make statements to the foreign press that embarrassed the Beijing government, the Communist leadership sent him back to Taiwan.

It is said that Hou's "Heirs of the Dragon" was "a kind of unofficial national anthem for Chinese in Taiwan and Hong Kong, and even on the mainland during the 1980s."[36] The students on the Square that morning in June were said to be singing "Heirs" with the final verse changed by Hou right before the troops arrived.

Heirs of the Dragon

In the far-off East flows a river called the Yangtze.
In the far-off East flows the Yellow River, too.
I've never seen the beauty of the Yangtze
Though often have I sailed it in my dreams.
And while I've never heard the roar of the Yellow River,
It pounds against its shores in my dreams.

In the ancient East there is a dragon;
China is its name.
In the ancient East there lives a people,
The dragon's heirs every one.
Under the claws of this mighty dragon I grew up
And its heirs I have become.
Like it or not—
Once and forever, an heir of the dragon.

It was a hundred years ago on a quiet night,
The deep dark night before the great changes,
A quiet night shattered by gunfire,
Enemies on all sides, the sword of the dictator.
For how many years did those gunshots resound?
So many years and so many years more.
Mighty dragon, open your eyes
For now and evermore, open your eyes.

Notes

[1] Quoted in Cyril Birch, "Literature under Communism" in MacFarquhar and Fairbank, p. 783.

[2] Quoted in Barmé, *In the Red* p. 159.

[3] Ding Ling, "Miss Sophie's Dairy," in *Miss Sophie's Diary and Other Stories* (Beijing: Panda Books, 1985), pp. 59–60.

[4] Leo Ou-fan Lee, "Literary Trends I: the Quest for Modernity, 1895–1927" in Fairbank, Ed., *The Cambridge History of China, Vol 12, Republican China 1912–1949, Part 1*, p. 473.

[5] Leo Ou-fan Lee, "Literary Trends: The Road to Revolution, 1927–1949" in Fairbank, Ed., *The Cambridge History of China, Vol 13, Republican China 1912–1949, Part 2*, p. 431.

[6] Ibid., pp. 441–442.

[7] Bonnie S. McDougall, "Writers and Performers, Their Works, and Their Audiences in the First Three Decades" in Bonnie S. McDougall, Ed., *Popular Chinese Literature and Performing Arts in the People's Republic of China, 1949–1979* (Berkeley: University of California Press, 1984), p. 269.

[8] Lee, "Literary Trends: The Road to Revolution, 1927–1949," p. 462.

[9] R. Keith Schoppa, *The Columbia Guide to Modern Chinese History* (New York, 2000), p. 203.

[10] Quoted in Gentzler, p. 233.

[11] Cyril Birch, "Literature under Communism," in MacFarquhar and Fairbank, pp. 774–775.

[12] Ibid., p. 789.

[13] Ibid., p. 791.

[14] Perry Link, Ed., *Stubborn Weeds* (Bloomington, In.: Indiana University Press, 1983), p. 20.

[15] Ibid., p. 188.

[16] Ibid., p. 185.

[17] Helen F. Siu and Zelda Stern, *Mao's Harvest* (New York: Oxford University Press, 1983), p. 19.

[18] Sha Yexin, Li Shoucheng, and Yao Mingde, *If I Were Genuine* (translated here as *What If I Really Were?*) in Link, pp. 248 and 250.

[19] Barmé, p. 287.

[20] Geremie Barmé and Linda Jaivin, Eds., *New Ghosts, Old Dreams* (New York: Times Books, 1992), p. 217.

[21] Barmé, *In the Red,* p. 73.

[22] Ibid., p. 184.

[23] The words are those of John Minford, quoted in Barmé and Jaivin, p. 248.

[24] Barmé, p. 360.

[25] Barmé and Jaivin, p. 252.

[26] Barmé, p. 135.

[27] Ibid., p. 130.

[28] Ibid., p. 360.

[29] Kristoff and Wudunn, p. 279.

[30] Sung-sheng Yvonne Chang, "Literature in Post-1949 Taiwan, 1950 to 1980s" in Murray A. Rubinstein, *Taiwan, A New History* (Armonk, N.Y.: M. E. Sharpe, 1999), p. 409.

[31] The phrase is from Birch, p. 794.

[32] Birch, p. 795.

[33] Ibid., p. 799.

[34] Barmé, p. 222.

[35] The phrase is from Joseph Bosco, "The Emergence of a Taiwanese Popular Culture" in Murray A. Rubinstein, *The Other Taiwan* (Armonk, N.Y.: M. E. Sharpe, 1994), p. 397.

[36] Barmé and Jaivin, pp. 153–154.

23

A Question of Identity: The Republic of China on Taiwan Since the 1970s

On the night of September 21, 1999, the strongest earthquake of the century rocked Taiwan. Ranking 7.6 on the Richter scale, it killed 2087 people and injured close to 9000 more; 13,000 buildings completely or partially collapsed, and over 100,000 people were homeless. Though a terrible nightmare—with long periods without electricity and with horrifyingly strong aftershocks, it did not derail Taiwan's bustling economy.

Just about six months later, on March 18, 2000, there was another earthquake of sorts, this one political. The Kuomintang, the party of Sun Yat-sen and Chiang Kai-shek, went down in a smashing political defeat in the presidential election. Little more than thirteen years after the first legal two-party election in Taiwan, the "rebel" Democratic Progressive Party won the election, sending the Kuomintang into shock and disarray. Former mayor of Taipei, Chen Shui-bian, who had been jailed in 1986 for opposition to the government, was elected president. His running mate and now new vice-president was Lu Hsiu-lien, a feminist activist who had herself been jailed in the 1979 incident in the southern city of Kaohsiung that one scholar called "a pivotal event in modern Taiwanese history."[1] What was the nature of the momentous changes that had swept over Taiwan after the death of Chiang Kaishek in 1975? This chapter looks at the changes in identity in the island state's politics, economy, society, and culture.

BIRTH OF A DEMOCRACY

As we have seen (Chapter 16), the government installed in the late 1940s by the Kuomintang mainlanders did not allow the 90 percent of the population composed of native Taiwanese any political role. The White Terror, aimed ostensibly against the Communists, actually targeted any dissent whatsoever. Chiang Ching-kuo became premier in 1971, and he was responsible for numerous crackdowns on dissidents. But Chiang was also responsible for beginning what has been called Taiwanization, that is, opening up the political system (slowly to be sure) to Taiwanese, as opposed to mainland immigrants and their descendants. By 1970 increasing numbers of Taiwanese were appointed to party posts at the county and municipal levels. It was the beginning of a policy of co-optation, of buying the opposition off by dangling political goodies before them. There were some Taiwanese who wanted more than simply being co-opted. In 1975 and 1976 Taiwanese opposition (known as "non-party" [*dangwai*]) tried to challenge the party in elections and demanded fundamental changes in the political system. The Kuomintang government reacted as it always had done on the mainland with repression and widespread arrests, determined to keep its monopoly of power.

At stake throughout these years was the identity of the state. Was the government headquartered in Taipei the Republic of China temporarily in exile? Or should the regime more appropriately be known as the Republic of Taiwan? The identity would always be determined by those who held the political and military power, the mainlander Kuomintang; they monopolized the military and security bureaucracy known as the Garrison Command.

The Challenges of the Late 1970s

Chiang Kai-shek was succeeded initially by his vice-president Yen Chia-kan, who was known as an economic planner; Chiang Ching-kuo continued to wield the iron fist in maintaining political control. In 1977, the *dangwai* took twenty-one of seventy-seven seats in the Taiwan Provincial Assembly. On election day in the northern city of Chungli a huge demonstration broke out over alleged fraud in vote counting. When police were sent in to calm the disturbance, fighting broke out. The angry demonstrators burned a police station, and there were a number of casualties. The episode became an inspiration to opponents of the government who were gearing up for more protests.

Chiang Ching-kuo took over the presidency in 1978 and met a heating up of the democratic protest movement. In 1979, the core of nonparty leaders published a political journal, in English called *Formosa,* in Chinese *Mei-li-tao.* The nonparty leaders hoped through its essays to inspire street demonstrations and mass rallies that could foster island-wide networks of politically active people. The government tried to keep the nonparty leaders "off balance, harassed them whenever possible, and leaked stories to the press about their personal lives that contained details of prurient interest"—a time-honored Chinese tactic to besmirch the opponents.[2] The leaders were subject to more and more intense surveillance: their telephones were tapped. With their control of the press, the Kuomintang government was always able to put its own "spin" on events as they occurred.

On December 10, 1979, nonparty leaders planned a rally in the southern port of Kaohsiung to celebrate the anniversary of the Universal Declaration of Human Rights. The attack on a *Mei-li-tao* staff member a day earlier by Kuomintang-hired thugs was a hint that the government clearly wanted to "do a number" on nonparty leaders by orchestrating a riot and then using it as an excuse to crack down on dissenters. Many like

Chiang Ching-kuo, son of Chiang Kai-shek and president of the Republic of China, 1978–1988

feminist Lu Hsiu-lien were aware that things were underfoot: "I sensed [she remembered] that something dangerous would happen that night. Things were out of control. If I were smart enough, I could have left right away, but of course I didn't . . . all we could do was wait and see."[3] Nonparty leaders riding on the platform of a truck and followed by their supporters, some thirty thousand strong, were met by attacking police who hemmed the crowd in, often keeping it from moving and sporadically firing tear gas. While the leaders urged calm from their truck platform microphones, "persons unknown to the rally organizers" and rumored to be hired by party rightists attacked the police, injuring over one hundred.[4]

Three days after the incident, the government, with President Chiang reportedly saying, "We cannot afford dissent," began a massive crackdown. Over 150 people were arrested; 41 nonparty leaders were tried and sentenced to prison terms. Among them was chief strategist for the movement, Shih Ming-teh, who had already served many years in prison for plotting against the government; he had initially avoided capture because he was hidden by leaders of the Presbyterian Church on Taiwan (PCT) which had been active in the Taiwanese cause. This time Shih was sentenced to life imprisonment in the notorious prison on Green Island, southeast of Taiwan; the general secretary of PCT was also sent there, for harboring Shih. Feminist Lu, who "could have left" before the rally but did not, was imprisoned. Many of those hauled in were subject to beatings and psychological torture. The government closed fifteen publications, including *Formosa*. All prisoners except for Shih were released in the 1980s while Chiang was still president; Shih was set free in 1990.

The Opening of the Breach

Street protests did not cease in the generally repressive early 1980s. But they were no longer simply the political theater of the nonparty Taiwanese. Advocates of other causes—ecology, women's rights, workers' rights, veterans' welfare, consumer rights—took to the streets. Aware that the proponents of all these issues simply could not be prosecuted and that the changing times required new policies, in 1986 Chiang initiated various reform efforts that, in retrospect, marked the "transition from authoritarian rule to some kind of participatory democracy."[5] Chiang's actions exhibited considerable courage given the continued strength of conservatives within his party and their opposition to many of the proposals that were being made. Yet he did agree to jail some opposition leaders, including Chen Shuibian, then a Taipei city councilman, as sacrificial lambs to the conservatives.

But the nonparty group was not to be intimidated. On September 28, 1986, shucking away forever their nonparty status, 135 of the nonparty leaders, in blaring defiance of the long-time ban on forming other parties, announced the establishment of their party, the Democratic Progressive Party (DPP). Chiang, the long-time repressor, became a supporter of the change. He pressured his party's conservatives to accede to an evolutionary change to greater democracy, contending that he himself had called for such changes. Specifically, he was able to get agreement on the abolition of martial law that had been in place since the late 1940s as well as the removal of the ban on the formation of opposition parties. Those remarkable changes came by October 15, little more than two weeks after the founding of the DPP was the first breach in the dike of authoritarian rule.

More breathtaking initiatives were underway. The Taipei government lifted all restrictions on travel to the PRC, making it possible for hundreds of thousands of mainlanders to return to visit their mainland homes for the first time since 1949. Many Taiwanese whose ancestral homes were in Fujian province across the Taiwan Strait also took advantage of the new opportunities.

The Presidency of Lee Teng-hui

Chiang died in January 1988. He passed on to his chosen successor, native Taiwanese Lee Teng-hui a Taiwan that "was a thriving economic entity that possessed a sophisticated and stable, but still evolving, political system."[6] Of Hakka background, Lee had studied agricultural economics, receiving a Ph.D. from Cornell University; he taught for many years at Taiwan National University (Taida) and served for two decades on the U.S.-ROC Joint Commission on Rural Reconstruction. He was mayor of Taipei from 1978 to 1981, governor of Taiwan province from 1981 to 1984, and became Chiang's vice-president in 1984. Lee took office at a time when the democratic changes initiated by Chiang were starting to flower. In December 1989 elections, the first of the full-fledged two party system, the DPP challenged the Kuomintang. Even though the Kuomintang won those elections, the DPP made a creditable showing, taking enough seats in the Legislative Yuan to be able to introduce legislation. The constitution of 1946, under which the government was operating, had established the Legislative Yuan as the national legislature.

Lee's leadership was remarkable in hastening the Taiwanization of the political system. Taiwanese made up 85 percent of the population but the number of official posts they held was like a drop in the bucket. Leadership in the military and police, for example, was almost monopolized by mainlanders. Taiwanese composed 75 percent of the rank and file of the military; but of the leaders, the Taiwanese generals numbered only about 17 percent and Taiwanese officers with a rank of lieutenant colonel or above made up only 4.3 percent of the total. Similarly, Taiwanese made up only 7.3 percent of 150 high-ranking police officers around the island. Lee began to remedy these paltry totals. In July 1988, when he was elected chair of the Kuomintang, he named thirty-one members to the party's central committee, sixteen of them being Taiwanese. Overall Taiwanese made up 40 percent of the new Central Committee compared to only 18 percent of the Central Committee formed in 1982. For his cabinet, he chose many younger Taiwanese; no fewer than fourteen held Ph.D.s, eleven from American institutions.

Lee had much trouble with various groups in the Kuomintang. His being Taiwanese was the first strike against him for many mainlanders; furthermore, they deeply resented his policy of Taiwanization, chalking it up simply to biased favoritism. Second-generation mainlanders were "young Turks" who did not want to submit to old Kuomintang procedures and policies, nor did they want Lee. Neanderthalic conservatives opposed Lee's domestic and foreign policy, especially his initiatives regarding the mainland. In the words of one scholar, they "seem[ed] not to have noticed that authoritarianism had gone out of fashion. Their passion for order and control, their willingness to manipulate the organs of government to execute their will, and their visceral distrust of anyone who disagree[d] with them reflect[ed] values that [ran] deeply in Chinese political history."[7] (That analysis also fit the conservative leaders in the PRC government of the 1980s and 1990s.) Kuomintang factions developed easily.

Under the constitution, the National Assembly was the parliamentary body established to elect the president and to adopt or amend the constitution. In the 1990 presidential election, anti-Lee forces in the National Assembly, having had enough of Lee's reforms, came together to try to block his election. Lee avoided being undone by the conservative mainlanders by naming as premier a mainlander, a career military man, and chief of staff from 1981 to 1989—Hau Pei-tsun. Hau quickly became the rallying point for mainlanders who generally tended to be far more conservative in their views of both domestic and foreign policy. In contrast to Lee's "mainstream" faction, they became known as the "non-mainstream" faction, the formation of which was encouraged by Madame Chiang Kai-shek, who maintained homes both in Taipei and New York City.

Taipei Spring

The wheeling and dealing of conservatives in the National Assembly to derail democratic reforms and to deny Lee the presidency brought an unexpected reaction from students from Taida and other universities. They copied a page from the student democracy movement in the PRC in 1989. From March 16 to March 22, 1990, they occupied the grounds of the Chiang Kai-shek Memorial in downtown Taipei, donned headbands with various political slogans, made demands, and even went on hunger strikes. In contrast to the generally unfocused Beijing student demands a year earlier, Taiwan students had much more specific and direct goals: "the disbanding of the electoral college [National Assembly], the suspension of the Temporary Provisions that freeze aging Mainlanders ["old thieves," as they were called by the students] in office, a timetable for full democratization, and a complete revamp of the Constitution."[8] But the chief difference from the Beijing Spring of a year earlier was that the government of Lee Teng-hui was open to talking about the issues; indeed, since most of the students' agenda coincided with his own, it was a pleasure for him to do so. One wonders what would have been the outcome had the non-mainstream faction and someone like Hau been in power.

On the day of his election, March 21, Lee himself went to the Chiang Kai-shek Memorial to talk with the students. He promised them that he would sponsor a "broad-based, high-level" conference to chart the course for the country's future. Four months later he convened a National Affairs Conference that brought together a diverse group of 136 political and academic leaders. From June 28 to July 4, 1990, they discussed and debated the course of "Taiwan's political development and offer[ed] recommendations for democratization."[9] Lee to his great political credit was able to take the recommendations of the National Affairs Conference as a mandate and a map to move to further democratization—at the heart of which was constitutional reform, a revamped National Assembly and Legislative Yuan, and other political changes.

Constitutional Change

In essence, because of the insistence of the Kuomintang that the National Assembly had to keep representatives from all Chinese provinces and that Taiwan was only one represented province, the current National Assembly represented China of 1947, not Taiwan in the early 1990s. Under the reforms envisioned in the National Affairs Conference, the 1991 National Assembly would convene and, amid its other work, would legislate itself out of existence. The question that emerged near the end of the assembly's session was whether it would play any role before its demise in charting constitutional changes. DPP representatives in both the Assembly and Legislative Yuan wanted no participation by the old-style Assembly because it was composed almost completely of mainlanders. They favored the new National Assembly taking up any constitutional changes. Relations between the Kuomintang and the DPP in the 1991 Assembly and the Legislative Yuan were notoriously rancorous. Name-calling, fist fights, hair-pulling, thrown ashtrays, and outright brawls frequently punctuated these sessions. A central issue that fueled the animosity was that of reunification with the mainland—the Kuomintang position—versus Taiwanese independence—the DPP position (see below).

In April 1991 when it became apparent that the Kuomintang was reneging on earlier pledges that only a new Assembly would take up constitutional issues, DPP representatives in the Assembly and the legislature walked out. Supported by ten thousand of their followers, they staged a huge demonstration march through Taipei, punctuated by frequent confrontations with police. DPP leaders called off any further action when the Kuomintang offered minor concessions, but they boycotted the remainder of the session.

It was a momentous session. The "Temporary Provisions," which had given the president the right to rule under emergency conditions during the state of war with the PRC and had been the basis for the Kuomintang's dictatorship, were abolished. Both the National Assembly and the Legislative Yuan were reduced in size, the first from 593 to 327, the second from 230 to 161. All senior deputies in the two bodies would retire at the end of the session. From that point on, two-thirds of the bodies would be composed of representatives elected on Taiwan and one-third would be made up of representatives of overseas Chinese. The latter arrangement originated with the ideas of Sun Yat-sen who stressed the help that overseas Chinese had provided in the Republican revolution and thus saw them as "part of the political community. According to ROC law, individuals who are born to Chinese parents are considered citizens of the republic regardless of where they actually were born, or where they reside."[10]

The quite remarkable democratic revolution of the late 1980s and 1990s continued with changes in the constitution in 1994. According to amendments, from that point on, presidents would be elected directly by voters; thus, the 1996 elections were the first under the new system. Presidential powers were strengthened with the decision that the premier's countersignature was no longer needed on presidential appointments. The terms of legislators were set at four years. The offices of speaker and deputy speaker were established for the National Assembly. In light of the frequent physical turmoil and unruliness in parliamentary bodies in the early years of the 1990s, the constitution was amended to limit parliamentary immunity of speech. In addition to the constitutional changes, the Legislative Yuan in the summer of 1994 passed legislation making the provincial governor and mayors of Taipei and Kaohsiung elected directly by the people.

The constitutional amendment that gave the people the right to elect the president directly took away from the National Assembly its primary task. After 1990, its main function was amending the constitution. Increasingly searching for things to do, in the late 1990s the Assembly more frequently clashed with the Legislative Yuan over power sharing and carrying out such responsibilities as budget review. Therefore, in April 2000, a constitutional amendment made the National Assembly a non-standing body with most of its powers transferred to the Legislative Yuan. The Legislature will initiate such items as constitutional amendments, impeachment of president or vice-president, and natural boundary changes. The Assembly will then be convened to vote on these matters. Most commentators believed the once-powerful Assembly will fade from the scene.

THE ISSUE: THE RELATIONSHIP WITH THE PRC

Apart from democratic reforms, the crucial issue of the 1990s and the early twenty-first century is Taiwan's identity. The position of the Taiwan government and the PRC is that there is one China; reunification of Taiwan and the mainland is simply a matter of time. The position of many Taiwanese and especially the Democratic Progressive Party is that there is one China and one Taiwan, or two Chinas; independence for Taiwan would be a ratification of the reality that has developed in fact if not in name since 1949—that Taiwan is a separate nation. The DPP position is anathema to the government in Beijing; even bringing it up throws Communist officials into something approaching apoplectic rage.

When constitutional reform was underway, firebrands in the DPP took the position that the 1946 constitution had to be discarded, not amended. "In their eyes, the entire po-litical system the constitution has been used to justify reflects the interest of the Mainlan-ders, with scant regard for the interests of the Taiwanese."[11] They set out to put together a constitution so that when the 1992 National Assembly met on constitutional matters, the DPP would not only be able to move to scrap the old constitution but have a proposal ready. The first article of the draft baldly set forth the party's position on the political identity of the island. It read, "Taiwan is a democratic republic of the people, by the people, and for the people whose name is the Republic of Taiwan."[12] They were scary words to many peo-ple, well aware that Beijing was thrown into war fever over even the hint of Taiwan think-ing of itself as independent. In a public opinion poll, 60 percent of the respondents disap-proved of the Republic of Taiwan language. The official *People's Daily* in Beijing bitterly condemned the DPP's draft. President Lee Teng-hui called it a "reckless and irresponsible move" and stressed that "there is only one China."[13] Election results for the National As-sembly in December 1991 also showed that the people did not favor the free Taiwan rhetoric at least: The Kuomintang took 71 percent of the vote, with the DPP garnering only 24 per-cent. Vote totals notwithstanding, the issue nevertheless would not go away.

Election Politics and the Issue

As a more open political system developed in the 1990s, there was a rift in the KMT, basi-cally over Lee Teng-hui's leadership. The New KMT Alliance developed early in the 1990s and transformed itself into another party, the New Party, in July 1993. In addition to being anti-Lee, they were pro-reform and pro-reunification. These three parties—the KMT, the New, and the DPP—continued to duke it out throughout the 1990s. In late 1994, under the new constitutional changes, there were campaigns for governor and provincial assembly and the mayors and city councils of Taipei and Kaohsiung. The New Party and the DPP cut into the KMT's provincial assembly and Taipei council's majorities; more striking, the New Party's Soong Chu-yu won the governorship and mayoralty of Kaohsiung, and pro-inde-pendence DPP firebrand, Chen Shui-bian won the mayoralty of Taipei.

   In early 1995, President Lee took action to lay to rest some of the bitterness that ex-isted among Taiwanese for mainlanders because of the February 28, 1947 incident (see Chapter 15). Three years earlier in winter 1992, Lee had had the official government report of the incident released with much fanfare in an attempt to "confront the ghosts of the past" and inaugurate a period of freer reporting among the media. On February 28, 1995, Lee ded-icated a memorial to the victims of the incident in the capital's New Park. In the ceremony, Lee, the Taiwanese Hakka, formally apologized to the victims' families in his capacity as KMT chairman and ROC president.

   One other issue that was political fodder for competing parties was government and party corruption. It was the New Party that especially targeted corruption in the DPP and in the KMT from which it had broken away. In 1991 the Minister of Communications was forced to resign in a stock scandal involving insider trading. In 1993 and 1994, there was the discovery of corruption in arms purchase deals in the Defense Ministry; naval officers had to step down in a scandal; and vote fraud was uncovered in the elections for both speak-ers and deputies. Members of the KMT were charged in a stock scandal. Even worse, the

DPP faced not only charges of corruption in the stock market but in a scandal involving the sale of heroin.

In a culture based on connections (*guanxi*), the nature of election campaigns can promote and exacerbate corruption. Big money for advertising and for campaign finances in general flow in from people who have agendas of their own and who believe that financial contributions will help them gain their ends. The line between contributions and bribes may be difficult to determine. The underworld became heavily involved in elections and put up its own candidates for the Legislative Yuan. As a measure of the extent of the system of patronage and payoffs that was called "black gold politics," in 2000 the new Minister of Justice set up an anti-corruption bureau, staffed by no fewer than *four thousand* people. In announcing the bureau's formation, he noted that "vote-buying during local-level elections and underworld involvement in politics have long repulsed the general public and they stand as obstacles to Taiwan's development."[14]

Lee Teng-hui's trip to the United States in the spring of 1995 and the impacts it had on PRC-Taiwan and PRC-United States relations were detailed in Chapter 21. Chinese missile tests off the Fujian coast 170 kilometers north of the island to try to intimidate voters in the December 1995 Legislative Yuan elections and the March 1996 presidential elections failed in their intent. In the elections for the legislature, the KMT won a little over 46 percent of the vote, almost 7 percent worse than in 1992; the DPP won over 33 percent of the vote, and the New Party about 13 percent. In the presidential elections in March, Beijing again used military threats and games to try to influence the elections. For nine days before the elections, they engaged in war games with live ammunition off the coast of Fujian. In addition, they fired surface-to-air missiles into two target zones, one thirty-five kilometers northeast of Taiwan, the other fifty-two kilometers southwest of Kaohsiung. Beijing was seemingly terrified that an advocate of independence might be elected, distrustful as they already were about Lee and his intent. Lee won 54 percent of the vote; the DPP candidate won 21 percent; and two renegade former KMTers polled 24.9 percent together. The tensions produced in the 1995–1996 election campaigns and the aggressiveness shown by the PRC did not bode well for the future.

The 2000 presidential elections were preceded in summer 1999 by Lee Teng-hui's inflammatory statement: "Since the introduction of its constitutional reforms in 1991 [the Republic of China] has redefined its relationship with mainland China as being state-to-state relations or at least special state-to-state relations."[15] Beijing turned livid once again, calling Taiwan a "rebel province" and denouncing Lee. But this time Beijing did not turn to blatant displays of military power; words sufficed. A casualty of the statement was the cessation of talks between non-official bodies established by both countries in the early 1990s to explore developing relations between the ROC and PRC.

The earthquake was soon coming—both the geological tremor and the political shocker. On March 18, 2000 DPP candidate Chen Shui-bian was elected president, winning over 39 percent of the vote to the New Party's candidate Soong Chu-yu's 37 percent and Lien Chan the KMT candidate with only 23 percent. The Kuomintang's fifty-five year dictatorship on Taiwan had ended. Chen hit the nail on the head: "This is the greatest victory of Taiwan's democracy movement," he said.[16] His electoral victory came despite (and perhaps also because of) Beijing's efforts to browbeat Taiwan's people. Three days before the election, the PRC's premier, Zhu Rongji ranted, "Let me give advice to all the people of Taiwan: Do not act on impulse . . . You will regret it very much, and it will be too late to repent."[17] Most assuredly, Beijing autocrats were well aware of Chen's statement given in a 1993 interview about the goal of the establishment of democracy in Taiwan: "[D]emocracy is the process and independence is the goal."[18]

One could almost call Chen's victory a storybook event in the history of Taiwan's democracy movement. Certainly it was a personal triumph over adversity. From the same 1993 interview as his linkage of democracy and independence:

> Basically, the road we took has been difficult in the past. Over the past forty years, to pursue party politics and democracy, our predecessors went through the 2–28 Incident, the period of white terror, the Kaohsiung Incident, and many bloody and horrifying assassinations. Even I have experienced this: my wife has to use a wheelchair for the rest of her life because of a "political car accident." [Chen's wife was paralyzed after being hit by a truck—an accident both believe was arranged for political purposes]. I have also been jailed. None of this matters. But, it has been a rough road. How many people sacrificed their lives? How many people were deprived of happiness? How many people were deprived of liberty? . . . We have given our blood and sweat for the lifting of martial law, for the easing of restrictions on the formation of political parties, for the liberalization of media restrictions, and the election of the legislature. It has not been easy to get what we have gotten, but we still have not achieved the ideals we expected.[19]

Perhaps in March 2000 the DPP did achieve what it may never have expected. To talk about the election as a storybook event is premature and naive, for Chen after the election had to govern with a party that had never been in power and thus did not have access to many of the accoutrements of power that the Kuomintang had. He had to deal with a legislature and a military still controlled by the Kuomintang; and he was faced with a bitterly hostile regime across the Taiwan Strait. Interesting times were ahead.

"PRAGMATIC DIPLOMACY"

A fully working democracy with a thriving economy (see below), infused by a national spirit: This description would naturally seem to conjure up the image of a modern, well-off nation state. This is a description of Taiwan, a nation-state in fact but not in name. Ousted from the United Nations in 1971 and with countless nations breaking diplomatic relations to embrace the PRC, Taiwan, like the American comedian Rodney Dangerfield, "gets no respect." What is such a country to do? Taiwan was trying to be readmitted to the United Nations. For the seventh time in September 1999, Taiwan's bid failed, supported by only thirteen countries, as opposed to fifteen in 1998 and twenty-two in 1997.

But the main answer was President Lee Teng-hui's "pragmatic diplomacy," which in essence meant linking up to other countries in any way possible. In many cases, perhaps most, pragmatic diplomacy should be called "checkbook diplomacy." Taiwan's "most faithful allies" are Central American countries, especially Panama, Costa Rica, and El Salvador. Not only are there diplomatic relations between them but Taiwan has given them huge quantities of financial aid. In 1999, for example, it set forth a seven-year plan during which time it would send to those countries "U.S. $10 billion of cooperation and investment funds."[20] Taiwan's relations with African countries have also been successful. In 1989 Liberia became the first country to re-establish diplomatic relations with Taiwan (while maintaining them with the PRC) since its 1971 expulsion from the United Nations. Other African countries—Swaziland, South Africa, the Central African Republic, and Niger—have also established diplomatic relations. Lee's trip to Nelson Mandela's South African inauguration in 1994 where he met some world leaders was a demonstration "to other nations that Lee's government was intent on finding a place for itself among the community of nations."[21]

In the 1990s, the ROC's relationship with Russia, the former states of the Soviet Union, and Western Europe have been primarily economic with the establishment of some air links. The focus with Russia, Latvia, Belarus (the native home of Chiang Ching-kuo's widow), Poland, and Bulgaria was on trade, business agreements, and investment. Air links were established with Latvia, Austria, and England. The possibility of using NATO's war in Kosovo in the late 1990s as an opportunity to assert itself in the international arena developed in 1999 when Taiwan offered a large aid package and low interest loans for the rebuilding of Macedonia. In the summer of that year, Taiwan's premier Vincent Siew (Hsiao Wan-chang) visited Skopje and offered yet more loans and aid. And so it went: Use money to make connections that one day might pay off for this aspiring nation. In this case, the hope was that establishing Taiwan as a force in the Balkans might offer "a diplomatic window and possibly a bridgehead in Europe."[22]

Record in Asia

Taiwan's record in Asia was hampered by the proximity of the PRC and the looming potential that the Chinese giant might play in the region. Thus, for example, when South Korea established diplomatic relations with the PRC in 1992, Taiwan simply broke off relations with South Korea. In 1993, non-official ties were reestablished when representative offices—"Taipei Mission in Korea" and "Korean Mission in Taipei"—were set up. Relations with Japan were dogged by the territorial claim of both over the Senkaku Islands (Diaoyutai, in Chinese) between Taiwan and the Ryukyu Islands, a dispute that, in the words of one scholar, is a "running sore on Chinese and Taiwanese nationalist sensitivities."[23] Taiwan's greatest Asian success in the 1990s came in Vietnam. Taiwan developed both diplomatic and extensive economic ties with Vietnam, becoming the largest foreign investor; Taiwanese have invested heavily in Vietnam's petroleum and textile industries. Taiwan also developed into Thailand's second biggest foreign investor and had substantial investments in the Philippines.

Relations with the United States

As we have seen, on January 1, 1979, the United States, one of Taiwan's closest allies and the one that had done most to have helped in the island's modern economic miracle, severed diplomatic relations with Taipei as it established relations with Beijing. The mutual defense treaty between Taiwan and the United States was also abolished. But in April 1979, the U.S. Congress passed the Taiwan Relations Act, which, in effect, accorded Taiwan "treatment equivalent to a sovereign state." Agreements over trade, fishing, copyrights, aviation, education, and defense technology between the two have been handled by two offices, the Taipei Economic and Cultural Representative Office in Washington, D.C. and the American Institute in Taiwan. Staffed by professional diplomats, these offices have been like the embassies of pre-1979. Indeed, Taiwan has twelve consular-like offices in U.S. cities—more than it had in 1979. With relations like this, who needs diplomatic relations?

Even more, the Taiwan Relations Act states that it is U.S. policy

> to consider any effort to determine the future of Taiwan by other than peaceful means . . . a threat to the peace and security of the Western Pacific area and of grave concern to the United States; to provide Taiwan with arms of a defensive character; [and] to maintain the capacity of the United States to resist any resort to force or other forms of coercion that would jeopardize the security or social or economic system of the people of Taiwan.[24]

Given the tense relationships between the PRC and Taiwan (one only needs to look at the PRC's missile firings and war games in 1996 and hostile talk in 2000 and Taiwan's provocative "state-to-state relations" statement in 1999), the Taiwan Relations Act may come back to haunt the United States. "Read literally, . . . the Act left open the possibility of renewed United States military protection and assistance to safeguard Taiwan's interests and deter mainland China if and when it was deemed necessary."[25] Thus, the United States continued to sell arms and planes to Taiwan—from George Bush's sale of F-16 fighter planes and surface-to-air missiles in 1992 to Bill Clinton's sale of long-range early-warning radar systems and advanced anti-missile systems like the Patriot and Aegis-class destroyers.

Cross-Strait Relations

Deng Xiaoping announced in 1979 that the PRC would no longer use the phrase "liberate Taiwan," would accept the reality of Taiwan's existence, and would support the "one country, two systems" approach for PRC-Taiwan relations. Lee Teng-hui in May 1991 announced the end of the civil war from Taiwan's perspective, an end to the "Period of Mobilisation for the Suppression of the Communist Rebellion," and an acceptance of the Beijing regime. Even before then, a thaw in cross-Strait relations had begun. A catalogue-like listing makes it clear.

> 1987—Ban on Taiwanese traveling to the PRC steadily relaxed.
> 1988—Indirect mail and indirect trade with PRC began.
> 1989—Indirect telephone links began.

1990—A National Unification Council was formed to plan and advise on policy.

1991—Taiwan (February) sets up Straits Exchange Foundation (SEF) and Beijing sets up counterpart Association for Relations Across the Taiwan Strait (ARATS) to deal with "commercial, legal, and administrative matters" emerging between the two.

1992—Between the two, 24.11 million items of mail, 14.72 million telephone calls, 62,000 telegrams. Officially declared indirect investment in PRC totaled 20 percent of all Taiwan investment—in enterprises numbering between 10,000 and 15,000. Delegations of PRC scientists visit Taiwan.

1993—First meeting (April 27) of SEF and ARATS in Singapore (see below)

1995—Direct shipping links established.

The first meeting of SEF and ARATs in April 1993 was in many ways like a summit meeting; it was the first "high-level" meeting between the PRC and Taiwan since 1949. While the SEF's deputy secretary-general perhaps hyperbolically called it "one of the historic moments of the century," the meeting was indeed "historic": it "symbolised the fundamental shift in the relationship between the two Chinas from one of confrontation between two sides engaged in an unfinished civil war to co-operative coexistence between complementary economies."[26] SEF and ARATS were to meet every three months, alternating between Beijing and Taipei, though that schedule was frequently altered by flare-ups in the relationship as in 1995–1996 and 1999–2000. An ongoing dialogue on issues like cultural, technological, and scientific exchanges, investment rights, fishing disputes, protecting intellectual property rights, resource and energy cooperation could not help but bring the region a greater sense of stability.

Ever more active cross-Strait economic ties have brought the island and the mainland closer almost year by year. The following table indicates that indirect exports from Taiwan to the PRC has risen over 300 percent from 1991 to 1999 and that indirect imports from the mainland has increased over 800 percent during that time.

Cross-Straits Trade*[27]

Year	Indirect exports	% Change	Indirect imports	% Change
1991	6,928.3	66.1	597.5	−21.94
1992	9,696.8	40.0	747.1	25.00
1993	12,727.8	31.3	1,015.5	35.90
1994	14,653.0	15.1	1,858.7	83.00
1995	17,898.2	22.1	3,091.3	66.30
1996	19,148.3	7.0	3,059.8	−1.00
1997	20,518.0	7.2	3,915.3	28.00
1998	18,380.1	−10.3	4,110.5	5.00
1999	21,221.3	15.5	4,526.3	10.10

*Unit = U.S. million

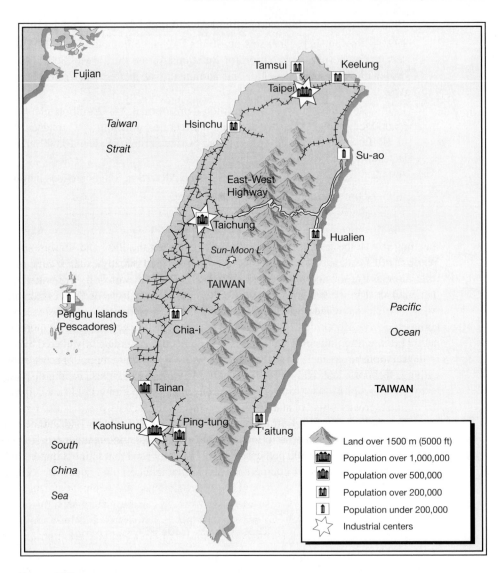

Taiwan, 2000

THE ECONOMIC MIRACLE

The expansion of exports was the engine that drove Taiwan's rapid economic growth; it was also the crucial source for its rapid industrialization. The brief tables below reveal the strikingly huge role that exports played in the overall economy.

Foreign Trade as a Ratio of GNP[28]

1951–1953	23%
1971–1973	81%
1988	88%
1989	78.8%
1990	75.5%

Exports as Percent of Total Output Growth

1956–1961	22.5%
1961–1966	35%
1966–1971	46%
1971–1976	67.7%

Export processing zones with their electronic industries and cheap labor (workers made 15 percent of what comparable workers made in the United States and 20 percent of those in Japan) were the cornerstones of economic success. And it was in the main American and Japanese investment that stimulated the electronic and electrical appliance industries. But electronics were only a part of the export success story. Beginning in the 1970s Taiwan moved into the machine tool industry and the transportation equipment industry, while in the 1980s it took great strides in the computer/information industry.

Supporting the expansion into these industries was a government commitment to fostering research and development. In 1979 the Kuomintang Legislative Yuan passed a law that set the guidelines for "science-based industrial parks" that would include residential accommodations, commercial enterprises, laboratories, and research units. The most famous such park that developed in the 1980s was the Hsinchu Technology Park. By 1990 it was generally acknowledged to be one of the most important research and development centers in East Asia. In 1995, it had 134 firms involved primarily with computers, telecommunications, integrated circuits, semiconductors, opto-electronics, biotechnology, and automation. But this is only one of a number of research and development efforts into which the government has poured money. Two other examples are the Chung-shan Institute of Science and Technology (established in 1971) to coordinate research and development related to defense and the Taiwan Aerospace Corporation (established in 1991) to transform Taiwan into an East Asian aerospace center.

A scholar has put the amazing success story into regional and world context.

For Taiwan, the core of the formula for its impressive rise has been its pivotal location at the center of a triangle of relationships between two constants (the United States and Japan) and one variable (China). From the United States came military protection, financial and material aid, capitalist ethics and advice, investment capital, technology, a huge market and strong political support. Japan provided markets, components, technology, investment, and work and management practices. China supplied the political and cultural values, the Kuomintang leadership, the threat factor, and, more recently, a huge new hinterland and market. The island of Taiwan supplied the central physical location, a defensible bastion, and a cheap, skilled labor force. Fortunately, the Kuomintang applied the right economic policies at the right time, managed the variable—China—in a masterly way and specialized in exporting to Japan and the United States.[29]

More and more people left the farms for involvement in this export-oriented economy. By 1980 the profile of the work force was 42 percent in industry, 33 percent in manufacturing, 38 percent in services, and only 20 percent in agriculture. As agriculture declined in importance, new forms of agriculture that could fit into the export market began to appear. The cultivation of flowers and decorative plants emerged in the 1970s and grew steadily into the 1990s. Live flowers, dried flowers, and potted plants were exported to Japan, the United States, Singapore, and Hong Kong. A hectare (2.47 acres) of flowers could bring a grower up to $24,000 U.S. while that same hectare producing rice would bring only $3,000 U.S. Aquaculture was another export oriented agricultural activity: carp, eel, tilapia, and sea cucumbers were grown in both brackish and fresh water ponds.

One other important aspect in the continuing economic success of the 1980s and 1990s was the money that the government poured into projects to shore up a sagging infrastructure. Chiang Ching-kuo committed the government to putting $8 billion U.S. toward what was called the "Ten Major Projects." In the crucial arena of transportation, monies were directed to the building of a superhighway connecting the island's north and south; to a new international airport; to the renovation of the country's railroad network, and to the construction of two new port facilities. To continue producing sufficient electric power, three nuclear power plants were constructed and at the turn of the century a fourth was being constructed. The government also sponsored several industrial plants, including a modern integrated steel mill, with the nuclear power plant erected on the island's southern tip. In 1991 President Lee Teng-hui announced a Six-Year National Development Plan also to focus on infrastructure. Specifics in this plan included a Taipei rapid transit system that would combine subways with elevated lines to connect the capital with suburban towns and cities and a high-speed train that would run from Taipei to Kaohsiung.

SOCIETY IN FLUX

Education

Seeming to reflect the economic vitality and rapid political change were changes in Taiwan's society. Undergirding both economic and political change was an expanding and successful educational system that provided a well-educated workforce and citizenry. As we have seen (Chapter 16), compulsory education was raised to nine years in 1968. Certainly as a result, the literacy rate shot from 45 percent in 1949 to 93 percent in 1990. Students could choose to go to academic or vocational high schools or go on the job market. As for higher education, in 1995, Taiwan had 42 universities and 75 polytechnic schools focusing on technical arts and applied science; together those graduated 37,000 engineers and over

135,000 technicians annually. In its support of education and students, the Kuomintang gave special consideration to fostering careers to help in the nation's construction—in engineering and the sciences, rather than, say, in the humanities or law. Thus of the 535,064 students (out of a total population or around 20 million) in Taiwanese higher education in 1989–1990, 34 percent were noted as studying engineering, 8 percent humanities or fine arts, and 1 percent law. In an interesting sidelight, 25 percent of all students studying for a Ph.D. in electrical engineering at American universities are Taiwanese.

In education as in all aspects of society and culture, the Kuomintang attempted to socialize the Taiwanese into being citizens of the Republic of China rather than citizens of Taiwan. Thus, only the Mandarin dialect, the "national language" of China, not Taiwanese, was used in schools, as well as on radio and television. Junior high and elementary students learned little about Taiwan. Reports showed that of about twelve hundred pages of required elementary social studies texts, only thirty mentioned Taiwan. In 1987 college entrance examinations, four of forty-two questions on geography were concerned with Taiwan and one of thirty-two questions on history was on Taiwan. The imbalance in curricular materials was an irritant among Taiwanese already upset by the attitudes and approaches of the mainlanders.

Women and Gender Roles

Education did allow women to emerge as they never had under traditional Chinese society. In the new Taiwan, women often started to enter the work force before marriage, thereby gaining independence from family before marriage. After marriage, their wages and salaries put them more on par with their husbands, and often led to situations where they participated more in decision making than in traditional marriages. Work after marriage also generally meant smaller families. It was not only in economic issues that the position of women rose. A more educated woman was more aware of legal rights (vis-à-vis men) and of political rights and opportunities in general; they were also more likely to participate in social causes.

The person most responsible for raising the issue of women's consciousness in Taiwan was Lu Hsiu-lien (Annette Lu) who was elected vice-president of the Republic of China in 2000. Educated at Harvard Law School, she became active on her return in women's issues. She dated the beginning of the feminist movement with essays she wrote in the early 1970s. One followed the 1972 murder of an adulteress by her Ph.D. candidate husband and the overwhelming sympathy that the public accorded the murderer. Lu said that the "sickness of society" compelled her to write "Which is More Important, Life or Chastity?"[30] Her major work, *New Feminism,* was published in 1974. At once a history of women's movements around the world and an account of the traditional role of women in China, the book argued that the real "glass ceiling" for women was not economic oppression but the "invisible concepts of patriarchal values [that] continue to control Chinese women's fates."[31] Lu was jailed for her participation in the 1979 Kaohsiung Incident, but many suspect her real "crime" was her strong feminist activity. She reported that during the interrogation following her arrest, one of her questioners said, "Your motivation to launch such a movement is to destabilize the society. . . ."[32]

The women's movement did not remain in the realm of the elites or the activists. From the mid-1970s to the mid-1990s no fewer than 96 popular magazines were published for women readers; they discussed women's roles, family issues, and sexuality. Often the "double standard" was evident in talking about husbands and wives, whether it had to do with who did the housework when both spouses had jobs or the permissibility of extramarital affairs for husbands but never wives. In the last decades of the twentieth century premarital sex was more common than ever before: a 1984 report of the Taiwan Family Planning Institute claimed that "34.4 percent of newlyweds had had sex before marriage, and, of these, 77 percent of the women were pregnant at the time of marriage."[33] Even though divorce was very possible, the divorce rate was very low. Why? Children were a part of the husband's family line; women who divorced were hardly ever given custody of the children. Divorce might mean that a woman would never see her children again. If a woman initiated a divorce, it is likely she would not be given alimony.

Social Problems

A 1990 survey queried respondents about their perceptions of the most serious social problems. They were, in this order, juvenile delinquency, transportation, public security, environmental pollution, and vice and prostitution. Statistics showed that crime by juveniles "increased in proportion to the population under eighteen."[34] In 1988, twenty-eight men per ten thousand under the age of eighteen were charged with a crime; just three years before, the number had been eighteen per ten thousand.

Transportation was a problem because of the excessive congestion. Traffic jams and gridlock were everywhere. The number of cars had surged forward to clog the streets and roadways: The 698 cars per 10,000 people in 1985 had gone up over 50 percent to 1,057 in 1988. In 1988, there was "one car for every ten citizens, and many times that number of motorcycles, with the numbers of both growing by the thousands each month."[35] The new rapid transit line was obviously meant to help with the problem in Taipei.

Concern with public security included fear of crime. Indeed, crime rates in the late 1980s seemed to be rising, though the figures were up-again, down-again. In 1985 there were thirty-two cases per ten thousand persons; that shot up to forty-nine per ten thousand in 1986 and down to forty-five per ten thousand in 1988. Judges seemed to be ordering severe sentences in an effort to reduce the rates of serious crime. More death sentences, for example, were handed out in the late 1980s and early 1990s than had been seen earlier. Public security also included freedom from social unrest. Demonstrations in the late 1980s and early 1990s clearly increased people's consciousness of security issues.

Environmental pollution of multiple kinds, as in the PRC, was one of the most serious, most abysmal problems faced by Taiwan in the last quarter of the twentieth century—the price of economic development. There were "biologically active wastes," including food wastes, human and animal wastes, and carcasses. The horrifying statistics were that "in all of Taiwan, less than 1 percent of human excrement receive[d] even primary sewage treatment; in Taipei City the figure [was] less than 3 percent. Not surprisingly, Taiwan had among the highest incidence of hepatitis B in the world."[36] There were pollutants that were "inert and semi-inert substances," that is, plastics, metal, glass in ordinary trash. These were usually dumped into land-fills, but it was no longer possible to find appropriate land-fill sites. Very serious, the most toxic of all pollutants, were hazardous wastes: pesticides, caustic chemicals, radioactive wastes, and chemicals used or produced by industry and agriculture. Air pollution was easily the most visible of all—"the ugly brown pall"—caused by an eye-watering mix of industrial pollution, motor vehicle emissions, the use of aerosols, and burning waste. Finally, there was noise pollution: noise levels of above eighty decibels were often registered on Taipei streets; the chief culprit here, having an overall negative effect on quality of life, was horn honking done indiscriminately and constantly.

In addition to these pollution problems, there were other serious environmental concerns. As in the PRC, the amount of land for agriculture was declining at an alarming rate; even worse than the outright decline was that close to half of what was now farmed was considered marginal. Soil erosion in many areas was a serious problem. There was also a potentially serious water shortage. Most island wildlife has been killed off. All in all, Taiwan, like the PRC, was an environmental nightmare.

The fifth serious problem mentioned by those Taiwanese surveyed was vice and prostitution. The government tried repeatedly to deal with the problem of prostitution, closing down a notorious center in the late 1970s. But that only made the problem worse, since businesses were then operated less openly. The numbers of those charged with crimes relating to pornography and prostitution rose dramatically—from 298 people in 1971 to 2088 in 1987. The problem is made worse by the involvement of the underworld seeking lucrative profits from the trade in flesh and sex.

A QUESTION OF IDENTITY

Always, always, always. In the background of every conversation and every situation is the undercurrent of identity—mainlander or Taiwanese. How did they see themselves? How did they see the Other? An American social scientist has suggested at least five separate identities for the people living on Taiwan.

The first three groups have a definite sense about their identity and what that identity means politically. There are mainlanders who identify themselves principally as Han Chinese and as one with the Kuomintang; they clearly see themselves "as part of the 'Chinese' nation."[37] Then there are those who might be seen as the polar opposite: Taiwanese who, though they recognize their cultural Chineseness, see themselves as part of nation of Taiwan. A third group is composed of Taiwanese who identify with a larger Chinese nation, but just do not want to become a part of the People's Republic of China as it is presently constituted. The other two groups wrestle with their identity, uncertain of exactly who they are in the unclear political situation. There are the offspring of mainlanders, born in Taiwan who feel a part neither of the Chinese nation or a Taiwanese nation. And there are Taiwanese who have been socialized under the Kuomintang umbrella, who speak Mandarin (and perhaps not Taiwanese), and who share with second or third generation mainlanders that sense of rootlessness.

The American social scientist setting forth these categories of identity left out the descendants of Taiwan's first people, the Austronesian-speaking aborigines that Han Chinese settlers had forced up into the central Taiwan mountains. Entering the twenty-first century there were over 360,000 aborigines, but they constituted less than 2 percent of Taiwan's population. Until the 1980s, they had either been gradually assimilated into the larger Han Chinese culture or were quiescently continuing to live separately in the mountains. In 1984 two dozen young aborigines formed the Alliance of Taiwan Aborigines (ATA) to begin to take action for the aboriginal community. By 1987, it was calling for aboriginal self-government. In the early 1990s, it established linkages with indigenous peoples in other countries, sending representatives in 1991 to the Geneva meeting of the UN Working Group on Indigenous Populations. The ATA's position was set forth by its leader, Yi-chiang Pallu-erh in 1992:

> Under the oppression of rulers from the outside, the collective vitality of Taiwan aboriginal peoples has grown weaker with each passing day, their national consciousness more and more insipid, and their culture almost wiped out. Only sufficient self-government rights can save their race from extinction.[38]

In July 1994, President Lee Teng-hui's meeting with ATA leaders to discuss their demands seemed a positive sign, though Lee rejected calls for self-government. But in November 1995 aboriginal interests received a blow when Yi-chiang and another ATA leader were jailed for leading demonstrations calling for aboriginal rights. Though the government established an Aboriginal Affairs Commission in 1996, its powers were significantly circumscribed. Perhaps the best hope for the aborigines in the early twenty-first century was the election victory of the Democratic Progressive Party, for that party has been more open to aboriginal concerns in the past than has the Kuomintang. Like all else on the island, the future remains problematic.

Notes

[1] Murray A. Rubinstein, "Political Taiwanization and Pragmatic Diplomacy: The Eras of Chiang Ching-kuo and Lee Teng-hui, 1971–1994" in Rubinstein, Ed., *Taiwan, A New History,* p. 441.

[2] Ibid.

[3] Quoted in ibid., p. 442.

[4] Marc J. Cohen, *Taiwan at the Crossroads* (Washington, D.C.: Asia Resource Center, 1988), p. 39.

[5] Hung-mao Tien, "Taiwan's Evolution Toward Democracy: A Historical Perspective," in Denis Fred Simon and Michael Y.M.Kau, Eds., *Taiwan, Beyond the Economic Miracle* (Armonk, N.Y.: M. E. Sharpe, 1992), p. 9.

[6] Rubinstein, p. 447.

[7] Alan M. Wachmann, "Competing Identities in Taiwan," in Rubinstein, Ed., *The Other Taiwan,* p. 24.

[8] Alan M. Wachmann, *Taiwan, National Identity and Democratization* (Armonk, N.Y.: M. E. Sharpe, 1994), pp. 151–152.

[9] Ibid., p. 152.

[10] Ibid., p. 200, n. 55.

[11] Ibid., p. 193.

[12] Quoted in Wachman, p. 194.

[13] *Free China Journal,* October 18, 1991, p. 1.

[14] Joe Hsu, "ROC Justice Minister Proposes Reforms Aimed at Halting Crime and Corruption," *Taipei Journal,* Vol. XVII, No. 22 (June 9, 2000), p. 2.

[15] Quoted in Jean-Pierre Cabestan, "Taiwan in 1999, A Difficult Year for the Island and the Kuomintang," *Asian Survey,* 40:1 (January/February 2000), p. 172.

[16] Terry McCarthy, "Taiwan Takes a Stand," *Time,* Vol. 155, No. 12 (March 27, 2000), p. 52.

[17] Ibid., p. 57.

[18] Wachmann, p. 162.

[19] Ibid., p. 256.

[20] Cabestan, p. 178.

[21] Rubinstein, p. 463.

[22] Cabestan, p. 177.

[23] Christopher Hughes, *Taiwan and Chinese Nationalism* (London: Routledge, 1997), p. 136.

[24] Quoted in Klintworth, p. 63.

[25] Ibid., p. 64.

[26] Ibid., p. 178.

[27] Source is Chiu Yueh-wen, "Cross-Strait Economic Ties Ready to Enter Next Phase," in *Taipei Journal,* Vol. 17, no. 21 (June 2, 2000), p. 3.

[28] Figures in tables from Klintworth, p. 122.

[29] Ibid., pp. 132–133.

[30] Hsiu-lien Annette Lu, "Women's Liberation: The Taiwanese Experience," in Rubinstein, Ed., *The Other Taiwan,* p. 293.

[31] Catherine S. Farris, "The Social Discourse on Women's Roles in Taiwan: A Textual Analysis" in *The Other Taiwan,* p. 311.

[32] Ibid.

[33] Ibid., p. 320.

[34] Hai-yuan Chu, "Taiwanese Society in Transition: Reconciling Confucianism and Pluralism," in *The Other Taiwan,* p. 89.

[35] Jack F. Williams, "Environmentalism in Taiwan," in Denis Fred Simon and Michael M.Y. Kau, *Taiwan, Beyond the Economic Miracle* (Armonk, N.Y.: M. E. Sharpe, 1992), p. 206.

[36] Jack F. Williams, "Paying the Price of Economic Development in Taiwan: Environmental Degradation," in *The Other Taiwan,* p. 241.

[37] Wachman, "Competing Identities," p. 61.

[38] Quoted in Michael Stainton, "Aboriginal Self-Government, Taiwan's Uncompleted Agenda" in Rubinstein, *Taiwan, A New History,* p. 425.

Epilogue

If one espoused a cyclical view of history, it would be fairly logical to see China in the period from the late eighteenth century to the early twenty-first century as going through a political and economic cycle from greatness to weakness and degradation back to near greatness. But such a view hides the dramatic contrasts in historical and global contexts between the late eighteenth century and the early twenty-first. It also hides the twists and turns in China's journey from multi-ethnic empire to modern nation state, changes in direction that were made not by forces of history but by people and their willful choices, whether rational or irrational. Throughout this journey, the Chinese state and the Chinese have repeatedly chosen, asserted, and had to deal with the implications of new identities for state, society, and culture. That is what this book has been about.

We have seen the various forces at work in China and among the Chinese at this end of the journey, the opening of the twenty-first century. Yet one more brief look—to the handling of religious diversity—reinforces the current picture of identities in the People's Republic of China and the Republic of China.

On April 25, 1999, outside the Communist party compound Zhongnanhai in Beijing over ten thousand members of the Buddhist Law Sect (Falun Gong) silently gathered and held a sit-in. It was a huge protest over the derogatory treatment of the founder of the sect, Li Hongzhi, in local magazines. The event itself scared the hell out of the Communist leaders: this sort of spontaneous happening had not occurred since 1989. But it was even scarier for the party-state leadership because Falun Gong had grown dramatically since its formation in 1992. While the sect claimed tens of millions of adherents, the government itself credited it with two million members. Even worse, during its seven years of existence, the identity of its founder had gone from recognized master of *qigong* (defined by one scholar as Chinese yoga—a routine emphasizing a form of calisthenics and breathing exercises) to being compared to great religious figures in world history. Shades of Hong Xiuquan and the Taipings!

Also shocking to the government leadership was the extent to which the sect had penetrated the party and government. Three of the five Falun Gong members who were selected to negotiate with Premier Zhu Rongji were high-ranking officials. In addition, one of the most vocal supporters of the movement was the former chief administrator of the hospital that treats top government leaders; he had the audacity to send Jiang Zemin a note suggesting that Falun Gong could accomplish things that Marxism could not. From the government's perspective, there simply had to be a crackdown. At a time when the "moral center" of the society was not clear, the consequences of allowing the sect to continue and perhaps mushroom out of control were unthinkable.

Thus, the government set out to spread widely details of the faults of the movement, pointing to how many people had died because they relied on the sect's teachings rather than seek proper medical care. They lambasted the founder of the sect, then residing in New York. They jailed sect members, many of whom continued periodically to protest the government persecution. In July 2000, the government announced that the struggle against the sect would be long. After over a year of political campaigns, harassment, and arrests, the New China News Agency reported that "the cult will not voluntarily step down from the historical stage." Thus, the fight against the sect will be a "long-lasting, complicated, and acute struggle."[1]

What does the Falun Gong and the government's reaction to it say about Chinese identity? First the flourishing of the sect and of so-called house churches of Protestant evangelical groups at a time when some believed that China had lost its soul suggested that the identity of China in the early twenty-first century is likely up for grabs. The revolution may be unfinished. The government was defensive about its position, still ambivalent toward its opening to the outside world, wanting desperately to continue its modern progress but fearful of all the baggage being brought into the country—hence also their ongoing deep concern with somehow controlling the Internet. The government reaction also suggested the continuation of the acute sense of history as part of Chinese political culture. The West looked at the government reaction to the sect with disbelieving eyes: How could the government so overreact? But Chinese leaders were well aware that the rise of religious-based sects had, more than once in the Chinese past, come at a time when the regime in power was starting to lose the Mandate. Historical memory made it absolutely essential that they nipped in the bud any such threat.

In sharp contrast to the PRC's response to the situation was the reaction of the Republic of China on Taiwan to a religious sect. The Yiguandao, a White Lotus-like sect, was established on the mainland in the 1920s. Brought to Taiwan by missionaries after World War II, the sect spread quickly. Its secrecy and ceremonies (only open to the initiated members) made it, in the time-honored word to describe the religious "Other," "heterodox." It was also illegal because of the existence of martial law. Still it spread. By the mid-1980s, it was said that up to 20 percent of the Taiwanese may have been initiated into the sect. By that time, many began to argue that the sect was simply an offshoot of Chinese popular religion. Scholars from the Institute of Ethnology of Academia Sinica lobbied for its being accepted as legal. In 1987, heeding the lobbying, the government lifted the ban on the sect as part of its democratization process and allowed it to register as a religion. The numbers in the sect increased, but the government did not seem to care.

The historic Chinese state has always insisted on control over religion, not so much for the propagation of religious ideas as for political control. But here, the reaction of the Taipei regime to Yiguandao could not have been more different from the reaction of Beijing to Falun Gong. The Taipei leadership saw it as illegal until 1987, but did not try to stop its growth and eliminate it. They did not react defensively and did not seem particularly threatened by the spread of this popular religious sect. They heeded the counsel of scholars who had studied the sect and were aware of its meaning. Despite Taiwan's lack of status in the world, its government acted with the confidence one might expect of the larger, more recognized, more powerful PRC.

At the turn of the century, the PRC and ROC were much alike—economically prospering, open to modern strains of popular culture, and dealing with similar problems (a polluted environment, the living conditions of their citizens, the location of society's moral center). But a chief difference in these two parts of China lay in their political identities. Given most of China's modern history where political rule tended to be conservative (except in the radical years of the 1950s to the 1970s), the situation on Taiwan perhaps seemed most anomalous. By 2000, Taiwan had become a clearly functioning democracy, the first such sustained regime in Chinese history. In sharp contrast stood the PRC's authoritarian rule. Perhaps by its very nature this kind of rule always seemed on the defensive, and political defensiveness tended to color all actions of the government in all arenas of life. This skittishness about its identity had only been exacerbated by the transforming modernizing reforms.

The monumental and most politically dicey question of identity, of course, is the future shape of a One China, that is the form that China will take after the People's Republic and the Republic join together (if that is indeed what will happen). That is an identity that the world is waiting to see, for it is certain that China, however it will be configured, will play an important role in shaping the world of the future.

Note

[1] *The Chicago Tribune,* July 20, 2000, Section 1, p. 9.

Index

Credits